MICROSOFT

EXCEL 7

COMPLETE CONCEPTS AND TECHNIQUES

MICROSOFT EXCEL 7

COMPLETE CONCEPTS AND TECHNIQUES

Gary B. Shelly
Thomas J. Cashman
James S. Quasney

boyd & fraser

bf

A DIVISION OF COURSE TECHNOLOGY
ONE MAIN STREET
CAMBRIDGE MA 02412

an International Thomson Publishing company ITP®

CAMBRIDGE • ALBANY • BONN • CINCINNATI • LONDON • MADRID • MELBOURNE
MEXICO CITY • NEW YORK • PARIS • SAN FRANCISCO • TOKYO • TORONTO • WA

A Division of Course Technology
One Main Street
Cambridge, Massachusetts 02142

I(T)P® International Thomson Publishing
boyd & fraser publishing company is an ITP company.
The ITP logo is a registered trademark of International Thomson Publishing.

Printed in the United States of America

For more information, contact boyd & fraser publishing company:

boyd & fraser publishing company
A Division of Course Technology
One Main Street
Cambridge, Massachusetts 02142, USA

International Thomson Editores
Campos Eliseos 385, Piso 7
Colonia Polanco
11560 Mexico D.F. Mexico

International Thomson Publishing Europe
Berkshire House
168-173 High Holborn
London, WC1V 7AA, United Kingdom

International Thomson Publishing GmbH
Konigswinterer Strasse 418
53227 Bonn, Germany

Thomas Nelson Australia
102 Dodds Street
South Melbourne
Victoria 3205 Australia

International Thomson Publishing Asia
Block 211, Henderson Road #08-03
Henderson Industrial Park
Singapore 0315

Nelson Canada
1120 Birchmont Road
Scarborough, Ontario
Canada M1K 5G4

International Thomson Publishing Japan
Hirakawa-cho Kyowa Building, 3F
2-2-1 Hirakawa-cho, Chiyoda-ku
Tokyo 102, Japan

ISBN 0-7895-0734-X

PHOTO CREDITS: *Project 1, page E 1.4,* Dan Bricklin and Bob Frankston, The Boston Computer Museum; *Project 2, page E 2.3,* Ferrari F50, John Lamm, *Road & Track*; *Project 4, page E 4.4,* Country Companies Insurance Group brochures, Courtesy of Country Life Insurance Company; *page E 4.5,* Insurance policy, Courtesy of MacGregor Insurance; *Project 5, page E 5.2,* Pencil image provided by PhotoDisc Inc. © 1996; Family provided by The STOCKMARKET/Michael Keller; *page E 5.3,* Hand shake and business meeting images provided by PhotoDisc Inc. © 1996; *Project 6, page E 6.2*; Two senior citizens image provided by PhotoDisc Inc. © 1996

6 7 8 9 10 BC 10 9 8 7

Microsoft Excel 7

Complete Concepts and Techniques

Contents

PROJECT THREE

What-If Analysis and Working with Large Worksheets

INTEGRATION FEATURE

Linking an Excel Worksheet to a Word Document

PROJECT FOUR

Working with Templates and Multiple Worksheets in a Workbook

PROJECT FIVE

Data Tables, Visual Basic for Applications, and Scenario Manager

PROJECT SIX

SORTING AND FILTERING A WORKSHEET DATABASE AND CREATING A DATA MAP

INTEGRATION FEATURE

EMBEDDING AN EXCEL WORKSHEET IN A WORD DOCUMENT USING DRAG AND DROP

Preface

Shelly Cashman Series® Microsoft Windows 95 Books

The Shelly Cashman Series Microsoft Windows 95 books reinforce the fact that you made the right choice when you use a Shelly Cashman Series book. The Shelly Cashman Series Microsoft Windows 3.1 books were used by more schools and more students than any other series in textbook publishing. Yet the Shelly Cashman Series team wanted to produce even better books for Windows 95, so the books were thoroughly redesigned to present material in an even easier to understand format and with more project-ending activities. Features such as Other Ways and More Abouts were added to give in-depth knowledge to the student. The opening of each project provides a fascinating perspective of the subject covered in the project. Completely redesigned student assignments include the unique Cases and Places. This book provides the finest educational experience for a student learning about computer software.

Objectives of This Textbook

Microsoft Excel 7: Complete Concepts and Techniques is intended for a two-unit course that presents Microsoft Excel 7. The objectives of this book are:

- To teach the fundamentals of Microsoft Excel 7
- To foster an appreciation of worksheets as a useful tool in the workplace
- To give students an in-depth understanding of worksheet design, charting, what-if analysis, worksheet database creation and manipulation, and OLE
- To provide a knowledge base of Microsoft Excel 7 on which students can build
- To help students who are working on their own

When students complete the course using this textbook, they will have a firm knowledge and understanding of Excel 7.

The Shelly Cashman Approach

Features of the Shelly Cashman Series Windows 95 books include:

- Project Orientation: Each project in the book uses the unique Shelly Cashman Series screen-by-screen, step-by-step approach.
- Screen-by-Screen, Step-by-Step Instructions: Each of the tasks required to complete a project is identified throughout the development of the project. Then, steps to accomplish the task are specified. The steps are accompanied by screens. The student is not told to perform a step without seeing the result of the step on a color screen. Hence, students learn from this book the same as if they were using a computer.

More *About* Scenario Manager

Worksheets are primarily used for what-if analysis. You enter values into cells and instantaneously the results change in the dependent cells. As you continue to change values in the key cells, you lose the previous results. If you want to go back, you have to reenter the data. Scenario manager allows you to store the different sets of values (called scenarios) so that you can easily redisplay them with a few clicks of the mouse button. Each scenario can have up to 32 sets of changing cells for each scenario.

*Other*Ways

1. Click Function Wizard button, select SUM in Function Name box, click OK button
2. Click Function on Insert menu, select SUM in Function Name box, click OK button

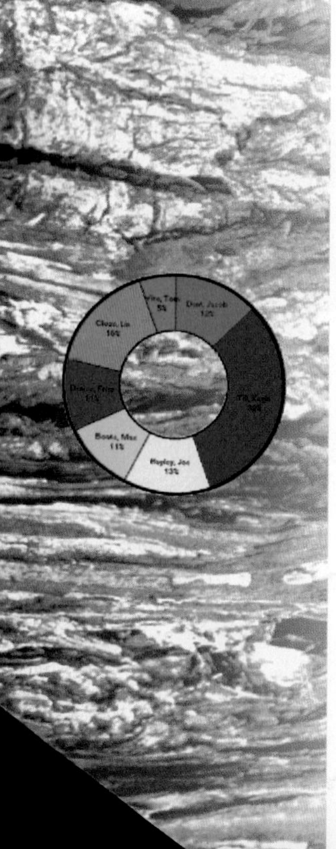

- **Thoroughly Tested Projects:** The computer screens in the Shelly Cashman Series Windows 95 books are shot directly from the author's computer. The screen is shot immediately after the author performs the step specified in the text. Therefore, every screen in the book is correct because it is produced only after performing a specific step, resulting in unprecedented quality in a computer textbook.
- **Multiple Ways to Use the Book:** The book can be used in a variety of ways, including: (a) Lecture and textbook approach – The instructor lectures on the material in the book. The student reads and studies the material and then applies the knowledge to an application on the computer; (b) Tutorial approach – The student performs each specified step on a computer. At the end of the project, the student has solved the problem and is ready to solve comparable student assignments; (c) Other approaches – Many teachers lecture on the material and then require their students to perform each step in the project, reinforcing the material lectured. The students then complete one or more of the In the Lab exercises; and (d) Reference – Each task in a project is clearly identified. Therefore, the material serves as a complete reference.
- **Windows/Graphical User Interface Approach:** Windows 95 provides a graphical user interface and all the examples in this book use this interface. Thus, the mouse is the preferred user communication tool. The secondary, or right, mouse button is used extensively.
- **Other Ways Boxes for Reference:** Windows 95 provides a wide variety of ways to carry out a given task. The Other Ways boxes displayed at the end of most of the step-by-step sequences specify the other ways to do the task completed in the steps. Thus, the steps and the Other Ways box make a comprehensive reference unit. You no longer have to reference tables at the end of a chapter or the end of a book.

Organization of This Textbook

Microsoft Excel 7: Complete Concepts and Techniques consists of six projects on Microsoft Excel 7 and two Integration Features. A short description of each follows.

Project 1 – Creating a Worksheet and Embedded Chart In Project 1, students are introduced to Excel terminology, the Excel window, and the basic characteristics of a worksheet and workbook. Topics include: starting and exiting Excel; entering text and numbers; selecting a range; using the AutoSum button; copying using the fill handle; changing font size; bolding; centering across columns; using the AutoFormat command; charting using the ChartWizard; saving and opening a workbook; editing a worksheet; using the AutoCalculate area; and obtaining online Help.

Project 2 – Formulas, Formatting, and Creating Charts students use formulas and functions to build a worksheet and learn more about formatting and printing a worksheet. Topics include: entering formulas; using functions; formatting text; formatting numbers; drawing borders and adding colors; changing the widths of columns and rows; spell checking; creating a 3-D pie chart on a separate sheet; previewing a worksheet; printing a section of a worksheet; and displaying and printing the formulas in a worksheet.

Project 3 – What-If Analysis and Working with Large Worksheets In Project 3, students learn how to work with larger worksheets, how to create a worksheet based on assumptions, how to use the IF function and absolute cell references, and how to perform what-if analysis. Topics include: assigning global formats; using the fill handle to create a series; deleting, inserting, copying, and moving data on a worksheet; displaying and docking toolbars; adding drop shadows to ranges; freezing titles; changing the magnification of worksheets; displaying different parts of the worksheet using panes; and simple what-if analysis and goal seeking.

Integration Feature 1 – Linking an Excel Worksheet to a Word Document In this section, students are introduced to linking a worksheet to a Word document. Topics include: a discussion of the differences among copying and pasting, copying and embedding, and copying and linking; opening multiple applications; saving and printing a document with a linked worksheet; and editing a linked worksheet in a Word document.

Project 4 – Working with Templates and Multiple Worksheets in a Workbook In Project 4, students learn to create a template and consolidate data into one worksheet. Topics include: building and copying a template; multiple worksheets; 3-D cell references; customized formats; comparison charts; adding notes to a cell; changing page setup characteristics; and finding and replacing data.

Project 5 – Data Tables, Visual Basic for Applications, and Scenario Manager In Project 5, students learn more about analyzing data in a worksheet and how to write macros using Visual Basic for Applications. Topics include: applying the PMT function to determine a monthly payment; using names to reference cells; analyzing data by (1) goal seeking, (2) creating a data table, and (3) creating a Scenario Summary Report worksheet; writing macros and recording macros that automate worksheet activities; creating a button and assigning a macro to it; and protecting a worksheet.

Project 6 – Sorting and Filtering a Worksheet Database and Creating a Data Map In Project 6, students learn how to create, sort, and filter a database. Topics include: using a data form to create and maintain a database; creating subtotals; finding, extracting, and deleting records that pass a test; applying database and lookup functions; creating a data map; and creating a pivot table.

Integration Feature 2 – Embedding an Excel Worksheet in a Word Document Using Drag and Drop In this section, students are introduced to embedding a worksheet into a Word document. Topics include: tiling applications on the desktop; embedding using drag and drop; untiling applications on the desktop; and editing an embedded object.

End-of-Project Student Activities

A notable strength of the Shelly Cashman Series Windows 95 books is the extensive student activities at the end of each project. Well-structured student activities can make the difference between students merely participating in a class and students retaining the information they learn. These activities include all of the following sections.

- What You Should Know A listing of the tasks completed within a project together with the pages where the step-by-step, screen-by-screen explanations appear. This section provides a perfect study review for the student.
- Test Your Knowledge Four pencil-and-paper activities designed to determine the student's understanding of the material in the project. Included are true/false questions, multiple-choice questions, and two short-answer exercises.

- **Use Help** Any user of Windows 95 must know how to use Help. Therefore, this book contains two Help exercises per project. These exercises alone distinguish the Shelly Cashman Series from any other set of Windows 95 instructional materials.
- **Apply Your Knowledge** This exercise requires the student to open and manipulate a file from the Student Floppy Disk that accompanies the book.
- **In the Lab** Three in-depth assignments per project that require the student to apply the knowledge gained in the project to solve problems on a computer.
- **Cases and Places** Seven unique case studies allow students to apply their knowledge to real-world situations.

Instructor's Resource Kit

A comprehensive Instructor's Resource Kit (IRK) accompanies this textbook in the form of a CD-ROM. The CD-ROM includes an electronic Instructor's Manual (called ElecMan) and teaching and testing aids. The CD-ROM (ISBN 0-7895-1179-7) is available through your Course Technology representative or by calling 1-800-648-7450. The contents of the CD-ROM are listed below.

- **ElecMan (*Elec*tronic Instructor's *Man*ual)** ElecMan is made up of Microsoft Word files. The files include lecture notes, solutions to laboratory assignments, and a large test bank. The files allow you to modify the lecture notes or generate quizzes and exams from the test bank using your own word processor. Where appropriate, solutions to laboratory assignments are embedded as icons in the files. When an icon appears, double-click it and the application will start and the solution will display on the screen. ElecMan includes the following for each project: project objectives; project overview; detailed lesson plans with page number references; teacher notes and activities; answers to the end-of-project exercises; test bank of 110 questions for every project (50 true/false, 25 multiple-choice, and 35 fill-in-the blank) with page number references; and transparency references. The transparencies are available through the Figures on CD-ROM described below. The test bank questions are numbered the same as in Course Test Manager. Thus, you can print out a copy of the project and use the printed test bank to select your questions in Course Test Manager.
- **Figures on CD-ROM** Illustrations for every screen in the textbook are available. Use this ancillary to create a slide show from the illustrations for lecture or to print transparencies for use in lecture with an overhead.
- **Course Test Manager** This cutting edge Windows-based testing software helps instructors design and administer tests and pre-tests. The full-featured online program permits students to take tests at the computer where their grades are computed immediately following completion of the exam. Automatic statistics collection, student guides customized to the student's performance, and printed tests are only a few of the features.
- **Lecture Success System** Lecture Success System files are for use with the application software, a personal computer, and projection device to explain and illustrate the step-by-step, screen-by-screen development of a project in the textbook without entering large amounts of data.
- **Lab Tests** Tests that parallel the In the Lab assignments are supplied for the purpose of testing students in the laboratory on the material covered in the project. You also can use these assignments as supplementary exercises.

- **Instructor's Lab Solutions** Solutions and required files for all the In the Lab assignments at the end of each project are available.
- **Student Files** All the files that are required by the student to complete the Apply Your Knowledge exercises and some of the later projects in the Office 95 textbook are included.
- **Interactive Labs** Fourteen hands-on interactive labs that take the student from ten to fifteen minutes to step through help solidify and reinforce computer concepts. Student assessment is available in each interactive lab by means of a Print button. The assessment requires the student to answer questions about the contents of the interactive lab.

Shelly Cashman Online

Shelly Cashman Online is a World Wide Web service available to instructors and students of computer education. Visit Shelly Cashman Online at http://www.bf.com/scseries.html. Shelly Cashman Online is divided into four areas:

- Series Information Information on the Shelly Cashman Series products.
- The Community Opportunities to discuss your course and your ideas with instructors in your field and with the Shelly Cashman Series team.
- Teaching Resources This area includes password-protected data from Instructor's Floppy Disks that can be downloaded, course outlines, teaching tips, and ancillaries such as ElecMan.
- Student Center Dedicated to students learning about computers with Shelly Cashman Series textbooks and software. This area includes cool links, data from Student Floppy Disks that can be downloaded, and much more.

Most of the instructor aids just described also are available to registered instructors on the Shelly Cashman Online home page (http://www.bf.com/scseries.html).

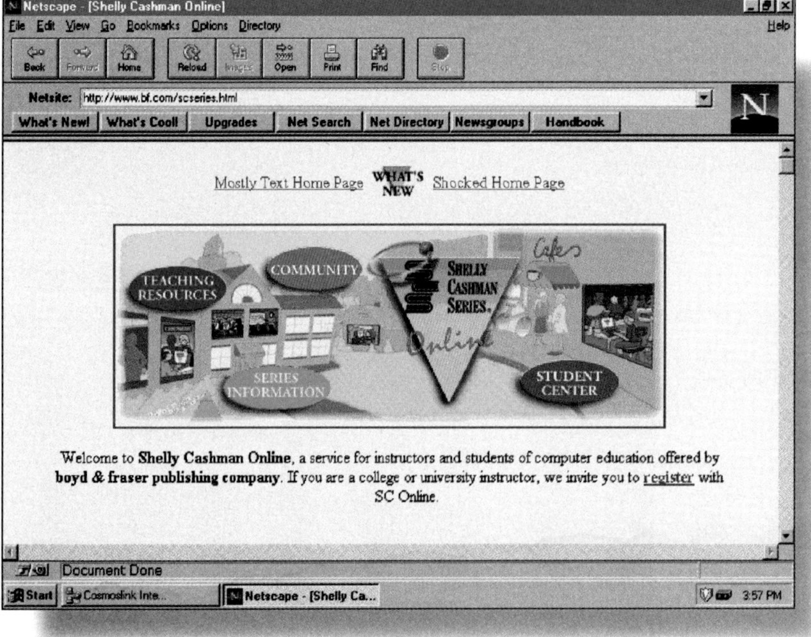

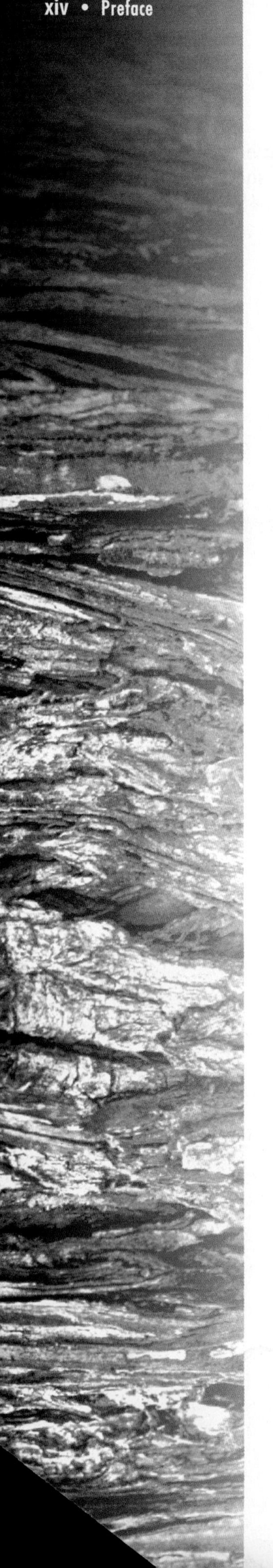

Acknowledgments

The Shelly Cashman Series would not be the leading computer education series without the contributions of outstanding publishing professionals. First, and foremost, among them is Becky Herrington, director of production and designer. She is the heart and soul of the Shelly Cashman Series, and it is only through her leadership, dedication, and tireless efforts that superior products are made possible. Becky created and produced the award-winning Windows 95 series of books.

Under Becky's direction, the following individuals made significant contributions to these books: Peter Schiller, production manager; Ginny Harvey, series administrator and manuscript editor; Lyn Markowicz, copy editor; Nancy Lamm and Debora Christy, proofreaders; Susan Sebok and Tim Walker, contributing writers; Ken Russo, senior illustrator and cover artist; Mike Bodnar, Stephanie Nance, Greg Herrington, and Dave Bonnewitz, Quark artists and illustrators; Patti Garbarino and Lora Wade, editorial assistants; Bill Lisowski, marketing director; Jeanne Black, Quark expert; Cristina Haley, indexer; Sarah Evertson of Image Quest, photo researcher; Henry Blackham, cover photographer; and Kent Lauer, cover glass work. Special mention must go to Suzanne Biron, Becky Herrington, and Michael Gregson for the outstanding book design, to Ken Russo for the cover design; and to Jim Quasney, series editor.

Gary B. Shelly
Thomas J. Cashman
James S. Quasney

Visit Shelly Cashman Online at
http://www.bf.com/scseries.html

Shelly Cashman Series - Traditionally Bound Textbooks

The Shelly Cashman Series presents computer textbooks across the entire spectrum including both Windows- and DOS-based personal computer applications in a variety of traditionally bound textbooks, as shown in the table below. For more information, see your Course Technology representative or call 1-800-648-7450.

COMPUTERS	
Computers	Using Computers: A Gateway to Information, World Wide Web Edition Using Computers: A Gateway to Information, World Wide Web Brief Edition Using Computers: A Gateway to Information, World Wide Web Edition and Exploring Computers: A Record of Discovery with CD-ROM Using Computers: A Gateway to Information Using Computers: A Gateway to Information, Brief Edition Exploring Computers: A Record of Discovery with CD-ROM A Record of Discovery for Exploring Computers Study Guide for Using Computers: A Gateway to Information, World Wide Web Edition Study Guide for Using Computers: A Gateway to Information
and Windows Apps	Using Computers: A Gateway to Information and Microsoft Office (also in spiral bound) Using Computers: A Gateway to Information and Microsoft Works 3.0 (also in spiral bound)
and Programming	Using Computers: A Gateway to Information and Programming in QBasic
WINDOWS APPLICATIONS	
Integrated Packages	Microsoft Office 95: Introductory Concepts and Techniques (also in spiral bound) Microsoft Office 95: Advanced Concepts and Techniques (also in spiral bound) Microsoft Office 4.3 running under Windows 95: Introductory Concepts and Techniques (also in spiral bound) Microsoft Office: Introductory Concepts and Techniques (also in spiral bound) Microsoft Office: Advanced Concepts and Techniques (also in spiral bound) Microsoft Works 4 for Windows 95* Microsoft Works 3.0 (also in spiral bound)* • Microsoft Works 2.0 (also in spiral bound) Microsoft Works 3.0—Short Course
Windows	Microsoft Windows 95: Introductory Concepts and Techniques (96-page) Introduction to Microsoft Windows 95 (224-page) Microsoft Windows 95: Complete Concepts and Techniques Microsoft Windows 3.1 Introductory Concepts and Techniques Microsoft Windows 3.1 Complete Concepts and Techniques
Windows Applications	Microsoft Word 2.0, Microsoft Excel 4, and Paradox 1.0 (also in spiral bound)
Word Processing	Microsoft Word 7* • Microsoft Word 6* • Microsoft Word 2.0 WordPerfect 6.1* • WordPerfect 6* • WordPerfect 5.2
Spreadsheets	Microsoft Excel 7* • Microsoft Excel 5* • Microsoft Excel 4 Lotus 1-2-3 Release 5* • Lotus 1-2-3 Release 4* • Quattro Pro 6 • Quattro Pro 5
Database Management	Microsoft Access 7* • Microsoft Access 2 Paradox 5 • Paradox 4.5 • Paradox 1.0 • Visual dBASE 5/5.5
Presentation Graphics	Microsoft PowerPoint 7* • Microsoft PowerPoint 4*
DOS APPLICATIONS	
Operating Systems	DOS 6 Introductory Concepts and Techniques DOS 6 and Microsoft Windows 3.1 Introductory Concepts and Techniques
Integrated Package	Microsoft Works 3.0 (also in spiral bound)
Word Processing	WordPerfect 6.1 • WordPerfect 6.0 WordPerfect 5.1 Step-by-Step Function Key Edition • WordPerfect 5.1 Function Key Edition
Spreadsheets	Lotus 1-2-3 Release 4 • Lotus 1-2-3 Release 2.4 • Lotus 1-2-3 Release 2.3 Lotus 1-2-3 Release 2.2 • Lotus 1-2-3 Release 2.01 Quattro Pro 3.0 • Quattro with 1-2-3 Menus (with Educational Software)
Database Management	dBASE 5 • dBASE IV Version 1.1 • dBASE III PLUS (with Educational Software) Paradox 4.5 • Paradox 3.5 (with Educational Software)
PROGRAMMING AND NETWORKING	
Programming	Introduction to Microsoft Visual Basic 4* (available with Student version of Visual Basic 4) Microsoft Visual Basic 3.0 for Windows* QBasic • QBasic: An Introduction to Programming • Microsoft BASIC Structured COBOL Programming
Networking	Novell NetWare for Users Business Data Communications: Introductory Concepts and Techniques
Internet	The Internet: Introductory Concepts and Techniques (UNIX) Netscape Navigator 3: An Introduction • Netscape Navigator 2 running under Windows 3.1 Netscape Navigator: An Introduction (Version 1.1) Netscape Navigator Gold: Creating Web Pages
SYSTEMS ANALYSIS	
Systems Analysis	Systems Analysis and Design, Second Edition

*Also available as a Double Diamond Edition, which is a shortened version of the complete book

Shelly Cashman Series - **Custom Edition**® Program

If you do not find a Shelly Cashman Series traditionally bound textbook to fit your needs, the Shelly Cashman Series' unique **Custom Edition** program allows you to choose from a number of options and create a textbook perfectly suited to your course. Features of the **Custom Edition** program are:

- Textbooks that match the content of your course
- Windows- and DOS-based materials for the latest versions of personal computer applications software
- Shelly Cashman Series quality, with the same full-color materials and Shelly Cashman Series pedagogy found in the traditionally bound books
- Affordable pricing so your students receive the **Custom Edition** at a cost similar to that of traditionally bound books

The table on the right summarizes the available materials.

For more information, see your Course Technology representative or call 1-800-648-7450.

For Shelly Cashman Series information, visit Shelly Cashman Online at http://www.bf.com/scseries.html

COMPUTERS	
Computers	Using Computers: A Gateway to Information, World Wide Web Edition Using Computers: A Gateway to Information, World Wide Web Brief Edition Using Computers: A Gateway to Information Using Computers: A Gateway to Information, Brief Edition A Record of Discovery for Exploring Computers (available with CD-ROM) Study Guide for Using Computers: A Gateway to Information, World Wide Web Edition Study Guide for Using Computers: A Gateway to Information Introduction to Computers (32-page)
OPERATING SYSTEMS	
Windows	Microsoft Windows 95: Introductory Concepts and Techniques (96-page) Introduction to Microsoft Windows 95 (224-page) Microsoft Windows 95: Complete Concepts and Techniques Microsoft Windows 3.1 Introductory Concepts and Techniques Microsoft Windows 3.1 Complete Concepts and Techniques
DOS	Introduction to DOS 6 (using DOS prompt) Introduction to DOS 5.0 or earlier (using DOS prompt)
WINDOWS APPLICATIONS	
Integrated Packages	Microsoft Works 4 for Windows 95* Microsoft Works 3.0* Microsoft Works 3.0—Short Course Microsoft Works 2.0
Microsoft Office	Using Microsoft Office (16-page) Object Linking and Embedding (OLE) (32-page) Schedule+ 7
Word Processing	Microsoft Word 7* • Microsoft Word 6* • Microsoft Word 2.0 WordPerfect 6.1* • WordPerfect 6* • WordPerfect 5.2
Spreadsheets	Microsoft Excel 7* • Microsoft Excel 5* • Microsoft Excel 4 Lotus 1-2-3 Release 5* • Lotus 1-2-3 Release 4* Quattro Pro 6 • Quattro Pro 5
Database Management	Microsoft Access 7* • Microsoft Access 2* Paradox 5 • Paradox 4.5 • Paradox 1.0 • Visual dBASE 5/5.5
Presentation Graphics	Microsoft PowerPoint 7* • Microsoft PowerPoint 4*
DOS APPLICATIONS	
Integrated Package	Microsoft Works 3.0
Word Processing	WordPerfect 6.1 • WordPerfect 6.0 WordPerfect 5.1 Step-by-Step Function Key Edition WordPerfect 5.1 Function Key Edition Microsoft Word 5.0
Spreadsheets	Lotus 1-2-3 Release 4 • Lotus 1-2-3 Release 2.4 • Lotus 1-2-3 Release 2.3 Lotus 1-2-3 Release 2.2 • Lotus 1-2-3 Release 2.01 Quattro Pro 3.0 • Quattro with 1-2-3 Menus
Database Management	dBASE 5 • dBASE IV Version 1.1 • dBASE III PLUS Paradox 4.5 • Paradox 3.5
PROGRAMMING AND NETWORKING	
Programming	Introduction to Microsoft Visual Basic 4* (available with Student version of Visual Basic 4) • Microsoft Visual Basic 3.0 for Windows* Microsoft BASIC QBasic
Networking	Novell NetWare for Users
Internet	The Internet: Introductory Concepts and Techniques (UNIX) Netscape Navigator 3: An Introduction Netscape Navigator 2 running under Windows 3.1 Netscape Navigator: An Introduction (Version 1.1) Netscape Navigator Gold: Creating Web Pages

*Also available as a mini-module

PROJECT ONE

Creating a Worksheet and Embedded Chart

PROJECT TWO

Formulas, Formatting, and Creating Charts

PROJECT THREE

What-If Analysis and Working with Large Worksheets

INTEGRATION FEATURE

Linking an Excel Worksheet to a Word Document

Microsoft *Excel 7*

Windows 95

Creating a Worksheet and Embedded Chart

Objectives:

You will have mastered the material in this project when you can:

- Start Excel
- Describe the Excel worksheet
- Select a cell or range of cells
- Enter text and numbers
- Use the AutoSum button to sum a range of cells
- Copy a cell to a range of cells using the fill handle
- Change the size of the font in a cell
- Bold cell entries
- Center cell contents over a series of columns
- Apply the AutoFormat command to format a range
- Use the Name box to select a cell
- Create a column chart using the ChartWizard
- Save a workbook
- Print a worksheet
- Exit Excel
- Open a workbook
- Use the AutoCalculate area to determine totals
- Correct errors on a worksheet
- Use online Help to answer your questions

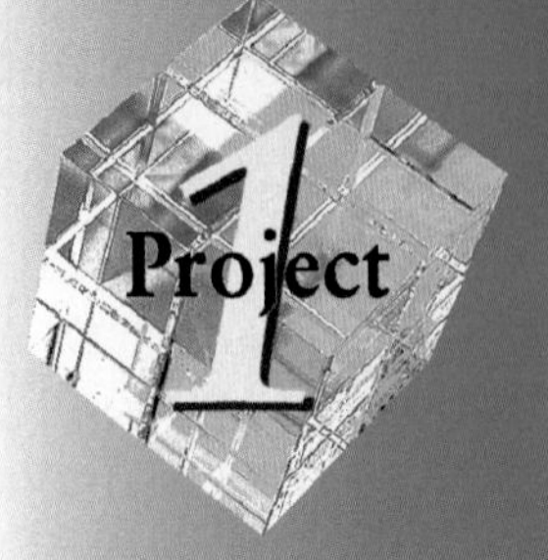

Electronic Spreadsheets *Launch* the Era of Personal Computers

Suppose Ebeneezer Scrooge had gone to Bob Cratchit an hour before quitting time on Christmas Eve and demanded a complete accounting of the business. Poor Cratchit, without calculator or computer, would have spent his Christmas Day laboring over his ledgers, doing the arithmetic in his head, scribing out the columns and rows of figures longhand, knowing that one math error meant he would be looking for work.

Fast-forward one hundred forty years from *A Christmas Carol* to a Harvard classroom, where graduate student Dan Bricklin watched his accounting professor laboriously erasing, re-entering, and then re-calculating tables of numbers in a worksheet. Suddenly, an idea took shape. Bricklin enlisted his friend Bob Frankston and together they designed the first electronic spreadsheet, called VisiCalc (for Visible Calculator). Many people credit VisiCalc with launching the era of the personal computer.

Since VisiCalc, designers have applied accelerating technology to produce increasingly more sophisticated versions of the computer spreadsheet. In simplest terms, an electronic spreadsheet, or worksheet, is a fast, accurate replacement for manual planning tools —

ACCOUNTING

BRICKLIN & FRANKSTON

pencil, accountant's ledger sheet, and calculator — allowing a user to make changes to rows and columns of variable numbers, then quickly to compare and summarize the results.

Microsoft's Excel 7 has taken the art and science of designing worksheets to the next level, providing tools for integrating powerful worksheets with impressive graphics. Excel's intuitive graphical user interface (GUI), hundreds of user features, built-in Wizards, and online demos and examples combine power and attractiveness with ease of creation.

During college years, when most students find themselves on squeaky-tight budgets, worksheets can help in a number of ways. A budget sheet can immediately show the impact if Mom's birthday present was forgotten or a must-see concert has to be squeezed in. A worksheet can amortize student loans to project the salary one needs after graduation to handle the monthly payments. The treasury function for student clubs and organizations can also benefit from worksheet management.

Industry, science, and government routinely use worksheets to build pro forma statements for business start-ups or search for the elusive neutrino or calculate the national debt, to cite a few examples. Sometimes worksheets are of such massive scale that only supercomputers can handle the number of inputs, especially in fields such as astronomy.

Fortunately for Tiny Tim, Scrooge did not ask the impossible of Cratchit. As for Dan Bricklin and Bob Frankston, their names may not be household terms, but for millions of people today, their contribution to personal computing has saved many a midnight dark and dreary. But that is yet another story . . .

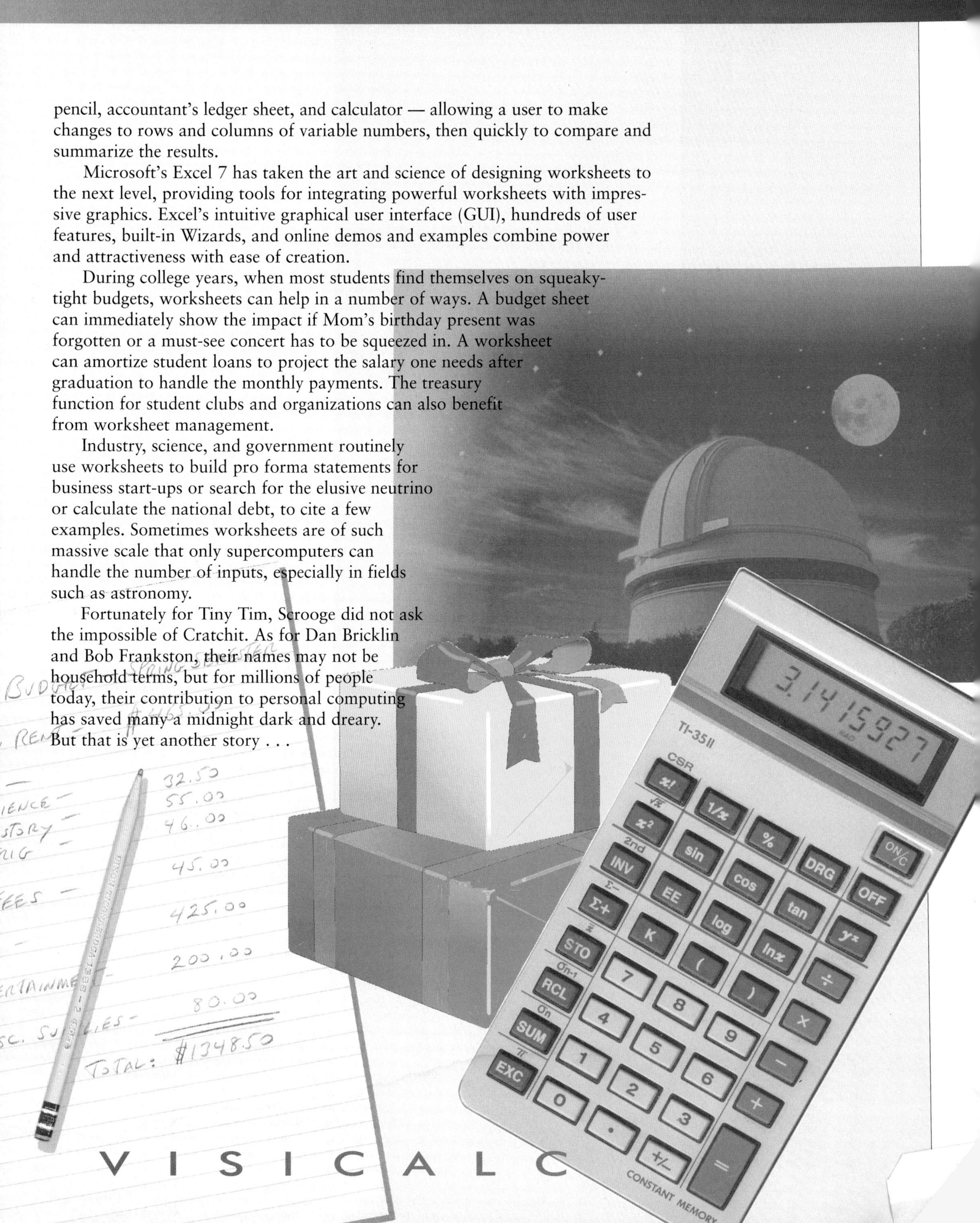

Microsoft
Excel 7
Windows 95

Creating a Worksheet and Embedded Chart

Case Perspective

The Rollablade Company has experienced explosive growth since its inception one year ago. With the popularity of inline skates, the company has grown faster than anyone could have imagined. But therein lies the problem. The management at Rollablade feels that Personnel expenses inside the company are within tolerances, but they are not sure what all the expenses are. They have asked you to prepare a worksheet that specifies company fourth-quarter personnel expenses.

In particular, they want to know the total expenses for Benefits, Travel, and Wages in the following four departments: Marketing, Finance, Sales, and Systems. They want the totals by department and they also want the totals by type of expenses (Benefits, Travel, and Wages).

Your task is to develop a worksheet to show these expenses. In addition, Max Trealer, the president, has asked to see a graphical representation of the expenses because he has little tolerance for lists of numbers.

What Is Microsoft Excel?

Microsoft Excel is a spreadsheet program that allows you to organize data, complete calculations, make decisions, graph data, and develop professional looking reports. The three major parts of Excel are:

- ***Worksheets*** Worksheets allow you to enter, calculate, manipulate, and analyze data such as numbers and text. The term worksheet means the same as spreadsheet.
- ***Charts*** Charts pictorially represent data. Excel can draw a variety of two-dimensional and three-dimensional charts.
- ***Databases*** Databases manage data. For example, once you enter data onto a worksheet, Excel can sort the data, search for specific data, and select data that meets a criteria.

Project One – Rollablade Fourth-Quarter Expenses

From your meeting with the Rollablade management, you have determined the following needs, source of data, calculations, and graph requirements.

Need: A worksheet (Figure 1-1) that shows Rollablade's fourth-quarter expenses (Benefits, Travel, and Wages) for four departments — Marketing, Finance, Sales, and Systems. The worksheet also includes total expenses for each department, each type of expense, and total company expenses for the quarter.

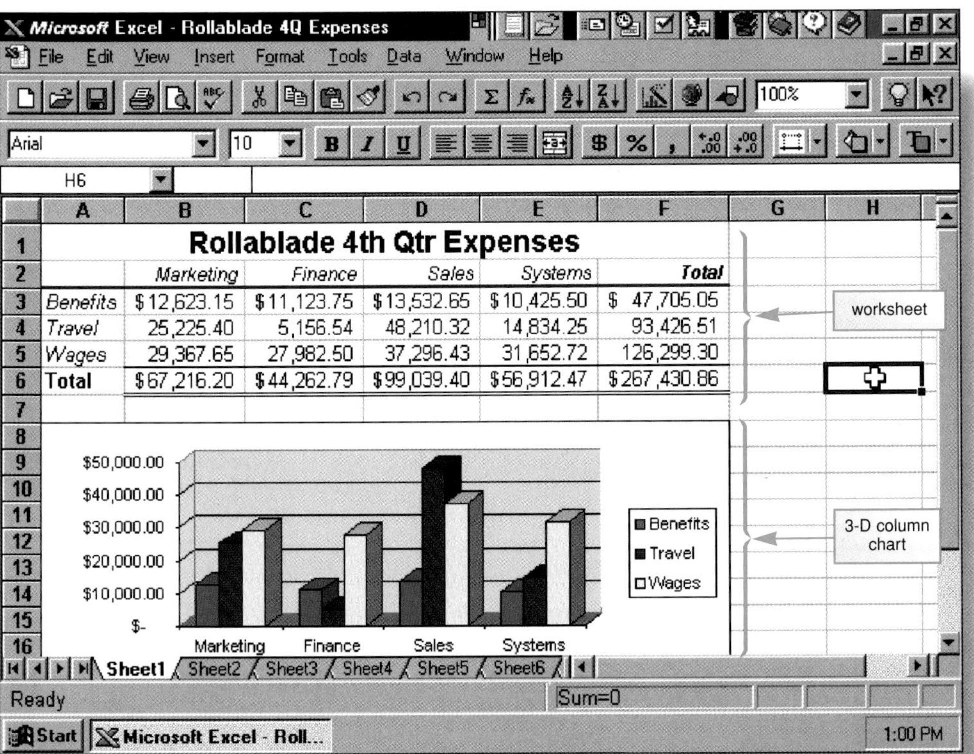

FIGURE 1-1

Source of Data: The data for the worksheet can be found in the personnel department of Rollablade. Harriet Latham, director of personnel, keeps the quarterly expense figures that are calculated by the company's accounting firm. They are typewritten on several different forms.

Calculations: You have determined that the following calculations must be made for the worksheet: (a) A sum for each of the departments (Marketing, Finance, Sales, and Systems) must be calculated; (b) A sum for each type of expense (Benefits, Travel, and Wages) must be calculated; and (c) A total for all expenses also must be calculated. In addition, management has asked that you format the worksheet so it is presentable to the board of directors at the next board meeting.

Graph Requirements: Beneath the worksheet, construct a 3-D column chart that compares the three expense categories for each of the four departments.

More *About* Excel's Ease and Power

Because of Excel's shortcut menus and toolbars, it is one of the easiest, and yet most powerful, worksheet packages available. Its easy-to-use formatting features allow you to produce professional-looking worksheets. Its powerful analytical features make it possible to answer complicated what-if questions with a few clicks of the mouse button.

More *About* Planning a Worksheet

Careful planning can significantly reduce your effort and result in a worksheet that is accurate, easy to read, flexible, and useful. In planning a worksheet, you should follow these steps: (1) define the problem, including need, source of data, calculations, and charting requirements; (2) design the worksheet; (3) enter the data and formulas; and, (4) test the worksheet.

Preparation Steps

The preparation steps below summarize how the worksheet and chart shown in Figure 1-1 will be developed in Project 1.

1. Start the Excel program.
2. Enter the worksheet title (Rollablade 4th Qtr Expenses), the column titles (Marketing, Finance, Sales, Systems, and Total), and the row titles (Benefits, Travel, Wages, and Total).
3. Enter the fourth-quarter expenses (Benefits, Travel, and Wages) for Marketing, Finance, Sales, and Systems.
4. Use the AutoSum button on the Standard toolbar to calculate the first-quarter totals for each department, for each type of expense, and the total quarterly expense for Rollablade.
5. Format the worksheet title (center it across the six columns, enlarge it, and make it bold).
6. Format the body of the worksheet (add underlines, display the numbers in dollars and cents, and add dollar signs).
7. Direct Excel to create the 3-D column chart.
8. Save the worksheet and 3-D column chart on a floppy disk.
9. Print the worksheet and 3-D column chart.
10. Exit Excel.

The following pages contain a detailed explanation of these tasks.

More *About* the Mouse

The mouse unit has been around as long as the personal computer itself. However, it had little use with earlier operating systems, such as MS-DOS. Few used the mouse or even attached it to their computer until recently when Windows began to dominant the market. Even with Windows 95, some former MS-DOS users prefer to use the keyboard over the mouse.

Mouse Usage

In this book, the mouse is the primary way to communicate with Excel. You can perform six operations with a mouse: point, click, right-click, double-click, drag, and right-drag.

Point means you move the mouse across a flat surface until the mouse pointer rests on the item of choice on the screen. As you move the mouse, the mouse pointer moves across the screen in the same direction. **Click** means you press and release the left mouse button. The terminology used in this book to direct you to point to a particular item and then click is, Click the particular item. For example, *Click the Bold button* means point to the Bold button and click.

Right-click means you press and release the right mouse button. As with the left mouse button, you normally will point to an item on the screen prior to right-clicking.

Double-click means you quickly press and release the left mouse button twice without moving the mouse. In most cases, you must point to an item before double-clicking. **Drag** means you point to an item, hold down the left mouse button, move the item to the desired location on the screen, and then release the left mouse button. **Right-drag** means you point to an item, hold down the right mouse button, move the item to the desired location, and then release the right mouse button.

The use of the mouse is an important skill when working with Microsoft Excel for Windows 95.

Starting Excel

To start Excel, Windows 95 must be running. Perform the following steps to start Excel.

Steps To Start Excel

1 **Click the Start button on the taskbar and then point to New Office Document (Figure 1-2).**

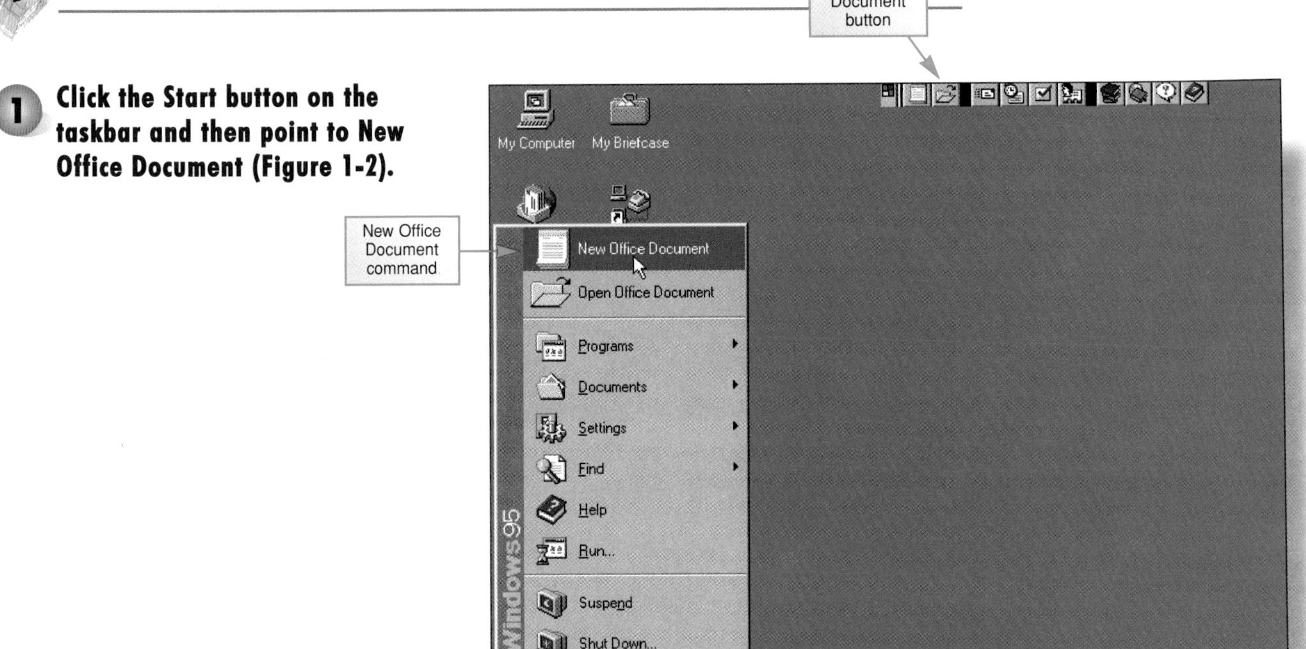

FIGURE 1-2

2 **Click New Office Document. If necessary, click the General tab in the New dialog box, and then point to the Blank Workbook icon (Figure 1-3).**

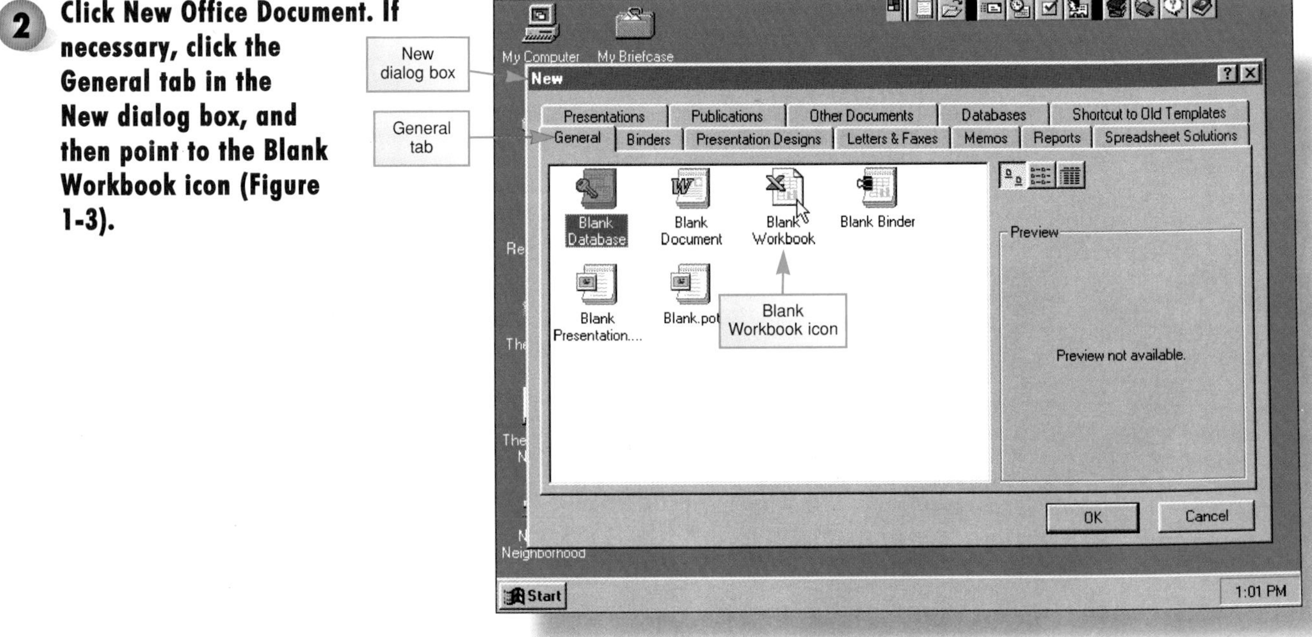

FIGURE 1-3

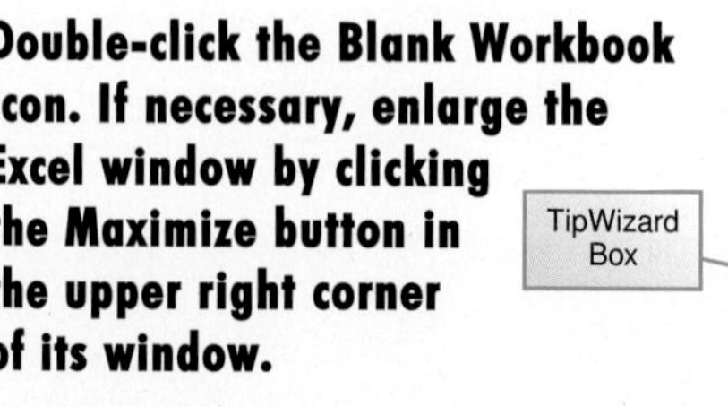

3 **Double-click the Blank Workbook icon. If necessary, enlarge the Excel window by clicking the Maximize button in the upper right corner of its window.**

Excel displays an empty workbook titled Book1 (Figure 1-4).

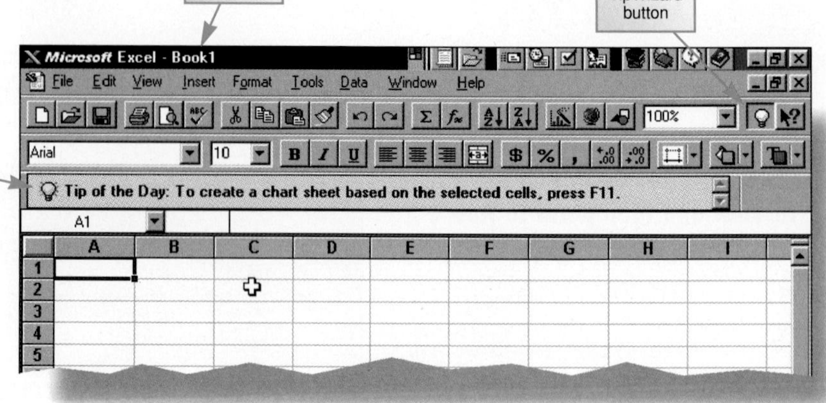

FIGURE 1-4

4 **If the TipWizard Box displays (Figure 1-4), click the TipWizard button on the Standard toolbar.**

Excel removes the TipWizard Box from the window and increases the display of the worksheet (Figure 1-5). The purpose of the TipWizard Box will be discussed later in this project.

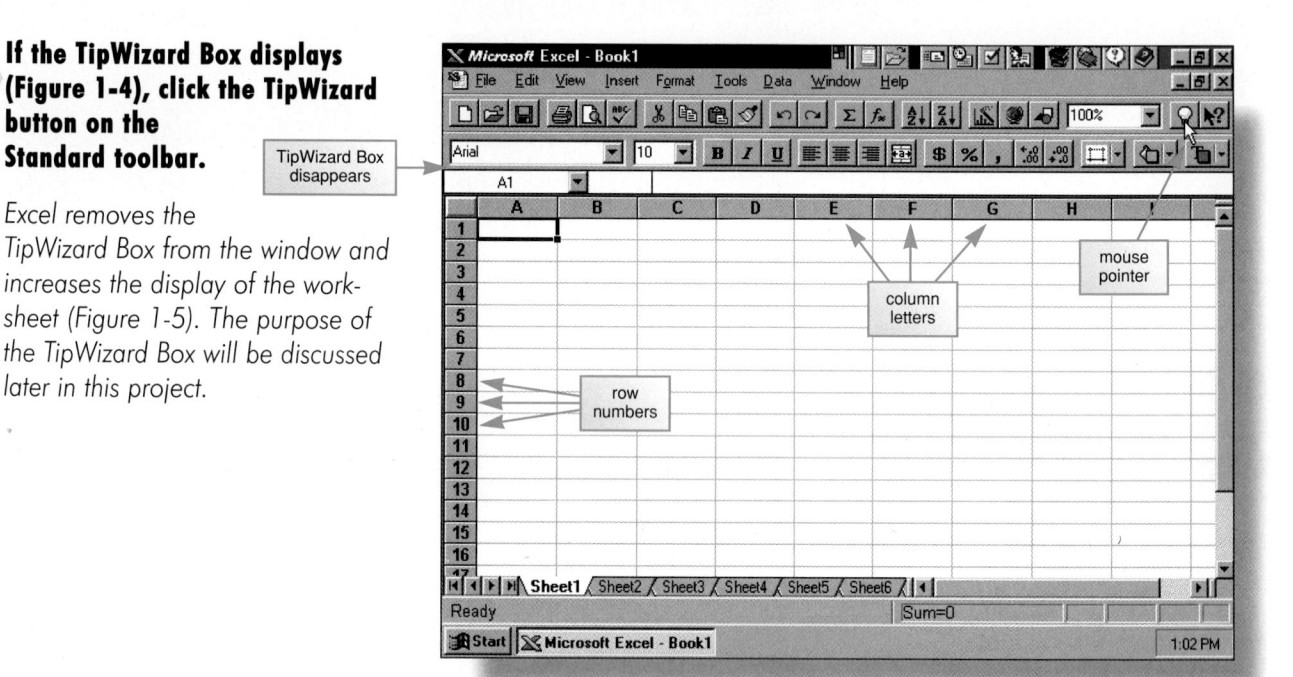

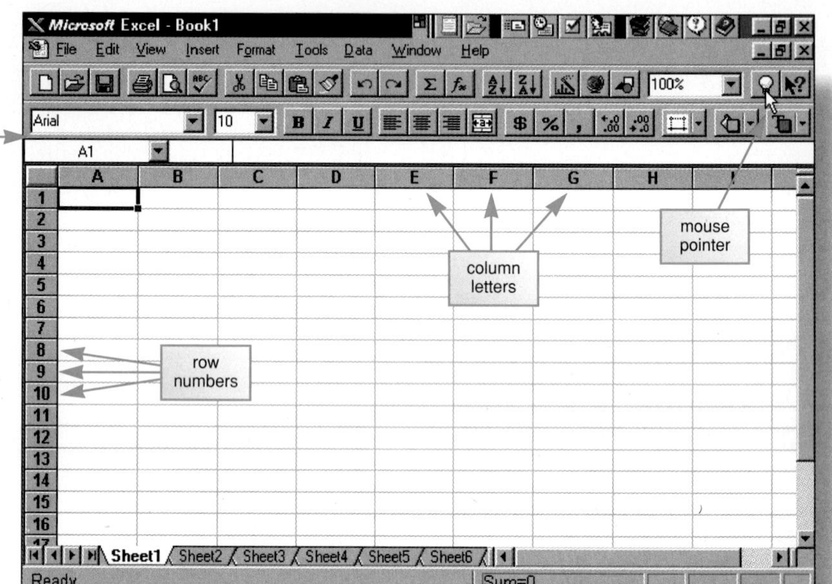

FIGURE 1-5

OtherWays

1. Right-click Start button, click Open, double-click New Office Document
2. On Microsoft Office Shortcut Bar, click Start a New Document button
3. On Start menu click Programs, click Microsoft Excel

The Excel Window

The **Excel window** consists of a variety of features to help you work more efficiently. It contains a title bar, menu bar, toolbars, formula bar, the worksheet window, sheet tabs, scroll bars, and the status bar. Each of these Excel window features and its components is described in this section.

The Workbook

When Excel starts, it creates a new empty workbook, called Book1. The **workbook** (Figure 1-6), is like a notebook. Inside the workbook are sheets, called **worksheets**. Each sheet name appears on a **sheet tab** at the bottom of the workbook. For example, Sheet1 is the name of the active worksheet displayed in the workbook called Book1. If you click on the tab labeled Sheet2, Excel displays the Sheet2 worksheet. A new workbook opens with 16 worksheets. If necessary, you can add additional worksheets to a maximum of 255. This project will use only the Sheet1 worksheet. Later projects will use multiple worksheets in a workbook.

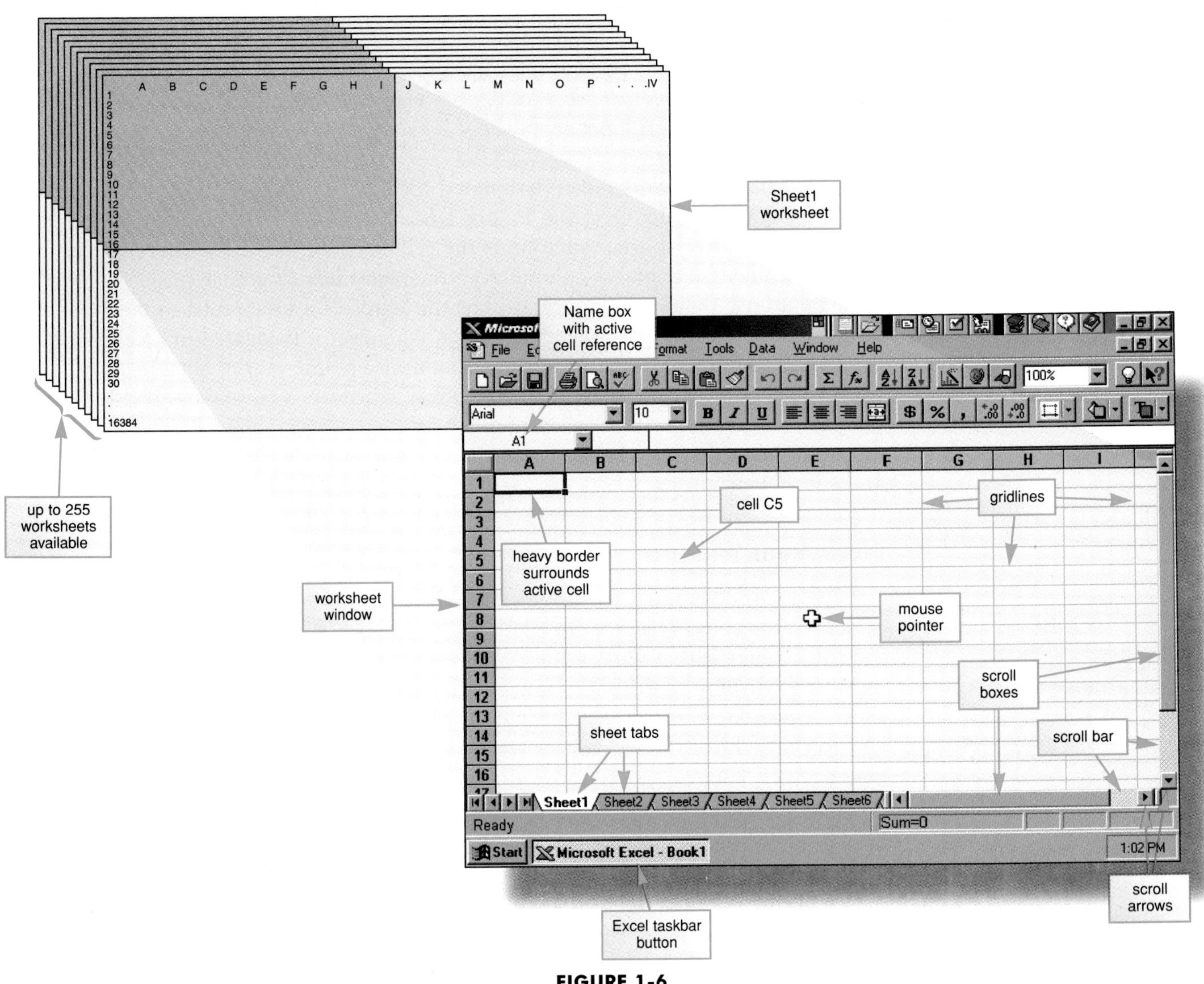

FIGURE 1-6

The Worksheet

The worksheet is organized into a rectangular grid containing columns (vertical) and rows (horizontal). A column letter above the grid, also called the column heading, identifies each **column**. A row number on the left side of the grid, also called the row heading, identifies each **row**. Nine complete columns (A through I) and sixteen complete rows (1 through 16) of the worksheet appear on the screen when the worksheet is maximized and the TipWizard Box is closed as shown earlier in Figure 1-5.

More *About* the TipWizard Box

Ever feel like you're being watched? You are when you use Excel. Excel keeps an eye on the way you work. If you complete a task and Excel knows a better way to carry out the task, it will inform you in the TipWizard Box. If the TipWizard Box is hidden, the light bulb icon on the TipWizard button (Figure 1-4) will light up when Excel adds a tip to the TipWizard Box. Click the TipWizard button to display or hide the TipWizard Box.

Cell, Gridlines, Active Cell, and Mouse Pointer

The intersection of each column and row is a **cell**. A cell is the basic unit of a worksheet into which you enter data. A cell is referred to by its unique address, or **cell reference**, which is the coordinates of the intersection of a column and a row. To identify a cell, specify the column letter first, followed by the row number. For example, cell reference C5 refers to the cell located at the intersection of column C and row 5 (see Figure 1-6 on the previous page).

The horizontal and vertical lines on the worksheet itself are called **gridlines**. Gridlines make it easier to see and identify each cell in the worksheet. If desired, you can remove the gridlines from the worksheet, but it is recommended that you leave the gridlines on.

More *About* the Mouse Pointer

The mouse pointer can become one of fourteen different shapes, such as an arrow, cross hair, or chart symbol, depending on the task you are performing in Excel and the mouse pointer's location on the screen.

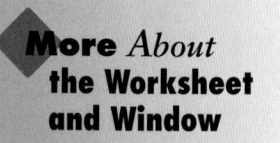

One cell on the worksheet, designated the **active cell**, is the one in which you can enter data. The active cell in Figure 1-6 is A1. Cell A1 is identified in two ways. First, a heavy border surrounds the cell. Second, the **active cell reference** displays immediately above column A in the **Name box** (Figure 1-6).

The mouse pointer in Figure 1-6 has the shape of a block plus sign. The mouse pointer displays as a **block plus sign** whenever it is located in a cell in the worksheet. Another common shape of the mouse pointer is the block arrow. The mouse pointer turns into the **block arrow** whenever you move it outside the window or when you drag cell contents between rows or columns. The other mouse pointer shapes are described when they appear on the screen during this and subsequent projects.

Worksheet Window

More *About* the Worksheet and Window

256 columns and 16,384 rows make for a gigantic worksheet! So big in fact that you might imagine it takes up the entire wall of a large room. Go one step further and imagine you can only view a small area of the worksheet on the wall at one time through your computer screen. The bad news is you can't see the entire worksheet at any one time. The good news is that you can quickly move the computer screen over the worksheet and view any part of it.

Each worksheet in a workbook has 256 columns and 16,384 rows for a total of 4,194,304 cells. The column headings begin with A and end with IV. The row headings begin with 1 and end with 16,384. Only a small fraction of the active worksheet displays on the screen at one time. You view the portion of the worksheet displayed on the screen through a **worksheet window** (Figure 1-6). Below and to the right of the worksheet window are **scroll bars**, **scroll arrows**, and **scroll boxes** which you can use to move the window around to view different parts of the active worksheet. To the right of the sheet tabs at the bottom of the screen is the tab split box. You can drag the **tab split box** (Figure 1-7) to increase or decrease the view of the sheet tabs.

Menu Bar, Standard Toolbar, Formatting Toolbar, Formula Bar, Sheet and Scroll Tabs, and Status Bar

The menu bar, Standard toolbar, Formatting toolbar, and formula bar appear at the top of the screen just below the title bar (Figure 1-7). The sheet tabs, tab scrolling buttons, and the status bar appear at the bottom of the screen, above the Windows 95 taskbar.

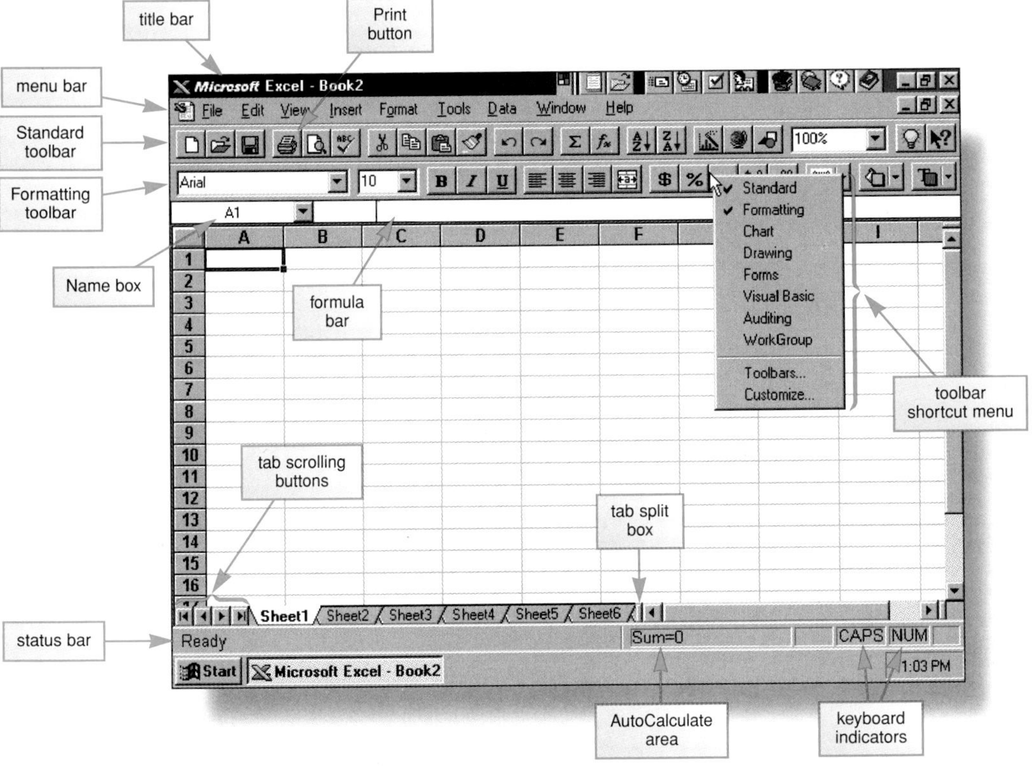

FIGURE 1-7

MENU BAR The **menu bar** displays the Excel menu names (Figure 1-7). Each menu name represents a menu of commands that you can use to retrieve, store, print, and manipulate data on the worksheet. To display a menu, such as the **File menu**, click the menu name File on the menu bar.

The menu bar can change to include other menu names depending on the type of work you are doing in Excel. For example, if you are working with a chart sheet rather than a worksheet, the menu bar names will reflect charting command options.

STANDARD TOOLBAR AND FORMATTING TOOLBAR The **Standard toolbar** and **Formatting toolbar** (Figure 1-7) contain buttons and drop-down list boxes that allow you to perform frequent tasks more quickly than when using the menu bar. For example, to print a worksheet, you click the Print button. Each button has a picture on the button face that helps you remember the button's function. Also, when you move the mouse pointer over a button or box, the name of the button or box appears below it. This is called a **ToolTip**.

Figure 1-8 on the next page illustrates the Standard and Formatting toolbars and describes the functions of the buttons. Each of the buttons and drop-down list boxes will be explained in detail when they are used in the projects.

More *About* **Your Screen Display**

If you're distracted by all the buttons and bars on your screen, you can increase the number of rows and columns displayed by clicking Full Screen on the View menu. Excel will immediately hide the buttons and bars, thus increasing the size of your window. Excel also displays a small toolbar with the Full Screen button on it. Click the Full Screen button to return to normal display.

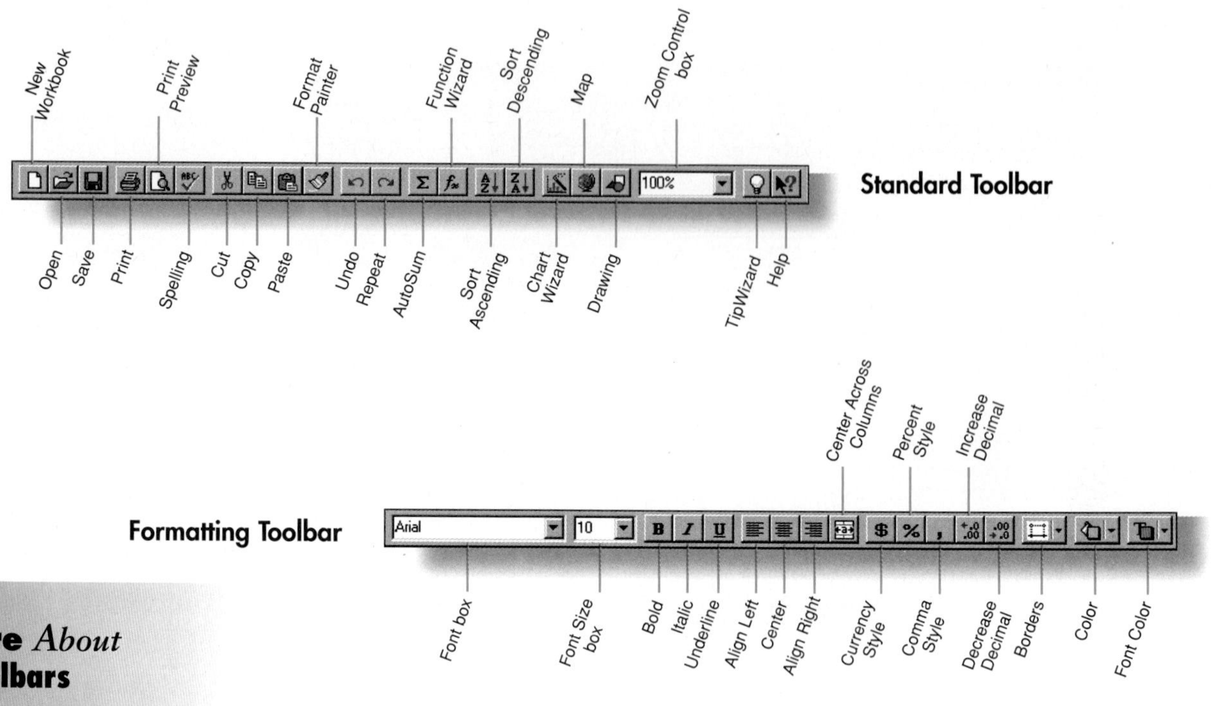

FIGURE 1-8

More *About* Toolbars

Do not be overly concerned if your toolbars have a different set of buttons. It probably means that a previous user changed the toolbars by using the Customize command on the shortcut menu (Figure 1-7) to add or delete buttons. To reset the Standard or Formatting toolbars so they appear as showin in Figure 1-8, right-click any toolbar, click Toolbars, click the toolbar name to reset, click the Reset button, and click the OK button.

Excel has several additional toolbars you can activate by clicking View on the menu bar. You can also point to a toolbar, such as the Formatting toolbar, and then right-click to display a shortcut menu, which lists the toolbars available (see Figure 1-7 on the previous page). A **shortcut menu** contains a list of commands or items to choose from that relate to the item you are pointing to when you right-click. Once a shortcut menu displays, you can click or right-click a command or item. The check mark to the left of Standard and Formatting in the shortcut menu in Figure 1-7 indicates they are displaying on the screen.

FORMULA BAR Below the Formatting toolbar is the **formula bar** (Figure 1-7). As you type, the data appears in the formula bar. Excel also displays the active cell reference on the left side of the formula bar in the Name box.

More *About* Shortcut Menus

Shortcut menus display the most frequently used commands that relate to the object the mouse pointer is pointing to. To display a shortcut menu, right-click the object. You can also display the shortcut menu by selecting the object and pressing SHIFT+F10. To hide a shortcut menu, click outside the shortcut menu or press ESC

STATUS BAR Immediately above the Windows 95 taskbar is the status bar. The **status bar** displays a brief description of the command selected (highlighted) in a menu, the function of the button the mouse pointer is on (Figure 1-7), or the current activity (mode) in progress (Figure 1-7). **Mode indicators**, such as Enter and Ready, specify the current mode of Excel. When the mode is Ready, Excel is ready to accept the next command or data entry. When the mode indicator is Enter, Excel is in the process of accepting data through the keyboard for the active cell.

In the middle of the status bar is the AutoCalculate area. The **AutoCalculate area** can be used in place of a calculator to view the sum or average or other types of totals of a group of numbers on the worksheet.

Keyboard indicators, such as CAPS (Caps Lock) and NUM (Num Lock), show which keys are engaged. Keyboard indicators display on the right side of the status bar within the small rectangular boxes (Figure 1-7).

Selecting a Cell

To enter data into a cell, you must first select it. The easiest way to **select a cell** (make active) is to use the mouse to move the block plus sign to the cell and click.

An alternative method is to use the **arrow keys** that are located just to the right of the typewriter keys on the keyboard. An arrow key selects the cell adjacent to the active cell in the direction of the arrow on the key.

You know a cell is selected (active) when a heavy border surrounds the cell and the active cell reference displays in the Name box on the left side of the formula bar.

Entering Text

In Excel, any set of characters containing a letter, hyphen (as in a telephone number) or space is considered **text**. Text is used to place titles on the worksheet, such as worksheet titles, column titles, and row titles. In Project 1 (Figure 1-9), the centered worksheet title, Rollablade 4th Qtr Expenses, in row 1 identifies the worksheet. The column titles in row 2 are the names of departments (Marketing, Finance, Sales, and Systems) and Total. The row titles in column A (Benefits, Travel, Wages, and Total) identify the data in each row.

More *About* **Entering Text**

A text entry in a cell can contain from 1 to 255 characters. Text entries are primarily used to identify parts of the worksheet, such as worksheet titles, column titles, and row titles. However, there are applications in which text entries are data that you dissect, string together, and manipulate using text functions.

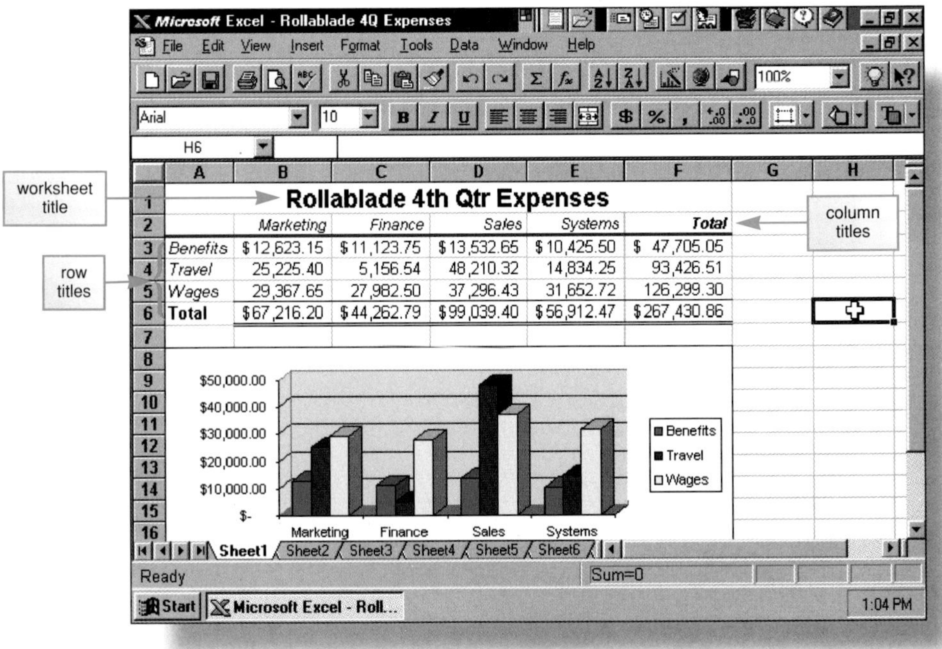

FIGURE 1-9

Entering the Worksheet Title

The following steps show how to enter the worksheet title (Rollablade 4th Qtr Expenses) into cell A1. Later in this project, the worksheet title will be centered over the column titles as shown in Figure 1-9.

To Enter the Worksheet Title

1 Click cell A1.

Cell A1 becomes the active cell and a heavy border surrounds it (Figure 1-10).

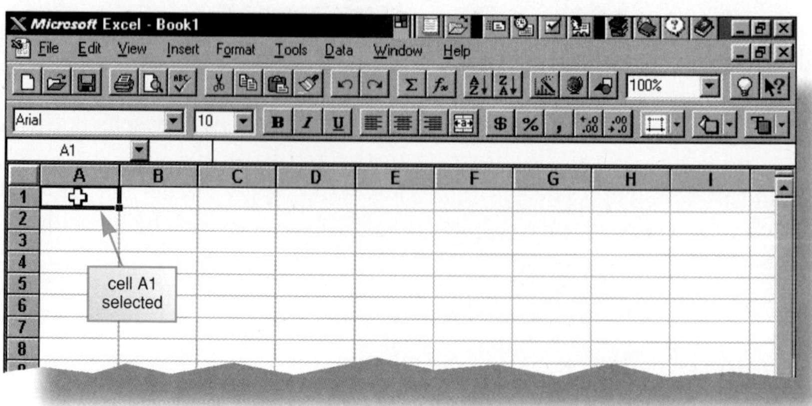

FIGURE 1-10

2 Type `Rollablade 4th Qtr Expenses` **in cell A1.**

When you type the first character, the mode indicator in the status bar changes from Ready to Enter and Excel displays three boxes: the ***cancel box****, the* ***enter box****, and the* ***Function Wizard box*** *in the formula bar (Figure 1-11). The entire title displays in the formula bar and the text also displays in cell A1 followed immediately by the insertion point. The* ***insertion point*** *is a blinking vertical line that indicates where the next character typed will appear.*

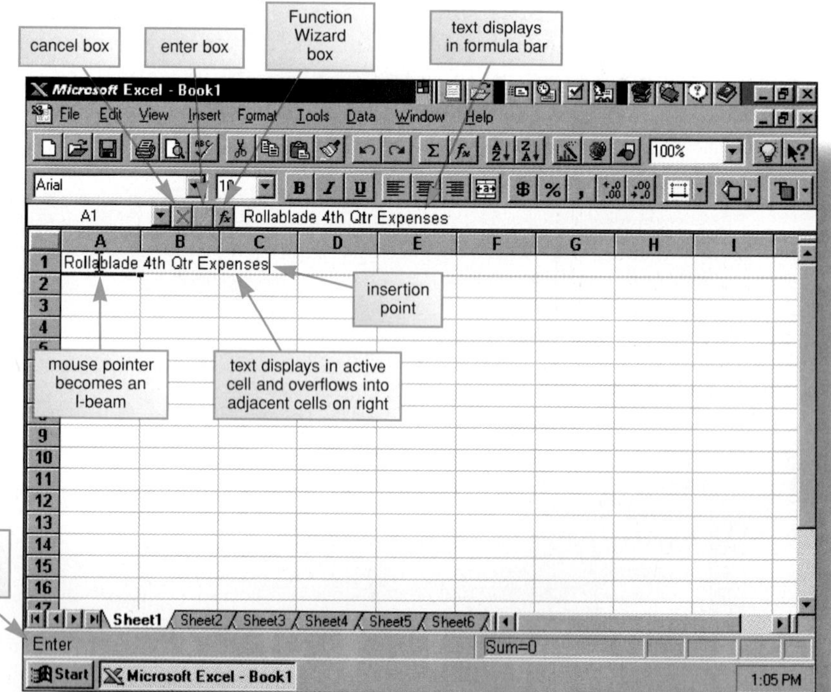

FIGURE 1-11

3 After you type the text, point to the enter box (Figure 1-12).

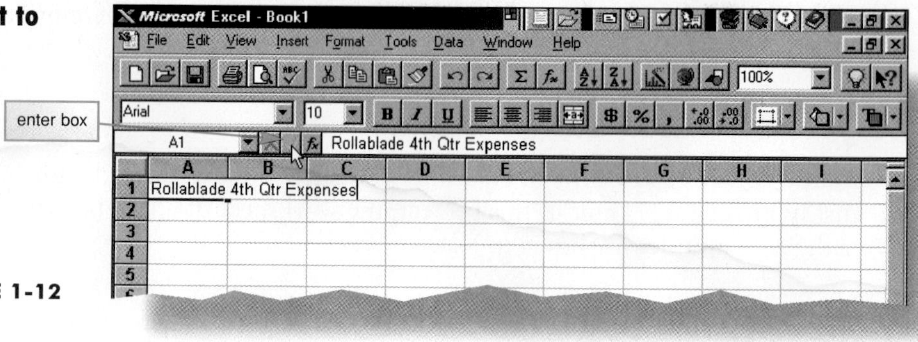

enter box

FIGURE 1-12

4 **Click the enter box to complete the entry.**

Excel enters the worksheet title in cell A1 (Figure 1-13).

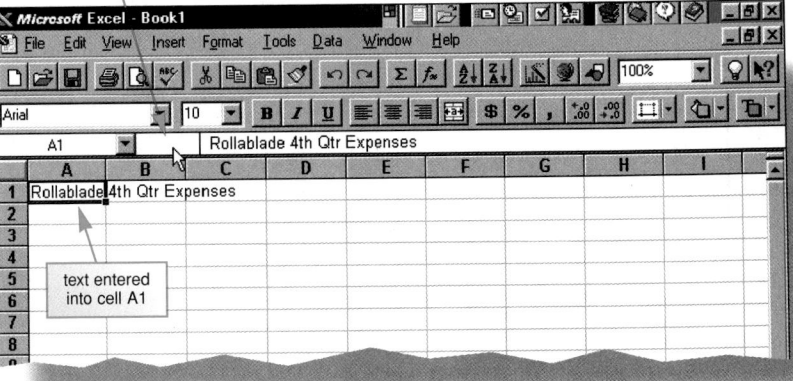

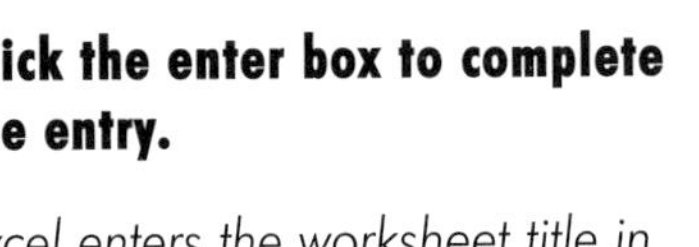

FIGURE 1-13

OtherWays

1. Click any cell other than active cell
2. Press ENTER
3. Press an arrow key
4. Press HOME, PAGE UP, PAGE DOWN, or END

When you complete a text entry into a cell, a series of events occurs. First, Excel positions the text left-justified in the active cell. **Left-justified** means the cell entry is to the far left in the cell. Therefore, the R in the company name Rollablade begins in the leftmost position of cell A1.

Second, when the text is longer than the width of a column, Excel displays the overflow characters in adjacent cells to the right as long as these adjacent cells contain no data. In Figure 1-13, the width of cell A1 is approximately nine characters. The text entered consists of 27 characters. Therefore, Excel displays the overflow characters in cells B1 and C1, because both cells are empty.

If cell B1 contained data, only the first nine characters of cell A1 would display on the worksheet. Excel would hide the overflow characters, but they would still remain stored in cell A1 and display in the formula bar whenever cell A1 was the active cell.

Third, when you complete an entry by clicking the enter box, the cell in which the text is entered remains the active cell.

More About the ENTER key

Unless you are entering large amounts of data onto a worksheet, you will probably want the ENTER key to complete an entry without changing the active cell location. If pressing the ENTER key changes the active cell location and you prefer for it to remain on the cell you entered data into, or you want it to move in another direction, click Options on the Tools menu, click the Edit tab, click the Move Selection after Enter check box to clear or select a new direction, and then click OK.

Correcting a Mistake While Typing

If you type the wrong letter and notice the error before clicking the enter box or pressing the ENTER key, use the **BACKSPACE key** to erase all the characters back to and including the one that is wrong. To cancel the entire entry before entering it into the cell, click the cancel box in the formula bar or press the **ESC key** . If you see an error in a cell, select the cell and retype the entry. Later in this project, additional error-correction techniques are covered.

AutoCorrect

The **AutoCorrect feature** of Excel works behind the scenes, correcting common mistakes when you complete text entry in a cell. AutoCorrect makes three types of corrections for you:

1. Corrects two initial capital letters by changing the second letter to lowercase.
2. Capitalizes the first letter in the names of days.

More About the AutoCorrect Feature

AutoCorrect is part of the IntelliSense™ technology that is built into Excel, which understands what you are trying to do and helps you do it.

3. Replaces commonly misspelled words with their correct spelling. For example, it will correct the misspelled word *recieve* to *receive* when you press the ENTER key, click the enter box, or press an arrow key to complete an entry. AutoCorrect will automatically correct the spelling of more than 400 words.

You can add to the list of misspelled words and their corresponding corrections or turn off any of the AutoCorrect features by clicking **AutoCorrect** on the Tools menu.

Entering Column Titles

To enter the column titles, select the appropriate cell and then enter the text, as described in the following steps.

Steps To Enter the Column Titles

1 Click cell B2.

Cell B2 becomes the active cell. The active cell reference in the Name box changes from A1 to B2 (Figure 1-14).

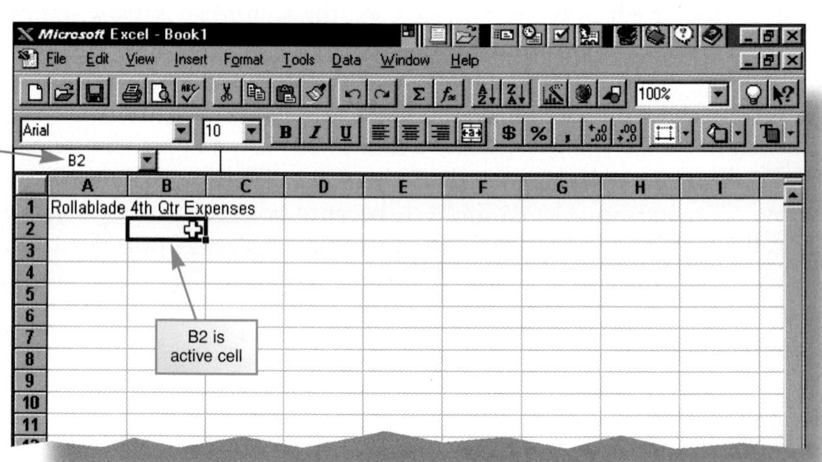

FIGURE 1-14

2 Type `Marketing` **in cell B2.**

Excel displays Marketing in the formula bar and in cell B2 (Figure 1-15).

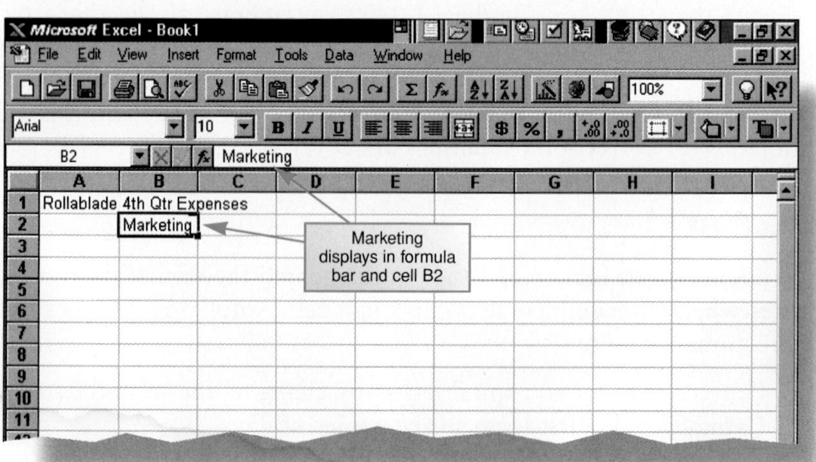

FIGURE 1-15

3 **Press the RIGHT ARROW key.**

Excel enters the column title, Marketing, in cell B2 and makes cell C2 the active cell (Figure 1-16). When you press an arrow key to complete an entry, the adjacent cell in the direction of the arrow (up, down, left, or right) becomes the active cell.

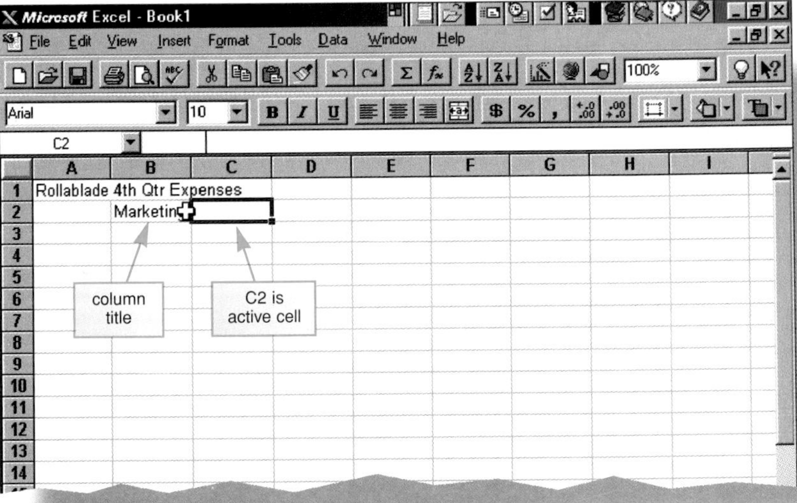

FIGURE 1-16

4 **Repeat Step 2 and Step 3 for the remaining column titles in row 2. That is, enter** `Finance` **in cell C2,** `Sales` **in cell D2,** `Systems` **in cell E2, and** `Total` **in cell F2. Complete the last column title entry in cell F2 by clicking the enter box or by pressing the ENTER key.**

The column titles display left-justified as shown in Figure 1-17.

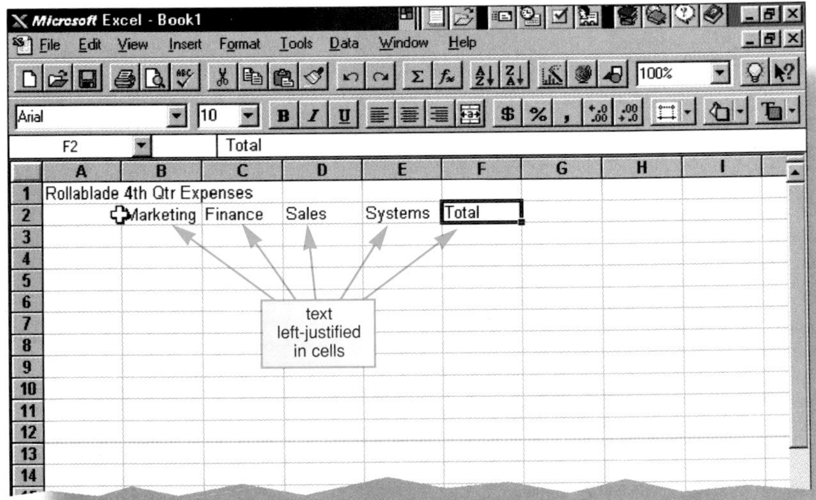

FIGURE 1-17

To complete an entry in a cell, use the arrow keys if the next entry is in an adjacent cell. If the next entry is not in an adjacent cell, click the next cell you plan to enter data in or click the enter box in the formula bar or press the ENTER key and then click the appropriate cell for the next entry.

Entering Row Titles

The next step in developing the worksheet in Project 1 is to enter the row titles in column A. This process is similar to entering the column titles and is described in the steps on the next page.

More *About* Entering Data

Tired of entering similar data? Excel remembers the data you have entered into consecutive cells in a column. Thus, if you enter the first few characters, Excel will handle the rest. This is called the AutoComplete feature. If you want to pick an entry from a list of column entries, right-click on a cell in the column and click Pick from List.

Steps To Enter Row Titles

1. **Click cell A3.**

   Cell A3 becomes the active cell (Figure 1-18). The active cell reference in the Name box changes from F2 to A3.

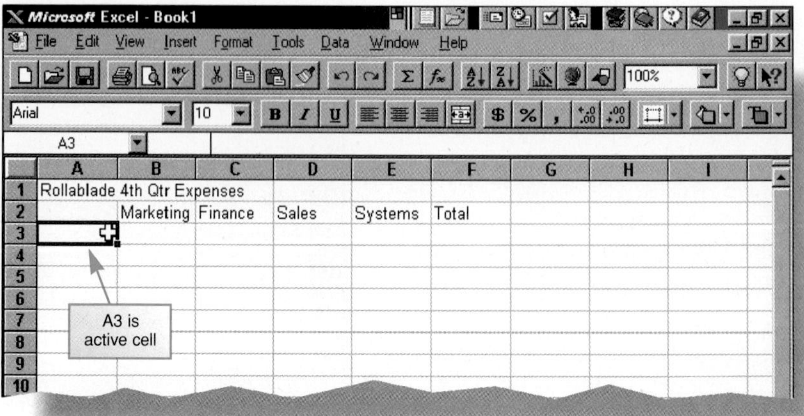

FIGURE 1-18

2. **Type** `Benefits` **and then press the DOWN ARROW key.**

   Excel enters the row title Benefits in cell A3 and cell A4 becomes the active cell (Figure 1-19).

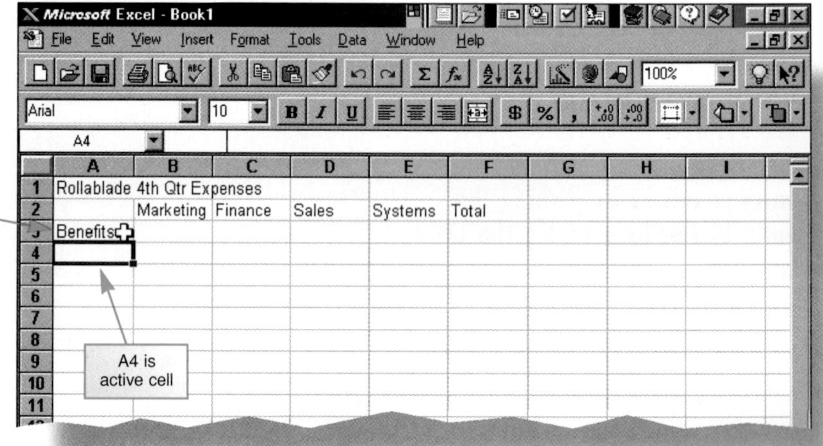

FIGURE 1-19

3. **Repeat Step 2 for the remaining row titles in column A. Enter** `Travel` **in cell A4,** `Wages` **in cell A5, and** `Total` **in cell A6. Complete the last row title in cell A6 by clicking the enter box or by pressing the ENTER key.**

   The row titles display as shown in Figure 1-20.

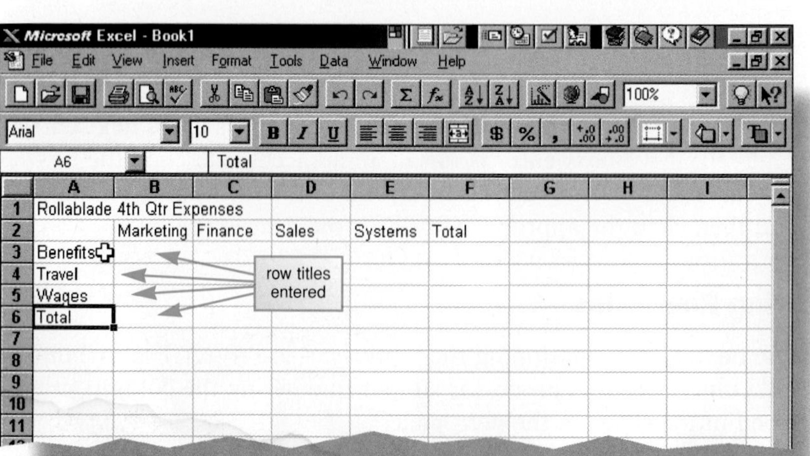

FIGURE 1-20

Entering Numbers

In Excel, you can enter numbers into cells to represent amounts. **Numbers** can include the digits zero through nine and any one of the following special characters:

+ - ( ) , / . $ % E e

If a cell entry contains any other character (including spaces) from the keyboard, Excel interprets the entry as text and treats it accordingly. The use of the special characters is explained when they are required in a project.

Table 1-1

	MARKETING	*FINANCE*	*SALES*	*SYSTEMS*
Benefits	**$12,623.15**	**$11,123.75**	**$13,532.65**	**$10,425.50**
Travel	**25,225.40**	**5,156.54**	**48,210.32**	**14,834.25**
Wages	**29,367.65**	**27,982.50**	**37,296.43**	**31,652.72**

In Project 1, the expenses for Benefits, Travel, and Wages for each of the four departments (Marketing, Finance, Sales, and Systems) obtained from Harriet Latham, director of personnel at Rollablade, are summarized in Table 1-1.

These numbers must be entered in rows 3, 4, and 5. The following steps illustrate how to enter these values one row at a time.

More *About* **Entering Numbers as Text**

There are times when you will want numbers, such as zip codes, to be handled by Excel as text. To enter a number as text, start the entry with an apostrophe (').

Steps To Enter Numeric Data

1 **Click cell B3.**

Cell B3 becomes the active cell (Figure 1-21).

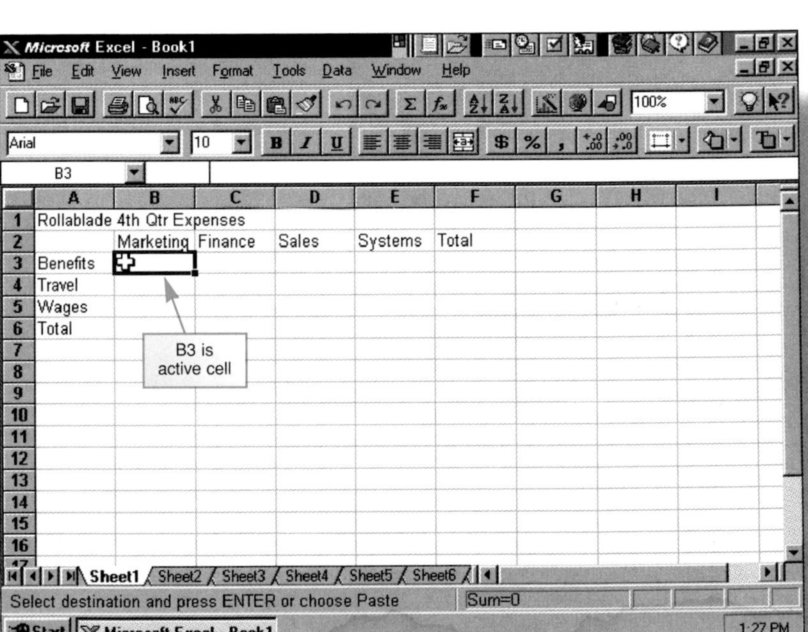

FIGURE 1-21

2 **Type** 12623.15 **and then press the RIGHT ARROW key.**

Excel enters the number 12623.15 right-justified in cell B3 and changes the active cell to cell C3 (Figure 1-22). The numbers on the worksheet are formatted with dollar signs and cents later in this project.

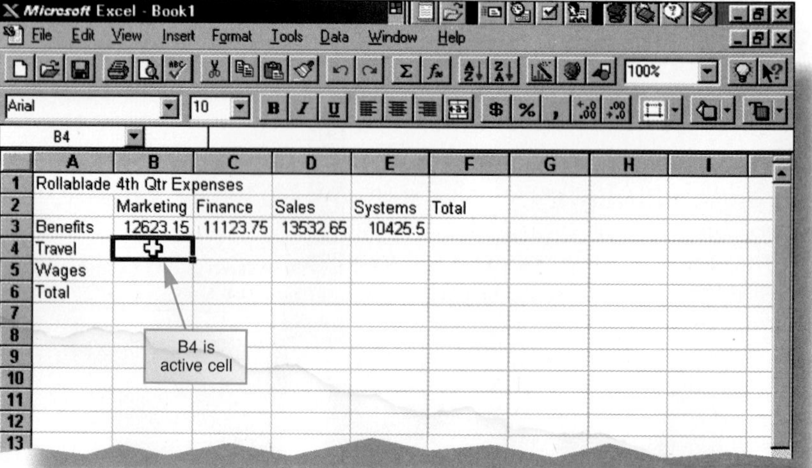

FIGURE 1-22

3 **Enter** 11123.75 **in cell C3,** 13532.65 **in cell D3, and** 10425.5 **in cell E3.**

Row 3 now contains the fourth-quarter benefit expenses all right-justified (Figure 1-23). ***Right-justified*** *means the cell entry is to the far right in the cell.*

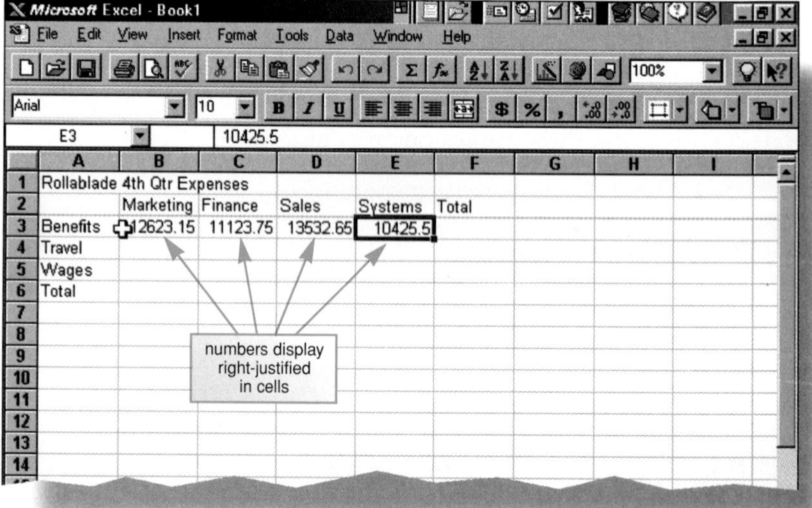

FIGURE 1-23

4 **Click cell B4 (Figure 1-24).**

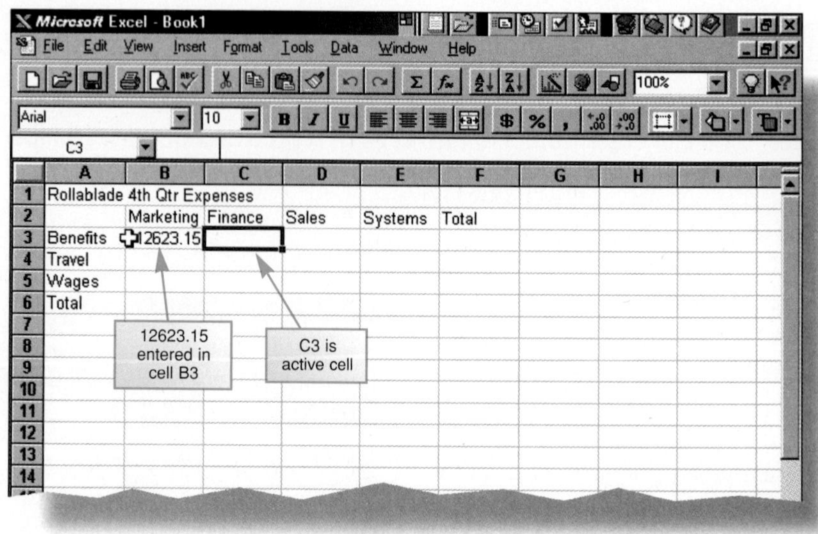

FIGURE 1-24

5 **Enter the fourth-quarter travel expenses for the four departments (**25225.4 **for Marketing,** 5156.54 **for Finance,** 48210.32 **for Sales, and** 14834.25 **for Systems) and the 4th quarter wage expenses for the four departments (**29367.65 **for Marketing,** 27982.5 **for Finance,** 37296.43 **for Sales, and** 31652.72 **for Systems).**

The fourth-quarter travel and wages expenses for the four departments display in row 4 and row 5 (Figure 1-25).

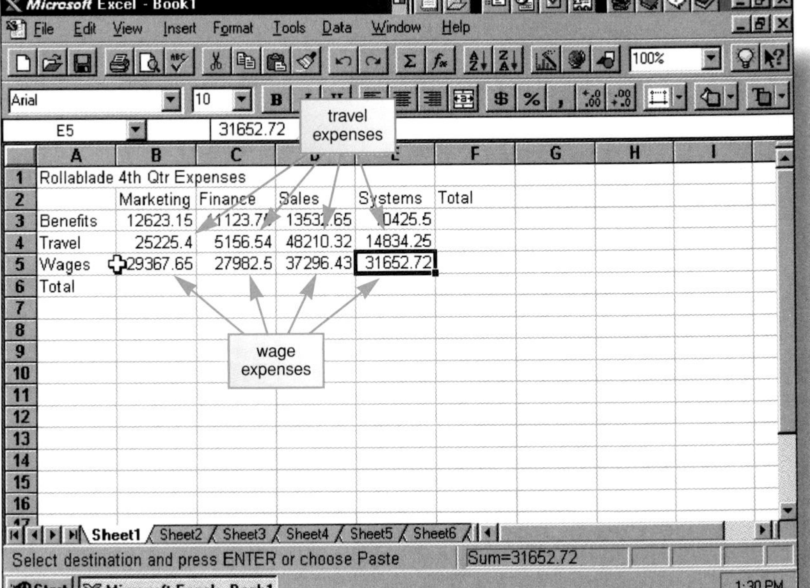

FIGURE 1-25

Steps 1 through 5 complete the numeric entries. Notice several important points. First, you are not required to type dollar signs and trailing zeros. Later, dollar signs will be added as previously described in Figure 1-1 on page E 1.7. When you enter a number that has cents, however, you must add the decimal point and the numbers representing the cents when you enter the number. You do not have to enter trailing zeros to the right of the decimal point. Second, Excel stores numbers right-justified in the cells. Third, the next section instructs Excel to calculate the totals in row 6 and in column F. Indeed, the capability of Excel to perform calculations is one of its major features.

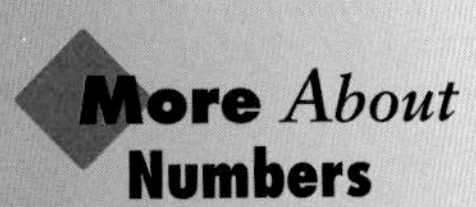

More *About* **Numbers**

How big can numbers get in Excel? A number in Excel can be between approximately -1 x 10^{307} and 1 x 10^{307}. To enter a number such as 93,000,000,000 you can enter the number as it is or type 9.3E10 which stands for 9.3 x 10^{10}. If the cell is not wide enough to display a number, Excel will display it in Scientific format if no format has been assigned to the cell. For example, the number 12,345,678,901 displays as 1.2346E+10. If a format has been assigned to a cell with a large number, Excel displays number signs (#) in the cell to indicate the number cannot display properly, unless you widen the cell.

Calculating a Sum

The next step in creating the expense worksheet is to determine the total expenses for the Marketing department. To calculate this value in cell B6, Excel must add the numbers in cells B3, B4, and B5. Excel's **SUM function** provides a convenient means to accomplish this task.

To use the SUM function, first you must identify the cell in which the sum will be stored after it is calculated. Then, you can use the **AutoSum button** on the Standard toolbar to enter the SUM function.

Although you can enter the SUM function in cell B6 through the keyboard as =SUM(B3:B6), the following steps illustrate how to use the AutoSum button to accomplish the same task.

Steps To Sum a Column of Numbers

1 Click cell B6.

Cell B6 becomes the active cell (Figure 1-26).

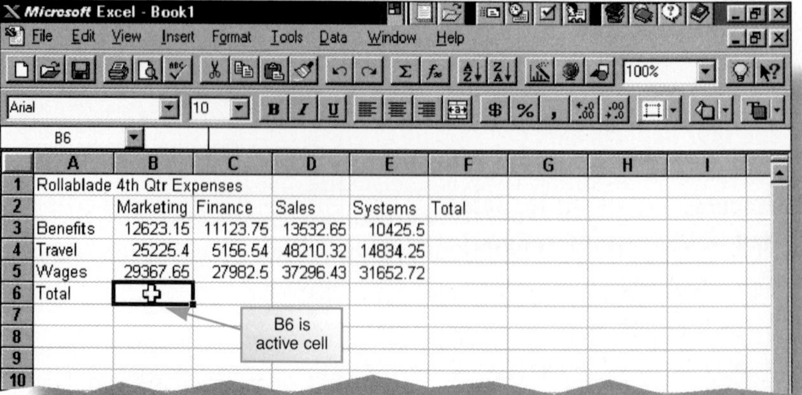

FIGURE 1-26

2 Click the AutoSum button on the Standard toolbar.

Excel responds by displaying =SUM(B3:B5) in the formula bar and in the active cell B6 (Figure 1-27). The =SUM entry identifies the SUM function. The B3:B5 within parentheses following the function name SUM is Excel's way of identifying the cells B3, B4, and B5. Excel also surrounds the proposed cells to sum with a moving border, also called a ***marquee****.*

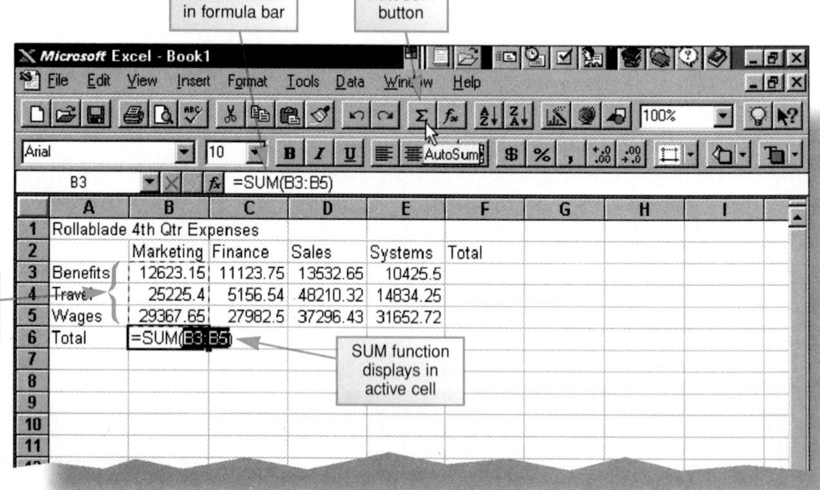

FIGURE 1-27

3 Click the AutoSum button a second time.

Excel enters the sum of the expenses for Marketing (67216.2 = 12623.15 + 25225.4+ 29367.65) in cell B6 (Figure 1-28). The SUM function assigned to cell B6 displays in the formula bar when B6 is the active cell.

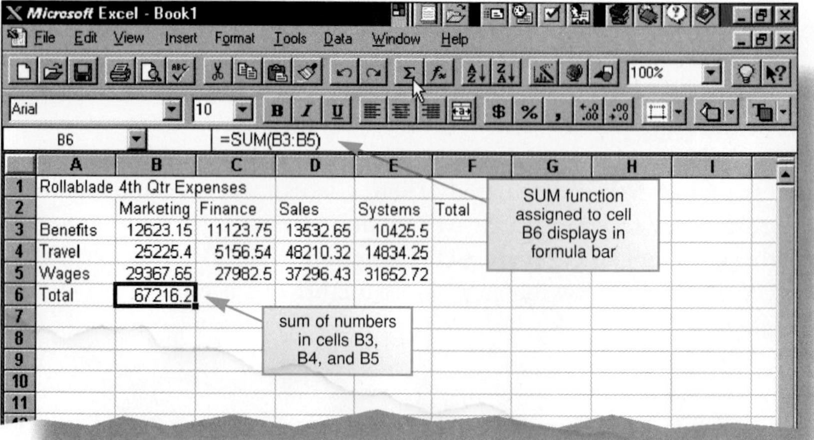

FIGURE 1-28

Other Ways

1. Press ALT+(=) for AutoSum

When you enter the SUM function using the AutoSum button, Excel automatically selects what it considers to be your choice of the group of cells to sum. The group of cells B3, B4, and B5 is called a range. A **range** is a series of two or more adjacent cells in a column or row or a rectangular group of cells. Many Excel operations, such as summing numbers, take place on cells within a range.

In proposing the range to sum, Excel first looks for a range of cells with numbers above the active cell and then to the left. If Excel proposes the wrong range, you can drag through the correct range anytime prior to clicking the AutoSum button a second time. You can also enter the correct range by typing the beginning cell reference, a colon (:), and the ending cell reference.

When using the AutoSum button, you can click it once and then click the enter box or press the ENTER key to complete the entry. Clicking the AutoSum button twice in succession, however, is the quickest way to enter the SUM function into a single cell.

Using the Fill Handle to Copy a Cell to Adjacent Cells

On the expense worksheet, Excel also must calculate the totals for Finance in cell C6, Sales in cell D6, and for Systems in cell E6. Table 1-2 illustrates the similarity between the entry in cell B6 and the entries required for the totals in cells C6, D6, and E6.

Table 1-2

CELL	SUM FUNCTION ENTRIES	REMARK
B6	=SUM(B3:B5)	Sums cells B3, B4, and B5
C6	=SUM(C3:C5)	Sums cells C3, C4, and C5
D6	=SUM(D3:D5)	Sums cells D3, D4, and D5
E6	=SUM(E3:E5)	Sums cells E3, E4, and E5

To place the SUM functions in cells C6, D6, and E6, you can follow the same steps shown in Figures 1-26 through 1-28. A second, more efficient method is to copy the SUM function from cell B6 to the range C6:E6. The cell being copied is called the **copy area**. The range of cells receiving the copy is called the **paste area**.

Notice from Table 1-2 that although the SUM function entries are similar, they are not exact copies. Each cell to the right of cell B6 has a range that is one column to the right of the previous column. When you copy cell addresses, Excel adjusts them for each new position, resulting in the SUM entries illustrated in Table 1-2. Each adjusted cell reference is called a **relative reference**.

The easiest way to copy the SUM formula from cell B6 to cells C6 and D6 is to use the fill handle. The **fill handle** is the small black square located in the lower right corner of the heavy border around the active cell (Figure 1-28). Perform the steps on the next page to use the fill handle to copy cell B6 to the adjacent cells C6:E6.

More *About* Copying and Moving Using the Mouse

Using the mouse and fill handle, you can quickly copy a cell or range of cells to an adjacent paste area as shown in the upcoming example. Another way to copy a cell or range of cells using the mouse is to select the copy area, point to the border of the copy area so the mouse pointer changes to a block arrow, and then while holding down the CTRL key, drag the copy area to the paste area. This second method requires that the paste area be the same size as the copy area. If you drag without holding down the CTRL key, Excel moves the data, rather than duplicates it.

To Copy a Cell to Adjacent Cells in a Row

1 With cell B6 active, point to the fill handle.

The mouse pointer changes to a cross hair (Figure 1-29).

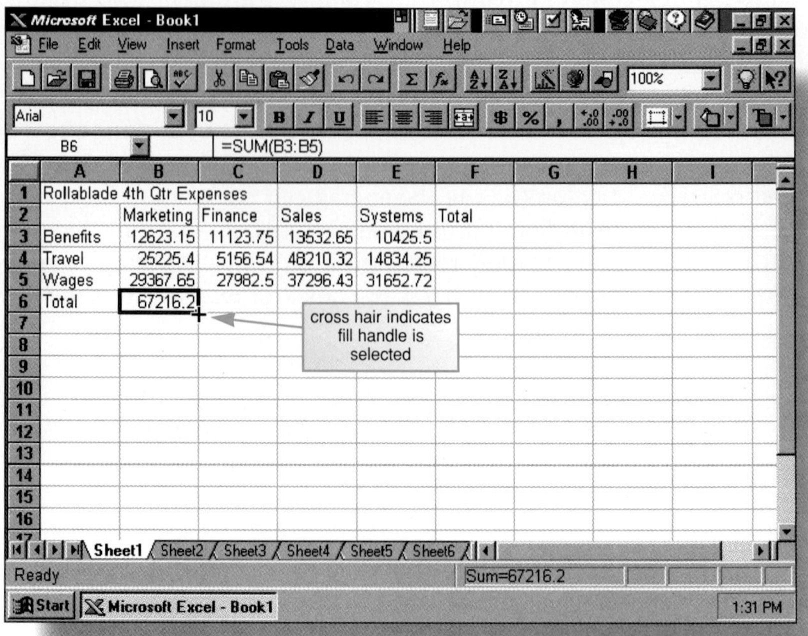

FIGURE 1-29

Drag the fill handle to select the paste area C6:E6.

Excel shades the border of the paste area C6:E6 (Figure 1-30).

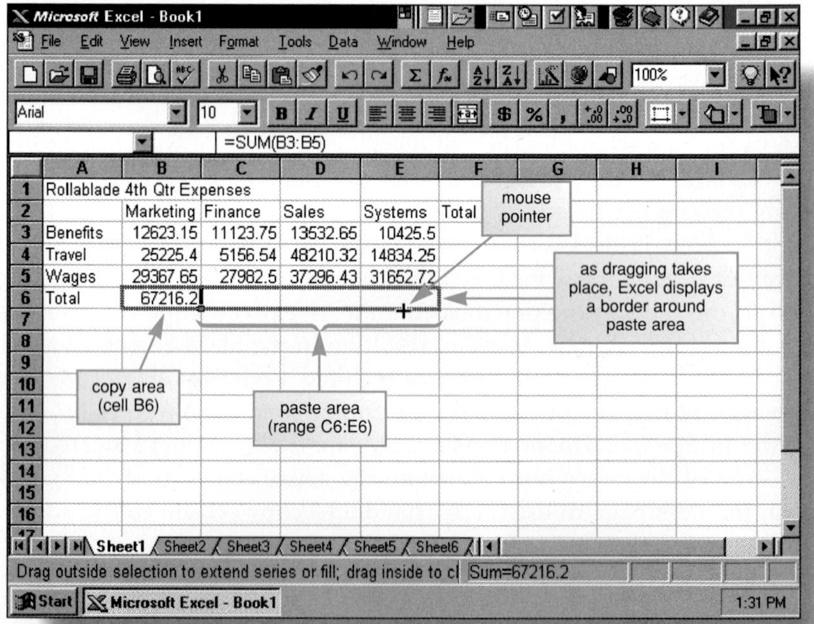

FIGURE 1-30

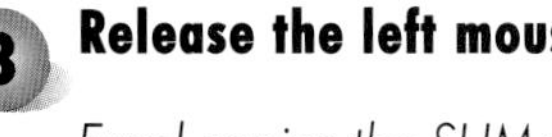

3 Release the left mouse button.

Excel copies the SUM function in cell B6 to the range C6:E6 (Figure 1-31). In addition, Excel calculates the sums and enters the results in cells C6, D6, and E6.

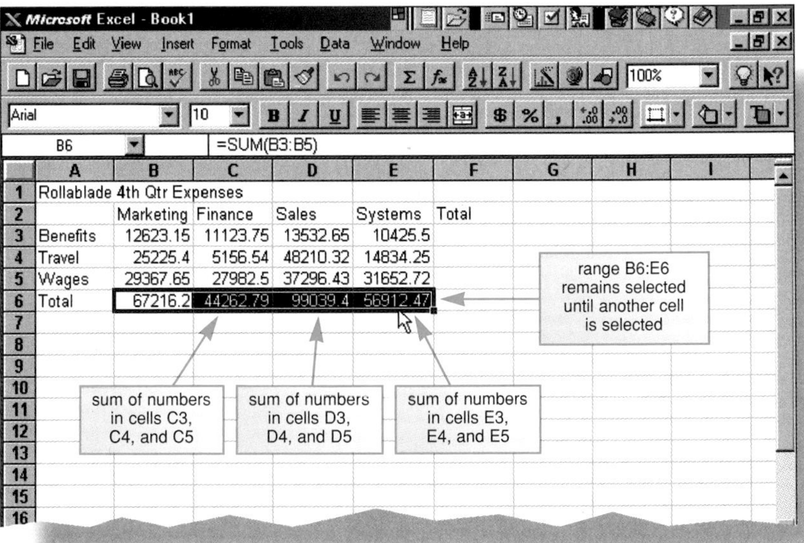

FIGURE 1-31

OtherWays

1. Right-click copy area, click Copy on shortcut menu, right-click paste area, click Paste on shortcut menu
2. Select copy area, click Copy button on Standard toolbar, select paste area, click Paste button on Standard toolbar to paste
3. Select copy area, on Edit menu click Copy, select paste area, on Edit menu click Paste
4. Select copy area, press CTRL+C, select paste area, press CTRL+V

After the copy is complete, the range remains selected. To remove the range selection, select any cell.

Determining Row Totals

The next step in building the expense worksheet is to total the individual Benefits, Travel, Wages, and company total expenses and place the sums in column F. Use the SUM function in the same manner as you did when the expenses by department were totaled in row 6. In this example, however, all the rows will be totaled at the same time. The following steps illustrate this process.

To Determine Multiple Totals at the Same Time

1 Click cell F3.

Cell F3 becomes the active cell (Figure 1-32).

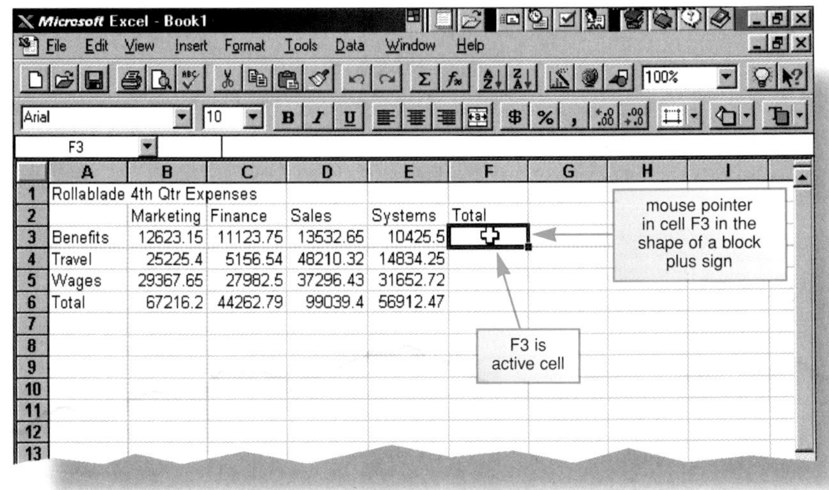

FIGURE 1-32

2 With the mouse pointer in cell F3 and in the shape of a block plus sign, drag the mouse pointer down to cell F6.

Excel highlights the range F3:F6 (Figure 1-33).

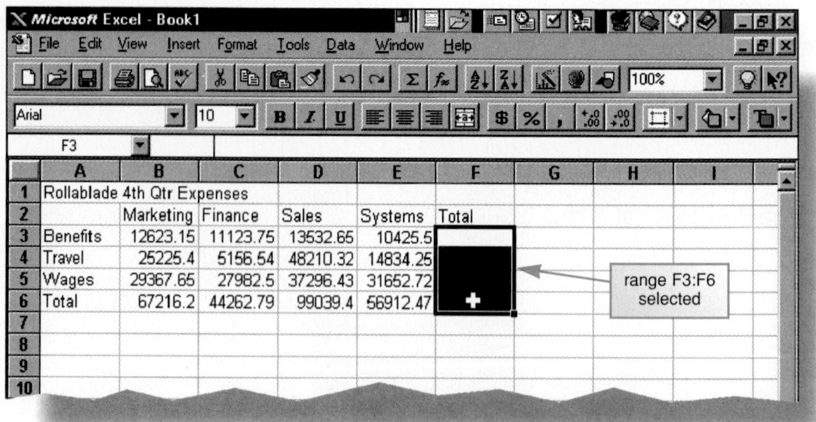

FIGURE 1-33

3 Click the AutoSum button on the Standard toolbar.

Excel assigns the functions =SUM(B3:E3) to cell F3, =SUM(B4:E4) to cell F4, =SUM(B5:E5) to cell F5, and =SUM(B6:E6) to cell F6, and then computes and displays the sums in the respective cells (Figure 1-34).

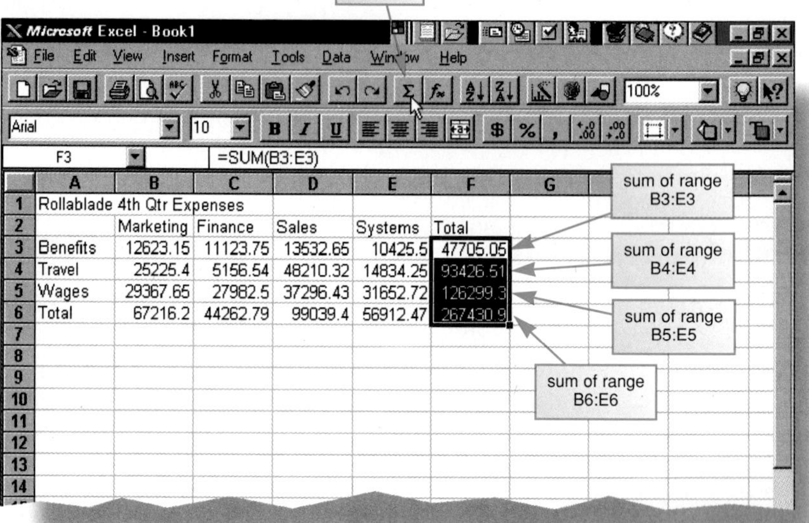

FIGURE 1-34

More *About* the AutoSum Button

In a hurry? Here's a quick way to determine all the totals in row 6 and column F in Figure 1-34 at once. Select the range (B3:F6) and click the AutoSum button. The range B3:F6 includes the numbers to sum plus an additional row (row 6) and an additional column (column F).

Because a range was selected next to rows of numbers and the AutoSum button was clicked, Excel assigned the SUM function to each cell in the selected range. Thus, four SUM functions with different ranges were assigned to the selected range, one for each row. This same procedure could have been used earlier to sum the columns. That is, rather than selecting cell B6 and clicking the AutoSum button twice and then copying the SUM function to the range C6:E6, you could have selected the range B6:E6 and then clicked the AutoSum button once.

Formatting the Worksheet

The text, numeric entries, and functions for the worksheet are now complete. The next step is to format the worksheet. You **format** a worksheet to emphasize certain entries and make the worksheet easier to read and understand.

Figure 1-35(a) shows the worksheet before formatting. Figure 1-35(b) shows the worksheet after formatting. As you can see from the two figures, a worksheet that is formatted not only is easier to read, but it also looks more professional.

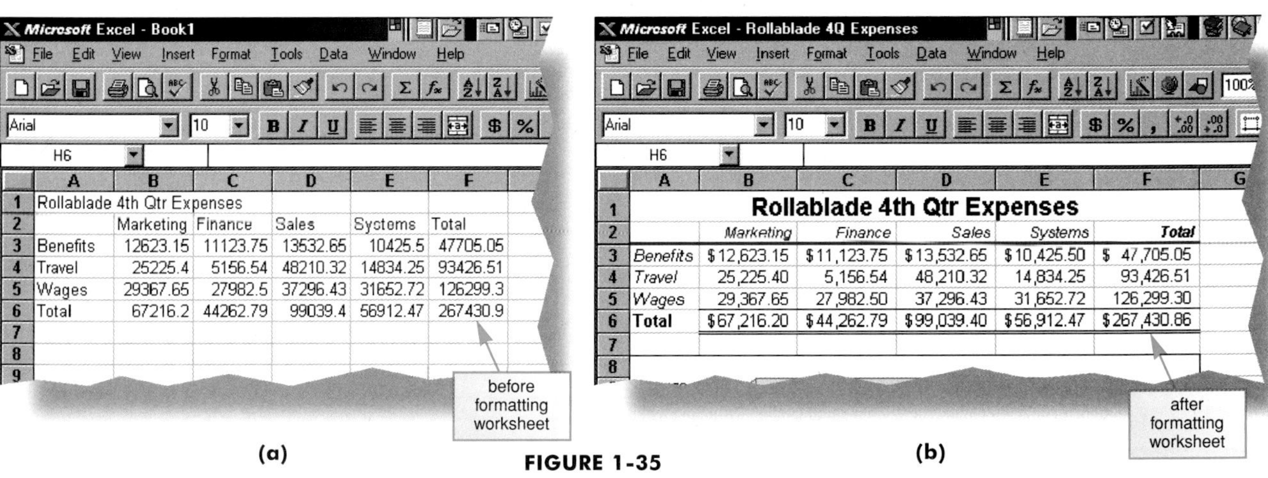

(a) FIGURE 1-35 (b)

To change the unformatted worksheet in Figure 1-35a to the formatted worksheet in Figure 1-35b, the following tasks must be completed:

1. Bold the worksheet title in cell A1.
2. Enlarge the worksheet title in cell A1.
3. Center the worksheet title in cell A1 across columns A through F.
4. Format the body of the worksheet. The body of the worksheet, range A2:F6, includes the column titles, row titles, and numbers. The result is numbers represented in a dollars-and-cents format, dollar signs in the first row of numbers and the total row, and underlines that emphasize portions of the worksheet.

The process required to format the expense spreadsheet is explained on the following pages. Although the format procedures will be carried out in the order presented, you should be aware that you can make these format changes in any order.

Fonts, Font Size, and Font Style

Characters that display on the screen are a specific shape and size. The **font type** defines the appearance and shape of the letters, numbers, and special characters. The **font size** specifies the size of the characters on the screen. Character size is gauged by a measurement system called points. A single **point** is about 1/72 of one inch in height. Thus, a character with a **point size** of ten is about 10/72 of one inch in height.

Font style indicates how the characters appear. They may be normal, bold, underlined, or italicized.

When Excel begins, the default font type for the entire spreadsheet is Arial with a size of 10 point, no bold, no underline, and no italic. With Excel you have the capability to change the font characteristics in a single cell, a range of cells, the entire worksheet, or the entire workbook.

Perform the steps on the next page to bold the worksheet title in cell A1.

More *About* **the Fonts**

In general, use no more than two font types and font styles in a worksheet.

Steps To Bold a Cell

1 Click cell A1 and then point to the Bold button on the Standard toolbar.

The ToolTip displays immediately below the Bold button identifying the function of the button (Figure 1-36).

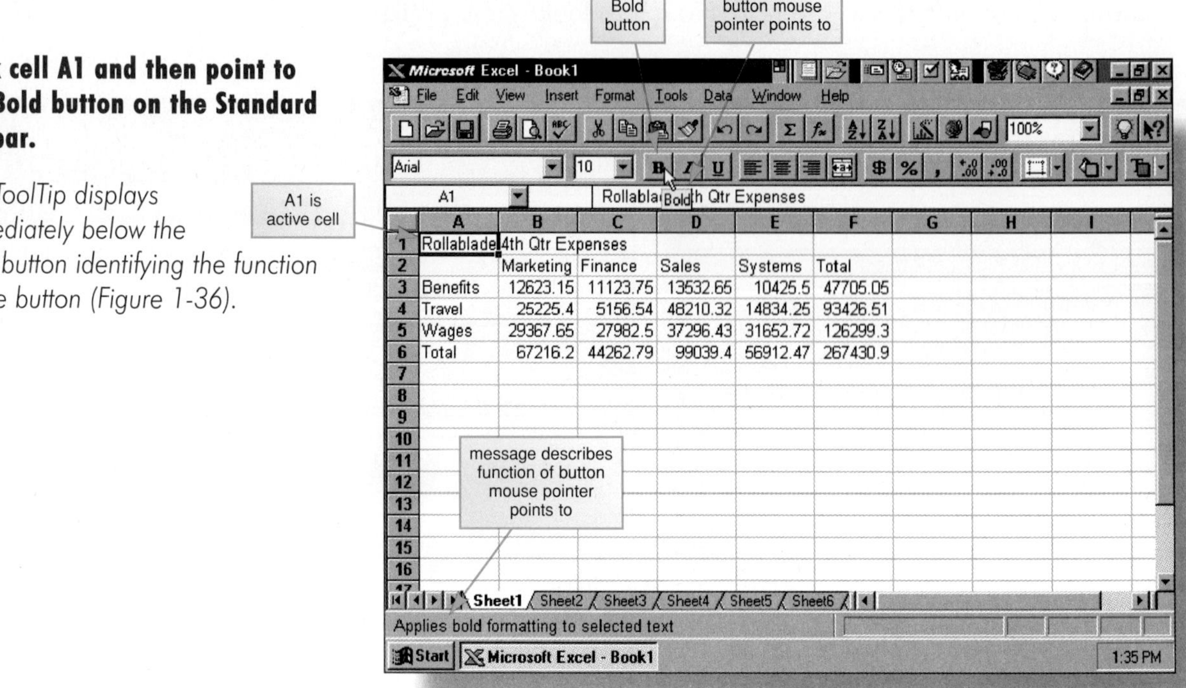

FIGURE 1-36

2 Click the Bold button.

Excel applies a bold format to the worksheet title Rollablade 4th Qtr Expenses (Figure 1-37).

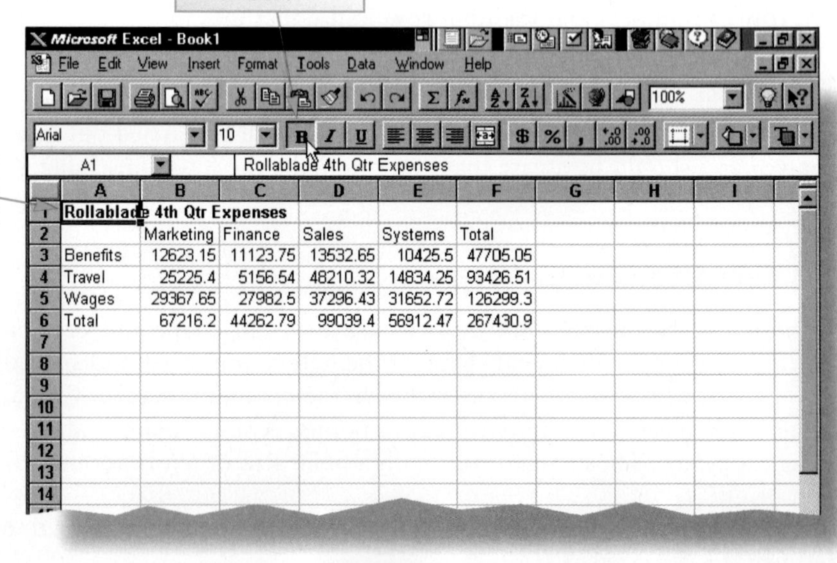

FIGURE 1-37

OtherWays

1. Right-click cell, click Format Cells on shortcut menu, click Font tab, click Bold, click OK button
2. On Format menu click Cells, click Font tab, click Bold, click OK button
3. Press CTRL+B

When the active cell is bold, the Bold button is recessed (Figure 1-37). Clicking the Bold button a second time removes the bold format.

Increasing the font size is the next step in formatting the worksheet title.

To Increase the Font Size of a Cell

1 With cell A1 selected, click the Font Size box arrow on the Formatting toolbar and point to 14 in the drop-down list box (Figure 1-38).

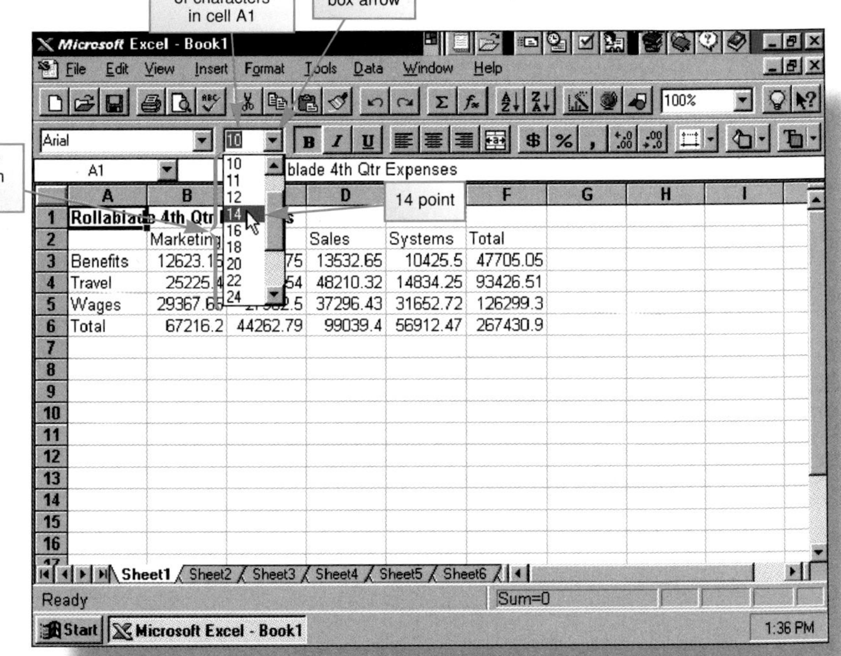

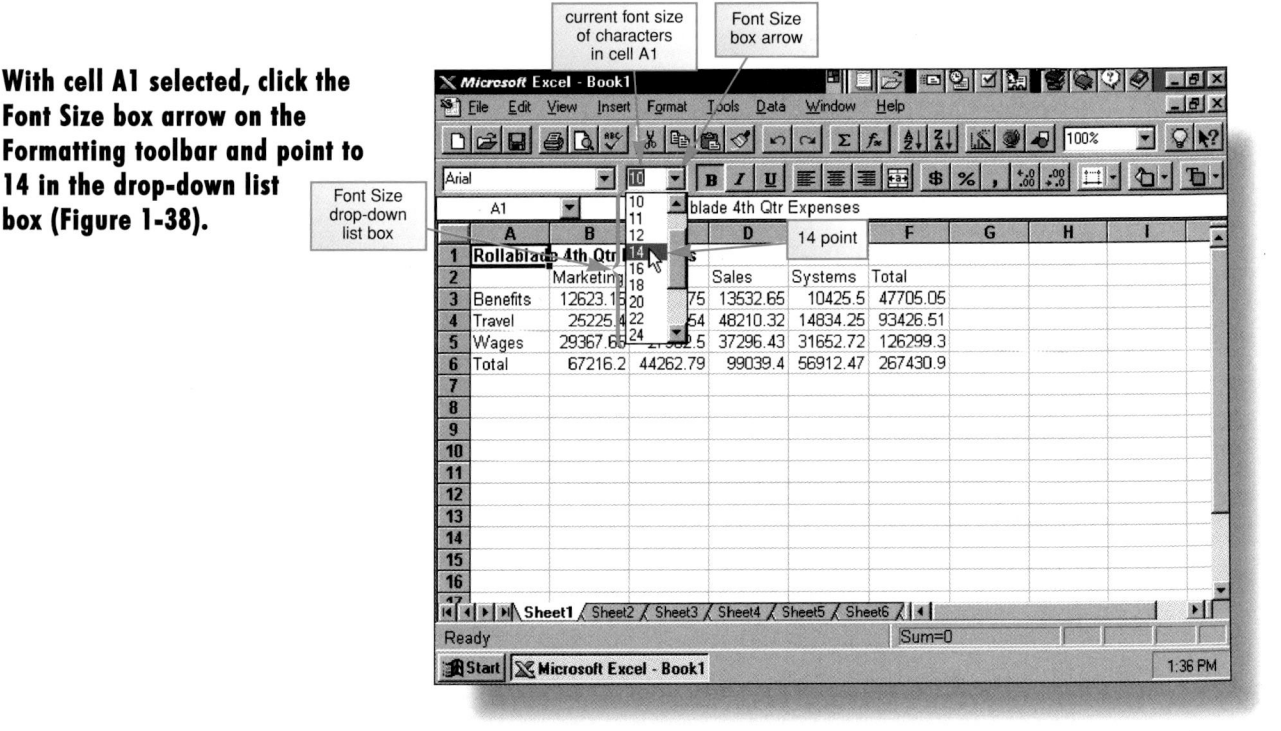

FIGURE 1-38

2 Click 14.

The characters in the worksheet title in cell A1 increase from 10 point to 14 point (Figure 1-39).

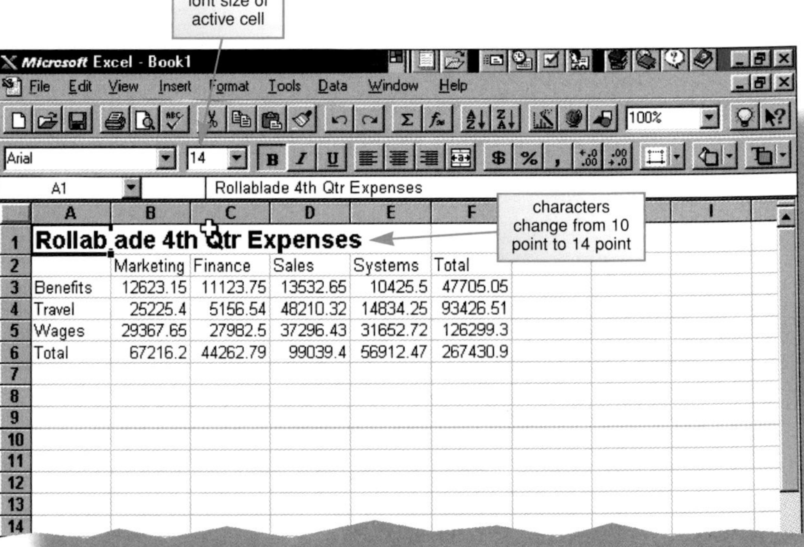

FIGURE 1-39

OtherWays

1. Right-click cell, click Format Cells on shortcut menu, click Font tab, select font size, click OK button
2. On Format menu click Cells, click Font tab, select font size, click OK button

The final step in formatting the worksheet title is to center it over columns A through F.

Steps To Center a Cell's Contents Across Columns

1 With cell A1 selected, drag the block plus sign to the rightmost cell (F1) in the range over which to center.

When you drag the mouse pointer over the range A1:F1, Excel highlights the cells (Figure 1-40).

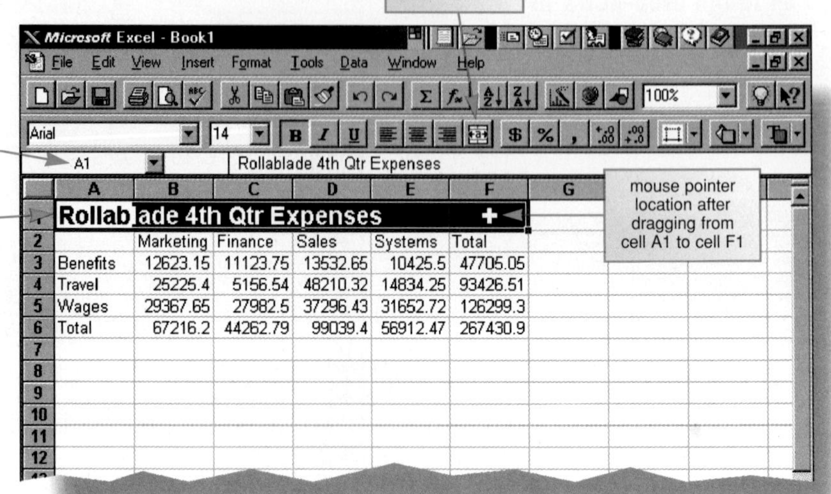

FIGURE 1-40

2 Click the Center Across Columns button on the Formatting toolbar.

Excel centers the contents of cell A1 across columns A through F (Figure 1-41). For the Center Across Columns button to work properly, all the cells except the leftmost cell in the range of cells must be empty.

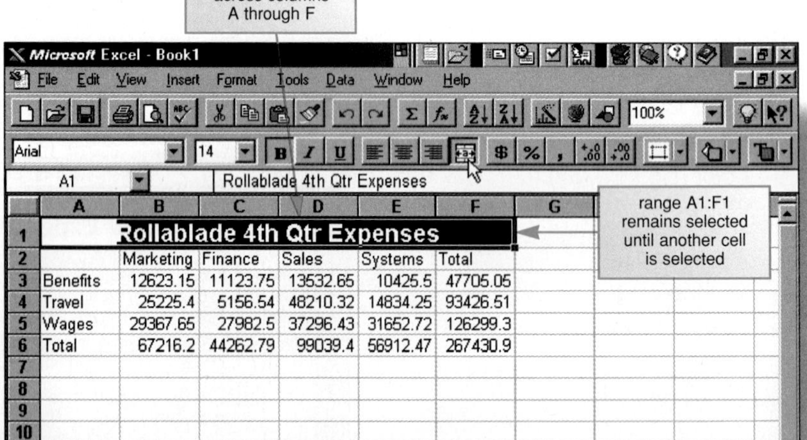

FIGURE 1-41

OtherWays

1. Right-click cell, click Format Cells on shortcut menu, click Alignment tab, click Center across selection, click OK button
2. On Format menu click Cells, click Font tab, click Alignment tab, click Center across selection, click OK button

To remove the selection from range A1:F1, select any cell in the worksheet. Most formats assigned to a cell will display on the Formatting toolbar when the cell is selected. For example, the font type and font size display in their appropriate boxes. Recessed buttons indicate an assigned format. To determine if less frequently used formats are assigned to a cell, point to the cell and right-click. Next, click **Format cells**, and then click each of the tabs in the **Format Cells dialog box**.

Using AutoFormat to Format the Body of a Worksheet

Excel has several customized format styles called **table formats** that allow you to format the body of the worksheet. The table formats can be used to give your worksheet a professional appearance. Follow these steps to automatically format the range A2:F6 in the expense worksheet using **AutoFormat** on the Format menu.

To Use AutoFormat to Format the Body of a Worksheet

1 **Select cell A2, the upper left corner cell of the rectangular range to format (Figure 1-42).**

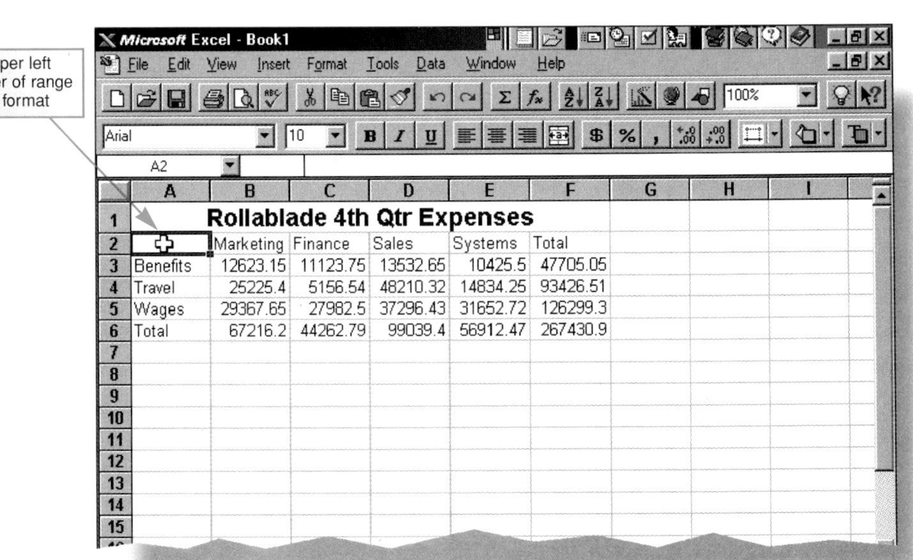

FIGURE 1-42

2 **Drag the mouse pointer to cell F6, the lower right corner cell of the range to format.**

Excel highlights the range to format (Figure 1-43).

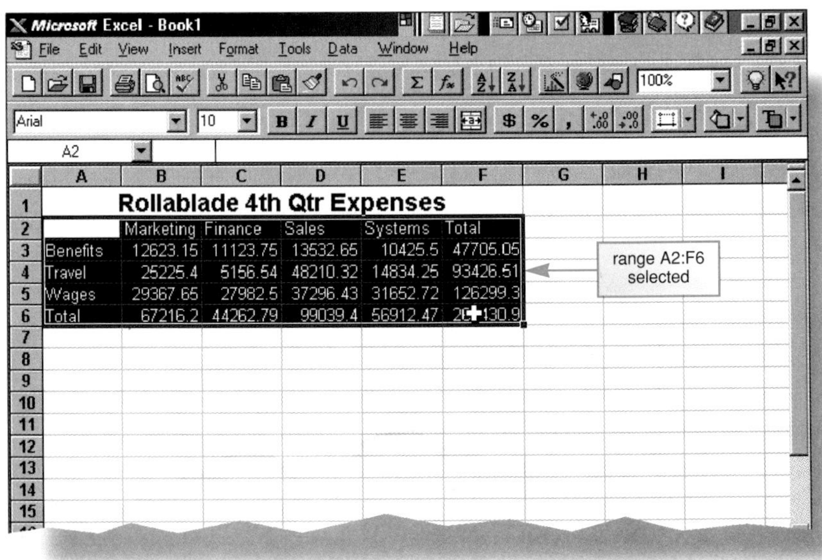

FIGURE 1-43

3 **Click Format on the menu bar and point to AutoFormat.**

The Format menu displays (Figure 1-44).

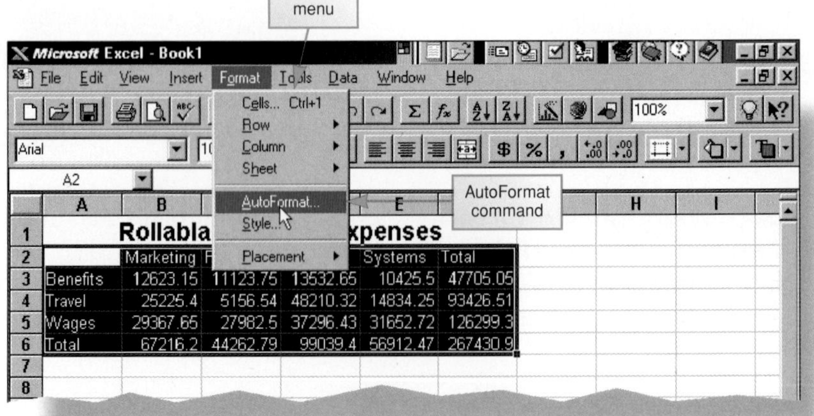

FIGURE 1-44

4 **Click AutoFormat.**

Excel displays the ***AutoFormat dialog box*** *(Figure 1-45). On the left side of the dialog box is the* ***Table Format list box*** *with the Table Format name, Simple, highlighted. In the Sample area of the dialog box is a sample of the format that corresponds to the highlighted Table Format name, Simple.*

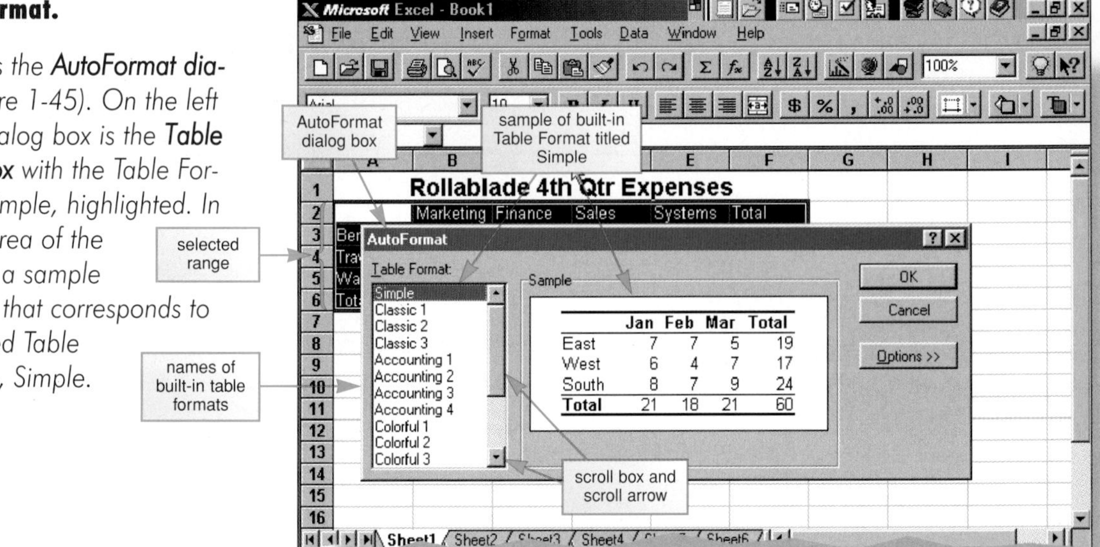

FIGURE 1-45

5 **Click Accounting 3 in the Table Format list box.**

The sample in the dialog box shows the Accounting 3 format selected (Figure 1-46).

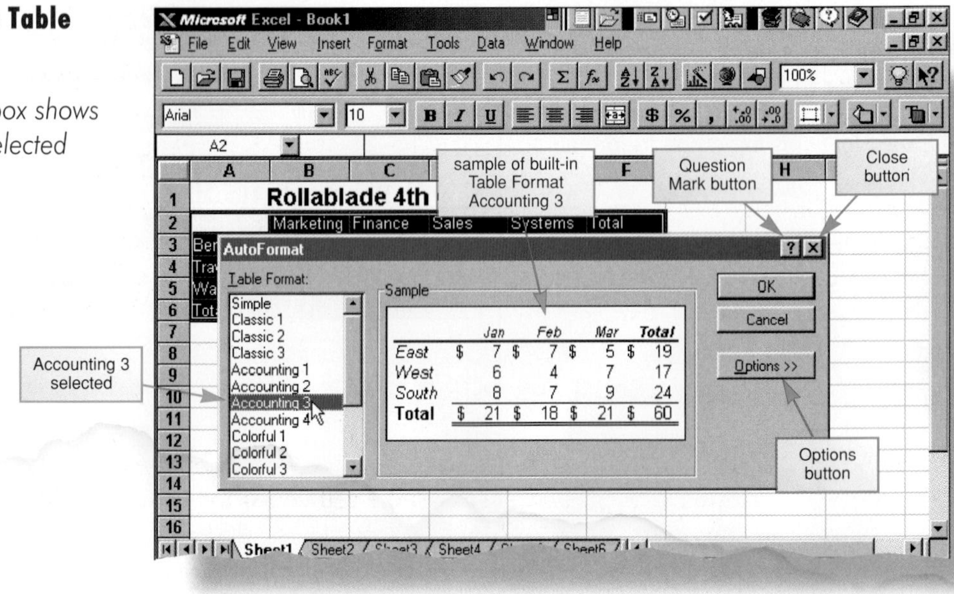

FIGURE 1-46

6 **Click the OK button in the AutoFormat dialog box. Select cell H6 to deselect the range A2:F6.**

Excel displays the worksheet with the range A2:F6 using the customized format, Accounting 3 (Figure 1-47).

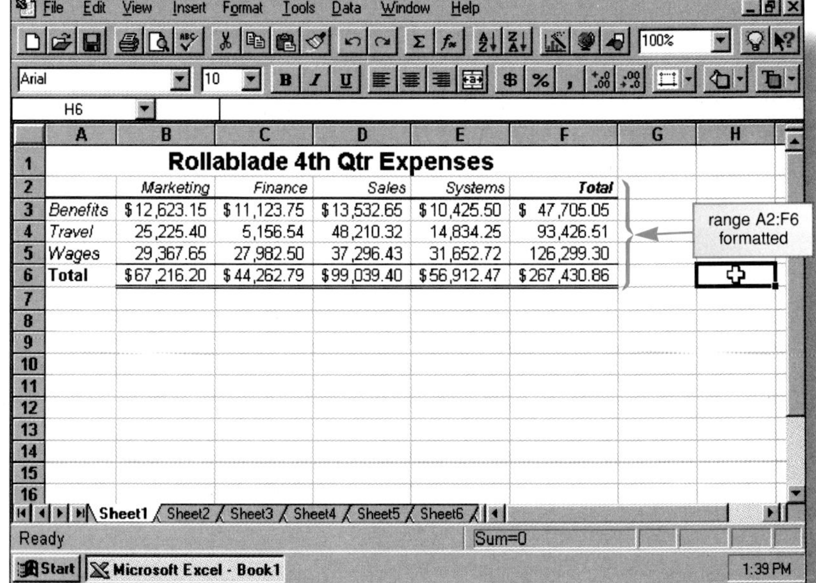

FIGURE 1-47

Excel provides seventeen customized format styles from which to choose. Each format style has different characteristics. The format characteristics associated with the customized format, Accounting 3 (Figure 1-47), include right-justification of column titles, numeric values displayed as dollars and cents, comma placement, numbers aligned on the decimal point, dollar signs in the first row of numbers and in the total row, and top and bottom borders emphasized. The width of column A has also been reduced so that the longest row title, Benefits, just fits in the column.

Notice the buttons in the AutoFormat dialog box in Figure 1-46. On the rightmost side of the title bar is the Close button. Use the **Close button** to terminate current activity without making changes. You can also use the **Cancel button** for this purpose. Use the **Question Mark button** to obtain Help on any box or button located in the dialog box. The **Options button** allows you to be selective in the formats assigned by the customized format.

The worksheet is now complete. The next step is to chart the expenses for the four departments. To create the chart, the active cell must be cell A2, the cell in the upper left corner of the range to chart. To select cell A2, you can move the mouse pointer to it and click. This is the procedure used in previous examples. You can also use the Name box to select a cell as described in the next section.

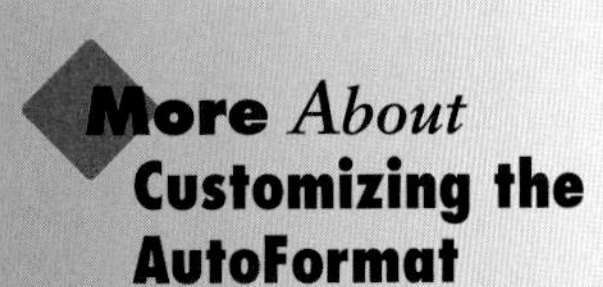

More *About* **Customizing the AutoFormat**

The Options button on the right side of the AutoFormat dialog box in Figure 1-46 allows you to modify the formats associated with any of the customized formats. If you assign two different customized formats to a range, Excel will add the formats of the second one to the formats of the first. Thus, if you decide to change a customized format, first select the range, then click Style on the Format menu. Then, with Normal style selected, click the OK button. This will remove all assigned formats except for the column-width changes. Next, assign the new customized format using the AutoFormat on the Format menu. Rather than using the Style command on the Format menu, you can also select the range and click Clear on the Edit menu, then click Formats on the submenu.

Using the Name Box to Select a Cell

The **Name box** is located on the left side of the formula bar. To select any cell, click the Name box and enter the cell reference of the cell you want to select. The following steps show how to select cell A2.

Steps To Use the Name Box to Select a Cell

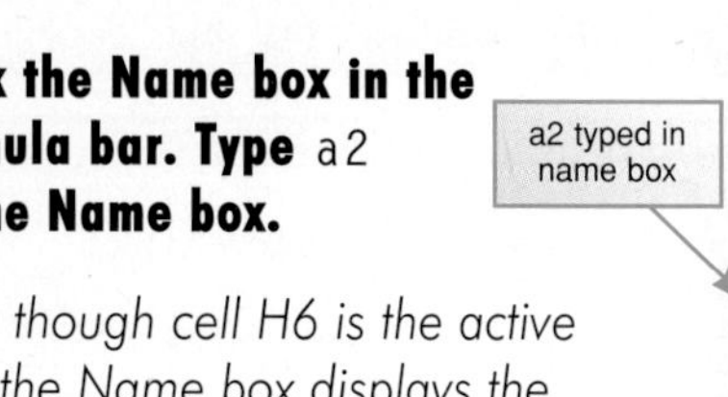

1 Click the Name box in the formula bar. Type a2 **in the Name box.**

Even though cell H6 is the active cell, the Name box displays the typed cell reference a2 (Figure 1-48).

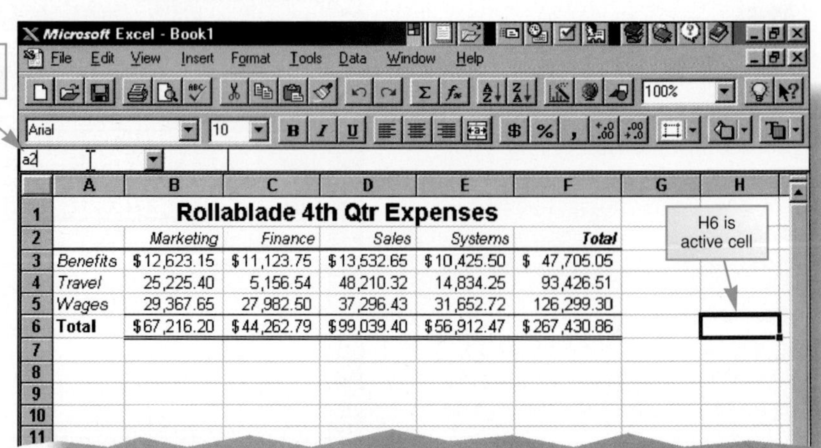

FIGURE 1-48

2 Press the ENTER key.

Excel changes the active cell from cell H6 to cell A2 (Figure 1-49).

FIGURE 1-49

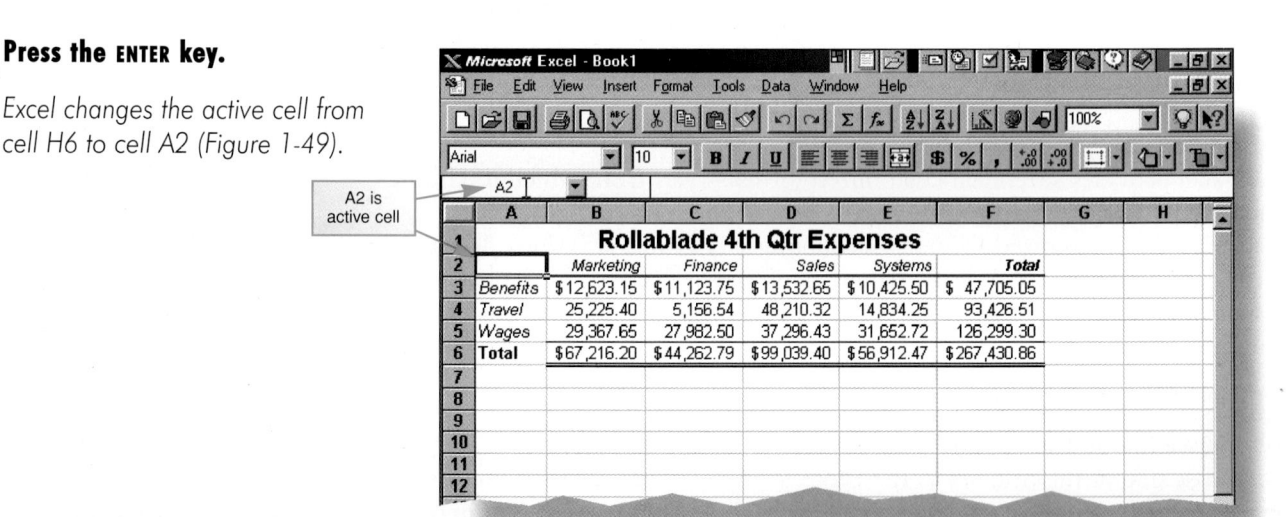

More About the Name Box

If you have cells in a worksheet that you find yourself continuously selecting for one reason or another, you can select the cells one at a time and type in a name for each in the Name Box, such as Company Total for cell F6 in Figure 1-49. Then when you want to select one of the named cells, click the Name Box arrow and click the cell name in the Name Box drop-down list box.

As you will see in later projects, besides using the Name box to select any cell, you can also use it to assign names to a cell or range of cells.

Excel supports several additional ways to select a cell, as summarized in Table 1-3 at the top of the next page.

Adding a 3-D Column Chart to the Worksheet

The 3-D column chart drawn by Excel in this project is based on the data in the expense worksheet (Figure 1-50). It is called an **embedded chart** because it is drawn on the same worksheet.

Table 1-3

KEY, NAME, BOX, OR COMMAND	FUNCTION
ALT+PAGE DOWN	Selects the cell one screenful to the right and moves the window accordingly.
ALT+PAGE UP	Selects the cell one screenful to the left and moves the window accordingly.
ARROW	Selects the adjacent cell in the direction of the arrow on the key.
CTRL+ARROW	Selects the border cell of the worksheet in combination with the arrow keys and moves the window accordingly. For example, to select the rightmost cell in the row that contains the active cell, press CTRL+RIGHT ARROW. You can also press the END key, release it, and then press the arrow key to accomplish the same task.
CTRL+HOME	Selects cell A1 or the cell below and to the right of frozen titles and moves the window to the upper left corner of the worksheet.
HOME	Selects the cell at the beginning of the row that contains the active cell and moves the window accordingly.
PAGE DOWN	Selects the cell down one window from the active cell and moves the window accordingly.
PAGE UP	Selects the cell up one window from the active cell and moves the window accordingly.
Name box	Selects the cell in the worksheet that corresponds to the cell reference you enter in the Name box.
Find command on Edit menu	Finds and selects a cell in the worksheet with specific contents that you enter in the Find dialog box. If necessary, Excel moves the window to display the cell. You can press SHIFT+F5 to display the Find dialog box.
F5 or Goto command on Edit menu	Selects the cell in the worksheet that corresponds to the cell reference you enter in the Goto dialog box and moves the window accordingly.

For Marketing, the light blue column represents the quarterly Benefits expense ($12,623.15), the purple column represents the quarterly traveling expense ($25,225.40), and the light yellow column represents the quarterly wage expense ($29,367.20). For Finance, Sales, and Systems, the same color columns represent the comparable expenses. Notice in this chart that the totals from the worksheet are not represented because the totals were not in the range specified for charting.

Excel derives the scale along the vertical axis (also called **y-axis**) of the chart on the basis of the values in the worksheet. For example, no value in the range A2:F5 is less than zero or greater than $50,000.00. It also determines automatically the $10,000.00 increments along the y-axis.

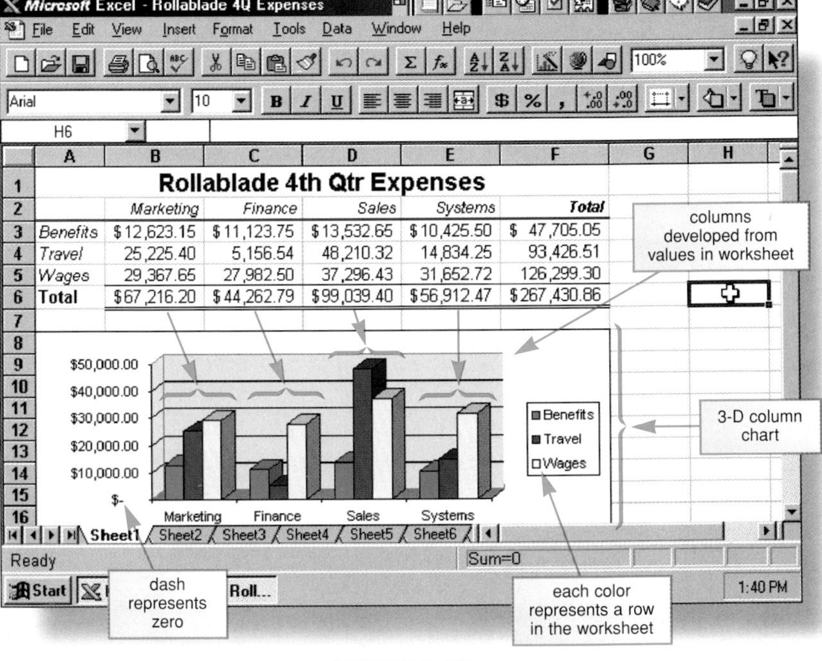

FIGURE 1-50

To draw a chart like the one in Figure 1-50 on the previous page, select the range to chart, click the **ChartWizard button** on the Standard toolbar, and select the area on the worksheet where you want the chart drawn. The area on the worksheet you select to draw the chart is called the **chart location**. In Figure 1-50, the chart is located immediately below the worksheet data. When you determine the location of the chart on the worksheet, you also determine its size by dragging the mouse pointer from the upper left corner of the chart location to the lower right corner of the chart location.

Follow these detailed steps to draw a 3-D column chart that compares the quarterly expenses for the four departments.

Steps To Add a 3-D Column Chart to the Worksheet

1 **With cell A2 selected, position the block plus sign within the cell's border (Figure 1-51).**

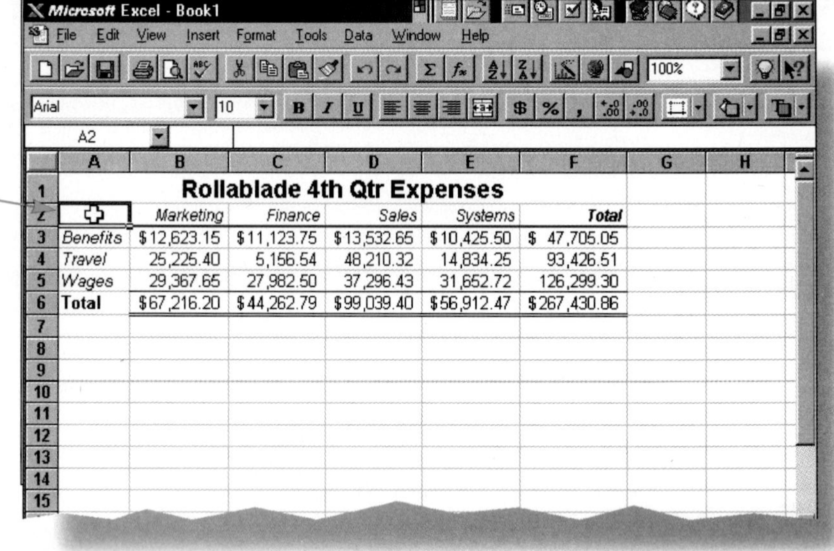

FIGURE 1-51

2 **Drag the mouse pointer to the lower right corner cell (cell E5) of the range to chart.**

Excel highlights the range to chart (Figure 1-52).

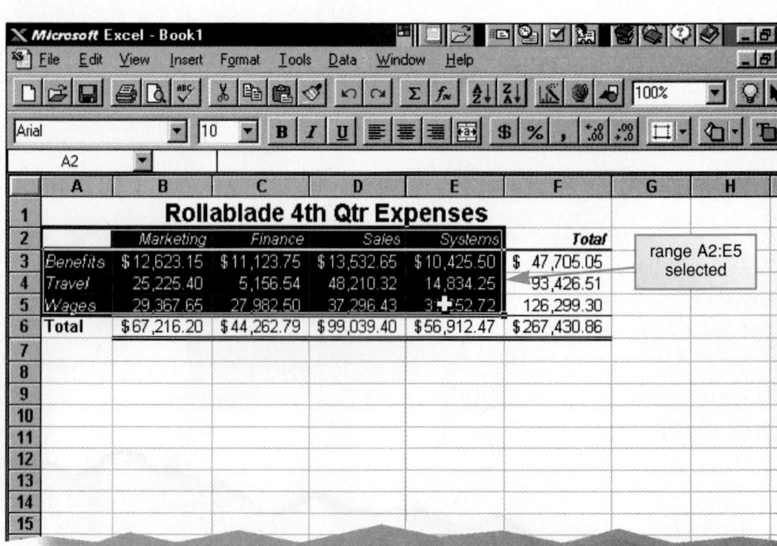

FIGURE 1-52

3 **Click the ChartWizard button on the Standard toolbar and then move the mouse pointer into the window.**

The mouse pointer changes to a cross hair with a chart symbol (Figure 1-53).

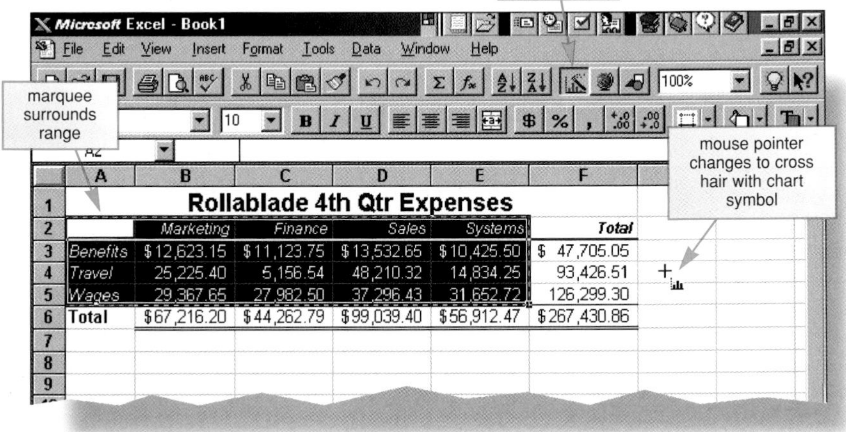

FIGURE 1-53

4 **Move the mouse pointer to the upper left corner of the desired chart location, immediately below the worksheet data (cell A8).**

A marquee surrounds the range to chart A2:E5 and the mouse pointer is in the upper left corner of cell A8. (Figure 1-54).

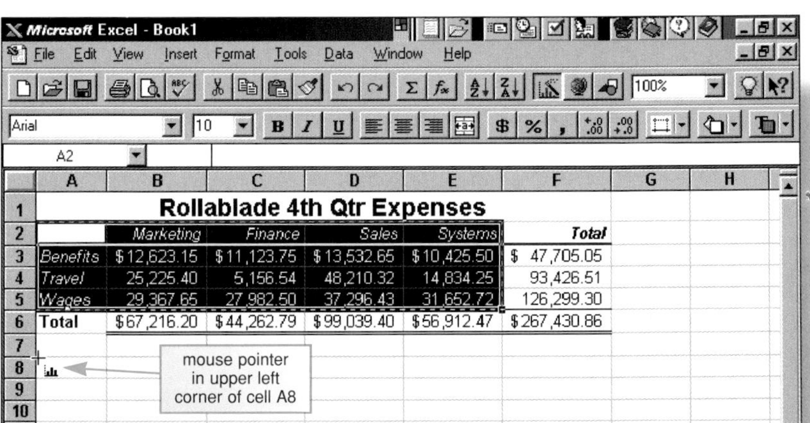

FIGURE 1-54

5 **Drag the mouse pointer to the lower right corner of the chart location (cell F17).**

The mouse pointer is positioned at the lower right corner of cell F17, and the chart location is surrounded by a solid line rectangle (Figure 1-55). You may want to hold down the ALT *key while you drag so the chart location snaps to the gridlines.*

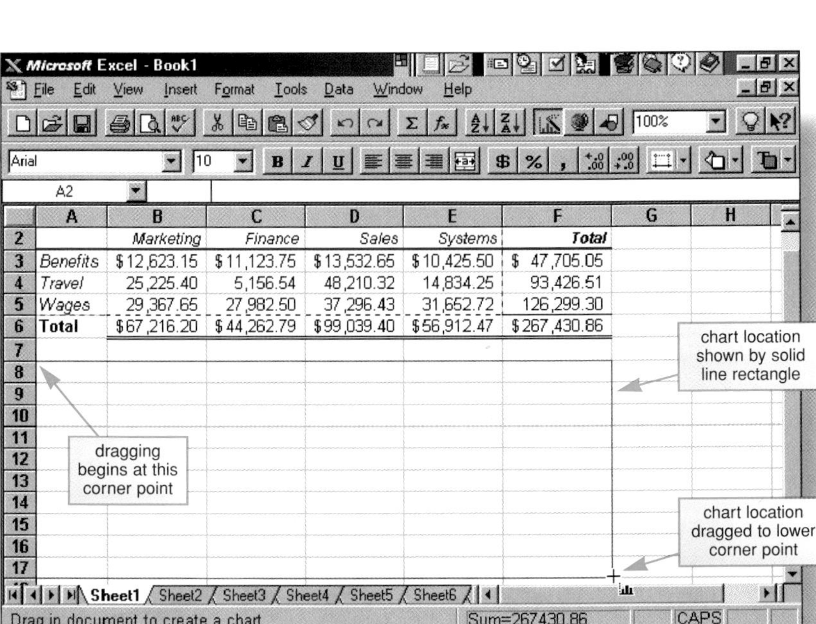

FIGURE 1-55

Release the left mouse button.

Excel responds by displaying the ChartWizard - Step 1 of 5 dialog box *when you release the mouse button after selecting the chart location (Figure 1-56).*

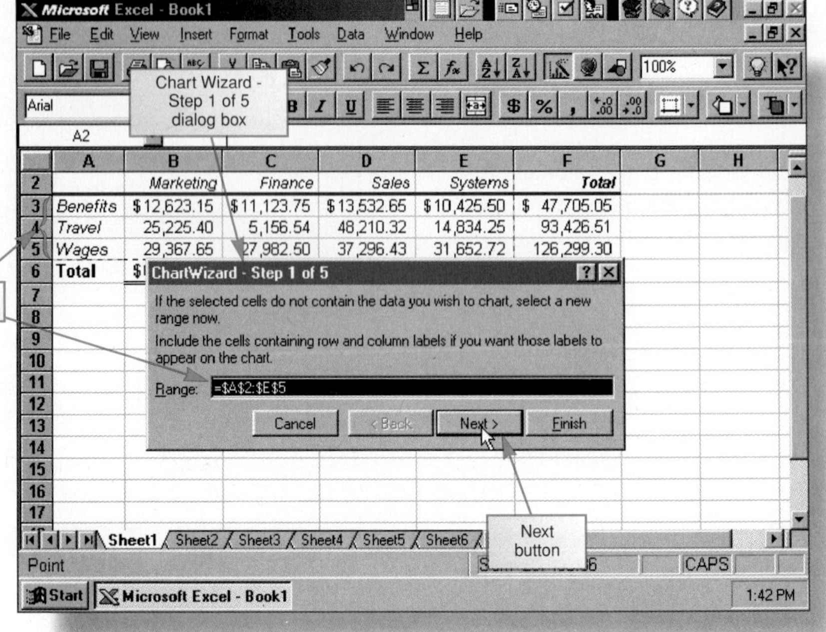

FIGURE 1-56

Click the Next button. When the ChartWizard - Step 2 of 5 dialog box displays, click 3-D Column (column 2, row 3) and then point to the Finish button (Figure 1-57).

Notice that the dialog box includes the fifteen different chart types from which you can choose.

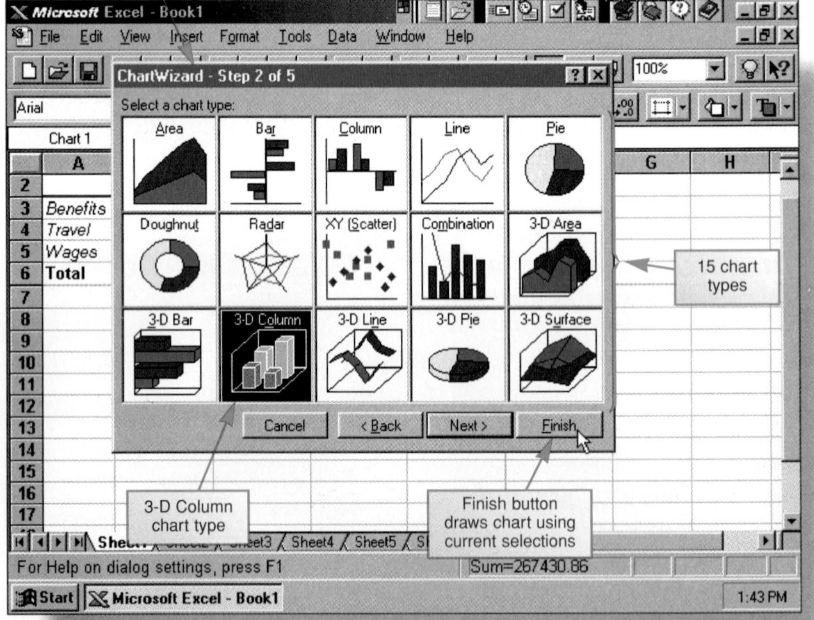

FIGURE 1-57

8 Click the Finish button.

Excel draws a 3-D column chart over the chart location comparing the quarterly expenses for the four departments (Figure 1-58). The small ***selection squares*** *(▪), or* ***handles****, on the border of the chart location indicate that the chart is selected. While the chart is selected, you can drag the chart to any location on the worksheet. You can also resize the chart by dragging the handles.*

9 Select a cell outside the chart location to remove the chart selection and use the vertical scroll bar to display the top of the worksheet.

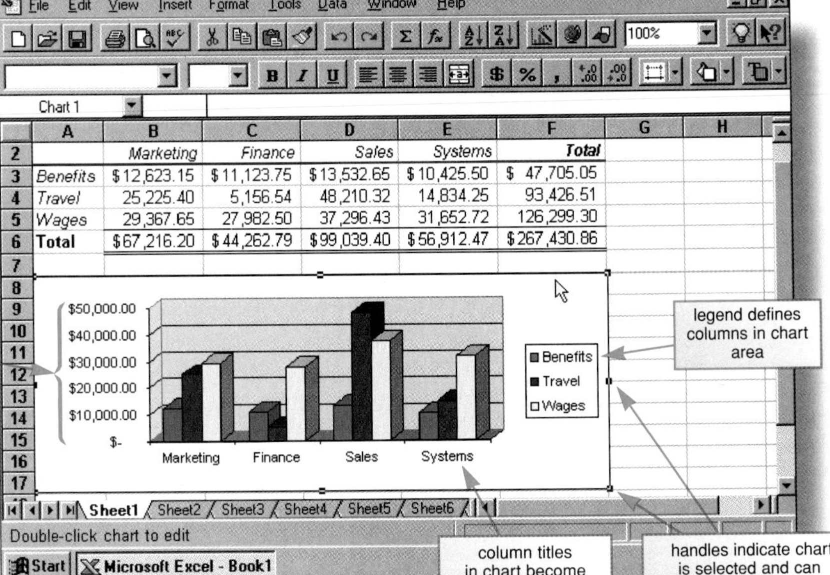

	A	B	C	D	E	F
2		Marketing	Finance	Sales	Systems	Total
3	Benefits	$12,623.15	$11,123.75	$13,532.65	$10,425.50	$ 47,705.05
4	Travel	25,225.40	5,156.54	48,210.32	14,834.25	93,426.51
5	Wages	29,367.65	27,982.50	37,296.43	31,652.72	126,299.30
6	Total	$67,216.20	$44,262.79	$99,039.40	$56,912.47	$267,430.86

FIGURE 1-58

OtherWays

1. On Insert menu click Chart, click On This Sheet

The embedded 3-D column chart in Figure 1-58 compares the three quarterly expenses within each department. It also allows you to compare expenses between the departments. Notice that Excel automatically selects the entries in the row at the top of the range (row 2) as the titles for the horizontal axis (also called the **x-axis**) and draws a column for each of the twelve cells containing numbers in the range. The small box to the right of the column chart in Figure 1-58 contains the legend. The **legend** identifies each bar in the chart. Excel automatically selects the leftmost column of the range (column A) as titles within the legend. As indicated earlier, Excel also automatically scales the y-axis on the basis of the magnitude of the numbers in the graph range.

Excel offers 15 different chart types (Figure 1-57). The **default chart type** is the chart Excel draws if you click the Finish button in the first ChartWizard dialog box. When you install Excel on a computer, the default chart type is the two-dimensional column chart.

More *About* **Changing the Chart Type**

Excel has more chart types than you can imagine. You can change the embedded chart to one of the other fourteen types by double-clicking the chart location. Once a heavy gray border surrounds the chart location, right-click the chart and right-click Chart Type on the shortcut menu. You can also use the shortcut menu to format the chart to make it look more professional. Subsequent projects will discuss changing charts, sizing charts, adding text to charts, and drawing a chart on a chart sheet.

Saving a Workbook

While you are building a workbook, the computer stores it in main memory. If the computer is turned off or if you lose electrical power, the workbook is lost. Hence, it is mandatory to save on disk any workbook that you will use later. A saved workbook is referred to as a **file** or **workbook**. The steps on the next page illustrate how to save a workbook to drive A using the Save button on the Standard toolbar.

Steps To Save a Workbook

1 **With a floppy disk in drive A, click the Save button on the Standard toolbar.**

Excel responds by displaying the *Save As dialog box* (Figure 1-59). The default folder is My Documents, the default filename is Book1, and the file type is Microsoft Excel Workbook. The buttons next to the Save in drop-down list box are used to select folders and change the display of filenames in the Save As dialog box.

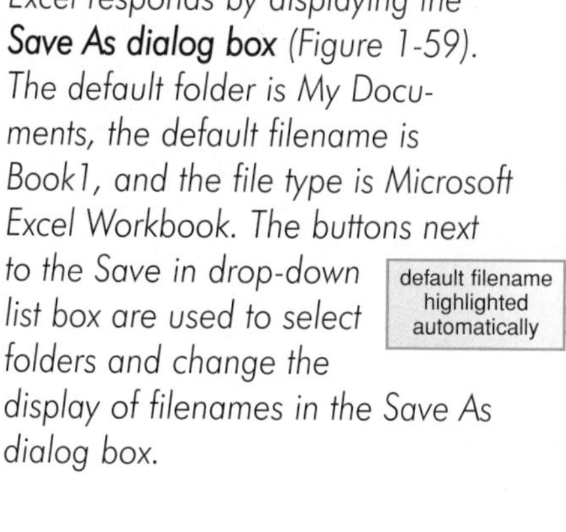

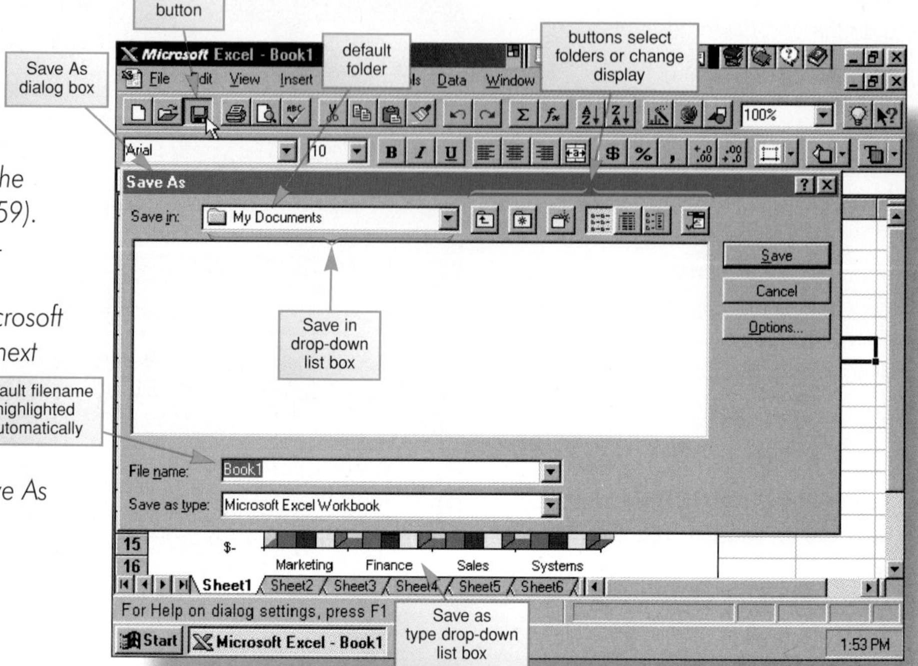

FIGURE 1-59

2 **Type** `Rollablade 4Q Expenses` **in the File name text box.**

The filename Rollablade 4Q Expenses replaces Book1 in the File name text box (Figure 1-60). A ***filename*** *can be up to 255 characters and can include spaces.*

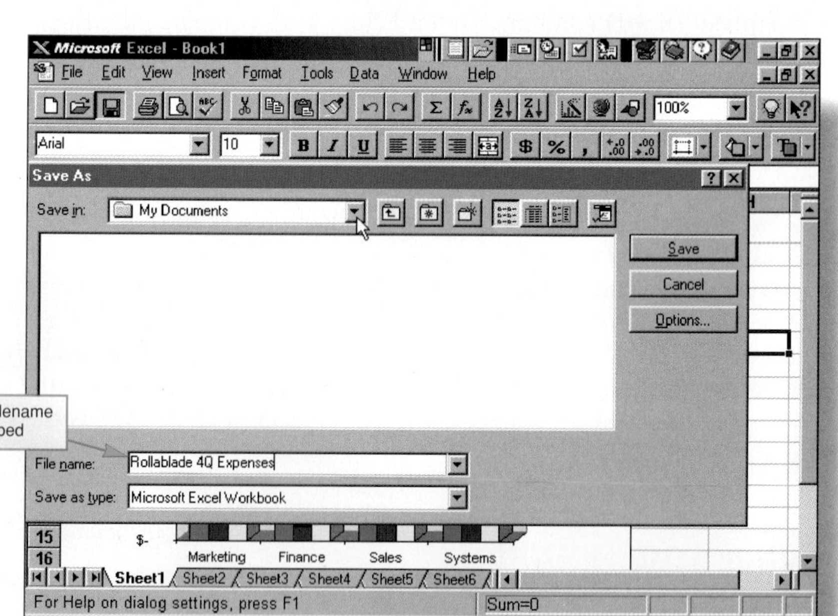

FIGURE 1-60

3 **Click the Save in box arrow and then point to the 3½ Floppy [A:] icon.**

A list of available drives and folders display (Figure 1-61).

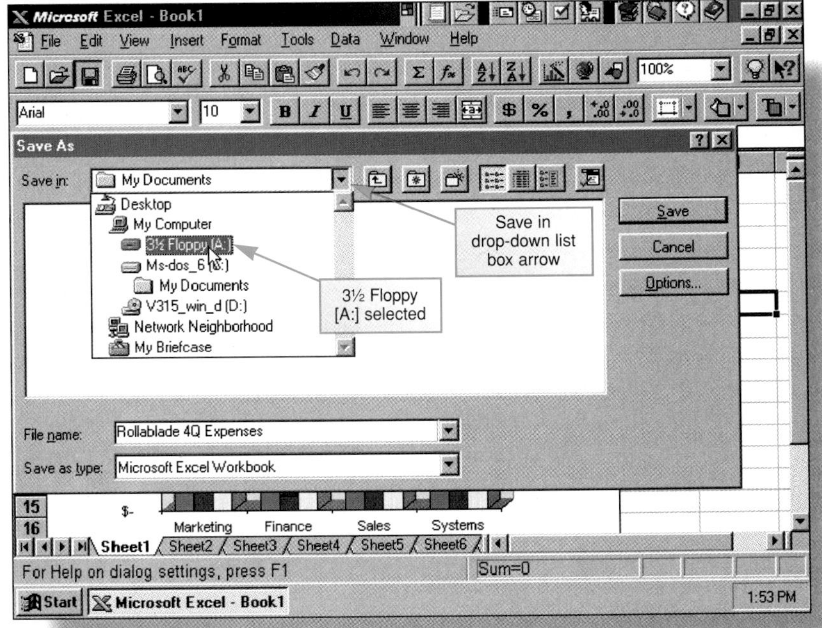

FIGURE 1-61

4 **Click 3½ Floppy [A:] icon and then point to the Save button.**

Drive A becomes the selected drive (Figure 1-62).

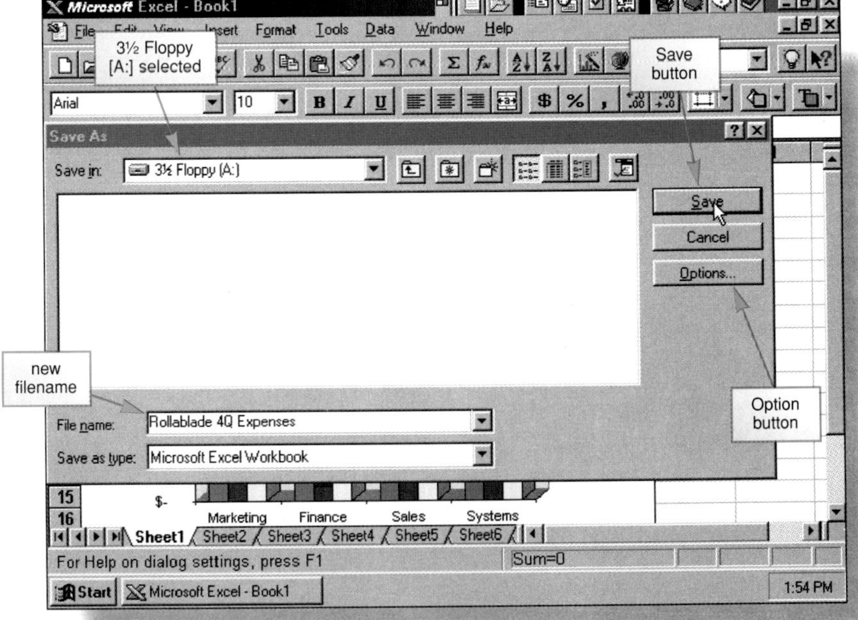

FIGURE 1-62

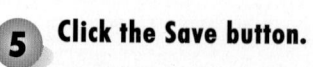

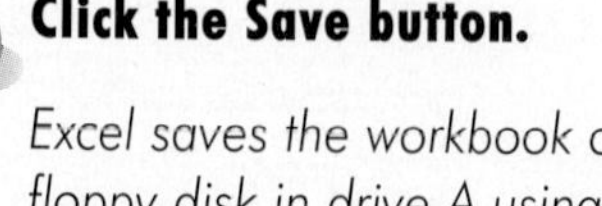

5 Click the Save button.

Excel saves the workbook on the floppy disk in drive A using the name Rollablade 4Q Expenses.xls. Excel automatically appends to the filename you entered in Step 2 the extension ***.xls****, which stands for Excel workbook. Although the Rollablade 4th Qtr Expenses workbook is saved on disk, it also remains in main memory and displays on the screen (Figure 1-63). Notice the filename in the title bar.*

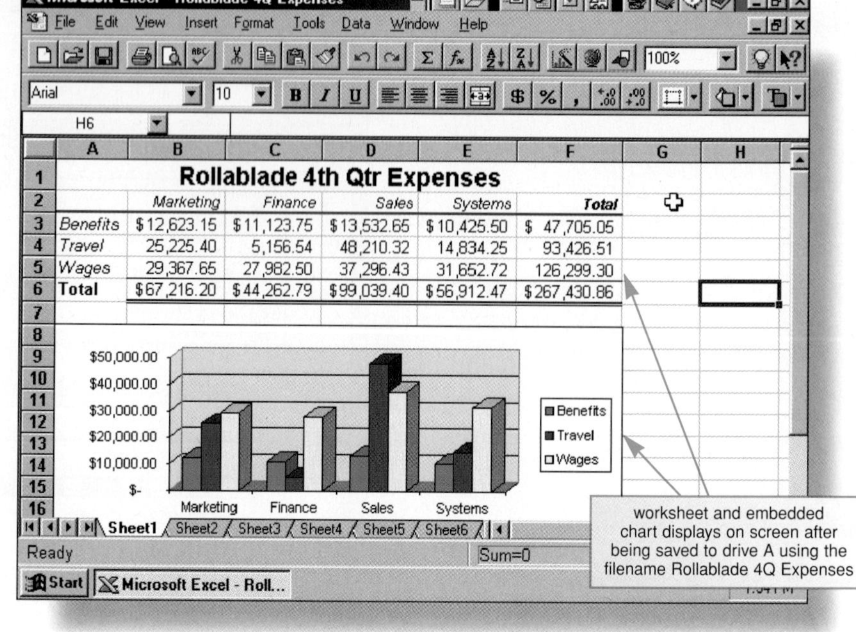

FIGURE 1-63

OtherWays

1. Right-click menu bar, click Save As, type filename, select drive or folder, click OK button
2. On File menu click Save As, type filename, select drive or folder, click OK button
3. Press CTRL+S, type filename, select drive or folder, click OK button

While Excel is saving the workbook, it momentarily changes the word Ready on the status bar to Saving. It also displays a horizontal bar on the status bar indicating the amount of the workbook saved. After the save operation is complete, Excel changes the name of the workbook in the title bar from Book1 to Rollablade 4Q Expenses (Figure 1-63).

The **Options button** in the Save As dialog box, as shown in Figure 1-62, allows you to save a backup copy of the workbook or limit access to the workbook. Saving a **backup workbook** means that each time you save a workbook, Excel copies the current version of the workbook on disk to a file with the same name with an extension of **.bak**. Thus, the second time you save a workbook, and thereafter, you will have two documents on disk with the same name, one with an extension of .xls and the other with an extension of .bak. In the case of a power failure or some other problem, use the (.bak) backup version of the document to restore your work.

You can also use the Options button to assign a password to your document. A password is case-sensitive and can be up to 15 characters long. **Case-sensitive** means Excel can differentiate between uppercase and lowercase letters If you assign a password and forget it, you cannot access the document.

The six buttons at the top of the Save As dialog box (Figure 1-62) and their functions are summarized in Table 1-4.

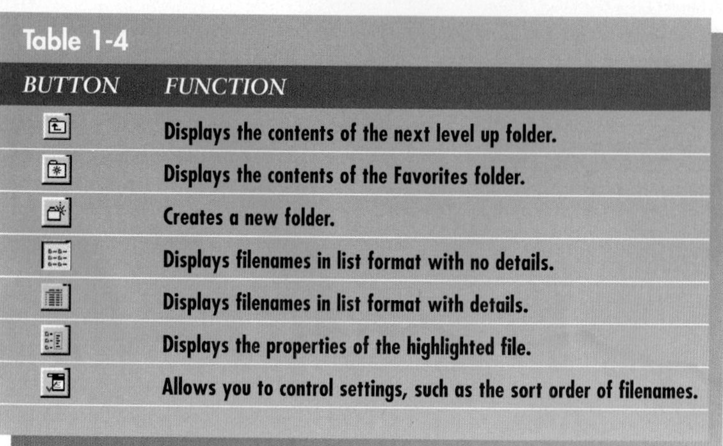

Table 1-4

BUTTON	FUNCTION
	Displays the contents of the next level up folder.
	Displays the contents of the Favorites folder.
	Creates a new folder.
	Displays filenames in list format with no details.
	Displays filenames in list format with details.
	Displays the properties of the highlighted file.
	Allows you to control settings, such as the sort order of filenames.

Printing the Worksheet

Once you have created the worksheet and saved it on disk, you might want to print it. A printed version of the worksheet is called a **hard copy** or **printout**.

There are several reasons why you would want a printout. First, to present the worksheet and chart to someone who does not have access to your computer, it must be in printed form. In addition, worksheets and charts are often kept for reference by persons other than those who prepare them. In many cases, the worksheets and charts are printed and kept in binders for use by others. This section describes how to print a worksheet and the embedded chart.

More About Printing

Interested in saving trees? Rather than printing a worksheet over and over until it's right, you can preview the printout on your screen, make adjustments to the worksheet, and then print only when it's exactly what you want. The Print Preview button is immediately to the right of the Print button on the Standard toolbar. Clicking it shows a perfect image on the screen of how the printout will appear on the printer. And each time you preview, rather than print, you save paper destined for the waste paper basket, which in turn saves trees.

Steps To Print a Worksheet

1. **Ready the printer according to the printer instructions.**

2. **Point to the Print button on the Standard toolbar (Figure 1-64).**

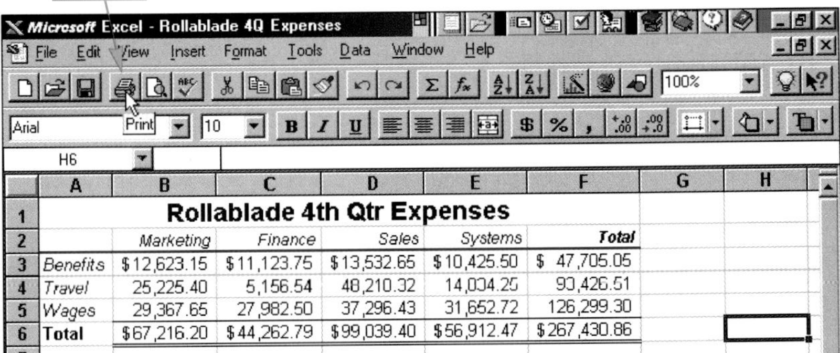

FIGURE 1-64

3. **Click the Print button.**

Excel displays the *Printing dialog box* (Figure 1-65) that allows you to cancel the print job at any time while the system is internally creating the worksheet and chart image to send to the printer. When the Printing dialog box disappears, the printing begins. Also, notice in Figure 1-65, the vertical dotted line along the right side of the worksheet. The dotted line indicates the right border of the area being printed.

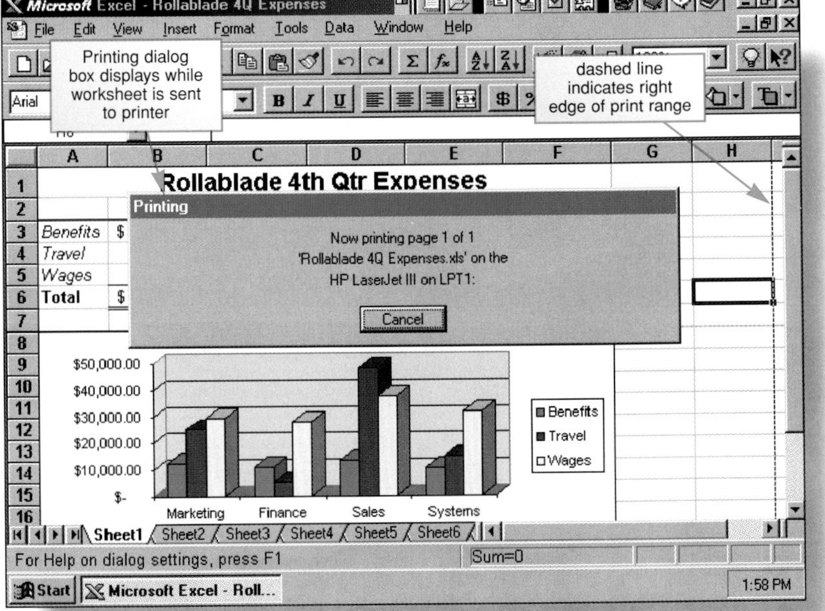

FIGURE 1-65

When the printer stops, retrieve the printout (Figure 1-66).

Sheet1

Rollablade 4th Qtr Expenses

	Marketing	*Finance*	*Sales*	*Systems*	*Total*
Benefits	$12,623.15	$11,123.75	$13,532.65	$10,425.50	$ 47,705.05
Travel	25,225.40	5,156.54	48,210.32	14,834.25	93,426.51
Wages	29,367.65	27,982.50	37,296.43	31,652.72	126,299.30
Total	$67,216.20	$44,262.79	$99,039.40	$56,912.47	$267,430.86

FIGURE 1-66

OtherWays

1. Right-click menu bar, click Print, click OK button
2. On File menu click Print, click OK button
3. Press CTRL+P, click OK button

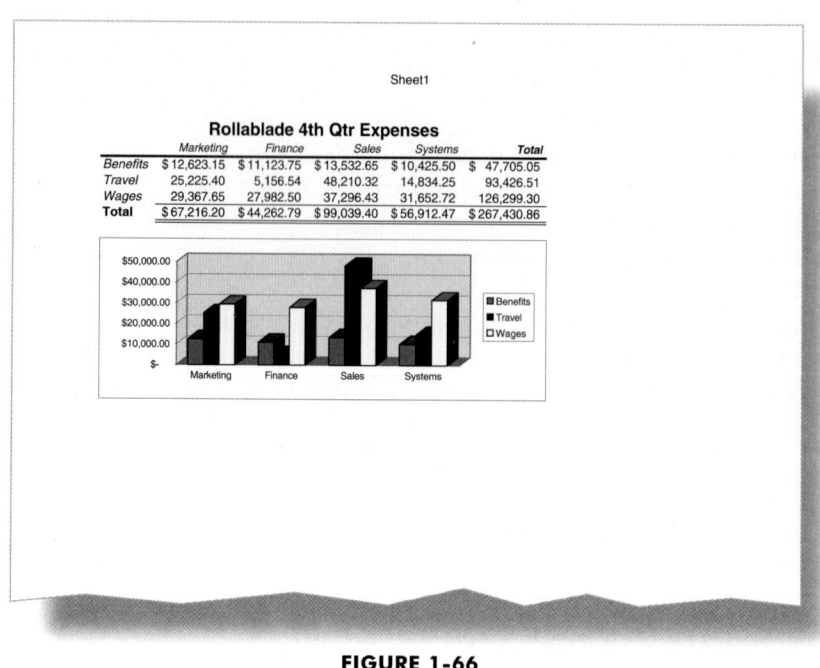

Notice in Figure 1-66 that Excel adds a header. A **header** is a line of text that prints at the top of each page. Although not shown in Figure 1-66, Excel also adds a footer. A **footer** is a line of text that prints at the bottom of each page. By default, Excel prints the name on the worksheet tab at the top of the screen as the header and the page number as the footer.

In Project 2, you will learn how to preview the printout on your screen before printing and how to print a selected range in a worksheet.

Exiting Excel

After you build, save, and print the worksheet and chart, Project 1 is complete. To exit Excel, complete the following steps.

Steps To Exit Excel

1. **Point to the Close button on the right side of the title bar (Figure 1-67).**

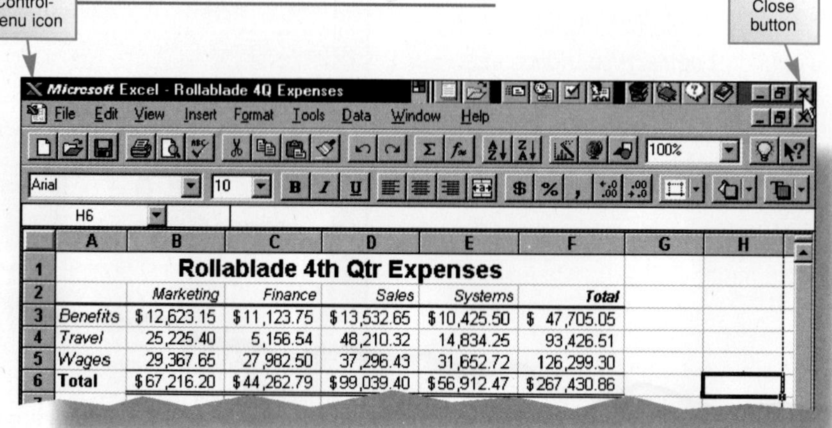

FIGURE 1-67

2 **Click the Close button.**

If you made changes to the workbook, Excel displays the question, "Save changes in 'Rollablade 4Q Expenses.xls'?" in the ***Microsoft Excel dialog box*** *(Figure 1-68). Click the Yes button to save the changes before exiting Excel. Click the No button to exit Excel without saving the changes. Click the Cancel button to terminate the Exit command and return to the worksheet.*

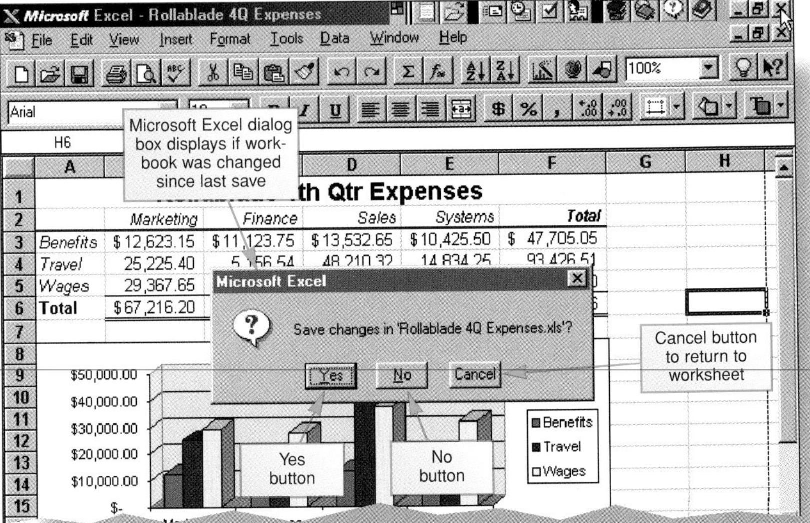

FIGURE 1-68

Starting Excel and Opening a Workbook

Once you have created and saved a workbook, often you will have reason to retrieve it from disk. For example, you might want to enter revised data, review the calculations on the worksheet, or add more data to it. The following steps assume Excel is not running.

OtherWays

1. Double-click Control-menu icon
2. Right-click Microsoft Excel taskbar button on taskbar, click Close
3. On File menu click Exit

Steps To Start Excel and Open a Workbook

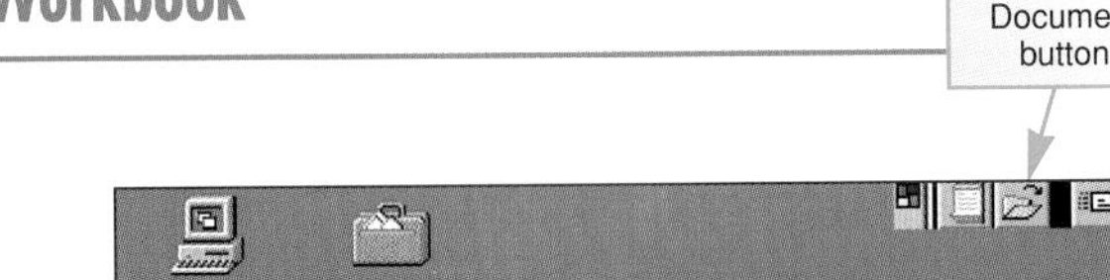

1 **With your floppy disk in drive A, click the Start button and then point to Open Office Document (Figure 1-69).**

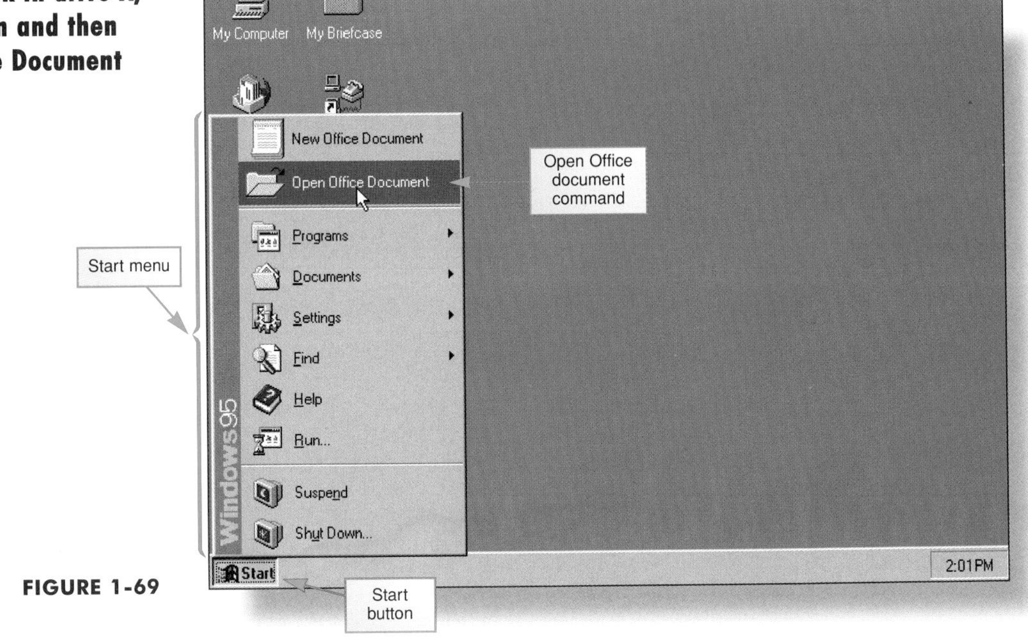

FIGURE 1-69

Click Open Office Document. If necessary, click the Look in box arrow and then double-click the 3½ Floppy [A:] icon.

*The **Open dialog box** displays (Figure 1-70).*

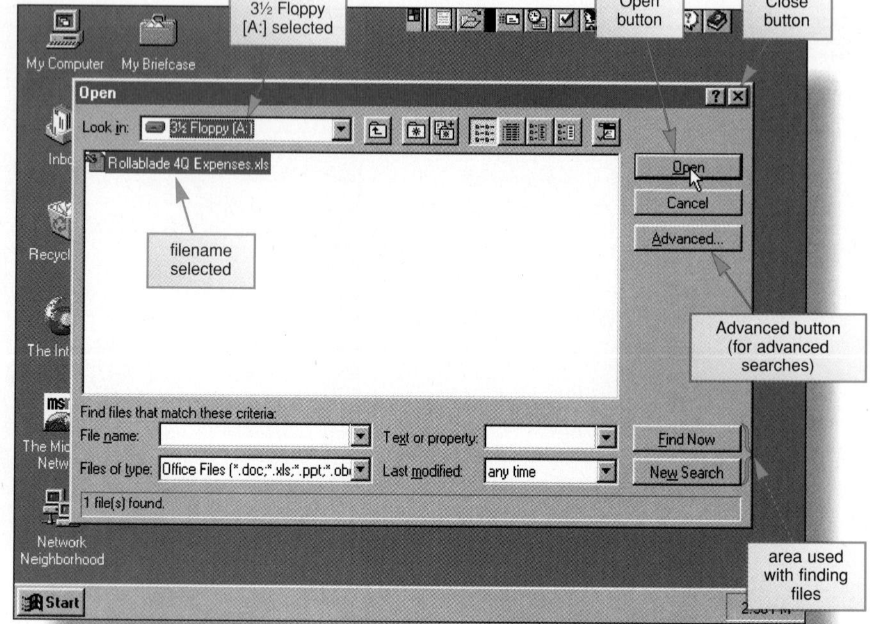

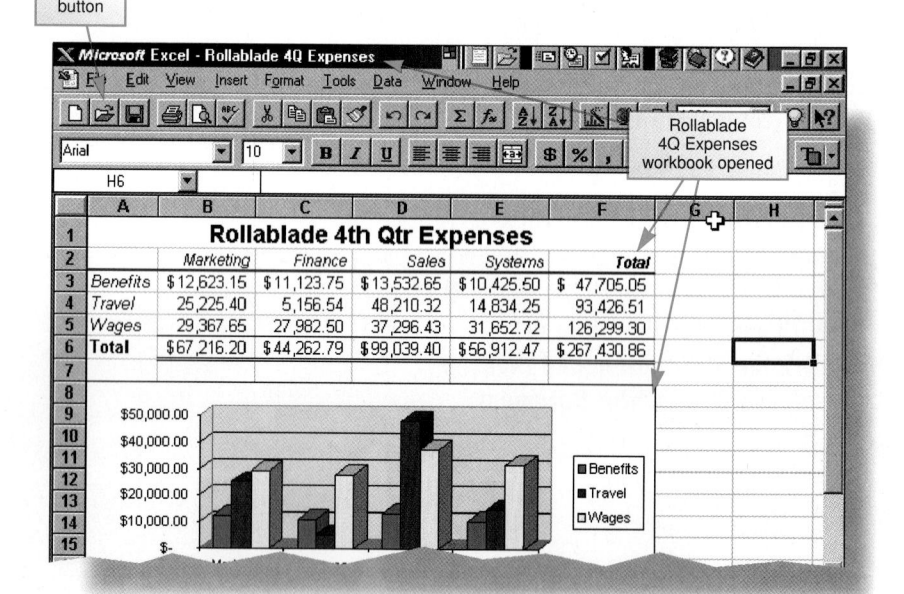

FIGURE 1-70

3 Double-click the filename Rollablade 4Q Expenses.

Excel starts and opens the document Rollablade 4Q Expenses.xls from drive A, and displays it on the screen (Figure 1-71). An alternative to double-clicking the filename is to click the filename and then click the Open button.

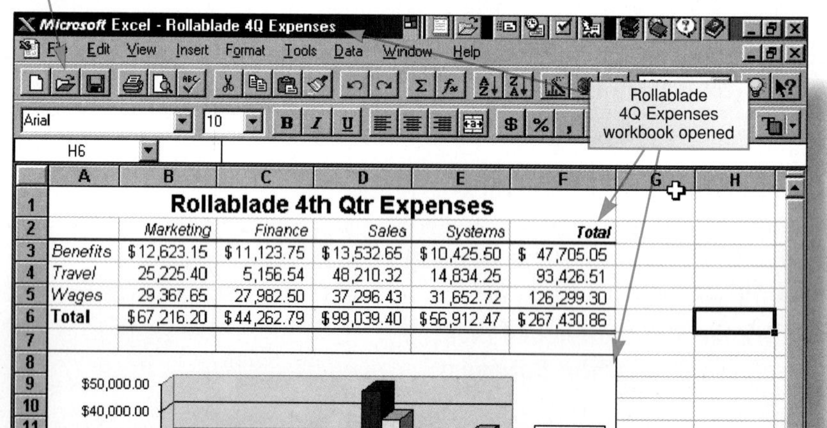

FIGURE 1-71

OtherWays

1. Double-click My Computer, click drive, click folder, double-click workbook icon
2. On Microsoft Office Shortcut Bar, click Open a Document button, select drive or folder, double-click filename
3. Click Start button, click Programs, click Microsoft Excel, click Open button on Standard toolbar, select drive or folder, double-click filename

AutoCalculate

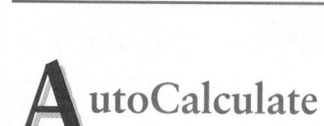

You can easily check a total of the numbers in a range by using the AutoCalculate area on the status bar (see Figure 1-72). All you need do is select the range of cells containing the numbers you want to total. Next, point to the AutoCalculate area and right-click to display the shortcut menu. The six totals on the AutoCalculate shortcut menu (Figure 1-72) are described in Table 1-5.

Table 1-5

TOTAL	FUNCTION
Average	Displays the average of the numbers in the selected range.
Count	Displays the number of nonblank cells in the selected range.
Count Nums	Displays the number of cells containing numbers in the selected range.
Max	Displays the greatest value in the selected range.
Min	Displays the least value in the selected range.
Sum	Displays the sum of the numbers in the selected range.

More *About* **Excel's Compatibility with Other Software Products**

Do you have files that were created using another software package? Excel has the capability to save or open Lotus 1-2-3, Quattro Pro, or dBASE files. It's easy. All you have to do is select the file type on the Save As or Open dialog boxes.

The following steps show how to display the average of the Benefits expenses in the range B3:E3.

To Use the AutoCalculate Area to Determine an Average

1 **Select the range B3:E3. Point to the AutoCalculate area on the status bar and then right-click.**

As shown in Figure 1-72, the sum of the numbers in the range B3:E3 displays ($47,705.05) because Sum is active in the AutoCalculate area (you may see a total other than the Sum on your screen). The shortcut menu listing the various types of totals displays next to the AutoCalculate area.

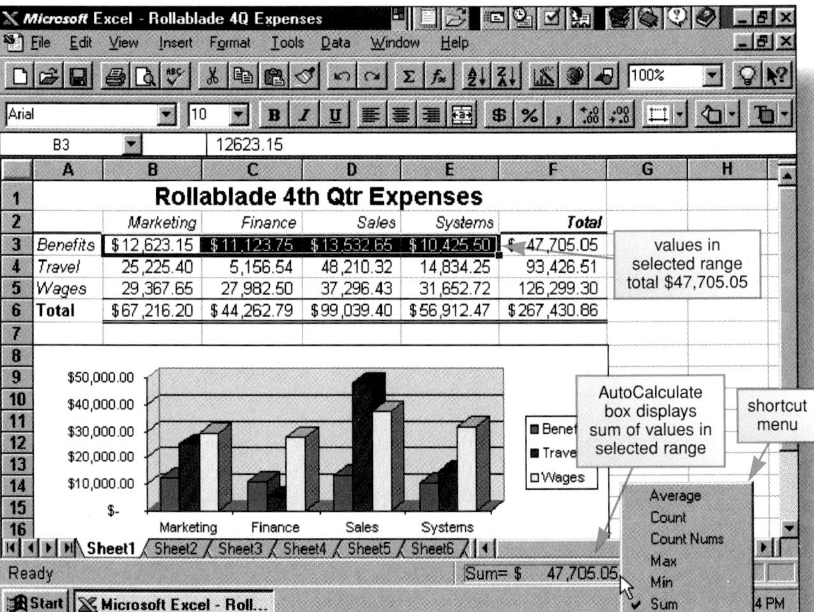

FIGURE 1-72

2 Right-click Average on the shortcut menu.

The average of the numbers in the range B3:E3 displays in the AutoCalculate area (Figure 1-73).

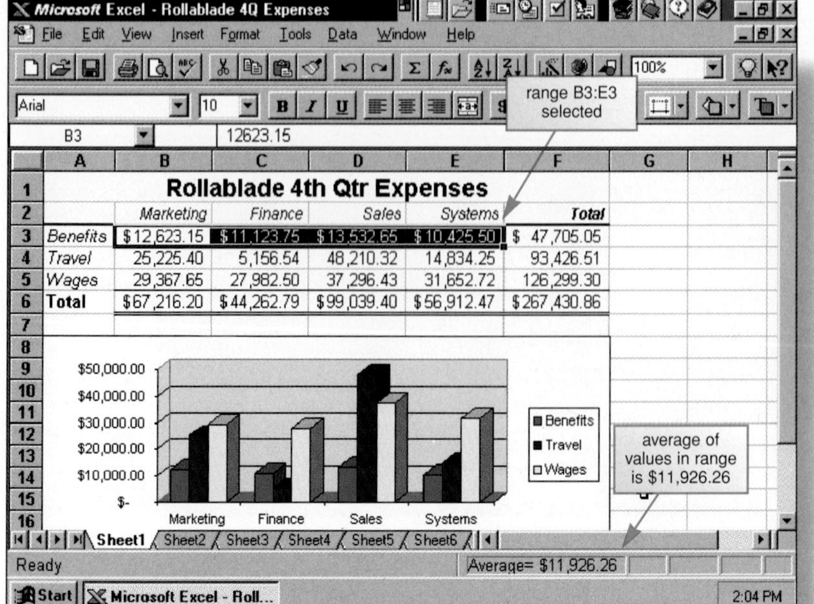

FIGURE 1-73

To change to any one of the other five totals for the range B3:E3, right-click the AutoCalculate area. Then right-click the desired total. You can see in Figure 1-72 on the previous page that a check mark to the left of the active total (Sum) indicates this total displays. Before continuing, change the total in the AutoCalculate area to Sum by pointing to it, right-clicking, and then clicking Sum on the shortcut menu.

Correcting Errors

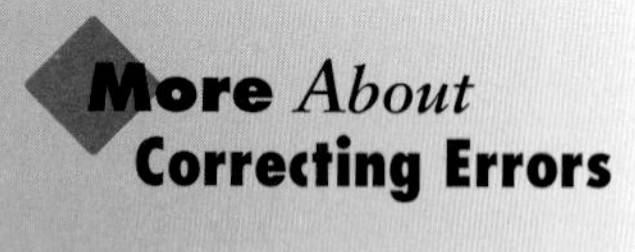

More *About* Correcting Errors

Learning how to correct errors in a worksheet is critical to becoming proficient in Excel. Thus, carefully review in this section how to correct errors prior to entering data in a cell, how to do in-cell editing, how to undo the last entry, and how to clear cells.

Several methods are available for correcting errors on a worksheet. The one you choose will depend on the severity of the error and whether you notice it while typing the data in the formula bar or after you have entered the incorrect data into the cell.

Correcting Errors Prior to Entering Data into a Cell

If you notice an error prior to entering data into a cell, use one of the following:

1. Press the BACKSPACE key to erase the portion in error and then type the correct characters; or
2. If the error is too severe, click the cancel box or press the ESC key to erase the entire entry in the formula bar and then reenter the data from the beginning.

In-Cell Editing

If you find an error in the worksheet after entering the data, you can correct the error in one of two ways:

1. If the entry is short, select the cell, retype the entry correctly, and click the enter box or press the ENTER key. The new entry will replace the old entry.
2. If the entry in the cell is long and the errors are minor, the **Edit mode** may be a better choice. Use the Edit mode as described below:
   a. Double-click the cell containing the error. Excel switches to Edit mode, the active cell contents display in the formula bar, and a flashing insertion point appears in the active cell (Figure 1-74). This editing procedure is called **in-cell editing** because you can edit the contents directly in the cell. The active cell contents also display in the formula bar.
   b. Make your changes, as specified below:
      (1) To insert between two characters, place the insertion point between the two characters and begin typing. Excel inserts the new characters at the location of the insertion point.
      (2) To delete a character in the cell, move the insertion point to the left of the character you want to delete and press the **DELETE key**, or place the insertion point to the right of the character you want to delete and press the **BACKSPACE key**. You can also use the mouse to drag over the character or adjacent characters to delete and press the DELETE key or click the Cut button on the Standard toolbar.

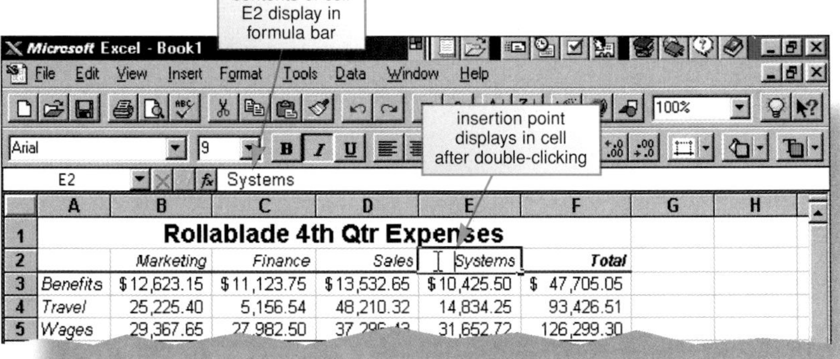

FIGURE 1-74

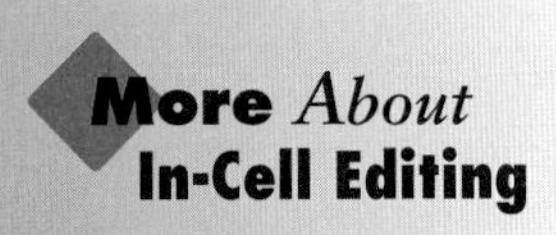

More *About* **In-Cell Editing**

An alternative to double-clicking the cell to edit is to select the cell and press function key F2.

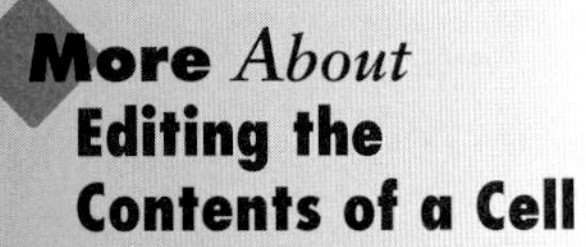

More *About* **Editing the Contents of a Cell**

Rather than in-cell editing, you can select the cell and click in the formula bar to edit the contents.

When you are finished editing an entry, click the enter box or press the ENTER key.

When Excel enters the Edit mode, the keyboard is usually in **Insert mode**. In Insert mode, as you type a character, Excel inserts the character and moves all characters to the right of the typed character one position to the right. You can change to **Overtype mode** by pressing the INSERT **key**. In Overtype mode, Excel overtypes the character to the right of the insertion point. The INSERT key toggles the keyboard between Insert mode and Overtype mode.

While in Edit mode, you may have occasion to move the insertion point to various points in the cell, select portions of the data in the cell, or switch from inserting characters to overtyping characters. Table 1-6 summarizes the most common tasks used during in-cell editing.

Table 1-6

TASK	*MOUSE*	*KEYBOARD*
Delete selected characters	Click the Cut button on the Standard toolbar	Press DELETE
Highlight one or more adjacent characters	Drag the mouse pointer over the adjacent characters	Press SHIFT+RIGHT ARROW or SHIFT+LEFT ARROW
Move the insertion point anywhere in a cell	Click the character at the appropriate position	Press RIGHT ARROW or LEFT ARROW
Move the insertion point to the beginning of data in a cell	Point to the left of the first character and click	Press HOME
Move the insertion point to the end of data in a cell	Point to the right of the last character and click	Press END
Select all data in a cell	Double-click cell with the insertion point in the cell	
Toggle between Insert and Overtype modes		Press INSERT

Undoing the Last Entry

Excel provides an **Undo button** on the Standard toolbar (Figure 1-75) that you can use to erase the most recent cell entry. Thus, if you enter incorrect data in a cell, click the Undo button and Excel changes the cell contents to what they were prior to entering the incorrect data.

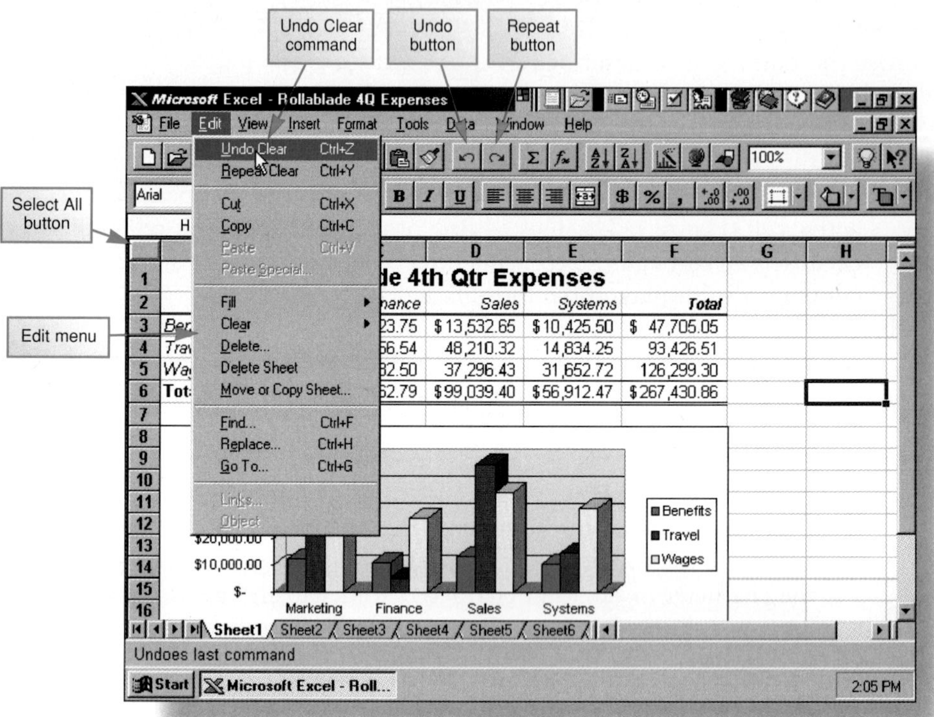

FIGURE 1-75

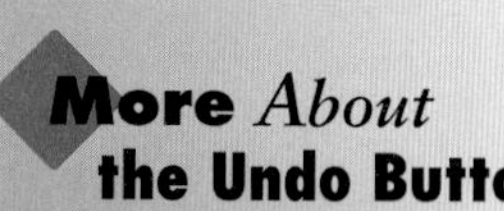

More *About* the Undo Button

The Undo button can undo more complicated worksheet activities than removing the latest entry from a cell. For example, most commands you issue can be undone if you click the Undo button before making another entry or issuing another command. You can't undo a save or print, but the general rule is that the Undo button can restore the worksheet data and settings to what they were the last time Excel was in Ready mode.

If Excel cannot undo an operation, then the button is inoperative. Next to the Undo button on the Standard toolbar is the Repeat button. The **Repeat button** allows you to repeat the last activity.

Finally, you can click **Undo** on the Edit menu (Figure 1-75) rather than using the Undo button. If Excel cannot undo an operation, then the words Can't Undo appear on the Edit menu in place of Undo.

Clearing a Cell or Range of Cells

It is not unusual to enter data into the wrong cell or range of cells. In such a case, to correct the error, you might want to erase or clear the data. ***Never press the SPACEBAR to enter a blank character to clear a cell.*** A blank character is text and is different from an empty cell, even though the cell may appear empty.

Excel provides three methods to clear the contents of a cell or a range of cells.

TO CLEAR CELL CONTENTS USING THE FILL HANDLE

Step 1: Select the cell or range of cells and point to the fill handle so the mouse pointer changes to a crosshair.

Step 2: Drag the fill handle back into the selected cell or range until a shadow covers the cell or cells you want to erase. Release the left mouse button.

TO CLEAR CELL CONTENTS USING THE SHORTCUT MENU

Step 1: Select the cell or range of cells to be cleared.
Step 2: Right-click the selection.
Step 3: Click Clear Contents.

TO CLEAR CELL CONTENTS USING THE DELETE KEY

Step 1: Select the cell or range of cells to be cleared.
Step 2: Press the DELETE key.

TO CLEAR CELL CONTENTS USING THE CLEAR COMMAND

Step 1: Select the cell or range of cells to be cleared.
Step 2: On the Edit menu, click Clear.
Step 3: Click All on the submenu.

You can also select a range of cells and click the Cut button on the Standard toolbar or click **Cut** on the Edit menu. Be aware, however, besides deleting the contents from the range, the Cut button or Cut command also copies the contents of the range to the clipboard.

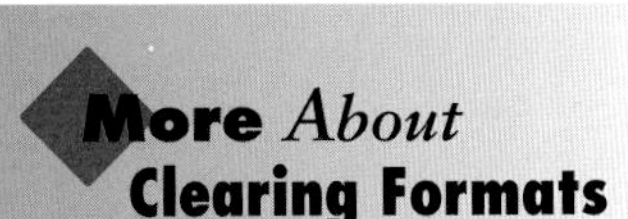

More *About* **Clearing Formats**

If you accidentally assign unwanted formats to a range of cells, you can use the Clear command on the Edit menu to delete the formats of a selected range. In this case, the format changes to normal. To view the characteristics of normal format, click Style on the Format menu or press ALT+' (APOSTROPHE).

Clearing the Entire Worksheet

Sometimes, everything goes wrong. If this happens, you may want to clear the worksheet entirely and start over. To clear the worksheet, follow these steps.

TO CLEAR THE ENTIRE WORKSHEET

Step 1: Click the Select All button (Figure 1-75).
Step 2: Press the DELETE key or click Clear on the Edit menu and then click All on the submenu.

An alternative to the Select All button in Step 1 is to press CTRL+A. You can also clear an entire worksheet by clicking **Close** on the File menu. If you use Close on the File menu, click the **New button** on the Standard toolbar to begin working on your next workbook.

More *About* **Global Activities**

Lotus 1-2-3 users may wonder how to carry out global activities in Excel, since there are no specific global commands. It's easy, simply click the Select All button or press CTRL+A before you issue a command, and the command will effect the entire worksheet.

TO DELETE AN EMBEDDED CHART

Step 1: Click the chart to select it.
Step 2: Press the DELETE key.

More *About*
Online Help

Prior versions of Excel came with several thick manuals. Most beginners had difficulty figuring out which manual contained the information they were after. The online Help feature of this latest version of Excel replaces the manuals with the tools described in Table 1-7.

Excel Online Help

At any time while you are using Excel, you can answer your Excel questions by using **online Help**. Used properly, this form of online assistance can increase your productivity and reduce your frustrations by minimizing the time you spend learning how to use Excel. Table 1-7 summarizes the six categories of online Help available to you.

Table 1-7

TYPE	DESCRIPTION	ACTIVATE BY CLICKING
Contents sheet	Groups Help topics by general categories; use when you know only the general category of the topic in question	Double-click the Help button on the Standard toolbar or click Microsoft Excel Help Topics on the Help menu, and then click the Contents tab.
Index sheet	Similar to an index in a book; use when you know exactly what you want	Double-click the Help button on the Standard toolbar or click Microsoft Excel Help Topics on the Help menu, and then click the Index tab.
Find sheet	Searches the index for all phrases that include the term in question	Double-click the Help button on the Standard toolbar or click Microsoft Excel Help Topics on the Help menu, and then click the Find tab.
Answer Wizard sheet	Allows you to enter English-type questions in your own words, such as "how do i save a workbook?"	Double-click the Help button on the Standard toolbar or click Answer Wizard or Microsoft Excel Help Topics on the Help menu, and then click the Answer Wizard tab.
Question button and Help button	Used to identify unfamiliar items on the screen	In a dialog box, click the Question mark button and then click an item in the dialog box. Click the Help button on the Standard toolbar, and then click an item on the screen.
TipWizard Box	Displays ways to do your work more quickly and easily	Click the TipWizard button on the Standard toolbar to display the TipWizard.

The following sections show examples of each type of online Help described in Table 1-7.

More *About*
the Contents Sheet

Use the Contents sheet in the same manner you would use a table of contents at the front of a textbook.

Using the Contents Sheet to Obtain Help

The **Contents sheet** in the **Help Topics dialog box** offers you assistance when you know the general category of the topic in question, but not the specifics. The following steps show how to use the Contents sheet tab to obtain information on editing the contents of cells.

To Obtain Help Using the Contents Sheet

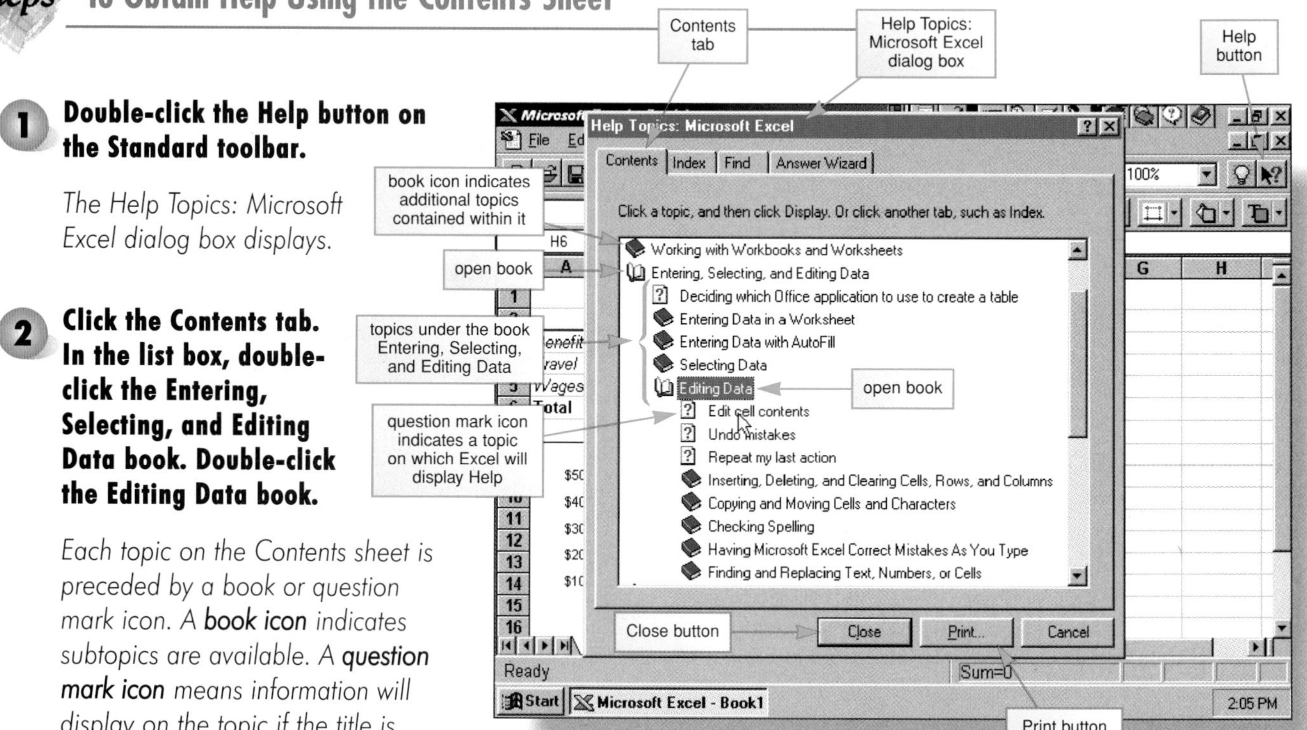

FIGURE 1-76

1 Double-click the Help button on the Standard toolbar.

The Help Topics: Microsoft Excel dialog box displays.

2 Click the Contents tab. In the list box, double-click the Entering, Selecting, and Editing Data book. Double-click the Editing Data book.

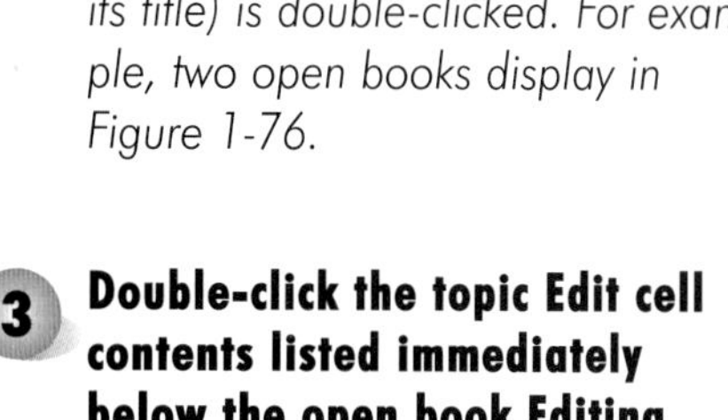

Each topic on the Contents sheet is preceded by a book or question mark icon. A **book icon** *indicates subtopics are available. A* **question mark icon** *means information will display on the topic if the title is double-clicked. Notice how the book icon opens when the book (or its title) is double-clicked. For example, two open books display in Figure 1-76.*

3 Double-click the topic Edit cell contents listed immediately below the open book Editing Data.

A Microsoft Excel Help window displays describing the steps for editing a cell's contents (Figure 1-77).

4 After reading the information, click the Close button in the Help Topics: Microsoft Excel dialog box.

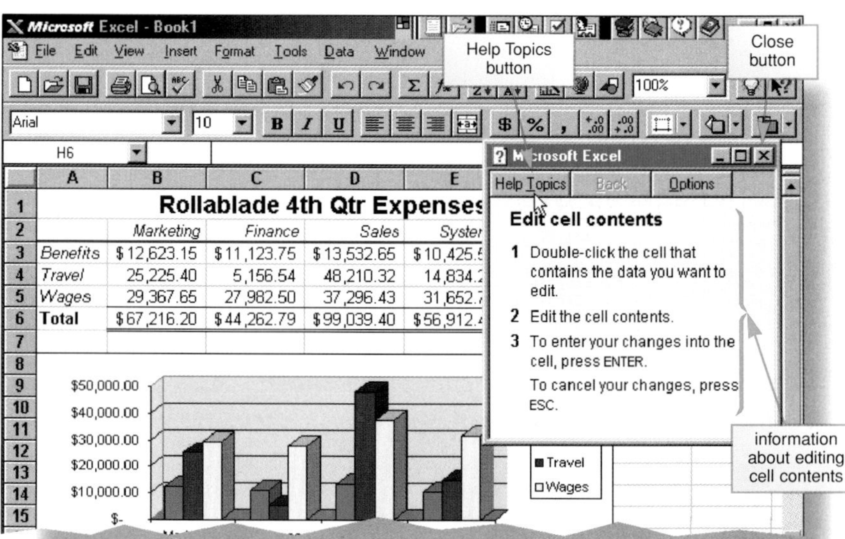

FIGURE 1-77

OtherWays

1. On Help menu click Microsoft Excel Help Topics, click Contents tab
2. Press F1, click Contents tab

Rather than double-clicking a topic in the list box, you can click it and then use the buttons at the bottom of the dialog box to open a book, display information on a topic, or print information on a topic (see Figure 1-76 on the previous page). You can also print the information by pointing to the dialog box and right-clicking (Figure 1-77) or clicking the Options button and then clicking Print Topic. To cancel the dialog box, click the Close button to return to Excel or click the Help Topics button to return to the Contents sheet.

More *About* the Index Sheet

If you have used the index of a book to look up terms, then you will feel comfortable with the Index sheet. It works the same way. Only you have to type the term you want information on, rather than look it up in an index.

Using the Index Sheet to Obtain Help

The next sheet in the Help Topics: Microsoft Excel dialog box is the Index sheet. Use the **Index sheet** when you know the term you want to find or at least the first few letters of the term. Use the Index sheet in the same manner you would an index at the back of a textbook.

The following steps show how to obtain information on the AutoCalculate area by using the Index sheet and entering auto, the first four letters of AutoCalculate.

Steps To Obtain Help Using the Index Sheet

1. **Double-click the Help button on the Standard toolbar.**

   The Help Topics: Microsoft Excel dialog box displays.

2. **Click the Index tab. Type** `auto` **in the top box labeled 1.**

   The term AutoCalculate is highlighted in the lower box labeled 2 (Figure 1-78). You may have to click AutoCalculate to highlight it.

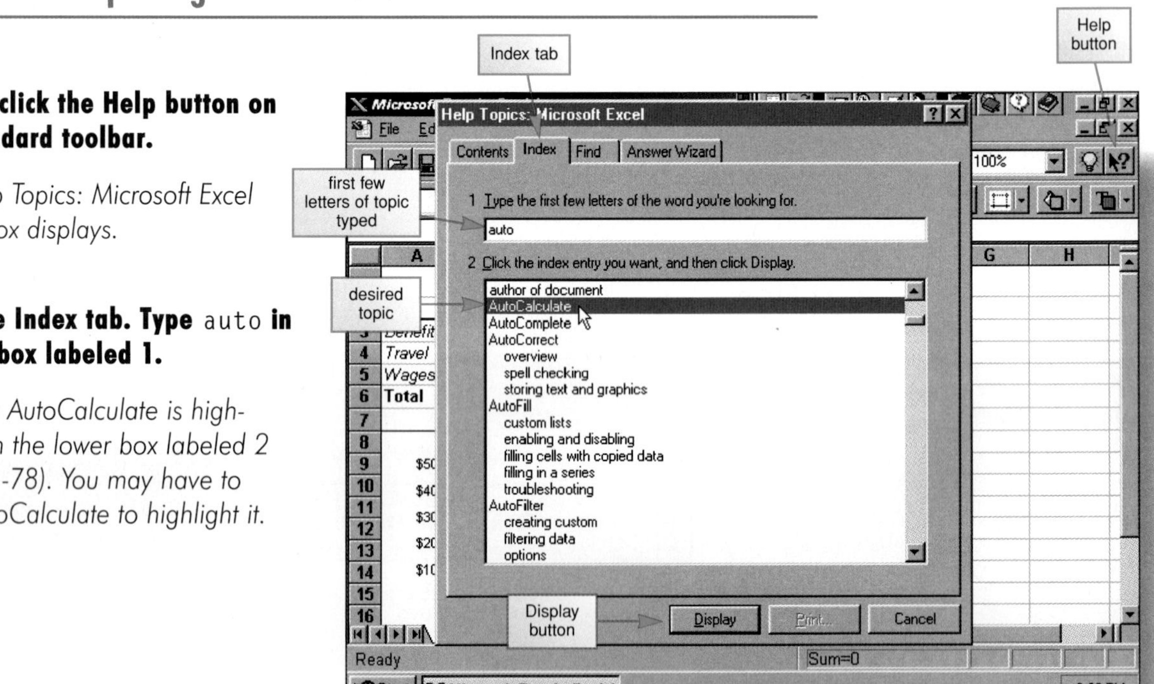

FIGURE 1-78

3 **Click the Display button. When the Microsoft Excel for Windows 95 Help window displays, click the AutoCalculate link.**

The information describing AutoCalculate displays above the AutoCalculate link (Figure 1-79). When you click a ***link****, which is a picture or phrase, Excel displays Help information.*

4 **Click the Close button in the upper right corner of the Microsoft Excel for Windows 95 Help window to close it.**

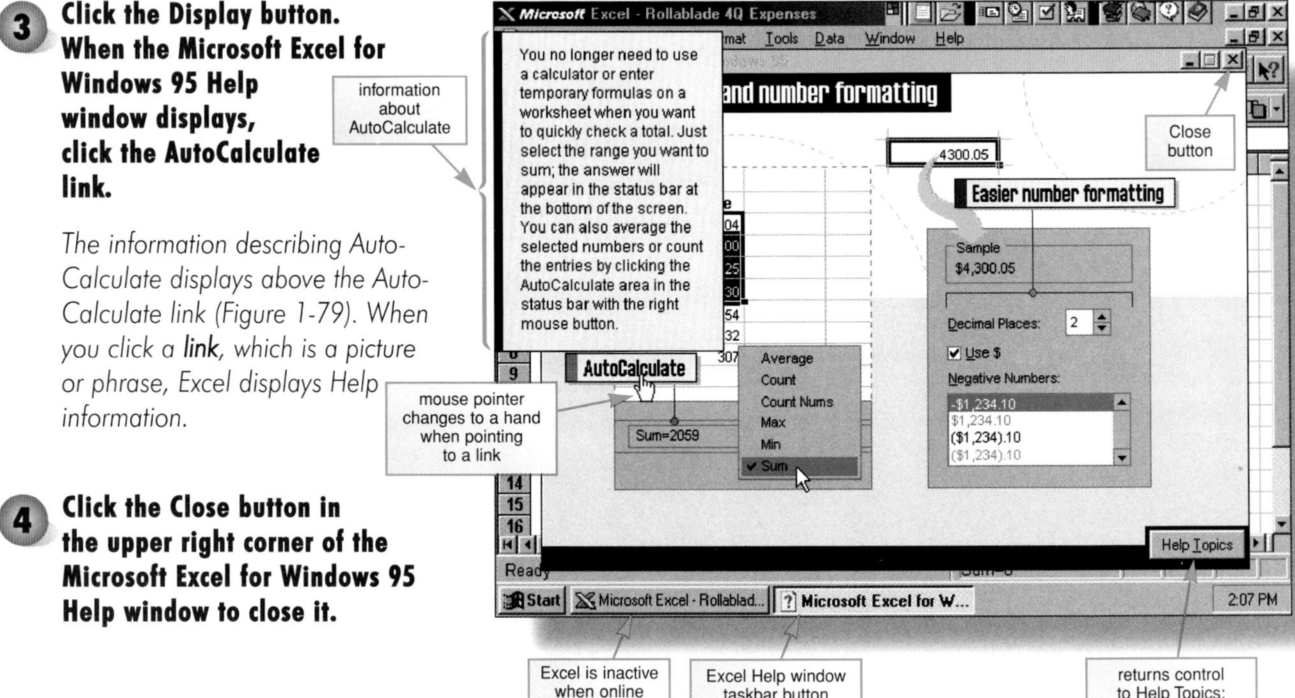

FIGURE 1-79

OtherWays

1. On Help menu click Microsoft Excel Help Topics, click Index tab
2. Press F1, click Index tab

Not all information you look up through online Help is printable. For example, it is not possible to print the information describing the AutoCalculate area on the status bar. Generally speaking, if the dialog box contains an Options button (see Figure 1-77 on page E 1.55), then you can print the information.

Using the Find Sheet to Obtain Help

The third sheet in the Help Topics: Microsoft Excel dialog box is the Find sheet. The **Find sheet** will return a list of all topics pertaining to the word. You can then further select words to narrow your search.

The steps on the next page show how to obtain information on using drag and drop methods to move or copy ranges in a worksheet.

More About the Find Sheet

Use the Find sheet when you know a word that is located anywhere in the term or phrase you want to look up.

Steps To Obtain Help Using the Find Sheet

1 **Double-click the Help button on the Standard toolbar.**

The Help Topics: Microsoft Excel dialog box displays.

2 **Click the Find tab. Type** `drag` **in the top box labeled 1.**

Matching words display in the middle box labeled 2 and 76 topics relating to the term drag are accessible in the lower box labeled 3 (Figure 1-80). The number of topics may be different on your computer.

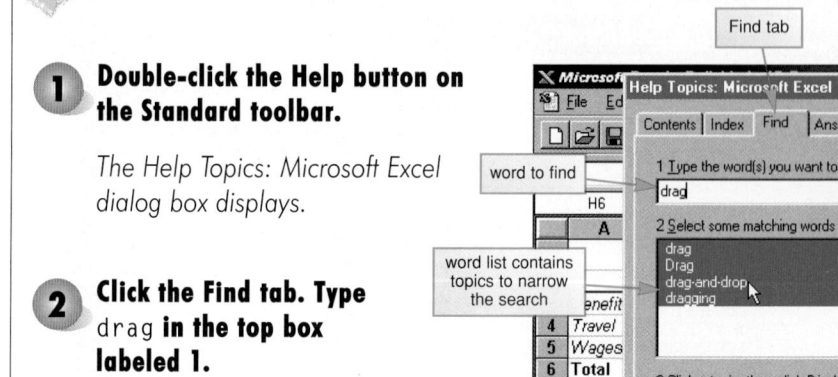

FIGURE 1-80

3 **Click the phrase, drag-and-drop, in the middle box labeled 2.**

The number of topics found changes from 76 to 3 in the lower box labeled 3 (Figure 1-81).

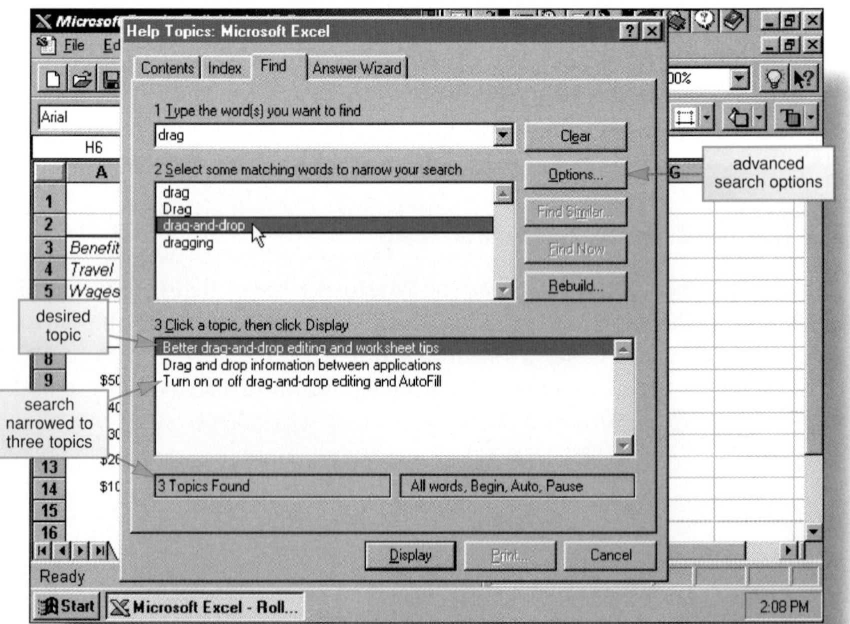

FIGURE 1-81

4 Double-click the topic Better drag-and-drop editing and worksheet tips in the lower box labeled 3 on the Find sheet. When the Microsoft Excel for Windows 95 Help window displays, click the Drag cells between worksheets link.

The information regarding dragging and dropping displays as shown in Figure 1-82.

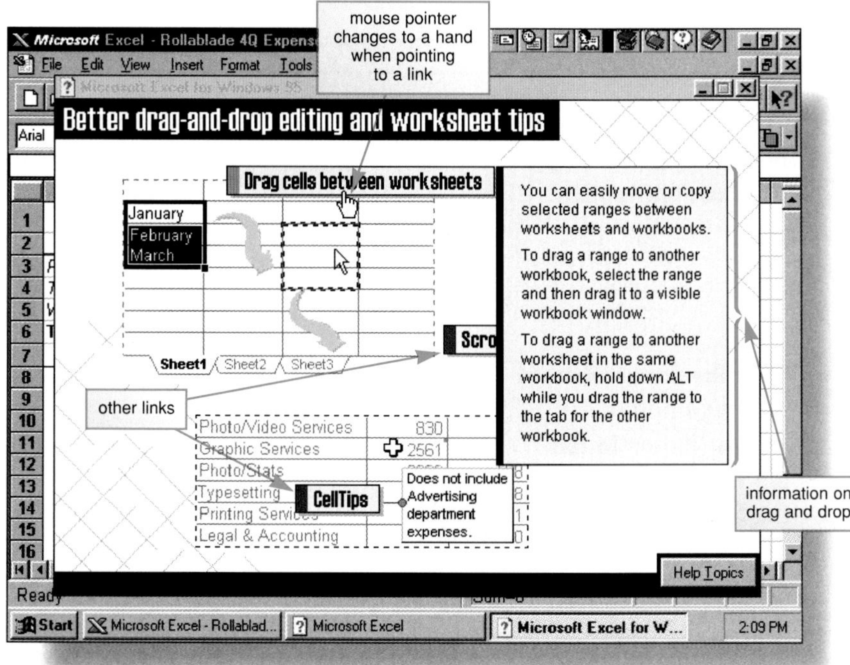

FIGURE 1-82

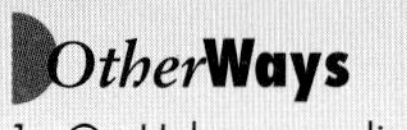
***Other*Ways**

1. On Help menu click Microsoft Excel Help Topics, click Find tab
2. Press F1, click Find tab

You can see from the previous steps that the Find sheet allows you to enter a word similar to the Index sheet, but instead of displaying an alphabetical listing, the Find sheet lists all the phrases that include the word entered. You then can choose the appropriate phrase to narrow your search.

Using the Answer Wizard Sheet to Obtain Help

The fourth and final sheet in the Help Topics: Microsoft Excel dialog box is the Answer Wizard sheet. Simply type a question in your own words and the **Answer Wizard** will assist you. For example, when you type a question, such as "How do I sum a range?" on the Answer Wizard sheet, it responds by displaying two categories of topics – *How Do I* and *Tell Me About*. The *How Do I* topics show how to complete a task, listing a step-by-step procedure or by example. The *Tell Me About* topics give you a better understanding of the task in question.

The steps on the next page show how to obtain information on summing multiple rows and columns by entering the question, "How do I sum a range?"

More *About* the Answer Wizard Sheet

Use the Answer Wizard sheet when you know what you want to do, but have no idea what the task is called.

Steps To Obtain Help Using the Answer Wizard

1 Double-click the Help button on the Standard toolbar.

The Help Topics: Microsoft Excel dialog box displays.

2 Click the Answer Wizard tab. Type `how do i sum a range` **in the top box labeled 1. Click the Search button on the Answer Wizard sheet.**

The Answer Wizard responds by displaying two categories (How Do I and Tell Me About) of topics in the lower box labeled 2 (Figure 1-83).

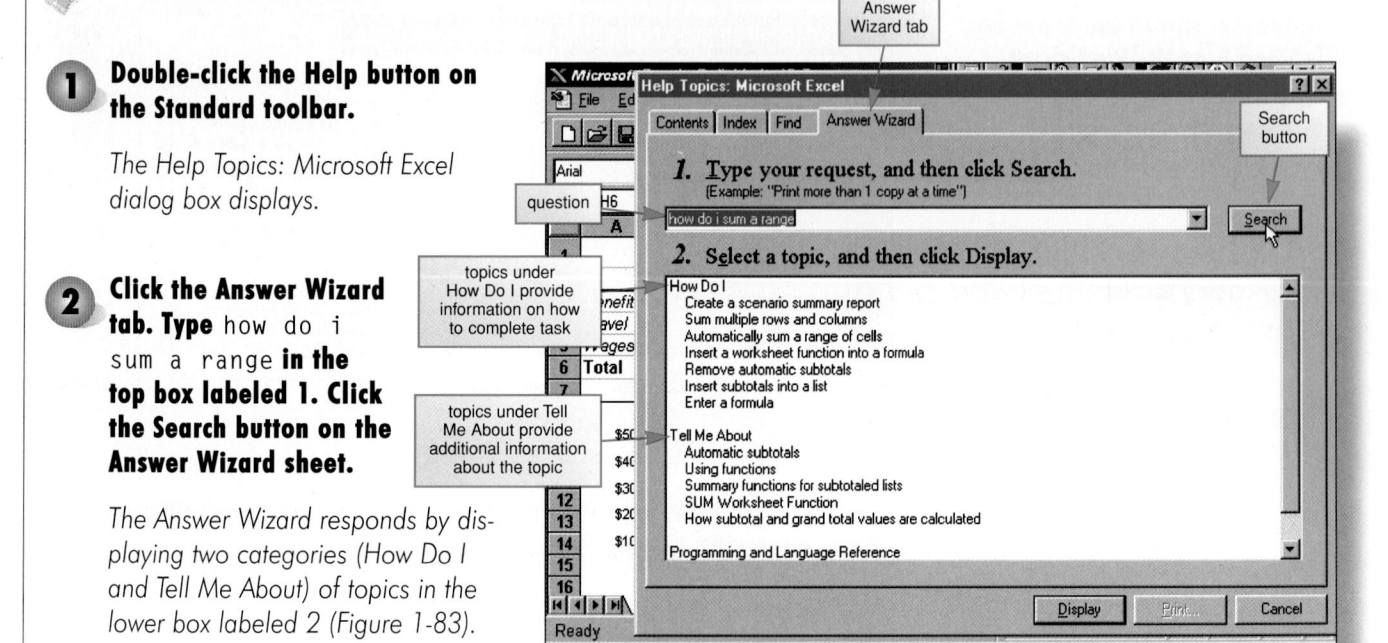

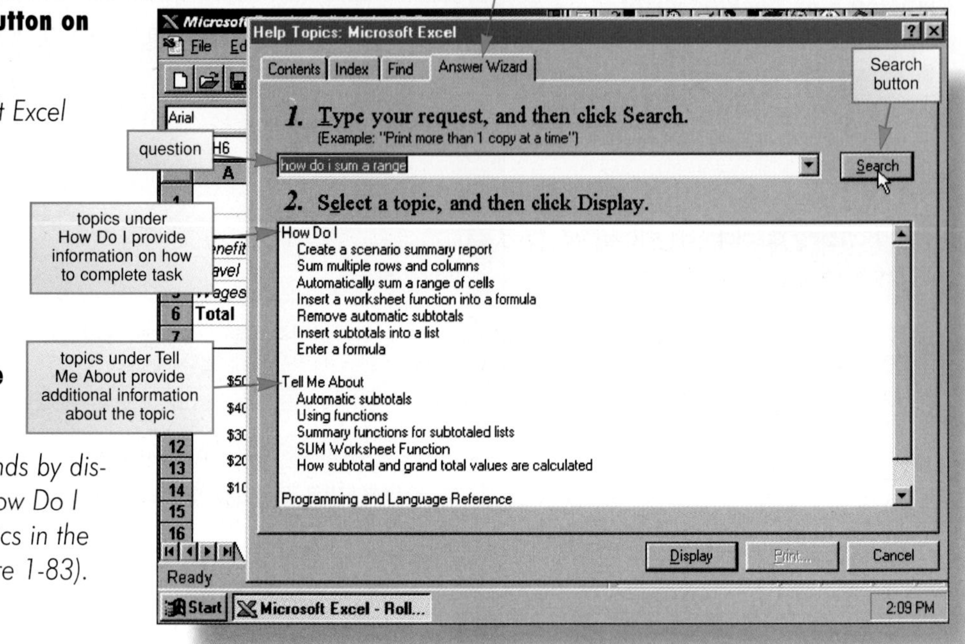

FIGURE 1-83

3 Double-click the topic, Sum multiple rows and columns, in the lower box labeled 2.

A Microsoft Excel Help window displays showing the step-by-step procedures for summing multiple rows and columns (Figure 1-84).

4 After reading the step-by-step procedures, click the Close button in the upper right corner of the dialog box to close it.

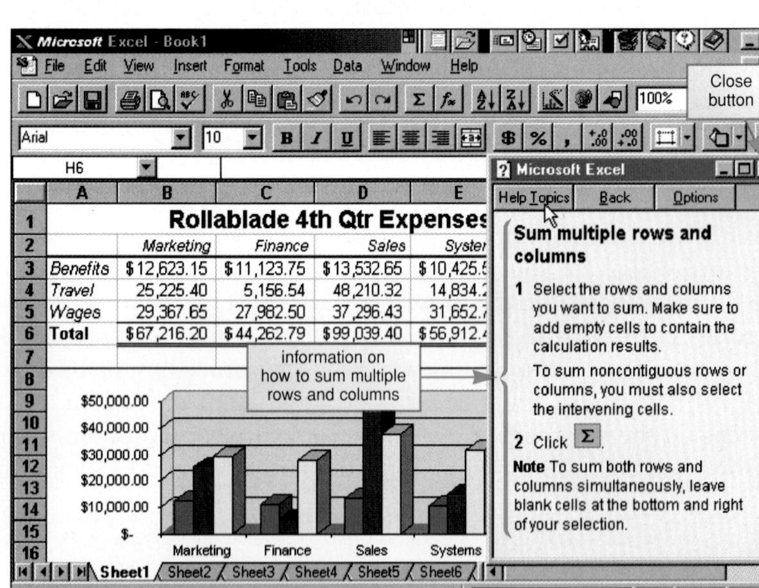

FIGURE 1-84

OtherWays

1. On Help menu click Answer Wizard
2. Press F1, click Answer Wizard tab

Here again, you can print the step-by-step procedures in Figure 1-84 by right-clicking in the Help window or by clicking the Options button. Instead of quitting online Help by clicking the Close button in Step 4, you can click the Help Topics button (Figure 1-84) to return to the Answer Wizard sheet shown in Figure 1-83.

The four online Help features (Contents, Index, Find, and Answer Wizard) of Excel presented thus far are powerful and easy to use. The best way to familiarize yourself with these Help tools is to use them. At the end of each project, there is a section titled Use Help. It is recommended that you step through these Help exercises to gain a better understanding of Excel online Help.

More *About* **Help**

The best way to familiarize yourself with the online Help features is to use them.

Using the Question Button or Help Button to Define Items on the Screen

Use the Question Mark button or Help button when you are not sure what an item on the screen is or what it does. Click either button and the mouse pointer changes to an arrow with a question mark. Next, click any item you want more information on. The **Question Mark button** displays in the upper right corner of dialog boxes, next to the Close button. For example, in Figure 1-85, the AutoFormat dialog box is on the screen. If you click the Question Mark button, and then click anywhere in the Table Format list box, an explanation of the Table Format list box displays.

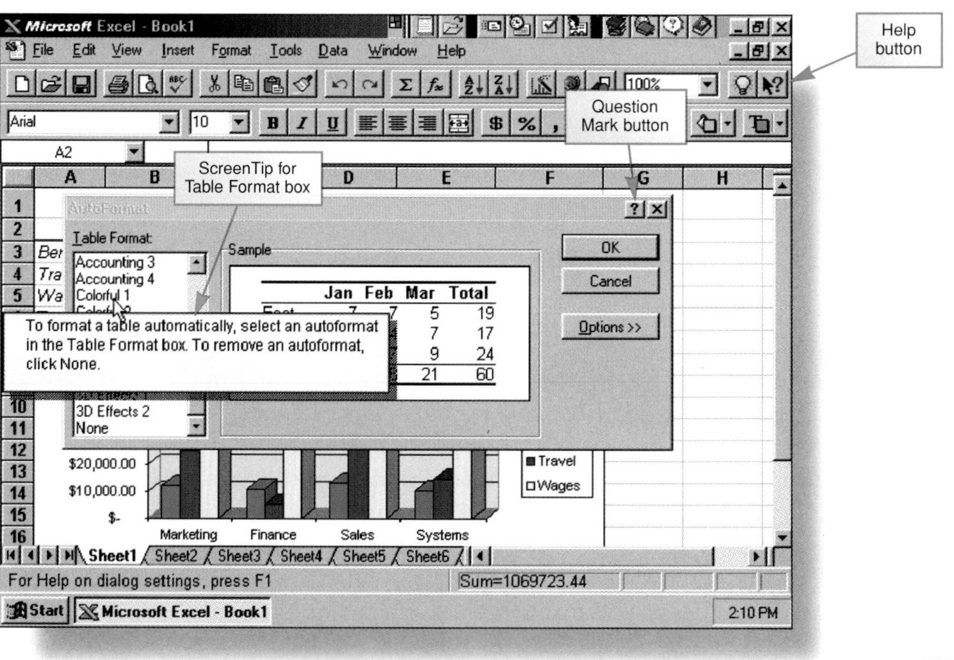

FIGURE 1-85

Whereas the Question mark button is used to display ScreenTips concerning items in a dialog box, the **Help button** on the Standard toolbar (Figure 1-85) is used to display ScreenTips concerning items on the Excel window. Once you click the Help button, you can move the arrow and question mark pointer to any menu name, button, or cell, and click to display a ScreenTip. For example, clicking the Center Across Columns button displays the ScreenTip shown in the bottom screen of Figure 1-86 on the next page. Click anywhere on the window to close the ScreenTip.

More *About* **the Question Mark Button and Help Button**

Both the Question Mark button on a dialog box and the Help button on the Standard toolbar display **ScreenTips**, which offer an explanation of the item you click when the mouse pointer changes to an arrow with a question mark.

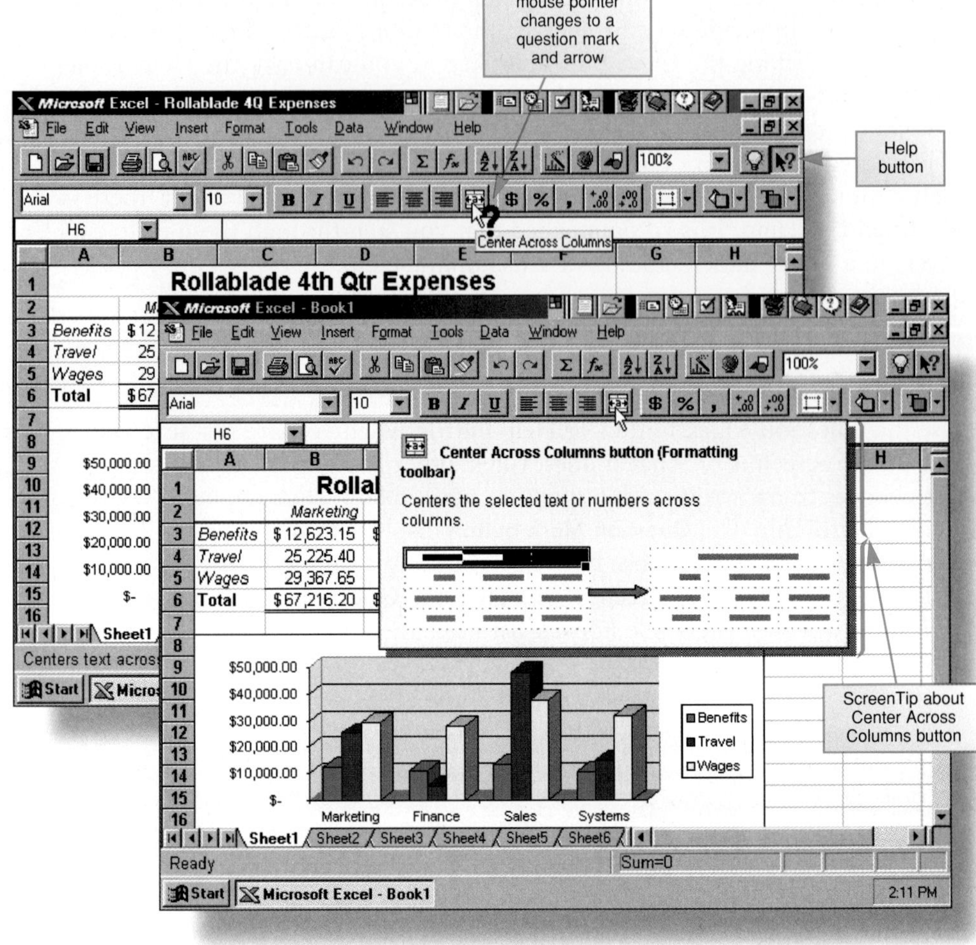

FIGURE 1-86

Information at Your Fingertips — TipWizard

Excel displays tips on how to work more efficiently in the **TipWizard Box**. When toggled on, the TipWizard Box displays at the top of the screen between the Formatting toolbar and formula bar (Figure 1-87). You toggle the TipWizard Box on or off by clicking the **TipWizard button** on the Standard toolbar. If toggled on when you start Excel, the TipWizard Box begins with a **tip of the day**. As you work through creating and editing a worksheet, Excel adds tips to the TipWizard box. The tips explain how to complete the activities you just performed more efficiently. You can scroll through these tips using the TipWizard Box.

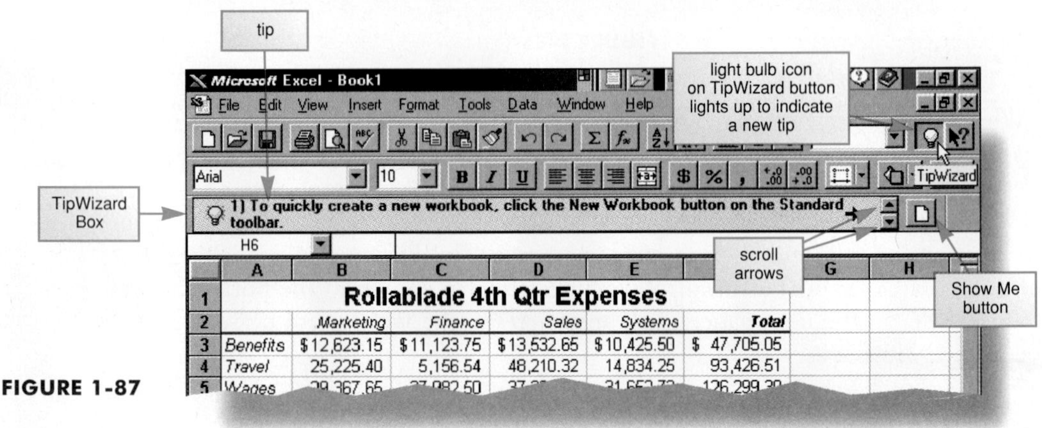

FIGURE 1-87

Exiting Excel

To exit Excel, complete the following steps.

TO EXIT EXCEL

Step 1: Click the Close button on the right side of the title bar.
Step 2: If the Microsoft Excel dialog box displays, click the No button.

More *About* **Exiting Excel**

Don't forget to remove your floppy disk from drive A after exiting Excel, especially if you are working in a laboratory environment. Nothing can be more frustrating than leaving all your hard work behind on a floppy disk for the next user.

Project Summary

The worksheet created in this project (Figure 1-1 on page E 1.7) allows the management of Rollablade to examine the Fourth-Quarter Expenses easily. Furthermore, the 3-D column chart should meet the needs of the president, Max Trealer, who as you recall from the Case Perspective has little tolerance for lists of numbers.

In creating the Rollablade Fourth-Quarter Expenses worksheet and chart in this project, you gained a broad knowledge about Excel. First, you were introduced to starting Excel. You learned about the Excel window and how to enter text and numbers to create a worksheet. You learned how to select a range and how to use the AutoSum button to sum numbers in a column or row. Using the fill handle, you learned how to copy a cell to adjacent cells.

Once the worksheet was built, you learned how to change the font size of the title, bold the title, and center the title over a range using buttons on the Formatting toolbar. Using the steps and techniques presented in the project, you formatted the body of the worksheet using the AutoFormat command, and you used the ChartWizard button to add a 3-D column chart. After completing the worksheet, you saved the workbook on disk and printed the worksheet. You learned how to edit data in cells. Finally, you learned how to use the six different online help tools to answer your questions.

What You Should Know

Having completed this project, you should be able to perform the following tasks:

- Add a 3-D Column Chart to the Worksheet *(E1.38)*
- Bold a Cell *(E1.30)*
- Center a Cell's Contents Across Columns *(E1.32)*
- Clear Cell Contents Using the Clear Command *(E1.53)*
- Clear Cell Contents Using the DELETE Key *(E1.53)*
- Clear Cell Contents Using the Fill Handle *(E1.52)*
- Clear Cell Contents Using the Shortcut Menu *(E1.53)*
- Clear the Entire Worksheet *(E1.53)*
- Copy a Cell to Adjacent Cells in a Row *(E1.26)*
- Delete an Embedded Chart *(E1.53)*
- Determine Multiple Totals at the Same Time *(E1.27)*
- Enter Numeric Data *(E1.21)*
- Enter Row Titles *(E1.20)*
- Enter the Column Titles *(E1.18)*
- Enter the Worksheet Title *(E1.8)*
- Exit Excel *(E1.46)*
- Increase the Font Size of a Cell *(E1.31)*
- Obtain Help Using the Answer Wizard *(E1.59)*
- Obtain Help Using the Contents Sheet *(E1.54)*
- Obtain Help Using the Find Sheet *(E1.57)*
- Obtain Help Using the Index Sheet *(E1.56)*
- Print a Worksheet *(E1.45)*
- Save a Workbook *(E1.42)*
- Start Excel *(E1.9)*
- Start Excel and Open a Workbook *(E1.47)*
- Sum a Column of Numbers *(E1.24)*
- Use AutoCalculate Area to Determine an Average *(E1.49)*
- Use AutoFormat to Format the Body of a Worksheet *(E1.33)*
- Use the Name Box to Select a Cell *(E1.36)*

A+ Test Your Knowledge

1 True/False

Instructions: Circle T if the statement is true or F if the statement is false.

T F 1. An Excel worksheet contains a total of 16,384 columns and 256 rows.

T F 2. Inside an Excel workbook are sheets, called worksheets.

T F 3. Each cell has a unique address made up of a row number followed by a column letter.

T F 4. The Excel taskbar button is in the title bar.

T F 5. You can use the fill handle to delete the contents of a cell.

T F 6. If you have not yet clicked the enter box or pressed the ENTER key or an arrow key to complete an entry in the formula bar, use the ESC key to erase the entry from the formula bar.

T F 7. To select the entire worksheet, click the Select All button or press CTRL+A.

T F 8. Text that contains more characters than the width of the column will always occupy two or more cells.

T F 9. The AutoCalculate area is used to enter a function, such as the SUM function, that is then assigned to the active cell when you press the ENTER key.

T F 10. Double-click the Help button on the Standard toolbar to initiate access to the Contents sheet.

2 Multiple Choice

Instructions: Circle the correct response.

1. To enlarge a reduced Excel window, click the __________ button.
   a. Maximize
   b. Undo
   c. Open
   d. Repeat
2. To enter text into a cell, the cell must be __________.
   a. defined as a text cell
   b. empty
   c. the active cell
   d. wide enough to display the entry
3. Which button do you click to display ScreenTips in a dialog box?
   a. Help button
   b. TipWizard button
   c. Question Mark button
   d. Open button

A+ Test Your Knowledge

4. When you enter a number into the active cell, the number is __________ in the cell.
   a. right-justified
   b. left-justified
   c. centered
   d. decimal-aligned
5. When defining the chart area, hold down the __________ key to snap to the gridlines.
   a. CTRL
   b. ALT
   c. SHIFT
   d. F1
6. If a single empty cell is selected and the Sum is active in the AutoCalculate area, then Sum = __________ displays in the AutoCalculate area.
   a. 0
   b. ?
   c. ERR
   d. 1
7. To display a shortcut menu, point to the object, such as the toolbar and __________.
   a. click the Select All button
   b. double-click
   c. click and right-click simultaneously
   d. right-click
8. The fill handle is located __________.
   a. on the taskbar
   b. on the status bar
   c. on the heavy border that surrounds the active cell
   d. on the title bar
9. Which one of the following will exit Excel?
   a. Double-click the title bar.
   b. Click the Close button on the title bar.
   c. Click Close on the File menu.
   d. Click the Minimize button on the title bar.
10. To display suggestions on how to complete tasks more efficiently, click the __________ button on the Standard toolbar.
    a. TipWizard
    b. Question Mark
    c. Help
    d. Paste

Test Your Knowledge

3 Understanding the Excel Worksheet

Instructions: In Figure 1-88, arrows point to the major components of the Excel window. Identify the various parts of the windows in the spaces provided.

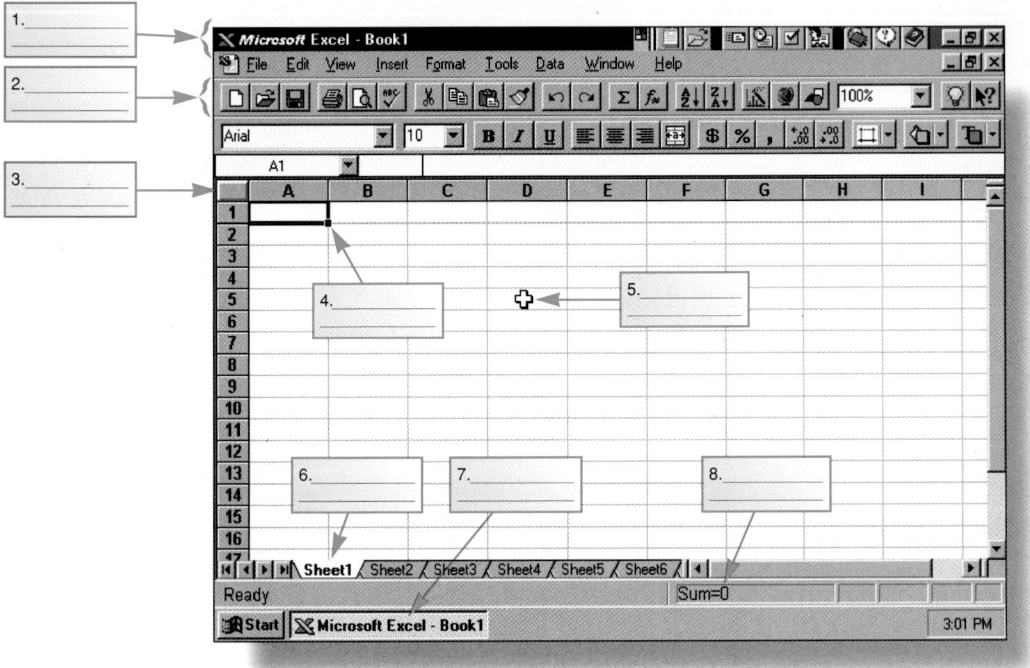

FIGURE 1-88

4 Understanding the Excel Toolbars and the Save As Dialog Box

Instructions: In the worksheet in Figure 1-89, arrows point to several of the buttons and boxes on the Standard and Formatting toolbars and in the Save As dialog box. In the spaces provided, identify each button and box.

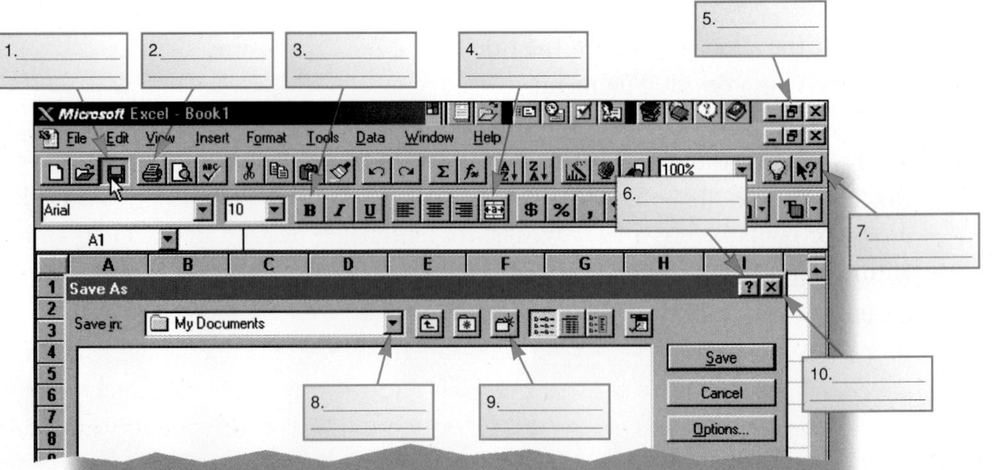

FIGURE 1-89

Use Help

1 Reviewing Project Activities

Instructions: Perform the following tasks using a computer.

1. Start Excel
2. Double-click the Help button on the Standard toolbar to display the Help Topics: Microsoft Excel dialog box.
3. Click the Contents tab. Double-click the Getting Help book. Double-click Getting assistance while you work.
4. Click the Answer Wizard link (Figure 1-90) and then read the Help information. Click the remaining four links and read their Help information. Click the Help Topics button in the lower right corner of the window to return to the Help Topics: Microsoft Excel dialog box.
5. Click the Index tab. Type `font` in the top box labeled 1 and then double-click font size under fonts in the lower box labeled 2 to display the Topics Found dialog box. Double-click Change the size of text and numbers. When the Help information displays, read it. Next, right-click within the box, and then click Print Topic. Click outside the ScreenTip. Hand in the printout to your instructor.

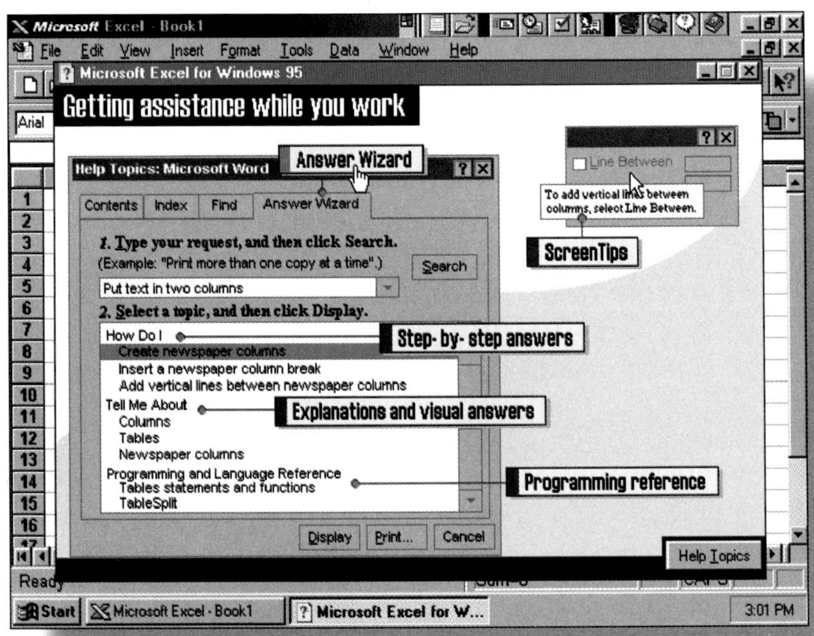

FIGURE 1-90

6. Double-click the Help button on the Standard toolbar. When the Help Topics: Microsoft Excel dialog box displays, click the Find tab. Type `chart` in the top box labeled 1. Click ChartWizard in the middle box labeled 2. Double-click create a chart in the lower box labeled 3. When the Microsoft Excel Help window displays, read it, ready the printer, right-click, and click Print Topic. Click the Insert or embed a chart on a worksheet link at the bottom of the Help window. Print the Help information. Click the Close button to close the Microsoft Excel dialog box with the Help information. Hand in the printouts to your instructor.
7. Double-click the Help button on the Standard toolbar. Click the Answer Wizard tab. Type `how do i open a workbook` in the top box labeled 1. Click the Search button. Double-click Create a new workbook in the lower box labeled 2 under How Do I. Read and print the Help information. Hand in the printout to your instructor

2 Expanding on the Basics

Instructions: Use Excel online Help to better understand the topics listed below. Begin each of the following by double-clicking the Help button on the Standard toolbar. If you are unable to print the Help information, then answer the questions on your own paper.

1. Using the Formatting book on the Contents sheet in the Help Topics: Microsoft Excel dialog box, answer the following questions:
   a. How would you use only parts of a customized format using AutoFormat?
   b. What are the five basic formats (Figure 1-91) available in Excel?
   c. What types of fast formatting techniques does Excel have?
2. Using the key term shortcut keys and the Index tab in the Help Topics: Microsoft Excel dialog box, display and print the shortcut keys to edit and move data. Then, answer the following questions:
   a. Which key or combination keys show or hide the Standard toolbar?
   b. Which key or combination keys select an entire row?
   c. Which key or combination keys select an entire column?

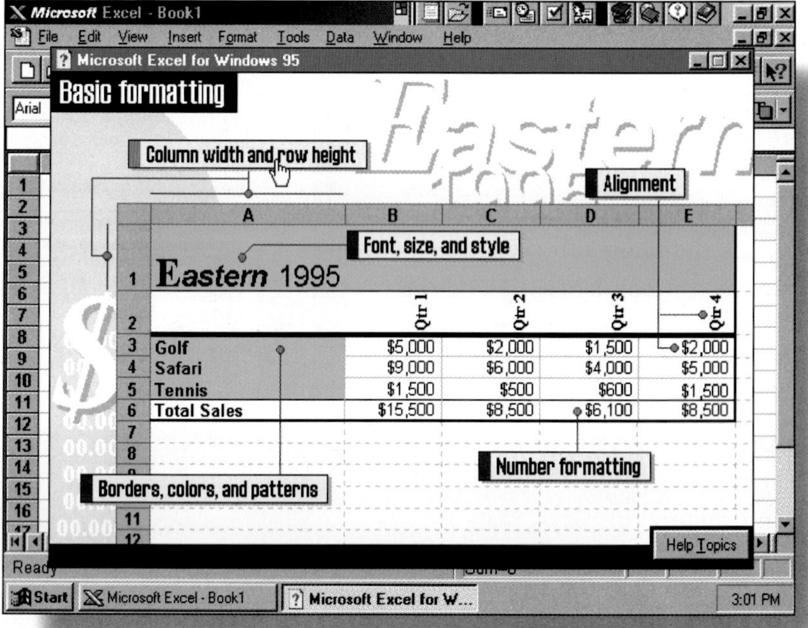

FIGURE 1-91

   d. Which key or combination keys extend the selection to the last cell in the worksheet?
   e. Which key or combination keys extend the selection by one cell?
3. Use the Find tab in the Help Topics: Microsoft Excel dialog box to display and then print information about the function keys. Then, answer the following questions:
   a. Which key or combination keys are used to display a shortcut menu?
   b. Which key or combination keys are used to create a chart?
   c. Which key or combination keys are used to restore the size of a window?
4. Use the Answer Wizard in the Help Topics: Microsoft Excel dialog box to display and print the application workspace specifications, worksheet and workbook specifications, and the charting specifications.

Apply Your Knowledge

CAUTION: It is recommended that you create a backup copy of the Student Floppy Disk that accompanies this book and then remove unneeded folders on the backup floppy disk to free up space. Do the following: (1) insert the Student Floppy Disk in drive A; (2) start Explorer; (3) right-click the 3½ Floppy [A:] folder in the All Folders side of the window; (4) click Copy Disk; (5) click Start and OK as required; (6) insert the backup floppy disk when requested; (7) delete folders on the backup floppy disk except the Excel folder.

1 Changing Data in a Worksheet

Instructions: Read the Caution box above and to the right. Start Excel. Open the workbook, Kevin's Lawn Care, from the Excel folder on the Student floppy disk that accompanies this book. As shown in Figure 1-92, the worksheet is a semiannual income and expense worksheet. Perform the following tasks:

1. Make the changes to the worksheet described in Table 1-8. As you edit the values in the cells containing numeric data, watch the total income (cells D6 and F6) and total expenses (cells D11 and F11). Each of the values in these four cells is based on the SUM function. When you enter a new value, Excel automatically recalculates the SUM functions. After you have successfully made the changes listed in the table, the total incomes in cells D6 and F6 should equal $106,077.50 and $110,420.78, respectively. The total expenses in cells D11 and F11 should equal $73,289.78 and $86,178.90, respectively.
2. Save the workbook. Use the filename Jacob's Lawn Care.
3. Print the revised worksheet.

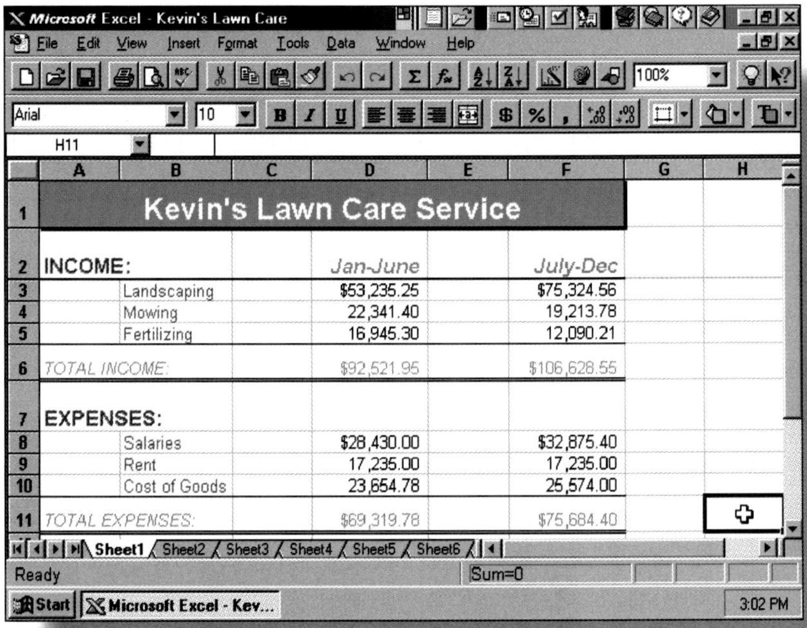

FIGURE 1-92

Table 1-8

CELL	CURRENT CELL CONTENTS	CHANGE CELL CONTENTS TO
A1	Kevin's Lawn Care Service	Jacob's Lawn Care Service
D3	53235.25	58753.20
F3	75324.56	82753.25
D5	16945.30	24982.90
F5	12090.21	8453.75
D8	28430.00	32400.00
F8	32875.40	43369.90

In the Lab

1 Building and Modifying a Sales Analysis Worksheet

Problem: As the assistant financial manager for Hayley's Pet Shop, Inc., you have been asked by your supervisor to analyze the third-quarter sales for the company, which has stores in four cities. The third-quarter sales are shown in Table 1-9.

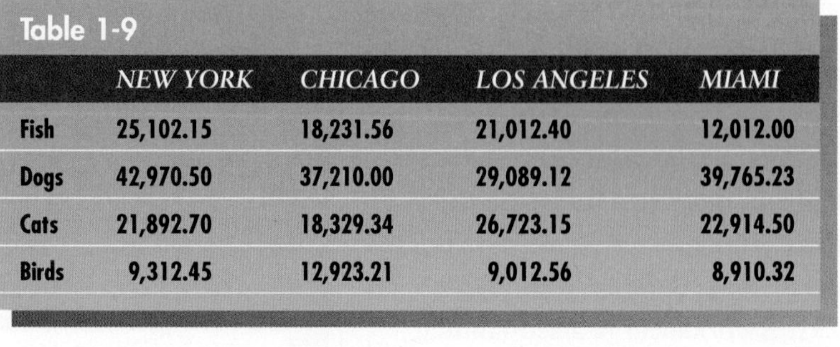

Table 1-9

	NEW YORK	CHICAGO	LOS ANGELES	MIAMI
Fish	25,102.15	18,231.56	21,012.40	12,012.00
Dogs	42,970.50	37,210.00	29,089.12	39,765.23
Cats	21,892.70	18,329.34	26,723.15	22,914.50
Birds	9,312.45	12,923.21	9,012.56	8,910.32

Instructions: Perform the following tasks:

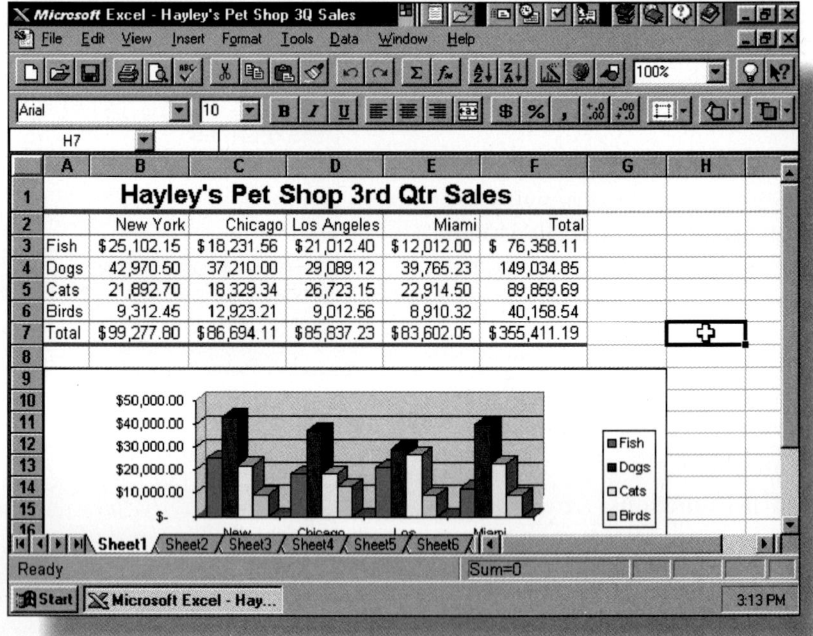

FIGURE 1-93

1. Create the worksheet shown in Figure 1-93 using the sales amounts in Table 1-9.
2. Direct Excel to determine the totals for the four store locations, the sales categories, and the company.
3. Format the worksheet title Hayley's Pet Shop 3rd Qtr Sales as 16 point, bold, and centered over columns A through F.
4. Format the range A2:F7 using the table format Accounting 2 as shown in the worksheet in Figure 1-93.
5. Use the ChartWizard button on the Standard toolbar to draw the 3-D column chart shown on the worksheet in Figure 1-93. Chart the range A2:E6.
6. Enter your name in cell A20. Enter your course, laboratory assignment number, date, and instructor name below in cells A21 through A24.
7. Save the workbook using the filename Hayley's Pet Shop 3Q Sales.
8. Print the worksheet.
9. Two corrections to the sales amounts were submitted. The correct sales amounts are: $18,567.23 for Birds in Miami and $39,598.25 for Dogs in Chicago. Enter the two corrections. After you enter the two corrections, the company total should equal $367,456.35 in cell F7. Print the worksheet containing the corrected values.

In the Lab

2 Creating an Annual College Expense Worksheet

Problem: You have decided to create an expense worksheet for the upcoming school year. The expenses you have determined are listed in Table 1-10.

Table 1-10

	SEMESTER 1	SEMESTER 2	SUMMER
Room & Board	1950	1950	750
Tuition	1750	1750	650
Books	350	400	125
Clothes	125	175	90
Entertainment	250	300	200
Miscellaneous	150	150	75

Instructions: Perform the following tasks:

1. Create the worksheet shown in Figure 1-94 using the expenses and category names in Table 1-10.
2. Direct Excel to determine the totals for each expense category, each semester, and the total annual expense.
3. Format the worksheet title Annual College Expenses to 18 point, bold, and centered over columns A through E.
4. Format the range A2:E9 using the table format Accounting 1 as shown in Figure 1-94.
5. Use the ChartWizard button to draw the 3-D area chart shown on the worksheet in Figure 1-94. Chart the range A2:D8 in the range A11:H24.
6. Enter your name in cell A26. Enter your course, laboratory assignment number, date, and instructor name below the chart in cells A27 through A30.
7. Save the workbook using the filename Annual College Expenses.
8. Print the worksheet.
9. Make the following changes to the Annual College Expense worksheet: Semester 1, Tuition — $3,000; Semester 2, Tuition — $3,000; and Summer, Entertainment — $1,500. The new three semester totals should be $5,825.00, $5,975.00, and $3,190.00, respectively.
10. Print the modified worksheet.

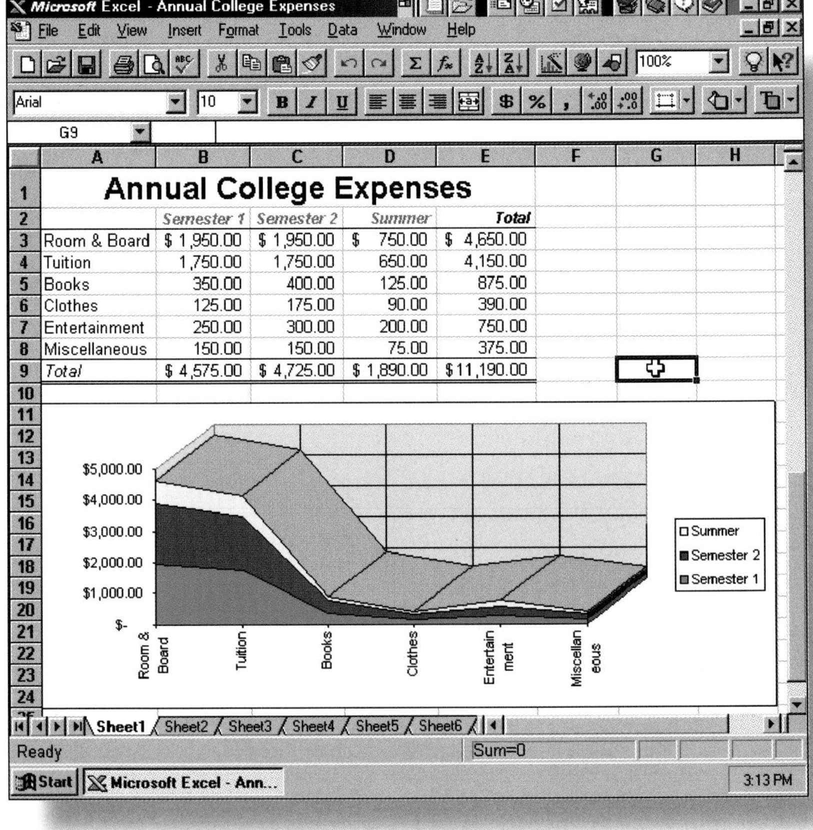

FIGURE 1-94

In the Lab

3 Creating a Personal Financial History Statement

Problem: For you to obtain a bank loan, the bank has requested you to supply a personal financial history statement. The statement is to include your average monthly income and all major expenses for the last seven years. The data required to prepare your financial statement is shown in Table 1-11.

Table 1-11

	1990	1991	1992	1993	1994	1995	1996
Income:							
Wages	1550	1600	1800	1850	1900	2200	2300
Tips	550	500	600	750	800	825	900
Expenses:							
Rent	850	875	900	925	975	990	1025
Utilities	160	165	175	180	180	190	210
Insurance	200	250	300	325	400	450	475
Other	290	325	375	400	425	430	435

Instructions: Using the numbers in Table 1-11, create the worksheet shown in Figure 1-95. Use the AutoSum button to calculate the total monthly income (row 7) and total monthly expenses (row 15) for each of the seven years. Make sure you begin each of the column titles with an apostrophe so the dates are not entered as numbers, or else they will be added into the totals when you apply the AutoSum button. Use the Answer Wizard and type in the question, `How do I sum`. Use the information to find all the Monthly Income totals in row 7 and column H by clicking the AutoSum button once. Apply the same techniques to find the Monthly Expenses totals in row 15 and column H.

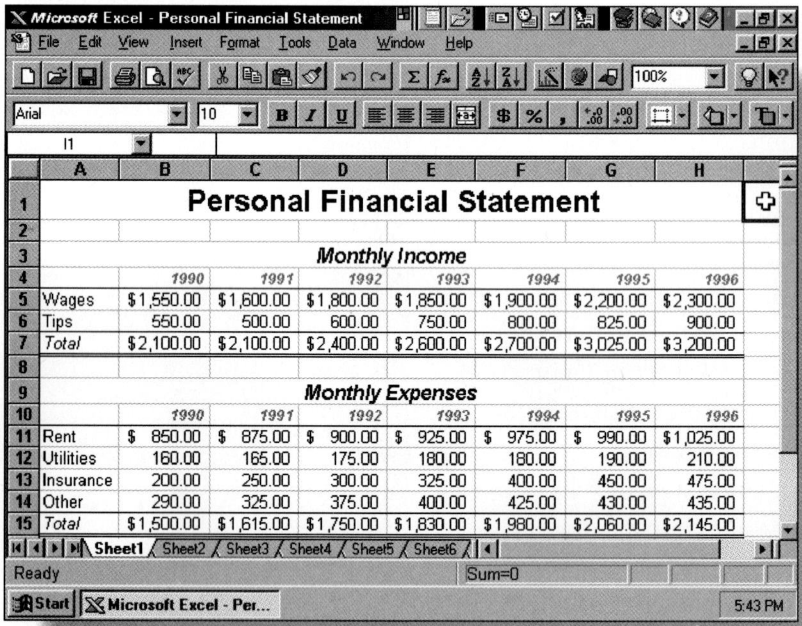

Microsoft Excel - Personal Financial Statement

Personal Financial Statement

Monthly Income

	1990	1991	1992	1993	1994	1995	1996
Wages	$1,550.00	$1,600.00	$1,800.00	$1,850.00	$1,900.00	$2,200.00	$2,300.00
Tips	550.00	500.00	600.00	750.00	800.00	825.00	900.00
Total	$2,100.00	$2,100.00	$2,400.00	$2,600.00	$2,700.00	$3,025.00	$3,200.00

Monthly Expenses

	1990	1991	1992	1993	1994	1995	1996
Rent	$ 850.00	$ 875.00	$ 900.00	$ 925.00	$ 975.00	$ 990.00	$1,025.00
Utilities	160.00	165.00	175.00	180.00	180.00	190.00	210.00
Insurance	200.00	250.00	300.00	325.00	400.00	450.00	475.00
Other	290.00	325.00	375.00	400.00	425.00	430.00	435.00
Total	$1,500.00	$1,615.00	$1,750.00	$1,830.00	$1,980.00	$2,060.00	$2,145.00

FIGURE 1-95

To format the worksheet, use the table format Accounting 1 for the Monthly Income table and then again for the Monthly Expenses table. Enter your name in cell A19 and your course, laboratory assignment number, date, and instructor name in cells A20 through A23.

Save the workbook using the filename Personal Financial Statement. Print the worksheet. Use online Help to understand and then print only the selection A1:H7 of the worksheet.

200 MHz

Cases and Places

The difficulty of these case studies varies:

◗ Case studies preceded by a single half moon are the least difficult. You are asked to create the required document based on information that has already been placed in an organized form.

◗◗ Case studies preceded by two half moons are more difficult. You must organize the information presented before using it to create the required worksheet.

◗◗◗ Case studies preceded by three half moons are the most difficult. You must choose a specific topic, and then obtain and organize the necessary information before using it to create the required worksheet.

1 ◗ Your school's football coach has compiled the number of yards gained by this week's opponent, the Hartford Hurricanes, in each quarter over the past six games (Figure 1-96).

With this data, along with the coach's requests, you have been asked to prepare a worksheet for meetings with assistant coaches and players. Use the concepts and techniques presented in this project to create the worksheet.

Hartford Hurricanes Offensive Production in the Last Six Games

	1st Quarter	2nd Quarter	3rd Quarter	4th Quarter
Rushing	360 yd.	262 yd.	300 yd.	139 yd.
Passing	134 yd.	156 yd.	195 yd.	246 yd.

Also show:
total yards gained each quarter
total yards gained passing
total yards gained rushing
bar chart with yards gained per quarter

FIGURE 1-96

2 ◗ As a newspaper reporter, you are preparing an article on the coming election based on a recent survey of the electorate, arranged by the age of those polled (Figure 1-97).

With this data, along with your editor's suggestions, you have been asked to produce a worksheet to accompany your article. Use the concepts and techniques presented in this project to create the worksheet.

Results of Election Poll--By Age of Respondent

	18-29	30-41	42-53	54-65	66+
Wilson	345	432	124	302	645
Taft	125	532	236	279	101
Undecided	409	132	382	248	76

Include total number of people surveyed in each age group, total number for each candidate, and total number undecided. Use a bar chart to illustrate polling data.
-Ed.

FIGURE 1-97

Cases and Places

3 ▶▶ The Palace Theater is a small movie house that shows almost-current releases. Three types of tickets are sold at each presentation: general admission, senior citizen, and children's. The theater management has asked you to prepare a worksheet that can be used in reevaluating its ticket structure. During an average week, weekday evening shows generate $4,500 from general admission ticket sales, $2,500 from senior citizen ticket sales, and $1,000 from children's ticket sales. Weekend matinee shows make $3,000 from general admission ticket sales, $800 from senior citizen ticket sales, and $2,100 from children's ticket sales. Weekend evening shows earn $6,720 from general admission ticket sales, $2,400 from senior citizen ticket sales, and $1,000 from children's ticket sales. Include total revenues for each type of ticket and for each presentation time, and a bar graph illustrating ticket revenues.

4 ▶▶ The Collegiate Academy, a private school where you are a consultant, has asked you to prepare a worksheet that can be used at the next meeting of its board of directors. The worksheet is to compare the school's expenditures last year to its anticipated expenditures this year. Last year, the school spent $960,000 on staff salaries and benefits, $13,500 on books and supplies, $8,100 on equipment, and $21,000 on building and grounds maintenance. This year, the school expects to spend $1,032,000 on staff salaries and benefits, $14,850 on books and supplies, $4,700 on equipment, and $23,500 on building and grounds maintenance. Include total expenditures in each category and for each school year, and a 3-D column chart illustrating yearly expenditures. After completing the worksheet, prepare a second worksheet showing how this year's expenditures would be affected if the amount spent on staff was changed to $1,104,000 (after hiring two new teachers) and the amount spent on equipment was changed to $11,500 (after purchasing three new computers).

5 ▶▶▶ Supermarkets often boast that they have the lowest prices. Make a list of seven items that can be purchased from any supermarket. Visit at least three supermarkets and obtain a price for each of the items listed. Make sure your prices are for similar items (same size, same or similar brand name, and so on). Create a worksheet showing the price of each individual item in the store and the total price for all seven items in a particular supermarket. Include a bar graph to illustrate your data.

6 ▶▶▶ Some academic disciplines appear to attract more students of one gender than the other. Visit at least five different academic departments in your school. Find out how many males and how many females have declared majors in that department. Using this information, create a worksheet showing the number of male majors and the number of female majors in each department, the total number of majors in the department, the total number of male majors in all five departments, and the total number of female majors in all five departments. Include a bar graph to illustrate your data.

7 ▶▶▶ Car dealerships order their inventories from the manufacturer based on the car models they have sold in the previous months. Visit a local dealership and make a list of the different types of car models that are offered from one manufacturer. Find out how many of each different model was purchased during the past three months. Using this information, create a worksheet showing the number of each car model that was sold every month, the total number sold of each car model, and the total number of cars sold each month. Include a bar graph to illustrate your data.

Microsoft *Excel 7*

Windows 95

Formulas, Formatting, and Creating Charts

Objectives:

You will have mastered the material in this project when you can:

- Enter multiple lines of text in the same cell
- Enter a formula
- Use Point mode to enter formulas
- Identify the arithmetic operators +, -, *, /, %, and ^
- Apply the AVERAGE, MAX, and MIN functions
- Change the font of a cell
- Change the font of individual characters in a cell
- Color the characters and background of a cell
- Add borders to a range
- Format numbers using the Format Cells dialog box
- Align text in cells
- Change the width of a column
- Change the height of a row
- Check the spelling of a worksheet
- Create a 3-D pie chart on a separate sheet
- Format chart items
- Rename sheet tabs
- Preview how a printed copy of the worksheet will look
- Print multiple sheets
- Print a partial or complete worksheet
- Display and print the formulas version of a worksheet
- Print to fit
- Distinguish between portrait and landscape orientation

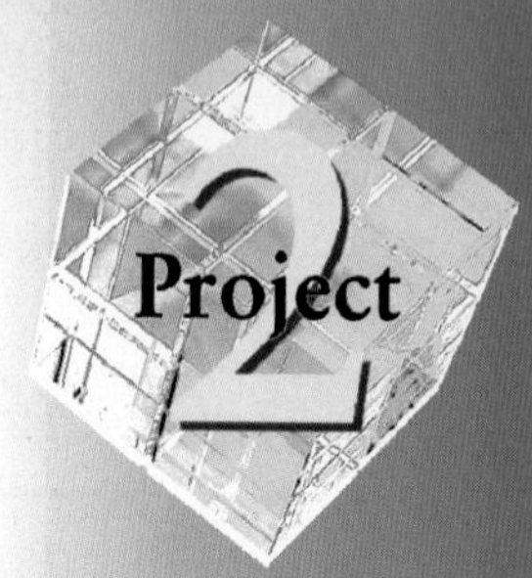

Recalculate the Formulas?

No Problem.

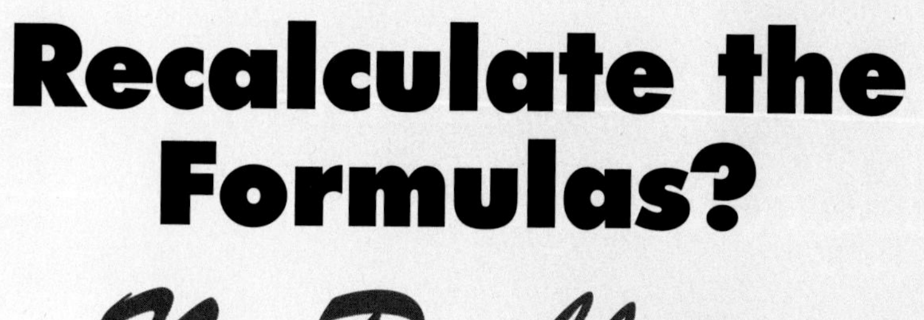

Imagine hugging the road in a red Formula One sports car with leather trimmed seats, triple-cool air conditioning, removable hardtop, and an aerodynamically sleek body conveying a haunting, exotic look. Imagine further that you own this street rocket. Impossible? Well, the car exists and you can figure out if you can afford it.

The car is a Ferrari F50, a Formula One racing car adapted for street use. The F50 is fast (202 MPH), incredibly expensive, and this year's ultimate fantasy machine. Only 349 of these cars will be built. Want one?

Here's the reality: Base price: $519,245. The price increases to $564,024 when you add the ten-speaker stereo system ($3,000) and sales tax ($41,779). Okay, you might say, but can I afford the monthly payments?

$$\text{Monthly Payment} = \frac{\text{Principal} \bullet \text{Monthly Interest Rate}}{\left[1 - \frac{1}{(1 + \text{Monthly Interest Rate})^{\text{Number of Payments}}}\right]}$$

After a standard down payment of 10% ($56,402), you must borrow $507,622. To determine your monthly payment, you can use the following formula:

$$\text{Monthly Payment} = \frac{\text{Principal} \bullet \text{Monthly Interest Rate}}{\left[1 - \frac{1}{(1 + \text{Monthly Interest Rate})^{\text{Number of Payments}}}\right]}$$

This baffling and confusing formula might cause you to throw your hands up and declare it is just not worth it. On the other hand, if you have an electronic spreadsheet program such as Excel 7, you can use it to perform the calculations quickly and easily. Assume for buying your new Ferrari you find a loan at 9% interest that you must pay off in five years (60 fixed monthly payments). When you enter this information, in less than a second Excel will provide you with your monthly payment ($10,537.40), the amount of principle and interest you pay each month, the ending balance at the end of each month, and the annual interest and annual principal you pay.

But what if you decide to save a little money by not buying the stereo, and you shop until you find a lender who will loan you the money at 8% interest? Must you go through the horror of manual calculations to determine your new monthly payment? Not if you are using Excel. Merely enter the new loan amount ($504,622) and interest rate (8%) and in a couple milliseconds, Excel will tell you your new monthly payment is only $10,231.91.

Worksheets such as Excel even enable you to work backwards. If you know how much you can afford as a monthly payment and at what interest rate, Excel can recalculate so you know the amount of money you can afford to borrow.

While it may be fantasy to own a Ferrari F50, with a few minor changes to the dollar amounts, Excel can help you decide exactly what car you can afford.

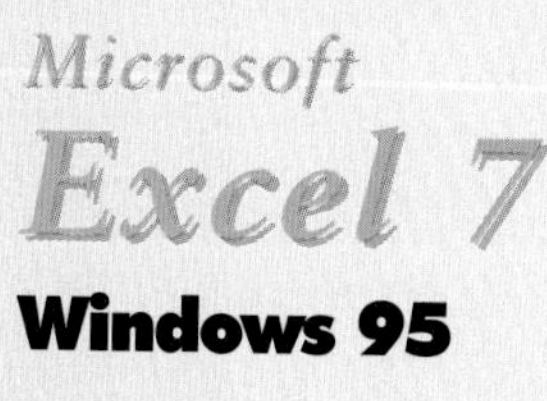

Windows 95

Formulas, Formatting, and Creating Charts

Case Perspective

Joe and Lisa Sabol own Ocean Air Art Institute, an art store that sells paintings and other art pieces. They have decided to expand their successful business by adding a second store in a neighboring town.

Joe and Lisa recently visited the loan department at the local savings and loan association and were told by Richard Leaman, the loan officer, to submit a report in the form of a worksheet that summarizes the profit potential of their current inventory. Mr. Leaman has also requested a pie chart showing the contribution of each art category to the total profit potential, so he can use it when he presents the loan request to the loan committee.

As a summer intern working for Ocean Air Art Institute, you have been assigned the task of designing and creating the worksheet and chart that satisfies the savings and loan association's requirements.

Introduction

In Project 1, you learned about entering data, summing values, how to make the worksheet easier to read, and how to draw a chart. You also learned about online Help and saving, printing, and loading a workbook from floppy disk into main memory. This project continues to emphasize these topics and presents some new ones.

The new topics include formulas, changing fonts, adding color to both characters and the background of a cell, adding borders, formatting numbers, changing the widths of columns and heights of rows, spell checking, additional charting techniques, and alternative types of worksheet displays and printouts. One alternative display and printout shows the formulas rather than the values in the worksheet. When you display the formulas in the worksheet, you see exactly what text, data, formulas, and functions you have entered into it.

Project Two – Ocean Air Art Institute

The summary notes from your meeting with Joe and Lisa, the owners of Ocean Air Art Institute, include the following: need, source of data, calculations, and graph requirements.

Need: An easy-to-read worksheet that summarizes the art pieces by category and shows the profit potential for each art category is needed. The worksheet is to include the units on hand, average unit cost, total cost, average unit selling price, total value, and profit potential for each art category. Also requested are totals and an average, maximum, and minimum for each of the calculations so the savings and loan association can, if necessary, base the loan on conditions that only certain types of art be sold in the new store.

Source of Data: The data for the inventory worksheet is available from George Kim, the part-time company controller. As part of his responsibilities as controller, Mr. Kim tracks inventory. He can supply the number of pieces of art in each art category (Oils, Watercolors, Sketches, and Acrylics) and the average unit price for each art category.

Calculations: The following calculations must be made for each of the four art categories as shown in Figure 2-1 on the next page.

1. Total Cost = Units On Hand × Average Unit Cost
   Joe and Lisa use a margin of 65%. The margin handles their overhead and profit. Thus, the Average Unit Price is calculated as follows:
   $$\text{Average Unit Price} = \text{Average Unit Cost} \times \left(\frac{1}{1 - .65}\right)$$
2. Total Value = Units On Hand × Average Unit Price
3. Profit Potential = Total Value – Total Cost
4. Compute the totals for Units On Hand, Total Cost, Total Value, and Profit Potential.
5. Use the Average, Maximum, and Minimum functions to determine the average, maximum, and minimum for the Units On Hand, Average Unit Cost, Total Cost, Average Unit Price, Total Value, and Profit Potential.

Graph Requirements: Draw a 3-D pie chart (Figure 2-1 on the next page) that shows the contribution of each of the four art categories to the total profit potential. Highlight the art category that has the greatest profit potential.

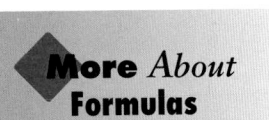

More *About* Formulas

To make full use of Excel, it is important that you understand the order in which multiple operations in a formula are carried out. Excel uses the same order as in algebra. That is, first all negations (–), then all percents (%), then all exponentiations (^), then all multiplications (*) and divisions (/) from left to right, and finally all additions (+) and subtractions (–) from left to right. Parentheses can be used to override the order of operations.

Preparation Steps

The preparation steps summarize how the worksheet and chart shown in Figure 2-1 will be developed in Project 2. The following tasks will be completed in this project.

1. Start the Excel program.
2. Enter the worksheet title, column titles, row titles, and the units on hand and average unit cost for each of the four art categories.
3. Compute the Total Cost, Average Unit Price, Total Value, and Profit Potential for the first art category, Oils.
4. Copy the formulas for the remaining three art categories.
5. Use the AutoSum button to display the totals for Units On Hand, Total Cost, Total Value, and Profit Potential.
6. Determine the average, maximum, and minimum for the Units On Hand, Average Unit Cost, Total Cost, Average Unit Price, Total Value, and Profit Potential.
7. Save an intermediate copy of the workbook.

FIGURE 2-1

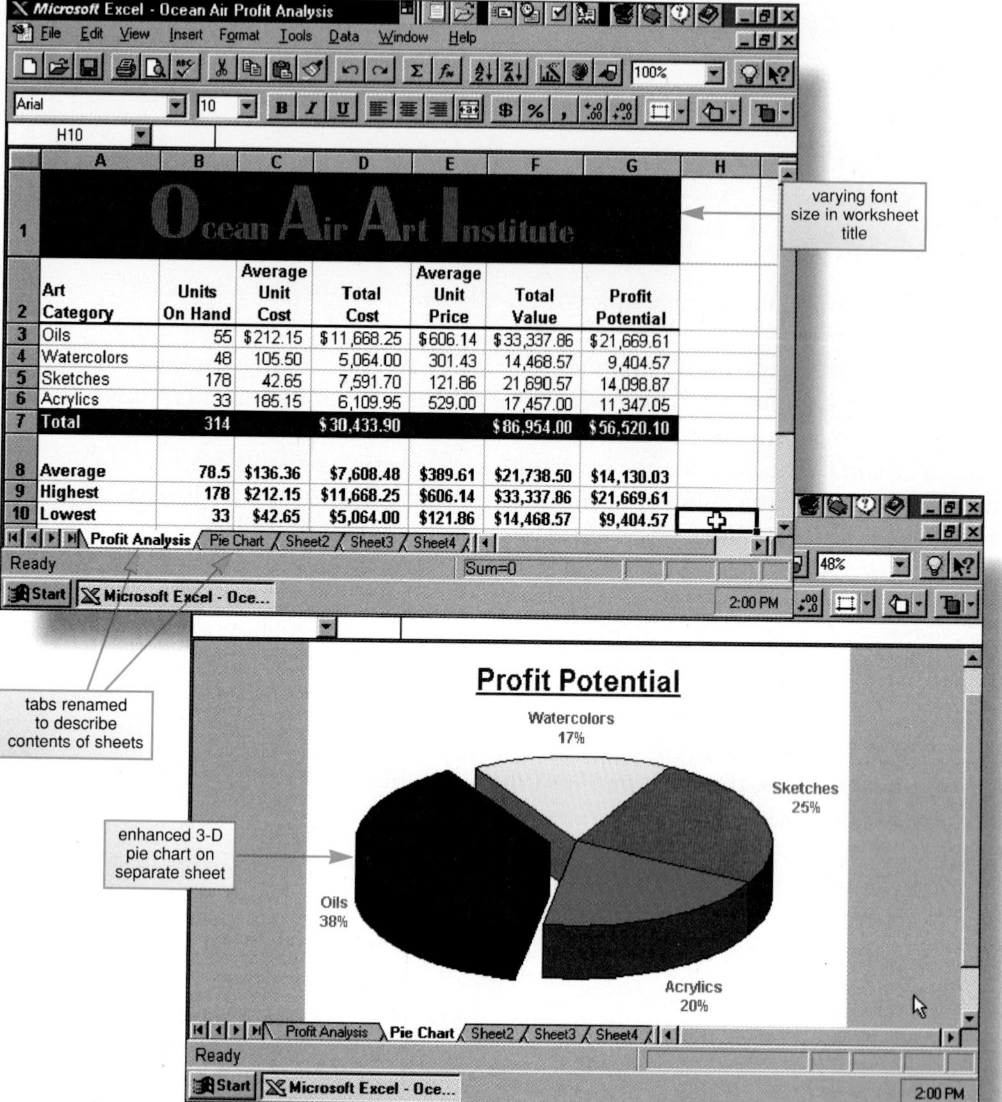

8. Format the worksheet so it has a professional appearance and is easy to read.
9. Draw the 3-D pie chart on a separate sheet. Highlight the largest slice. Improve the readability of the pie chart by using colors to emphasize the chart title and pie slice labels.
10. Rename the sheet tabs.
11. Save the workbook.
12. Preview and print the worksheet and 3-D pie chart.
13. Print the formulas version of the worksheet so the formulas can be verified.

The following pages contain a detailed explanation of these tasks.

Starting Excel

To start Excel, Windows 95 must be running. Perform the steps at the top of the next page to start Excel.

TO START EXCEL

Step 1: Click the Start button on the taskbar.
Step 2: Click New Office Document. If necessary, click the General tab in the New dialog box.
Step 3: Double-click the Blank Workbook icon.

An alternative to Steps 1 and 2 is to click the Start a New Document button on the Microsoft Office Shortcut Bar.

Entering the Titles and Numbers into the Worksheet

The worksheet title in Figure 2-1 is centered over columns A through G in row 1. Because the centered text first must be entered into the leftmost column of the area over which it is centered, it will be entered into cell A1.

The column headings in row 2 begin in cell A2 and extend through cell G2. Notice in row 2 of Figure 2-1 that multiple lines of text in each cell make up the column titles. You start a new line in a cell by pressing ALT+ENTER at the conclusion of each line, except for the last line, which is completed by clicking the enter box, pressing the ENTER key, or pressing one of the arrow keys. When you see ALT+ENTER in a step, hold down the ALT key, and while holding it down, press the ENTER key, then release both keys.

The row titles in column A begin in cell A3 and continue down to cell A10. The numbers, submitted by George Kim, the company controller, are summarized in Table 2-1. These numbers are entered into the range B3:C6. The steps required to enter the worksheet title, column titles, row titles, and numbers are outlined in the remainder of this section and are shown in Figure 2-2 on the next page.

Table 2-1

ART CATEGORY	UNITS ON HAND	AVERAGE UNIT COST
Oils	55	212.15
Watercolors	48	105.50
Sketches	178	42.65
Acrylics	33	185.15

TO ENTER THE WORKSHEET TITLE

Step 1: Select cell A1. Type `Ocean Air Art Institute` as the cell entry.
Step 2: Press the DOWN ARROW key.

The worksheet title displays as shown in cell A1 of Figure 2-2 on the next page.

TO ENTER THE COLUMN TITLES

Step 1: With cell A2 active, type `Art`, press ALT+ENTER, type `Category`, and press the RIGHT ARROW key.
Step 2: Type `Units`, press ALT+ENTER, type `On Hand`, and press the RIGHT ARROW key.
Step 3: Type `Average`, press ALT+ENTER, type `Unit`, press ALT+ENTER, type `Cost`, and press the RIGHT ARROW key.
Step 4: Type `Total`, press ALT+ENTER, type `Cost`, and press the RIGHT ARROW key.

More *About* **Designing a Worksheet**

With early spreadsheet packages, users often skipped rows to improve the appearance of the worksheet. With Excel it is not necessary to skip rows because you can increase the height of rows to add white space between information.

Step 5: Type `Average`, press ALT+ENTER, type `Unit`, press ALT+ENTER, type `Price`, and press the RIGHT ARROW key.
Step 6: Type `Total`, press ALT+ENTER, type `Value`, and press the RIGHT ARROW key.
Step 7: Type `Profit`, press ALT+ENTER, type `Potential`, and press the RIGHT ARROW key.

The column titles display as shown in row 2 of Figure 2-2. As you add more lines to a cell through the use of the ALT+ENTER key, Excel increases the height of the entire row.

More About Wrapping Lengthy Text in a Cell

If you have a long text entry, such as a paragraph, you can instruct Excel to wrap the text in a cell, rather than pressing ALT+ENTER to end a line. To wrap text, click Format Cells on the shortcut menu, click the Alignment tab, and click the Wrap Text check box. Excel will automatically increase the height of the cell so the additional lines will fit. However, if you want to control the contents of a line in a cell, rather than letting Excel wrap based on the width of a cell, then you must end a line with ALT+ENTER.

TO ENTER THE ROW TITLES

Step 1: Select cell A3. Type `Oils` and then press the DOWN ARROW key.
Step 2: Enter the row titles `Watercolors`, `Sketches`, `Acrylics`, `Total`, `Average`, `Highest`, and `Lowest` in cells A4 through A10.

The row titles display as shown in column A of Figure 2-2.

TO ENTER THE NUMBERS

Step 1: Enter `55` in cell B3 and `212.15` in cell C3.
Step 2: Enter `48` in cell B4 and `105.5` in cell C4.
Step 3: Enter `178` in cell B5 and `42.65` in cell C5.
Step 4: Enter `33` in cell B6 and `185.15` in cell C6.

The numeric entries display as shown in the range B3:C6 of Figure 2-2. Later in this project the numbers will be formatted so they are easier to read.

More About Entering Numbers into a Range

An efficient way to enter a set of numbers into a range of cells, such as B3:C6 in Figure 2-2, is to select the range by dragging from cell B3 to cell C6 prior to entering the numbers. After initially selecting the range, cell B3 remains the active cell. Thus, type the value for cell B3 and press the ENTER key. Excel responds by entering the number and moving the active cell selection down one cell. When you enter the last value in the first column, Excel will move the active cell selection to the top of the next column and then precede downward.

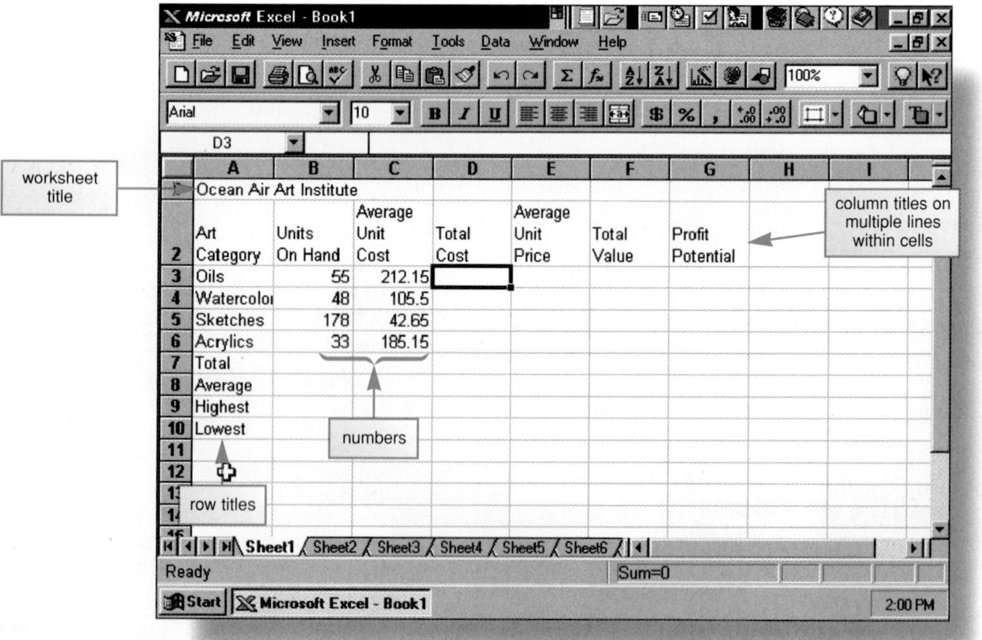

FIGURE 2-2

Entering Formulas

The total cost for each art category, which displays in column D, is equal to the corresponding units on hand in column B times the corresponding average unit cost in column C. Thus, the total cost for Oils in row 3 is obtained by multiplying 55 (cell B3) times 212.15 (cell C3).

One of the reasons Excel is such a valuable tool is because you can assign a **formula** to a cell and Excel will calculate the result. In this example, the formula in cell D3 multiplies the values in cells B3 and C3 and displays the result in cell D3.

The worksheet would be of little value if you had to manually multiply 55 x 212.15 and then enter the result, 11668.25, in cell D3, because every time the values in cells B3 and C3 change, you would have to recalculate the product and enter the new value in cell D3. By entering a formula, Excel recalculates the formula whenever a new value is entered into the worksheet. Complete the following steps to enter the formula using the keyboard.

More *About* **Recalculation of Formulas**

Every time you enter a value into a cell in the worksheet, Excel recalculates all formulas. It makes no difference if there is one formula or hundreds of formulas in the worksheet. Excel recalculates the formulas instantaneously. This is one of the reasons why a spreadsheet package, such as Excel, is so heavily used in business.

To Enter a Simple Formula Using the Keyboard

1 **Select cell D4. Type** =b3*c3 **as the cell entry.**

The formula displays in the formula bar and in cell D3 (Figure 2-3).

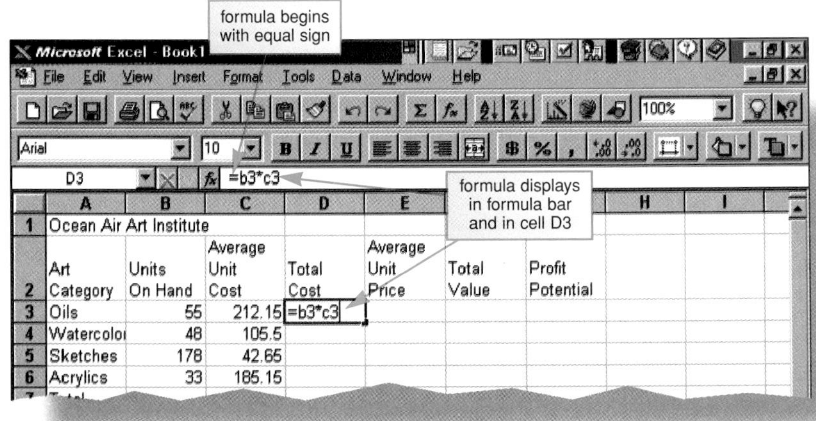

FIGURE 2-3

2 **Press the RIGHT ARROW key.**

Instead of displaying the formula in cell D3, Excel completes the arithmetic indicated by the formula and displays the result, 11668.25 (Figure 2-4).

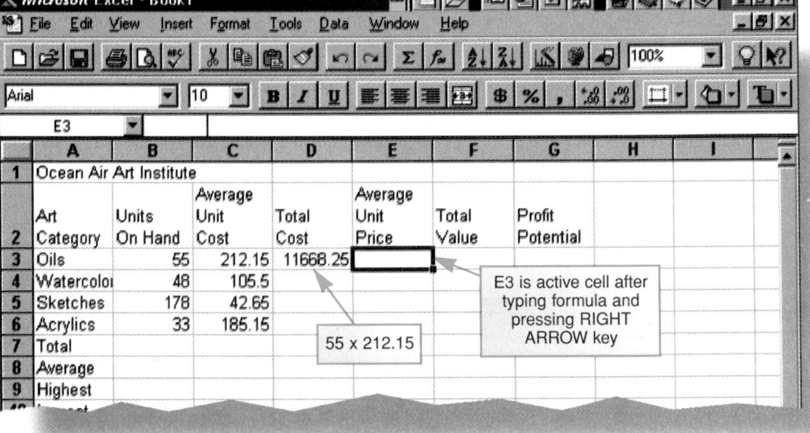

FIGURE 2-4

More *About* Entering Formulas

Besides the equal sign (=), you can start a formula with a plus sign (+) or a minus sign (–). However, don't forget to start with one of these three characters or the formula will be interpreted by Excel as text.

The equal sign (=) preceding b3*c3 is an important part of the formula. It alerts Excel that you are entering a formula or function and not text. The asterisk (*) following b3 is the arithmetic operator, which directs Excel to perform the **multiplication operation**. Other valid Excel arithmetic operators include + (**addition**), – (**subtraction**), / (**division**), % (**percentage**), and ^ (**exponentiation**).

You can enter formulas in uppercase or lowercase and you can add spaces between the arithmetic operators to make the formulas easier to read. That is, =b3*c3 is the same as =b3 * c3, =B3 * c3, =B3 * C3, or = b3*c3.

Order of Operations

When more than one operator is involved in a formula, Excel uses the same order of operations as in algebra. Moving from left to right in a formula, **the order of operations** is as follows: first negation (–), then all percents (%), then all exponentiations (^), then all multiplications (*) and divisions (/), and finally all additions (+) and subtractions (–). You can use **parentheses** to override the order of operations. For example, following the order of operations, 8 * 5 – 2 is equal to 38. With use of parentheses, however, 8 * (5 – 2) is equal to 24 because the parentheses instruct Excel to subtract 2 from 5 before multiplying by 8. Table 2-2 illustrates several examples of valid formulas.

Table 2-2

FORMULA	REMARK
=F6	Assigns the value in cell F6 to the active cell.
=3 + -2^2	Assigns the sum of 3 plus 4 (or 7) to the active cell.
=2 * R3 or =R3 * 2 or =(2 * R3)	Assigns two times the contents of cell R3 to the active cell.
=12 * 25%	Assigns the product of 12 times 0.25 (or 3) to the active cell.
=-A12 * A45	Assigns the negative value of the product of the values contained in cells A12 and A45 to the active cell.
=3 * (K12 - D2)	Assigns the product of three times the difference between the values contained in cells K12 and D2 to the active cell.
=A1 / C6 - A3 * A4 + A5 ^ A6	From left to right: first exponentiation (A5 ^ A6), then division (A1 / C6), then multiplication (A3 * A4), then subtraction (A1 / C6) – (A3 * A4), and finally addition (A1 / C6 – A3 * A4) + (A5 ^ A6). If cell A1 = 10, A3 = 6, A4 = 2, A5 = 5, A6 = 2, and C6 = 2, then Excel assigns the active cell the value 10 / 2 – 6 * 2 + 5 ^ 2 = 18.

Entering a Complex Formula

As indicated in the previous section, you can assign to a cell as complex a formula as required. In the Ocean Air Art Institute worksheet, the formula

$$\text{Average Unit Cost} \times \left(\frac{1}{1 - .65}\right) \qquad \text{or} \qquad c3 * (1/(1 - .65))$$

must be assigned to cell E3. The average unit cost is the value in cell C3. The formula requires that the quantity in the denominator, 1 – .65, be determined first because the difference must be divided into 1 before the multiplication takes place. Parentheses are used to control the order of operations or Excel would multiply the value in cell C3 by 1 and then divide by 1 before subtracting .65. With cell C3 equal to 212.15 (see Figure 2-4 on page E 2.9), Excel completes the operations for cell E3 as shown below:

Step 1	=c3 * (1 / (1 – .65))	=212.15 * (1 / (.35))
Step 2		=212.15 * (2.857142857)
Step 3		=606.1429

Perform the following steps to enter a complex formula using the keyboard.

More *About* Troubling Formulas

If Excel will not accept a formula, remove the equal sign from the left side and complete the entry as text. Later, after entering additional data or after you have determined the error, reinsert the equal sign.

Steps To Enter a Complex Formula Using the Keyboard

1 **With cell E3 selected, type** `=c3*(1/(1-.65))` **as the cell entry.**

The formula displays in cell E3 as shown in Figure 2-5.

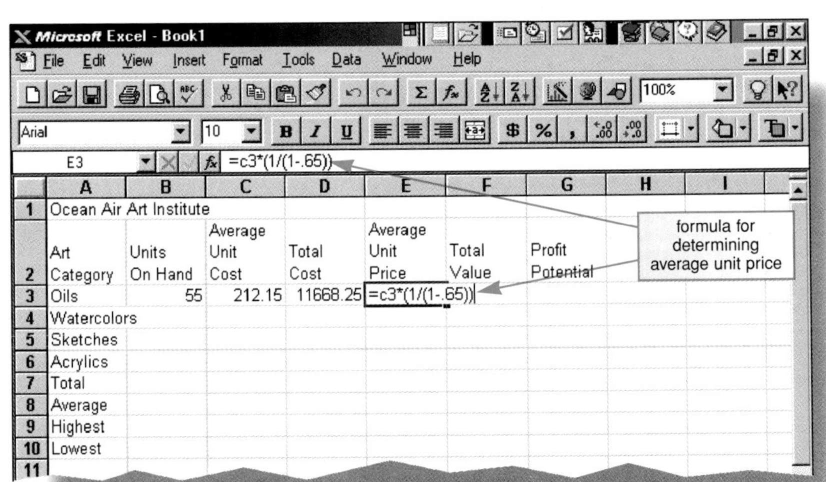

FIGURE 2-5

2 **Press the RIGHT ARROW key.**

The average unit cost for Oils displays in cell E3 (Figure 2-6).

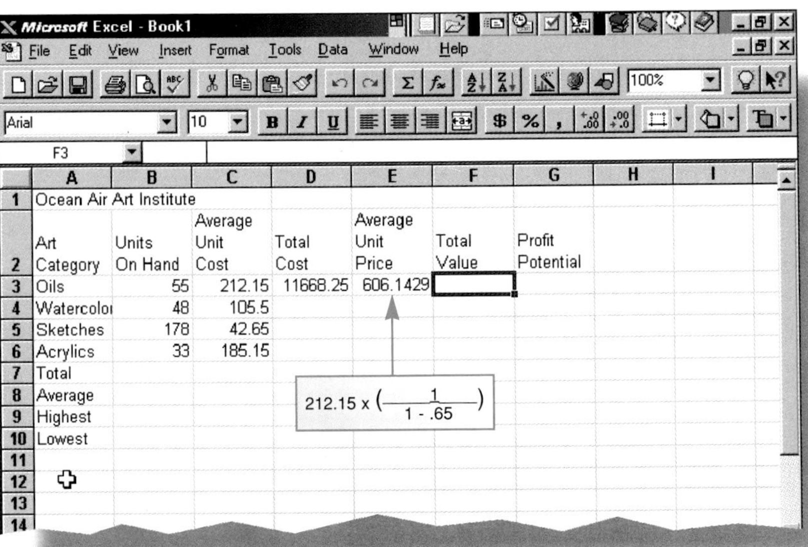

FIGURE 2-6

More About Using Point Mode

Point mode allows you to create formulas using the mouse. Instead of typing a cell reference in a formula, simply click a cell and Excel will append the corresponding cell reference at the location of the insertion point. You can also use the Customize command on the shortcut menu. It displays when you right-click a toolbar to create a new toolbar made up of buttons that represent the operators. Thus, with Excel you can enter entire formulas without ever touching the keyboard.

The first two formulas were entered into cells D3 and E3 using the keyboard. The next section shows you how to enter the formulas in cells F3 and G3 using the mouse to select cell references in a formula.

Entering Formulas Using Point Mode

In the worksheet shown in Figure 2-1 on page E 2.6, the total value of each art category displays in column F. The total value for Oils in cell F3 is equal to the units on hand (cell B3) times the average unit price (cell E3). The result in cell F3 indicates the worth of the Oil paintings inventory if all paintings were sold. The profit potential for Oils in cell G3 is equal to the total value in cell F3 minus the total cost in cell D3.

Instead of entering the formulas =b3*e3 in cell F3 and =f3 – d3 in cell G3 by using the keyboard as in the first two formulas, you can use the following steps to use the mouse and Point mode to enter the last two formulas. **Point mode** allows you to select cells for use in a formula by using the mouse.

Steps To Enter Formulas Using Point Mode

1 With cell F3 selected, type the equal sign (=) to begin the formula and then click cell B3.

Excel responds by highlighting cell B3 with a marquee and by appending B3 to the equal sign in cell F3 (Figure 2-7).

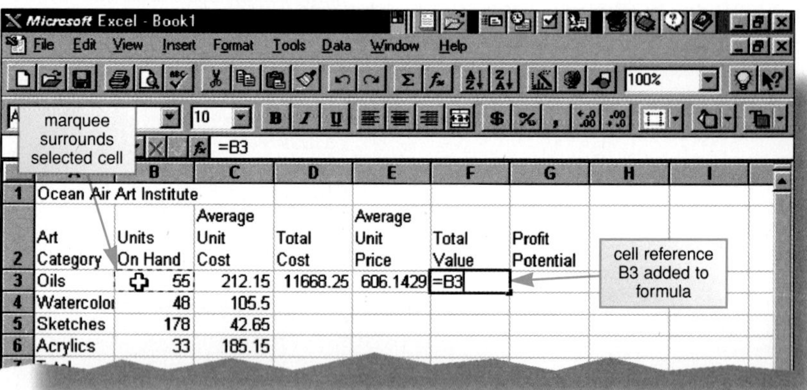

FIGURE 2-7

2 Type the asterisk (*) and then click cell E3.

Excel highlights cell E3 with a marquee and appends E3 to the asterisk (*) in cell F3 (Figure 2-8).

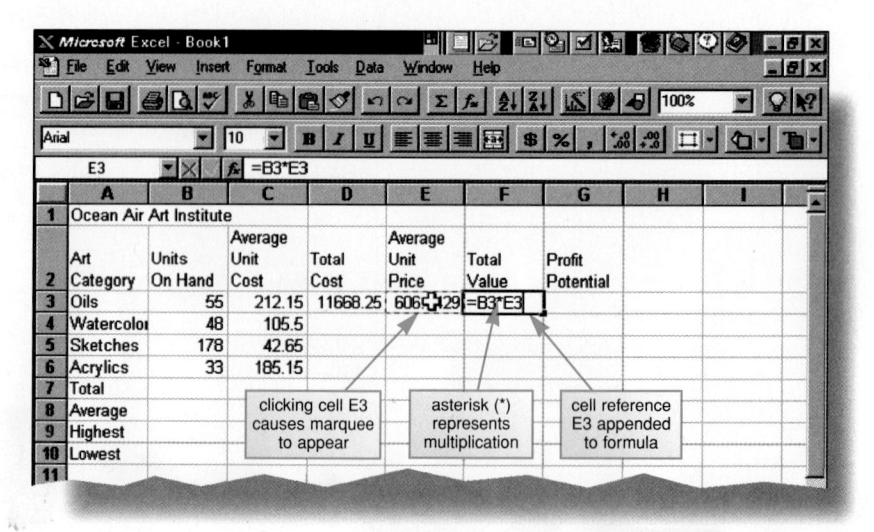

FIGURE 2-8

3 **Click the enter box or press the ENTER key. Click cell G3.**

*Excel determines the product of =B3*E3 and displays the result, 33337.86, in cell F3 (Figure 2-9).*

4 **With cell G3 selected, type = and then click cell F3. Type - and then click cell D3.**

The formula =F3 – D3 displays in cell G3 and in the formula bar (Figure 2-9).

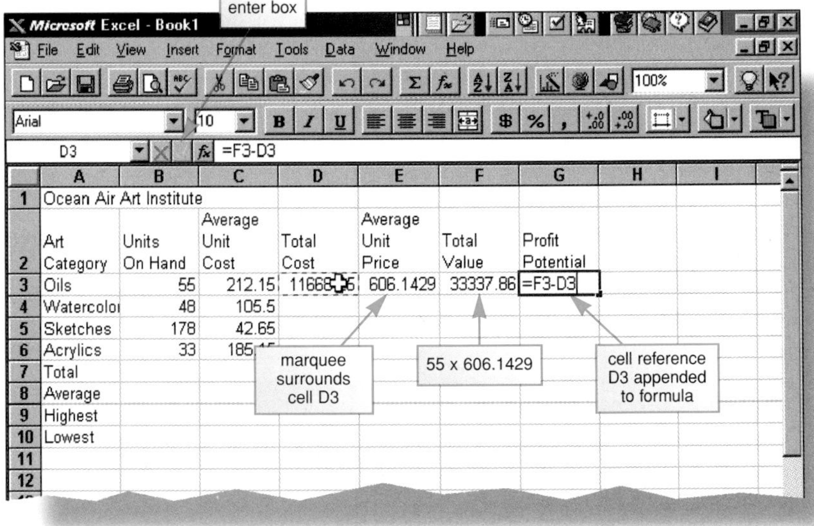
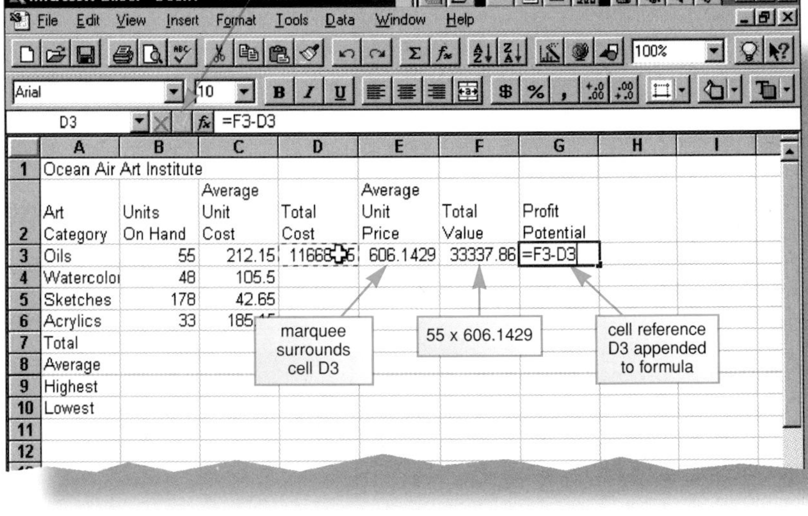

FIGURE 2-9

5 **Click the enter box or press the enter key.**

The profit potential for Oils, 21669.61, displays in cell G3 (Figure 2-10).

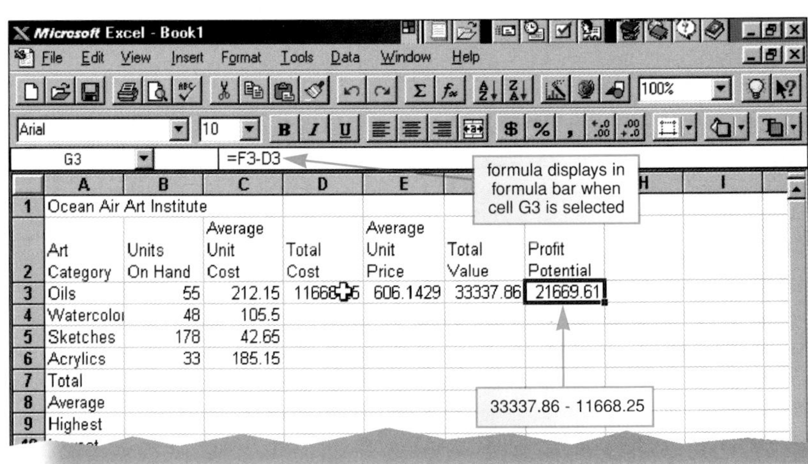

FIGURE 2-10

The four formulas for the Oils category in cells D3 through G3 are now complete. The same four formulas could be entered one at a time for Watercolors, Sketches, and Acrylics. An easier method of entering the formulas, however, is to select the four formulas in cells D3 through G3 and use the fill handle to copy them to the range D4:G6.

Copying a Range of Cells Down Rows to an Adjacent Range Using the Fill Handle

In Project 1, you learned how to copy a cell to a range of adjacent cells using the fill handle. This section shows you how to copy a range of cells to an adjacent range. Recall that when you copy a formula, Excel adjusts the cell references so the new formulas reflect computations using their respective values. Thus, if you copy downward, Excel adjusts the row portion of cell references. If you copy across, then Excel adjusts the column portion of cell references.

Perform the following steps to copy a range of cells.

To Copy a Range of Cells Down Rows to an Adjacent Range Using the Fill Handle

1 Click cell D3 and then drag to the right to select the range D3:G3. Point to the fill handle.

The range D3:G3 is highlighted and the mouse pointer changes to the cross hair (Figure 2-11).

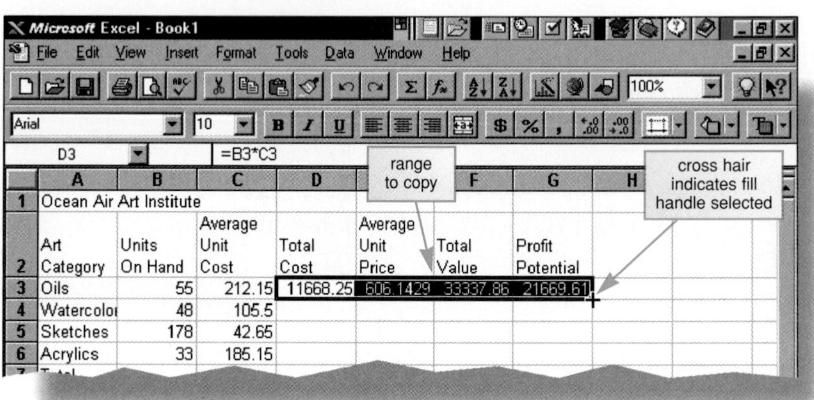

FIGURE 2-11

2 Drag the fill handle down to highlight the range D4:G6.

After you release the left mouse button, Excel copies the four formulas in the range D3:G3 to the range D4:G6 and displays the total cost, average unit price, total value, and profit potential for the remaining art categories (Figure 2-12).

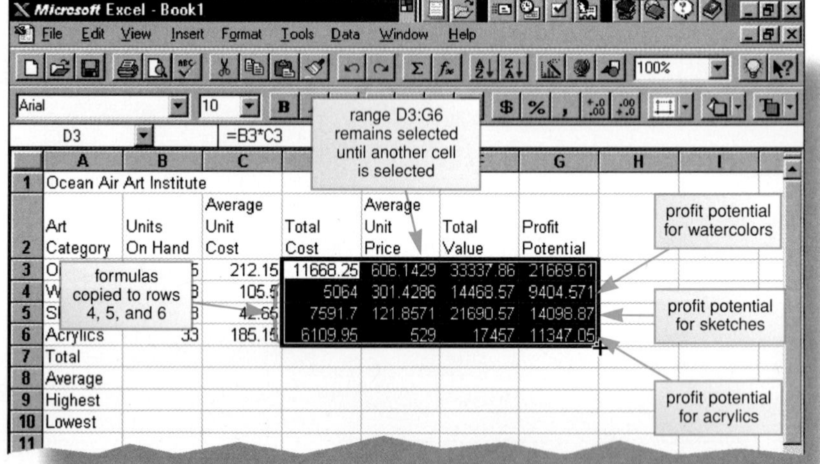

FIGURE 2-12

Other Ways

1. Select copy area, right-click copy area, click Copy on shortcut menu, right-click paste area, click Paste on shortcut menu
2. Select copy area, click Copy button on Standard toolbar, select paste area, click Paste button on Standard toolbar
3. Select copy area, on Edit menu click Copy, select paste area, on Edit menu click Paste
4. Select copy area, press CTRL+C, select paste area, press CTRL+V

Select any cell to remove the selection from the range D3:G6.

As indicated earlier, when Excel copies the four formulas in the range D3:G3 to the range D4:G6, the row references in the formula are adjusted as the formula is copied downward. For example, in column D the formula assigned to cell D4 is =B4*C4. Similarly, Excel assigns cell D5 the formula =B5*C5, and cell D6 the formula =B6*C6. When you copy downward, the row reference changes in the formula.

Calculating the Totals Using the AutoSum Button

The next step is to determine the totals in row 7 for the units on hand in column B, the total cost in column D, the total value in column F, and the profit potentialin column G. To determine the total in column B, cells B3 through B6 must be summed. You can enter the function =sum(b3:b6) in cell B7, or you can select cell B7 and then click the AutoSum button twice. Similar SUM functions or the AutoSum button can be used in cells D7, F7, and G7. The most efficient method is to use the AutoSum button as shown in the following steps.

More *About* **Selecting a Range**

If you dislike dragging to select a range, press F8 and use the arrow keys to select one corner of the range and then the cell diagonally opposite it in the proposed range. Make sure you press F8 to turn selection off after you are finished with the range or you will continue to select ranges.

TO CACULATE TOTALS USING THE AUTOSUM BUTTON

Step 1: Select cell B7. Click the AutoSum button twice. (Do not double-click.)
Step 2: Select cell D7. Click the AutoSum button twice.
Step 3: Select the range F7:G7. Click the AutoSum button once.

The four totals display in row 7 as shown in Figure 2-13.

An alternative method to calculating the totals using the AutoSum function is to select all four cells before clicking the AutoSum button. To select the nonadjacent range B7, D7, F7, and G7, select cell B7, and then hold down the CTRL key and click the remaining three cells one at a time. Next, click the AutoSum button.

AutoSum button

Microsoft Excel - Book1

F7 =SUM(F3:F6)

	A	B	C	D	E	F	G
1	Ocean Air Art Institute						
2	Art Category	Units On Hand	Average Unit Cost	Total Cost	Average Unit Price	Total Value	Profit Potential
3	Oils	55	212.15	11668.25	606.1429	33337.86	21669.61
4	Watercolor	48	105.5	5064	301.4286	14468.57	9404.571
5	Sketches	178	42.65	7591.7	121.8571	21690.57	14098.87
6	Acrylics	33	185.15	6109.95	529	17457	11347.05
7	Total	314		30433.9		86954	56520.1
8	Average						
9	Highest						
10	Lowest						

sum of units on hand in range B3:B6
sum of individual total costs in range D3:D6
sum of individual total values in range F3:F6
sum of individual profit potentials in range G3:G6

Inserts SUM function and proposes sum range — Sum=143474.1

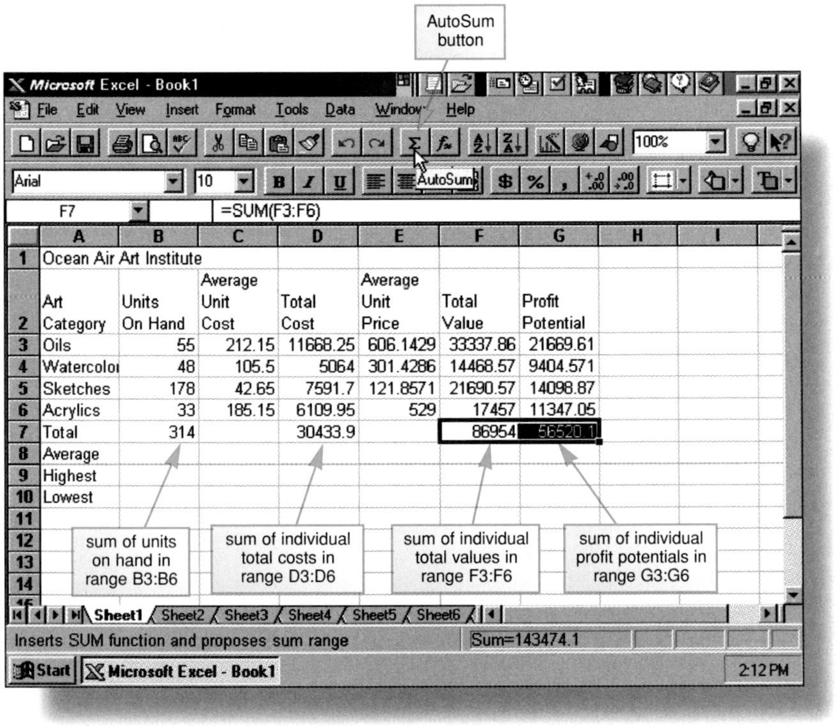

FIGURE 2-13

Using the AVERAGE, MAX, and MIN Functions

The next step in creating the Ocean Air Art Institute worksheet is to compute the average, maximum value, and minimum value for the units on hand in column B. Once the values are determined, the entries can be copied across to the other columns.

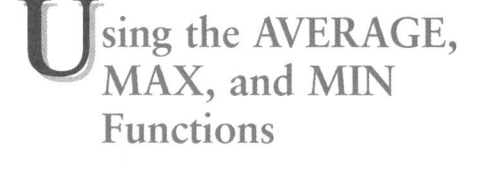

Excel includes functions to compute these statistics. A **function** is a prewritten formula that takes a value or values, performs an operation, and returns a value or values. The values that you give to a function to perform operations on are called the **arguments**. All functions begin with an equal sign and include the arguments in parentheses after the function name. For example, in the function =AVERAGE(B3:B6), the function name is AVERAGE and the argument is the range B3:B6.

Computing the Average

To determine the average of the numbers in the range B3:B6, perform the steps on the next page.

To Find the Average of a Group of Numbers

1 Select cell B8. Type =average(**in the cell.**

Excel displays the beginning of the AVERAGE function in the formula bar and in cell B8 (Figure 2-14).

AVERAGE function without range displayed in formula bar and in cell B8

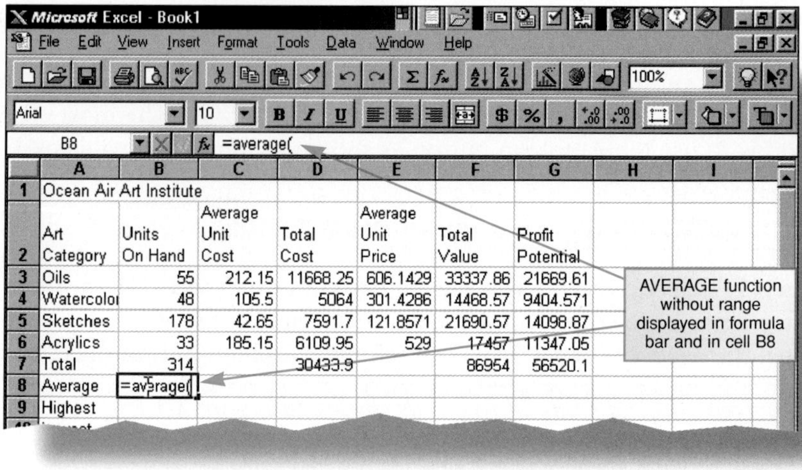

FIGURE 2-14

2 Click cell B3, the first endpoint of the range to average. Drag down to cell B6, the second endpoint of the range to average.

A marquee surrounds the range B3:B6. When you click cell B3, Excel appends cell B3 to the left parenthesis in the formula bar and highlights cell B3 with a marquee. When you begin dragging, Excel appends a colon (:) to the function and also the cell reference of the cell where the mouse pointer is located (Figure 2-15).

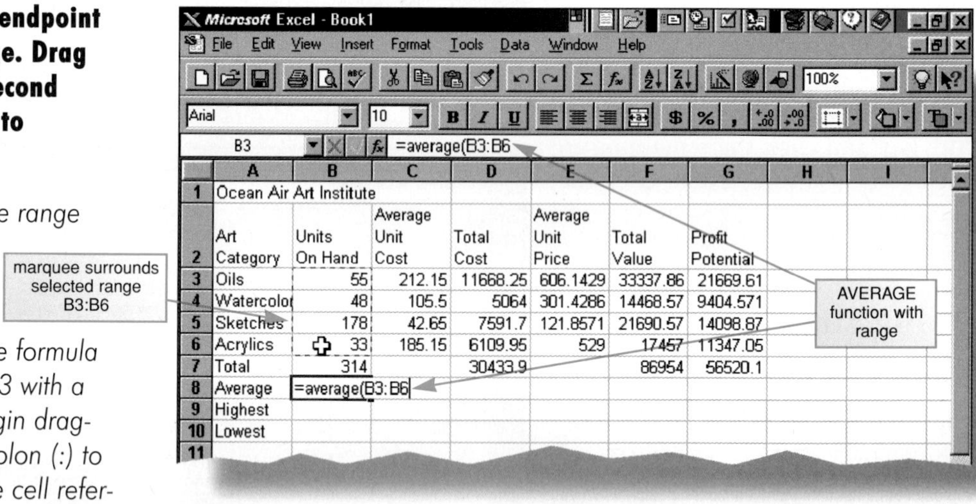

marquee surrounds selected range B3:B6

AVERAGE function with range

FIGURE 2-15

3 Release the left mouse button and then click the enter box or press the ENTER key.

Excel computes the average, 78.5, of the three numbers in the range B3:B6 and assigns it to cell B8 (Figure 2-16).

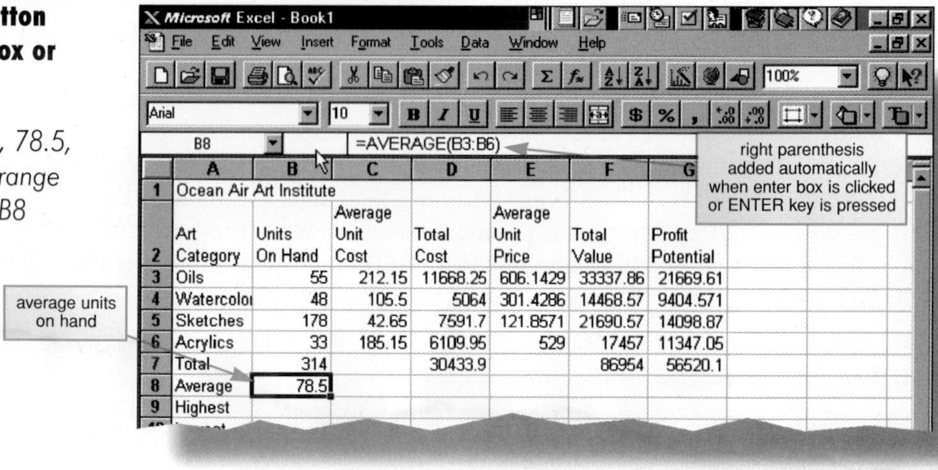

right parenthesis added automatically when enter box is clicked or ENTER key is pressed

average units on hand

FIGURE 2-16

*Other*Ways

1. Click Function Wizard button on Standard toolbar, select desired function, respond in dialog boxes
2. Type =, click the function wizard box in formula bar, select desired function, respond in dialog boxes

Notice that Excel appends the right parenthesis automatically to complete the AVERAGE function when you click the enter box or press the ENTER key. The AVERAGE function requires that the range (the argument) be included within parentheses following the function name. Also, when you use the Point mode as in the previous steps, you cannot use the arrow keys to complete the entry. While in Point mode, the arrow keys change the selected cell reference in the formula being created.

In the example just illustrated, Point mode was used to select the range following the left parenthesis. Rather than use Point mode, you can type the range. If you decide to type a range, remember that the colon (:) separating the endpoints of the range is required punctuation.

More *About* **Excel's Add-Ins**

Excel comes with add-ins that can simplify your work. Add-ins are installed during or after the installation and activated through the Add-Ins command on the Tools menu. Some add-ins add commands to menus or controls to dialog boxes. Some of the more popular add-ins are View Manager (name and save frequently used worksheet locations), Analysis ToolPak (new function category), Engineering (engineering functions), Report Manager (additional printing capabilities), and Solver (linear and nonlinear optimization).

Calculating the Highest Value in a Range Using the MAX Function

The next step is to select cell B9 and determine the highest value in the range B3:B6. Excel has a function for displaying the highest value in a range called the **MAX function**. Enter the function name and use Point mode as described below.

TO FIND THE HIGHEST NUMBER IN A RANGE

Step 1: Select cell B9. Type `=max(` as the entry.
Step 2: Click cell B3, the first endpoint of the desired range. Drag down to cell B6, the second endpoint of the desired range.
Step 3: Release the left mouse button and then click the enter box or press the ENTER key.

Excel determines the highest value in the range B3:B6 as 178 (cell B5) and displays it in cell B9 (Figure 2-17).

Certainly it would be as easy as entering the MAX function to scan the range B3:B6 to determine the highest value in the range B4:B8 and enter the number 178 as a constant in cell B9. The display would be the same as Figure 2-17. If the values in the range B3:B6 change, however, cell B9 would continue to display 178. By using the MAX function, you are guaranteed that Excel will recalculate the highest value in the range B3:B6 each time a new value is entered into the worksheet. Scanning the range manually for the highest value also would be much more time-consuming if the worksheet contained more categories.

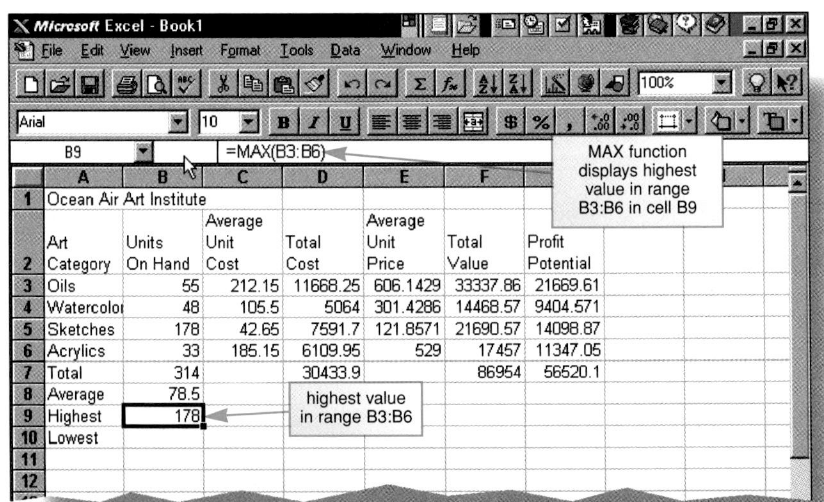

FIGURE 2-17

Entering the MIN Function Using the Function Wizard Button

The next step is to enter the **MIN function** in cell B10 to determine the lowest value in the range B3:B6. Although you could enter the MIN function in the same fashion as the MAX function, the following steps show an alternative using Excel's **Function Wizard button** on the Standard toolbar.

Steps: To Enter the MIN Function Using the Function Wizard Button

1 Select cell B10. Click the Function Wizard button on the Standard toolbar. Click MIN in the Function Name list box in the Function Wizard - Step 1 of 2 dialog box, and then point to the Next button.

*Excel displays the **Function Wizard - Step 1 of 2 dialog box** with Most Recently Used selected in the **Function Category list box** and MIN selected in the **Function Name list box** (Figure 2-18).*

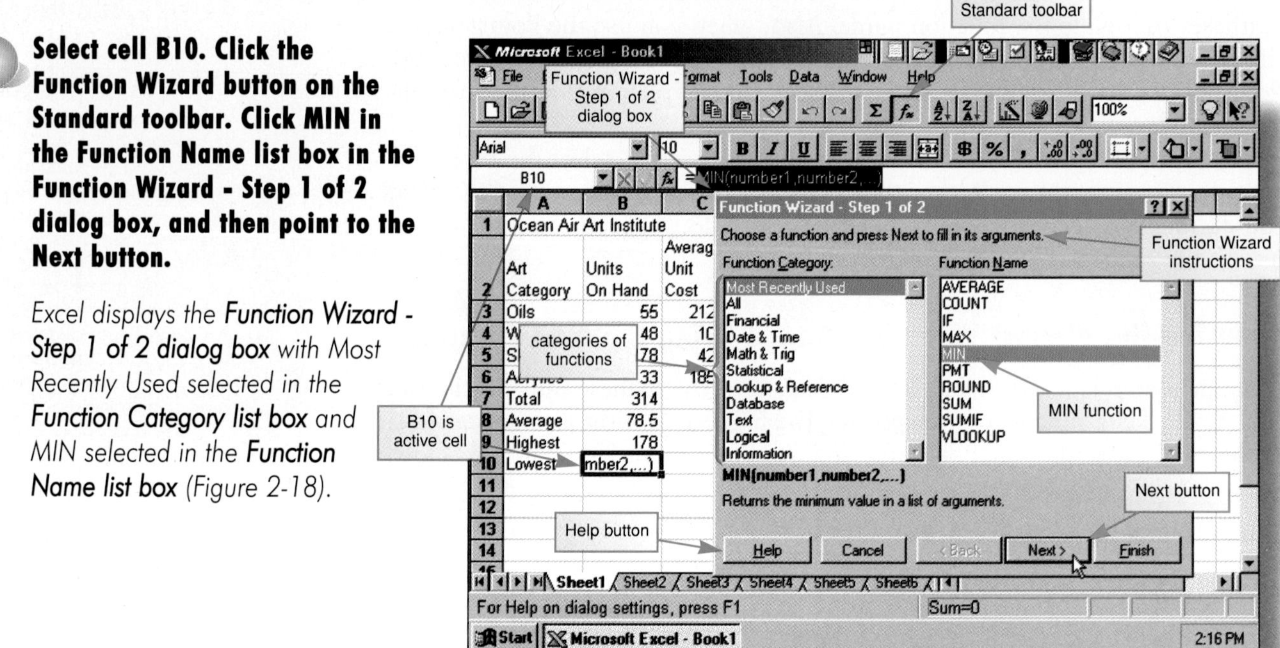

FIGURE 2-18

2 Click the Next button in the Function Wizard - Step 1 of 2 dialog box.

Excel displays the Function Wizard Step 2 of 2 dialog box.

3 Use the mouse to select the range B3:B6 on the worksheet.

Excel enters the range in the number 1 box and displays the result of =MIN(B3:B6) in the Value box (33) in the Function Wizard - Step 2 of 2 dialog box (Figure 2-19).

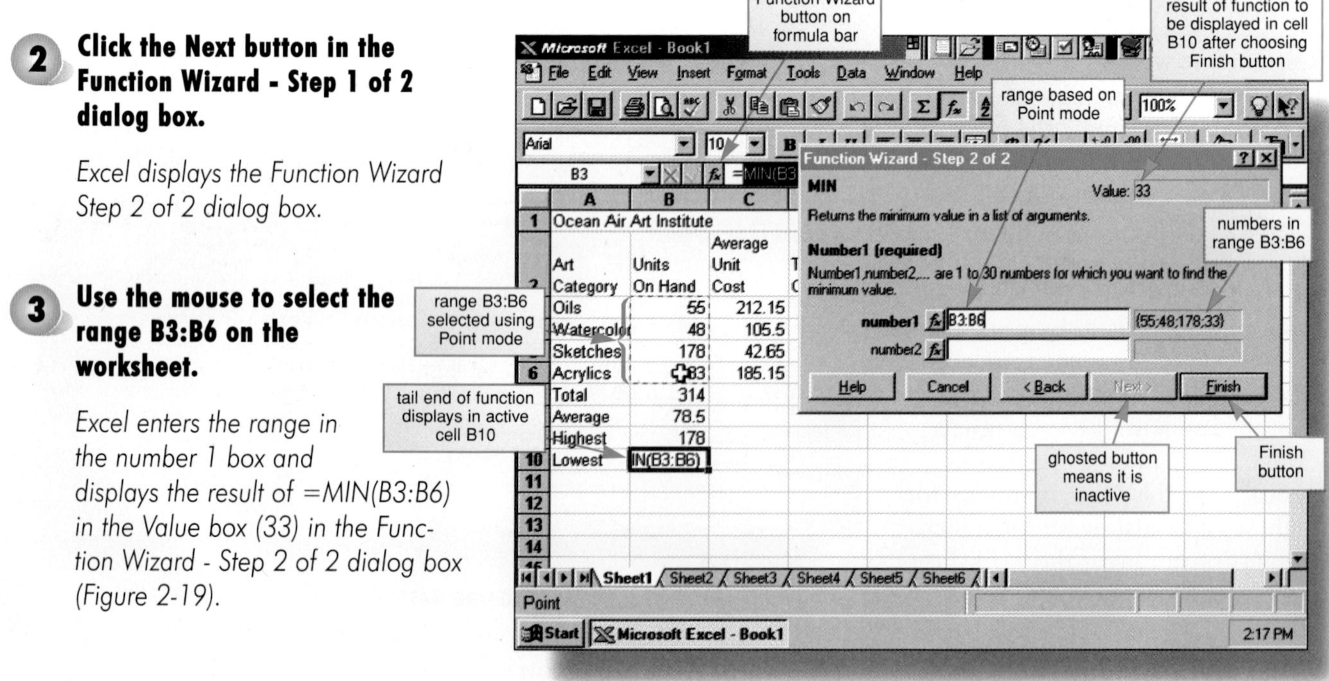

FIGURE 2-19

Click the Finish button.

Excel determines the lowest value in the range B3:B6 and displays it in cell B10 (Figure 2-20).

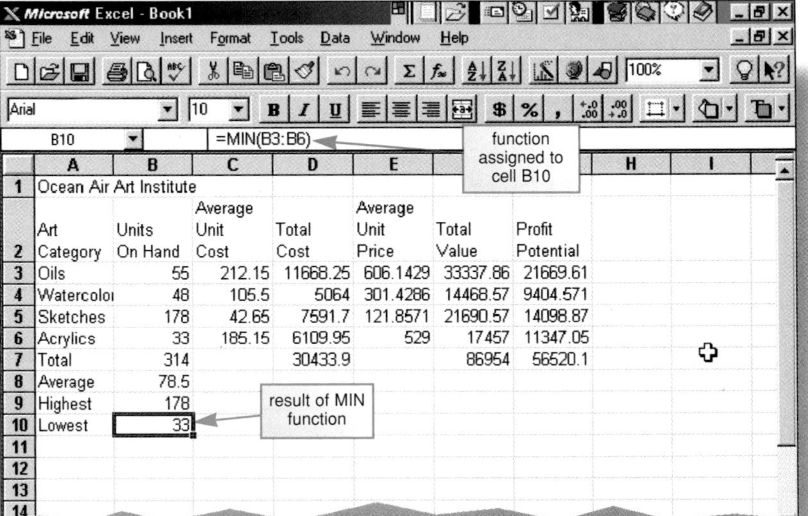

FIGURE 2-20

OtherWays

1. Press SHIFT+F3

You can see from the previous example that using the Function Wizard button on the Standard toolbar allows you to enter a function into a cell easily without requiring you to memorize its format. Anytime you desire to enter a function, simply click the Function Wizard button on the Standard toolbar, select the desired function, and enter the arguments.

An alternative to using the Function Wizard button on the Standard toolbar is to use the function wizard button on the formula bar, next to the enter box. This button displays only when the formula bar is active (see Figure 2-19) and is primarily used to enter a function in the middle of a formula you are entering into a cell. A third alternative for entering a function into a cell is to click Function on the Insert menu.

Thus far, you have learned to use the SUM, AVERAGE, MAX, and MIN functions. Besides these four functions, Excel has more than 400 additional functions that perform just about every type of calculation you can imagine. These functions are categorized as shown in the Function Category box in Figure 2-18. To obtain a list and description of the available functions, click Microsoft Excel Help Topics on the Help menu. When Excel displays the Help Topics: Microsoft Excel dialog box, click the Index tab, and type `functions` in the top box labeled 1. Under functions in the lower box labeled 2, scroll down and then double-click worksheet function index. One-by-one, click each category. To obtain a hard copy of any desired listing, click the Optionsbutton and then click Print Topic.

In the Function Wizard dialog box in Figure 2-19, five buttons are available. If a button is ghosted (dimmed), it means you cannot choose it. The functions of the five Function Wizard buttons are described in Table 2-3.

Table 2-3

BUTTON	FUNCTION
Help	Displays Help on the Function Wizard.
Cancel	Cancels the Function Wizard and returns to the worksheet.
< Back	Displays the previous dialog box.
Next >	Displays the next dialog box.
Finish	Assigns the selections made to the cell thus far.

More About Ranges

If you are an experienced Lotus 1-2-3 user and find it difficult to change your ways, you can enter a range using two periods. For example, Excel interprets B5..B10 as B5:B10.

More About Using Point Mode

In Step 3 and Figure 2-19 the range is entered in the number 1 box in the Function Wizard - Step 2 of 2 dialog box by dragging through the range on the worksheet. If part of the range is hidden by the dialog box, point to the title bar of the dialog box and drag it out of the way.

Copying the AVERAGE, MAX, and MIN Functions

The final step before formatting the worksheet is to copy the AVERAGE, MAX, and MIN functions in the range B8:B10 to the range C8:G10. Here again, the fill handle will be used to complete the copy.

Steps To Copy a Range of Cells Across Columns to an Adjacent Range Using the Fill Handle

1. **Select the range B8:B10. Drag the fill handle in the lower right corner of cell B10 and drag across to cell G10.**

   Excel highlights the copy area (range B8:B10) and displays a rectangle around the paste area (range C8:G10) (Figure 2-21).

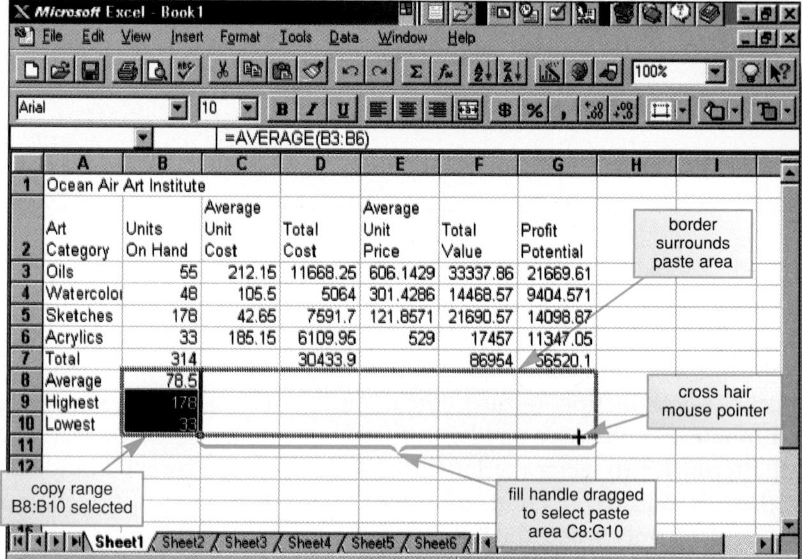

FIGURE 2-21

2. **Release the left mouse button.**

   Excel copies the three functions across the range C8:G10 (Figure 2-22).

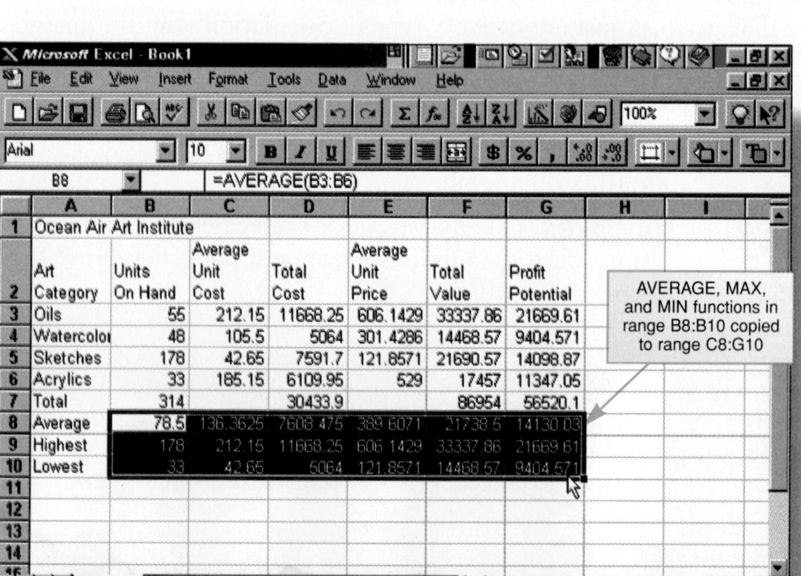

FIGURE 2-22

Here again, you must remember that Excel adjusts the ranges in the copied functions so that each function refers to the column of numbers above it. Review the numbers in rows 8 through 10 in Figure 2-22. You should see that each function is determining the appropriate value in the column above it for the numbers in rows 3 through 6.

Select any cell in the worksheet to remove the selection from the range B8:G10. This concludes entering the data and formulas into the worksheet. The next step is to format the worksheet so it is easier to read. Before proceeding, however, it is best to save an intermediate copy of the workbook.

Saving an Intermediate Copy of the Workbook

A good practice is to save intermediate copies of your work. That way, if your computer loses power or you make a serious mistake, you can always retrieve the latest copy from disk. Use the Save button on the Standard toolbar often, because you can save typing time later if the unexpected happens. For the following steps, it is assumed you have a floppy disk in drive A.

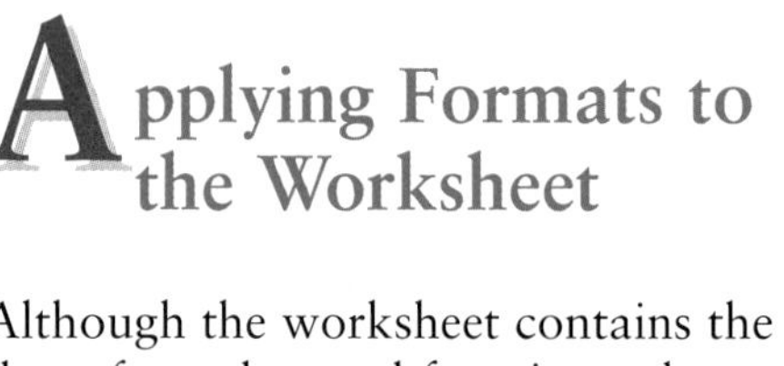

More *About* **Saving a Workbook**

You should save your workbooks every 5 to 10 minutes so that if the system fails you can retrieve a copy without a major loss of work. You can instruct Excel to automatically save a workbook.

TO SAVE AN INTERMEDIATE COPY OF THE WORKBOOK

Step 1: Click the Save button on the Standard toolbar.

Step 2: Type `Ocean Air Profit Analysis` in the File name text box. If necessary, change to 3½ floppy [A:] in the Save in drop-down list box.

The Save As dialog box displays as shown in Figure 2-23.

Step 3: Click the Save button in the Save As dialog box.

After Excel completes the save, the worksheet remains on the screen with Ocean Air Profit Analysis in the title bar. You can immediately continue with the next activity.

Applying Formats to the Worksheet

Although the worksheet contains the data, formulas, and functions, the text and numbers need to be formatted to improve their appearance and readability.

In Project 1, you used the AutoFormat command to format the majority of the worksheet. This section describes how to change the unformatted worksheet in Figure 2-24a to the formatted worksheet in Figure 2-24b (on the next page) without using the AutoFormat command.

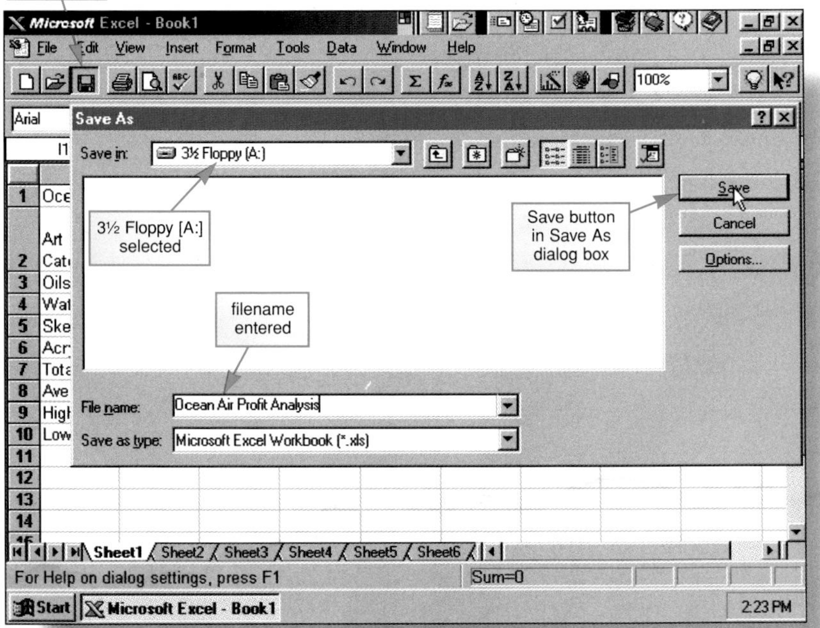

FIGURE 2-23

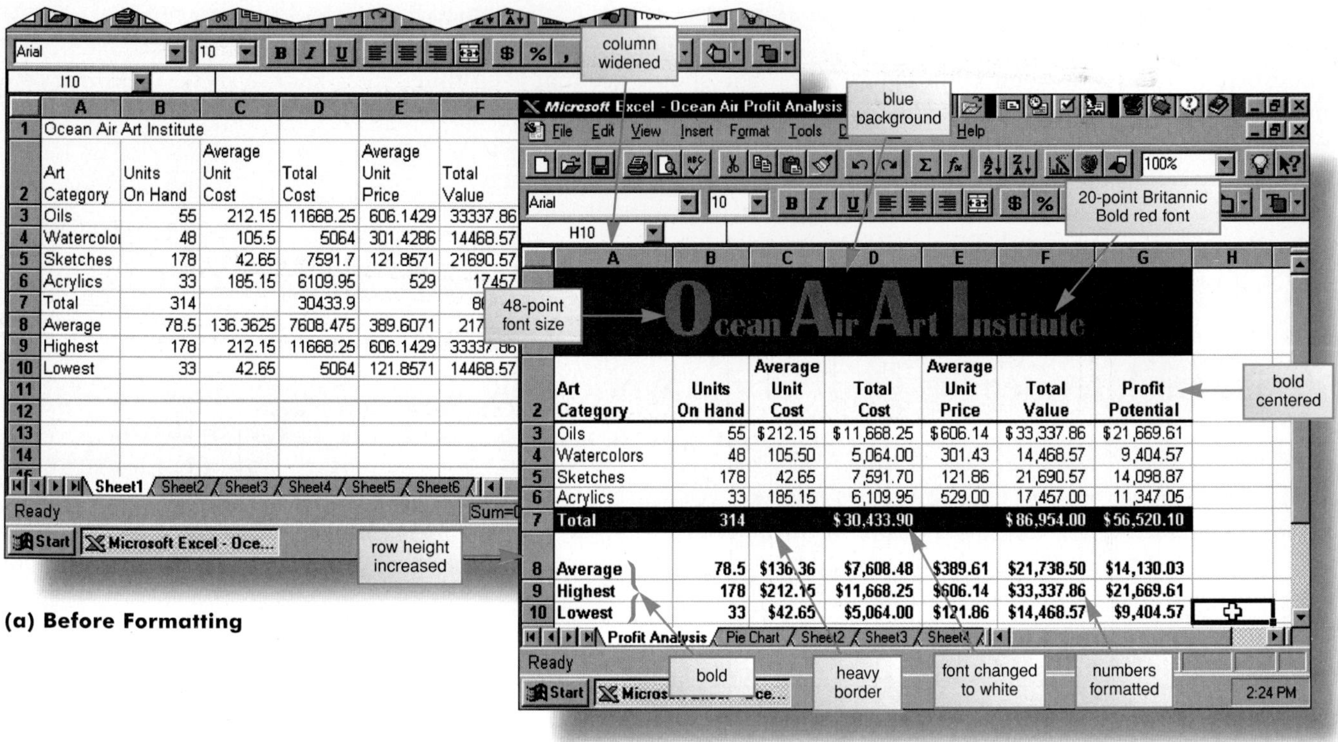

(a) Before Formatting

FIGURE 2-24

(b) After Formatting

The following outlines the type of formatting that is required in Project 2:

1. Worksheet title
   a. Font type — TrueType (TT) Britannic Bold (or TT Courier New if your system does not have TT Britannic Bold)
   b. Font size — 48 for first character in each word; 20 for subsequent characters
   c. Font color — red
   d. Background color (range A1:G1) — blue
   e. Alignment — center across columns A through G
   f. Border — outline A1:G1
2. Column titles
   a. Font style — bold
   b. Alignment — column A title left, columns B through G centered
   c. Border — underline
3. Row titles
   a. Font style — bold total titles
4. Total line
   a. Font style — bold
   b. Font color — white
   c. Background color — blue
   d. Border — outline A7:G7
5. Monetary amounts in rows 3 and 7 through 10
   a. Currency style with two decimal places
   b. Bold totals in rows 8 through 10
6. Numbers in range C4:G6
   a. Comma style with two decimal places
7. Column widths
   a. Increase column A to 13.00 characters; columns B through G to best fit

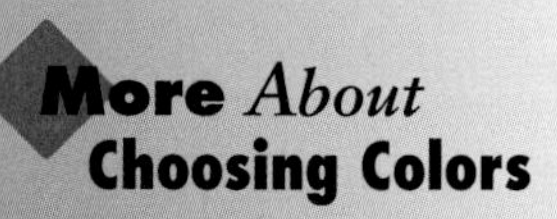

More *About*
Choosing Colors

Knowing how people perceive colors helps you emphasize parts of your worksheet. Warmer colors (red and orange) tend to reach toward the reader. Cooler colors (blue, green, and violet) tend to pull away from the reader. Bright colors jump out of a dark background and are easiest to see. White or yellow text on a dark blue, green, purple, or black background is ideal.

8. Row heights
   a. Change row 1 to 51.00 points; row 8 to 27.75 points

Except for the Currency style assigned to the totals in rows 8 through 10, all of the above formatting can be accomplished by using the mouse and Formatting toolbar.

More *About* Adding Colors and Borders

Colors and borders can change a boring worksheet into an interesting and easy-to-read worksheet. Colors and borders can also be used to make important information stand out.

Applying Formats to the Worksheet Title

To emphasize the worksheet title in cell A1, the font type, size, style, and color are changed as described in the following steps. The background color blue and a border will be added later with row 7, which calls for the same background color and border.

Steps To Format the Characters in the Worksheet Title

1 **Click cell A1.**

2 **Click the Font box arrow on the Formatting toolbar and point to TT Britannic Bold (or TT Courier New if your system does not have TT Britannic Bold).**

The Font drop-down list box displays (Figure 2-25).

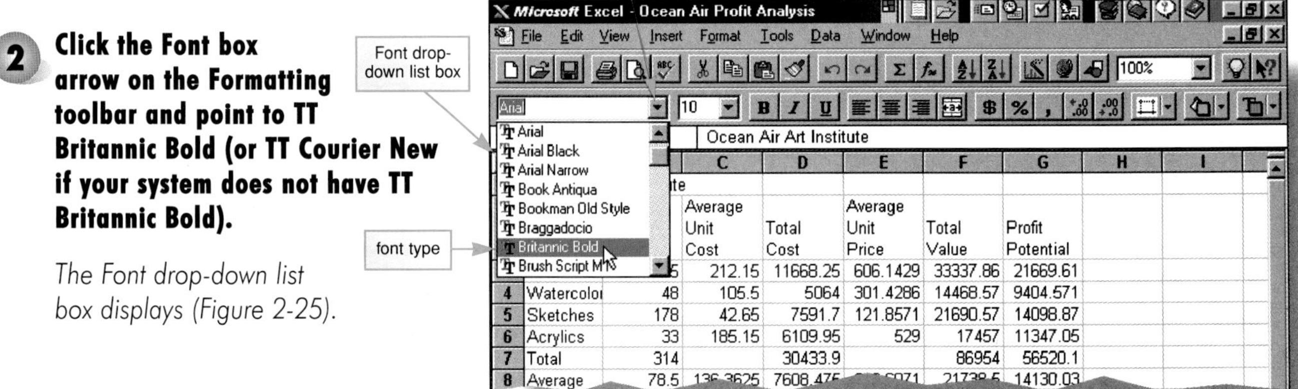

FIGURE 2-25

3 **Click TT Britannic Bold (or TT Courier New). Click the Font Size box arrow on the Formatting toolbar and point to 20.**

The characters in cell A1 display using TT Britannic Bold (or TT Courier New). The font size 20 is highlighted in the Font Size drop-down list box (Figure 2-26).

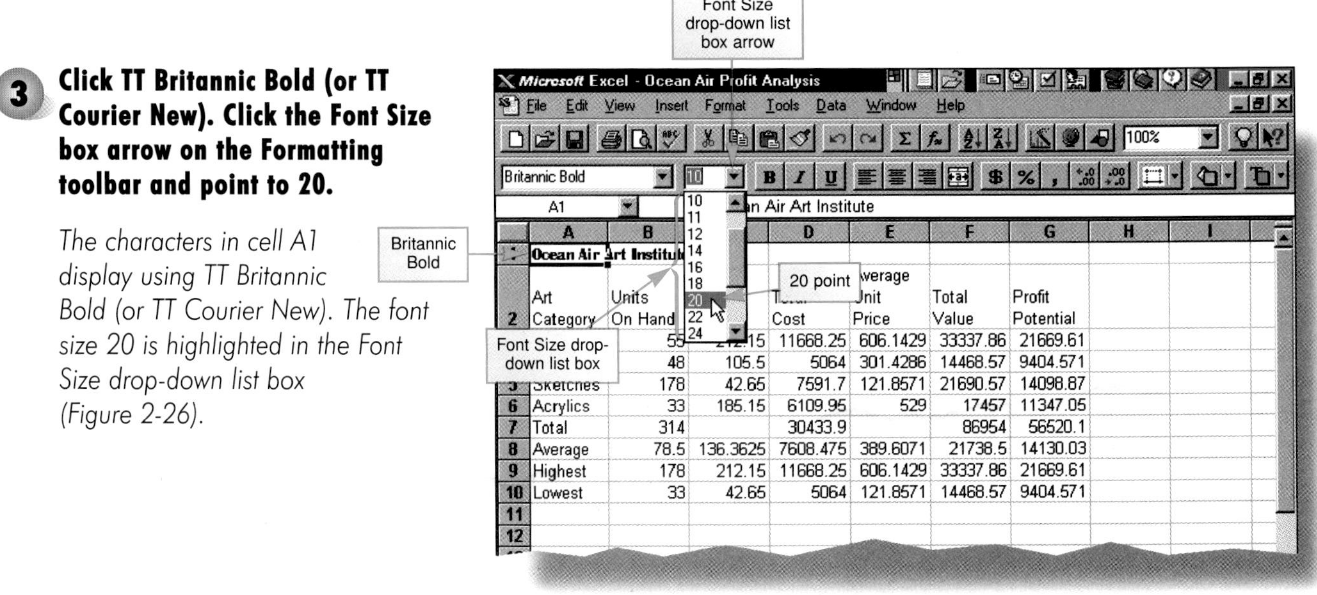

FIGURE 2-26

4 **Click 20 in the Font Size drop-down list box. Double-click cell A1 to edit the cell contents. Drag across the first character O in Ocean, and then point to the Font Size box arrow.**

The font in cell A1 displays in 20 point. Excel enters the Edit mode and the letter O in Ocean is selected (Figure 2-27). Excel increases the row heights of rows 1 and 2 automatically so the larger characters fit in the cells.

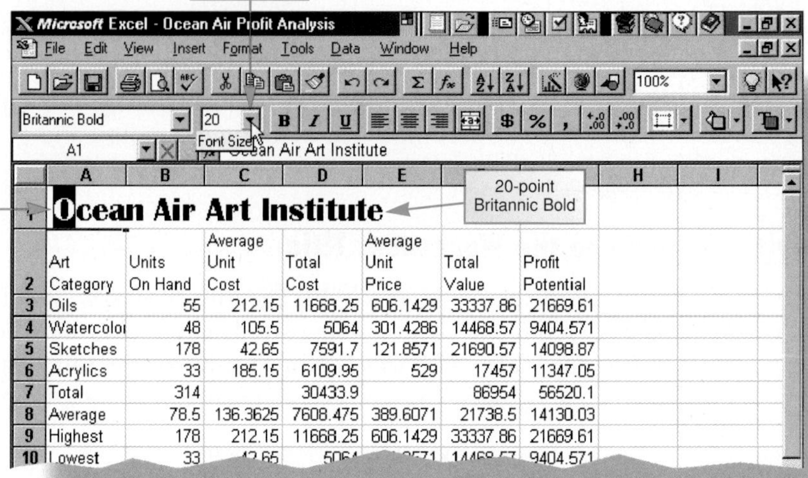

FIGURE 2-27

5 **Click the Font Size box arrow and then point to 48 (Figure 2-28).**

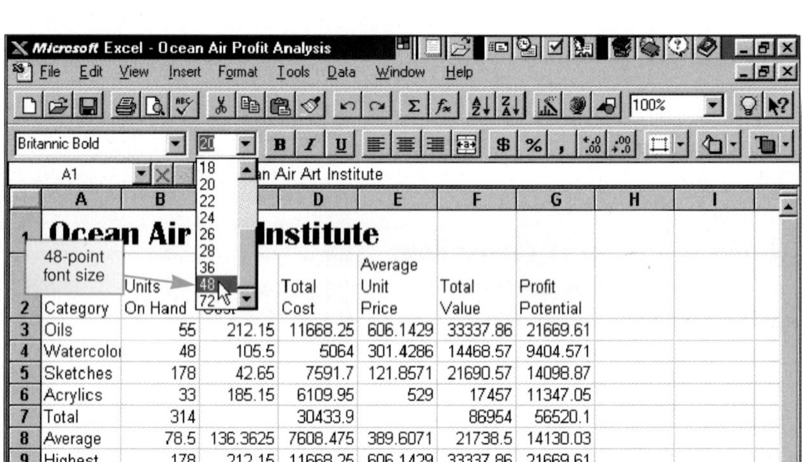

FIGURE 2-28

6 **Click 48 in the Font Size box. While in Edit mode, drag across the first letter of the remaining words in the worksheet title one at a time and change their font size to 48.**

The first letter of each word in the worksheet title appears larger than the other characters (Figure 2-29).

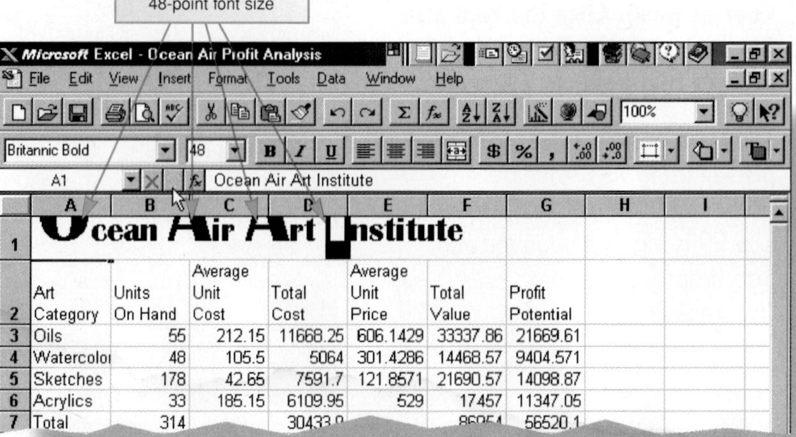

FIGURE 2-29

7 **Click the enter box or press the ENTER key to complete editing the contents of cell A1. Click the Font Color button arrow on the Formatting toolbar and point to the color red (column 3, row 1 on the Font Color palette).**

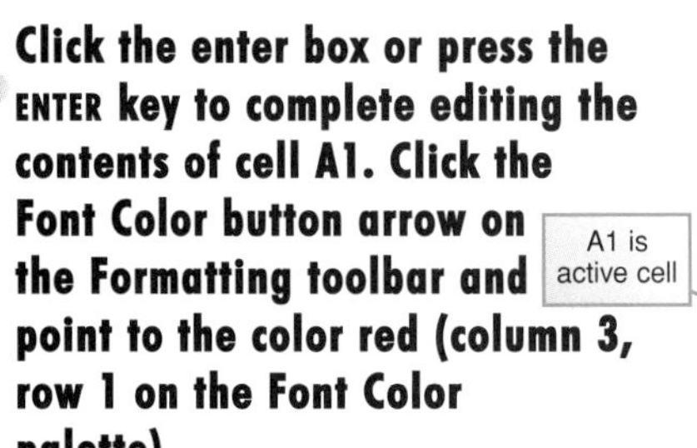

Excel displays the worksheet title with the new font sizes and increases the row height so the larger characters display in their entirety. The Font Color palette displays in the upper right corner of the screen (Figure 2-30).

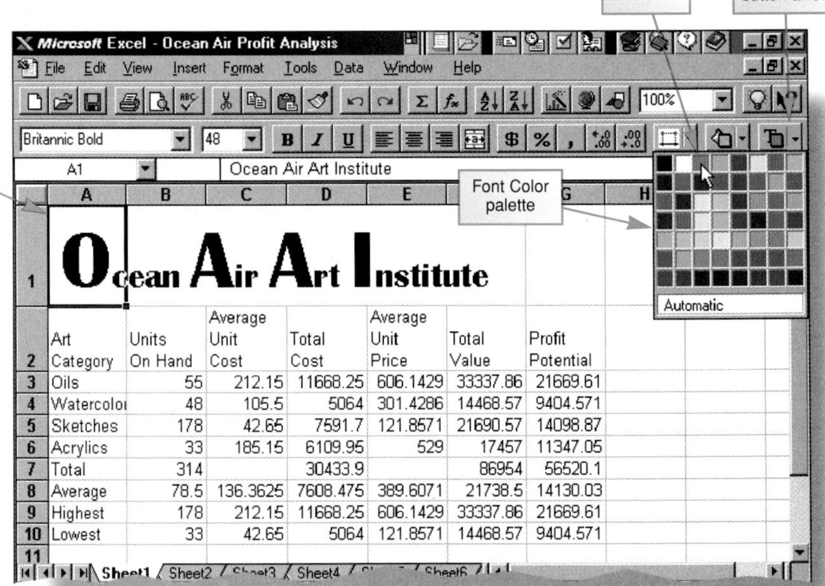

FIGURE 2-30

8 **Click the color red on the Font Color palette.**

The worksheet title is red (Figure 2-31).

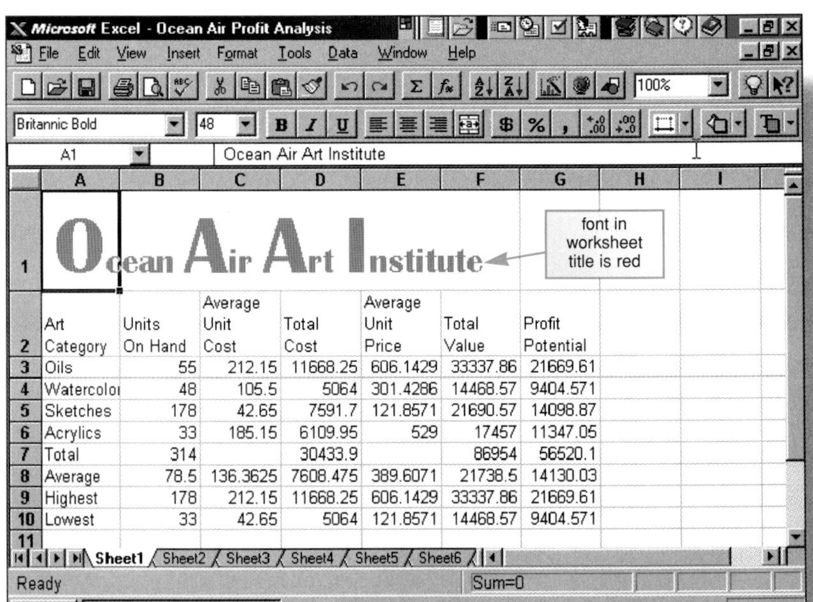

FIGURE 2-31

OtherWays

1. Right-click cell, click Format Cells, click Font tab, select font formats, click OK button
2. On the File menu click Cells, click Font tab, select font formats, click OK button
3. Press CTRL+1, click Font tab, select font formats, click OK button

When developing presentation-quality worksheets, different fonts often are used in the same worksheet. Excel allows you to change the font of individual characters in a cell or all the characters in a cell, in a range of cells, or in the entire worksheet. You can also change the font any time while the worksheet is active. For example, some Excel users prefer to change the font before they enter any data. Others change the font while they are building the worksheet or after they have entered all the data.

The next step is to center the worksheet title across columns A through G.

More *About*
Centering Across Columns

To deselect Centering Across Columns, select the cell the title was assigned to and click the recessed Center Across Columns button on the Formatting toolbar.

TO CENTER THE WORKSHEET TITLE

Step 1: Click cell A1.
Step 2: Select the range A1:G1.
Step 3: Click the Center Across Columns button on the Formatting toolbar.

Excel centers the worksheet title in cell A1 across columns A through G (Figure 2-32).

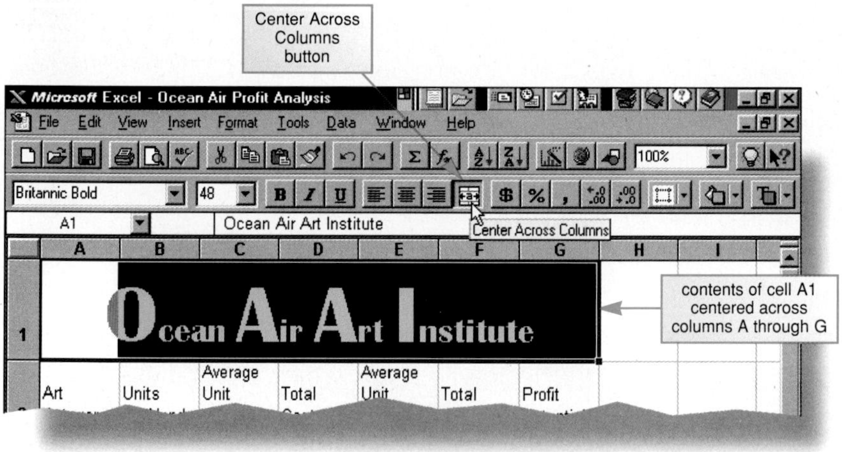

FIGURE 2-32

The final formats to be assigned to the worksheet title are the blue background color and outline border (Figure 2-24b on page E 2.22). These same formats also must be assigned to the totals in row 7. Thus, both ranges will be formatted at the same time by selecting nonadjacent ranges. You select nonadjacent ranges by selecting the first range (A1:G1) and then, while holding down the CTRL key, selecting the second range (A7:G7). Perform the following steps to change the background colors and apply an outline border.

Steps To Change the Background Colors and Apply an Outline Border

1 **Select the range A1:G1. Hold down the CTRL key and select the nonadjacent range A7:G7. Click the Color button arrow on the Formatting toolbar and then point to the color blue (column 1, row 4 on the Color palette).**

The nonadjacent ranges A1:G1 and A7:G7 are highlighted and the Color palette displays (Figure 2-33).

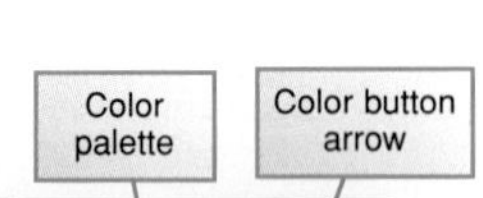

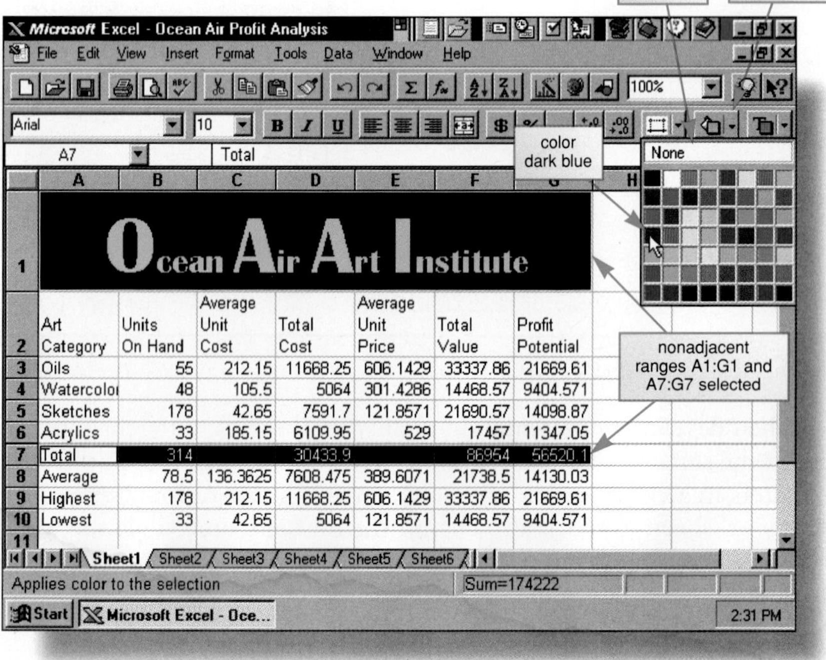

FIGURE 2-33

2 **Click the color blue on the Color palette. Click the Borders button arrow on the Formatting toolbar and then point to the heavy outline border (column 4, row 3).**

The background color of the ranges A1:G1 and A7:G7 appear yellow because they are selected and the Borders palette displays (Figure 2-34). When a cell is selected on the worksheet in the next step, the background color of the two ranges will change to blue.

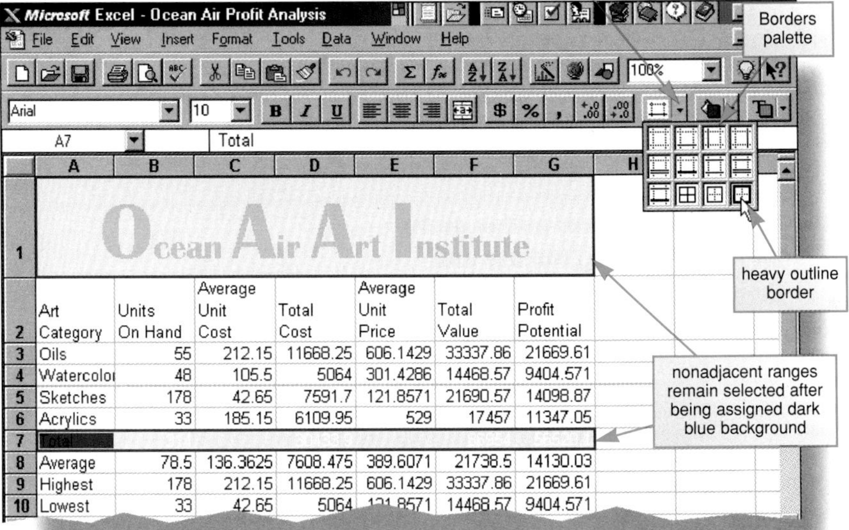

FIGURE 2-34

3 **Click the heavy outline border (column 4, row 3 on the Borders palette). Select any cell on the worksheet.**

The background color of the ranges A1:G1 and A7:G7 changes to blue and both ranges have a heavy outline border (Figure 2-35).

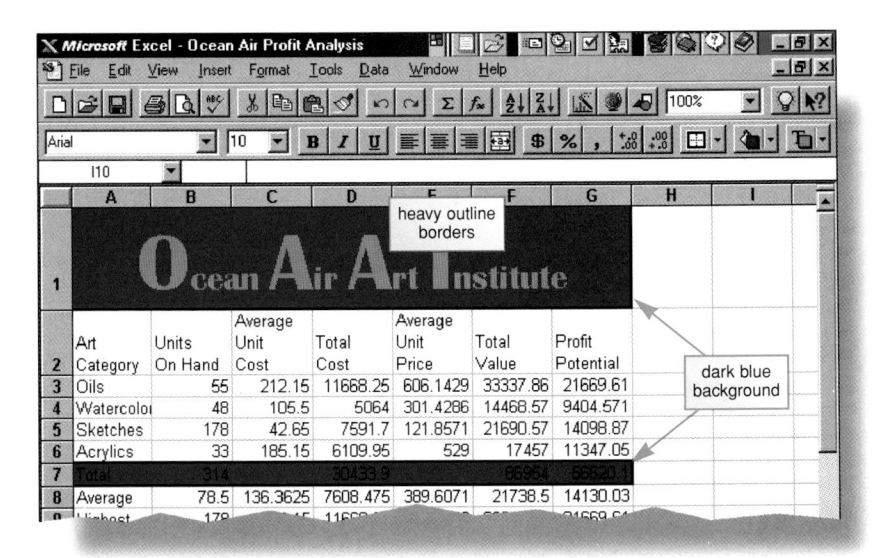

FIGURE 2-35

OtherWays

1. Right-click range, click Format Cells on shortcut menu, click Font tab, click Color arrow, click desired color, click OK button
2. On Format menu click Cells, click Font tab, click Color arrow, click desired color, click OK button
3. Right-click range, click Format Cells on shortcut menu, click Border tab, click a style, click desired border type, click OK button
4. On Format menu click Cells, click Border tab, click a style, click desired border type, click OK button

You can remove borders, such as the outline around the range A1:G1, by selecting the range and pressing CTRL+SHIFT+_. You can remove a background color by clicking the arrow on the Color button on the Formatting toolbar and clicking None on the Color palette.

Changing the Font Color and Bolding Nonadjacent Ranges

As you can see in the range A7:G7 in Figure 2-35, it is difficult to read black characters on a blue background. Complete the following steps to change the font color in the range A7:G7 to white and to bold the column titles in row 2 and totals in the range A7:G10.

Steps To Change the Font Color and Bold Nonadjacent Ranges

1. **Select the range A7:G7.**

2. **Click the Font Color button arrow on the Formatting toolbar and then point to the color white (column 2, row 1 on the Font Color palette).**

   The Font Color palette displays as shown in Figure 2-36.

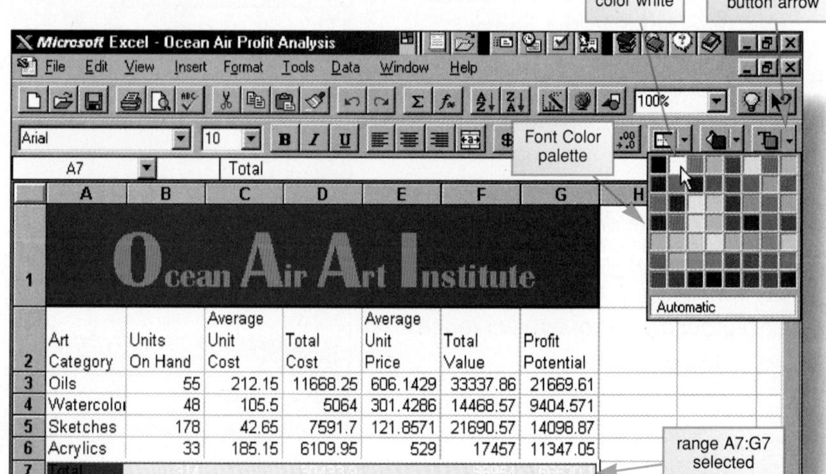

FIGURE 2-36

3. **Click the color white on the Font Color palette.**

4. **Select the range A2:G2. Hold down the CTRL key and select the nonadjacent range A7:G10. Click the Bold button on the Formatting toolbar.**

   The worksheet column titles in row 2 and the totals in the range A7:G10 display as shown in Figure 2-37.

5. **Select any cell on the worksheet to deselect the nonadjacent ranges.**

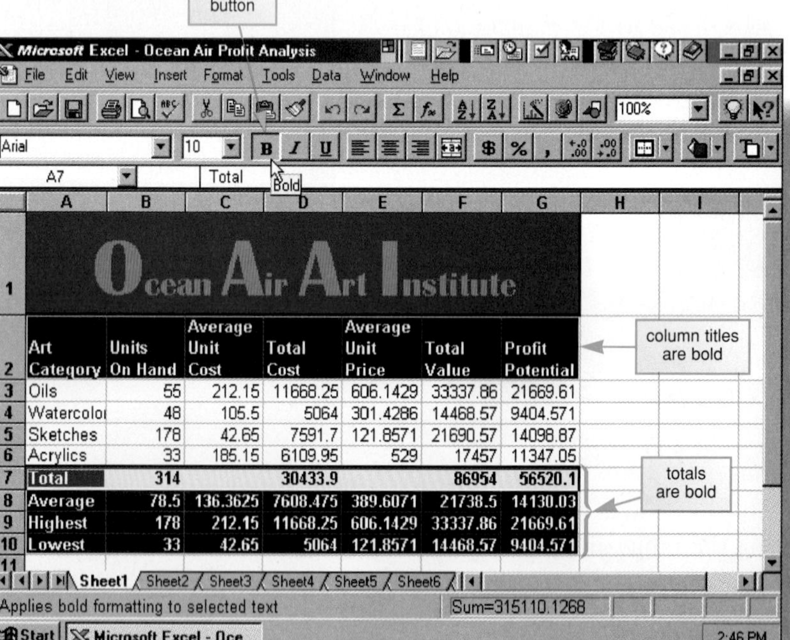

FIGURE 2-37

You can see in Figure 2-37 that the bold white characters on a blue background stand out and are much easier to read than the black characters on a blue background.

Applying Formats to the Column Titles

According to Figure 2-24b on page E 2.22, the column titles have a heavy underline. Furthermore, the title in column A is left-aligned in cell A2 and the column titles in cells B2:G2 are centered. The following steps assign these formats to the column titles.

Steps To Underline and Center the Column Titles

1 **Select the range A2:G2. Click the Borders button arrow on the Formatting toolbar and then point to the heavy bottom border (column 2, row 2 on the Borders palette).**

The Borders palette displays (Figure 2-38).

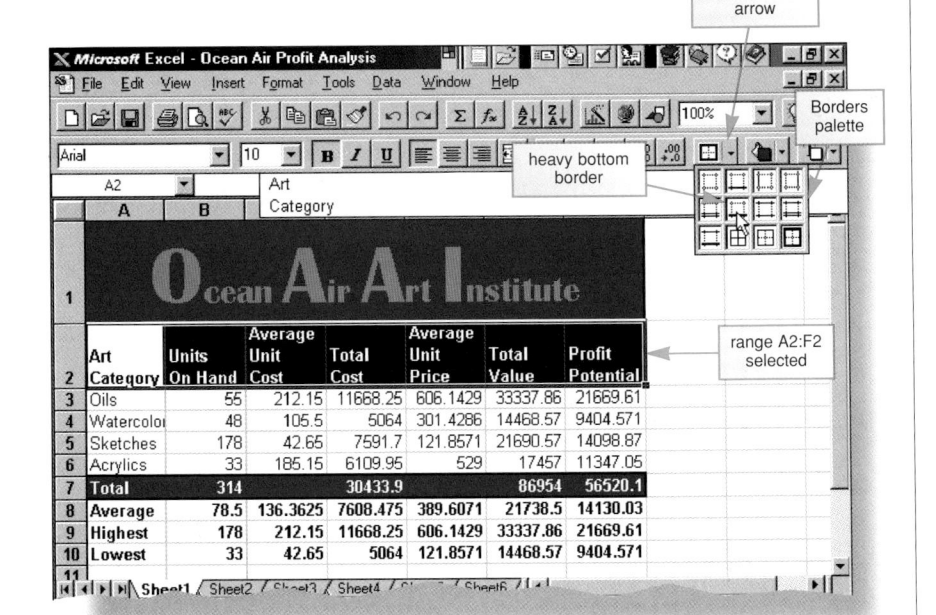

FIGURE 2-38

Click the heavy bottom border. Select the range B2:G2 and then point to the Center button on the Formatting toolbar.

The selected range B2:G2 is highlighted (Figure 2-39).

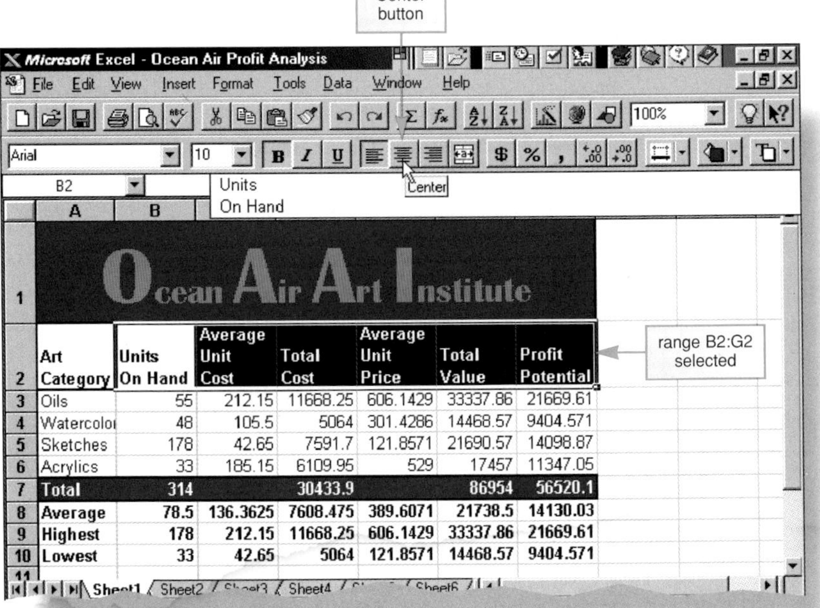

FIGURE 2-39

Click the Center button and then select any cell in the worksheet.

The column titles display as shown in Figure 2-40.

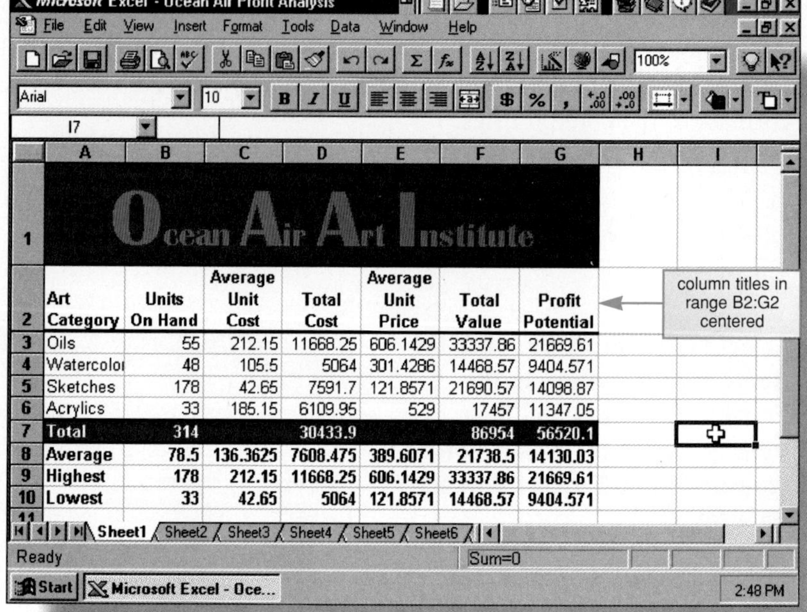

	A	B	C	D	E	F	G
2	Art Category	Units On Hand	Average Unit Cost	Total Cost	Average Unit Price	Total Value	Profit Potential
3	Oils	55	212.15	11668.25	606.1429	33337.86	21669.61
4	Watercolor	48	105.5	5064	301.4286	14468.57	9404.571
5	Sketches	178	42.65	7591.7	121.8571	21690.57	14098.87
6	Acrylics	33	185.15	6109.95	529	17457	11347.05
7	Total	314		30433.9		86954	56520.1
8	Average	78.5	136.3625	7608.475	389.6071	21738.5	14130.03
9	Highest	178	212.15	11668.25	606.1429	33337.86	21669.61
10	Lowest	33	42.65	5064	121.8571	14468.57	9404.571

FIGURE 2-40

OtherWays

1. Right-click range, click Format Cells on shortcut menu, click Alignment tab, click desired alignment, click OK button
2. On Format menu click Cells, click Alignment tab, click desired alignment, click OK button

You can align the contents of cells several different ways. The more common alignments are left-align, center, and right-align. These three alignments are used so often that Microsoft includes them on the Formatting toolbar. Most worksheet users left-align a column title over text as shown in column A in Figure 2-40 and center or right-align column titles over numbers. In Figure 2-40, the column titles over numbers in the range B2:G2 are centered.

You can also align text when you initially enter it into a cell by appending a special character to the front. An apostrophe (') instructs Excel to left-align the text. A caret (^) centers the text and a quotation mark (") right-aligns the text.

More *About* Aligning and Rotating Text in Cells

Besides aligning text horizontally in a cell, you can align text vertically (top, center, bottom, or justify). You can also rotate text so that the characters are below one another rather than side-by-side. To align vertically or rotate the text, click Format Cells on the shortcut menu, click the Alignment tab, and then select the type of alignment you want.

Formatting Numbers

When using Excel, you can format numbers to represent dollar amounts, whole numbers with comma placement, and percentages through the use of buttons on the Formatting toolbar. Customized format styles can be assigned using the Cells command on the Format menu or the Format Cells command on the shortcut menu.

According to Figure 2-24(b) on page E 2.22, the worksheet has an accounting report look to it in that the first row of numbers (row 3) and the monetary totals (rows 7 through 10) have dollar signs and the numbers between the first row and totals do not have dollar signs. To display a dollar sign in a number you will want to use the Currency style format.

The **Currency style** appends a dollar sign to the left of the number, inserts a comma every three positions to the left of the decimal point, and displays numbers to the nearest cent (hundredths place). The **Currency Style button** on the Formatting toolbar will assign the desired format. The dollar sign appended to the left of the number, however, is a fixed dollar sign. A **fixed dollar sign** displays to the far left in the cell, often with spaces between it and the first digit. To append a dollar sign that displays immediately to the left of the number (called a **floating dollar sign**), you need to use the Cells command on the Format menu or the Format Cells command on the shortcut menu. According to the project specifications, a fixed dollar sign is to be assigned to the numbers in rows 3 and 7. A floating dollar sign is to be assigned to the monetary totals in rows 8 through 10.

To display monetary amounts without dollar signs, you will want to use the Comma style format. The **Comma style** inserts a comma every three positions to the left of the decimal point.

The remainder of this section describes how to format the numbers in the desired fashion.

More *About* **Formatting Numbers as You Enter Them**

You can format numbers when you enter them by entering a dollar sign ($), comma (,) or percent sign (%) as part of the number. For example, if you enter 1500, Excel displays 1500. However, if you enter $1500, Excel displays $1,500.

Formatting Numbers Using Buttons on the Formatting Toolbar

The following steps show how to assign the Currency style format and Comma style format using the Currency Style button and Comma Style button on the Formatting toolbar.

To Apply a Currency Style Format and Comma Style Format Using Buttons on the Formatting Toolbar

1 **Select the range C3:G3. Hold down the CTRL key and select the nonadjacent range D7:G7. Point to the Currency Style button on the Formatting toolbar.**

The nonadjacent ranges display as shown in Figure 2-41.

	Art Category	Units On Hand	Average Unit Cost	Total Cost	Average Unit Price	Total Value	Profit Potential
3	Oils	55	212.15	11668.25	606.1429	33337.86	21669.61
4	Watercolor	48	105.5	5064	301.4286	14468.57	9404.571
5	Sketches	178	42.65	7591.7	121.8571	21690.57	14098.87
6	Acrylics	33	185.15	6109.95	529	17457	11347.05
7	Total	314		30433.9		86954	56520.1
8	Average	78.5	136.3625	7608.475	389.6071	21738.5	14130.03
9	Highest	178	212.15	11668.25	606.1429	33337.86	21669.61
10	Lowest	33	42.65	5064	121.8571	14468.57	9404.571

FIGURE 2-41

2 **Click the Currency Style button on the Formatting toolbar. Select the range C4:G6 and then click the Comma Style button on the Formatting toolbar.**

Several numbers in the range C3:G6 display as a sequence of number signs (#) indicating they are too large to fit in the width of the cells (Figure 2-42). Some of the smaller numbers display with the appropriate format. Later the column widths will be increased so the numbers will display in place of the number signs.

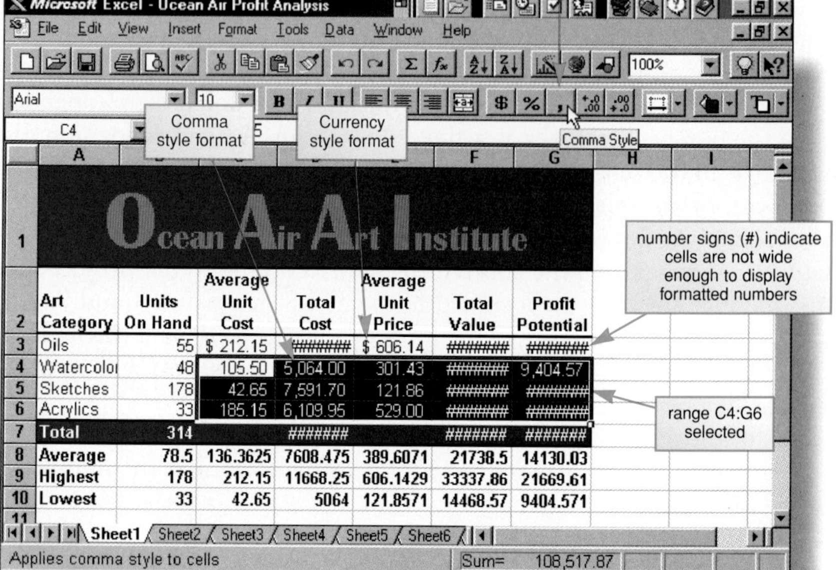

FIGURE 2-42

OtherWays

1. Right-click range, click Format Cells on shortcut menu, click Number tab, click Currency in Category list box, click OK button
2. On Format menu click Cells, click Number tab, click Currency in Category list box, click OK button

In cell C3, the dollar sign displays to the far left with spaces between it and the first digit in the cell. Thus, the Currency Style button assigns a fixed dollar sign to the number.

Excel rounds a number to fit the format selected. For example, in cell E3, Excel rounds the actual value 606.1429 down to 606.14. In cell E4, Excel rounds the actual value 301.4286 up to 301.43.

Formatting Numbers Using the Format Cells Command on the Shortcut Menu

Thus far, you have been introduced to two ways to format numbers in a worksheet. In Project 1, you formatted the numbers using the AutoFormat command on the Format menu. In the previous section, you were introduced to using the Formatting toolbar as a means of selecting a format style. A third way to format numbers is to use the Cells command on the Format menu or the Format Cells command on the shortcut menu. Using either command allows you to display numbers in any desired format you can imagine. The following steps show you how to apply the Currency style with a floating dollar sign to the totals in the range C8:G10 using the Format Cells command on the shortcut menu.

More *About* **Formatting Numbers in Calculations**

The numbers you see on your screen may not be the same ones used in calculations. When a number has more decimal places than are displayed because of your formatting, the actual number is used in the computation. For example, 32.368 is the actual number but 32.37 displays because you formatted with two decimal places.

To Apply a Currency Style with a Floating Dollar Sign Using the Format Cells Command on the Shortcut Menu

1 **Select the range C8:G10. Right-click within the selected range. Point to Format Cells.**

The shortcut menu displays as shown in Figure 2-43.

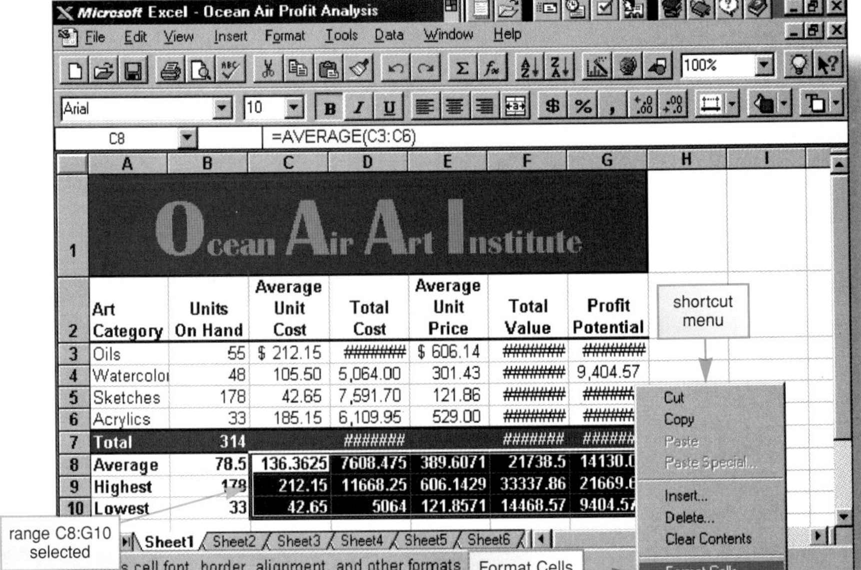

FIGURE 2-43

2 **Click Format Cells on the shortcut menu. Click the Number tab in the Format Cells dialog box.**

3 **Click Currency in the Category list box, click ($1,234.10) in the Negative Numbers list box, and then point to the OK button.**

The Format Cells dialog box *displays as shown in Figure 2-44.*

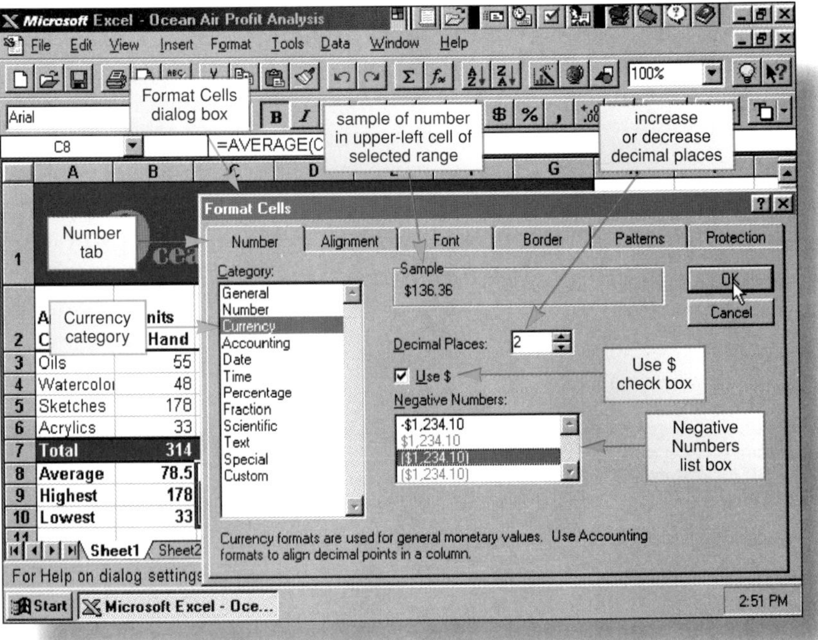

FIGURE 2-44

4 Click the OK button. click any cell outside the selected range.

The worksheet displays with the totals in rows 7 through 10 assigned the Currency style format with a floating dollar sign as shown in Figure 2-45. Here again, the number signs (#) indicate that the columns are not wide enough to display the formatted numbers.

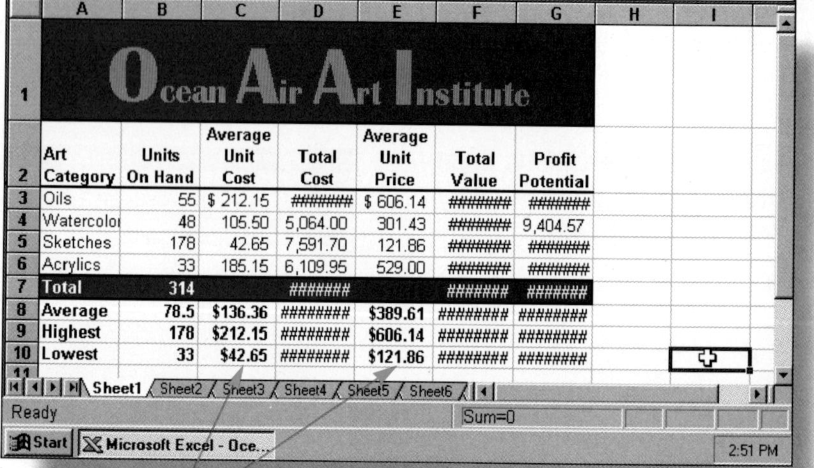

FIGURE 2-45

Other Ways

1. On Format menu click Cells, click Number tab, click Currency in Category list box, click OK button
2. Press CTRL+SHIFT+$

You can see the difference in the Currency style formats assigned to cells C3 and C8. The Currency style was assigned to cell C3 using the Currency Style button on the Formatting toolbar and the result is a fixed dollar sign. The Currency style was assigned to cell C8 using the Format Cells dialog box and the result is a floating dollar sign. Recall that the floating dollar sign will always display immediately to the left of the first digit and the fixed dollar sign will always display on the left side of the cell.

Figure 2-44 on the previous page shows there are 12 categories of formats from which you can choose. Once you select a category, you can select the number of decimal places, whether a dollar sign should display, and how you want negative numbers to display.

It is important to select the Negative Numbers format in Step 3 (on the previous page) because it adds a space to the right of the number as do the Currency Style and Comma Style buttons. If you do not select the proper Negative Numbers format, then the numbers will not be aligned on the decimal points in the worksheet. You can verify this by clicking one of the formatted cells and assigning the Currency category with the first Negative Numbers format (–$1,234.10) instead of ($1,234.10).

With the number formatting complete, the next step is to increase the column widths so the numbers display, rather than the number signs as is the case in Figure 2-45. The next section shows you how to increase the column widths.

More About Painting Formats

Painting is not an envious chore. But in Excel, if you know how to paint you can save yourself time and effort when formatting a worksheet. For example, if you see a cell that has the format you want to assign to another cell or range of cells, click the cell with the desired format, click the Format Painter button (the paintbrush on the Standard toolbar), and then click the cell or drag through the cells you want to paint the format with.

Changing the Widths of Columns and Heights of Rows

When Excel begins and the blank worksheet displays on the screen, all the columns have a default width of 8.43 characters and all the rows have a height of 12.75 points. A **character** is defined as TT Arial 10 point, the default font used by Excel. At any time, you can change the width of the columns or height of the rows to make the worksheet easier to read or to ensure that entries will display properly in the cells to which they are assigned.

Changing the Widths of Columns

When changing the column width, you can manually set the width or you can instruct Excel to size the column to best fit. **Best fit** means that the width of the column will be increased or decreased so the widest entry will fit in the column. The width of column A will be set manually because more space is preferred between columns A and B to improve the appearance of the report. Columns B through G will be set to best fit after widening column A. Complete the following steps to change the width of column A from 8.43 to 13.00.

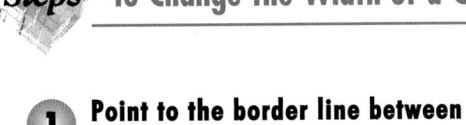

Steps To Change the Width of a Column by Dragging

1 Point to the border line between the column A and column B headings above row 1.

The mouse pointer becomes a split double arrow (Figure 2-46).

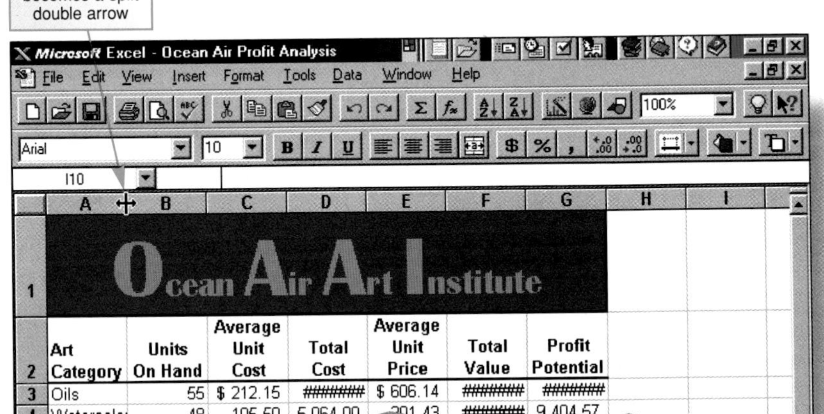

FIGURE 2-46

2 Drag to the right until the number 13.00 displays in the Name box on the left side of the formula bar.

A dotted line shows the new right border of column A and the number 13.00 displays in the Name box (Figure 2-47).

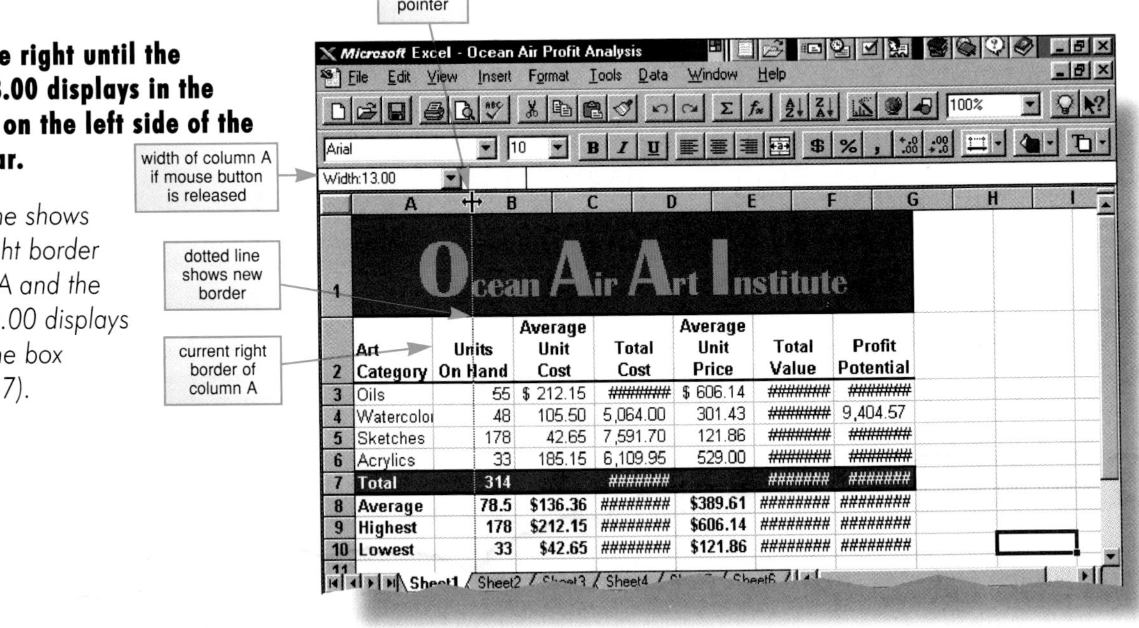

FIGURE 2-47

3 **Release the left mouse button.**

Excel sets the width of column A to 13.00 (Figure 2-48).

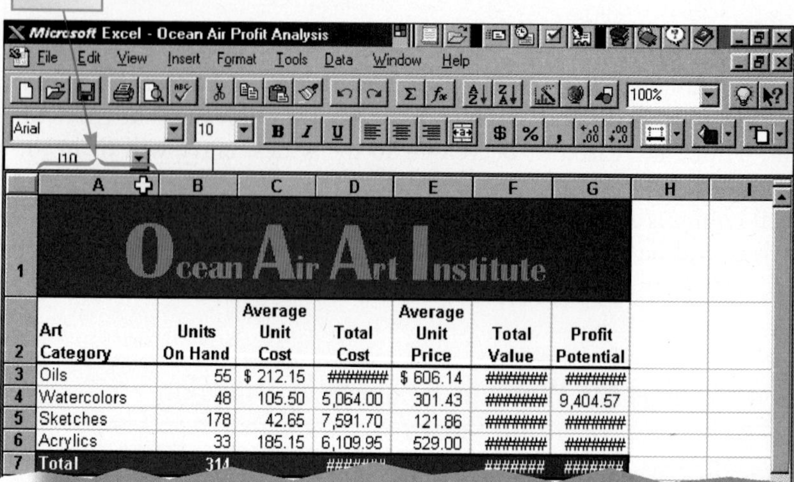

FIGURE 2-48

OtherWays

1. Right-click column heading above row 1 or drag through multiple column headings and right-click, click Column Width, enter new column width, click OK button
2. Select cell in column or select range of cells across columns, on Format menu click Column, click Width, enter new column width, click OK button

Compare the entries in column A of Figure 2-48 to Figure 2-46 on the previous page. Notice how the row title, Watercolors, displays in its entirety in Figure 2-48. Furthermore, the additional space to the right improves the worksheet's appearance.

You can also use the Column Width command on the shortcut menu. The command appears on the shortcut menu only when one or more entire columns are selected, however. You select entire columns by dragging through the column headings. Use the Column Width command instead of the mouse when you want to increase or decrease the column width significantly.

The following steps change the column widths of columns B through G to best fit.

Steps To Change the Widths of Columns to Best Fit

1 **Drag the mouse pointer from column heading B through column heading G. Move the mouse pointer to the right border of column heading G.**

Columns B through G are highlighted and the mouse pointer changes to a split double arrow (Figure 2-49).

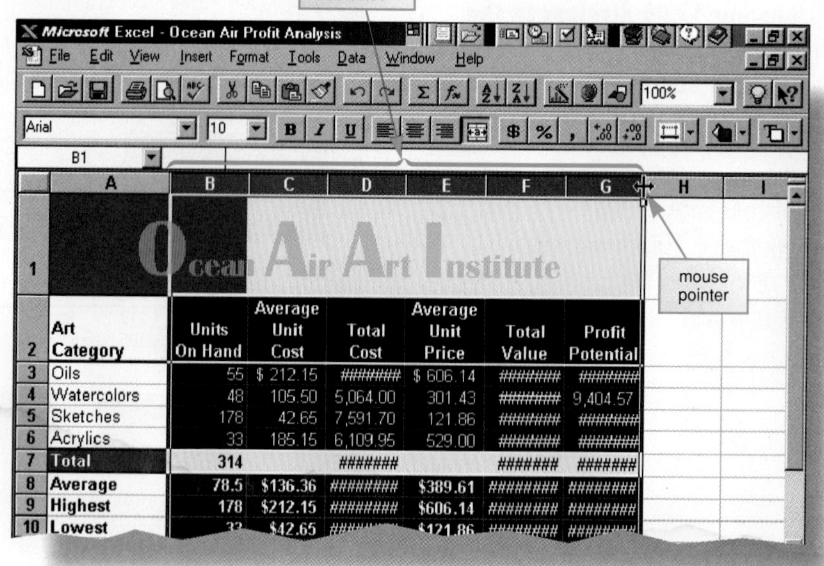

FIGURE 2-49

2 **Double-click the right border of column heading G and then click any cell in the worksheet.**

The width of columns B through G increase just enough so the widest entries in each column display completely (Figure 2-50).

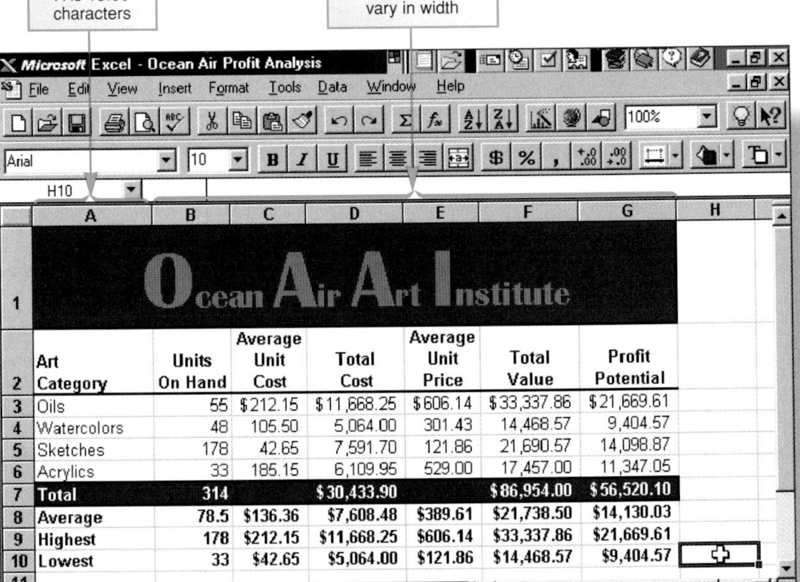

FIGURE 2-50

Compare Figure 2-50 to Figure 2-49. Columns B through G are wider in Figure 2-50 and the number signs in Figure 2-49 have been replaced with numeric values. Excel has increased the width of columns B through G just enough so all the characters in each column display. To determine the exact width of a column, move the mouse pointer to the right border line of the column heading. When the mouse pointer changes to a split double arrow, hold down the left mouse button. Excel displays the new column width in place of the cell reference in the Name box in the formula bar.

The column width can vary between zero and 255 characters. When you decrease the column width to zero, the column is hidden. **Hiding columns** is a technique you can use to hide sensitive data on the screen that you do not want others to see. When you print a worksheet, hidden columns do not print. To display a hidden column, position the mouse pointer to the left of the heading border where the hidden column is located and drag to the right.

More *About* **Best Fit**

Spreadsheet specialists often use best fit twice to increase the widths of columns in a worksheet, once immediately after entering the column titles, and then again after entering and formatting the numbers in the columns.

Changing the Heights of Rows

When you increase the font size of a cell entry, such as Ocean Air Art Institute in cell A1, Excel increases the row height automatically so the characters display properly. You also can manually adjust the height of a row to increase or decrease space to improve the appearance of the worksheet. The row height is measured in point size. The default row height is 12.75 points. Recall from Project 1 that a point is equal to 1/72 of an inch. Thus, 12.75 points is equal to about one-sixth of an inch.

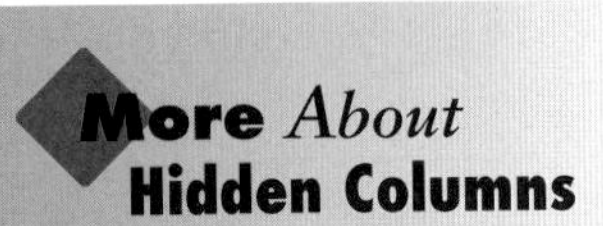

More *About* **Hidden Columns**

It often gets frustrating trying to use the mouse to unhide a range of columns. An alternative is to unhide columns using the keyboard. First select the columns to the right and left of the hidden ones and then press CTRL+SHIFT+). To use the keyboard to hide a range of columns, select the columns to hide, press CTRL+O.

The following steps show how to use the mouse to decrease the height of row 1 from 60.75 points to 51.00 points and increase the height of row 8 from the default 12.75 points to 27.75 points. Recall that the height of row 1 was increased automatically earlier from the default 12.75 points to 60.75 points when the font size was increased. So that all rows of numbers display on the screen at one time and to allow for the increase in the height of row 8, the height of row 1 will be decreased to 51.00 points. Perform the following steps to change the heights of rows by dragging.

To Change the Heights of Rows by Dragging

1 **Move the mouse pointer to the border line between row headings 1 and 2.**

The mouse pointer changes to a split double arrow (Figure 2-51).

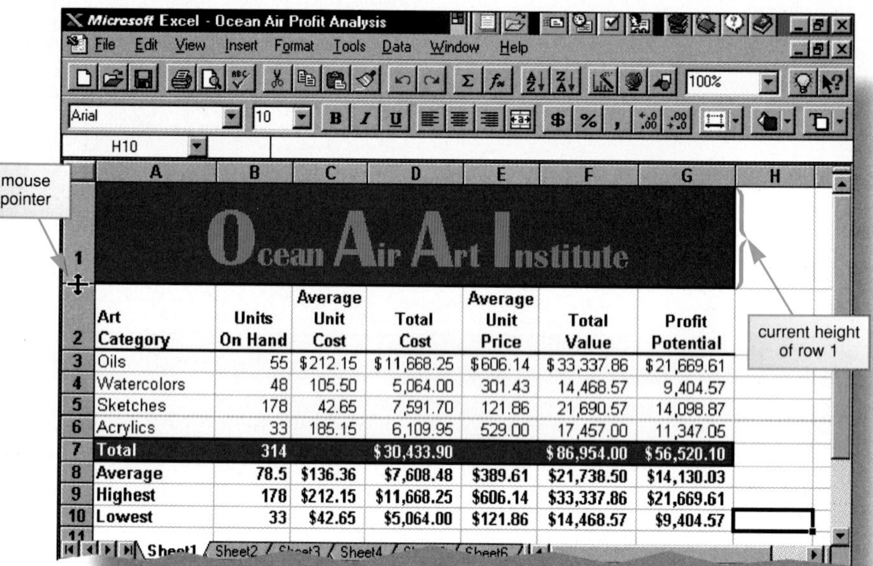

FIGURE 2-51

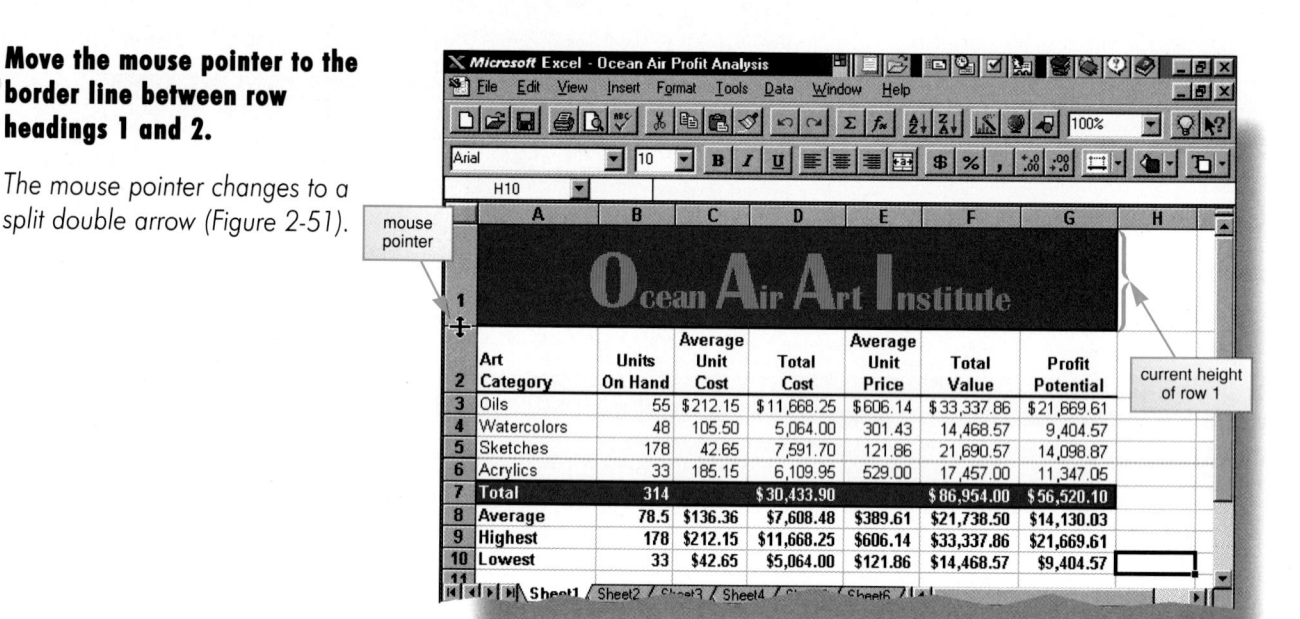

2 **Drag upward until 51.00 displays in the Name box on the left side of the formula bar.**

Excel displays a horizontal dotted line (Figure 2-52). The distance between the dotted line and the top of row 1 indicates the new row height for row 1.

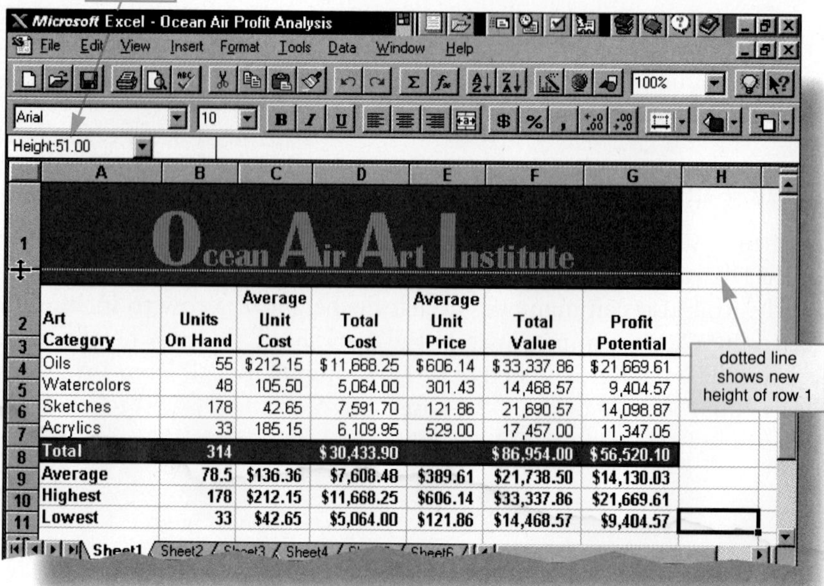

FIGURE 2-52

3 **Release the left mouse button. Move the mouse pointer to the border line between row headings 8 and 9 and then drag down until 27.75 shows in the Name box on the left side of the formula bar.**

The height of row 1 is changed to 51.00. The dotted line indicates the new height of row 8 (Figure 2-53).

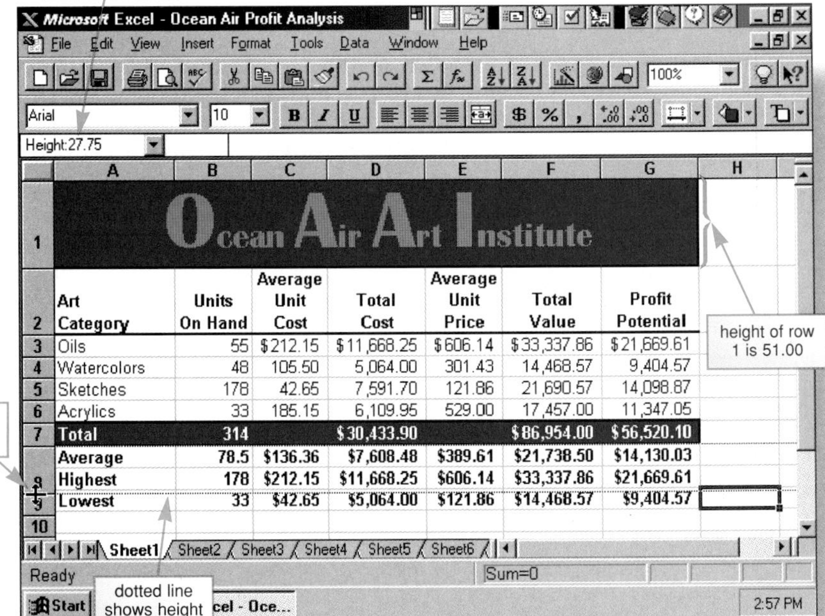

FIGURE 2-53

4 **Release the left mouse button.**

The height of row 8 changes to 27.75 points (Figure 2-54).

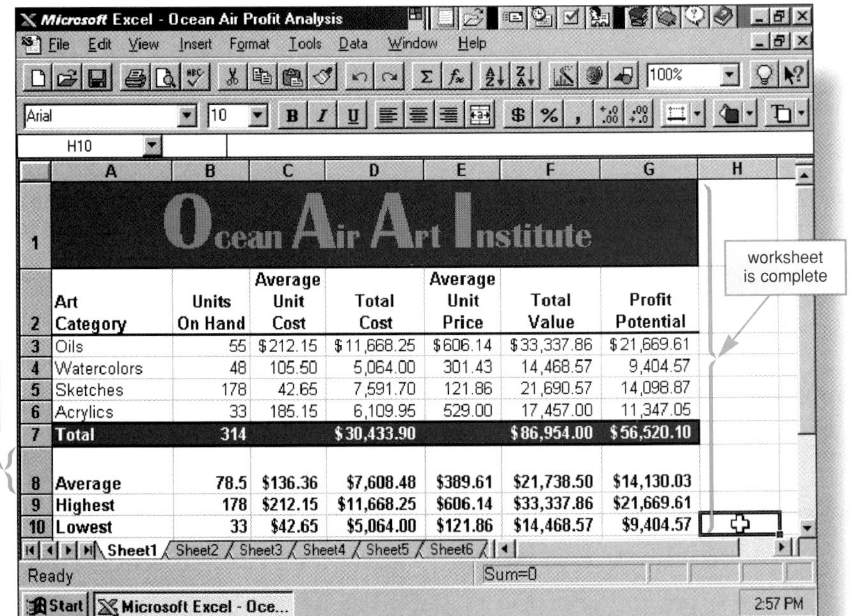

FIGURE 2-54

The row height can vary between zero and 409 points. When you decrease the row height to zero, the row is hidden. To show a hidden row, point just below the row heading border where the row is hidden and drag down.

If for some reason you want to switch back to the default row height, simply move the mouse pointer to the row border and double-click.

OtherWays

1. Right-click row heading to the left of column 1 or drag through multiple row headings and right-click, click Row Height, enter new row height, click OK button
2. Select cell in row or select range of cells down through rows, on Format menu click Row, click Height, enter new row height, click OK button

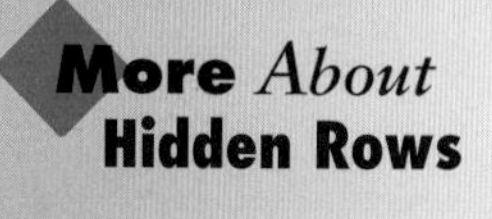

More *About* **Hidden Rows**

You can use the keyboard to unhide a range of rows. First select the rows immediately above and below the hidden ones and press CTRL+SHIFT+(. To use the keyboard to hide a range of rows, select the rows to hide, press CTRL+9.

The task of formatting the spreadsheet is complete. The next step is to check the spelling of the spreadsheet.

Checking Spelling

Excel has a spell checker you can use to check the worksheet for spelling errors. The spell checker looks for spelling errors by comparing words on the worksheet against words contained in its standard dictionary. If you have any specialized terms that are not in the **standard dictionary**, you can add them to a **custom dictionary** through the **Spelling dialog box**.

When the spell checker finds a word that is not in the dictionaries, it displays the word in the Spelling dialog box so you can correct it if it is misspelled.

You invoke the spell checker by clicking the **Spelling button** on the Standard toolbar. To illustrate Excel's reaction to a misspelled word, the word Highest in cell A9 is purposely misspelled as Higest, as shown in Figure 2-55.

Steps To Check Spelling in the Worksheet

1 Select cell A1. Click the Spelling button on the Standard toolbar.

The spell checker begins checking the spelling of the text in the worksheet with the active cell (cell A1) and continues checking to the right and down row by row. If the spell checker comes across a word that is not in the standard or custom dictionaries, the Spelling dialog box displays (Figure 2-55).

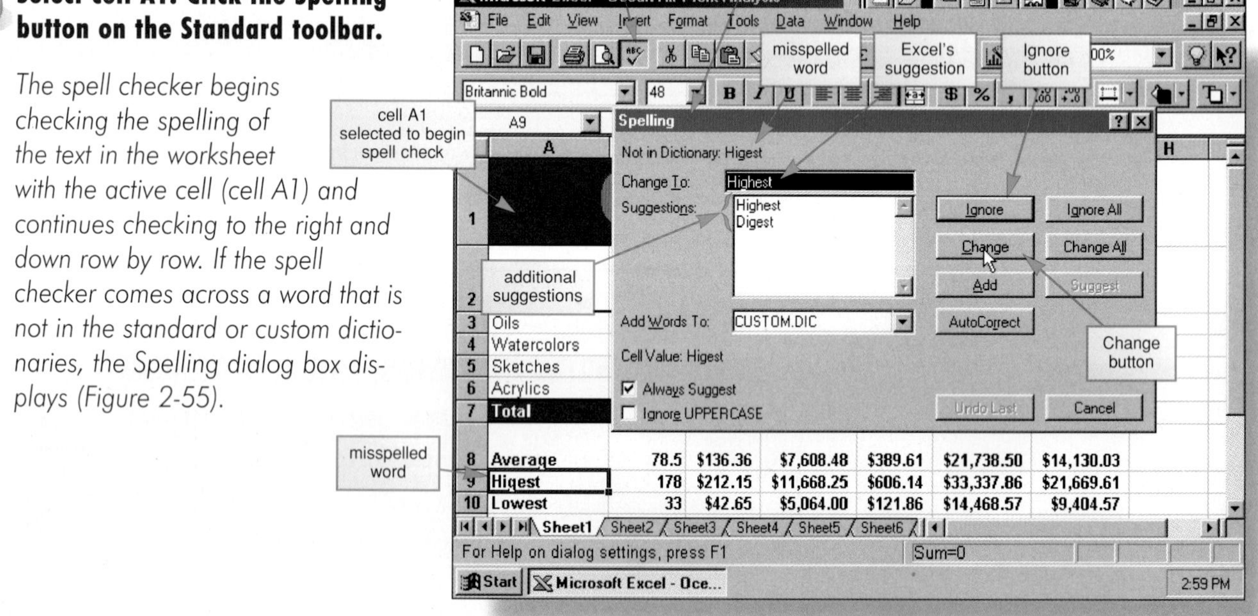

FIGURE 2-55

2 **When the spell checker displays a word in the Change To box, select one of the seven buttons to the right of the Suggestions box in the Spelling dialog box.**

In Figure 2-55 the word Highest in cell A9 is misspelled as Higest. The spell checker displays its best guess of the word you wanted (Highest) in the Change To box. Because Highest is in fact the correct spelling, click the Change button.

3 **Click the OK button when Excel displays the Microsoft Excel dialog box to indicate the spell checking is complete (Figure 2-56).**

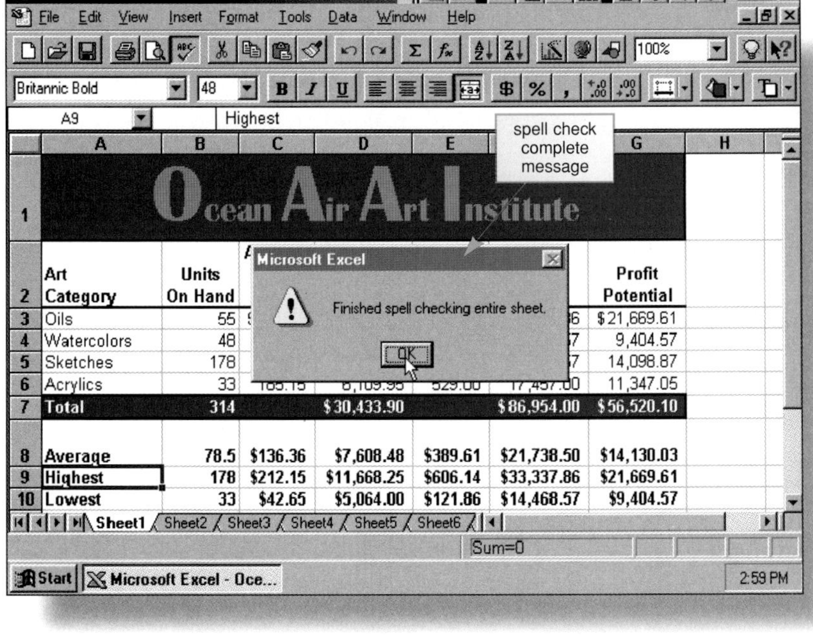

FIGURE 2-56

OtherWays

1. Right-click menu bar, click spelling
2. On the Tools menu click Spelling
3. Press F7

When the spell checker identifies a word not in the dictionaries, it changes the active cell to the cell containing the word not in the dictionaries. The Spelling dialog box (Figure 2-55) lists the word not in the dictionaries, a suggested correction, and a list of alternative spellings. If you agree with the suggested correction in the Change To box, click the Change button. To change the word throughout the worksheet, click the **Change All button**.

If one of the words in the Suggestions list box is correct, click the word and then click the Change button or double-click the word. If none of the listed words is correct, type the correct word and then click the Change button. To skip correcting the word, click the **Ignore button**. To have Excel ignore the word for the remainder of the worksheet, click the **Ignore All button**.

Consider these additional points regarding the spell checker:

- To check the spelling of the text in a single cell, double-click the cell and click the Spelling button on the Standard toolbar.
- When you select a single cell and the formula bar is not active before invoking the spell checker, Excel checks the entire worksheet including notes and embedded charts.
- If you select a range of cells before invoking the spell checker, Excel checks only the spelling of the words in the selected range.
- To check the spelling of a chart, select the chart before invoking the spell checker.
- To check the spelling of all the sheets in a workbook, click Select All Sheets from a sheet tab shortcut menu, and then invoke the spell checker. You display the sheet tab shortcut menu by right-clicking the sheet tab.
- If you select a cell other than cell A1 before you start the spell checker, a dialog box displays after Excel checks to the end of the worksheet asking if you want to continue checking at the beginning.

More *About* Checking Spelling

Always take the time to check the spelling of a worksheet before submitting it to your supervisor. Nothing deflates an impression more than a professional-looking report with misspelled words.

- To add words that are not in the standard dictionary to the custom dictionary, click the **Add button** in the Spelling dialog box (Figure 2-55) when Excel identifies the word.
- Click the **AutoCorrect** button (Figure 2-55) to add the misspelled word and its equivalent word in the Change To box to the AutoCorrect list. For example, if the misspelled word is *dox* and you mean *do*, then with *do* in the Change To box and *dox* the misspelled word, click the AutoCorrect button. Then, anytime in the future that you type *dox*, Excel will change it to *do*.

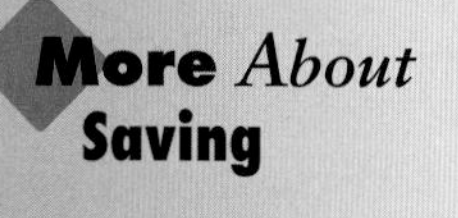

More *About* **Saving**

If you want to save the workbook under a new name, click the Save As command on the File menu or shortcut menu that displays when you right-click the menu. Some Excel users feel better if they save workbooks to two different drives. They use the Save button on the Standard toolbar to save the latest version of the workbook to the default drive. Then, they use the Save As command to save a second copy to another drive.

Saving the Workbook a Second Time Using the Same Filename

Earlier in this project, you saved an intermediate version of the workbook using the filename Ocean Air Profit Analysis. To save the workbook a second time using the same filename, click the Save button on the Standard toolbar. Excel automatically stores the latest version of the workbook under the same filename Ocean Air Profit Analysis without displaying the Save As dialog box as it did when you saved the workbook the first time.

If you want to save the workbook under a new name, choose the **Save As command** from the File menu or shortcut menu. For example, some Excel users use the Save button to save the latest version of the workbook to the default drive. Then, they use the Save As command to save a second copy to another drive.

You can also click Save on the File menu or shortcut menu or press SHIFT+F12 or CTRL+S to save a workbook a second time under the same filename. The shortcut menu that contains the Save command displays when you point to the menu bar.

Adding a Pie Chart to the Workbook

The next step in this project is to draw the three-dimensional pie chart on a separate sheet as shown in Figure 2-57. A **pie chart** is used to show how 100% of an amount is divided. Each **slice** (or wedge) of the pie represents a contribution to the whole. The pie chart in Figure 2-57 shows the contribution of each art category to the company's profit potential. It is easy to see from the pie chart that Oils has the greatest profit potential and Watercolors has the least profit potential.

The pie chart in Figure 2-57 differs from the 3-D column chart in Project 1 in that it is not embedded in the worksheet. Instead, it is created on a separate sheet, called a **chart sheet**.

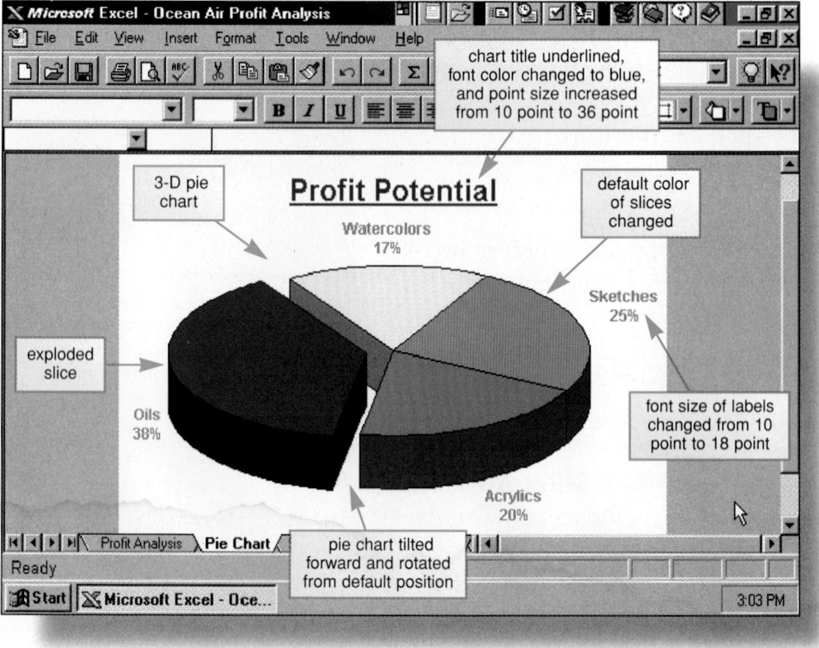

FIGURE 2-57

The range in the worksheet to graph is the nonadjacent ranges A3:A6 and G3:G6 (Figure 2-58). The art category names in the range A3:A6 will identify the slices. The entries in column A are called the **category names**. The range G3:G6 contains the data that determines the size of the slices in the pie. The entries in column G are called the **data series**. Because there are four art categories, the pie chart contains four slices.

This project also calls for emphasizing the art category with the greatest profit potential (Oils) by offsetting its slice from the main portion. A pie chart with one or more slices offset is called an **exploded pie chart**.

As described in Figure 2-57, the pie chart has also been enhanced from the default pie chart that is first drawn by rotating and tilting the pie forward, changing the colors of the slices, and modifying the chart title and labels that identify the slices.

More *About* **Charting**

Line chart, bar chart, pie chart – which chart will best describe your worksheet data? For answers, double-click the Help button on the Standard toolbar. Click the Contents tab. Double-click the following books: Working with Charts and Maps; Formatting a Chart book; and Changing the Type of Chart book. Finally, double-click the link titled, The best chart type for my data. One at a time, click the nine chart types and read the information.

Drawing the Pie Chart

To draw the pie chart on a separate sheet, you select the nonadjacent range and use the **Chart command** from the **Insert menu**. Once the chart is created, it will be formatted as shown in Figure 2-57 in the following fashion:

1. Chart title — increase the font size to 36 and change the font color to blue
2. Slice labels — increase the font size to 18 and change the font color to red
3. Explode the Oils slice
4. Rotate and tilt the pie chart so the Oils slice will display more prominently
5. Change the color of the slices of the pie chart

To Draw a Pie Chart

1. **Select the range A3:A6. Hold down the CTRL key and select the range G3:G6. On the Insert menu, click Chart and then point to As New Sheet.**

The nonadjacent ranges are selected and the Chart menu displays (Figure 2-58).

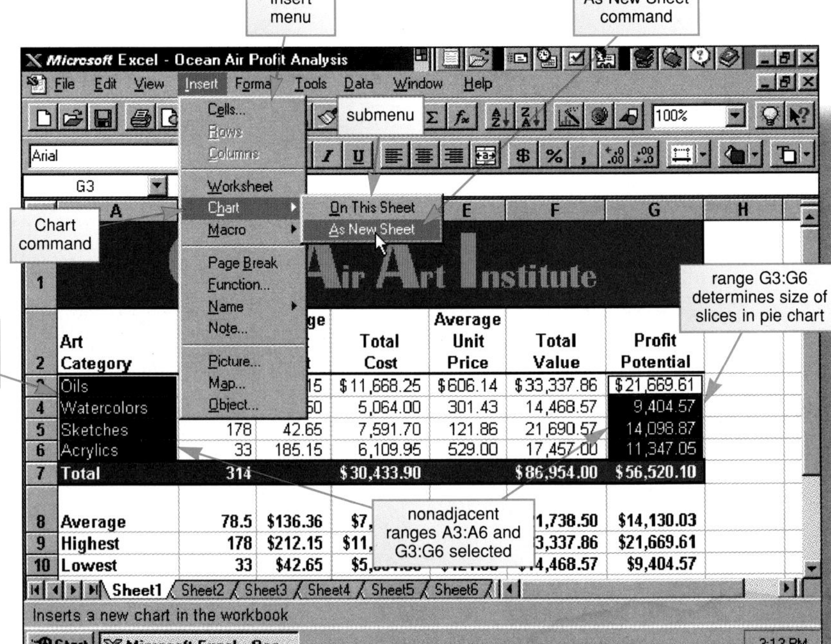

FIGURE 2-58

2 **Click As New Sheet on the Chart menu.**

Excel displays the ChartWizard – Step 1 of 5 dialog box, which shows the selected range to chart (Figure 2-59). If necessary, you can modify the range to chart in this dialog box.

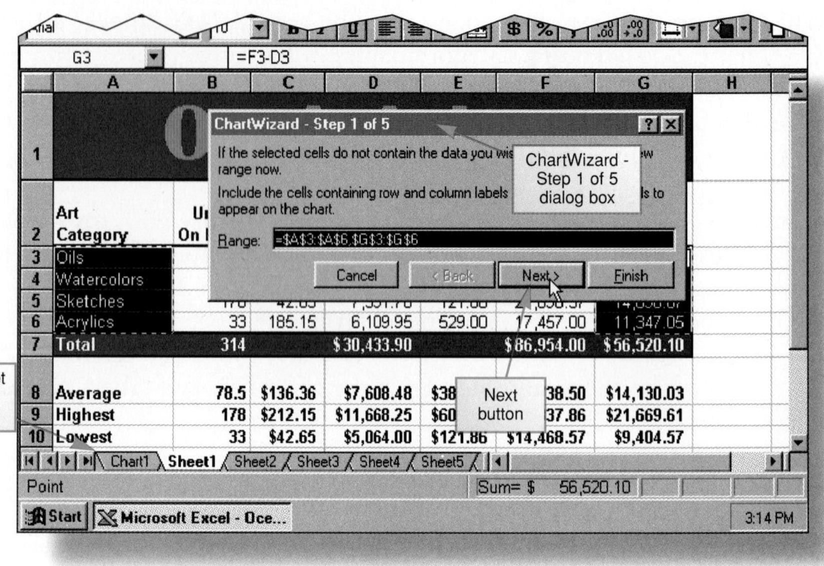

FIGURE 2-59

3 **Click the Next button. Click 3-D Pie in the ChartWizard - Step 2 of 5 dialog box.**

The ChartWizard - Step 2 of 5 dialog box displays available with 15 charts (Figure 2-60). The first nine charts in the dialog box are two-dimensional. The last six charts are three-dimensional. The 3-D Pie chart type is selected.

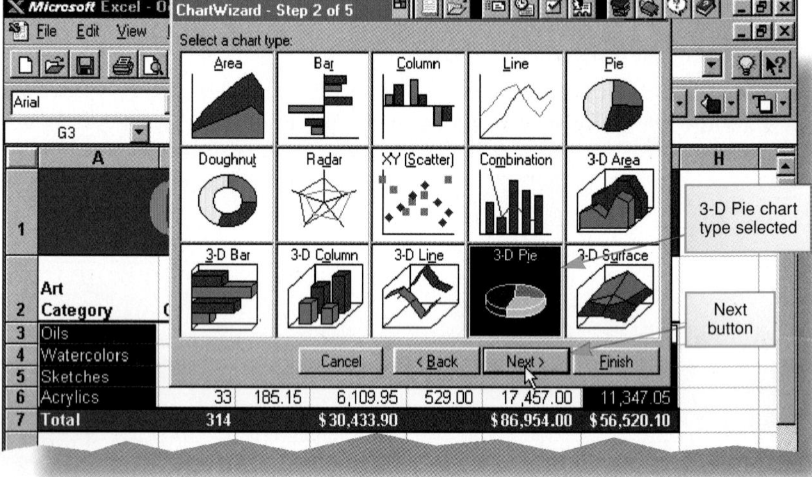

FIGURE 2-60

4 **Click the Next button. When the ChartWizard - Step 3 of 5 dialog box displays, click the last format, format 7.**

The ChartWizard - Step 3 of 5 dialog box displays with seven different 3-D pie chart formats (Figure 2-61). Format 7 with the labels and percents outside the pie chart is selected.

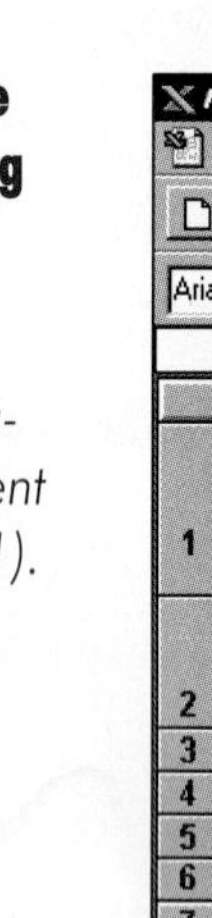

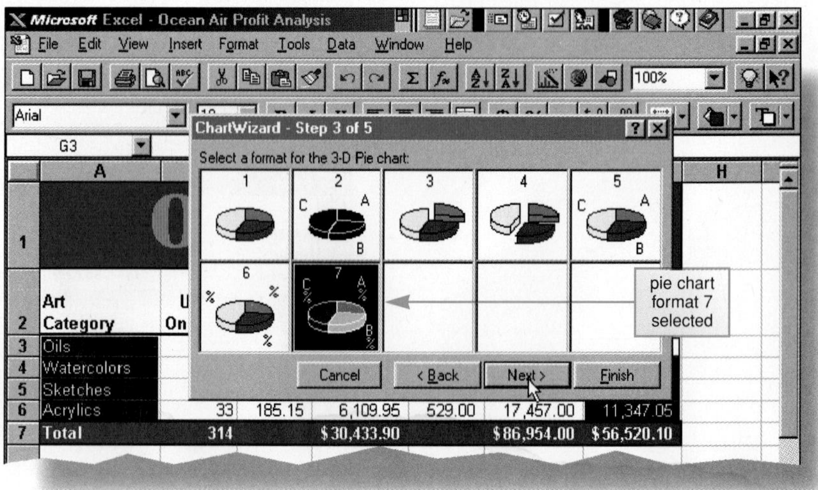

FIGURE 2-61

5 **Click the Next button. If a Microsoft Excel dialog box displays, click the OK button and then change the settings on the ChartWizard - Step 4 of 5 dialog box to agree with those shown in Figure 2-62.**

The ChartWizard - Step 4 of 5 dialog box shows a sample 3-D pie chart (Figure 2-62).

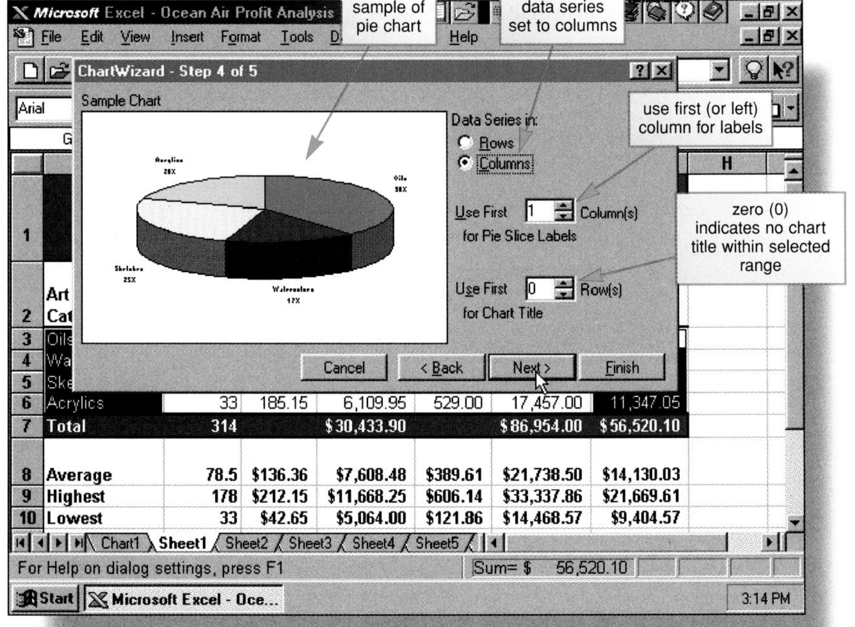

FIGURE 2-62

6 **Click the Next button. Type** `Profit Potential` **in the Chart Title box in the ChartWizard - Step 5 of 5 dialog box.**

The ChartWizard - Step 5 of 5 dialog box displays on the screen (Figure 2-63). The dialog box gives you the opportunity to add a legend and add a chart title. The chart title you enter shows in the Sample Chart area. In this case, a legend is not required to clarify the slices. Thus, the No option button is selected.

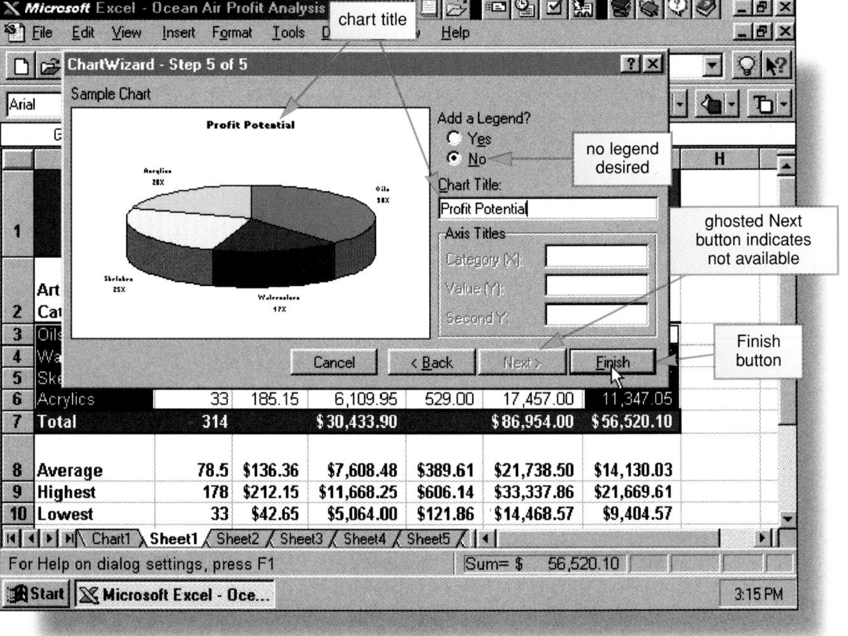

FIGURE 2-63

7 Click the Finish button in the ChartWizard - Step 5 of 5 dialog box.

Excel draws the three-dimensional pie chart and displays it on a sheet titled Chart1 (Figure 2-64).

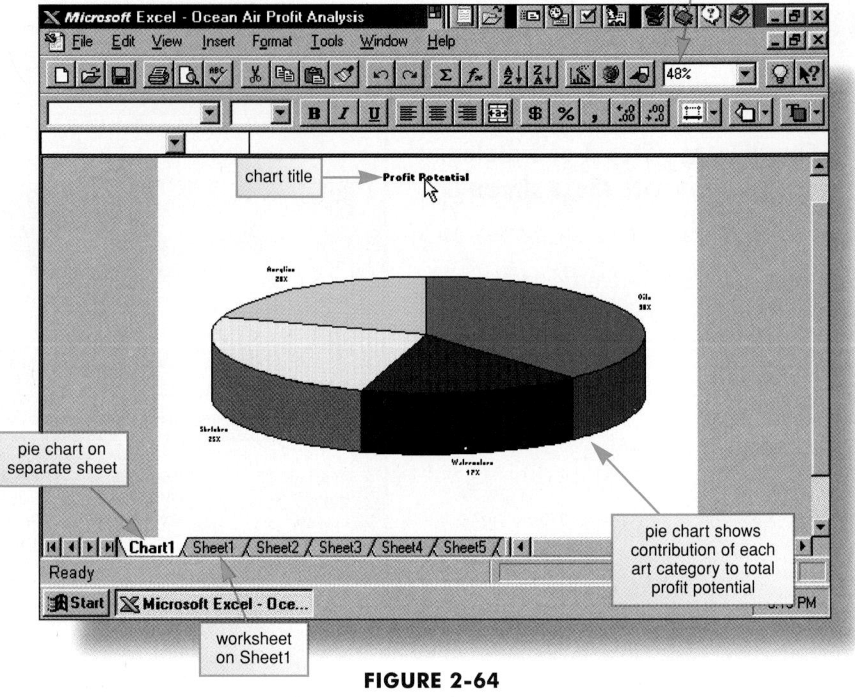

FIGURE 2-64

OtherWays

1. Select range to chart and Press F11

Each slice of the pie chart represents one of the four art categories – Oils, Watercolors, Sketches, and Acrylics. The names of the art categories and the percent contribution to the total profit potential display outside the slices. The chart title, Profit Potential, displays immediately above the pie chart.

Excel determines the direction of the data series range (down a column or across a row) on the basis of the selected range. Because the selection for the pie chart is down the worksheet (ranges A3:A7 and G3:G7), Excel sets the Data Series to Columns automatically as shown in Figure 2-62 on the previous page.

Notice in the five ChartWizard dialog boxes (Figure 2-59 through Figure 2-63) that you can return to the previous ChartWizard dialog box, return to the beginning of the ChartWizard, or create the chart with the options selected thus far while any one of the five ChartWizard dialog boxes is on the screen.

Formatting the Chart Title and Chart Labels

The next step is to format the chart title and labels that identify the slices. Before you can format a **chart item**, such as the chart title or labels, you must select it. Once a chart item is selected, you can format it using the Formatting toolbar, shortcut menu, special keys, or the Format menu. The Formatting toolbar will be used to format the chart title, similar to the way the cell entries were formatted earlier in this project. The labels will be formatted using the shortcut menu. Complete the following steps to format the chart title and labels.

To Format the Chart Title and Labels

1. **Click the chart title. Click the Font Size arrow on the Formatting toolbar and then click 36. Click the Underline button on the Formatting toolbar.**

   Excel displays a box with handles around the chart title, increases the size of the characters in the chart title, and underlines the chart title.

2. **Click the Font Color button arrow on the Formatting toolbar and then point to the color blue (column 1, row 4 on the font Color palette).**

   The Chart1 sheet displays as shown in Figure 2-65.

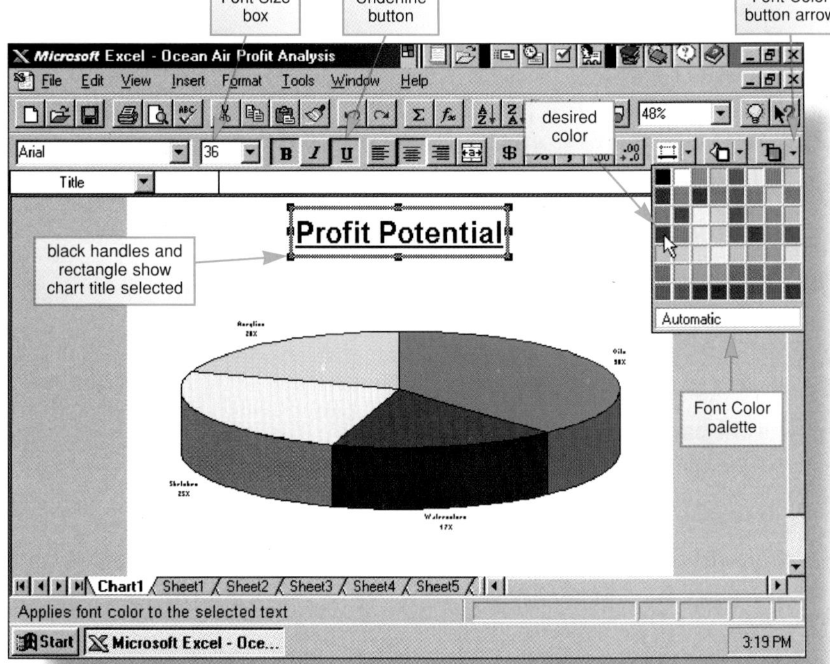

FIGURE 2-65

3. **Click the color blue on the Font Color palette. Right-click one of the four labels that identify the slices. Point to Format Data Labels on the shortcut menu.**

   The chart title displays as shown in Figure 2-66. The labels are selected and the shortcut menu displays.

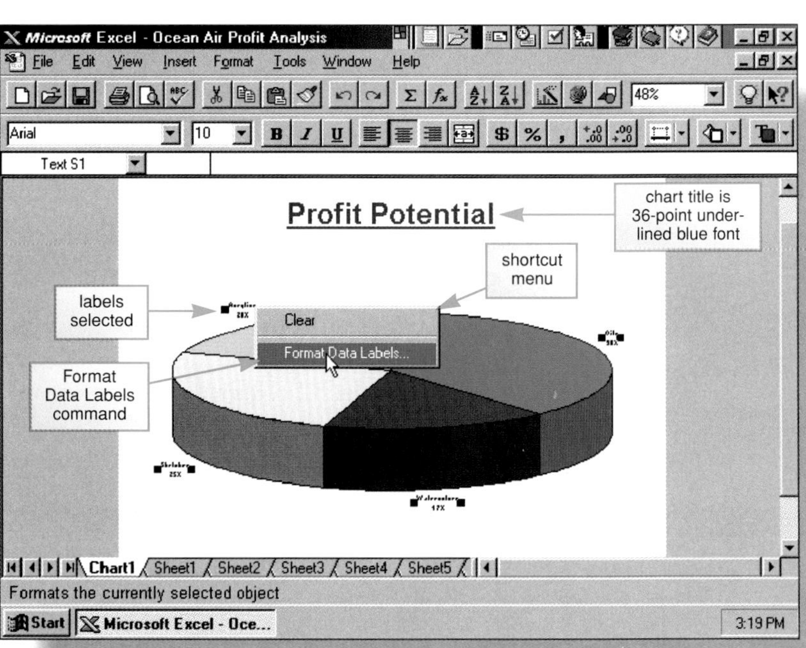

FIGURE 2-66

4 Click Format Data Labels on the shortcut menu. When the Format Data Labels dialog box displays, click the Font tab, click Bold in the Font Style list box, click 18 in the Size list box, click the Color arrow and point to the color red (column 3, row 1 on the Color palette).

The Format Data Labels dialog box displays as shown in Figure 2-67.

5 Click the color red and then click the OK button.

The labels that identify the slices are bold, larger, and red as shown in Figure 2-68.

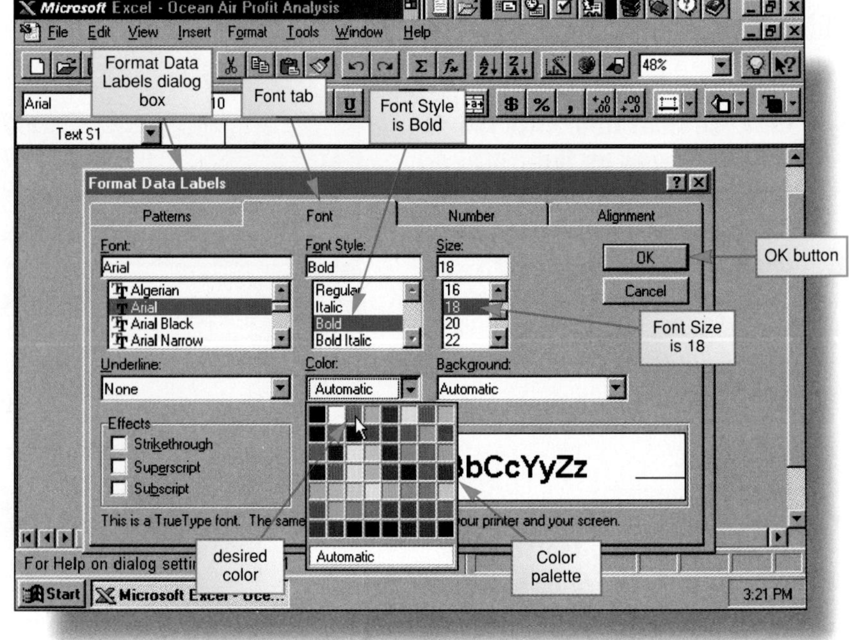

FIGURE 2-67

OtherWays

1. Right-click title or labels, click Format Chart Title or click Format Data Labels
2. Press CTRL+B to bold, CTRL+U to underline

Compare Figure 2-68 to Figure 2-65 on the previous page. You can see in Figure 2-68 that the labels and chart title are easier to read and make the chart sheet look more professional when compared to Figure 2-65.

Notice the labels in Figure 2-66 have black handles. This means that if you want to, you can move and resize them. You can also select and format individual labels by clicking a label after all the labels have been selected. For example, to emphasize a small or large slice in a pie chart, you could make its label larger or a different color.

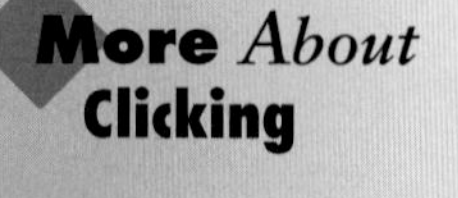

More *About* **Clicking**

There are a few Excel formatting activities, especially with charts, that require you to click the object twice before selecting a format. Clicking an object twice is not the same as double-clicking. For double-clicking the clicking sequence is rapid. When you are asked to click an object twice, pause before clicking a second time.

Changing the Colors of the Slices

The next step is to change the colors of the slices of the pie. The colors you see in Figure 2-68 are the default colors Excel uses when you first create a pie chart. Project 2 requires that the colors be changed to those shown earlier in Figure 2-57 on page E 2.42. To change the colors of the slices, you select them one at a time and use the Color button on the Formatting toolbar as shown in the following steps.

Steps To Change the Colors of the Pie Slices

1 **Click the Oils slice twice, once to select all the slices and once to select the individual slice. (Do not double-click.) Click the Color button arrow on the Formatting toolbar and then point to the color blue (column 1, row 4 on the color palette).**

Excel displays black handles around the Oils slice and the Color palette displays (Figure 2-68).

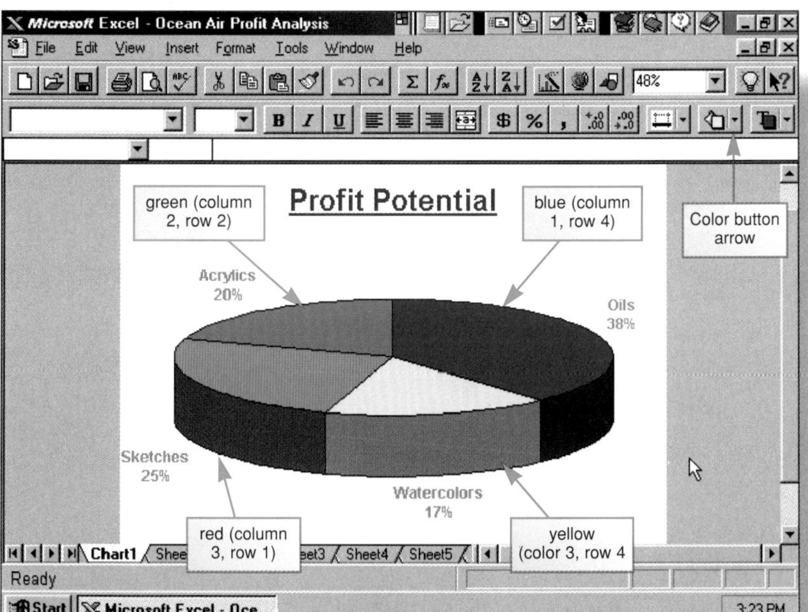

FIGURE 2-68

2 **Click the color blue.**

Excel changes the Oils slice to the color blue.

3 **One at a time, click the remaining slices and use the following colors on the Color palette for the art categories specified: Acrylics - green (column 2, row 2); Sketches - red (column 3, row 1); Watercolors - yellow (column 3, row 4). Click outside the chart area.**

The pie chart displays as shown in Figure 2-69.

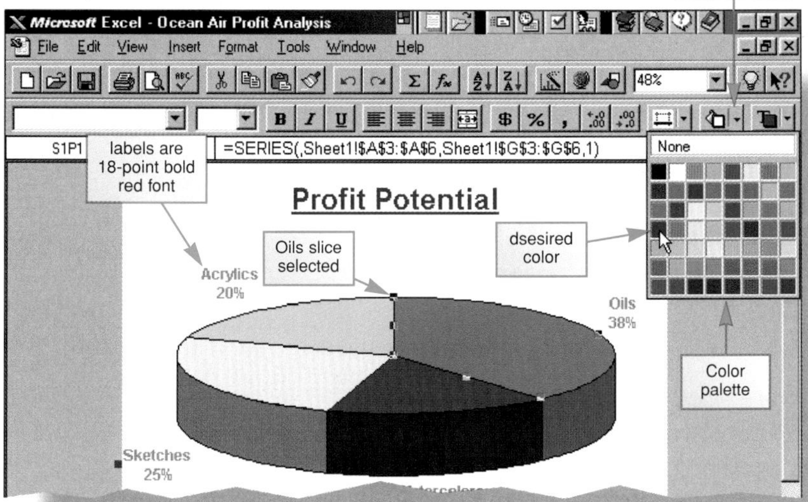

FIGURE 2-69

OtherWays

1. Right-click selected slice, click Format Data Point on shortcut menu, click Patterns tab, click color, click OK button
2. On Format menu click Selected Data Point, click Patterns tab, click color, click OK button

Exploding the Pie Chart

The next step is to emphasize the slice representing the Oils painting category by offsetting, or **exploding,** it from the rest of the slices. The reason for exploding the Oils slice is because it represents the greatest profit potential and by exploding it, the slice will be stand out. Perform the steps on the next page to offset a slice of the pie chart.

To Explode the Pie Chart

1 **Click the slice labeled Oils twice. (Do not double-click.)**

Excel surrounds the Oils slice with handles.

2 **Drag the slice to the desired position, and then release the left mouse button.**

Excel redraws the pie chart with the Oils slice offset from the rest of the pie chart (Figure 2-70).

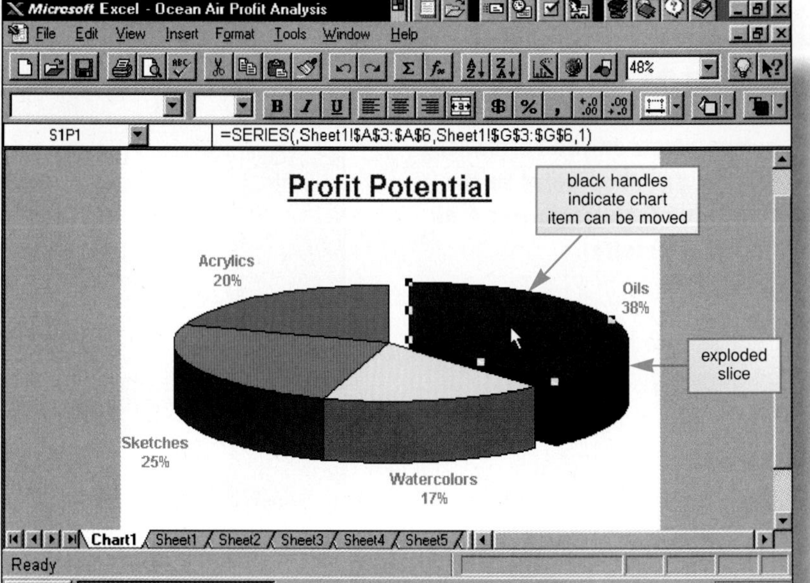

FIGURE 2-70

Although you can offset as many slices as you want, as you drag more slices away from the main portion of the pie chart, the slices become smaller. If you continue to offset slices, the pie chart becomes too small to have an impact on the reader.

Rotating and Tilting the Pie Chart

In a three-dimensional chart, you can change the view to better display the section of the chart you are trying to emphasize. Excel allows you to control the rotation angle, elevation, perspective, height, and angle of the axes by using the **3-D View command** on the Format menu or shortcut menu.

To obtain a better view of the offset for the Oils slice, you can rotate the pie chart 190 degrees to the left. The rotation angle of a pie chart is defined by the line that divides the Oils and Acrylics slices. Excel initially draws a pie chart with one of the dividing lines pointing to twelve o'clock (or zero degrees). Besides rotating the pie chart, the following steps also tilt, or change, the elevation so the pie chart is at less of an angle to the viewer.

To Rotate and Tilt the Pie Chart

1 **With the Oils slice selected, right-click the Oils slice and then point to 3-D View on the shortcut menu.**

The shortcut menu displays as shown in Figure 2-71.

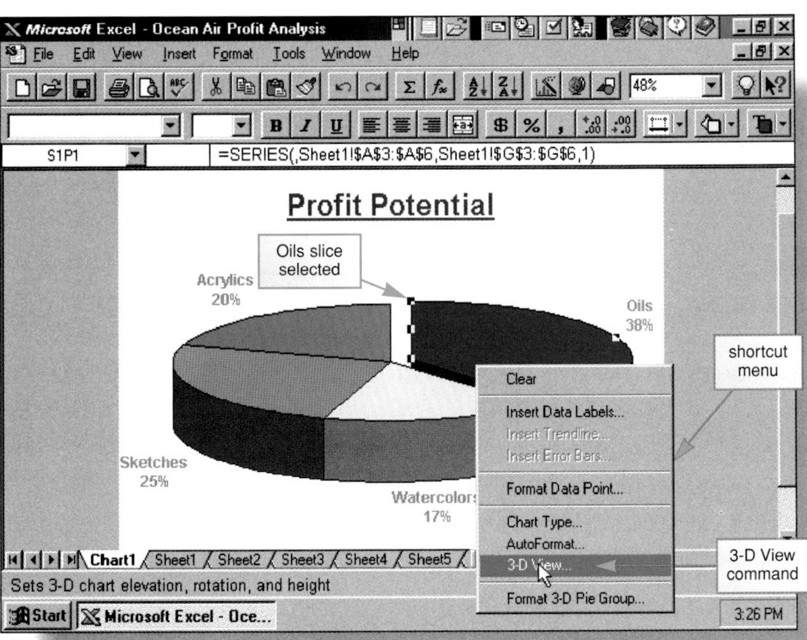

FIGURE 2-71

2 **Click 3-D View on the shortcut menu. When the Format 3-D View dialog box displays, click the up arrow button in the Format 3-D View dialog box until 25 displays in the Elevation box.**

The 3-D View dialog box displays (Figure 2-72). A sample of the pie chart displays in the dialog box. The result of increasing the elevation of the pie chart is to tilt it forward.

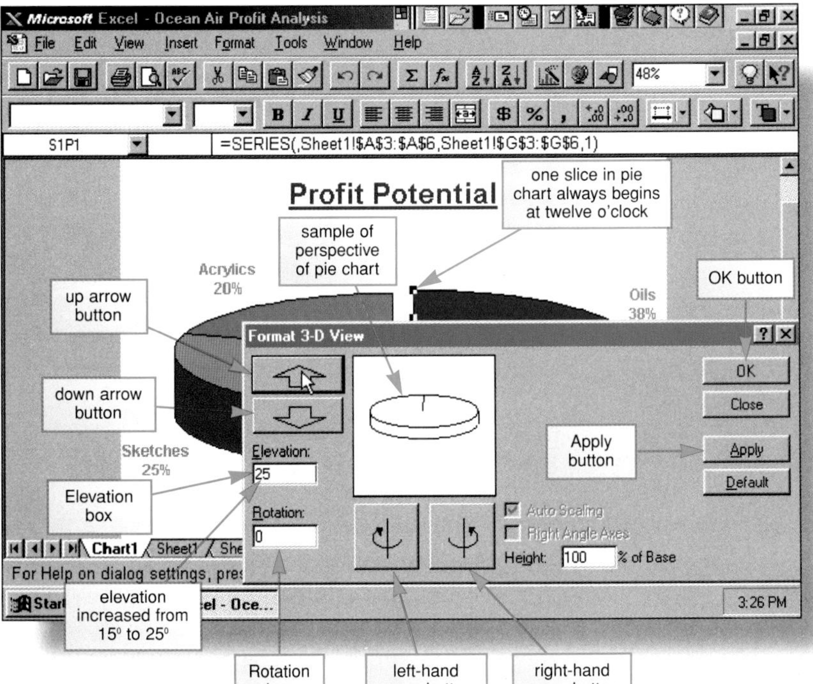

FIGURE 2-72

3 **Rotate the pie chart by clicking the right-hand arrow button until the Rotation box displays 190.**

The new rotation setting (190) displays in the Rotation box as shown in Figure 2-73. A sample of the rotated pie chart displays in the dialog box.

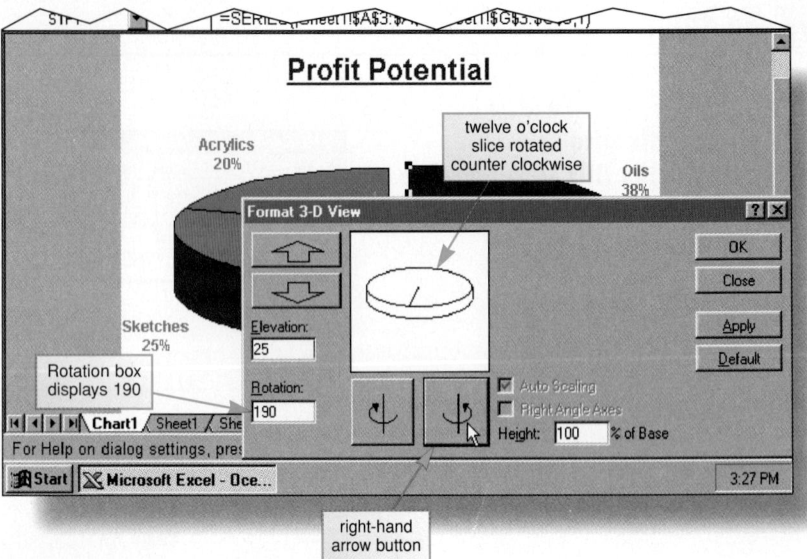

FIGURE 2-73

4 **Click the OK button on the Format 3-D View dialog box.**

Excel displays the pie chart tilted forward and rotated to the left so the space between the Oils slice and the main portion of the pie is more prominent (Figure 2-74).

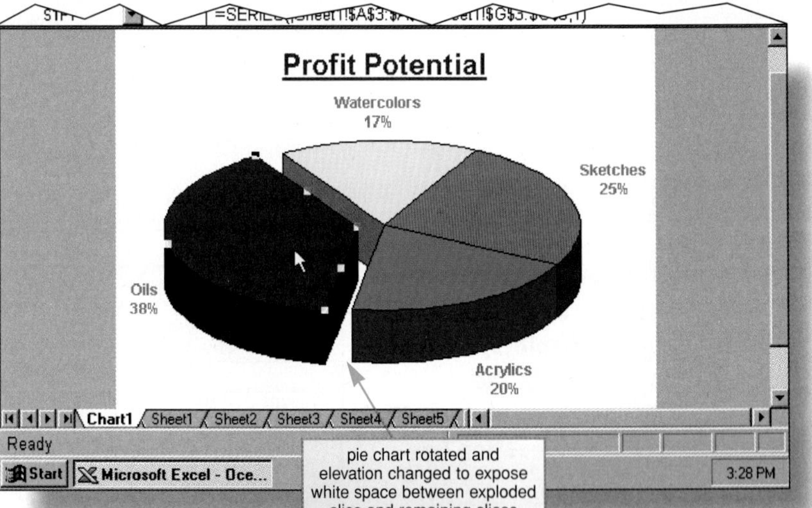

FIGURE 2-74

OtherWays

1. On the Format menu click 3-D View, select settings on Format 3-D View dialog box, click OK button

More *About* **Changing a Pie Chart's Perspective**

You can increase or decrease the base height (thickness) of the pie chart by changing the height to base ratio in the Format 3-D View dialog box.

Compare Figure 2-74 to Figure 2-70 on page E 2.50. The offset of the Oils slice is more noticeable in Figure 2-74 because the pie chart has been tilted and rotated to expose the white space between the Oils slice and the main portion of the pie chart.

Besides controlling the rotation angle and elevation, you also can control the thickness of the pie chart by entering smaller or larger percents than the default 100% in the Height box (Figure 2-73).

The pie chart is complete. The next step is to change the names on the sheet tabs and rearrange the order of the sheets so the worksheet is first, followed by the chart. If you look at the sheet tabs below the pie chart in Figure 2-74, you will see that Sheet1, which contains the worksheet is behind the sheet labeled Chart1.

Changing the Names on the Sheet Tabs and Rearranging the Order of the Sheets

At the bottom of the screen (Figure 2-75) are the tabs that allow you to display any sheet in the workbook. By default, the tab names are Sheet1, Sheet2,and so on. When you draw a chart on a separate sheet, Excel assigns the name Chart1 to the sheet tab. The following steps show you how to rename the sheet tabs and reorder the sheets so the worksheet comes before the chart sheet.

More About Sheets

To move from sheet to sheet in a workbook, you click the sheet tabs at the bottom of the window. The name of the active sheet is always bold on a white background. You can rename the sheets, add and delete sheets, and move or copy sheets within a workbook or to another workbook.

Steps To Rename the Sheet Tabs and Rearrange the Order of the Sheets

1 Double-click the tab named Chart1 in the lower left corner of the window.

Excel displays the Rename Sheet dialog box.

2 Type `Pie Chart` **in the Name box.**

The Rename Sheet dialog box displays as shown in Figure 2-75.

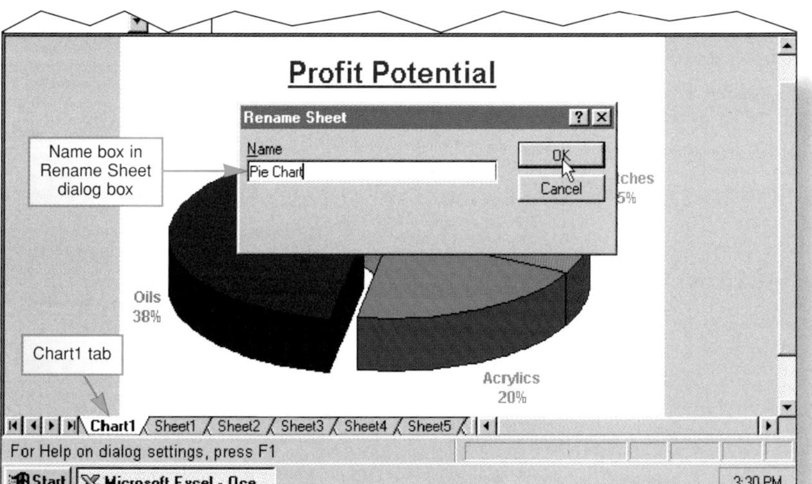

FIGURE 2-75

3 Click the OK button in the Rename Sheet dialog box. Double-click the Sheet1 tab. Type `Profit Analysis` **in the Name box.**

Excel renames the Chart1 tab Pie Chart and redisplays the Rename Sheet dialog box with the new title for the Sheet1 tab (Figure 2-76).

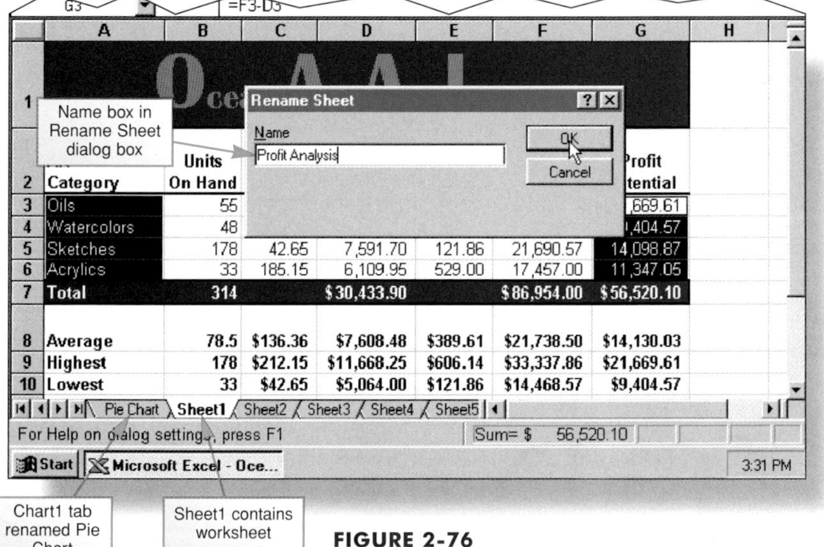

FIGURE 2-76

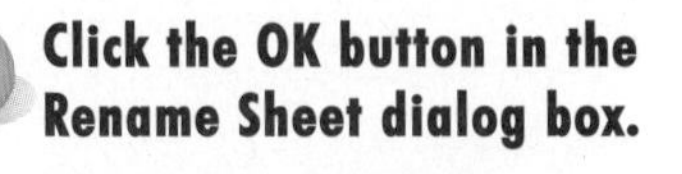

4 **Click the OK button in the Rename Sheet dialog box.**

Excel renames the Sheet1 tab Profit Analysis.

5 **Point to the Profit Analysis tab and drag it over the Pie Chart tab.**

The mouse pointer changes to a pointer and a document (Figure 2-77).

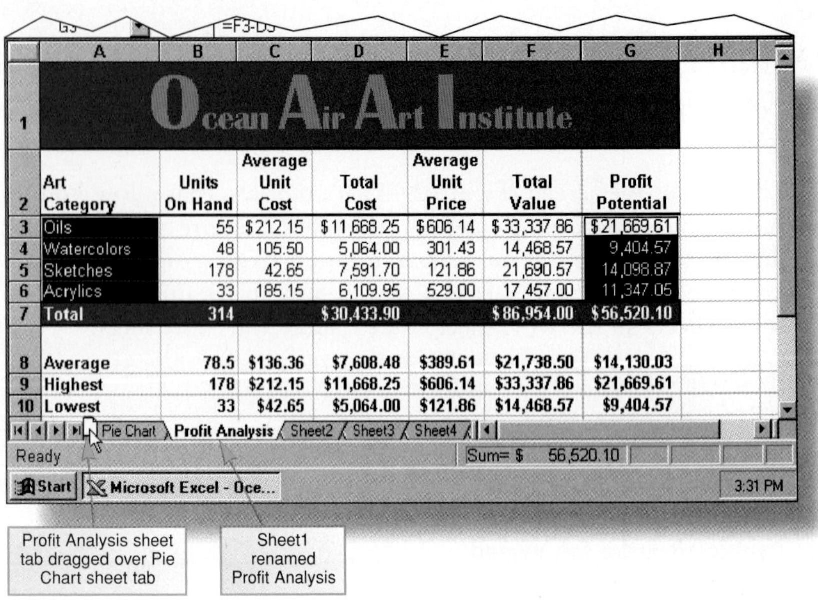

FIGURE 2-77

6 **Release the left mouse button.**

Excel moves the sheet named Profit Analysis in front of the sheet named Pie Chart. The workbook for Project 2 is complete (Figure 2-78).

7 **Click the Save button on the Standard toolbar to save the workbook to disk using the filename Ocean Air Profit Analysis.**

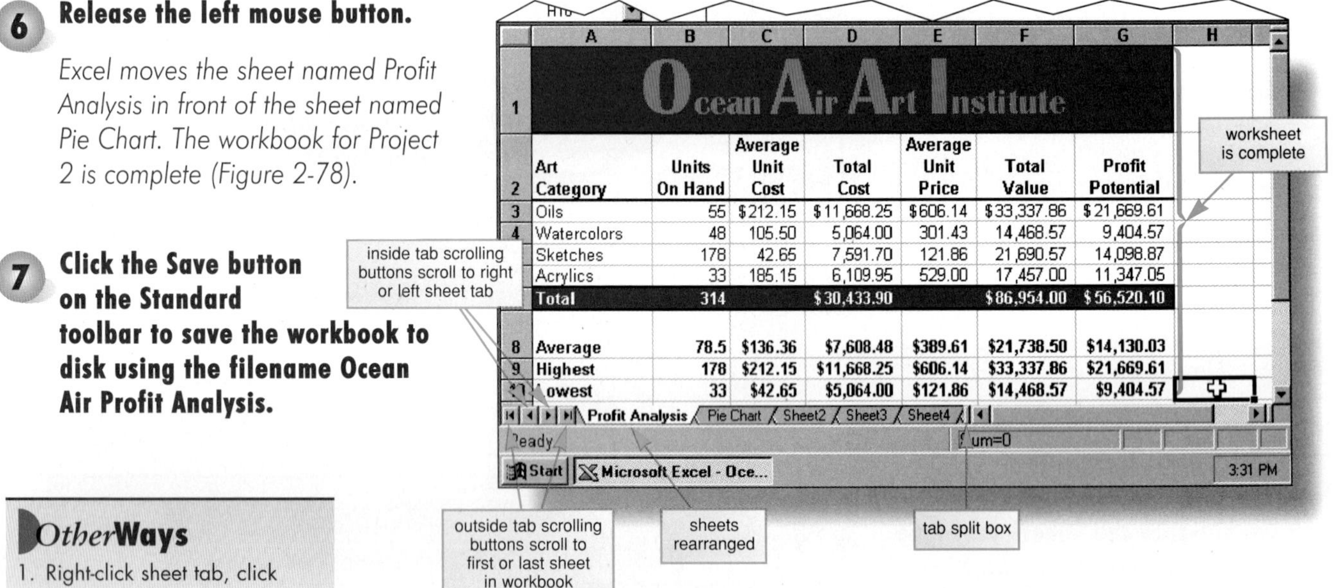

FIGURE 2-78

Other **Ways**

1. Right-click sheet tab, click Rename
2. Right-click sheet tab, click Move or Copy
3. On the Edit menu click Move or Copy

More *About* **Sheet Tabs**

You can use the keyboard to move from sheet to sheet in a workbook. Press CTRL+PGUP to move to the next sheet. Press CTRL+PGDN to move to the previous sheet.

The previous steps showed you how to rename the sheet tabs at the bottom of the screen and how to resequence them. Sheet names can be up to 31 characters (including spaces) in length. The longer the tab names, the fewer tabs will show. You can increase the number of tabs that show, however, by dragging the **tab split box** next to the scroll arrow (Figure 2-78) to the right. This will reduce the size of the scroll bar at the bottom of the screen. Double-click the tab split box to reset it to its normal position.

You can also use the **scroll buttons** to the left of the sheet tabs (Figure 2-78) to move between sheets. The leftmost and rightmost scroll buttons move to the first or last sheet in the workbook. The two middle scroll buttons move one sheet to the left or right.

Previewing and Printing Selected Sheets in a Workbook

In Project 1, you printed the worksheet without previewing it on the screen. By previewing the worksheet, you see exactly how it will look without generating a hard copy. Previewing a workbook can save time, paper, and the frustration of waiting for a printout only to find out it is not what you want.

The Print Preview command, as well as the Print command, will preview only selected sheets. You know a sheet is selected when the tab at the bottom of the screen is white. Thus, in Figure 2-78, the Profit Analysis sheet is selected, but the Pie Chart sheet is not. To select additional sheets, hold down the CTRL key and click any sheet tabs you want included in the preview or printout.

> **More About**
> **Selecting Additional Sheets**
>
> To select several consecutive sheets in a workbook, hold down the SHIFT key and click the sheet tab at the opposite end of the group to select. Thus, if Sheet1 is active and you want to select Sheet1 through Sheet5, hold down the SHIFT key and click Sheet5. Excel will select Sheet1, Sheet2, Sheet3, Sheet4, and Sheet5.

Steps To Preview Selected Sheets in a Workbook

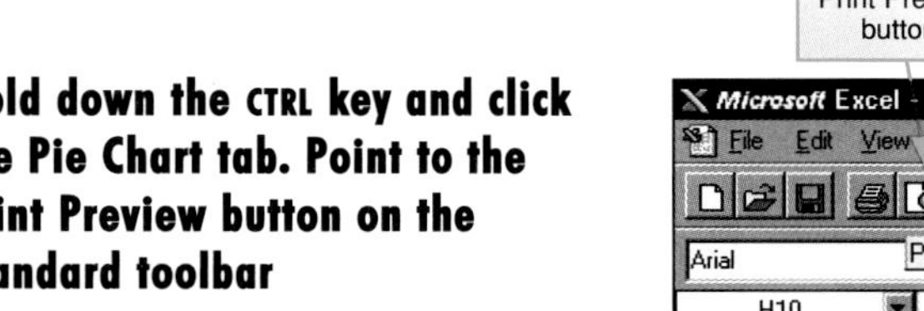

1 Hold down the CTRL key and click the Pie Chart tab. Point to the Print Preview button on the Standard toolbar

Both sheets are selected (Figure 2-79).

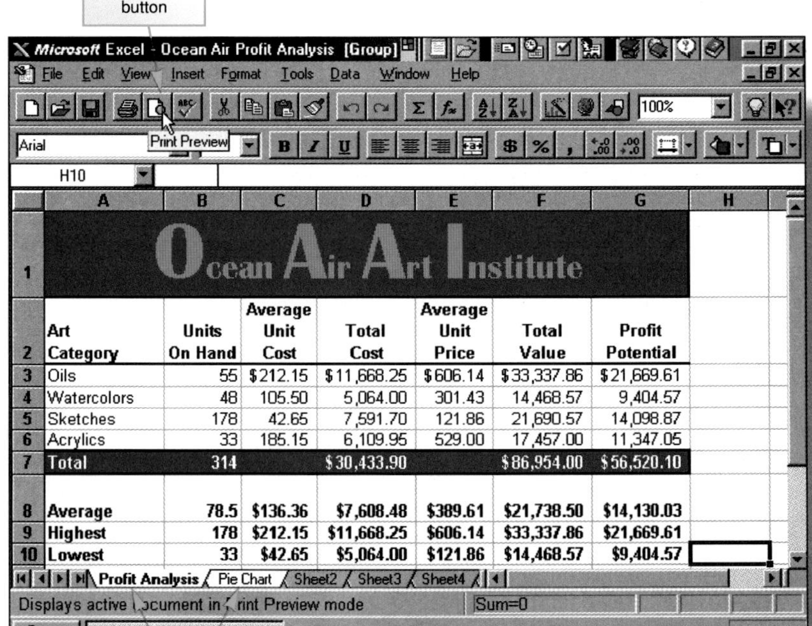

FIGURE 2-79

2 **Click the Print Preview button on the Standard toolbar.**

Excel displays a preview of the worksheet in the ***preview window*** *and the mouse pointer changes to a magnifying glass (Figure 2-80).*

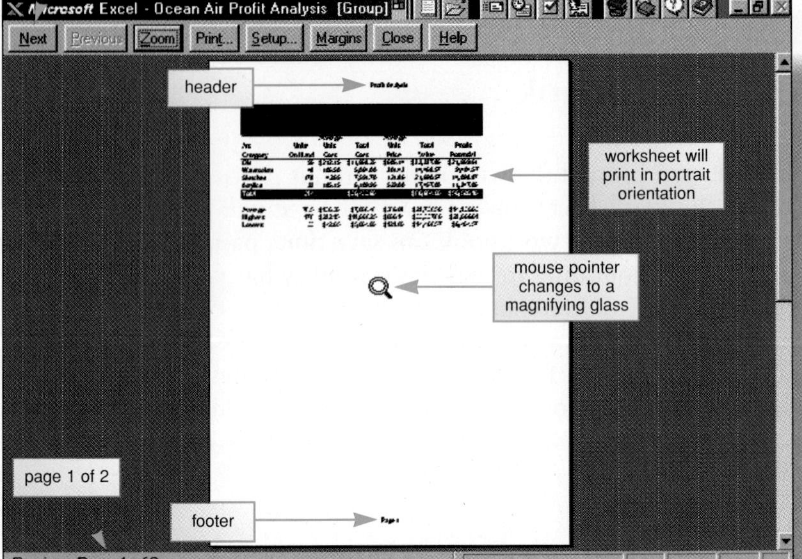

FIGURE 2-80

3 **Click the Next button to display a preview of the chart.**

A preview of the pie chart displays (Figure 2-81).

4 **Click the Close button in the preview window to return to the workbook.**

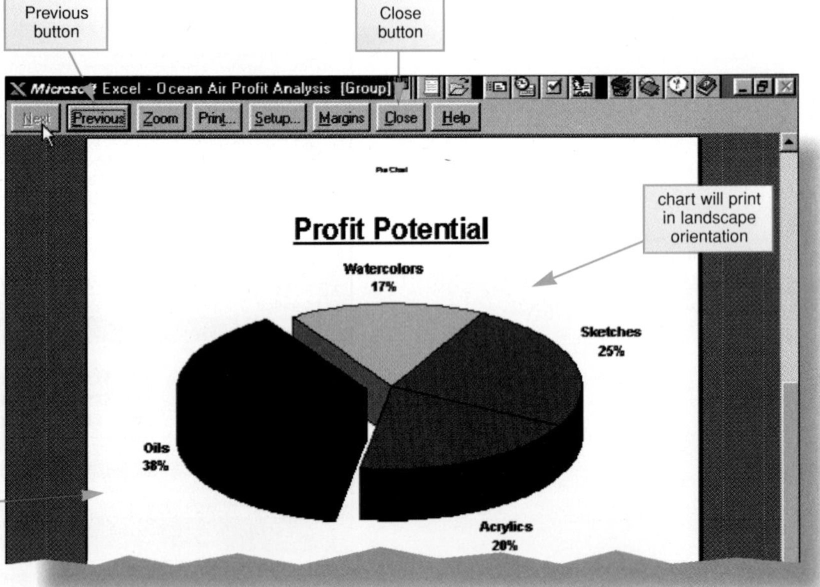

FIGURE 2-81

Other **Ways**

1. On File menu click Print Preview
2. On File menu click Page Setup, click Print Preview
3. Right-click menu, click Page Setup, click Print Preview

More *About* **Print Preview**

A popular button in the preview window (Figure 2-80) is the Margins button, which allows you to adjust the columns and margins. This is important, because the preview window shows the worksheet as it will print (WYSIWYG – What You See Is What You Get), whereas the screen may not.

Excel displays several buttons at the top of the preview window (Figure 2-81). The functions of these buttons are summarized in Table 2-4.

Rather than click the Next and Previous buttons to move from page to page as described in Table 2-4, you can press the PAGE UP and PAGE DOWN keys to do the same. You can also click the page in the preview window when the mouse pointer is a magnifying glass to carry out the function of the Zoom button.

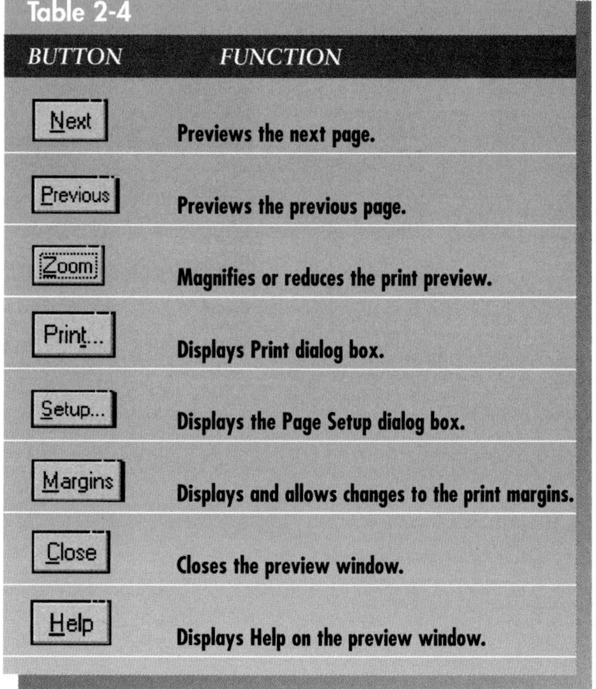

Table 2-4

BUTTON	FUNCTION
Next	Previews the next page.
Previous	Previews the previous page.
Zoom	Magnifies or reduces the print preview.
Print...	Displays Print dialog box.
Setup...	Displays the Page Setup dialog box.
Margins	Displays and allows changes to the print margins.
Close	Closes the preview window.
Help	Displays Help on the preview window.

Printing Selected Sheets in a Workbook

Although the two selected sheets could have been printed from the preview window, the following steps show how to print them using the Print button on the Standard toolbar.

Steps To Print Selected Sheets in a Workbook

1. **If both sheets are not selected, hold down the CTRL key and click the inactive sheet tab.**

2. **Point to the Print button on the Standard toolbar (Figure 2-82).**

3. **Click the Print button.**

   Excel prints the worksheet and pie chart on the printer (Figure 2-83 on the next page).

4. **Right-click the Profit Analysis tab at the bottom of the window and then click Ungroup Sheets to deselect the Pie Chart tab.**

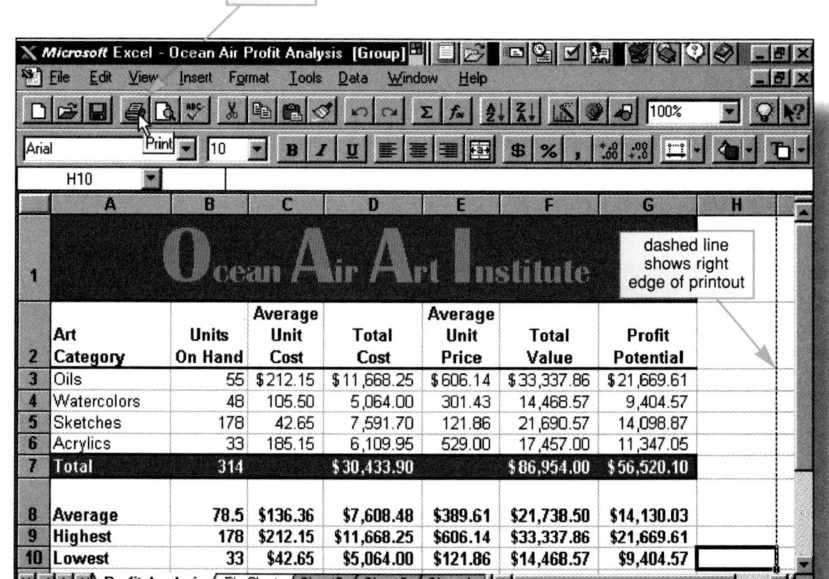

FIGURE 2-82

OtherWays

1. To print all nonblank worksheets, right-click tab, click Select All Sheets, click Print button on Standard toolbar

Notice that the worksheet is printed in portrait orientation and the chart is printed in landscape orientation (see Figure 2-83 on the next page). **Portrait orientation** means the printout is across the page width of 8.5 inches. **Landscape orientation** means the printout is across the page length of 11 inches. Excel selects landscape orientation automatically to print any chart created on a separate sheet.

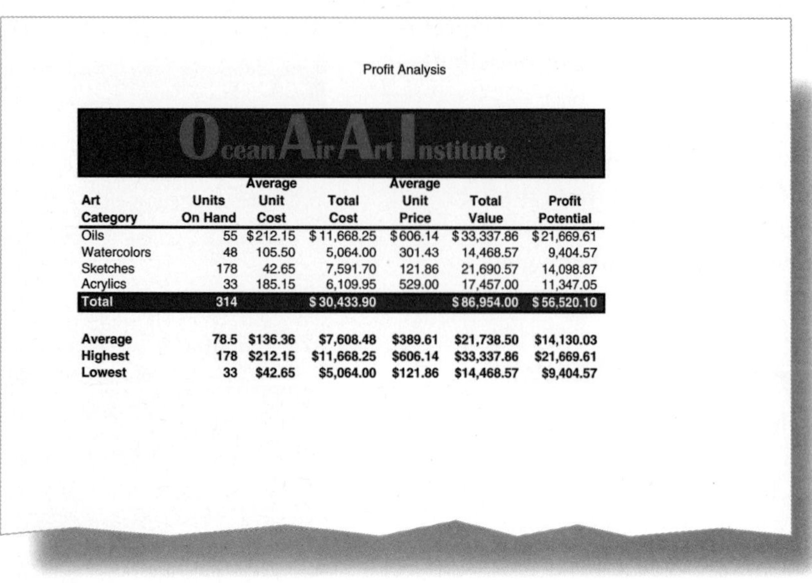

Profit Analysis

Ocean Air Art Institute

Art Category	Units On Hand	Average Unit Cost	Total Cost	Average Unit Price	Total Value	Profit Potential
Oils	55	$212.15	$ 11,668.25	$606.14	$ 33,337.86	$ 21,669.61
Watercolors	48	105.50	5,064.00	301.43	14,468.57	9,404.57
Sketches	178	42.65	7,591.70	121.86	21,690.57	14,098.87
Acrylics	33	185.15	6,109.95	529.00	17,457.00	11,347.05
Total	314		$ 30,433.90		$ 86,954.00	$ 56,520.10
Average	78.5	$136.36	$7,608.48	$389.61	$21,738.50	$14,130.03
Highest	178	$212.15	$11,668.25	$606.14	$33,337.86	$21,669.61
Lowest	33	$42.65	$5,064.00	$121.86	$14,468.57	$9,404.57

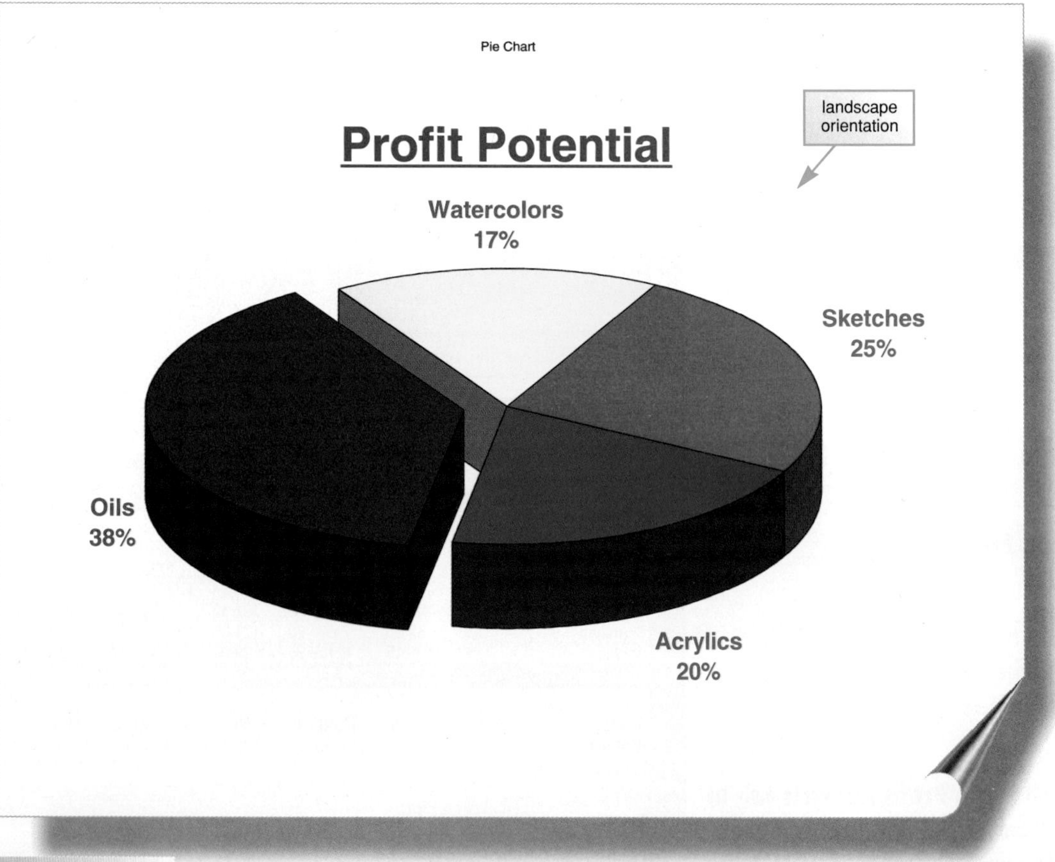

FIGURE 2-83

More *About* **Printing**

A dark font on a dark background, such as the red on blue title for Ocean Air Art Institute, will not print properly on a black and white printer. For b lack and white printing, use a light colored font for a dark background and a dark font for a light colored background.

Printing a Section of the Worksheet

You might not always want to print the entire worksheet. You can print portions of the worksheet by selecting the range of cells to print and then click Selection in the Print dialog box. The following steps show how to print the range A2:C6.

To Print a Section of the Worksheet

1 Select the range A2:C6. Right-click the menu bar.

The shortcut menu displays (Figure 2-84).

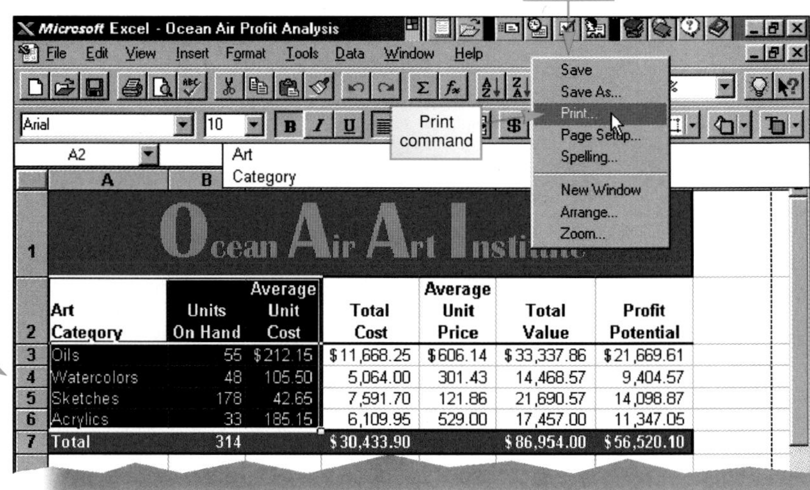

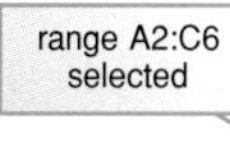

FIGURE 2-84

2 Click Print on the shortcut menu. Click Selection in the Print dialog box.

Excel displays the Print dialog box (Figure 2-85).

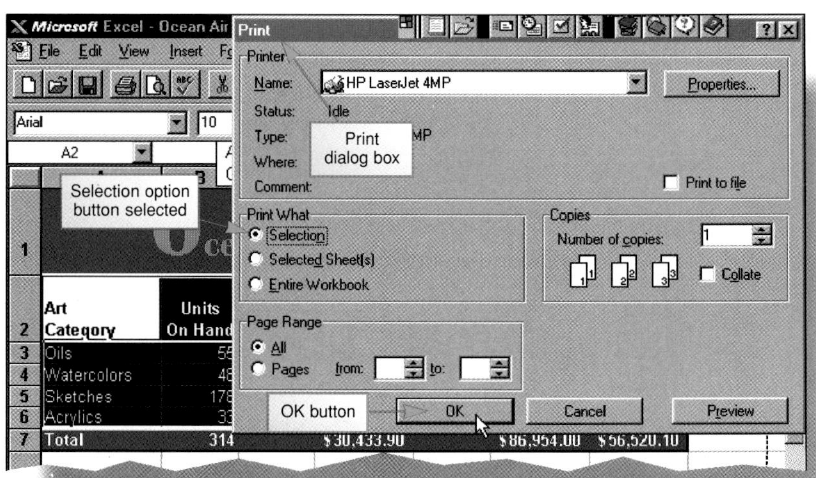

FIGURE 2-85

3 Click the OK button in the Print dialog box.

Excel prints the selected range of the worksheet on the printer (Figure 2-86).

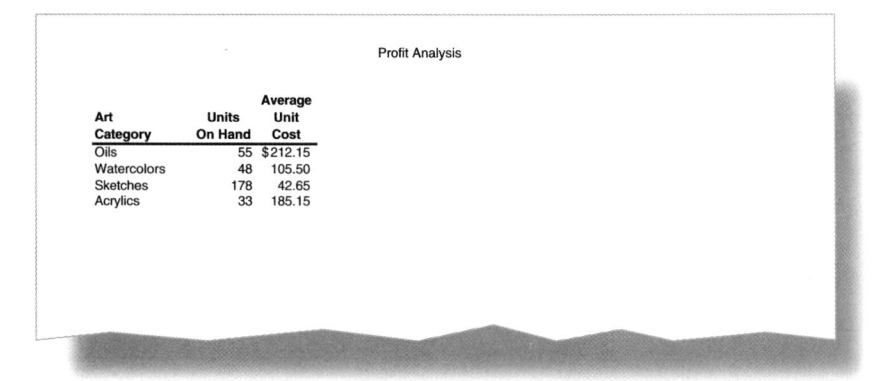

Profit Analysis

Art Category	Units On Hand	Average Unit Cost
Oils	55	$212.15
Watercolors	48	105.50
Sketches	178	42.65
Acrylics	33	185.15

FIGURE 2-86

OtherWays

1. Select range, on File menu click Print Area, click Set Print Area, click Print button on Standard toolbar; on File menu click Print Area, click Clear Print Area

There are three option buttons in the Print What area on the Print dialog box (Figure 2-85 on the previous page). The Selection option button instructs Excel to print the selected range. The Selected Sheet(s) option button instructs Excel to print the active sheet (the one displaying on the screen) or the selected sheets. Finally, the Entire Workbook option button instructs Excel to print all the sheets in the workbook. Selecting Entire Workbook is an alternative to selecting tabs by holding down the SHIFT or CTRL keys and clicking tabs to make their sheets active. The Selected Sheet option is the default.

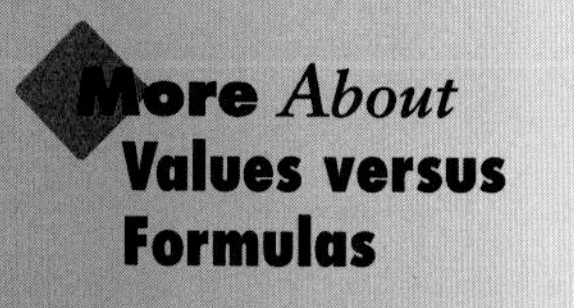

More *About* **Values versus Formulas**

When completing class assignments, don't enter numbers in cells that require formulas. Most instructors require their students to hand in both the values version and formulas version of the worksheet. The formulas version verifies that you entered formulas, rather than numbers in formula-based cells.

Displaying and Printing the Formulas in the Worksheet

Thus far, the worksheet has been printed exactly as it displays on the screen. This is called the **values version** of the worksheet. Another variation that you can display and print is called the formulas version. The **formulas version** displays and prints what was originally entered into the cells instead of the values in the cells. You can toggle between the values version and formulas version by pressing CTRL+` (LEFT SINGLE QUOTATION MARK to the left of the number 1 key).

The formulas version is useful for debugging a worksheet because the formulas and functions, rather than the numeric results, display and print. **Debugging** is the process of finding and correcting errors in the worksheet.

When you change from values to formulas, Excel increases the width of the columns so the formulas and text do not overflow into adjacent cells on the right. Thus, the worksheet usually becomes significantly wider when the formulas display. To fit the wide printout on one page you can use landscape orientation and the Fit to option on the Sheet sheet in the Page Setup dialog box. To change from values to formulas and print the formulas on one page, perform the following steps.

To Display the Formulas in the Worksheet and Fit the Printout on One Page

1 Press CTRL+` (LEFT SINGLE QUOTATION MARK to the left of the number 1 key).

Excel changes the display of the worksheet from values to formulas (Figure 2-87). The formulas in the worksheet display showing unformatted numbers, formulas, and functions that were assigned to the cells. Excel increases the widths of the columns automatically.

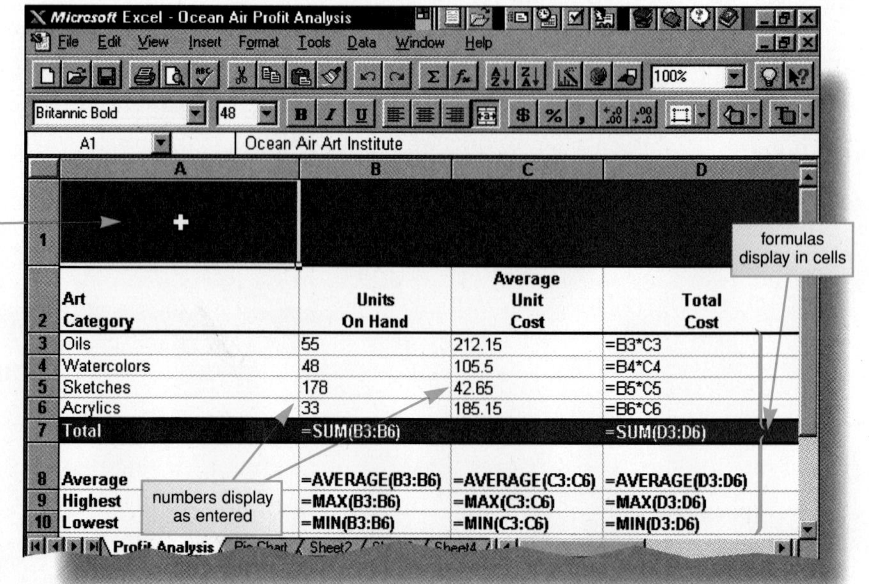

FIGURE 2-87

2 **Right-click the menu bar and then click Page Setup on the shortcut menu. When the Page Setup dialog box displays, click the Page tab, click Landscape and Fit to so the wide printout fits on one page in landscape orientation.**

Excel displays the Page Setup dialog box with the Landscape and Fit to selected (Figure 2-88).

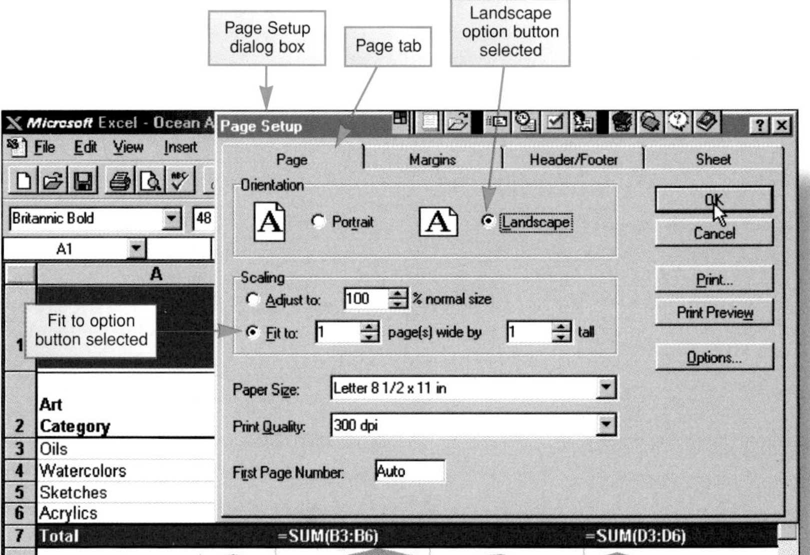

FIGURE 2-88

3 **Click the OK button in the Page Setup dialog box. Ready the printer and then click the Print button on the Standard toolbar. When you are finished with the formulas version, press CTRL+` to display the values version.**

Excel prints the formulas in the worksheet on one page in landscape orientation (Figure 2-89).

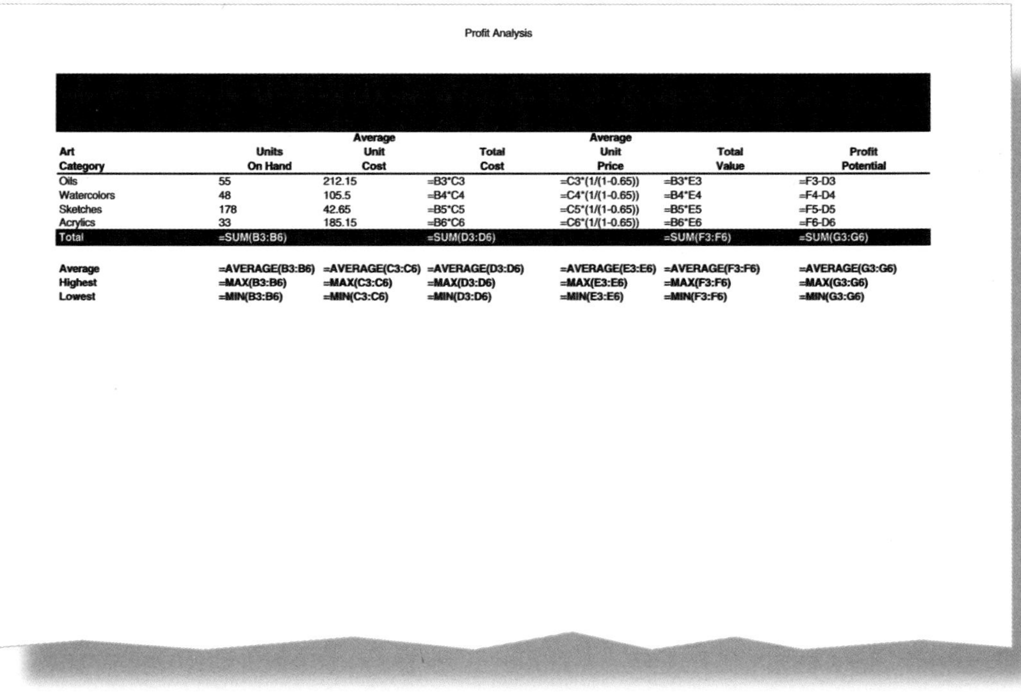
Profit Analysis

Art Category	Units On Hand	Average Unit Cost	Total Cost	Average Unit Price	Total Value	Profit Potential
Oils	55	212.15	=B3*C3	=C3*(1/(1-0.65))	=B3*E3	=F3-D3
Watercolors	48	105.5	=B4*C4	=C4*(1/(1-0.65))	=B4*E4	=F4-D4
Sketches	178	42.65	=B5*C5	=C5*(1/(1-0.65))	=B5*E5	=F5-D5
Acrylics	33	185.15	=B6*C6	=C6*(1/(1-0.65))	=B6*E6	=F6-D6
Total	=SUM(B3:B6)		=SUM(D3:D6)		=SUM(F3:F6)	=SUM(G3:G6)
Average	=AVERAGE(B3:B6)	=AVERAGE(C3:C6)	=AVERAGE(D3:D6)	=AVERAGE(E3:E6)	=AVERAGE(F3:F6)	=AVERAGE(G3:G6)
Highest	=MAX(B3:B6)	=MAX(C3:C6)	=MAX(D3:D6)	=MAX(E3:E6)	=MAX(F3:F6)	=MAX(G3:G6)
Lowest	=MIN(B3:B6)	=MIN(C3:C6)	=MIN(D3:D6)	=MIN(E3:E6)	=MIN(F3:F6)	=MIN(G3:G6)

FIGURE 2-89

OtherWays

1. On Tools menu click Options, click View tab, click Formulas check box, click OK button

Although the formulas in the worksheet were printed in the previous example, you can see from Figure 2-87 that the display on the screen can also be used for debugging errors in the worksheet.

The formulas in the worksheet were printed using the Fit to option so they would fit on one page. Anytime characters extend past the dashed line that represents the rightmost edge of the printed worksheet, the printout will be made up of multiple pages. If you prefer to print the worksheet on one page, click Fit to in the Page Setup dialog box (Figure 2-88) before you print.

More *About* the Fit To Option

Don't take the Fit To option lightly. Most applications involve worksheets that extend beyond the 8½-by-11-inch page. Most users want the information on one page, however, at least with respect to the width of the worksheet. Thus, the landscape orientation with the Fit To option is a common choice among Excel users.

Changing the Print Scaling Option Back to 100%

Depending on your printer driver, you may have to change the Print Scaling option back to 100% after using the Fit to option. Complete the following steps to reset the Print Scaling option so future worksheets print at 100%, instead of being squeezed on one page.

TO CHANGE THE PRINT SCALING OPTION BACK TO 100%

Step 1: Right-click the menu bar and then click the Page Setup command.
Step 2: Click the Page tab in the Page Setup dialog box. Click Adjust to in the Scaling box.
Step 3: If necessary, type 100 in the Adjust to box.
Step 4: Click the OK button in the Page Setup dialog box.

Using the Adjust to box, you can specify the percentage of reduction or enlargement in the printout of a worksheet. The default percentage is 100%. The 100% automatically changes to the percentage required whenever you click the Fit to option.

Exiting Excel

After completing the worksheet and pie chart, you can exit Excel, by performing the following steps.

TO EXIT EXCEL

Step 1: Click the Close button on the upper right side of the title bar.
Step 2: If the Microsoft Excel dialog box displays, click the Yes button.

Project Summary

The worksheet and accompanying pie chart (Figure 2-1 on page E 2.6) you created for Lisa and Joe Sabol meet the requirements set by the loan officer, Mr. Leaman, at the local savings and loan association. The report includes the units on hand, average unit cost, total cost, average unit selling price, total value, and profit potential for each art category sold by Ocean Air Art Institute, as well as the requested statistics. Finally, the pie chart dramatically shows the contribution of each art category to the total profit potential.

In creating the Ocean Air Art Institute workbook, you learned how to enter formulas, calculate an average, find the highest and lowest numbers in a range, change the font, draw borders, format numbers, and change column widths and row heights. You also learned how to create a pie chart on a separate sheet, format the pie chart, rename sheet tabs, preview a worksheet, print a workbook, print a section of a worksheet and display and print the formulas in the worksheet using the Fit to option.

What You Should Know

Having completed this project, you should be able to perform the following tasks:

- Apply Currency Style and Comma Style Formats Using the Formatting Toolbar *(E 2.31)*
- Apply a Currency Style with a Floating Dollar Sign Using the Format Cells Command on the Shortcut Menu *(E 2.33)*
- Calculate Totals Using the AutoSum Button *(E 2.14)*
- Center the Worksheet Title *(E 2.26)*
- Change the Background Colors and Apply an Outline Border *(E 2.26)*
- Change the Colors of the Pie Slices *(E 2.49)*
- Change the Font Color and Bold Nonadjacent Ranges *(E 2.28)*
- Change the Heights of Rows by Dragging *(E 2.37)*
- Change the Print Scaling Option Back to 100% *(E 2.62)*
- Change the Width of Columns by Dragging *(E 2.35)*
- Change the Widths of Columns to Best Fit *(E 2.36)*
- Check Spelling in the Worksheet *(E 2.40)*
- Copy a Range of Cells Across Columns to an Adjacent Range Using the Fill Handle *(E 2.20)*
- Copy a Range of Cells Down Rows to an Adjacent Range Using the Fill Handle *(E 2.14)*
- Display The Formulas in the Worksheet and Fit the Printout on One Page *(E 2.60)*
- Draw a Pie Chart *(E 2.43)*
- Enter a Complex Formula Using the Keyboard *(E 2.11)*
- Enter a Simple Formula Using the Keyboard *(E 2.9)*
- Enter Formulas Using Point Mode *(E 2.12)*
- Enter the Column Titles *(E 2.7)*
- Enter the MIN Function Using the Function Wizard Button *(E 2.17)*
- Enter the Numbers *(E 2.8)*
- Enter the Row Titles *(E 2.8)*
- Enter the Worksheet Title *(E 2.7)*
- Explode the Pie Chart *(E 2.50)*
- Find the Average of a Group of Numbers *(E 2.16)*
- Find the Highest Number in a Range *(E 2.17)*
- Format the Characters in the Worksheet Title *(E 2.23)*
- Format the Chart Title and Labels *(E 2.47)*
- Preview Selected Sheets in a Workbook *(E 2.55)*
- Print a Section of the Worksheet *(E 2.58)*
- Print Selected Sheets in a Workbook *(E 2.57)*
- Rename the Sheet Tabs and Rearrange the Order of the Sheets *(E 2.53)*
- Rotate and Tilt the Pie Chart *(E 2.51)*
- Save an Intermediate Copy of the Workbook *(E 2.21)*
- Start Excel *(E 2.7)*
- Underline and Center the Column Titles *(E 2.29)*

A+ Test Your Knowledge

1 True/False

Instructions: Circle T if the statement is true or F if the statement is false.

T F 1. Use the Currency Style button on the Formatting toolbar to change the entry in a cell to different international monetary values.

T F 2. The minimum column width is zero.

T F 3. If you assign a cell the formula =12 / 3, the number 4 displays in the cell.

T F 4. In the formula =9 / 3 + 2, the addition operation (+) is completed before the division operation (/).

T F 5. The formulas =C4 * c3, =c4 * c3, and =C4*C3 result in the same value being assigned to the active cell.

T F 6. You can assign a function to a cell by typing it in the formula bar or using the Function Wizard button on the Standard toolbar.

T F 7. If you use the Point mode to enter a formula or select a range, you must click the enter box to complete the entry.

T F 8. If the function =AVERAGE(G5:G8) assigns a value of 20 to cell H10, and cell H10 is copied to cell G10, cell G10 may or may not equal 10.

T F 9. When a number is too large to fit in a cell, Excel displays at signs (@) in place of each digit in the cell.

T F 10. To increase or decrease the width of a column, use the mouse to point at the column heading right border and drag it.

2 Multiple Choice

Instructions: Circle the correct response.

1. Which one of the following arithmetic operations is completed first if they are all found in a formula with no parentheses?
   a. ^ c. /
   b. – d. *
2. The __________ preceding a formula is important because it alerts Excel that you are entering a formula and not text, such as words.
   a. exclamation point (!) c. equal sign (=)
   b. number sign (#) d. asterisk (*)
3. When you copy a formula with relative cell references across columns, __________.
   a. the row references change in the formula
   b. the column references change in the formula
   c. no references are changed in the formula
   d. the result of the formula remains the same
4. When you point to the fill handle, the mouse pointer becomes a(n) __________.
   a. cross hair c. dark plus sign with two arrowheads
   b. magnifying glass d. arrow

A+ Test Your Knowledge

5. The maximum width of a column is __________ characters.
   a. 31 c. 193
   b. 63 d. 256
6. When Excel starts and the worksheet displays, all the columns have a default width of __________ and a row height of __________.
   a. 9 characters, 9.00 points
   b. 8.43 characters, 12.75 points
   c. 6 characters, 15.00 points
   d. 12.75 characters, 9.00 points
7. Which one of the following describes a column width where the user has requested that Excel determine the width to use?
   a. custom fit c. close fit
   b. usual fit d. best fit
8. When Excel displays what you actually entered into the cells, it is called the __________ version.
   a. formulas c. formatted
   b. displayed d. values
9. A sheet tab name can be up to __________ characters in length.
   a. 8 c. 31
   b. 255 d. 48
10. To rotate a selected pie chart, use the __________ command on the shortcut menu.
   a. Format Data Series c. 3-D View
   b. Chart Type d. Format 3-D Pie Group

3 Entering Formulas

Instructions: Using the values in the worksheet in Figure 2-90, write the formula that accomplishes the task for each of the following items and compute the value assigned to the specified cell.

1. Assign cell G1 the difference between cells C2 and F3.
   Formula: __________
   Result: __________
2. Assign cell A2 cell D2 divided by F5.
   Formula: __________
   Result: __________

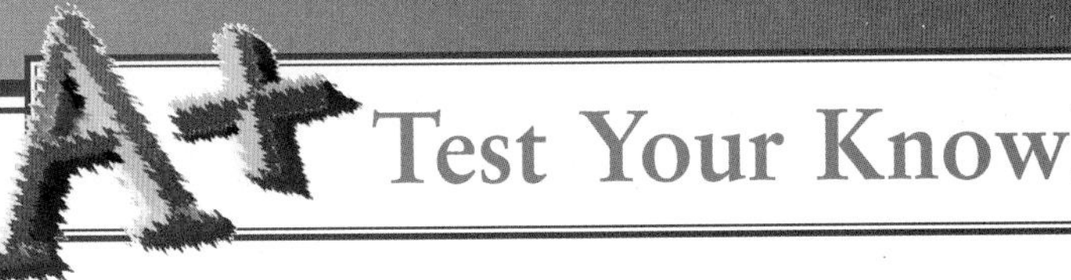

	A	B	C	D	E	F	G	H	I
1			3	5	7	9			
2			12	10	3	4			
3			5	2	1	6			
4			21	18	30	35			
5			2	0	3	2			
6									
7									

FIGURE 2-90

(continued)

Test Your Knowledge

Entering Formulas *(continued)*

3. Assign cell D6 the sum of the range E1:F2, less cell C4.

   Formula: ____________________ Result ____________________

4. Assign cell H6 three times the product of cell E4 and cell E2.

   Formula: ____________________ Result: ____________________

5. Assign cell H1 the sum of the range of cells C2:C5 minus the product of cells F1 and F2.

   Formula: ____________________ Result: ____________________

6. Assign cell G2 the result of cell C5 less cell C3 raised to cell E5.

   Formula: ____________________ Result: ____________________

7. Assign cell H2 the expression (A ^ 3 - 6 * B * C) / (4 * B) where the value of A is in cell C5, the value of B is in cell D2, and the value of C is in cell F5.

   Formula: ____________________ Result: ____________________

4 Understanding Formulas

Instructions: Figure 2-91 displays the formulas version of a worksheet. In the spaces provided, indicate the numeric value assigned to the cells if the numbers display instead of the formulas.

1. D1 ____________________
2. D2 ____________________
3. D3 ____________________
4. A4 ____________________
5. B4 ____________________
6. C4 ____________________
7. D4 ____________________

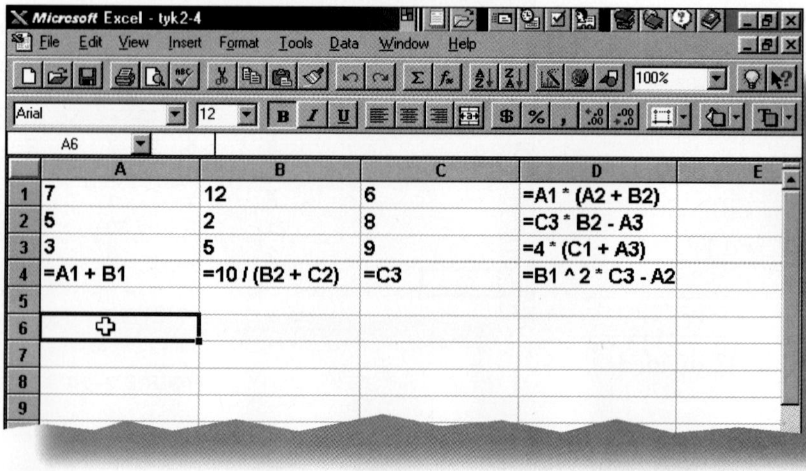

Microsoft Excel - tyk2-4

	A	B	C	D	E
1	7	12	6	=A1 * (A2 + B2)	
2	5	2	8	=C3 * B2 - A3	
3	3	5	9	=4 * (C1 + A3)	
4	=A1 + B1	=10 / (B2 + C2)	=C3	=B1 ^ 2 * C3 - A2	
5					
6					
7					
8					
9					

FIGURE 2-91

Use Help

1 Reviewing Project Activities

Instructions: Perform the following tasks using a computer.

1. Start Excel. Double-click the Help button on the Standard toolbar to display the Help Topics: Microsoft Excel dialog box. Click the Contents tab. Double-click the Creating Formulas and Auditing Workbooks book.
2. Double-click the Entering Formulas book. One at a time, double-click each of the six links in the Entering Formulas book. Read and print the information for each link. To print the information click the Print Topic command on the shortcut menu. To return to the previous dialog box, click the Help Topics button. Hand in the printouts to your instructor.
3. Repeat Step 4 for the Using Functions book.
4. If the Help Topics: Microsoft Excel dialog box is not on the screen, double-click the Help button on the Standard toolbar. Click the Find tab. Type `row height` in the top box labeled 1. Double-click Adjust row height in the lower box labeled 3, read it, and click Print Topic on the shortcut menu. Click the Close button to close the Microsoft Excel Help window. Hand in the printout.
5. Double-click the Help button on the Standard toolbar. Click the Answer Wizard tab. Type `how do i format numbers` in the top box labeled 1. Click the Search button. Double-click Number formatting in the lower box labeled 2 under Tell Me About. One at a time, click the three links.

2 Expanding on the Basics

Instructions: Use Excel online Help to better understand the topics listed below. Begin each of the following by double-clicking the Help button on the Standard toolbar. If you are unable to print the help information, then answer the questions on your own paper.

1. Double-click the Working with Charts and Maps book on the Contents sheet in the Help Topics: Microsoft Excel dialog box. Double-click the Formatting a Chart book. Double-click Changing the Type of a Chart book. Double-click the link titled, The best chart type for my data. One at a time, click each type of chart and write down when the selected chart type would be the preferred one to use. When you are finished, click the Close button and hand in your answers to your instructor.
2. Use the Find sheet in the Help Topics: Microsoft Excel dialog box to display and then print information about operator precedence. Indicate which operators are at the same level.
3. Use the Answer Wizard sheet in the Help Topics: Microsoft Excel dialog box to answer the question, *how do I use sheet tabs?* Answer the following related questions:
   a. How do I switch to another sheet?
   b. How do I select sheets in a workbook?
   c. How do I add a worksheet?
   d. How do I display more or fewer sheet tabs?
   e. How do I rename a sheet tab?

Apply Your Knowledge

1 Changing the Appearance of a Pie Chart

Instructions: Start Excel. Open the workbook Wally's Warehouse Cost Analysis from the Excel folder on the Student Floppy Disk that accompanies this book. Perform the following tasks to change the appearance of the pie chart that accompanies the worksheet to make it look like Figure 2-92.

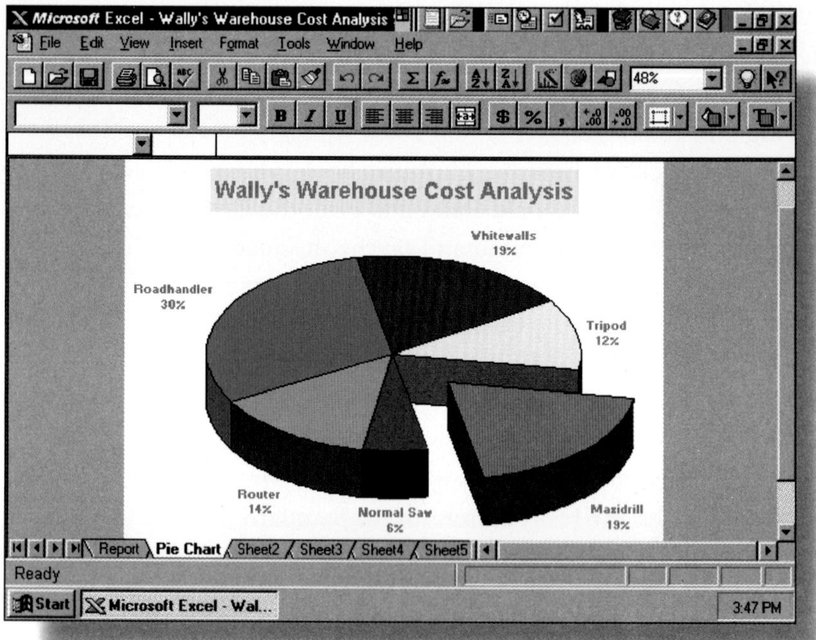

FIGURE 2-92

1. Double-click the Chart1 tab in the lower left corner of the window and rename it Pie Chart. Drag the tab titled Report to the left of the tab titled Pie Chart. Click the Pie Chart tab to display the pie chart.
2. Click the pie chart title and change the font to 28-point red (column 3, row 1). Change the title background to tan (column 4, row 5).
3. Click one of the labels that identify the slices. Change the font to 14-point bold red (column 3, row 1).
4. Click the Maxidrill slice twice. Drag it away from the other slices.
5. Right-click one of the slices. Click 3-D View. Change the elevation to 40° and the rotation to 230°.
6. If the Maxidrill slice is not selected, click it twice. (Do not double-click.) Change the color of the slice to red (column 3, row 1).
7. Print the pie chart. Save the workbook using the filename Wally's Warehouse Inventory Report 2.
8. Click the Report tab. Change the quantity on hand (column F) for Roadhandler, Tripod, and Normal Saw by incrementing each by 50 units. After the changes, the total cost in cell G9 should be $19,624.68. Click the Pie Chart tab. Notice how the slices changed size on the basis of the new entries. Hold down the CTRL key and click the Report tab. Print the selected sheets.

In the Lab

1 Planet Earth Sales Analysis Worksheet and 3-D Column Chart

Problem: The computer consulting firm you and a friend started recently on a part-time basis has received its first contract. The client, Planet Solutions Inc., has specified in the contract that you are to build a sales analysis worksheet that determines the sales quota and percentage of quota met for the sales representatives in Table 2-5. The desired worksheet is shown in Figure 2-93. The client has also requested a 3-D column chart (Figure 2-94 on page E2.71) that compares the net sales by sales representative.

Table 2-5

NAME	SALES AMOUNT	SALES RETURN	SALES QUOTA
Lora Wade	$692,500	$122,500	$500,000
Scott Tisooh	359,250	63,500	300,000
Max Beagle	472,099	57,100	375,000
Mandi Nice	256,350	24,950	275,000

Instructions Part 1: Perform the following tasks to build the worksheet shown in Figure 2-93.

1. Use the Select All button and the Bold button to bold the entire worksheet.
2. Increase the width of column A to 14.00 points and the width of columns B through F to 13.00 points.
3. Enter the worksheet title, Planet Solutions, in cell A1, column titles in row 2, using ALT+ENTER to start a new line in the cells, and the row titles in column A as shown in Figure 2-93.
4. Enter the sales data described in Table 2-5 in columns B, C, and E as shown in Figure 2-93. Enter the numbers without dollar signs or commas.

Microsoft Excel - Planet Solutions 1

	A	B	C	D	E	F
1	Planet Solutions					
2	Sales Representative	Sales Amount	Sales Returns	Net Sales	Sales Quota	Above Quota
3	Lora Wade	$692,500.00	$122,500.00	$570,000.00	$500,000.00	$70,000.00
4	Scott Tisooh	359,250.00	63,500.00	295,750.00	300,000.00	(4,250.00)
5	Max Beagle	472,099.00	57,100.00	414,999.00	375,000.00	39,999.00
6	Mandi Nice	256,350.00	24,950.00	231,400.00	275,000.00	(43,600.00)
7	Totals	$1,780,199.00	$268,050.00	$1,512,149.00	$1,450,000.00	$62,149.00
8	Average	$445,049.75	$67,012.50	$378,037.25	$362,500.00	
9	% of Quota Sold ====>		104.29%			
10						

Sales Analysis / Bar Chart / Sheet2 / Sheet3 / Sheet4

FIGURE 2-93

5. Obtain the net sales in column D by subtracting the sales returns in column C from the sales amount in column B. Enter the formula in cell D3 and copy it to the range D4:D6.
6. Obtain the above quota amounts in column F by subtracting the sales quota in column E from the net sales in column D. Enter the formula in cell F3 and copy it to the range F4:F6.

(continued)

In the Lab

Planet Earth Sales Analysis Worksheet and 3-D Column Chart *(continued)*

7. Obtain the totals in row 7 by adding the column values for each salesperson. In row 8, use the AVERAGE function to determine the column averages.
8. Obtain the percent of quota sold in cell C9 by dividing the total net sales amount in cell D7 by the total sales quota amount in cell E7.
9. Change the worksheet title font in cell A1 to yellow (column 6, row 1 on the Font Color palette), Footlight MT Light (or a font that is similar), and increase its size to 36 point. Edit cell A1 and increase the font size of the first letter in each word to 48 point. Center the title across columns A through F. Color the background of the ranges A1:F1, A7:F7, and C9 purple (column 1, row 2 on the Color palette). Assign a heavy outline border (column 4, row 3 on the Borders palette) to the ranges A1:F1, A7:F7, and C9.
10. Use the Italic button on the Formatting toolbar to italicize the column titles in row 2. Draw a heavy bottom border (column 2, row 2 on the Borders palette) in the range A2:F2. Center the titles in columns B through F.
11. Change the font color in the range A7:F7 and cell C9 to white (column 2, row 1 on the Font Color palette).
12. Change the row heights as follows: row 1 to 57.00 points; and rows 8 and 9 to 24.00 points.
13. Assign the Currency style with a floating dollar sign to the ranges B3:F3, B7:F7, and B8:E8. To assign the format, select a range and then right-click. Click Format Cells on the shortcut menu. Click the Number tab in the Format Cells dialog box, and then click Currency in the Category list. Click Use $. Select two decimal places and parentheses to represent negative numbers. Select the range B4:F6 and then click the Comma Style button on the Standard toolbar. Select cell C9. Click the Percent Style button on the Standard toolbar. Click the Increase Decimal button on the Standard toolbar twice to display the percent in cell C9 to hundredths.
14. Enter your name, course, laboratory assignment number (Lab 2-1), date, and instructor name below the entries in column A in separate cells.
15. Save the workbook using the filename Planet Solutions 1. Print the entire worksheet. Print only the range A2:B8.
16. Display the formulas by pressing CTRL+`. Print the formulas using Fit to in the Scaling box on the Page sheet in the Page Setup dialog box. After printing the worksheet, reset the Scaling option by clicking the Adjust to on the Page sheet in the Page Setup dialog box and then changing the percent value to 100%. Change the display from formulas to values by pressing CTRL+`.

Instructions Part 2: Increment each of the four values in the sales quota column by $5,000.00 until the percent of quota sold in cell C9 is below, yet as close as possible to, 100%. All four values in column E must be incremented the same number of times. The percent of quota sold in C9 should equal 98.83%. Save the workbook as Planet Solutions 2. Print the worksheet.

Instructions Part 3: With the percent of quota sold in cell C9 equal to 98.83% from Part 2, decrement each of the four values in the sales return column by $1,500.00 until the percent of quota sold in cell C9 is above, yet as close as possible to, 100%. Decrement all four values in column C the same number of times. Your worksheet is correct when the percent of quota sold in cell C9 is equal to 100.01%. Save the workbook as Planet Solutions 3. Print the worksheet.

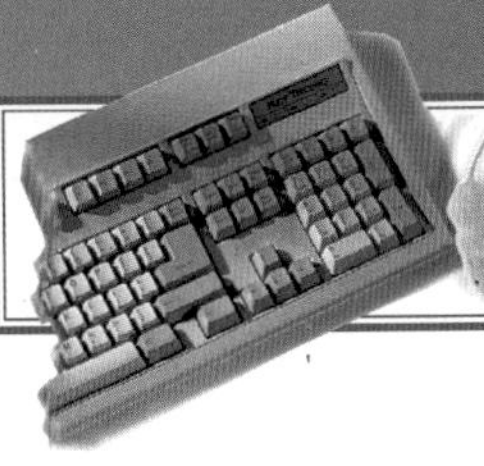

In the Lab

Instructions Part 4: Open Planet Solutions 1 from Part 1. Select the range A3:A6. Use the CTRL key to select the nonadjacent range D3:D6. Click Chart on the Insert menu to create a chart as a new sheet. Draw a 3-D column chart using format number 4 (Figure 2-94). Notice the following about the chart:(a) the Data Series for this chart is in columns; (b) there is no legend on the chart; and (c) the chart does have a title of Sales by Representative.

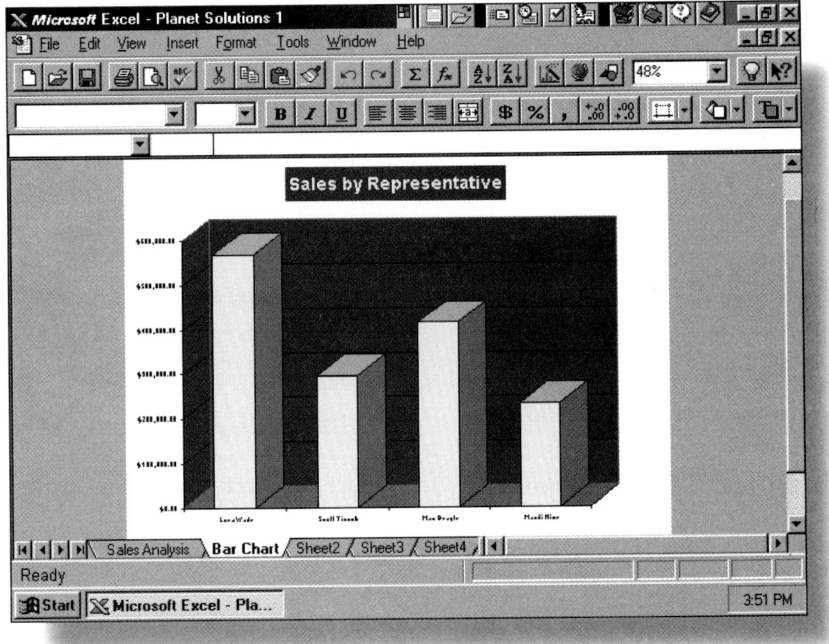

FIGURE 2-94

Once the chart displays, change the chart title as follows: font — yellow (column 6, row 1), 22 point; background purple (column 1, row 2). Change the color of the chart background to purple (column 1, row 2) and change the color of the columns to yellow (column 6, row 1). Rename the sheet tabs at the bottom of the screen to read Sales Analysis for the sheet tab corresponding to the worksheet and Bar Chart for the sheet tab corresponding to the chart. Rearrange the order of the sheet tabs so the worksheet appears first with the chart following it. Save the workbook as Planet Solutions 4. Preview and then print the entire workbook.

2 Steel Frame House Weekly Payroll Worksheet

Problem: You are enrolled in a sophomore Office Information Systems course in which the students are given projects in the local business community. You have been assigned to the Steel Frame House Company. You have been asked to prepare a weekly payroll report for the six employees in Table 2-6.

Table 2-6

EMPLOYEE	RATE PER HOUR	HOURS	DEPENDENTS
Dent, Jacob	22.50	39.5	4
Till, Kevin	28.00	64	3
Hayley, Joe	23.00	40	4
Boate, Max	14.50	46.25	1
Suzi, Jeff	13.35	12	3
Dense, Fritz	15.40	43	5

(continued)

In the Lab

Steel Frame House Weekly Payroll Worksheet *(continued)*

Instructions: Perform the following tasks to create a worksheet similar to the one in Figure 2-95:

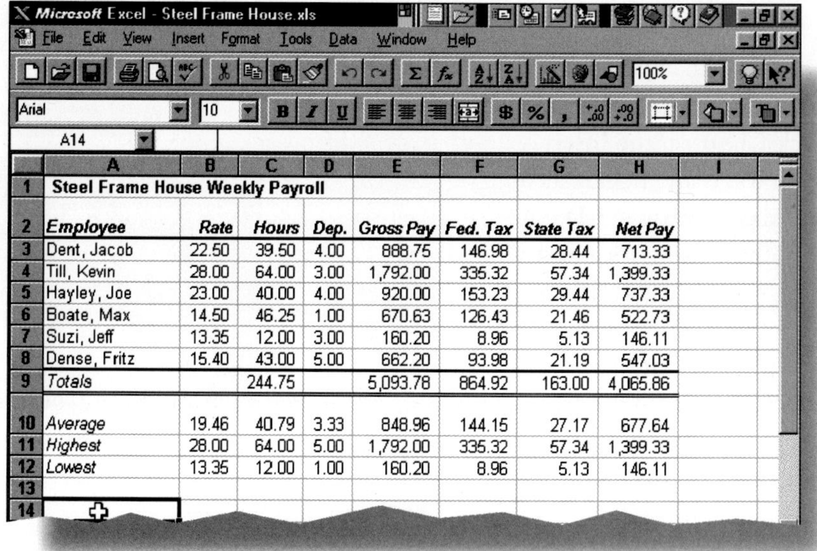

	A	B	C	D	E	F	G	H
1	**Steel Frame House Weekly Payroll**							
2	***Employee***	***Rate***	***Hours***	***Dep.***	***Gross Pay***	***Fed. Tax***	***State Tax***	***Net Pay***
3	Dent, Jacob	22.50	39.50	4.00	888.75	146.98	28.44	713.33
4	Till, Kevin	28.00	64.00	3.00	1,792.00	335.32	57.34	1,399.33
5	Hayley, Joe	23.00	40.00	4.00	920.00	153.23	29.44	737.33
6	Boate, Max	14.50	46.25	1.00	670.63	126.43	21.46	522.73
7	Suzi, Jeff	13.35	12.00	3.00	160.20	8.96	5.13	146.11
8	Dense, Fritz	15.40	43.00	5.00	662.20	93.98	21.19	547.03
9	*Totals*		244.75		5,093.78	864.92	163.00	4,065.86
10	*Average*	19.46	40.79	3.33	848.96	144.15	27.17	677.64
11	*Highest*	28.00	64.00	5.00	1,792.00	335.32	57.34	1,399.33
12	*Lowest*	13.35	12.00	1.00	160.20	8.96	5.13	146.11

FIGURE 2-95

1. Enter the worksheet title, Steel Frame House Weekly Payroll, in cell A1. Enter the column titles in row 2, the row titles in column A, and the data in columns B through D from Table 2-6 as shown in Figure 2-95.
2. Use the following formulas to determine the gross pay, federal tax, state tax, and net pay:
   a. Gross Pay = Rate*Hours (Hint: Assign the first employee in cell E3 the formula =B3*C3, and copy the formula in E3 to the range E4:E8 for the remaining employee).
   b. Federal Tax = 20%*(Gross Pay–Dependents*38. 46)
   c. State Tax = 3.2%*Gross Pay
   d. Net Pay = Gross Pay–(Federal Tax+State Tax)
3. Show totals for the gross pay, federal tax, state tax, and net pay in row 9.
4. Determine the average, highest, and lowest values of each column in rows 10 through 12 by using the appropriate functions.
5. Bold the worksheet title.
6. Using the buttons on the Formatting toolbar, assign the Comma style with two decimal places to the range B3:H12.
7. Bold, italicize, and draw a heavy border under the column titles in the range A2:H2. Right-align the column titles in the range B2:H2.
8. Italicize the range A9:A12. Draw a heavy top border and a light double bottom border in the range A9:H9.
9. Change the height of row 10 to 24.00 points, the width of column A to 15.00 characters, and the width of columns B through H to best fit.
10. Enter your name, course, laboratory assignment number (Lab 2-2), date, and instructor name below the entries in column A in separate but adjacent cells.
11. Save the workbook using the filename, Steel Frame House.
12. Preview and then print the worksheet.

In the Lab

13. Press CTRL+` to change the display from values to formulas. Print the formulas version of the worksheet using the Fit to option on the Page sheet in the Page Setup dialog box. After the printer is finished, reset the worksheet to display the numbers by pressing CTRL+`. Reset the Scaling option to 100% by clicking Adjust to on the Page sheet in the Page Setup dialog box and setting the percent value to 100%.
14. Increase the number of hours worked for each employee by 8.25 hours. Total Net Pay in cell H9 should equal $4,805.59. Increase the width of column F to best fit to view the new federal tax total. Print the worksheet with the new values. Do not save the worksheet with the new values.

3 Annie's Antiques Monthly Accounts Receivable Balance Sheet

Problem: You were recently hired as a summer intern in the Accounting department of Annie's Antiques, a prosperous antique company with several outlets on the east coast. Your supervisor noticed that you had taken an Excel spreadsheet course the previous semester and approached you about an accounting project. The project she has in mind involves using Excel to generate a much-needed report that summarizes the monthly accounts receivable balance. A graphic breakdown of the data is also desired. The customer accounts receivable data in Table 2-7 is available for test purposes.

Instructions Part 1: Construct a worksheet similar to the one shown in Figure 2-96 on the next page. Include all six fields in Table 2-7 in the report plus the service charge and new balance. (Assume no negative unpaid monthly balances.)

Perform the following tasks:

1. Use the Select All button and Bold button on the Formatting toolbar to bold the entire worksheet.
2. Assign the worksheet title, Annie's Antiques, to cell A1. Assign the worksheet subtitle Monthly Accounts Receivable to cell A2.
3. Enter the column titles in the range A3:H3 as shown in Figure 2-96. Change the widths of columns A through H to best fit.
4. Enter the account numbers and row titles in column A. Enter the account numbers as text. To learn how to enter numbers as text, click the Index tab in the Help Topics: Microsoft Excel Help dialog box and look up the term, number. Select the subphrase, entering as text. Enter the remaining data in Table 2-7.

Table 2-7

ACCOUNT NUMBER	CUSTOMER NAME	BEGINNING BALANCE	PURCHASES	PAYMENTS	RETURNS
1623	Abbot, Jim	2,923.15	589.50	375.00	312.00
2245	Zell, Mary	1,298.34	237.12	125.00	0.00
3314	Hart, Ed	3,523.00	98.75	10.00	22.65
4523	Flint, Fred	2,218.75	5.50	223.00	23.10
6712	Fogs, Trina	1,625.00	89.43	10.00	0.00

(continued)

In the Lab

Annie's Antiques Monthly Accounts Receivable Balance Sheet *(continued)*

5. Use the following formulas to determine the service charge in column G and the new balance at the end of month in column H for each account:
   a. Service Charge = 2.25%*(Beginning Balance–Payments–Returns)
   b. New Balance = Beginning Balance+Purchases–Payments–Returns+Service Charge
6. Compute totals for the numeric columns in row 9.
7. Cell C10 should contain the appropriate function to calculate the maximum value in the range C4:C8. Copy cell C10 to the range D10:H10.

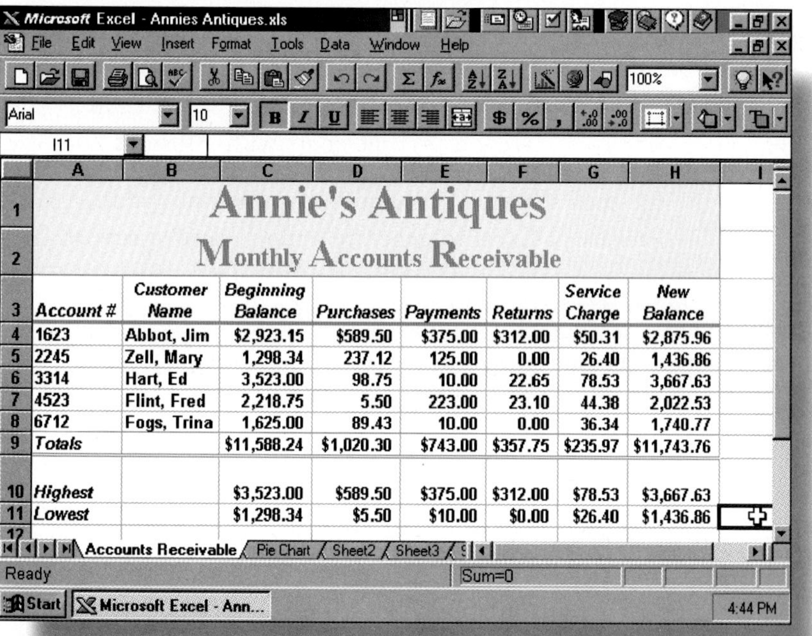

	A	B	C	D	E	F	G	H
3	Account #	Customer Name	Beginning Balance	Purchases	Payments	Returns	Service Charge	New Balance
4	1623	Abbot, Jim	$2,923.15	$589.50	$375.00	$312.00	$50.31	$2,875.96
5	2245	Zell, Mary	1,298.34	237.12	125.00	0.00	26.40	1,436.86
6	3314	Hart, Ed	3,523.00	98.75	10.00	22.65	78.53	3,667.63
7	4523	Flint, Fred	2,218.75	5.50	223.00	23.10	44.38	2,022.53
8	6712	Fogs, Trina	1,625.00	89.43	10.00	0.00	36.34	1,740.77
9	Totals		$11,588.24	$1,020.30	$743.00	$357.75	$235.97	$11,743.76
10	Highest		$3,523.00	$589.50	$375.00	$312.00	$78.53	$3,667.63
11	Lowest		$1,298.34	$5.50	$10.00	$0.00	$26.40	$1,436.86

FIGURE 2-96

8. Cell C11 should contain the appropriate function to calculate the minimum value in the range C4:C8. Copy cell C11 to the range D11:H11.
9. Change the worksheet title font in cell A1, to 28-point CG Times. Format the worksheet subtitle font in cell A2 to 16-point CG Times and the first letter of each word in the subtitle to 24 point. Center the worksheet titles in cells A1 and A2 across the range A1:H2. Change the heights of rows 1 through 3 and row 10 to 27.75. Add a red light border to the range A1:H2 by using the Border tab in the Format Cells dialog box.
10. Select the range A1:H2 and change the background color to light brown (column 4, row 5 of the Color palette). Change the font color in the range A1:H2 to red (column 3, row 1 of the Font Color palette).
11. Italicize the column titles and place a red heavy border below them. Center the column titles in the range A3:H3. Italicize the titles in rows 9, 10, and 11. Add a single, red light upper border and red double underline border to the range A9:H9.
12. Use the Format Cells command on the shortcut menu to format the numbers in row 4 and rows 9 through 11 to Currency style with a floating dollar sign. Use the same command to assign the Comma style (currency with no dollar sign) to the range C5:H8. The Format Cells command is preferred over the Comma Style button because the worksheet specifications call for displaying zero as 0.00 rather than as a dash (-), as shown in Figure 2-96.
13. Change the widths of columns B through H again to best fit.

14. Rename the sheet tab Accounts Receivable.
15. Enter your name, course, laboratory assignment number (LAB2-3), date, and instructor name below the entries in column A in separate but adjacent cells.
16. Save the workbook using the filename Annies Antiques.
17. Print the worksheet in landscape orientation. Print the range A3:C9 in portrait orientation.
18. Press CTRL+` to change the display from values to formulas, and then print to fit on one page in landscape orientation. After the printer is finished, reset the worksheet to display values by pressing CTRL+`. Reset the Scaling option to 100% by clicking Adjust to on the Page sheet in the Page Setup dialog box and setting the percent value to 100%.

Instructions Part 2: Draw the pie chart showing the contribution of each customer to the total new balance as shown in Figure 2-97. Select the nonadjacent chart ranges B4:B8 and H4:H8. The range B4:B8 will identify the slices while the range H4:H8 will determine the size of the slices. Use the Chart command on the Insert menu to create a chart on a new sheet. Draw a 3-D pie chart with a format 7 (Figure 2-97). Notice the following about the chart: (a) the Data Series for this pie chart is in columns; (b) there is no legend on the chart; and (c) the chart does have a title of Contributions to Accounts Receivable. The chart title has a light brown background and 28-point bold red font. Change the font of the data labels to 16-point bold blue, font. Change the colors of the slices to those shown in Figure 2-97. Explode the slice representing the greatest contribution. Use the 3-D View command on the shortcut menu to change the rotation to 290^0 and the elevation to 40^0. Rename the Chart1 tab Pie Chart. Rearrange the order of the sheet tabs so the worksheet appears first with the chart following it. Save the workbook using the same filename as in Part 1. Print the chart.

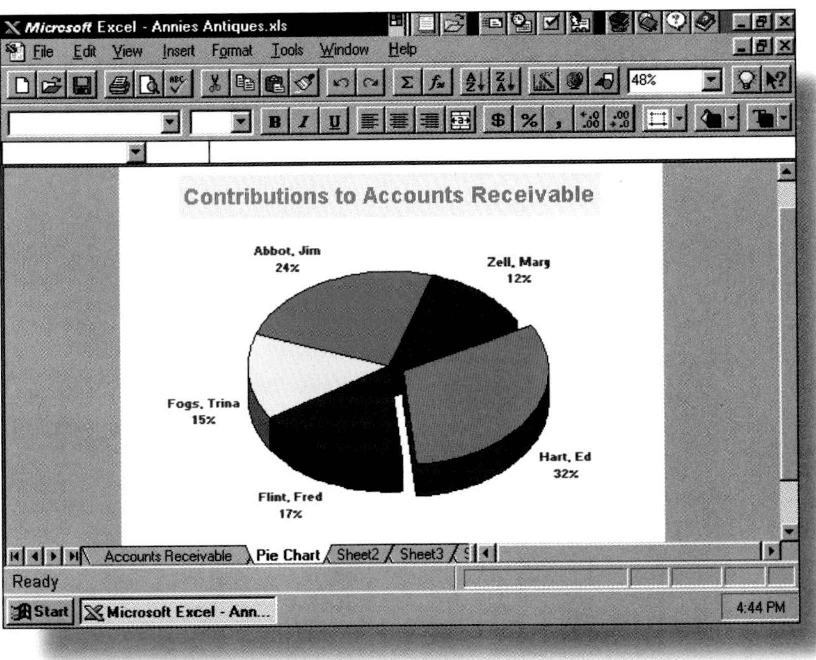

FIGURE 2-97

200 MHz

Cases and Places

The difficulty of these case studies varies:

◗ Case studies preceded by a single half moon are the least difficult. You are asked to create the required worksheet based on information that has already been placed in an organized form.

◗◗ Case studies preceded by two half moons are more difficult. You must organize the information presented before using it to create the desired worksheet.

◗◗◗ Case studies preceded by three half moons are the most difficult. You must choose a specific topic, and then obtain and organize the necessary information before using it to create the required worksheet.

1 ◗ Several naturalists are conducting a study of the interrelationships among five animal species on an island. The naturalists trapped animals, determined their ages, tagged the animals, and released them. Later, a second collection of animals was caught and the number of tagged animals was counted. The naturalists then tabulated their data. (Figure 2-98).

Otter Creek Island Wildlife Survey

Animal	First Catch	Animals over Median Age	Second Catch	Tagged Animals in Second Catch
Moose	32	18	25	4
Deer	326	146	95	24
Fox	148	42	114	21
Wolf	26	7	18	5
Otter	406	142	146	38

FIGURE 2-98

With these facts, you have been asked to prepare a work sheet for the naturalists that determines an estimated population for each species, the estimated number of older animals in each species, and the percentage of older animals in each species. The following formulas can be used to obtain this information:

Estimated Population = (First Catch x Second Catch) ÷ Tagged Animals

Estimated Older Animals = (Animals over Median Age ÷ First Catch) x Estimated Population

Percentage Older Animals = Estimated Older Animals ÷ Estimated Total Population

Include a total, maximum value, and minimum value for Estimated Populations and Estimated Older Animals. On a separate sheet, create an appropriate chart comparing the Estimated Populations. Use the concepts and techniques presented in this project to create and format the worksheet and chart.

Cases and Places

200 MHz

2 ◗ The Student Aid Committee at Hoover College offers short-term loans at simple interest. Loans are provided in five categories (tuition assistance, academic supplies, room and board, personal emergency, and travel expenses), for varying lengths of time and diverse rates of interest. At the end of the semester, the Student Aid Committee summarized their loan activity (Figure 2-99).

Hoover College Student Loans

Loan Type	Principal	Rate	Time (Years)
Tuition Assistance	$48,000.00	10%	0.33
Academic Supplies	$16,000.00	12%	0.25
Room and Board	$26,500.00	15%	0.33
Personal Emergency	$5,500.00	8%	0.17
Travel Expenses	$4,000.00	17%	0.17

FIGURE 2-99

With this data, the committee has asked you to develop a worksheet they can use at their next meeting. The worksheet should determine the interest accrued, amount due, and percentage of the total budget used for each loan type. The following formulas can be applied to obtain this information:

Interest = Principal x Rate x Time

Amount Due = Principal + Interest

Percentage of Budget = Principal ÷ Total Principal

Include a total, maximum value, and minimum value for Principal, Interest, and Amount Due. On a separate sheet, create an appropriate chart that shows the portion of the total principal each loan type uses. Use the concepts and techniques presented in this project to create and format the worksheet and chart.

3 ◗ Newton Elementary School selects students for its gifted program based on teacher recommendations and IQ (intelligence quotient) scores. The IQ scores are ascertained using the formula

$$IQ = \frac{100m}{c}$$

where *m* represents mental age (determined by a standardized test) and *c* represents chronological age. This year, eight third-graders were tested for the program. The test results were: Banks, F. (mental age 9.8, chronological age 8.2); Danko, M. (mental age 9.6, chronological age 7.8); Frieze, B. (mental age 10.0, chronological age 8.4); Hunt, N. (mental age 11.8, chronological age 8.8); Jewls, B. (mental age 11.4, chronological age 8.2); Lawson, I. (mental age 10.2, chronological age 8.6); Meyers, N. (mental age 12.4, chronological age 9.0); and Podarski, P. (mental age 11.4, chronological age 8.1). Using these figures, you have been asked to create a worksheet for the selection committee's next meeting. The worksheet should show mental age, chronological age, and IQ for each child. Include the average, maximum, and minimum for each value. On a separate sheet, make an appropriate chart illustrating every student's IQ. Use the concepts and techniques presented in this project to create and format the worksheet and chart.

Cases and Places

4 ▶▶ Driving the Back Roads is a small company that rents a fleet of six vintage cars: a 1906 Packard "S 24" Victoria, a 1907 S & M Simplex Limousine, a 1908 Pierce Great Arrow Touring Car, a 1908 Stanley Roadster, a 1911 Mercer Raceabout, and a 1915 Locomobile Town Coupe. The charge for renting a car is determined by the formula $c = 1000d + 8.5m$, where c is the rental charge, d is the number of days the car is rented, and m is the number of miles the car is driven. Over the past month, the Packard was rented for 13 days and driven 120.4 miles, the Simplex was rented for 16 days and driven 150.8 miles, the Pierce Arrow was rented for 14 days and driven 224.6 miles, the Stanley was rented for 15 days and driven 90.6 miles, the Mercer was rented for 24 days and driven 408.6 miles, and the Locomobile was rented for 18 days and driven 262.6 miles. Using these figures, Driving the Back Roads has asked you to create a worksheet for its monthly meeting showing the number of days each car was rented, the miles each car was driven, the net proceeds from each car, and the percentage of the company's total net proceeds each car represents. Include totals, averages, maximum, and minimum where appropriate. On a separate sheet, make a suitable chart comparing the income from each car.

5 ▶▶▶ Realtors often use a formula to determine how much money prospective buyers can afford to spend on a house. Visit a real estate office to learn how agents analyze the financial status of their clients. With their formulas and estimates of your future income, create a worksheet showing how expensive a house you could manage to buy today and five, ten, fifteen, twenty, and twenty-five years from now. Assuming you purchase a house for the amount indicated by the realtor's formula and make a down payment of 10%, ascertain the amount of money you would have to put down for each house and the amount of money you would have to borrow.

6 ▶▶▶ Veterinarians sometimes use formulas to vary the amount of medicine they prescribe based on factors such as an animal's weight or age. Visit a veterinarian's office and learn the formulas used in prescribing at least two different medications. With these formulas and the relevant information from eight animals (your pets or the pets of friends), prepare a worksheet showing how much medication each animal could be given. Where appropriate, show average, maximum, and minimum values. Include a chart illustrating how the amount of medication varies based on a relevant factor, and a formulas version of the worksheet.

7 ▶▶▶ Retailers occasionally use formulas to determine the selling price of an item based on that item's wholesale cost. Visit a store and find out any formulas that are used to price items. Ask to see a list of the wholesale costs and determine the cost of a at least six individual items that are priced on the basis of the formula you are given. With this information, prepare a worksheet showing each item's wholesale cost, retail price, and the retailer's profit. Find the retail price and retailer's profit if the items were put on sale at a 10% discount. Show totals, averages, maximums, and minimums. Include a chart illustrating what part of the profit is represented by each item when all six items are sold.

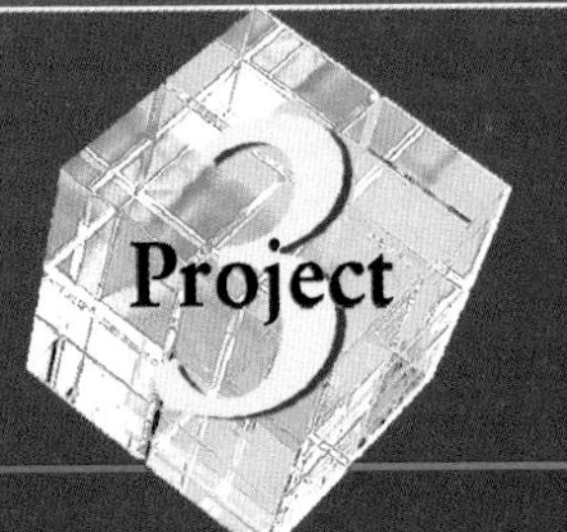

Microsoft Excel 7

Windows 95

What-If Analysis and Working with Large Worksheets

Objectives:

You will have mastered the material in this project when you can:

- Use the fill handle to create a series of month names
- Copy a cell's format to another cell using the Format Painter button
- Copy a range of cells to a nonadjacent paste area
- Freeze the column and row titles
- Insert and delete cells
- Format numbers by entering them with a format symbol
- Display the system date using the NOW function and format it
- Use the IF function to enter one value or another in a cell on the basis of a logical test
- Copy absolute cell references
- Italicize text
- Add a drop shadow to a range of cells
- Display and dock toolbars
- Create a 3-D column chart on a separate sheet
- Format the 3-D column chart
- Use the Zoom Control box to change the appearance of the worksheet
- View different parts of the worksheet through window panes
- Use Excel to answer what-if questions
- Analyze worksheet data by using the Goal Seek command

Could You Spend $1 Trillion in Your Lifetime?

Can you imagine spending a trillion dollars; that is, ten times $100 billion? It is hard even to imagine what a trillion dollars is. If you were given a trillion $1 bills, just counting them would take you 32,000 years at a rate of one per second, twenty-four hours a day. You would break several records if you accomplished that feat.

The world is still waiting for its first trillionaire – speculated to be Asia's Richard Li, 27, or Brunei's Sultan Hassanal Bolkiah, 48. The current U.S. national debt, however, exceeds 5 trillion dollars ($5,000,000,000,000) with projected annual interest payments of $235 billion. Italy, Japan, and Australia also face debts in trillions of dollars. It is no wonder that financial counselors encourage sound fiscal control and budgeting to avoid deficit spending or debt. People who borrow are expected both to be able and willing to pay back what they owe along with an appropriate amount of interest. When working with any sum of money – whether an individual's thousands, the more than 125 American billionaires' billions, or even the nation's trillions – creating a realistic budget indeed can be difficult. Budgets provide a sense of perspective that makes it possible to

keep debt at a minimum. Although you are not responsible for preparing a national $1.64 trillion budget, knowing where your money goes is the first step in planning a sound personal budget.

Personal budgeting helps reconcile income and expenses. For instance, based on a loan calculation and budget, you could determine the Ferrari F50 you wanted to buy is out of the question. A monthly payment of $10,231.91 is just too high. The Toyota Celica, however, with a monthly payment of $570.33 is manageable. Now for the rest of your personal expenses. As a recent college graduate with a master's degree, your first job grosses $31,000 annually. Personal expenses to consider include: utilities, insurances, living expenses (such as housing, loans, transportation costs, groceries, and so on), car payments, entertainment, and credit card payments. A personal budget can help you determine if you are able to buy the condo you want on your yearly salary, and if so, how much you should borrow and realistically can afford to repay. Personal budgets track your income, expenses, net worth, and cash flow changes while organizing and analyzing your financial data in a logical format.

Electronic spreadsheet software can ease your calculations and show exactly how your money is being spent. Based on your input, a budget summary (indicating both surplus/(shortfall) and with/without contingencies) and a budget graph can be generated automatically. You can pose what-if questions to speculate on the results of budget changes or goal seek to determine what to eliminate or cut back to arrive at a month-end surplus with contingencies.

Just as the nation must examine line by line how its money is spent, personal budget calculations allow you to do the same. Initially, living within a budget may appear restrictive but it can provide a sound perspective on your fiscal management and goals. The alternative — you could easily exceed the average debt-to-asset ratio of 30 percent and end up joining the world's trillionaire debt club.

Personal Expenses

Microsoft
Excel 7
Windows 95

What-If Analysis and Working with Large Worksheets

Case Perspective

Each day millions of people connect to the World Wide Web using providers that charge a small monthly access fee. Information Mining is the premier provider in the Midwest. Each January and July, the chief financial officer (CFO), Marissa Gold, submits a report to the board of directors, titled Six-Month Projected Net Sales, Expenses, and Net Income.

In the past, Marissa manually completed the report and drew a column chart comparing projected monthly net income. When she presented her last report, several directors wanted to know the effect on the net income if the expense percent allocations were changed slightly.

While the directors waited impatiently, it took an embarrassed Marissa several minutes to calculate the answers. Marissa knew the next time she presented the semi-annual projections, she would have to use a PC and an electronic worksheet to address the what-if questions. As lead worksheet specialist for Information Mining, you are to meet with Marissa, determine her needs, and create the worksheet and chart.

Introduction

This project introduces you to techniques that will enhance your capabilities to create worksheets and draw charts. You will learn about other methods for entering values in cells and formatting them. You also will learn how to use absolute cell references and how to use the IF function to assign one value or another to a cell based on a logic test.

In the previous projects, you learned how to use the Standard and Formatting toolbars. Excel has several other toolbars that can make your work easier. One such toolbar is the **Drawing toolbar**, which allows you to draw shapes, arrows, and drop shadows around cells you want to emphasize in the worksheet.

Worksheets normally are much larger than those created in the previous projects. Worksheets that extend beyond the size of the window present a viewing problem because you cannot see the entire worksheet at one time. For this reason, Excel provides several commands that allow you to rearrange the view on the screen to display critical parts of a large worksheet. These commands allow you to maintain the row and column titles on the screen at all times by freezing the titles so they always display and to view different parts of a spreadsheet through window panes.

From your work in Projects 1 and 2, you are aware of how easily charts are created. This project continues to develop new charting techniques that allow you to convey your message in a dramatic pictorial fashion.

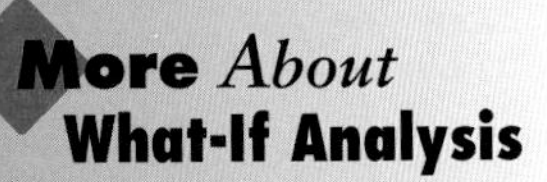

The ability of Excel to instantaneously answer what-if questions is the single most important reason why millions of business people use this software. Just a few short years ago, what-if questions of any complexity could only be answered by large expensive computers programmed by highly-paid computer professionals. And then you might have to wait days for the turnaround. Excel and its equivalents give the non-computer professional the capability of getting complex business-related questions answered quickly and economically.

When you set up a worksheet, you should use as many cell references in formulas as possible, rather than constant values. The cell references in a formula often are called assumptions. **Assumptions** are cells whose values you can change to determine new values for formulas. This project emphasizes the use of assumptions and introduces you to answering what-if questions such as, What if you decrease the advertising expenses assumption (cell B16 in Figure 3-1a) by 1% — how would the decrease affect the projected six-month net income (cell H13 in Figure 3-1a)? This capability of quickly analyzing the effect of changing values in a worksheet is important in making business decisions.

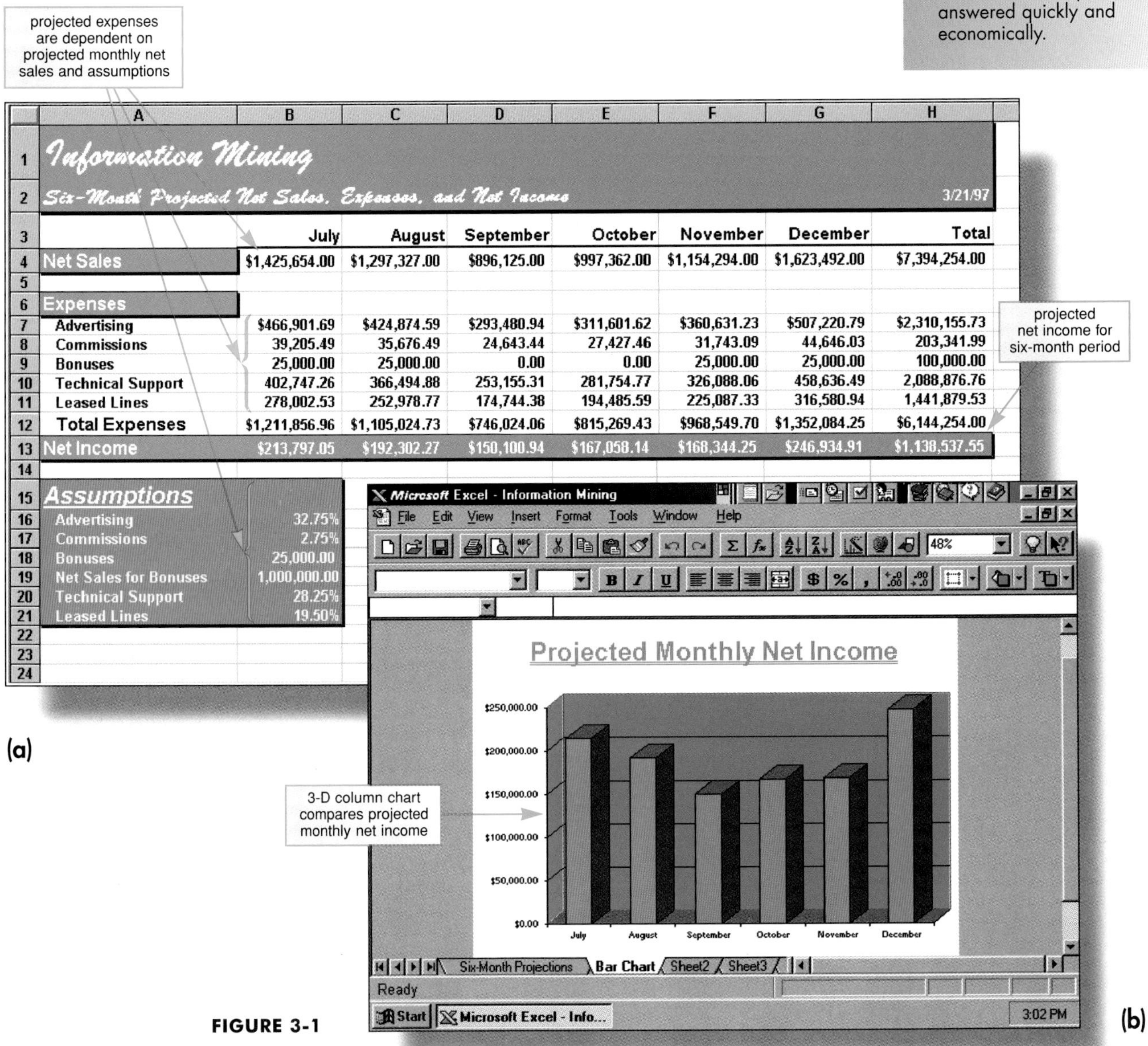

projected expenses are dependent on projected monthly net sales and assumptions

	A	B	C	D	E	F	G	H
1	Information Mining							
2	Six-Month Projected Net Sales, Expenses, and Net Income							3/21/97
3		July	August	September	October	November	December	Total
4	Net Sales	$1,425,654.00	$1,297,327.00	$896,125.00	$997,362.00	$1,154,294.00	$1,623,492.00	$7,394,254.00
5								
6	Expenses							
7	Advertising	$466,901.69	$424,874.59	$293,480.94	$311,601.62	$360,631.23	$507,220.79	$2,310,155.73
8	Commissions	39,205.49	35,676.49	24,643.44	27,427.46	31,743.09	44,646.03	203,341.99
9	Bonuses	25,000.00	25,000.00	0.00	0.00	25,000.00	25,000.00	100,000.00
10	Technical Support	402,747.26	366,494.88	253,155.31	281,754.77	326,088.06	458,636.49	2,088,876.76
11	Leased Lines	278,002.53	252,978.77	174,744.38	194,485.59	225,087.33	316,580.94	1,441,879.53
12	Total Expenses	$1,211,856.96	$1,105,024.73	$746,024.06	$815,269.43	$968,549.70	$1,352,084.25	$6,144,254.00
13	Net Income	$213,797.05	$192,302.27	$150,100.94	$167,058.14	$168,344.25	$246,934.91	$1,138,537.55
14								
15	Assumptions							
16	Advertising	32.75%						
17	Commissions	2.75%						
18	Bonuses	25,000.00						
19	Net Sales for Bonuses	1,000,000.00						
20	Technical Support	28.25%						
21	Leased Lines	19.50%						

projected net income for six-month period

(a)

Microsoft Excel - Information Mining

Projected Monthly Net Income

$250,000.00
$200,000.00
$150,000.00
$100,000.00
$50,000.00
$0.00

July August September October November December

3-D column chart compares projected monthly net income

Six-Month Projections | Bar Chart | Sheet2 | Sheet3

Ready

Start | Microsoft Excel - Info... | 3:02 PM

(b)

FIGURE 3-1

Project Three – Information Mining Six-Month Projected Net Sales, Expenses, and Net Income

Studies have shown that over 25% of all business worksheets have errors. You can ensure correctness by using the Auditing command on the Tools menu. The Auditing command indicates relationships among formulas.

You took the following notes regarding the required worksheet and chart in your meeting with the CFO, Marissa Gold.

Need: A worksheet (Figure 3-1a) and 3-D column chart (Figure 3-1b) are required. The worksheet is to show Information Mining's projected monthly net sales, expenses, and net income for a six-month period. The 3-D column chart is to compare the projected monthly net incomes.

Source of Data: The projected monthly net sales (row 4 of Figure 3-1a) and the six assumptions (range A15:B21) that are used to determine the projected monthly expenses are available from the CFO.

Calculations: Each of the projected monthly expenses in the range B7:G11 of Figure 3-1a — advertising, commissions, bonuses, technical support, and leased lines — is determined by taking a percentage of the corresponding projected monthly net sales in row 4. The assumptions in the range A15:B21 are as follows:

1. The projected monthly advertising expenses are 32.75% of the projected net sales.
2. The projected monthly commissions are 2.75% of the projected net sales.
3. The projected monthly bonuses are $25,000.00 if the projected monthly net sales exceeds the net sales for bonus in cell B19 ($1,000,000.00).
4. The projected monthly technical support expenses are 28.25% of the projected sales.
5. The projected monthly leased lines expenses are 19.50% of the projected sales.

The projected total expenses for each month in row 12 of Figure 3-1a are the sum of the corresponding projected monthly expenses in rows 7 through 11. The projected monthly net income in row 13 is equal to the corresponding projected monthly net sales minus the projected monthly total expenses.

Because the projected expenses in rows 7 through 11 are dependent on the assumptions in the range A15:B21 of Figure 3-1a, you can use the what-if capability of Excel to determine the impact of changing these percent expenses on the projected monthly total expenses in row 12.

Graph Requirements: A 3-D column chart on a separate sheet (Figure 3-1b) that compares the contribution of each month to the projected net income for the six-month period.

Preparation Steps

The following tasks will be completed in this project to create the worksheet and chart shown in Figure 3-1a and b.

1. Start the Excel program.
2. Bold all cells in the worksheet.
3. Enter the worksheet titles, column titles, and row titles. Increase the column widths.
4. Save the workbook.
5. Enter the assumptions in the range B16:B21.
6. Enter the projected net sales for each of the six months in row 4.
7. Display the system date in cell H2.

8. Enter the formulas that determine the monthly projected expenses and monthly projected net income in the range B7:G13. Determine the totals in column H.
9. Format the worksheet so it appears as shown in Figure 3-1a on page E 3.5.
10. Create the 3-D column chart that compares the monthly net incomes using the nonadjacent selection of ranges B3:G3 and B13:G13.
11. Format the 3-D column chart.
12. Check spelling, preview, print, and save the workbook.
13. Use the Zoom Control box on the Standard toolbar to change the appearance of the worksheet.
14. Divide the window into panes.
15. Analyze the data in the worksheet by changing the assumptions in the range A15:B21 and by goal seeking.

The following sections contain a detailed explanation of each of these steps.

Starting Excel

To start Excel, Windows 95 must be running. Perform the following steps to start Excel.

More *About* **Readability**

Bolding the entire worksheet makes it easier for people with less than average eyesight to read the worksheet. An alternative is to increase the font size of the entire worksheet from 10-point to 12- or 14-point.

TO START EXCEL

Step 1: Click the Start button on the taskbar.
Step 2: Click New Office Document. If necessary, click the General tab in the New dialog box.
Step 3: Double-click the Blank Workbook icon.

An alternative to Steps 1 and 2 is to click the Start a New Document button on the Microsoft Office Shortcut Bar.

Changing the Font of the Entire Worksheet to Bold

The first step is to change the font of the entire worksheet to bold so all entries are emphasized.

TO CHANGE THE FONT OF THE ENTIRE WORKSHEET TO BOLD

Step 1: Click the Select All button immediately above row heading 1 and to the left of column heading A.
Step 2: Click the Bold button on the Standard toolbar.

No immediate change takes place on the screen. As you enter text and numbers into the worksheet, however, Excel will display them in bold.

Entering the Worksheet Titles

The worksheet contains two titles, one in cell A1 and another in cell A2. In the previous projects, the titles were centered over the worksheet. With large worksheets that extend beyond the width of a window, it is best to display them in the upper left corner as shown in Figure 3-1a.

TO ENTER THE WORKSHEET TITLES

Step 1: Select cell A1 and type `Information Mining` to enter the title.
Step 2: Select cell A2 and type `Six-Month Projected Net Sales, Expenses, and Net Income` to enter the second title.
Step 3: Select cell B3.

Excel responds by displaying the worksheet titles in cells A1 and A2 in bold (Figure 3-2).

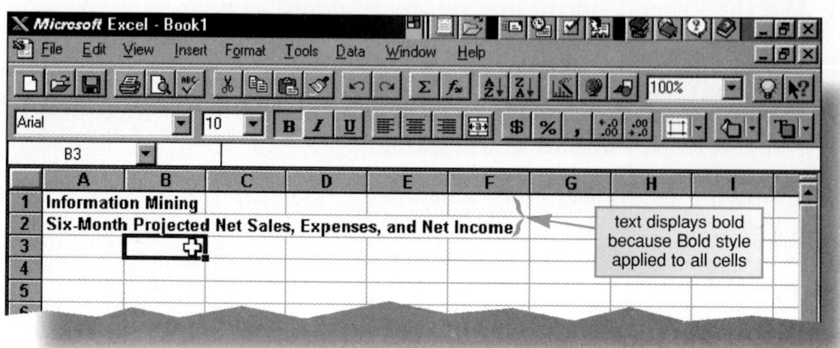

FIGURE 3-2

Using the Fill Handle to Create a Series

In Projects 1 and 2, you used the fill handle to copy a cell or a range of cells to adjacent cells. You can also use the fill handle to create a series of numbers, dates, or month names automatically. Perform the following steps to enter the month name July in cell B3, format cell B3, and then using the fill handle, create the remaining five month names August, September, October, November, and December in the range C3:G3 (see Figure 3-5).

Steps To Use the Fill Handle to Create a Series of Month Names

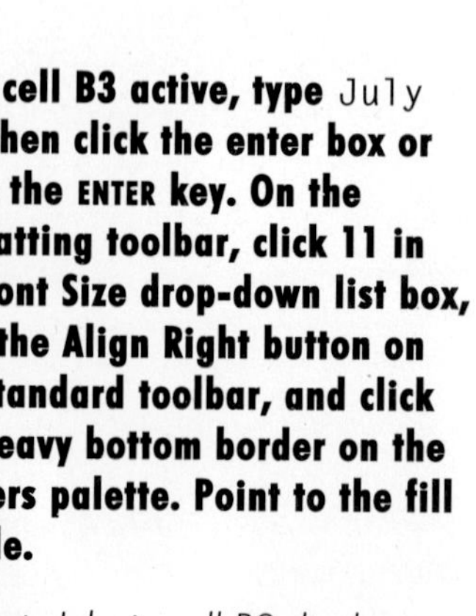

1 With cell B3 active, type `July` and then click the enter box or press the ENTER key. On the Formatting toolbar, click 11 in the Font Size drop-down list box, click the Align Right button on the Standard toolbar, and click the heavy bottom border on the Borders palette. Point to the fill handle.

The text, July, in cell B3 displays using the assigned formats (Figure 3-3). The mouse pointer changes to a cross hair when positioned on the fill handle.

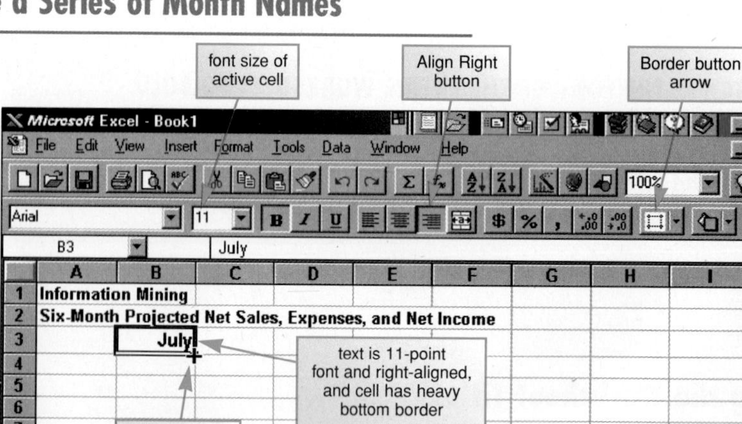

FIGURE 3-3

2 Drag the fill handle to the right to select the range C3:G3.

Excel displays a light border that surrounds the range selected (Figure 3-4).

FIGURE 3-4

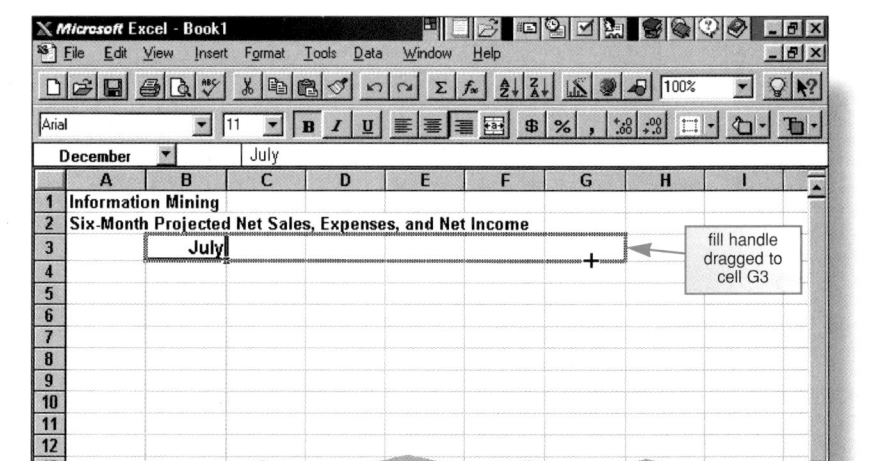

3 Release the left mouse button.

Using July in cell B3 as the basis, Excel creates the month name series August through December in the range C3:G3 (Figure 3-5). The formats assigned earlier to cell B3 (11-point font, right-aligned, and heavy bottom border) in Step 1 are copied to the range C3:G3.

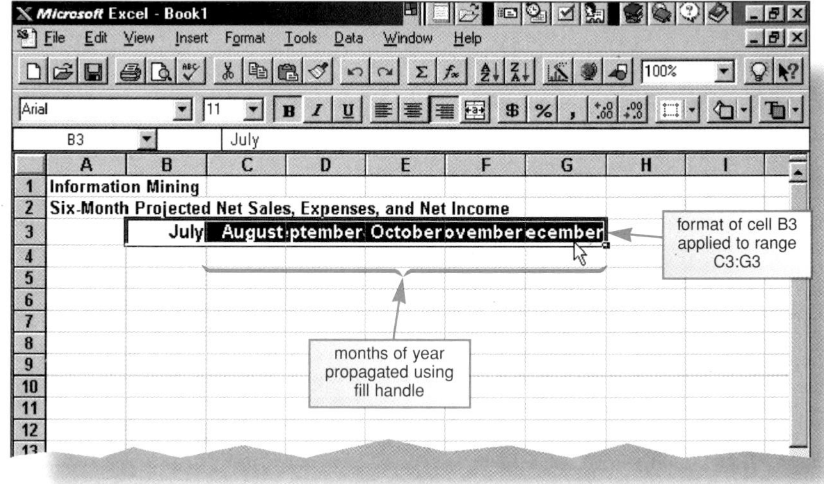

FIGURE 3-5

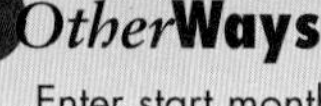

OtherWays

1. Enter start month in cell, right-drag fill handle in the direction you want to fill, click Fill Months on shortcut menu

Besides creating a series of values, the fill handle also copies the format of cell B3 (11-point font, right-aligned, and a heavy bottom border) to the range C3:G3. If you drag the fill handle past cell G3 in Step 2 to June, Excel continues to increment the months and will logically repeat July, August, and so on.

You can create different types of series using the fill handle. Table 3-1 on the next page illustrates several examples. Notice in Examples 4 through 7 in Table 3-1 that if you use the fill handle to create a series of numbers or non-sequential months, you are required to enter the first number in the series in one cell and the second number in the series in an adjacent cell. You then select both cells and drag the fill handle across the paste area.

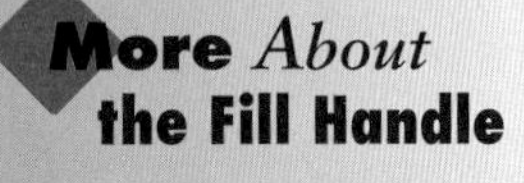

More About the Fill Handle

The fill handle is one of the most popular and impressive tools available with Excel. Use it to copy or to create a data series. To use it to copy a potential series initiator, like the word January, to a paste area, hold down the CTRL key while you drag. You can also establish a custom series by dragging the fill handle with the right mouse button. If you create the wrong series, choose the Undo button on the Standard toolbar or the Undo command on the Edit menu.

Table 3-1

EXAMPLE	CONTENTS OF CELL(S) COPIED USING THE FILL HANDLE	NEXT THREE VALUES OF EXTENDED SERIES
1	6:00	7:00, 8:00, 9:00
2	Qtr3	Qtr4, Qtr1, Qtr2
3	Quarter 1	Quarter 2, Quarter 3, Quarter 4
4	Jul-97, Oct-97	Jan-98, Apr-98, Jul-98
5	1999, 2000	2001, 2002, 2003
6	1, 2	3, 4, 5
7	200, 195	190, 185, 180
8	Sun	Mon, Tue, Wed
9	Tuesday	Wednesday, Thursday, Friday
10	1st Part	2nd Part, 3rd Part, 4th Part
11	-1, -3	-5, -7, -9

Copying a Cell's Format Using the Format Painter Button

Because it is not part of the series, the last column title, Total, in cell H3 must be entered separately. Furthermore, to ensure that it appears the same as the other column titles, the same formats as the months (11-point font, right-aligned, and a heavy bottom border) must be applied to cell H3. The **Format Painter button** on the Standard toolbar allows you to copy a cell's format to another cell. The following steps enter the column title, Total, in cell H3 and format the cell using the Format Painter button.

Steps To Copy a Cell's Format Using the Format Painter Button

1. **Select cell H3. Type** `Total` **and then press the LEFT ARROW key.**

2. **With cell G3 selected, click the Format Painter button on the Standard toolbar. Move the mouse pointer over cell H3.**

   The mouse pointer changes to a block plus sign with a paint brush (Figure 3-6).

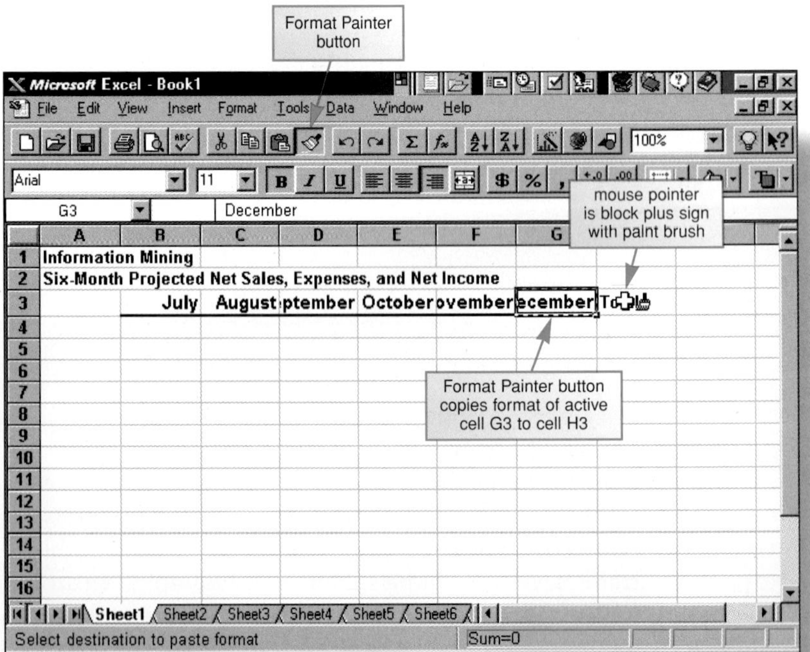

FIGURE 3-6

3 Click cell H3 to assign the format of cell G3 to cell H3. Click cell A4.

Cell H3 is assigned the same format (11-point font, right-aligned, and a heavy bottom border) as cell G3 (Figure 3-7).

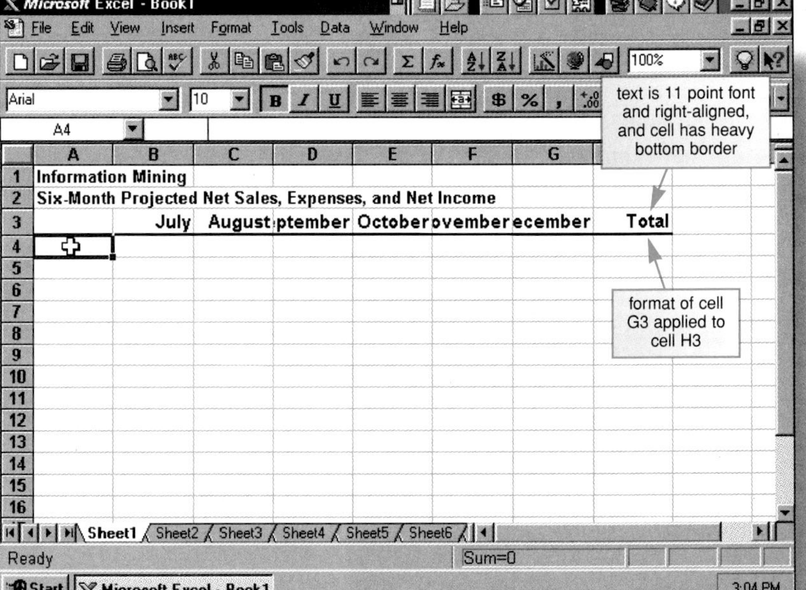

FIGURE 3-7

OtherWays

1. Click Copy button, select paste area, on Edit menu click Paste Special, click Formats, click OK button

The Format Painter button can also be used to copy the formats of a cell to a range or to copy a range to another range. To copy formats to a range of cells, select the cell or range to copy from, click the Format Painter button, and then drag through the range to which you want to paste the formats.

More *About* the Format Painter Button

Double-click, rather than click, the Format Painter button to copy the formats to non-adjacent ranges. After double-clicking, one-by-one, drag through the ranges. Finally, click the Format Painter button to deactivate it.

Increasing the Column Widths and Entering Row Titles

In Project 2, the column widths were increased after the values were entered into the worksheet. Sometimes, you may want to increase the column widths before you enter the values and then, if necessary, adjust them later. The following steps increase the column widths and add the row titles in column A down to Assumptions in cell A15.

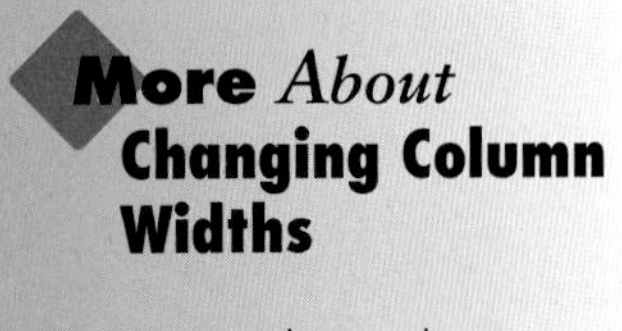

More *About* Changing Column Widths

You can use the CTRL key to select nonadjacent columns before increasing the column width or assigning a common format.

To Increase Column Widths and Enter Row Titles

1 **Move the mouse pointer to the border between column heading A and column heading B so the pointer changes to a split double arrow. Drag the mouse pointer to the right until the width displayed in the Name box on the left side of the formula bar equals 25.00.**

The distance between the left edge of column A and the vertical dotted line below the mouse pointer shows the proposed column width, and 25.00 displays in the Name box (Figure 3-8).

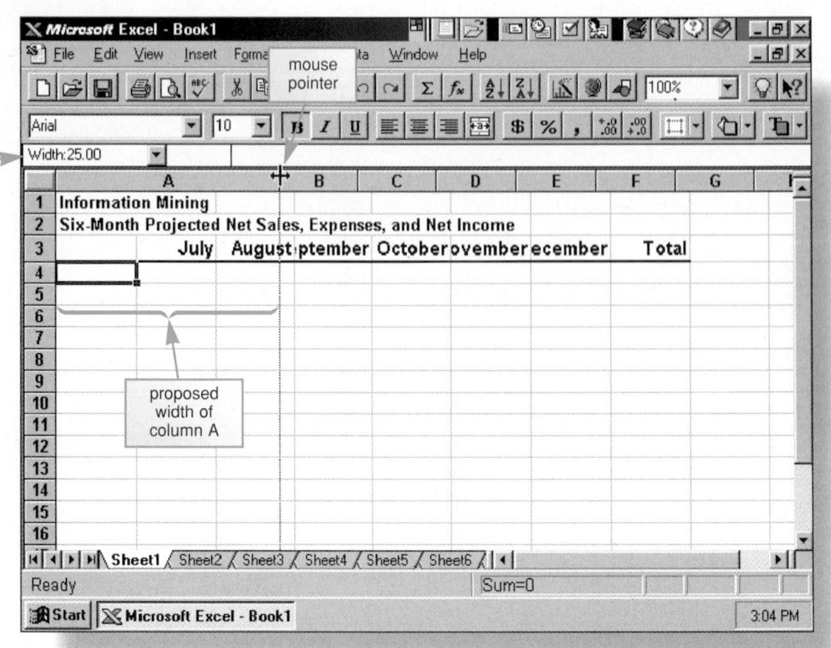

FIGURE 3-8

Release the left mouse button. Select columns B through G by pointing to column heading B and dragging though column heading G. Move the mouse pointer to the borderline between column headings B and C and drag the mouse to the right until the width displayed in the Name box is 13.00.

The distance between the left edge of column B and the vertical line below the mouse pointer shows the proposed column width of columns B through G, and 13.00 displays in the Name box (Figure 3-9).

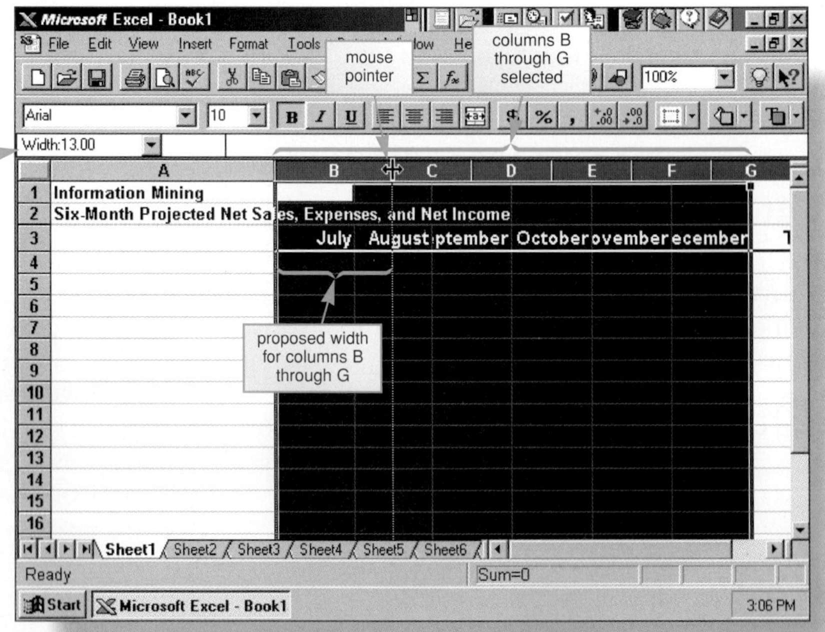

FIGURE 3-9

3 **Release the left mouse button. Use the same technique described in Step 1 to increase the width of column H to 15.00.**

4 **Enter** Net Sales **in cell A4,** Expenses **in cell A6,** bbbAdvertising **in cell A7 (where bbb represents three spaces), and** bbbCommissions **in cell A8. Enter** bbbBonuses **in cell A9,** bbbTechnical Support **in cell A10,** bbbLeased Lines **in cell A11,** bbbTotal Expenses **in cell A12,** Net Income **in cell A13, and** Assumptions **in cell A15 as shown in Figure 3-10.**

The row titles display as shown in Figure 3-10.

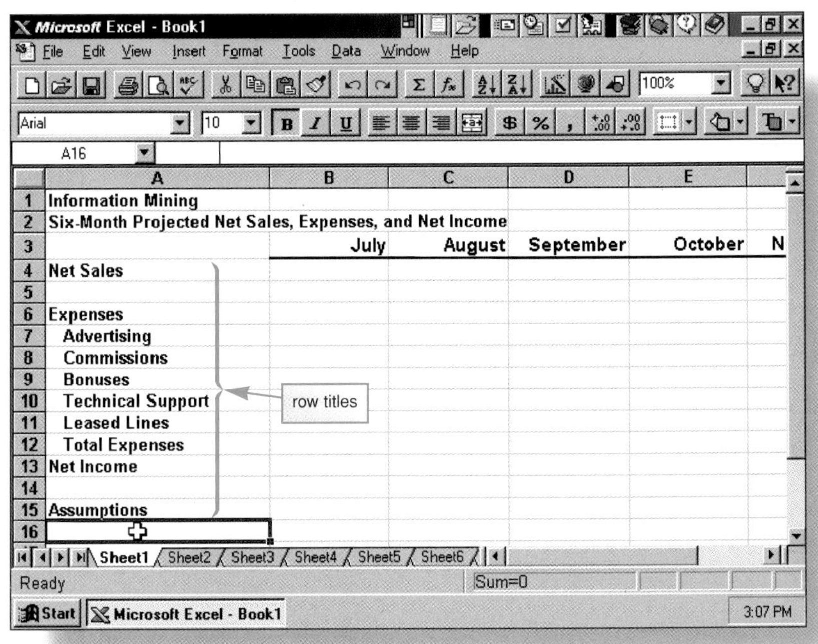

FIGURE 3-10

Copying a Range of Cells to a Nonadjacent Paste Area

According to Figure 3-1a on page E 3.5, the row titles in the Assumptions table in the range A16:A21 are the same as the row titles in the range A7:A11, except for the additional entry in cell A19. Hence, the range A7:A11 can be copied to the range A16:A20 and the additional entry in cell A19 can be inserted. Notice that the range to copy (range A7:A11) is not adjacent to the paste area (range A16:A20). In the first two projects, the fill handle worked well for copying a range of cells to an adjacent paste area, but you cannot use the fill handle to copy a range of cells to a nonadjacent paste area.

A more versatile method of copying a cell or range of cells is to use the Copy button and Paste button on the Standard toolbar. You can use these two buttons to copy a range of cells to an adjacent or nonadjacent paste area.

When you click the **Copy button**, it copies the contents and format of the selected range and places the entries on the Clipboard, replacing the Clipboard's contents. The **Copy command** on the Edit menu or shortcut menu works the same as the Copy button.

The **Paste button** copies the contents of the Clipboard to the paste area. The Paste command on the Edit menu or shortcut menu works the same as the Paste button. Use the Paste button when you are copying to more than one cell or range. Complete a single paste by pressing the ENTER key.

More *About* **Copying**

If you have a range of cells in another workbook that you want to copy into the current workbook, open the source workbook, select the range, and then click the Copy button to place the range of cells on the Clipboard. Next, activate the destination workbook by clicking its filename on the Window menu. Finally, select the paste area and press ENTER.

To Copy a Range of Cells to a Nonadjacent Paste Area

1 Select the range A7:A11 and click the Copy button on the Standard toolbar. Scroll down until row 20 is visible and then click cell A16, the top cell of the paste area.

Excel surrounds the range A7:A11 with a marquee when you click the Copy button (Figure 3-11). Excel also copies the values and formats of the range A7:A11 onto the Clipboard.

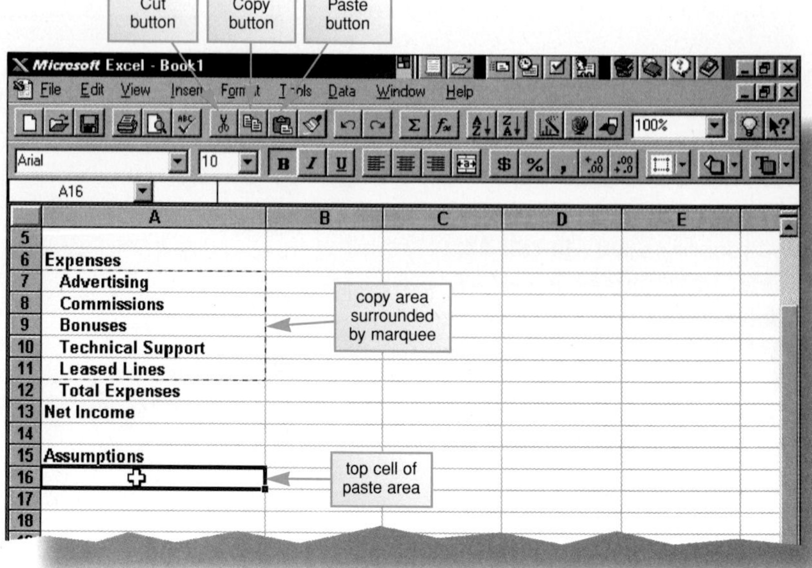

FIGURE 3-11

2 Press the ENTER key to complete the copy.

Excel copies the contents of the Clipboard (range A7:A11) to the paste area A16:A20 (Figure 3-12).

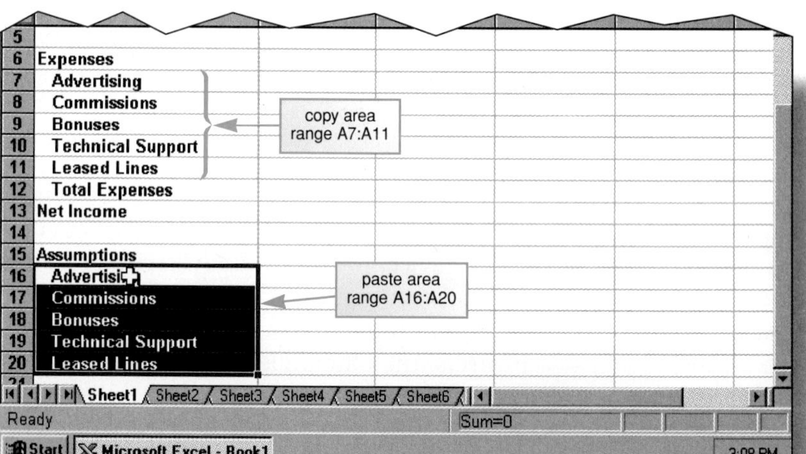

FIGURE 3-12

OtherWays

1. Select copy area, while holding down CTRL key, drag copy area to paste area
2. Right-click copy area, click Copy on shortcut menu, right-click paste area, click Paste on shortcut menu
3. Select copy area, click Copy button on Standard toolbar, select paste area, click Paste button on Standard toolbar to paste, press ESC
4. Select copy area, on Edit menu click Copy, select paste area, on Edit menu click Paste
5. Select copy area, press CTRL+C, select paste area, press CTRL+V

In Step 1 and Figure 3-11, you can see that you are not required to highlight the entire paste area (range A16:A20) before pressing the ENTER key to complete the copy. Because the paste area is exactly the same size as the range you are copying, you need only select the top left cell of the paste area. In the case of a single column range such as A16:A20, the top cell of the paste area (cell A16) is the upper left cell of the paste area.

When you complete a copy, the values and formats in the paste area are replaced with the values and formats on the Clipboard. Any data contained in the paste area prior to the copy and paste is lost. If you accidentally delete valuable data, immediately click the Undo button on the Standard toolbar or click the **Undo Paste command** on the Edit menu to undo the paste.

When you use the ENTER key to paste, the contents on the Clipboard are erased after the copy is complete. When you paste using the Paste button or Paste command on the Edit menu or shortcut menu, the contents of the Clipboard remain available for additional copying. Thus, if you plan to copy the cells to more than one paste area, click the Paste button or click Paste on the Edit menu or shortcut menu instead of pressing the ENTER key. Then, select the next paste area and invoke the Paste command again. If you paste using the Paste button or the Paste command from the Edit menu or shortcut menu, the marquee remains around the range to copy to remind you that the copied range is still on the Clipboard. To erase the marquee, press the ESC key.

More *About* **Moving Cells versus Copying Cells**

You may hear someone say, "move it or copy it , its all the same." No, its not the same! When you move cells, the original location is blanked and the format is reset to the default. When you copy cells, the copy area remains intact. In short, copy cells to duplicate and move cells to rearrange.

Using Drag and Drop to Move or Copy Cells

You can use the mouse to move or copy cells. First, you select the copy area and point to the border of the range. You know you are pointing to the border of a range when the mouse pointer changes to a block arrow. To move the selected cells, drag the selection to its new location. To copy a range, hold down the CTRL key while dragging. Then release the mouse button before you release the CTRL key. Using the mouse to move or copy cells is called **drag and drop.**

Another way to move cells is to select them, click the Cut button on the Standard toolbar (Figure 3.11), select the new area, and then click the Paste button on the Standard toolbar or press the ENTER key. You can also use the **Cut command** on the Edit menu or shortcut menu.

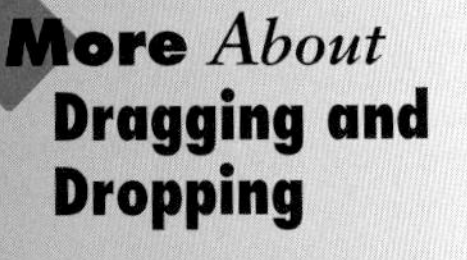

More *About* **Dragging and Dropping**

If the mouse pointer does not change to an arrow when you point to the border of the range to copy, then the Drag and Drop option is turned off. To turn it on, click Options on the Tools menu, click the Edit tab, click Allow Cell Drag and Drop check box.

Inserting and Deleting Cells in a Worksheet

At any time while the worksheet is on the screen, you can add cells to insert new data or delete cells to remove unwanted data. You can insert or delete individual cells, a range of cells, entire rows, entire columns, or entire worksheets.

Inserting Rows

The **Rows command** on the Edit menu or the **Insert command** on the shortcut menu allows you to insert rows between rows that already contain values. In the Assumptions table at the bottom of the worksheet, room must be made between rows 18 and 19 to add a row for the Net Sales for Bonuses assumption (see Figure 3-1a on page E 3.5). The following steps show how to accomplish the task of inserting a new row into the worksheet.

Steps To Insert Rows

1 Right-click row heading 19.

Row 19 is selected and the shortcut menu displays as shown in Figure 3-13.

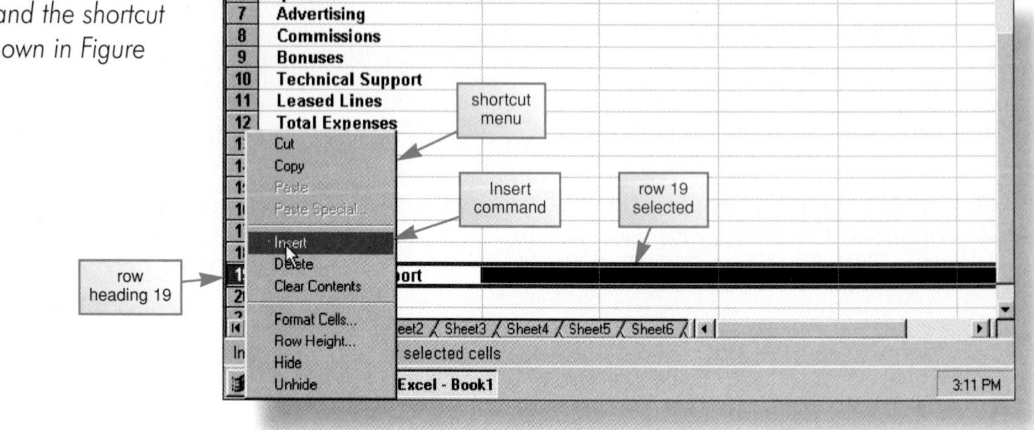

FIGURE 3-13

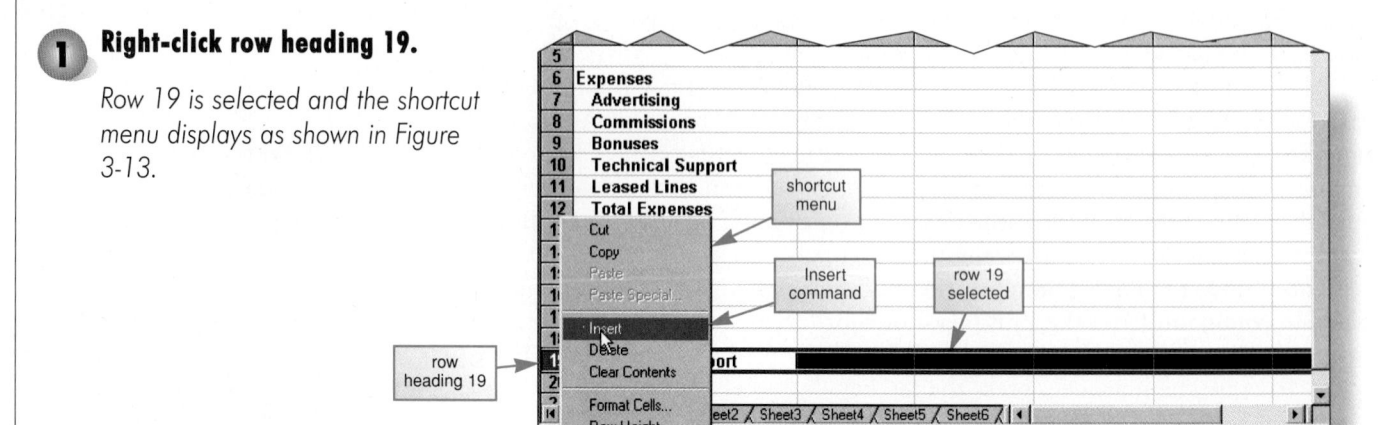

2 Click the Insert command. Click cell A19.

Excel inserts a new row by pushing down all rows below and including row 19, the one originally selected (Figure 3-14).

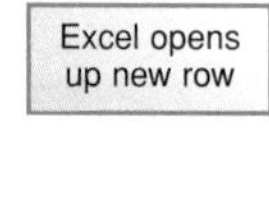

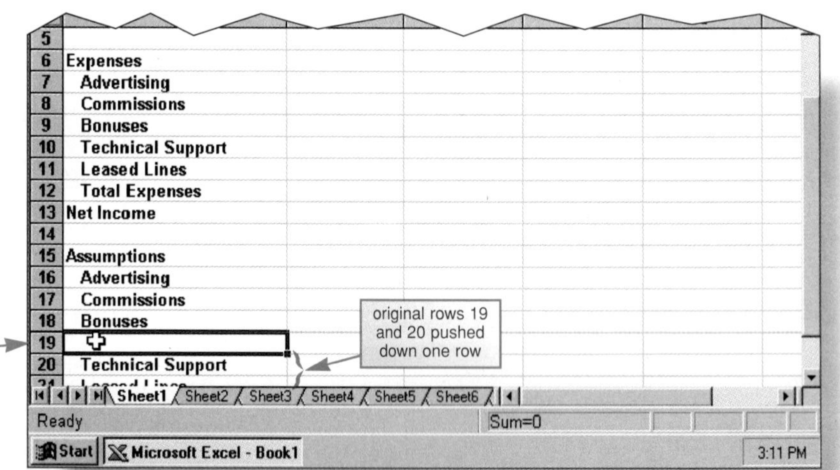

FIGURE 3-14

OtherWays

1. Select cell in row, on Insert menu click Rows
2. Select cell in row, press CTRL+SHIFT+PLUS SIGN, click Entire Row, click OK button

If the rows pushed down include any formulas, Excel adjusts the cell references to the new locations. Thus, if a formula in the worksheet references a cell in row 19 before the insert, then after the insert, the cell reference in the formula is adjusted to row 20.

The primary difference between the Insert command on the shortcut menu and the Rows command on the Insert menu is this: The Insert command on the shortcut menu requires that you select an entire row (or rows) in order to insert a row (or rows). The Rows command on the Insert menu requires that you select a single cell in a row to insert one row or a range of cells to indicate more than one row to insert. Inserted rows duplicate the format (including colors) of the row above them.

Inserting Columns

You insert columns into a worksheet in the same way you insert rows. To insert columns, begin your column selection immediately to the right of where you want Excel to insert the new blank columns. Select the number of columns you want to insert. Next, choose the Columns command from the Insert menu or the Insert command from the shortcut menu. Here again, if you use the **Columns command**, you need only select cells in the columns to push to the right, whereas you must select entire columns to use the Insert command on the shortcut menu. Inserted columns duplicate the format of the column to their left.

Inserting Individual Cells or a Range of Cells

The Insert command on the shortcut menu or the Cells command on the Insert menu allows you to insert a single cell or a range of cells. You should be aware that if you shift a single cell or a range of cells, however, they no longer may be lined up with their associated cells. To ensure that the values in the worksheet do not get out of order, it is recommended that you insert only entire rows or entire columns.

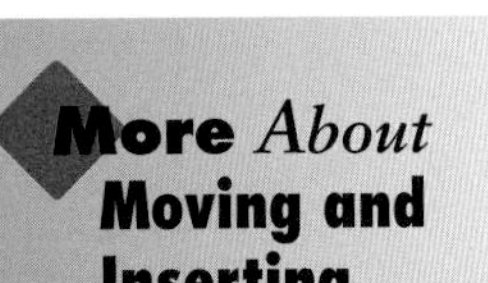

More *About* **Moving and Inserting**

You can move and insert between existing cells by holding down the SHIFT key while you drag the selection to the gridline where you want to insert. You can also copy and insert by holding down the CTRL and SHIFT keys while you drag the selection to the desired gridline.

Deleting Columns and Rows

The **Delete command** on the Edit menu or shortcut menu removes cells (including the data and format) from the worksheet. Deleting cells is not the same as clearing cells. The Clear command described earlier in Project 1 on page E 1.53, clears the data out of the cells, but the cells remain in the worksheet. The Delete command removes the cells from the worksheet and moves rows up when you delete rows or moves columns to the left when you delete columns.

Excel does not adjust cell references to the deleted row or column in formulas located in other cells. Excel displays the error message **#REF!** (meaning cell reference error) in those cells containing formulas that reference cells in the deleted area. For example, if cell A7 contains the formula =A4+A5 and you delete row 5, then Excel assigns the formula =A4+#REF! to cell A6 (originally cell A7) and displays the error message #REF! in cell A6, which originally was cell A7.

Deleting Individual Cells or a Range of Cells

Although Excel allows you to delete an individual cell or range of cells, you should be aware that if you shift a cell or range of cells on the worksheet, they no longer may be lined up with their associated cells. For this reason, it is recommended that you delete only entire rows or entire columns.

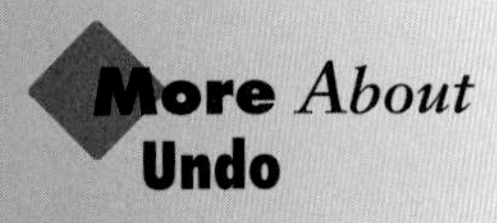

More *About* **Undo**

Inserting, copying, deleting, and moving have the potential to render a worksheet useless. Carefully review these actions before continuing on to the next task. If your not sure the action is correct, click the Undo button on the Standard toolbar.

Entering Numbers with a Format Symbol

The next step is to enter the row title, Net Sales for Bonuses, in cell A19 and enter the assumption values in the range B16:B21. The assumption numbers can be entered as decimal numbers as was done in Projects 1 and 2 and then format them later, or you can enter them with format symbols. When you enter a number with a **format symbol**, Excel immediately formats the number when it is assigned to the cell. Valid format symbols include the dollar sign ($), comma (,), and percent sign (%). If the number entered is a whole number, then it displays without any decimal places.

Table 3-2

FORMAT SYMBOL	ENTERED IN FORMULA BAR	DISPLAYS IN CELL	COMPARABLE FORMAT
$	$352	$352	Currency (0)
	$5798.62	$5,798.62	Currency (2)
	$64,123.3	$64,123.30	Currency (2)
,	9,876	9,876	Comma (0)
	7,913.3	7,913.30	Comma (2)
%	9%	9%	Percent (0)
	7.3%	7.30%	Percent (2)
	2.33%	2.33%	Percent (2)

If the number entered with a format symbol has one or more decimal places, then Excel displays the number with two decimal places. Table 3-2 illustrates several examples of numbers entered with format symbols. The number in parentheses in column 3 indicates the number of decimal places.

The following steps describe how to complete the entries in the Assumptions table and save an intermediate version of the workbook.

Steps To Enter a Number with a Format Symbol

1. **Click cell A19 and enter the text** ~~bbb~~`Net Sales for Bonuses` **(where** ~~**bbb**~~ **represents three spaces).**

2. **Enter** `32.75%` **in cell B16,** `2.75%` **in cell B17,** `25,000.00` **in cell B18,** `1,000,000.00` **in cell B19,** `28.25%` **in cell B20, and** `19.5%` **in cell B21.**

   The entries display in a format based on the format symbols entered with the numbers (Figure 3-15).

3. **Click the Save button on the Standard toolbar. Type the filename** `Information Mining` **in the File name text box. Click the Save in box arrow and then click the 3½ Floppy [A:] icon. Click the Save button in the Save As dialog box.**

   The workbook name in the title bar changes from Book1 to Information Mining.

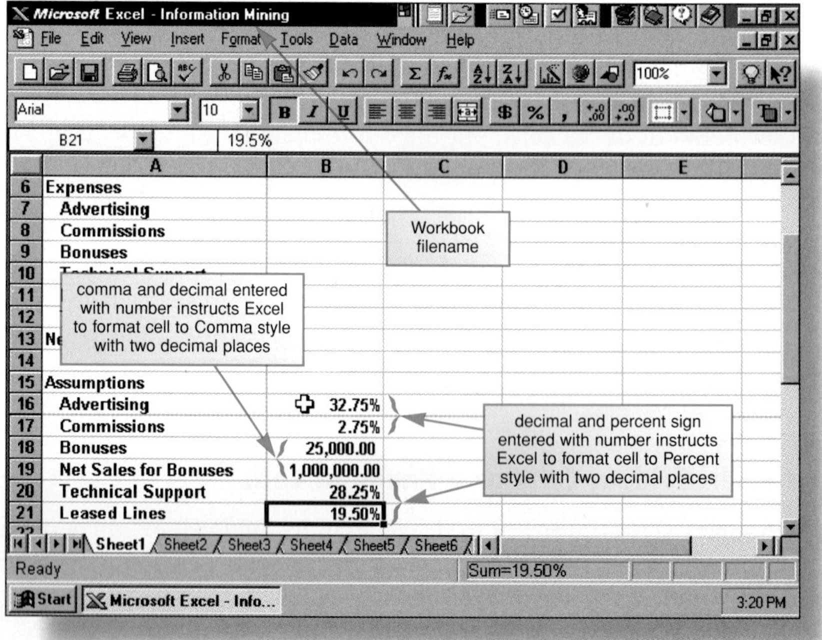

FIGURE 3-15

Freezing Worksheet Titles

Freezing worksheet titles is a useful technique for viewing large worksheets that extend beyond the window. For example, when you scroll down or to the right, the column titles in row 3 and the row titles in column A that define the numbers disappear off the screen. This makes it difficult to remember what the numbers represent. To alleviate this problem, Excel allows you to freeze the titles so they remain on the screen no matter how far down or to the right you scroll.

Complete the following steps to freeze the worksheet title and column titles in rows 1, 2, and 3, and the row titles in column A using the **Freeze Panes command** on the **Window menu**.

More *About* **Freezing Titles**

If you only want to freeze column headings, then select the appropriate cell in column A before you click the Freeze Panes command on the Window menu. If you only want to freeze row titles, then select the appropriate cell in row 1. To freeze both column and row titles, select the cell that is the intersection of the column and row titles.

Steps To Freeze Column and Row Titles

1 Click cell B4, the cell below the column headings you want to freeze and to the right of the row titles you want to freeze. Click Window on the menu bar and then point to Freeze Panes (Figure 3-16).

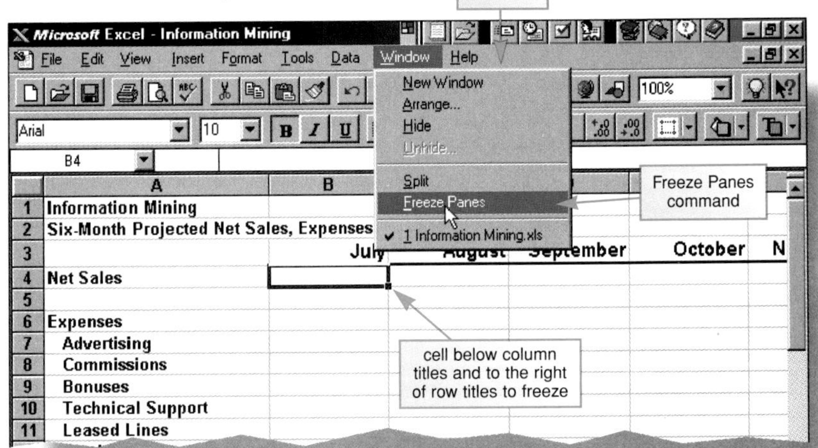

FIGURE 3-16

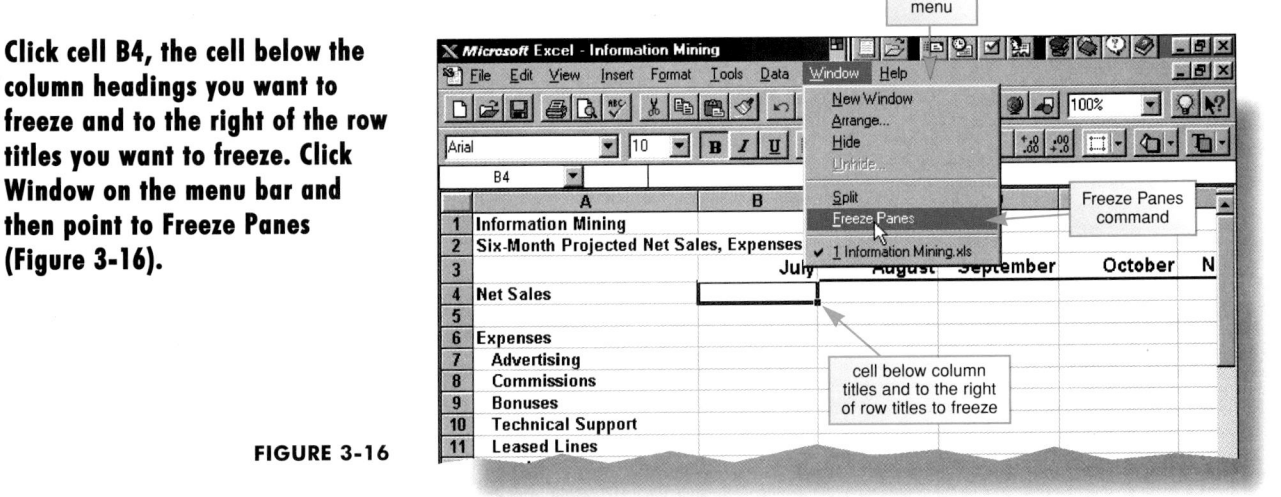

2 Click Freeze Panes on the Window menu.

Excel splits the window into two parts. The right border along column A changes to a thin black line indicating the split between the frozen row titles in column A and the rest of the worksheet. The bottom border in row 3 changes to a thin black line indicating the split between the frozen column titles in rows 1 through 3 and the rest of the worksheet (Figure 3-17).

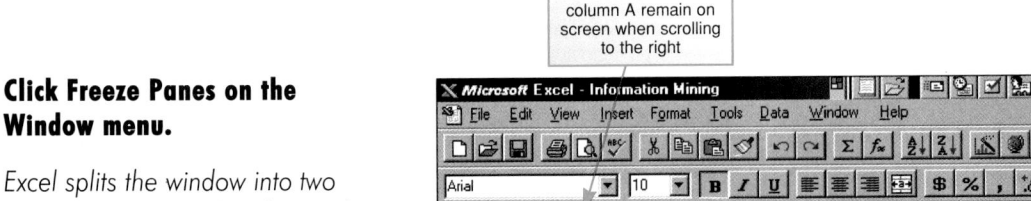

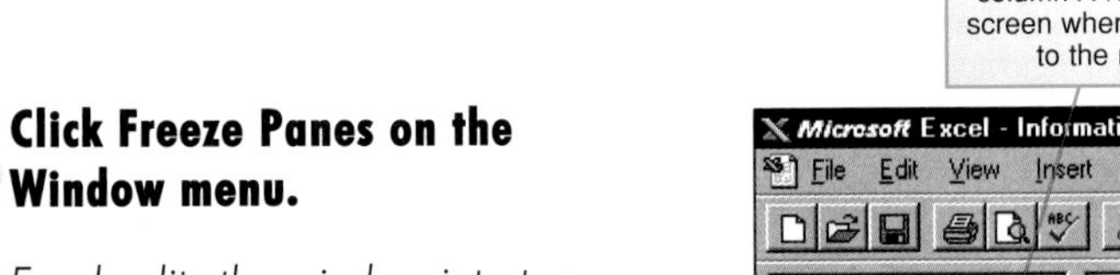

FIGURE 3-17

The row titles in column A remain on the screen even when you use the right scroll arrow to move the window to the right to display column G.

The titles are frozen until you unfreeze them. You unfreeze the titles by clicking Unfreeze Panes on the Window menu. Later steps in this project show you how to use the Unfreeze Panes command.

Entering the Projected Sales

The next step is to enter the projected sales and their total in row 4. Enter these numbers without any format symbols as shown in the following steps.

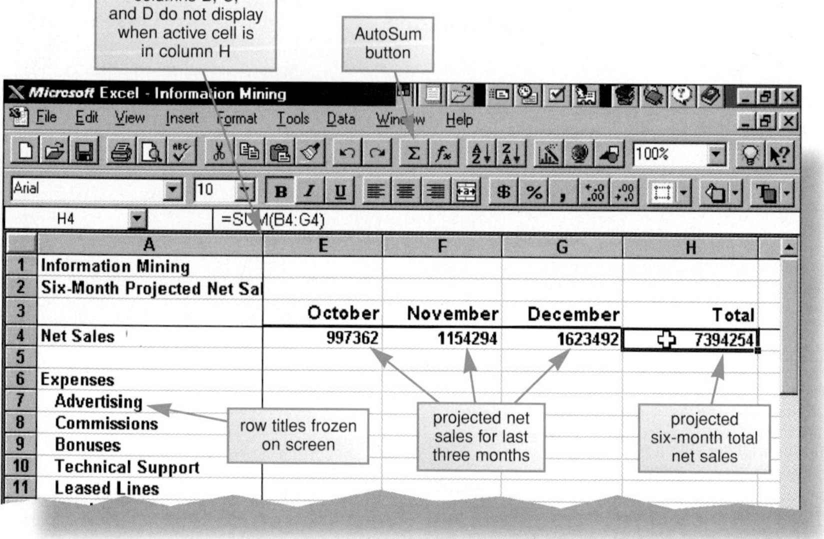

FIGURE 3-18

TO ENTER THE PROJECTED SALES

Step 1: With cell B4 selected, enter 1425654 in cell B4, 1297327 in cell C4, 896125 in cell D4, 997362 in cell E4, 1154294 in cell F4, 1623492 in cell G4.

Step 2: Click cell H4 and then click the AutoSum button on the Standard toolbar twice.

The projected six-month total net sales displays in cell H4 as shown in Figure 3-18. Notice that columns B, C, and D have scrolled off the screen, but column A remains because it was frozen earlier.

Displaying the System Date

The worksheet in Figure 3-1a on page E 3.5 includes a date stamp in cell H2. A **date stamp** is the system date of which your computer keeps track. If the computer's system date is set to the current date, which normally it is, then the date stamp is equivalent to the current date.

In information processing, a report such as a printout of the worksheet is often meaningless without a date stamp. For example, the date stamp in Project 3 is useful for showing when the six-month projections were made.

To enter the system date in a cell in the worksheet use the **NOW function**. The NOW function is one of fourteen date functions available in Excel. When assigned to a cell, the NOW function returns a decimal number in the range 1 to 65,380, corresponding to the dates January 1, 1900 through December 31, 2078 and the time of day. Excel formats the number representing the system's date and time automatically to the date and time format m/d/yy h:mm where the first m is the month, d is the day of the month, yy is the last two digits of the year, h is the hour of the day, and mm is the minutes past the hour.

The following steps show how to enter the NOW function and change the format from m/d/yy h:mm to m/d/yy where m is the month number, d is day of the month, and yy is the last two digits of the year.

More *About* **Dates**

How many days have you been alive? Enter today's date (i.e., 3/29/97) in cell A1. Next, enter your birthdate (i.e., 6/22/40) in cell A2. Finally, select cell A3 and enter the formula =A1 - A2. Cell A3 will display the number of days you have been alive.

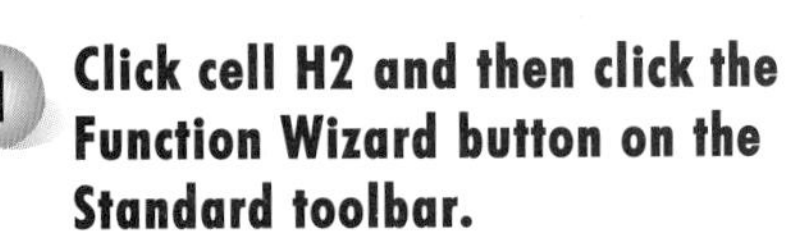

To Enter and Format the System Date

1 Click cell H2 and then click the Function Wizard button on the Standard toolbar.

2 Click Date & Time in the Function Category box and then click NOW in the Function Name box.

The Function Wizard - Step 1 of 2 dialog box displays as shown in Figure 3-19.

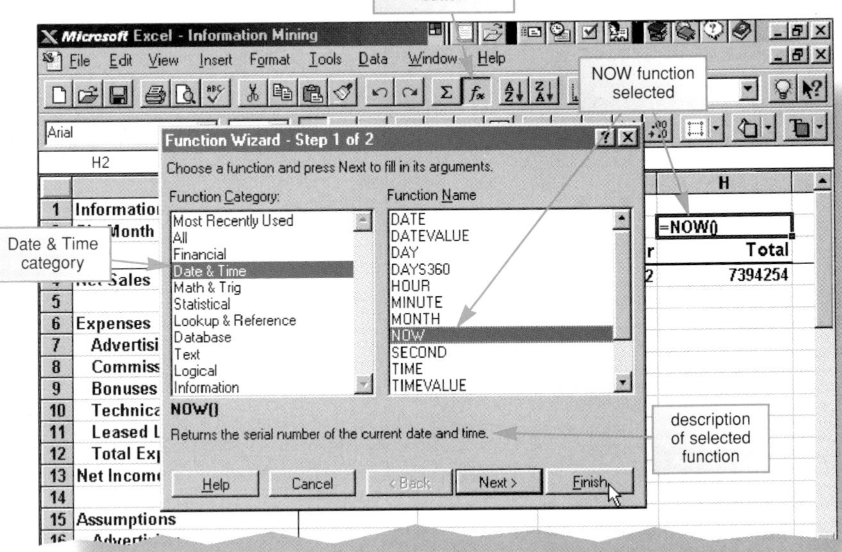

FIGURE 3-19

3 Click the Finish button.

Excel displays the system date and system time in cell H2 using the default date and time format m/d/yy h:mm (Figure 3-20).

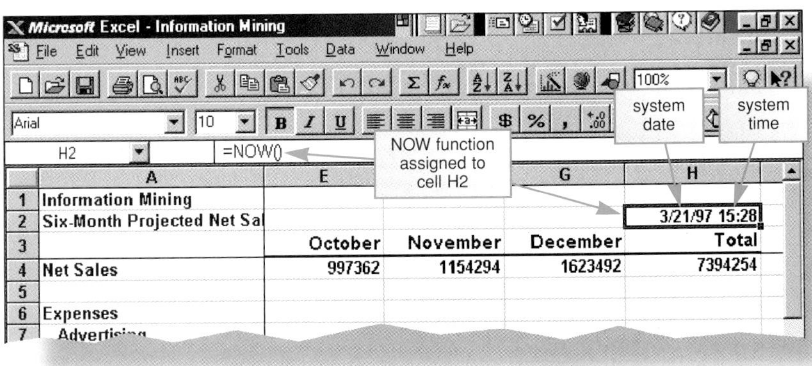

FIGURE 3-20

4 Right-click cell H2 and then point to Format Cells.

Excel displays the shortcut menu (Figure 3-21).

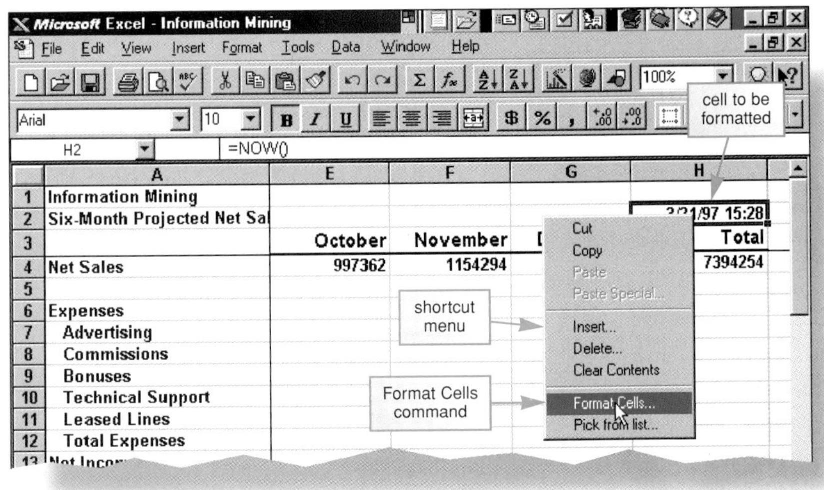

FIGURE 3-21

5 Click the Format Cells command and then click the Number tab in the Format Cells dialog box. Click Date in the Category box and then click 3/4/95 in the Type box.

Excel displays the Format Cells dialog box with Date and m/d/yy (3/4/95) highlighted (Figure 3-22).

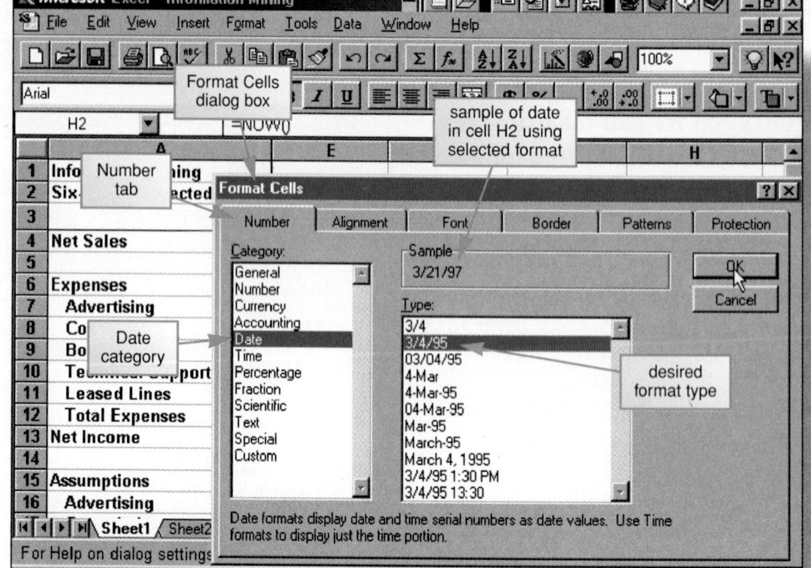

FIGURE 3-22

6 Click the OK button in the Format Cells dialog box.

Excel displays the date in the form m/d/yy (Figure 3-23). The date on your computer may different.

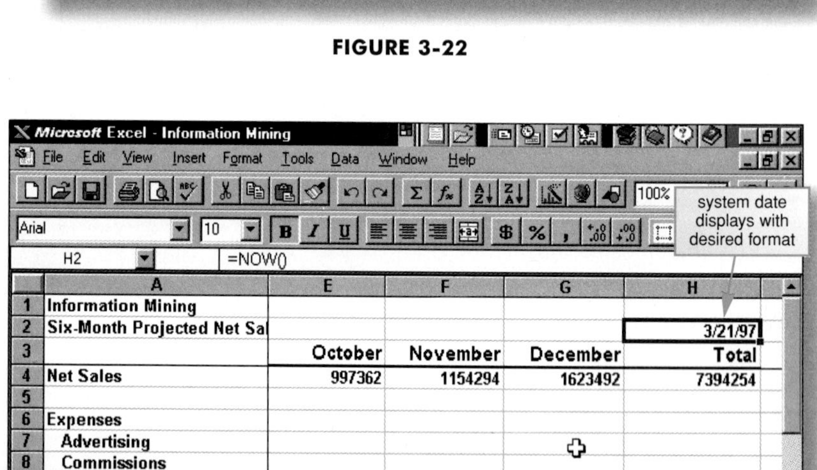

FIGURE 3-23

OtherWays

1. On Insert menu click Function, click Date & Time, click NOW, click Next button, click Finish button
2. Press CTRL+SEMICOLON (not a volatile date)

In Figure 3-23, the date displays in the cell right-aligned because Excel treats a date as a number. If you format the date by applying the **General format** (Excel's default for numbers), the date displays as a number. To format a cell to General, select the General category in the Format Cells dialog box. For example, if the system time and date is 12:00 noon on January 21, 1997 and the cell containing the NOW function is assigned the General format, then Excel displays the following number in the cell:

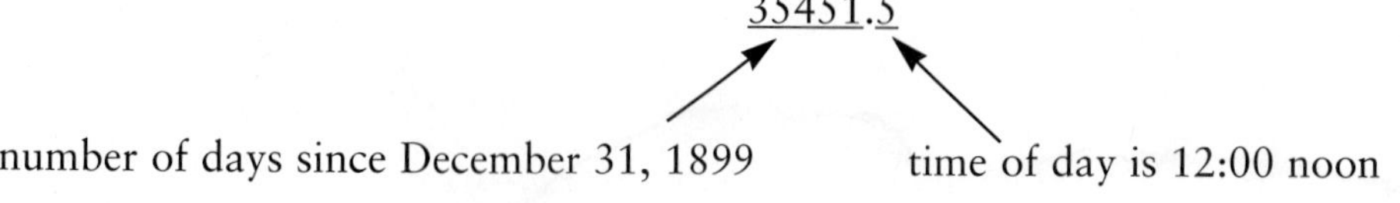

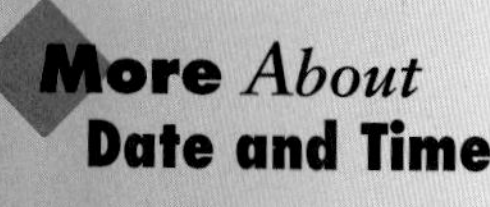

More About Date and Time

You can enter any date or time into a cell in a variety of formats such as 3/5/9, Feb-95, and 8:45 PM, and Excel will consider the entry to be a number. Excel automatically formats the entry in the same form you enter it.

The whole number portion of the number (35451) represents the number of days since December 31, 1899. The decimal portion (.5) represents the time of day (12:00 noon).

Absolute Versus Relative Addressing

The next step is to enter the formulas that determine the projected payroll expenses in the range B7:G13 (Figure 3-1a on page E 3.5). The projected monthly expenses are based on the projected monthly net sales in row 4 and the assumptions in the range B16:B21. The formulas for each column are the same, except for the sales in row 4. Thus, the formulas can be entered for July in column B and copied to columns C through G. The formulas for determining the July projected payroll expenses are shown in Table 3-3.

If you enter in column B the formulas as they appear in Table 3-3 and then copy them to columns C through G, Excel will adjust the cell references for each column automatically. Thus, after the copy, the August advertising in cell C7 would be =C16*C4. The cell reference C4 (August Net Sales) is correct. Cell C16 is empty, however. The need here is a way to keep a cell reference in a formula the same when it is copied. The formula for cell C7 should read =B16*C4 rather than =C16*C4.

Table 3-3

CELL	EXPENSE	FORMULA	COMMENT
B7	Advertising	=B16 * B4	Advertising % times July Net Sales
B8	Commissions	=B17 * B4	Commissions % times July Net Sales
B9	Bonuses	=IF(B4 >= B19, B18, 0)	Bonuses equals value in cell B18 or zero
B10	Technical Support	=B20 * B4	Technical Support % times July Net Sales
B11	Leased Lines	=B21 * B4	Leased Lines % times July Net Sales
B12	Total Expenses	=SUM(B7:B11)	Sum of expenses
B13	Net Income	=B4 - B12	Net Sales minus Expenses

Excel has the capability to keep a cell reference constant when it copies a formula or function by using a technique called **absolute referencing**. To specify an absolute reference in a formula, add a dollar sign ($) to the beginning of the column name, row name, or both in formulas you plan to copy. For example, $B$16 is an absolute reference and B16 is a relative reference. Both reference the same cell. The difference shows when they are copied. A formula using $B$16 instructs Excel to use the same cell (B16) as it copies the formula to a new location. A formula using B16 instructs Excel to adjust the cell reference as it copies. Table 3-4 gives some additional examples of absolute references. A cell reference with one dollar sign before either the column or the row is called a **mixed cell reference**.

Table 3-4

CELL REFERENCE	MEANING
$B$16	Both column and row references remain the same when you copy this cell reference because they are absolute.
B$16	The column reference changes when you copy this cell reference to another column because it is relative. The row reference does not change because it is absolute.
$B16	The row reference changes when you copy this cell reference to another row because it is relative. The column reference does not change because it is absolute.
B16	Both column and row references are relative. When copied to another row and column, both the row and column in the cell reference are adjusted to reflect the new location.

More *About*
Entering Fractions

How do you enter fractions? To enter a fraction, such as ½, type .5 or 0 1/2 (i.e., type zero, followed by a space, followed by the number 1, followed by a slash, followed by the number 2). If you type 1/2, Excel will store the value in the cell as the date January 2.

Entering the July Advertising and Commissions Formulas

The following steps show how to enter the advertising formula (=$B$16*B4) in cell B7 and the commissions formula (=$B$17*B4) in cell B8 for the month of January using Point mode. When you enter an absolute reference, you can type the $ or you can press F4 with the insertion point in or to the right of the cell reference you want to change to absolute.

Steps To Enter Formulas Containing Absolute Cell References

1. **Click cell B7. Type the equal sign (=) to begin a formula and then click cell B16. Press F4 to change B16 to an absolute reference in the formula. Type the asterisk (*) and then click cell B4.**

   The formula displays in cell B7 and in the formula bar (Figure 3-24).

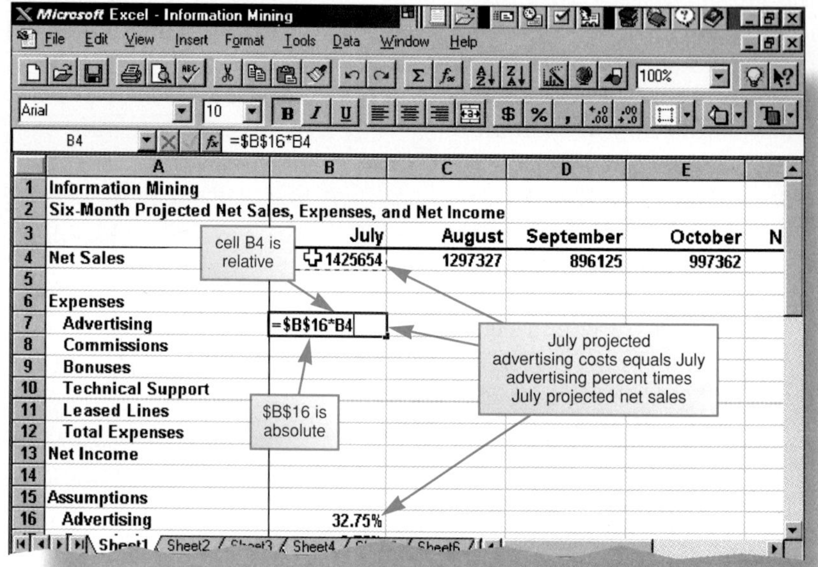

FIGURE 3-24

2. **Click the enter box or press the ENTER key to complete the entry in cell B7. Click B8, type the equal sign (=) to begin a formula and then click cell B17. Press F4 to change B17 to an absolute reference in the formula. Type the asterisk (*) and click cell B4. Click the enter box or press the ENTER key.**

   Excel displays the results of the projected July advertising expense formula (466901.685) in cell B7 and the projected July commissions expense formula (39205.485) in cell B8 (Figure 3-25).

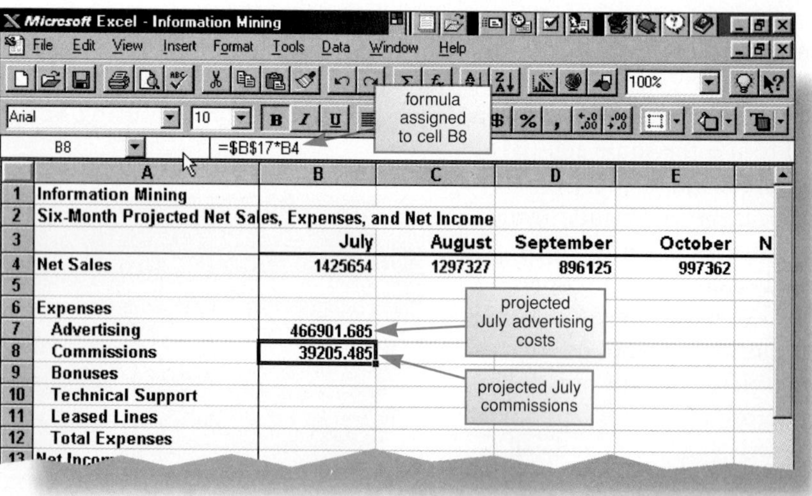

FIGURE 3-25

Making Decisions – The IF Function

If the projected July net sales in cell B4 is greater than or equal to the net sales for bonuses in cell B19, then the projected July bonuses in cell B9 is equal to the amount in cell B18 (25,000.00); otherwise, cell B9 is equal to zero. One way to assign the projected monthly bonuses in row 9 is to manually compare the projected net sales for each month in row 4 to the net sales for bonuses in cell B19 and then enter 25,000 when the corresponding projected month net sales equals or exceeds the amount in cell B19. Because the data in the worksheet changes each time you prepare the report or adjust the figures, however, you will find it preferable to have Excel assign automatically the projected monthly bonus to the entries in the appropriate cells. What you need in cell B9 is an entry that displays 25,000 or 0 (zero), depending on whether the projected July net sales in cell B4 is greater than or equal to or less than the number in cell B19.

Excel has the **IF function** that is useful when the value you want to assign to a cell is dependent on a logical test. A **logical test** is made up of two expressions and a relational operator. Each expression can be a cell reference, a number, text, a function, or a formula. A **comparison operator** is one of the following: > (greater than), < (less than), = (equal to), >= (greater than or equal to), <= (less than or equal to), <> (not equal to). For example, assume you assign cell B9 the IF function:

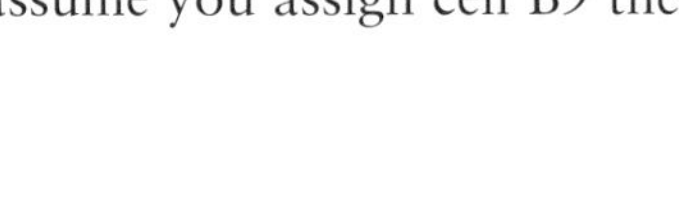

If the projected July net sales in cell B4 is greater than or equal to the value in cell B18, then 25,000 displays in cell B9. If the projected July sales in cell B4 is less than the value in cell B18, then cell B9 displays a zero.

The general form of the IF function is:

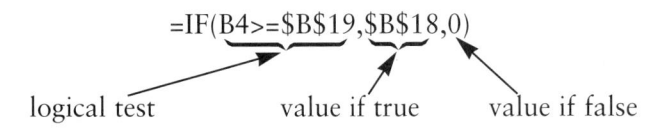

=IF(logical-test, value-if-true, value-if-false)

The argument, value-if-true, is the value you want displayed in the cell when the logical test is true. The argument, value-if-false, is the value you want displayed in the cell when the logical test is false.

Table 3-5 lists the valid relational operators and examples of their use in IF functions.

Table 3-5

RELATIONAL OPERATOR	MEANING	EXAMPLE
=	Equal to	=IF(C5 = K7, B29 - F3, K5 + S3)
<	Less than	=IF(J17 / B5 < 12, B15, B13 - 5)
>	Greater than	=IF(=SUM(T4:T9) > 300, 0, 1)
>=	Greater than or equal to	=IF(A15 >= $R$2, C4 * H5, 6)
<=	Less than or equal to	=IF(H5 + F5 <= 10, H10, 9 * B3)
<>	Not equal to	=IF(C5 <> B$5, "OK", "Not OK")

More About Absolute Referencing

Absolute referencing is one of the most difficult worksheet concepts to understand. One point to keep in mind is that there is only one command, the Copy command, that is affected by an absolute cell reference. An absolute cell reference instructs Excel to keep the same cell reference as it copies a formula from one cell to another.

More About the IF Function

Assume you want to assign the formula =F4*G6 to the active cell, but display an empty cell (blank) when the formula is equal to zero. Try this: enter =IF(F4*G6 = 0, " ", F4*G6) into the cell. This IF function assigns the blank between the quotation marks to the cell when F4*G6 is equal to zero, otherwise, it assigns the value of F4*G6 to the cell.

The following steps assign the IF function =IF(B4>=$B$19,$B$18,0) to cell B9. This function will determine whether or not the spreadsheet projects a bonus for July.

To Enter an IF Function

1 **Click cell B9, and then type** `=if(b4>=$b$19,$b$18,0` **in the cell.**

The IF function displays in cell B9 and in the formula bar (Figure 3-26).

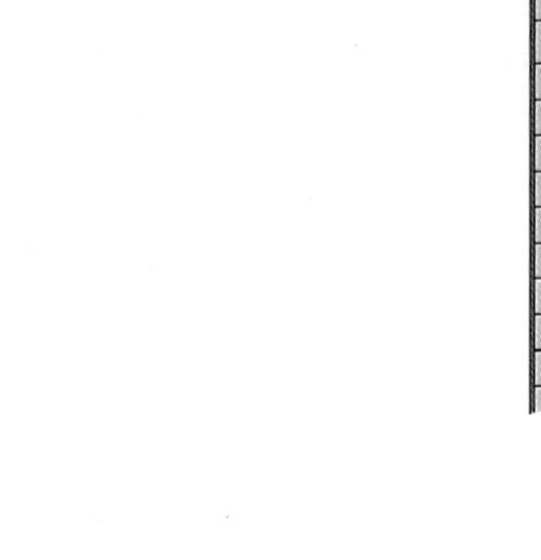

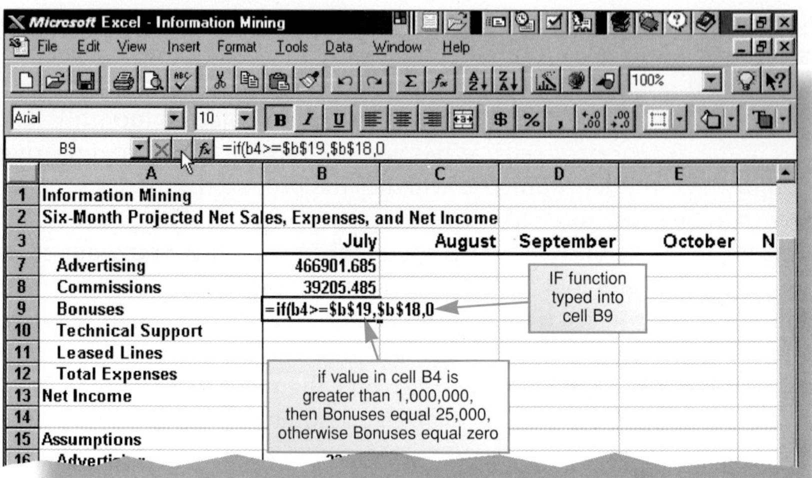

FIGURE 3-26

2 **Click the enter box or press the ENTER key.**

Excel displays 25000 in cell B9 because the value in cell B4 (1,425,654.00) is greater than or equal to the value in cell B19 (1,000,000.00) (Figure 3-27). Recall that it is not necessary to type the closing parenthesis when you enter a function.

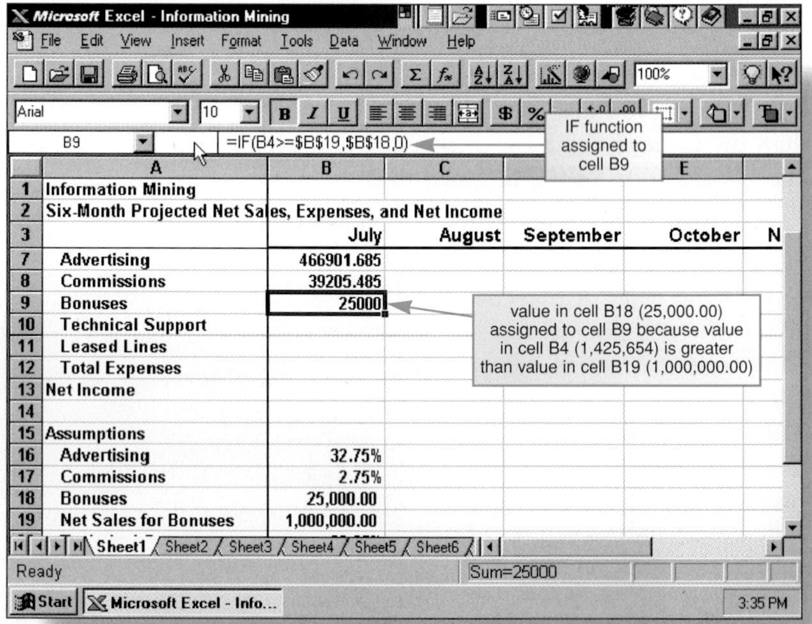

FIGURE 3-27

The value that Excel displays in cell B9 depends on the values assigned to cells B4, B18, and B19. For example, if the projected sales in cell B4 is reduced below 1,000,000.00, then the IF function in cell B9 will change the display to zero. Changing the net sales for bonuses in cell B19 to a greater amount has the same effect.

Entering the Remaining Projected Expense and Net Income Formulas for July

The projected July technical support expense in cell B10 is equal to the technical support percent in cell B20 times the projected July net sales in cell B4. Likewise, the projected July leased lines expenses in cell B11 is equal to the leased line percent in cell B21 times the projected July net sales. The projected total expenses for July in cell B12 is equal to the sum of the July expenses in the range B7:B11. The projected July net income in cell B13 is equal to the projected net sales minus the projected total expenses for July. The following steps enter the four formulas into the worksheet.

TO ENTER THE REMAINING PROJECTED EXPENSE AND NET INCOME FORMULAS FOR JULY

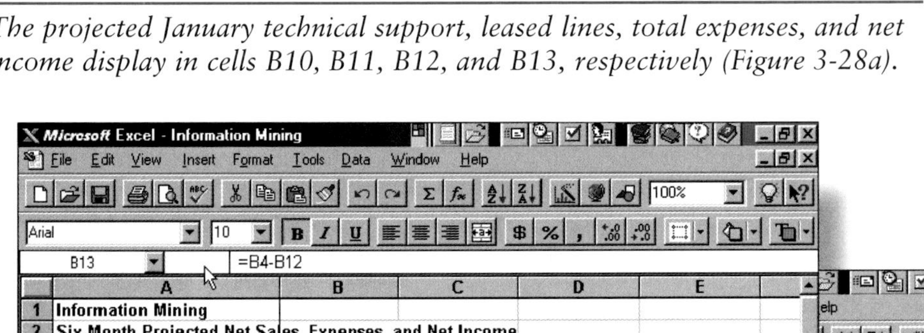

Step 1: Click cell B10. Type =b20*b4 and then press the DOWN ARROW key.
Step 2: Type =b21*b4 and then press the DOWN ARROW key.
Step 3: Click the AutoSum button on the Standard toolbar twice.
Step 4: Click cell B13. Type =b4-b12 and then click the enter box or press the ENTER key.

The projected January technical support, leased lines, total expenses, and net income display in cells B10, B11, B12, and B13, respectively (Figure 3-28a).

More *About* **Freezing Formula Values**

You can freeze the value of a formula by replacing the formula with the frozen value. Do the following: (1) click the cell with the formula; (2) press F2 or click in the formula bar; (3) press F9 to display the value in the formula bar; (4) click the enter box or press the ENTER key.

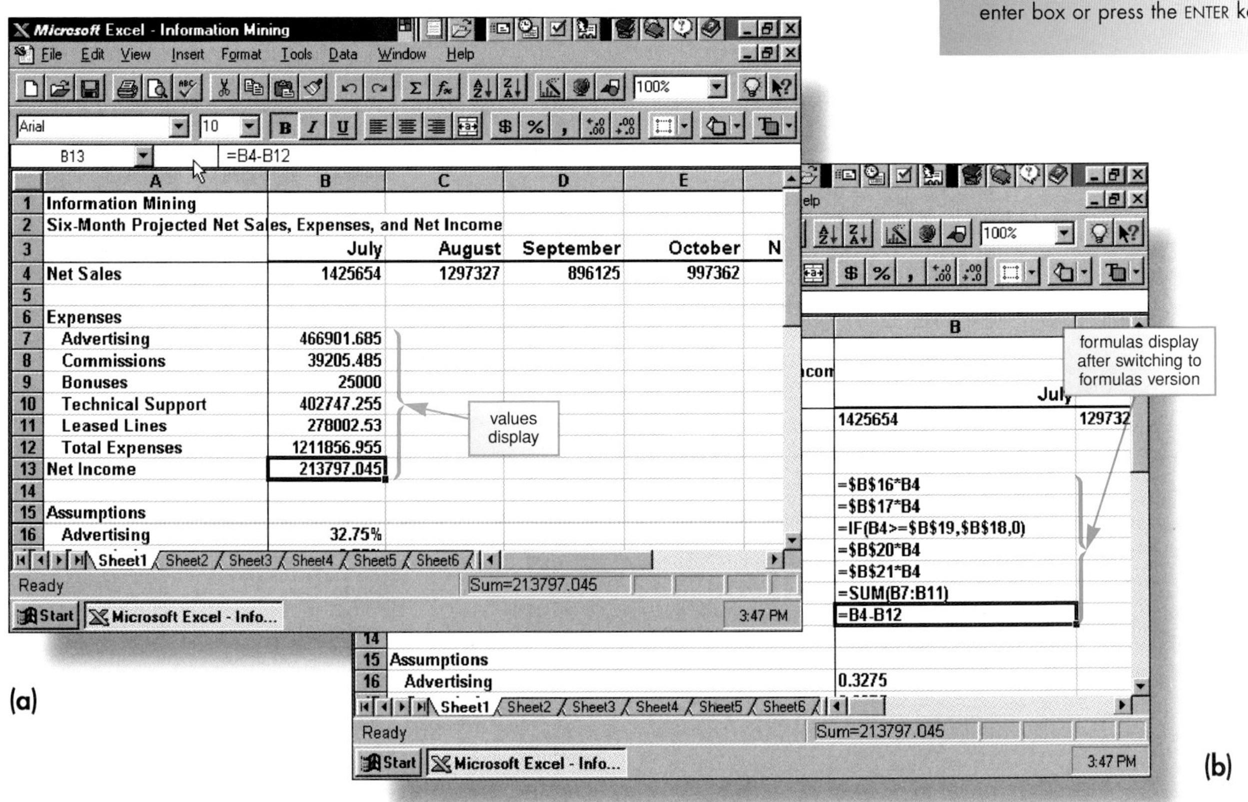

FIGURE 3-28

You can view the formulas in the worksheet by pressing CTRL+`. The display changes from Figure 3-28a to Figure 3-28b. Press CTRL+` to display the values again.

To copy the projected expenses and totals, complete the following steps using the fill handle.

Steps To Copy the Projected Expenses and Totals Using the Fill Handle

1 Select the range B7:B13. Point to the fill handle near the lower right corner of cell B13.

The range B7:B13 is selected and the mouse pointer changes to a cross hair (Figure 3-29).

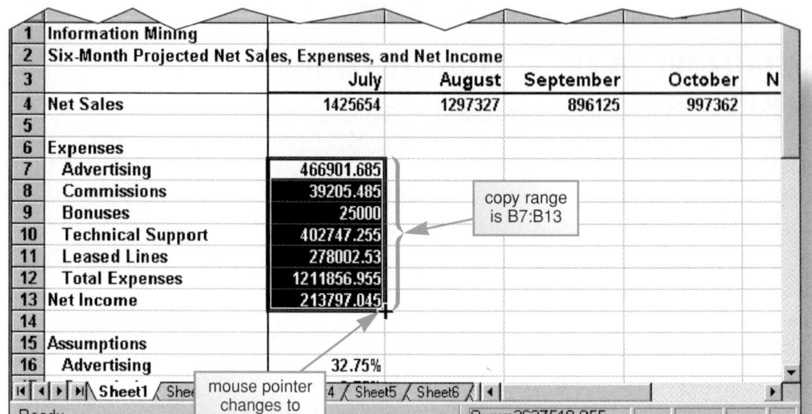

FIGURE 3-29

2 Drag the fill handle to select the paste area C7:G13 and then release the left mouse button.

Excel copies the formulas in the range B7:B13 to the paste area C7:G13. The last three columns of the paste area display as shown in Figure 3-30.

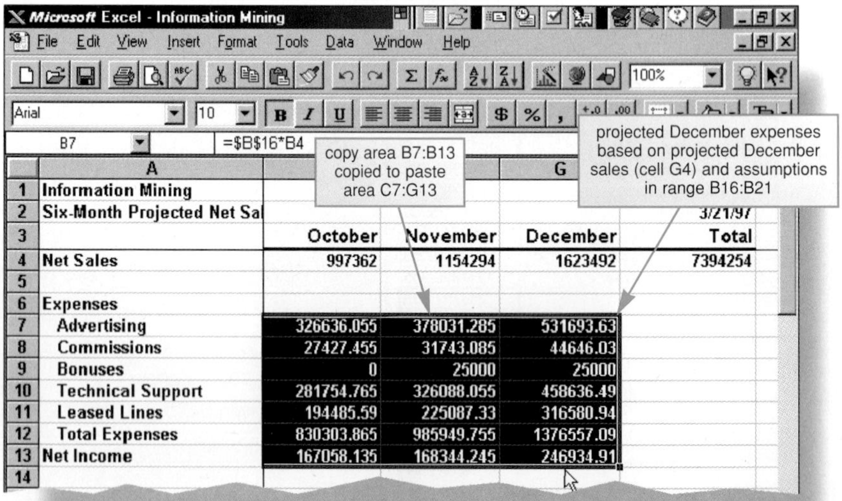

FIGURE 3-30

Determining the Projected Total Expenses by Category and Total Net Income

Follow the steps at the top of the next page to determine the total projected expenses by category and total net income in the range H7:H13.

TO DETERMINE THE PROJECTED TOTAL EXPENSES BY CATEGORY AND TOTAL NET INCOME

Step 1: Select the range H7:H13.
Step 2: Click the AutoSum button on the Standard toolbar.

The projected total payroll expenses by category and total net income display in the range H7:H13 (Figure 3-31).

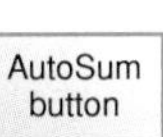

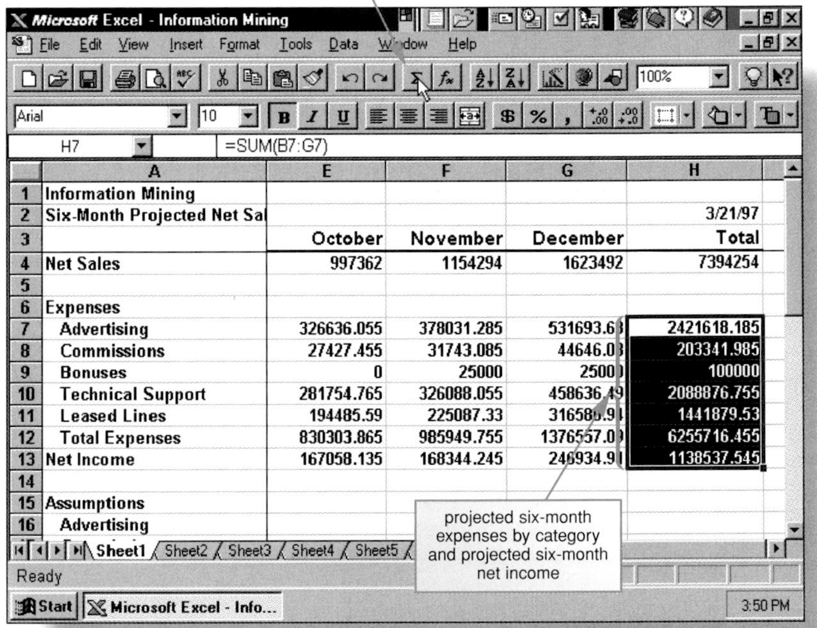

FIGURE 3-31

Unfreezing Worksheet Titles and Saving the Workbook

All the text, data, and formulas have been entered into the worksheet. The next step is to improve the appearance of the worksheet. Before modifying the worksheet's appearance, the following steps unfreeze the titles and save the workbook under its current filename Information Mining.

TO UNFREEZE THE WORKSHEET TITLES AND SAVE THE WORKBOOK

Step 1: Click cell B4 to clear the range selection from the previous steps.
Step 2: Click Window on the menu bar and then point to Unfreeze Panes (Figure 3-32).
Step 3: Click Unfreeze Panes.
Step 4: Click the Save button on the Standard toolbar.

Excel unfreezes the titles so that column A scrolls off the screen when you scroll to the right and the first three rows scroll off the screen when you scroll down. The workbook is saved using the filename Information Mining.

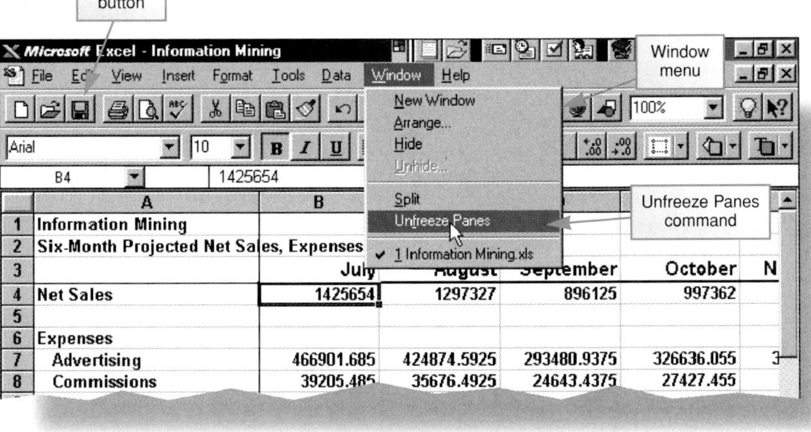

FIGURE 3-32

Formatting the Worksheet

The worksheet in Figure 3-31 determines the projected monthly expenses and net incomes. Its appearance is uninteresting, however, even though some minimal formatting was done earlier. This section will complete the formatting of the worksheet so the numbers are easier to read and to emphasize the titles, assumptions, categories, and totals (Figure 3-33 on the next page).

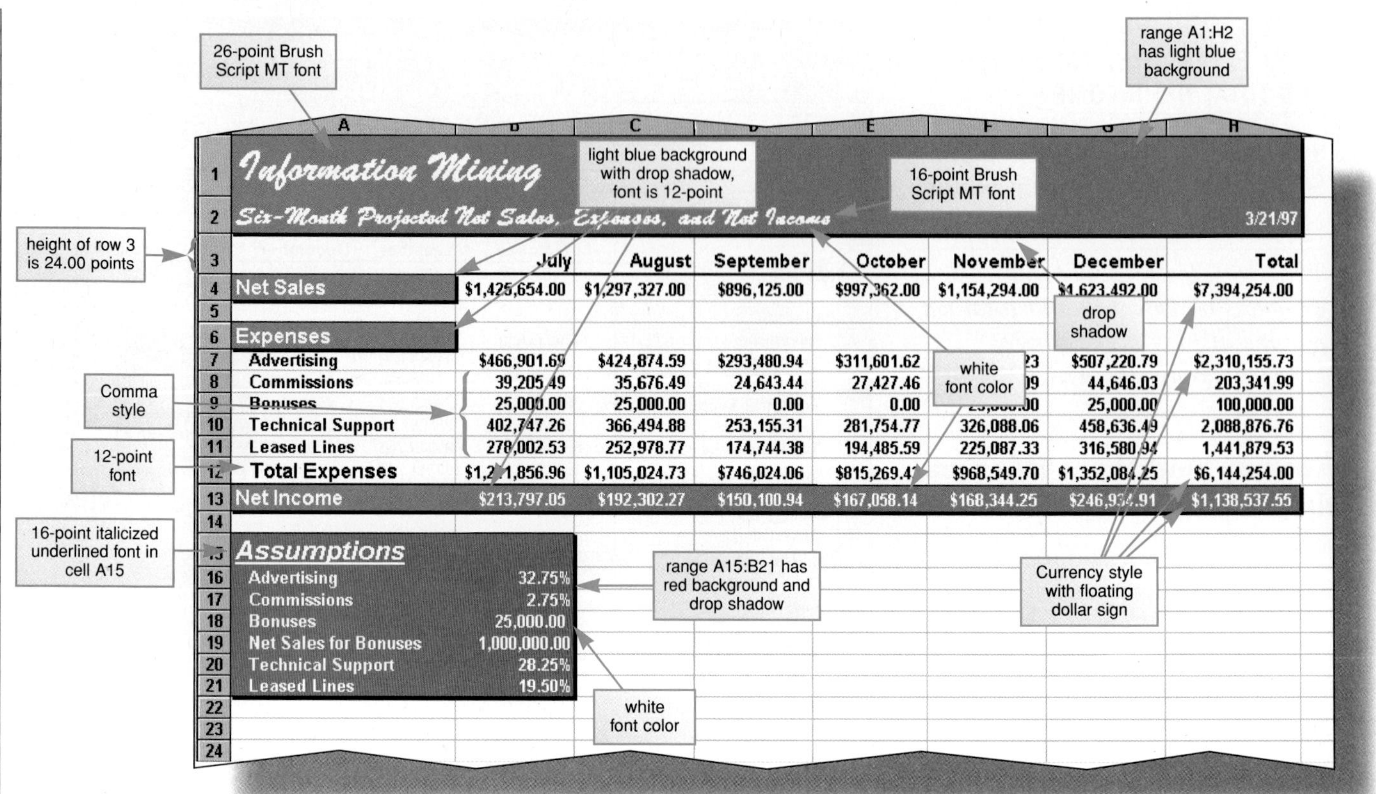

FIGURE 3-33

Formatting the Projected Sales and Payroll Expenses

Format the projected monthly net sales and expenses as follows:

1. Assign the Currency style with a floating dollar sign to rows 4, 7, 12, and 13.
2. Assign a customized Comma style to rows 8 through 11.

Assigning a Currency style with a floating dollar sign requires that you use the Format Cells command, rather than the Currency Style button on the Formatting toolbar because the button assigns a fixed dollar sign. The Comma style must also be assigned using the Format Cells command because the Comma Style button on the Formatting toolbar displays a dash (-) when a cell has a value of zero. The specifications for this worksheet call for displaying a value of zero as 0.00 (see cell D9 in Figure 3-33). The following steps format the numbers in rows 4 and 7 through 13.

To Assign Formats to the Projected Net Sales, Expenses, and Net Income

1. **Select the range B4:H4. Hold down the CTRL and select the nonadjacent ranges B7:H7 and B12:H13. Release the CTRL key. Right-click the selected range and then point to Format Cells.**

   The selected range is highlighted and the shortcut menu displays as shown in Figure 3-34.

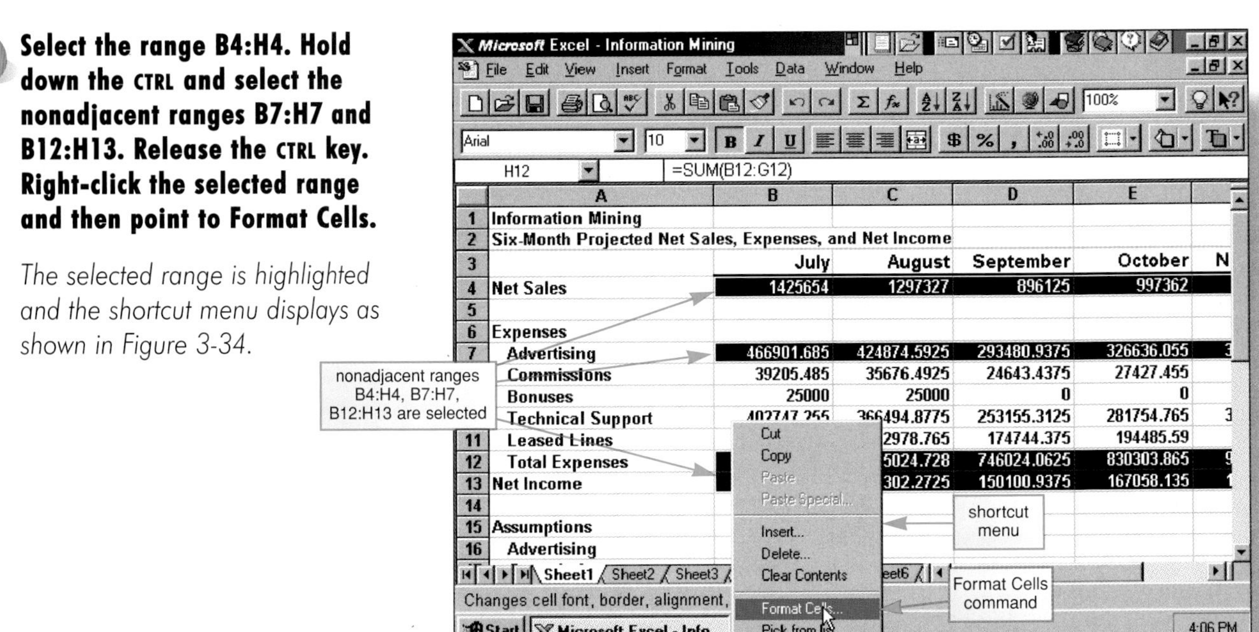

FIGURE 3-34

2. **Click Format Cells. When the Format Cells dialog box displays, click the Number tab, click Currency in the Category box, select two decimal places in the Decimal Places box, click the Use $ check box to ensure a dollar sign displays, and click ($1,234.10) in the Negative Numbers box.**

   The format settings display on the Number sheet in the Format Cells dialog box as shown in Figure 3-35.

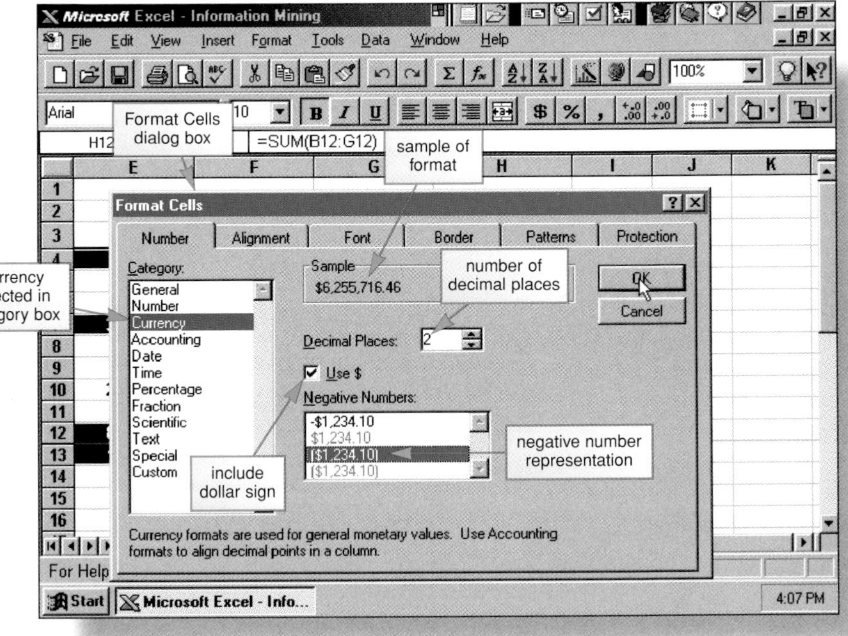

FIGURE 3-35

3 **Click the OK button on the Format Cells dialog box.**

4 **Select the range B8:H11. Right-click within the selected range. Click Format Cells on the shortcut menu. Click Currency in the Category box, select 2 in the Decimal Places box, click the Use $ check box so a dollar sign does not display, click (1,234.10) in the Negative Numbers box.**

The format settings display on the Numbers sheet in the Format Cells dialog box as shown in Figure 3-36.

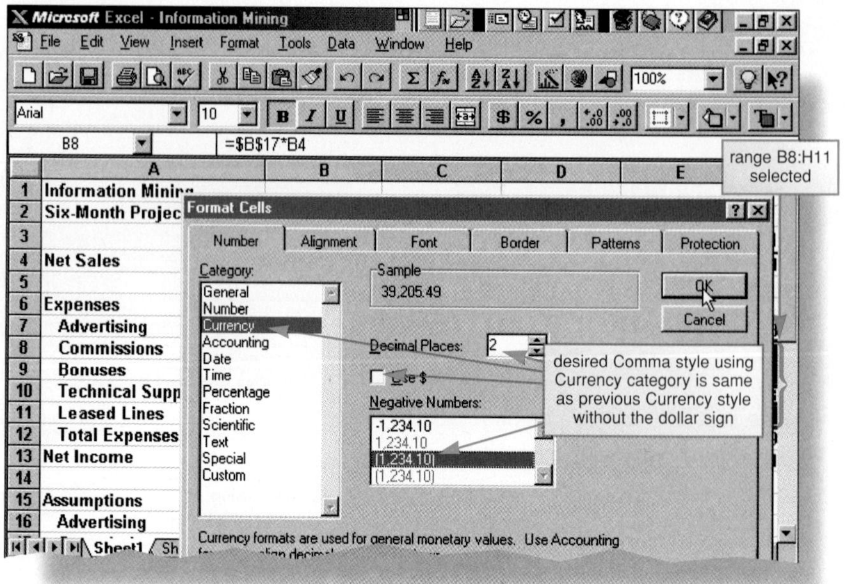

FIGURE 3-36

5 **Click the OK button on the Format Cells dialog box.**

The Currency style and Comma style formats display as shown in Figure 3-37.

	A	B	C	D	E
1	Information Mining				
2	Six-Month Projected Net Sales, Expenses, and Net Income				
3		July	August	September	October
4	Net Sales	$1,425,654.00	$1,297,327.00	$896,125.00	$997,362.00
5					
6	Expenses				
7	Advertising	$466,901.69	$424,874.59	$293,480.94	$326,636.06
8	Commissions	39,205.49	35,676.49	24,643.44	27,427.46
9	Bonuses	25,000.00	25,000.00	0.00	0.00
10	Technical Support	402,747.26	366,494.88	253,155.31	281,754.77
11	Leased Lines	278,002.53	252,978.77	174,744.38	1_4,485.59
12	Total Expenses	$1,211,856.96	$1,105,024.73	$746,024.06	$830,303.87
13	Net Income	$213,797.05	$192,302.27	$150,100.94	$167,058.14
14					
15	Assumptions				
16	Advertising	32.75%			

Currency style with floating dollar sign

Comma style

FIGURE 3-37

Instead of selecting Currency in the Category box in Step 4 (Figure 3-36), you could have selected Accounting to generate the same Comma style format. You should review the formats available under each category title. Thousands of combinations of format styles are available when you use the Format Cells dialog box to assign formats.

The next step is to format the titles at the top of the worksheet.

Formatting the Titles

To emphasize the worksheet titles in cells A1 and A2, the font type, size, and color are changed as described in the following steps.

To Format the Titles

1 **Select the range A1:A2. Click the Font box arrow. Scroll down and point to TT Brush Script MT (or a similar font).**

The Font drop-down list box displays (Figure 3-38).

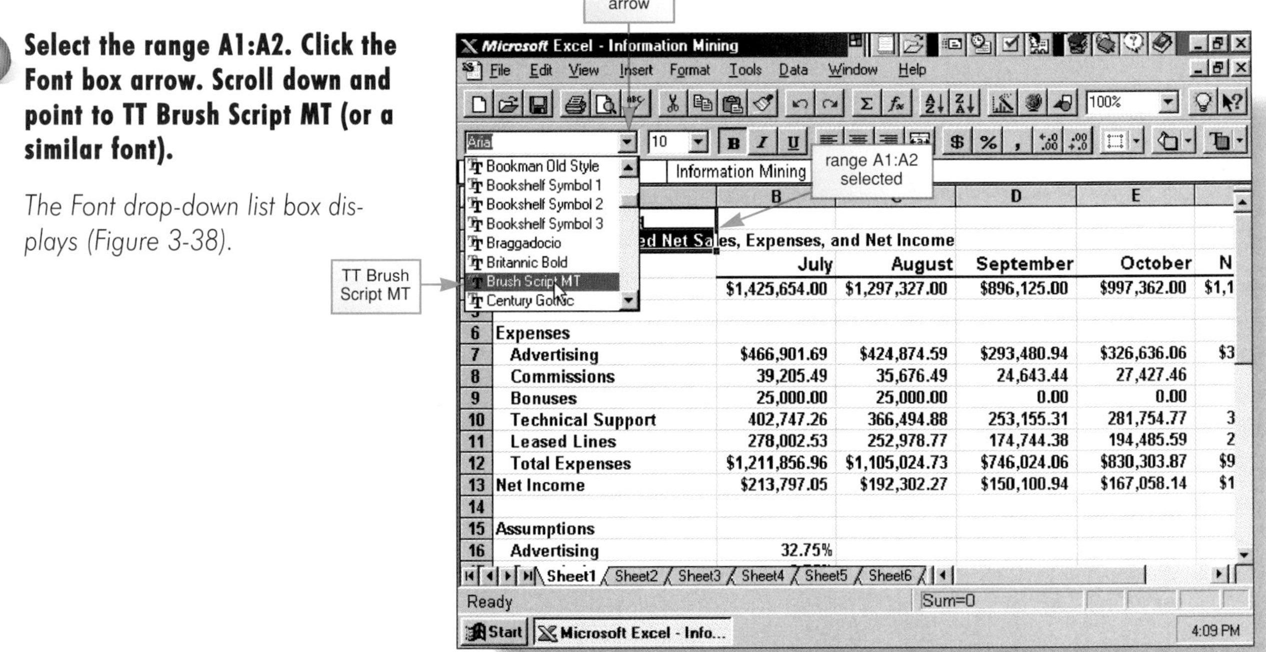

FIGURE 3-38

2 **Click TT Brush Script MT. Click cell A1. Click the Font Size box arrow and then click 26. Click cell A2. Click the Font Size box arrow and then click 16.**

The titles in the range A1:A2 display as shown in Figure 3-39.

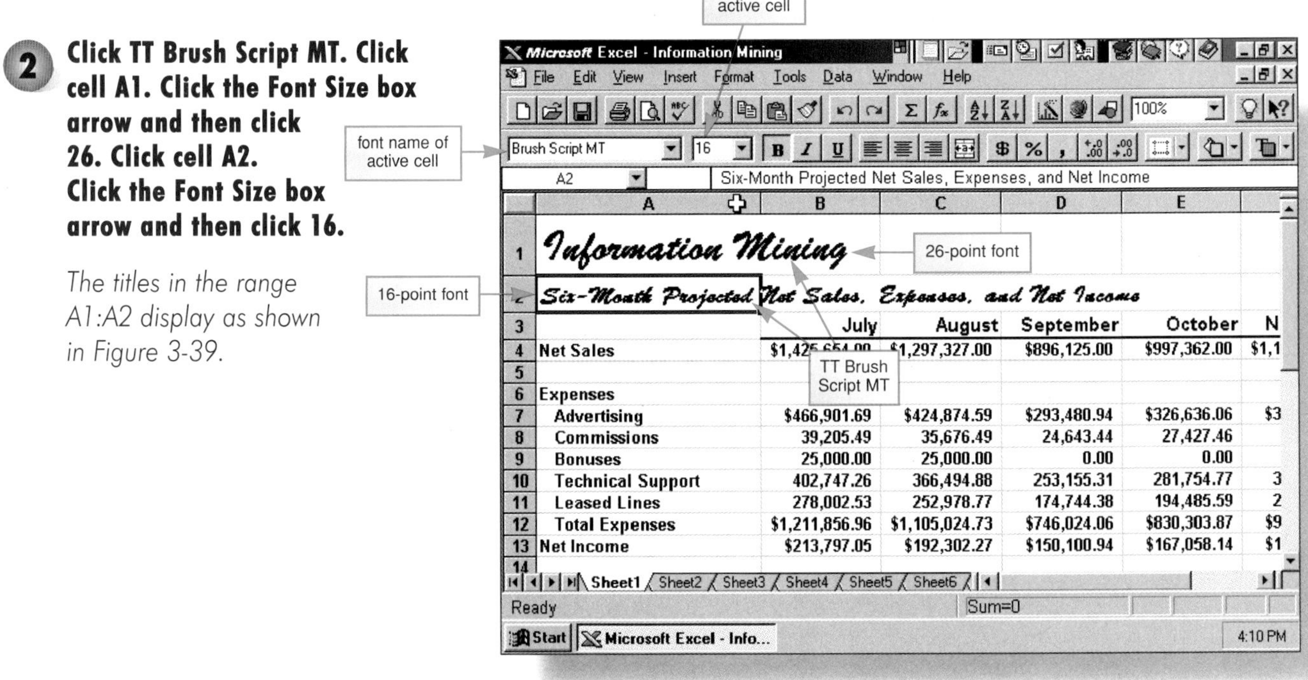

FIGURE 3-39

3 **Select the range A1:H2. Click the Color button arrow on the Formatting toolbar. Click light blue (column 1, row 3 on the Color palette). Click the Font Color button arrow on the Formatting toolbar. Point to white (column 2, row 1 on the Font Color palette).**

The selected range and Font Color palette display as shown in Figure 3-40.

4 **Click white.**

Excel changes the color of the font in the titles from black to white (see Figure 3-33 on page E 3.30).

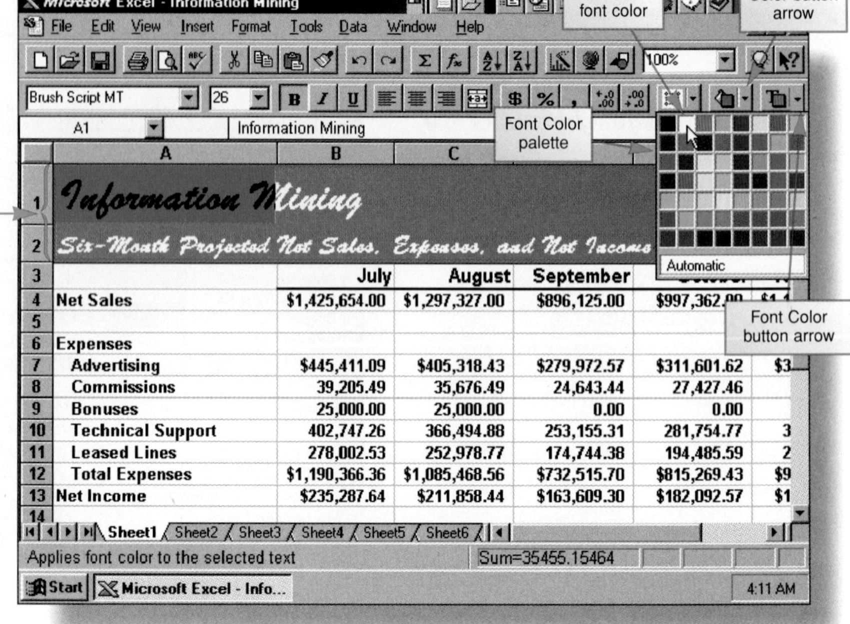

FIGURE 3-40

***Other* Ways**

1. Right-click range, click Format Cells, click Patterns tab to color background or click Font tab to color font

With the range A1:H2 selected, the next step is to add a drop shadow. To add a drop shadow, the Drawing toolbar must display on the screen. The following section describes how to display and dock an inactive (hidden) toolbar.

Displaying the Drawing Toolbar

Excel has more than 200 buttons that you can display on toolbars. Most of the buttons display on thirteen built-in toolbars. You can also create customized toolbars containing the buttons that you often use. Two of the thirteen built-in toolbars are the Standard toolbar and Formatting toolbar that usually display at the top of the screen. Another built-in toolbar is the Drawing toolbar. The **Drawing toolbar** provides tools that can simplify adding lines, boxes, and other geometric figures to a worksheet.

You can use the shortcut menu or the Toolbars command on the View menu to display or hide any one of the thirteen toolbars. The Drawing toolbar can also be displayed or hidden by clicking the Drawing button on the Standard toolbar. Perform the steps that follow to display the Drawing toolbar, obtain information on the functions of buttons, and then dock the Drawing toolbar at the bottom of the screen.

More *About* **Color Palettes**

If your Color palette has less colors than shown on the Color palette in Figure 3-40, then your system is using a different Color palette setting. The figures in this book were created using High Color (16 bit). To check your Color palette setting, minimize all applications, right-click the desktop, click Properties, click the Settings tab, and locate the Color palette box. If you change the settings, you must restart Windows 95.

Steps To Display the Drawing Toolbar

1 Click the Drawing button on the Standard toolbar.

The Drawing toolbar displays (Figure 3-41). Excel locates the Drawing toolbar on the screen wherever it displayed and in whatever shape it displayed the last time it was used.

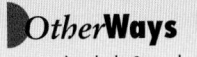

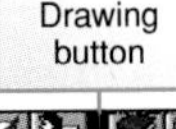

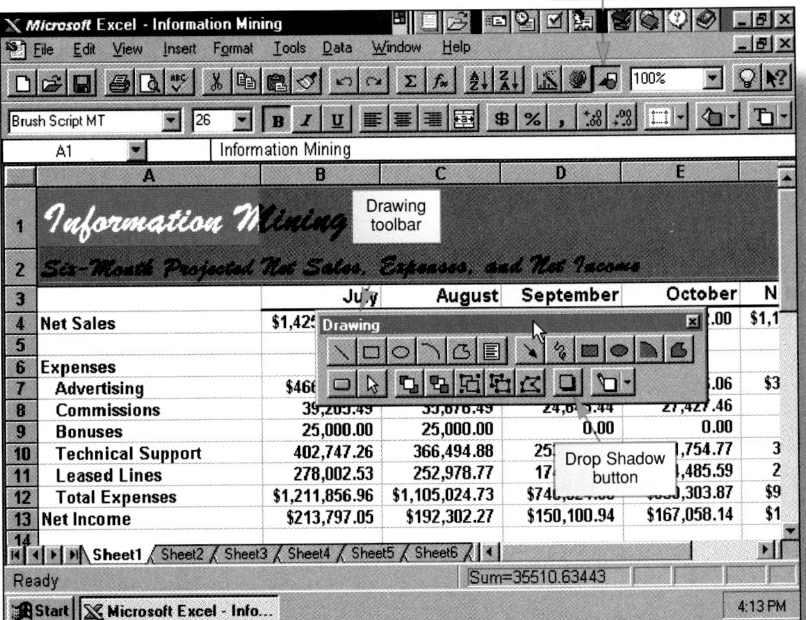

FIGURE 3-41

OtherWays

1. Right-click Standard or Formatting toolbar, click Drawing
2. On View menu click Toolbars, click Drawing check box, click OK button

In addition to moving the mouse across the textbar buttons and reading the ToolTips, you can also obtain information on any button by performing the following steps.

TO LIST THE FUNCTIONS OF BUTTONS ON A TOOLBAR

Step 1: Right-click any toolbar.
Step 2: Click Customize on the shortcut menu.
Step 3: Click a toolbar name in the Categories box.
Step 4: One at a time, click the buttons in the Buttons area and read the descriptions of the buttons at the bottom of the Customize dialog box.

Moving and Shaping a Toolbar

The Drawing toolbar in Figure 3-41 is called a **floating toolbar** because you can move it anywhere in the window. You move the toolbar by positioning the mouse pointer in a blank area within the toolbar (not on a button) and dragging it to its new location. A floating toolbar always displays in its own window with a title bar. As with any window, you can drag the toolbar window borders to resize it and you can click the Close box in the title bar to hide a floating toolbar.

Sometimes a floating toolbar gets in the way no matter where you move it. Hiding the toolbar is one solution. At times, however, you will want to keep it active as you use it. For this reason, Excel allows you to locate toolbars on the edge of its window. If you drag the toolbar close to the edge of the window, Excel positions the toolbar in a **toolbar dock**.

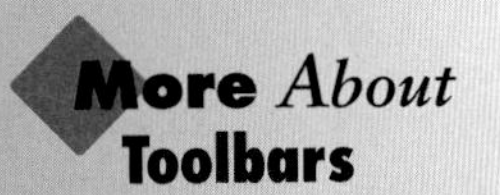

More About Toolbars

You can create your own toolbar and assemble the buttons you want on it by using the Customize command on the shortcut menu that displays when you right-click a toolbar.

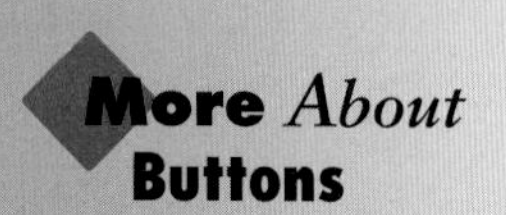

More About Buttons

You can think of buttons as being assigned instructions that execute whenever a button is clicked.

Excel provides four toolbar docks, one on each of the four sides of the window. You can add as many toolbars to a dock as you want. However, each time you dock a toolbar, the window decreases slightly in size to compensate for the room taken up by the toolbar. The following steps show how to dock the Drawing toolbar at the bottom of the screen below the scroll bar.

Steps To Dock a Toolbar at the Bottom of the Screen

1. **Position the mouse pointer in the title bar or a blank area in the Drawing toolbar.**

2. **Drag the Drawing toolbar below the scroll bar at the bottom of the screen and release the left mouse button.**

   Excel docks the Drawing toolbar at the bottom of the screen (Figure 3-42).

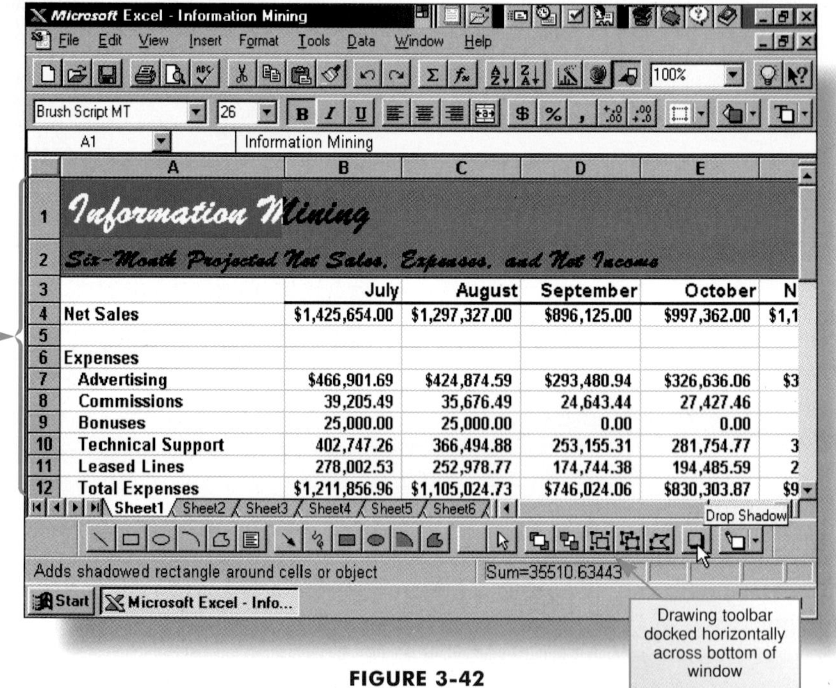

FIGURE 3-42

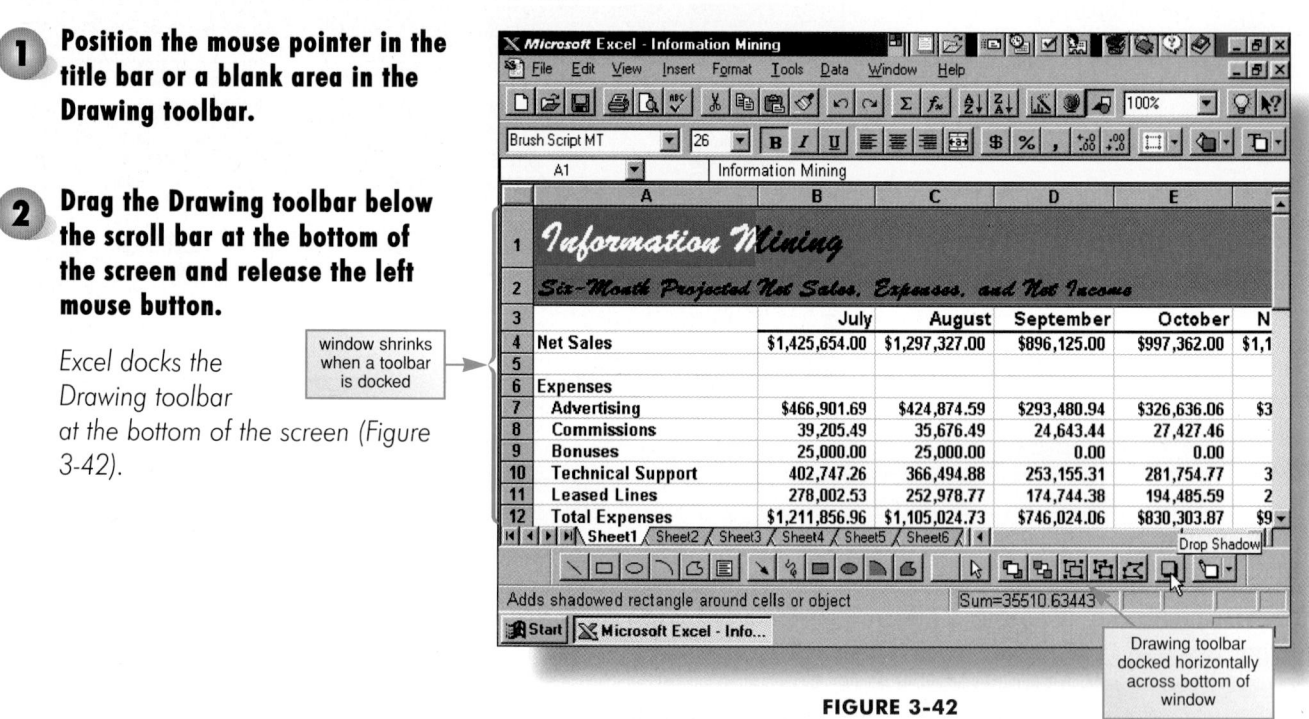

More About Docking Toolbars

A toolbar button that has a drop-down list box, such as the Pattern button on the far right side of the Drawing toolbar in Figure 3-42, cannot be docked on the left or right edge of the window.

Compare Figure 3-42 to Figure 3-41. Excel resizes the Drawing toolbar automatically to fit across the window and between the scroll bar and status bar. Also, the heavy window border that surrounded the floating toolbar has changed to a light border. To move a toolbar to any of the other three docks, drag the toolbar to the desired edge before releasing the left mouse button.

Adding a Drop Shadow to the Title Area

With the Drawing toolbar at the bottom of the screen, the next step is to add the drop shadow to the selected title area in the range A1:H2.

Steps To Add a Drop Shadow

1 With the range A1:H2 selected, click the Drop Shadow button on the Drawing toolbar. Click cell A5.

Excel adds a drop shadow to the range A1:H2 (Figure 3-43).

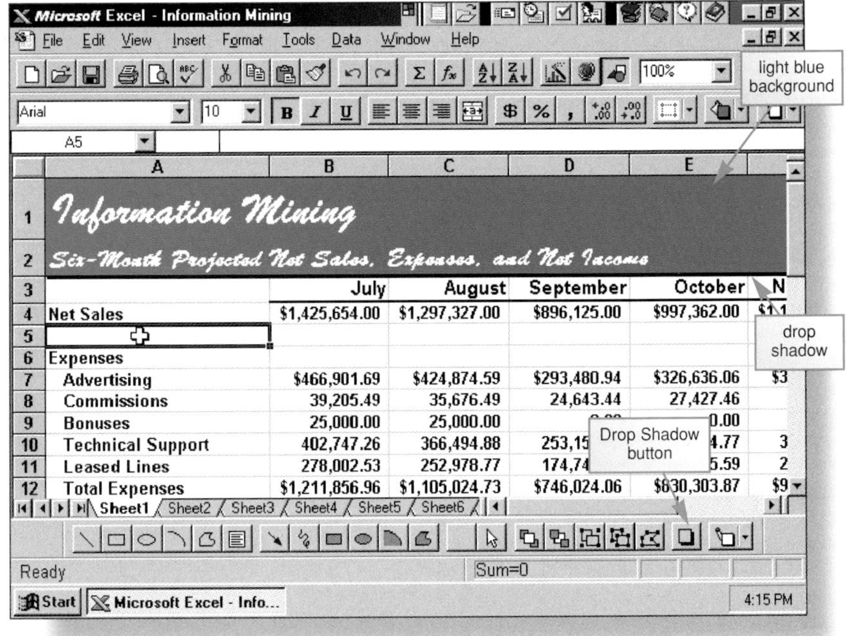

FIGURE 3-43

When you add a drop shadow to a range of cells, Excel also selects the drop shadow and surrounds it with black handles. To deselect the drop shadow, select any cell (cell A5 in Step 1 above)

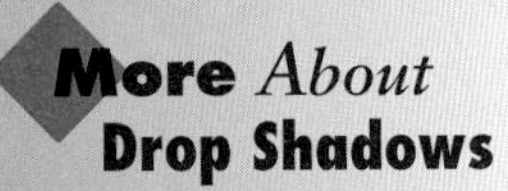

More *About* **Drop Shadows**

To remove an unwanted drop shadow, click it so the handles appear on the drop shadow, and then press the DELETE key. Also, a drop shadow is a shape and not a format. Thus, if you used the Format Painter button to apply formats from a range with a drop shadow, then the drop shadow will not be copied.

Increasing the Height of the Row Containing the Column Headings

Row 3 contains the column headings. The next step is to increase the white space between the worksheet title and the column titles by increasing the height of row 3 to 24.00 points.

TO INCREASE THE HEIGHT OF A ROW

Step 1: Point to the border line between row headings 3 and 4. Drag the mouse down until a height of 24.00 displays in the Name box in the formula bar (Figure 3-44 on the next page).

Step 2: Release the left mouse button.

Excel increases the height of row 3 to 24.00 points (see Figure 3-45 on page E 3.39).

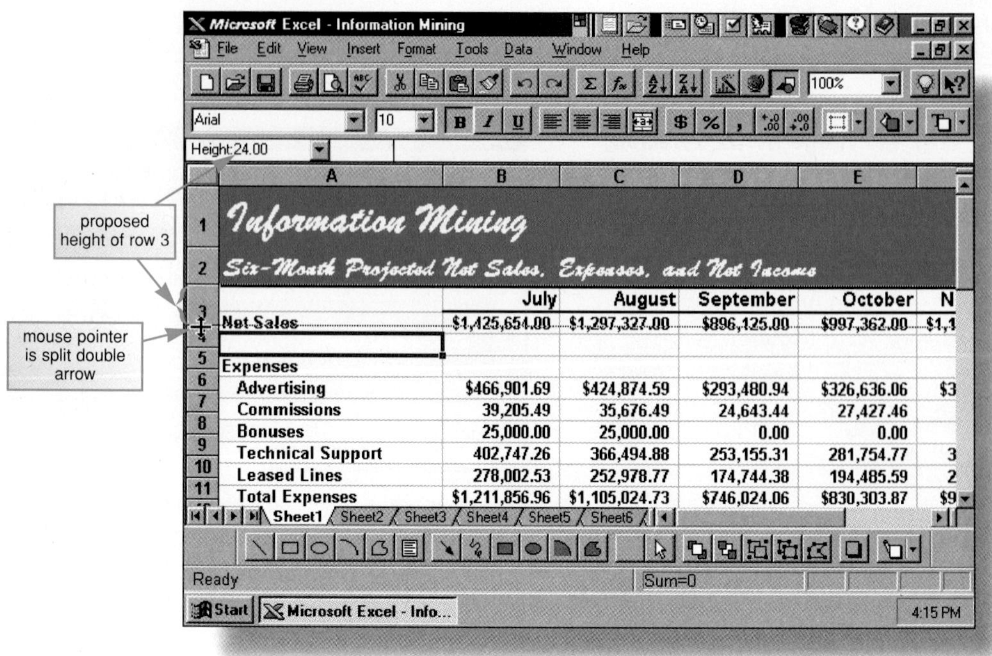

FIGURE 3-44

Formatting the Category Row Titles and Net Income Row

The specifications in Figure 3-33 on page E 3.30 requires a font size of 12 in cells A4, A6, A12, and A13. Also, cells A4, A6, and the range A13:H13 all require the same background color, font color, and drop shadows assigned earlier to the worksheet titles in the range A1:H2. If you look at the Color and Font Color buttons on the formatting toolbar in Figure 3-45 you will notice that the last colors selected and assigned to the worksheet titles are on the buttons. This means that after selecting a range to format, simply click the Color button to assign the light blue background to the range and click the Font Color button to assign the color white to the font in the range. The following steps change the font size in cells A4, A6, A12, and A13, and then add the light blue background color, white font color, and drop shadows to cells A4, A6, and the range A13:H13.

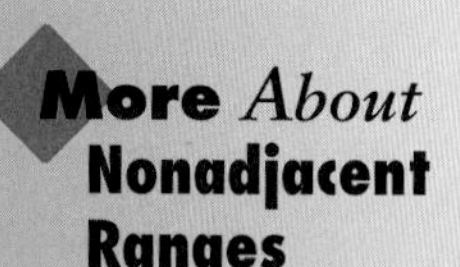

More *About* **Nonadjacent Ranges**

One of the more difficult tasks to learn is selecting nonadjacent ranges. To complete this task, do not hold down the CRTL key when you select the first range because Excel will consider the current active cell to be the first selection. Once the first range is selected, hold down the CRTL key and drag through the ranges. If a desired range is not in the window, use the scroll arrows to move the window over the range. It is not necessary to hold down the CRTL key while you move the window.

To Change Font Size, Add Background and Font Colors, and Add Drop Shadows to Nonadjacent Selections

1 **Click cell A4. Hold down the CTRL key and click cells A6, A12, and A13. Click the Font Size box arrow on the Formatting toolbar and then click 12 in the drop-down list.**

The font size in cells A4, A6, A12, and A13 changes to 12 points.

2 **Click cell A4. Hold down the CTRL key and click cell A6 and select the range A13:H13. Click the Color button to assign the nonadjacent range the light blue background color. Click the Font Color button to change the font to white.**

The nonadjacent ranges are selected and the background and font colors are changed (Figure 3-45).

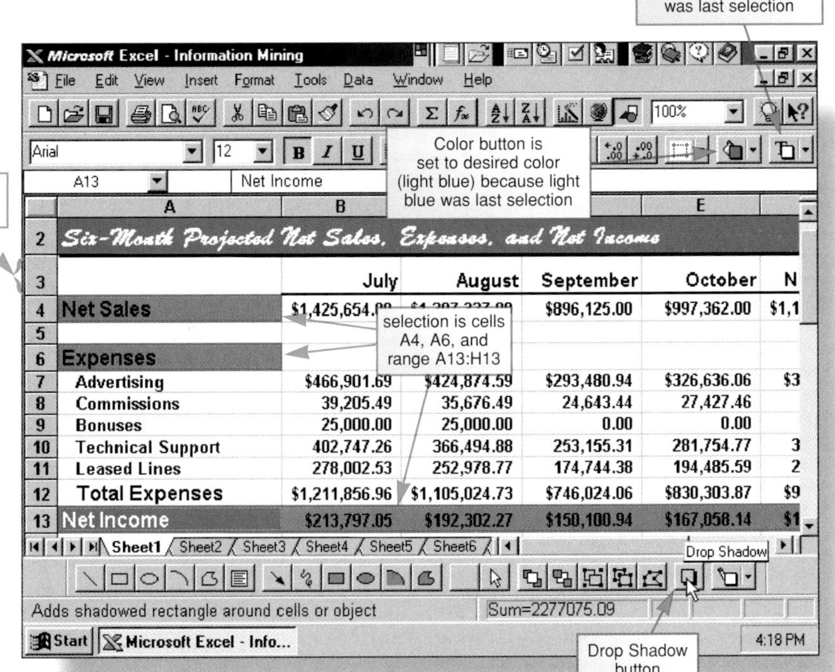

FIGURE 3-45

3 **Click the Drop Shadow button on the Drawing toolbar.**

Excel colors the nonadjacent selection and adds a drop shadow to cells A4, A6, and the range A13:H13. The drop shadow on the range A13:H13 remains selected (Figure 3-46).

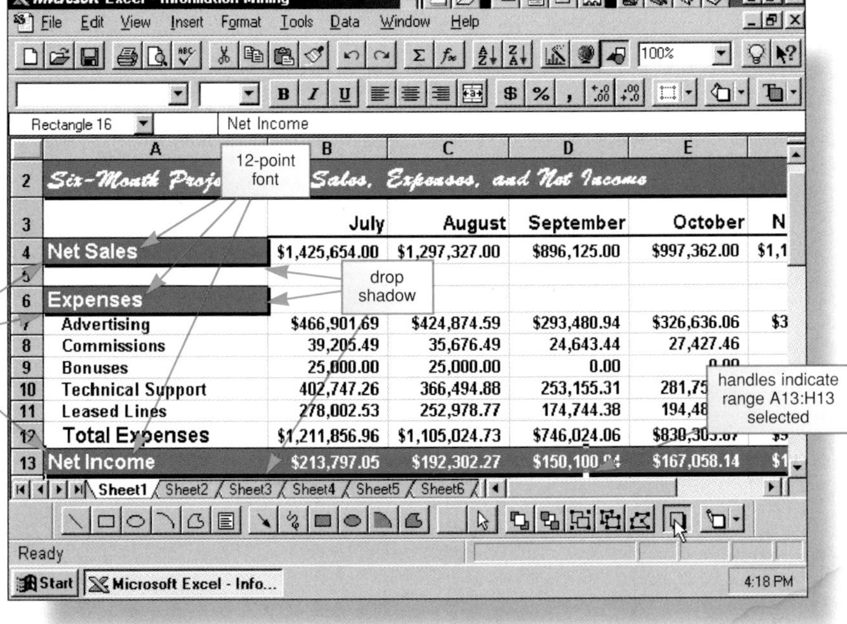

FIGURE 3-46

An alternative to formatting all three areas at once is to select each one separately and apply the formats. Although formatting cell A4 first and then using the Format Painter button on the Standard toolbar may sound like a good idea, the drop shadow is considered a shape and not a format. Thus, Excel would not paint the drop shadow on cell A6 and the range A13:H13. It would paint the background and font colors, however.

Formatting the Assumptions Table

The last step to improving the appearance of the worksheet is to format the Assumptions table in the range A15:B21. The specifications in Figure 3-33 on page E 3.30 require a 16-point italicized underlined font for the title in cell A15. The range A15:B21 has a red background color with a white font and a drop shadow surrounds it. The following steps format the Assumptions table.

To Format the Assumptions Table

1. **Click cell A15. Click the Font Size box arrow on the Formatting toolbar and click 16 point. Click the Italics button and Underline button on the Formatting toolbar.**

   The table heading Assumptions displays as shown in Figure 3-47.

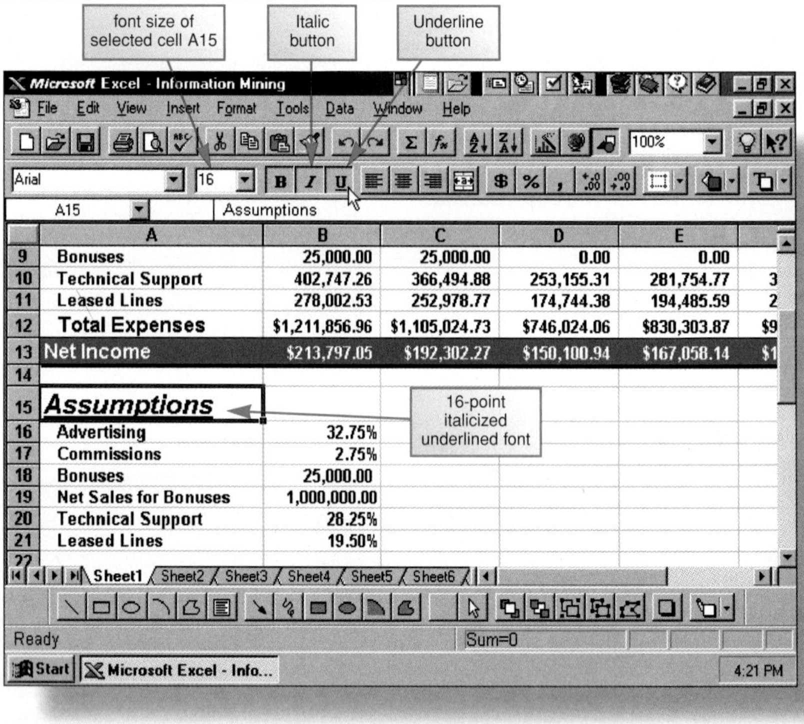

FIGURE 3-47

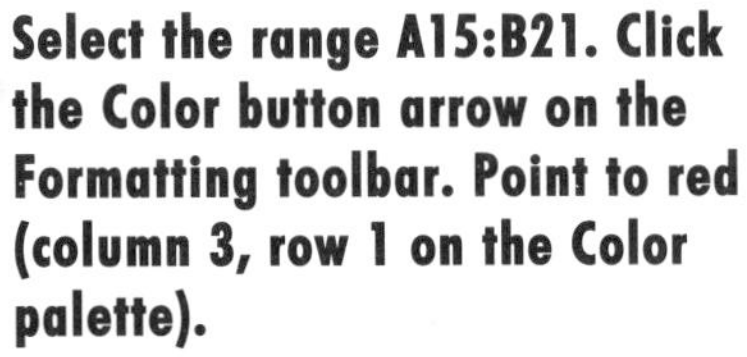

2 **Select the range A15:B21. Click the Color button arrow on the Formatting toolbar. Point to red (column 3, row 1 on the Color palette).**

The Color palette displays as shown in Figure 3-48.

FIGURE 3-48

3 **Click red on the Color palette. Click the Font Color button on the Formatting toolbar.**

The background color of the Assumptions table is red and the font color is white.

4 **Click the Drop Shadow button on the Drawing toolbar. Select cell D21.**

The Assumptions table displays as shown in Figure 3-49.

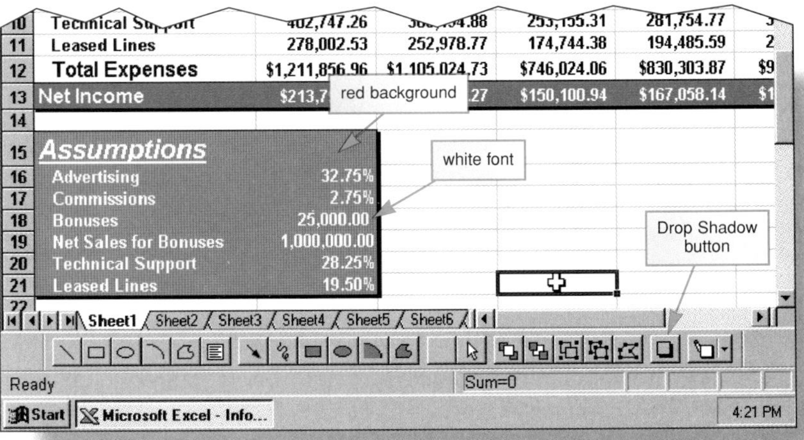

FIGURE 3-49

Notice when you assign the **italic** font style to a cell, Excel slants the characters slightly to the right as shown in cell A15 in Figure 3-49.

Hiding a Toolbar

With the formatting of the worksheet complete, the next step is to hide the Drawing toolbar docked at the bottom of the screen. As shown in the following step, you can hide the Drawing toolbar by clicking the Drawing button on the Standard toolbar.

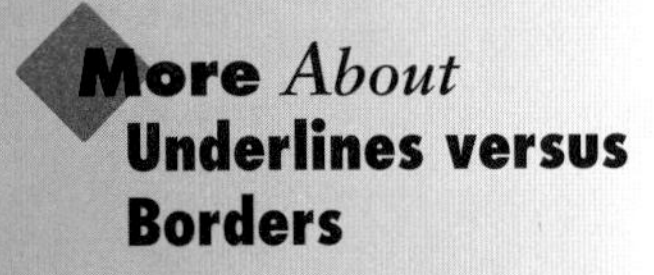

More *About* **Underlines versus Borders**

An underline is different from a bottom border. An underline only underlines the characters in a cell. A bottom border encompasses the width of the entire cell and shows whether or not the cell contains characters.

Steps To Hide the Drawing Toolbar

1. **Click the Drawing button on the Standard toolbar.**

   The Drawing toolbar is removed from the screen (Figure 3-50).

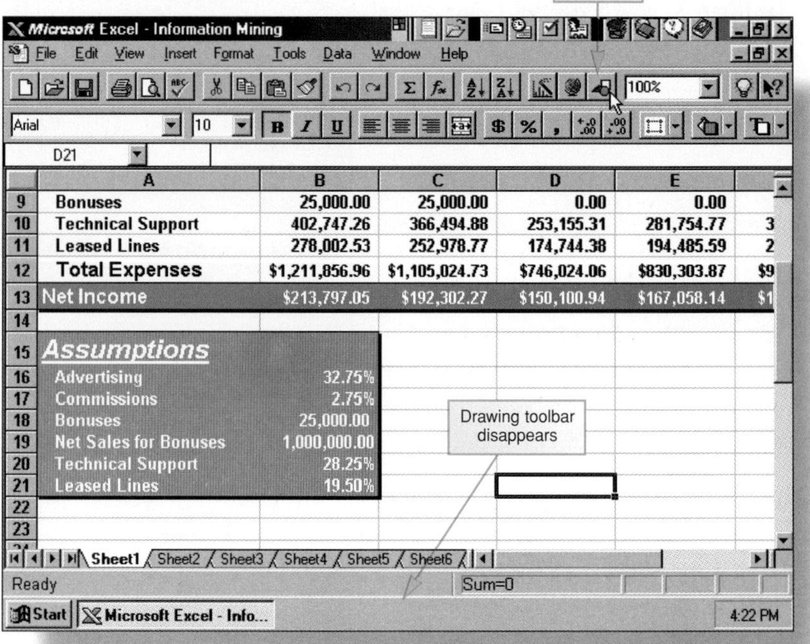

FIGURE 3-50

OtherWays

1. Drag docked toolbar onto screen, click its Close box
2. On View menu click Toolbars, click check box of toolbar to hide, click OK button
3. Right-click toolbar to hide, click its name on shortcut menu

The worksheet is complete. Before moving on to create the 3-D column chart, save the workbook by clicking the Save button on the Standard toolbar.

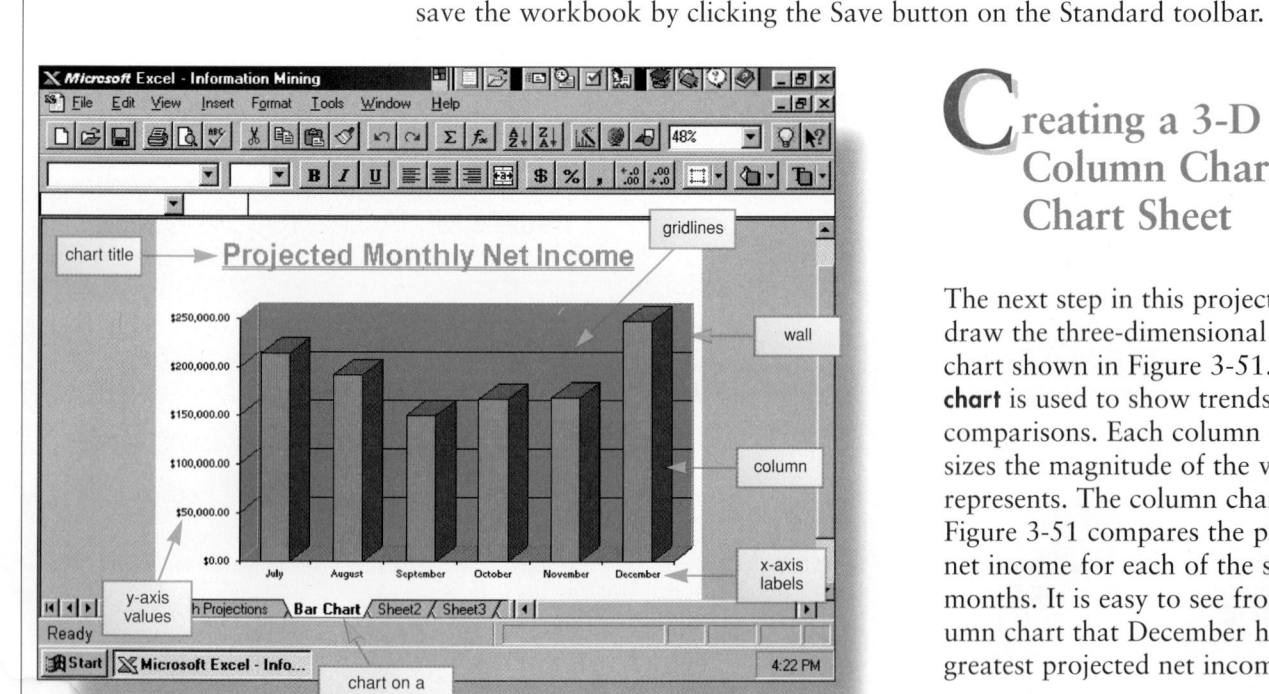

Creating a 3-D Column Chart on a Chart Sheet

The next step in this project is to draw the three-dimensional column chart shown in Figure 3-51. A **column chart** is used to show trends and comparisons. Each column emphasizes the magnitude of the value it represents. The column chart in Figure 3-51 compares the projected net income for each of the six months. It is easy to see from the column chart that December has the greatest projected net income.

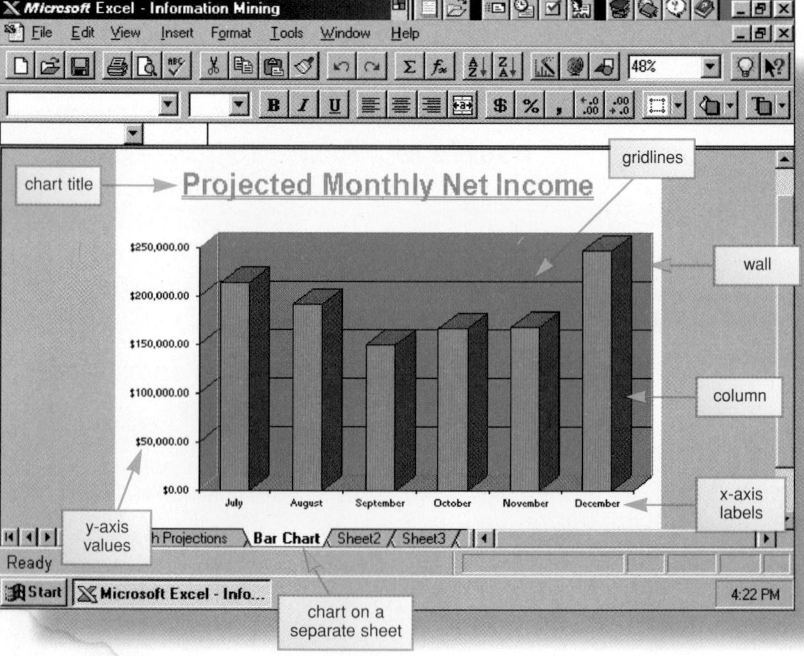

FIGURE 3-51

The column chart in Figure 3-51 differs from the one in Project 1 in that it is not embedded in the worksheet. Rather, it is created on a separate chart sheet as was the pie chart in Project 2.

The ranges of the worksheet to graph are B3:G3 and B13:G13 (Figure 3-52). The month names in the range B3:G3 identify the columns and show at the bottom of the column chart. The month names in the range B3:G3 are called category names. The range B13:G13 contains the data that determines the magnitude of the columns. The values in the range are called the data series. Because six category names and six numbers are included in the data series, the column chart contains six columns.

Drawing the 3-D Column Chart

In Project 1, you used the ChartWizard button on the Standard toolbar to draw an embedded 3-D column chart. **Embedded** means the chart is on the same sheet with the worksheet. Anytime you want to create an embedded chart, the ChartWizard button is the best choice. To create a chart on a separate sheet, use the Chart command on the Insert menu as you did in Project 2 to create the pie chart. This command takes you into the ChartWizard, but first asks you if you want to create the chart on the same sheet or a separate sheet.

The following steps illustrate how to create a 3-D column chart on a separate sheet.

More *About* **the Zoom Control Box**

The chart size in Figure 3-51 is only 48% of the actual printed size. If you want to increase the size on the screen, click the Zoom Control box arrow on the Standard toolbar and click one of the larger percents. You can also type a percent in the Zoom Control box. Once you get the chart built in this project, try zooming to 75%, 100%, 200%, and Selection (default size).

To Draw a 3-D Column Chart on a Chart Sheet

1 **Select the range B3:G3. Hold down the CTRL key and select the nonadjacent range B13:G13. Click Chart on the Insert menu. Point to As New Sheet on the Chart submenu.**

Excel displays the Chart submenu, which allows you to choose where in the workbook you want to create the chart (Figure 3-52).

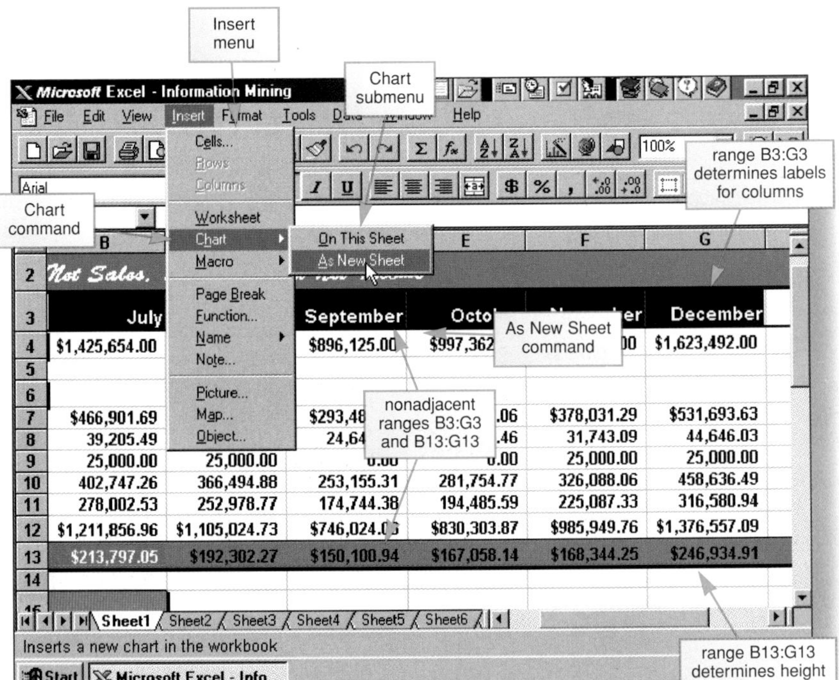

FIGURE 3-52

2 Click As New Sheet on the Chart submenu.

Excel displays the ChartWizard - Step 1 of 5 dialog box, which displays the selected range in the worksheet (Figure 3-53). You can type a new range or use the mouse to change the range in the worksheet if you decide you want to alter your original selection.

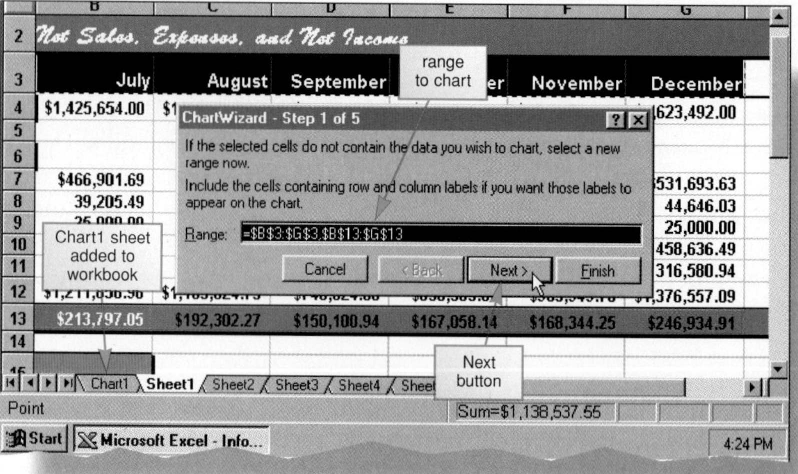

FIGURE 3-53

3 Click the Next button. Select 3-D Column in the ChartWizard - Step 2 of 5 dialog box (Figure 3-54).

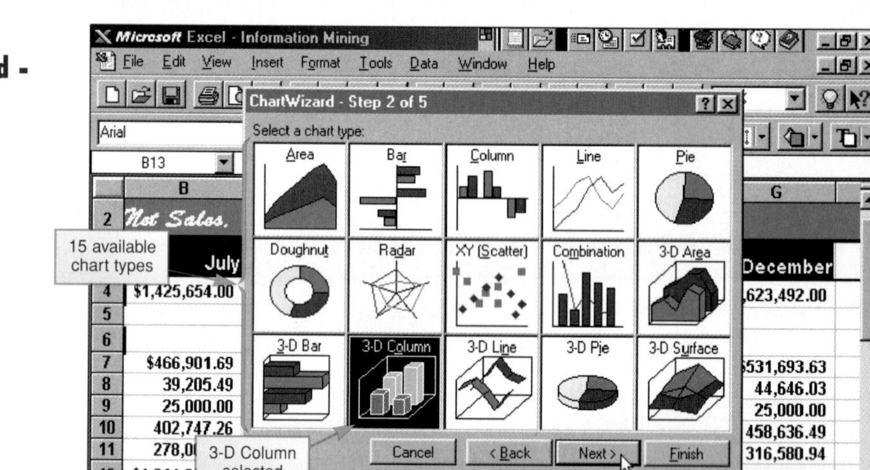

FIGURE 3-54

4 Click the Next button. Select format 4 for the chart.

The ChartWizard - Step 3 of 5 dialog box displays with a selection of eight different 3-D Column chart formats (Figure 3-55).

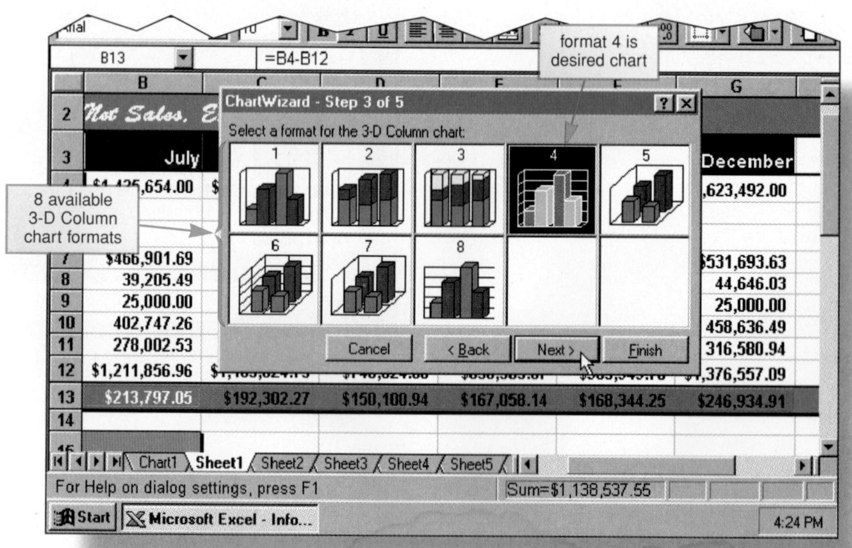

FIGURE 3-55

5 **Click the Next button.**

The ChartWizard - Step 4 of 5 dialog box displays with a sample of the 3-D column chart. (Figure 3-56).

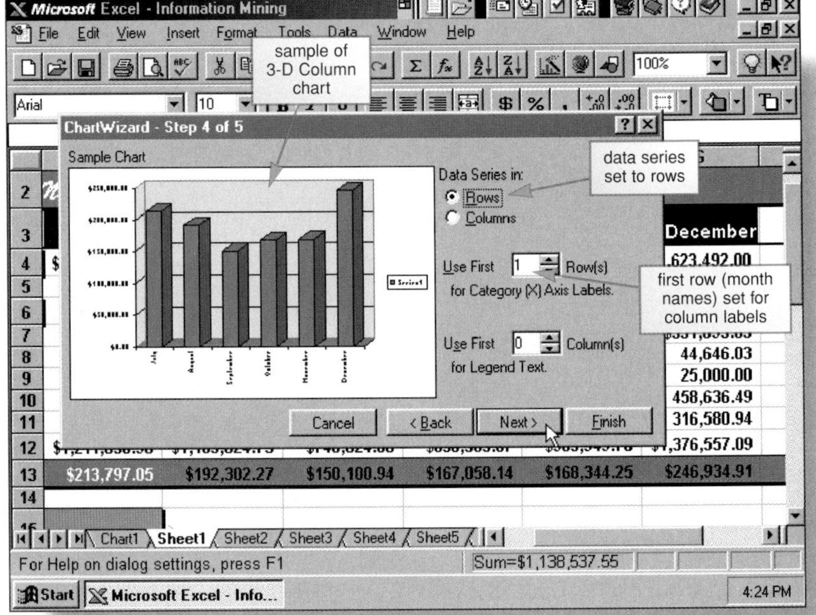

FIGURE 3-56

6 **Click the Next button. Click No under Add a Legend? Click the Chart Title box. Type** `Projected Monthly Net Income` **in the Chart Title box.**

The ChartWizard - Step 5 of 5 dialog box displays. You have the opportunity in this dialog box to add a chart title, y-axis title, x-axis title, and select whether or not you want legends to display alongside the chart. Excel changes the sample chart dynamically in the dialog box as you enter titles (Figure 3-57).

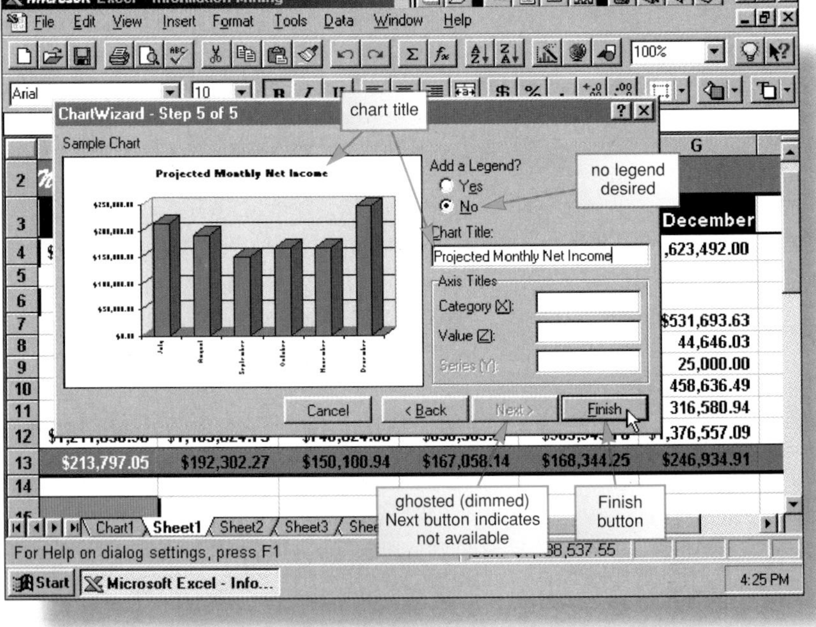

FIGURE 3-57

7 Click the Finish button.

Excel displays the 3-D column chart on a separate sheet (Figure 3-58).

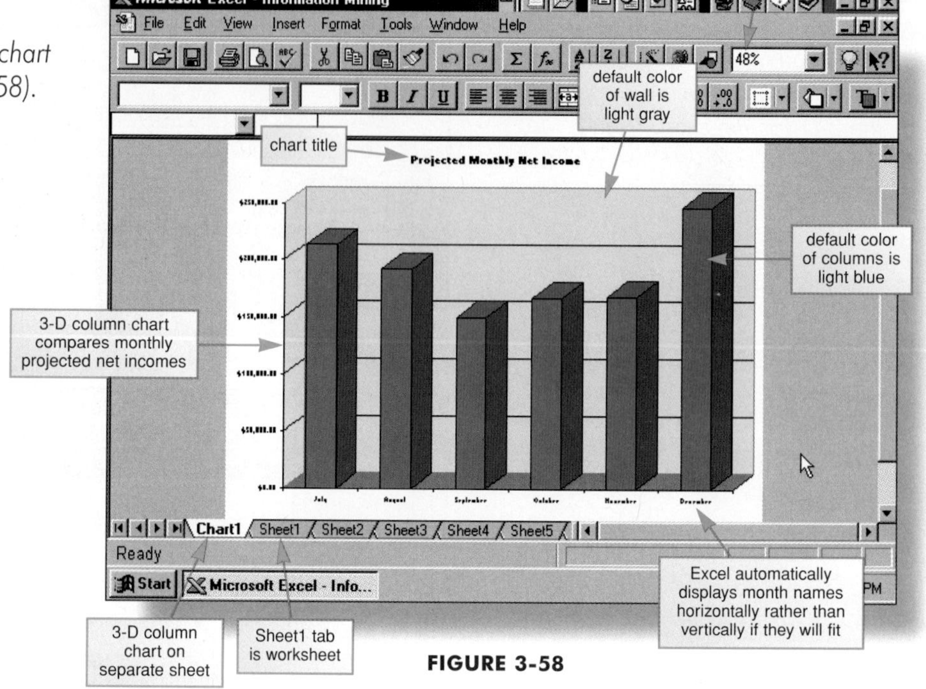

FIGURE 3-58

Each column in the chart in Figure 3-58 represents one of the last six months of the year. The names of the months (range B3:G3) display below the corresponding columns on the x-axis. The values along the y-axis (the vertical line to the left of the columns) are determined automatically by Excel from the highest and lowest projected net incomes in the range B13:G13 of the worksheet.

In the five ChartWizard dialog boxes (Figures 3-53 through 3-57) you can return to the previous ChartWizard dialog box by clicking the Back button.

If you compare the sample chart in Figure 3-57 and the chart in Figure 3-58, you will notice that Excel automatically displays the month names horizontally when they will fit, rather than vertically as shown in Figure 3-57.

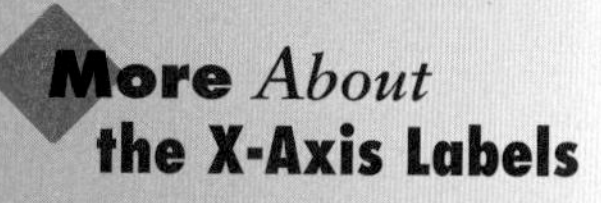

More *About* the X-Axis Labels

If the labels along the x-axis display vertically (see sample chart in Figure 3-57) rather than horizontally (Figure 3-58), reduce their font size by right-clicking one of the labels and clicking Format Axis. Remember, what you see on the screen is reduced by over 50% of the printed version.

Enhancing the 3-D Column Chart

Excel allows you to change any chart item labeled in Figure 3-51 on page E 3.42. All you have to do is double-click the chart item you want to change and Excel displays a dialog box containing the changeable characteristics. To change the 3-D column chart in Figure 3-58 so it looks like the one in Figure 3-51, the following changes must be made:

1. Chart title — increase font size to 36-point, double underline, change the font color to red
2. Columns — change color to red
3. Wall — change color to light blue
4. Data labels – increase font size from 10- to 12-point

Perform the following steps to enhance the 3-D column chart.

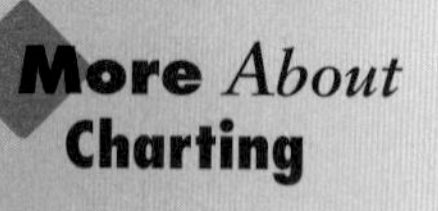

More *About* Charting

Press the ESC key to deselect a chart item.

To Enhance the 3-D Column Chart

1 **Right-click the chart title. Point to Format Chart Title on the shortcut menu.**

Black handles and a gray rectangle surround the chart title, and Excel displays a shortcut menu (Figure 3-59).

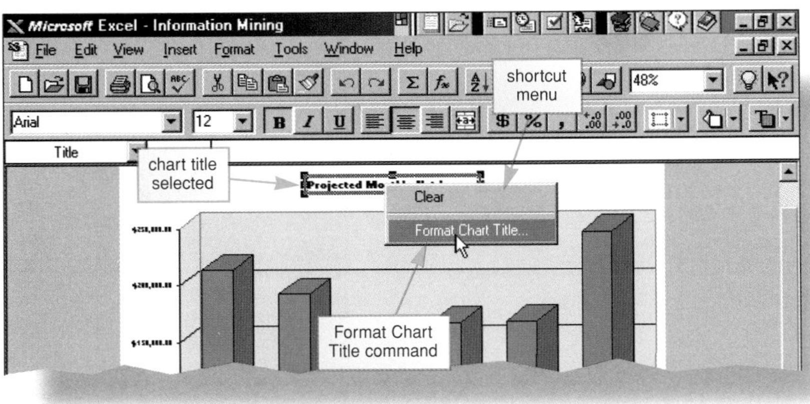

FIGURE 3-59

2 **Click Format Chart Title on the shortcut menu. When the Format Chart Title dialog box displays, click the Font tab. Click 36 in the Size box, click the Underline box arrow and click Double, and click the Color box arrow and select red (column 3, row 1 on the Color palette).**

The Format Chart Title dialog box displays as shown in Figure 3-60.

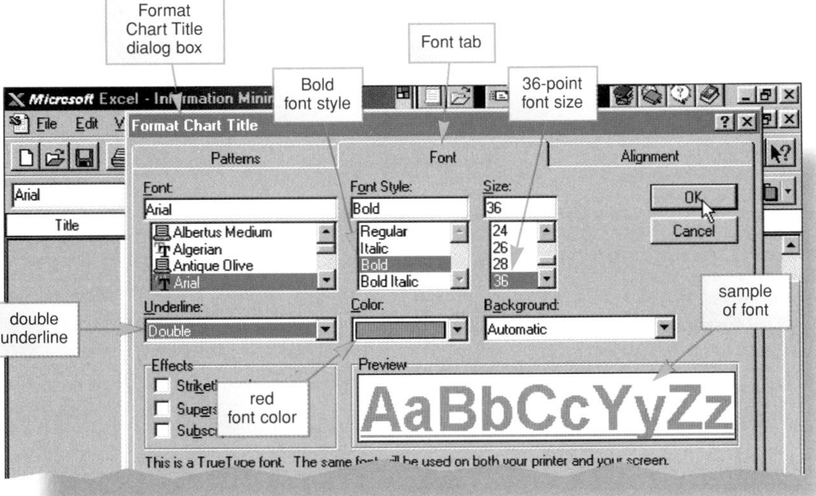

FIGURE 3-60

3 **Click the OK button. Click one of the six columns in the chart. Click the Color button arrow on the Formatting toolbar.**

Excel displays the formatted chart title. Handles appear at the corner points of the six columns and the Color palette displays (Figure 3-61).

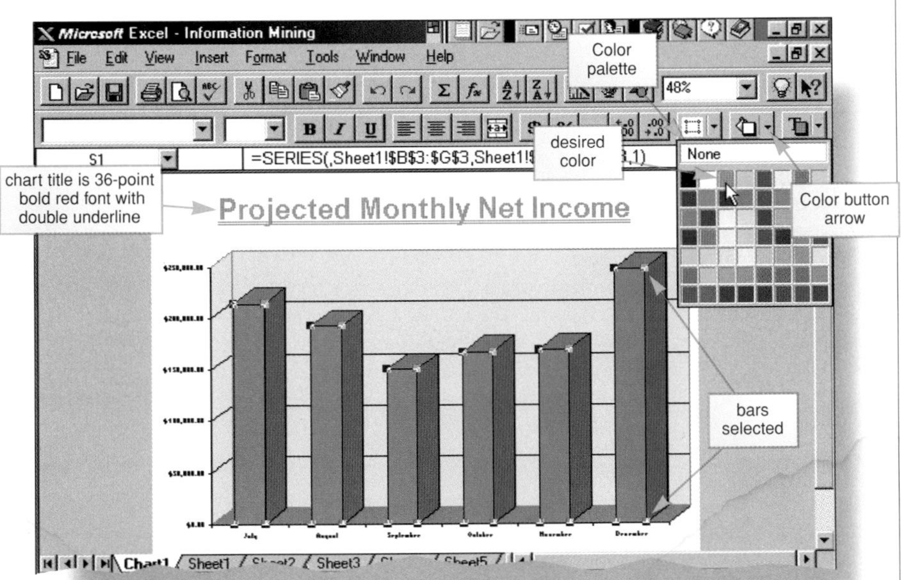

FIGURE 3-61

Click red (column 3, row 1 on the Color palette). Click the wall (not the gridlines) behind the columns. Click the Color button arrow on the Formatting toolbar.

The color of the columns are changed to red, the walls are selected, and the Color palette displays (Figure 3-62).

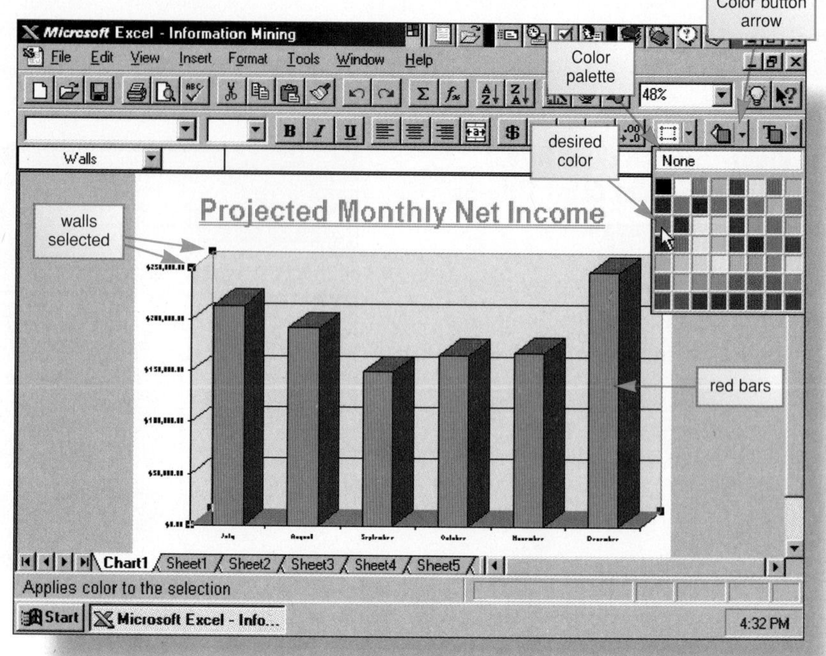

FIGURE 3-62

5 Click light blue (column 1, row 3 on the Color palette). Click one of the labels on the y-axis. Click the Font size box arrow. Point to 12 in the Font Size drop-down list box.

The color of the walls behind the columns changes to light blue. The vertical axis has black handles on its endpoints. The Font Size drop-down list box displays (Figure 3-63).

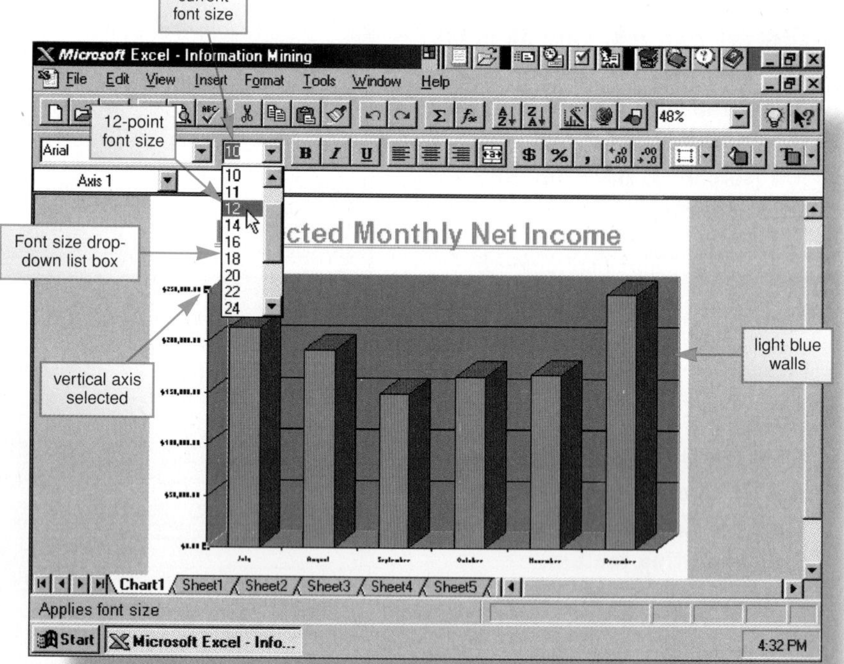

FIGURE 3-63

6 **Click 12 in the Font Size drop-down list box. Click one of the month names on the x-axis. Click the Font Size box arrow. Click 12 in the Font Size drop-down list box.**

The enhanced 3-D column chart displays as shown in Figure 3-64.

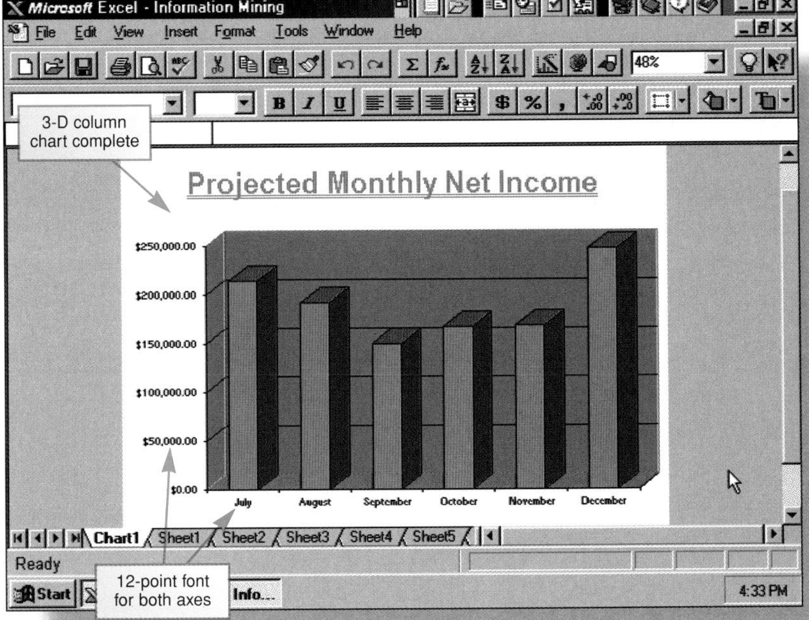

FIGURE 3-64

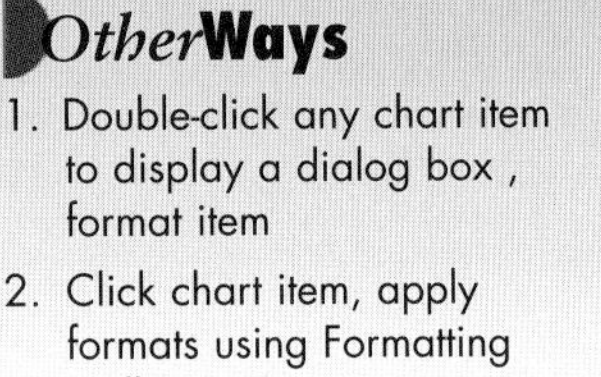

OtherWays

1. Double-click any chart item to display a dialog box , format item
2. Click chart item, apply formats using Formatting toolbar

Compare the chart title in Figure 3-58 on page E 3.46 to the one in Figure 3-64. You can see that the chart title stands out after being formatted. One of the drawbacks to increasing the font size of the chart title is that Excel decreases the size of the chart itself to make room for the larger font. You can select the chart, however, and increase its size if you so desire.

Changing the Name of the Sheet Tabs and Rearranging the Order of the Sheets

The final step in creating the worksheet and 3-D column chart in Project 3 is to change the names of the tabs at the bottom of the screen. The steps on the next page show you how to rename the sheet tabs and reorder the sheets so the worksheet comes before the chart sheet.

More About Highlighting

You can use the Text Box button on the Drawing toolbar to add text to highlight parts of a worksheet or chart.

Steps To Rename the Sheet Tabs and Rearrange the Order of the Sheets

1. **Double-click the tab named Chart1 at the bottom of the screen. When the Rename Sheet dialog box displays, type** `Bar Chart` **as shown in Figure 3-65.**

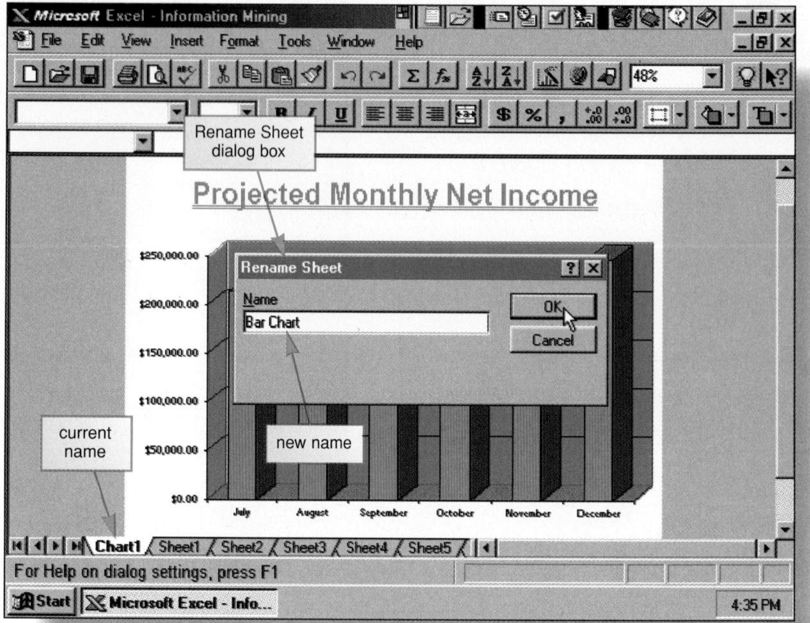

FIGURE 3-65

2. **Click the OK button in the Rename Sheet dialog box.**

3. **Repeat Steps 1 and 2 for the Sheet1 tab. Type** `Six-Month Projections` **for the tab name.**

4. **Drag the Six-Month Projections tab to the left over the Bar Chart tab.**

Excel rearranges the sequence of the sheets and displays the worksheet (Figure 3-66).

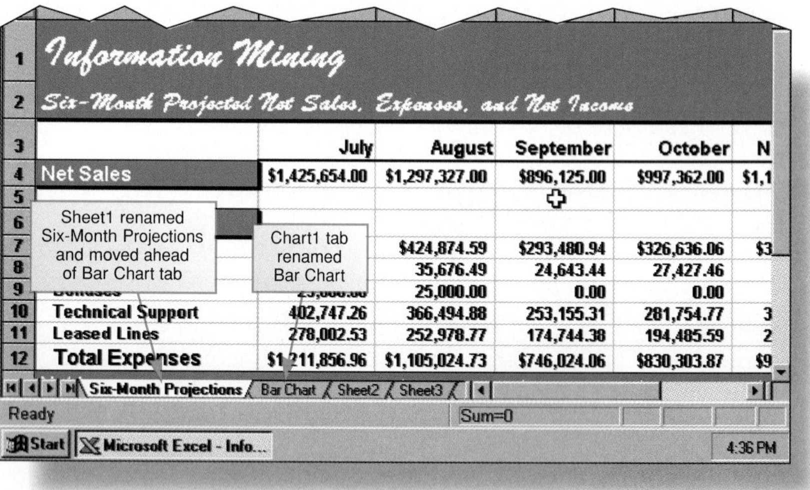

FIGURE 3-66

OtherWays

1. Right-click sheet tab, click Rename
2. Right-click sheet tab, click Move or Copy
3. On Edit menu click Move or Copy

Checking Spelling, Saving, Previewing, and Printing the Workbook

With the workbook complete, the next series of steps is to check spelling, save, preview, and print the workbook. Each series of steps concludes with saving the workbook to ensure the latest changes are saved to disk.

Checking Spelling of Multiple Sheets

The spell checker checks the spelling of only the selected sheets. Thus, before checking the spelling, hold down the CTRL key and click the Bar Chart tab as described in the following steps.

TO CHECK SPELLING OF MULTIPLE SHEETS

Step 1: With the Six-Month Projections sheet active, hold down the CTRL key and click the Bar Chart tab.
Step 2: Click the spelling button on the Standard toolbar. Correct any errors.
Step 3: Click the Save button on the Standard toolbar.

Previewing and Printing the Workbook

With the worksheet and chart complete, the next step is to preview and print them. Recall that Excel only previews and prints selected sheets. Because the worksheet is too wide to print in portrait, you must change the orientation to landscape.

TO PREVIEW AND PRINT THE WORKBOOK IN LANDSCAPE ORIENTATION

Step 1: If both sheets are not selected, select the inactive one by holding down the CTRL key and clicking the tab of the inactive sheet.
Step 2: Right-click the menu bar, click Page Setup, click the Page tab, click the Landscape option button, click the OK button.
Step 3: Click the Print Preview button on the Standard toolbar. When you are finished previewing, click the Close button.
Step 4: Ready the printer.
Step 5: Click the Print button on the Standard toolbar.
Step 6: Right-click the Six-Month Projections tab. Click Ungroup Sheets on the shortcut menu to deselect the Bar Chart tab.
Step 7: Click the Save button on the Standard toolbar.

The worksheet and bar chart print as shown in Figure 3-67 on the next page.

Six-Month Projections

Information Mining

Six-Month Projected Net Sales, Expenses, and Net Income 4/23/97

	July	August	September	October	November	December	Total
Net Sales	$1,425,654.00	$1,297,327.00	$896,125.00	$997,362.00	$1,154,294.00	$1,623,492.00	$7,394,254.00
Expenses							
Advertising	$466,901.69	$424,874.59	$293,480.94	$326,636.06	$378,031.29	$531,693.63	$2,421,618.19
Commissions	39,205.49	35,676.49	24,643.44	27,427.46	31,743.09	44,646.03	203,341.99
Bonuses	25,000.00	25,000.00	0.00	0.00	25,000.00	25,000.00	100,000.00
Technical Support	402,747.26	366,494.88	253,155.31	281,754.77	326,088.06	458,636.49	2,088,876.76
Leased Lines	278,002.53	252,978.77	174,744.38	194,485.59	225,087.33	316,580.94	1,441,879.53
Total Expenses	$1,211,856.96	$1,105,024.73	$746,024.06	$830,303.87	$985,949.76	$1,376,557.09	$6,255,716.46
Net Income	$213,797.05	$192,302.27	$150,100.94	$167,058.14	$168,344.25	$246,934.91	$1,138,537.55

Assumptions	
Advertising	32.75%
Commissions	2.75%
Bonuses	25,000.00
Net Sales for Bonuses	1,000,000.00
Technical Support	28.25%
Leased Lines	19.50%

Page 1

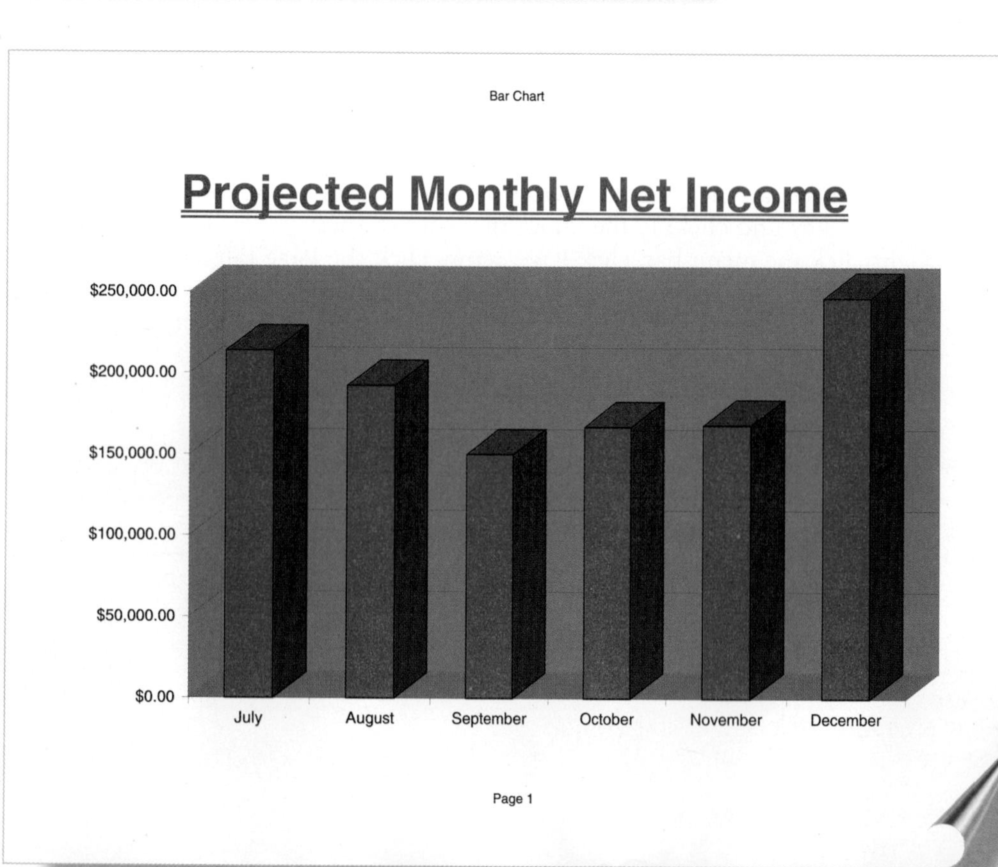

FIGURE 3-67

Changing the View of the Worksheet

With Excel, you can easily change the view of the worksheet. For example, you can magnify or shrink the worksheet on the screen. You can also view different parts of the worksheet through **window panes**.

Shrinking and Magnifying the View of a Worksheet or Chart

You can magnify (zoom in) or shrink (zoom out) the display of a worksheet or chart by using the **Zoom Control box** on the Standard toolbar. When you magnify a worksheet, the characters on the screen become large and fewer columns and rows display. Alternatively, when you shrink a worksheet, more columns and rows display. Magnifying or shrinking a worksheet affects only the view; it does not change the window size or printout of the worksheet or chart. Perform the following steps to shrink and magnify the view of the worksheet.

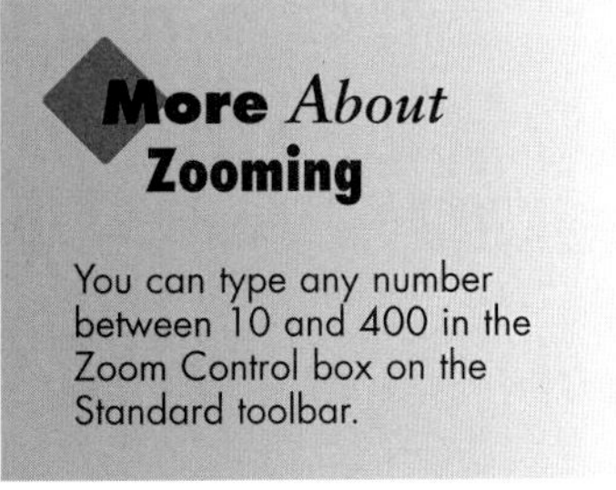

More *About* **Zooming**

You can type any number between 10 and 400 in the Zoom Control box on the Standard toolbar.

Steps To Shrink and Magnify the Display of a Worksheet or Chart

1. **Click the Zoom Control box arrow on the Standard toolbar.**

   A drop-down list of percentages displays (Figure 3-68).

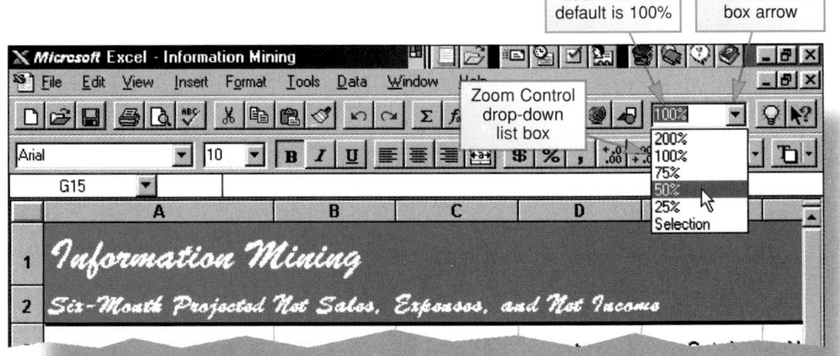

FIGURE 3-68

2. **Click 50% in the drop-down list.**

   Excel shrinks the display of the worksheet to a magnification of 50% of its normal display (Figure 3-69). With the worksheet zoomed to 50%, you can see more rows and columns than you did at 100% magnification.

3. **Click the Zoom Control box arrow on the Standard toolbar and then click 100%.**

   Excel returns to a normal display.

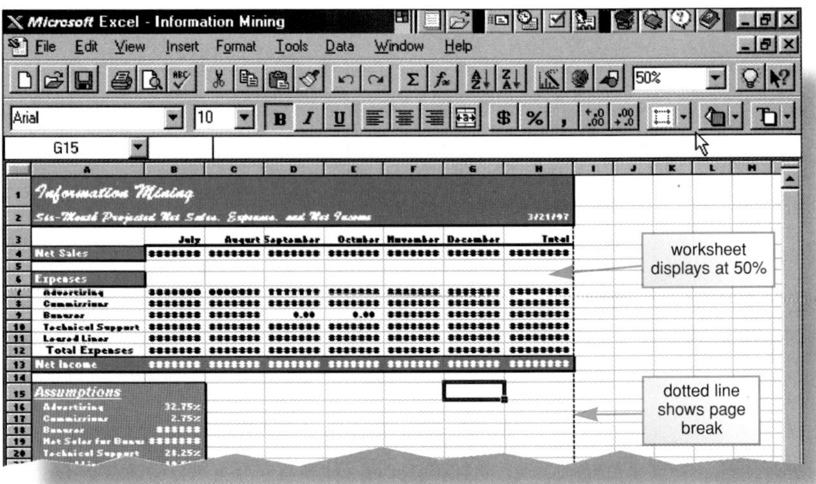

FIGURE 3-69

Other Ways

1. On View menu click Zoom, click desired magnification, click OK button

Notice in Figure 3-69 on the previous page how you get a better view of the page breaks (dotted lines) when you shrink the display of the worksheet. Depending on the type of printer you have, you can end up with the dotted lines representing the page breaks at different locations on the worksheet.

Splitting the Window into Panes

In Excel, you can split the window into two or four window panes and view different parts of a large worksheet at the same time. To split the window into four panes, select the cell where you want the four panes to intersect. Next, click the **Split command** on the Window menu. Follow the steps below to split the window into four panes.

Steps To Split a Window into Four Panes

1 **Click cell D5, the intersection of the proposed four panes. Click Window on the menu bar and then point to Split.**

The Window menu displays as shown in Figure 3-70.

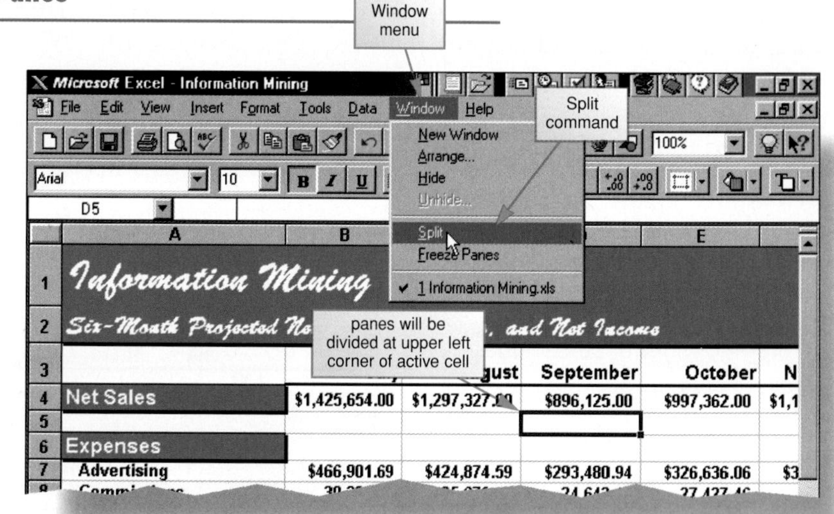

FIGURE 3-70

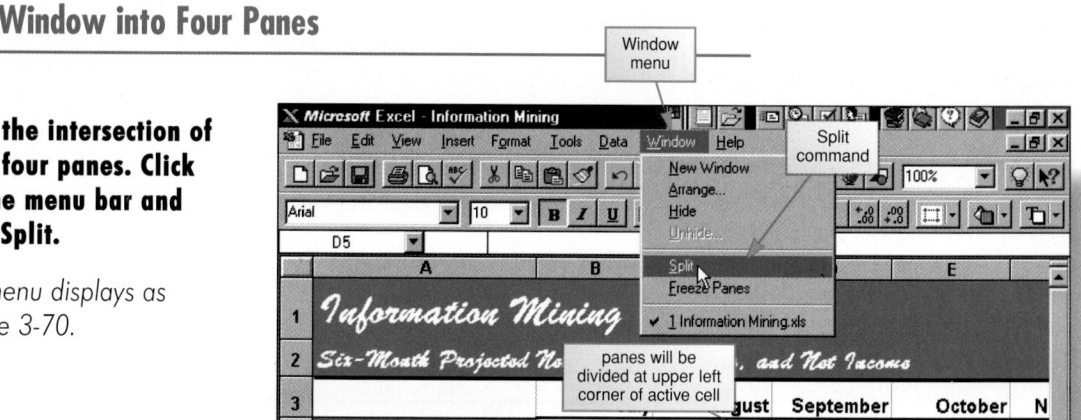

2 **Click Split on the Window menu. Use the scroll arrows to display the four corners of the worksheet.**

Excel divides the window into four panes and the four corners of the worksheet display (Figure 3-71).

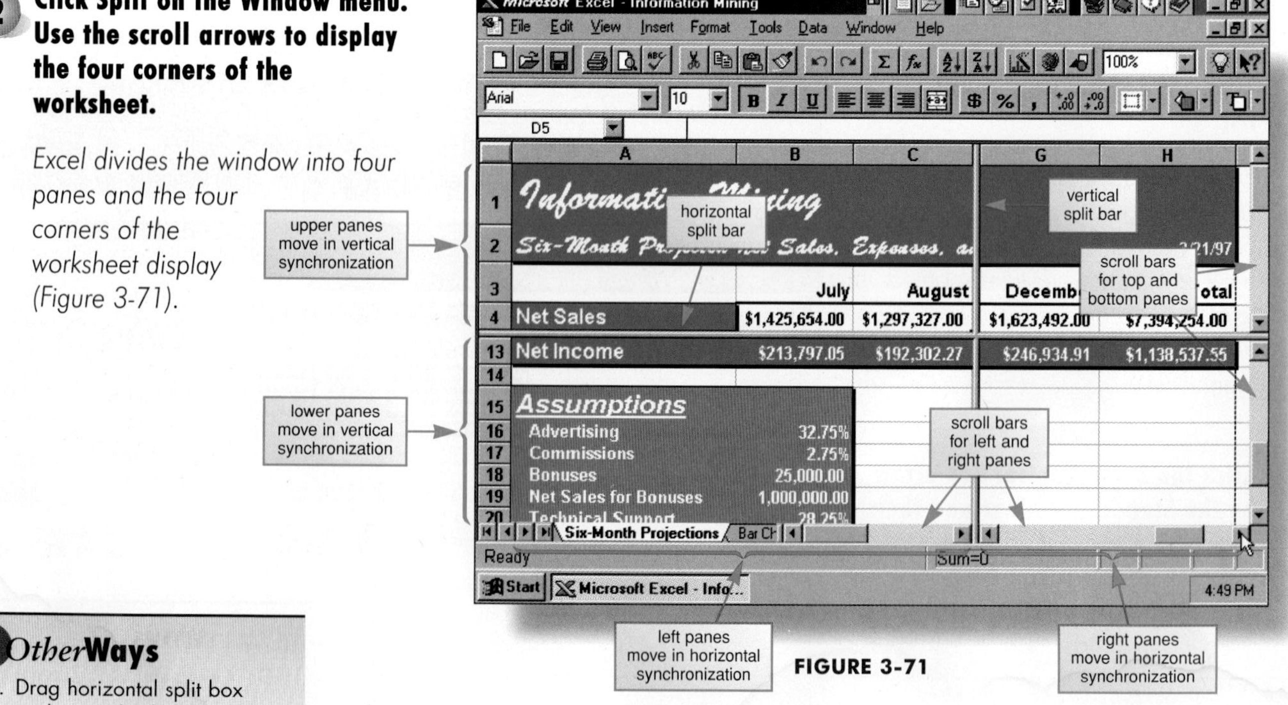

FIGURE 3-71

Other Ways

1. Drag horizontal split box and vertical split box to desired locations

The four panes in Figure 3-71 are used to display the following: (1) the upper left pane displays the range A1:C4; (2) the upper right pane displays the range G1:H4; (3) the lower left pane displays A13:C20; and (4) the lower right pane displays the range G13:H20.

The vertical bar going up and down the middle of the window is called the **vertical split bar**. The horizontal bar going across the middle of the window is called the **horizontal split bar**. If you look closely at the scroll bars below the window and to the right of the window, you will see that the panes split by the horizontal split bar scroll together vertically. The panes split by the vertical split bar scroll together horizontally. To resize the panes, drag either split bar to the desired location in the window.

You can change the values of cells in any of the four panes. Any change you make in one pane also takes effect in the other panes.

To remove one of the split bars from the window, drag the split box to the edge of the window or double-click the split bar. Follow these steps to remove both split bars.

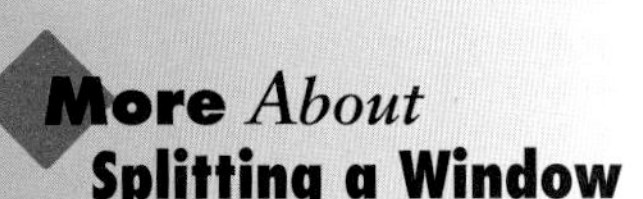

More About Splitting a Window

If you want to split the window into two panes, rather than four, drag the vertical split box or horizontal split box (Figure 3-72 on the next page) to the desired location.

TO REMOVE THE FOUR PANES FROM THE WINDOW

Step 1: Position the mouse pointer at the intersection of the horizontal and vertical split bars.

Step 2: Double-click the split four-headed arrow.

Excel removes the four panes from the window.

What-If Analysis

The automatic recalculation feature of Excel is a powerful tool that can be used to analyze worksheet data. Recall in the Case Perspective on page E 3.4 the problem Marissa Gold had when members of the board of directors suggested she change her assumptions to generate new projections. Because she had to perform this task manually, it took her several minutes. The recalculations then rendered her chart useless.

Using Excel to scrutinize the impact of changing values in cells that are referenced by a formula in another cell is called **what-if analysis** or **sensitivity analysis**. Not only does Excel recalculate all formulas in a worksheet when new data is entered, it also redraws any associated charts.

In Project 3, the projected monthly expenses and net incomes in the range A7:G13 are dependent on the **assumptions** in the range A15:B21. Thus, if you change any of the assumptions, Excel immediately recalculates the projected monthly expenses in rows 7 through 12 and the projected monthly net incomes in row 13. Finally, because the projected monthly net incomes in row 13 change, Excel redraws the 3-D column chart, which is based on these numbers.

More About What-If Analysis

Worksheets are the ultimate tool for what-if-analysis. You enter values into key cells, such as B16:B21 in the Assumptions table, and then see what happens to the dependent cells. Besides manually changing assumptions in a worksheet, Excel has additional methods for answering what-if questions, including Goal Seeking, Solver, Pivot Tables, Scenario Manager, and the Analysis ToolPak.

A what-if question for the worksheet in Project 3 might be, What if the first three assumptions in the range A15:B21 are changed as follows: Advertising 32.75% to 25.00%; Commissions 2.75% to 1.25%; Bonuses $25,000.00 to $10,000.00 — how would these changes affect the projected six-month net income in cell H13? To answer questions like this, you need only change the first three values in the assumptions table. Excel immediately answers the question regarding the projected six-month net income in cell H13 by instantaneously recalculating the worksheet and redrawing the 3-D column chart.

The following steps change the first three assumptions as indicated in the previous paragraph and determine the new projected six-month net income in cell H13. To ensure that the Assumptions table (range A15:B21) and the projected six-month net income in cell H13 show on the screen at the same time, the following steps also divide the window into two vertical panes.

Steps To Analyze Data in a Worksheet by Changing Values

1 Use the vertical scroll bar to move the window so cell A4 is in the upper left corner of the screen.

2 Drag the vertical split box from the lower right corner of the screen so that the vertical split bar is positioned immediately to the right of column D. Use the right scroll arrow in the right pane to display the totals in column H.

Excel divides the window into two vertical panes and shows the totals in column H in the pane on the right side of the window (Figure 3-72).

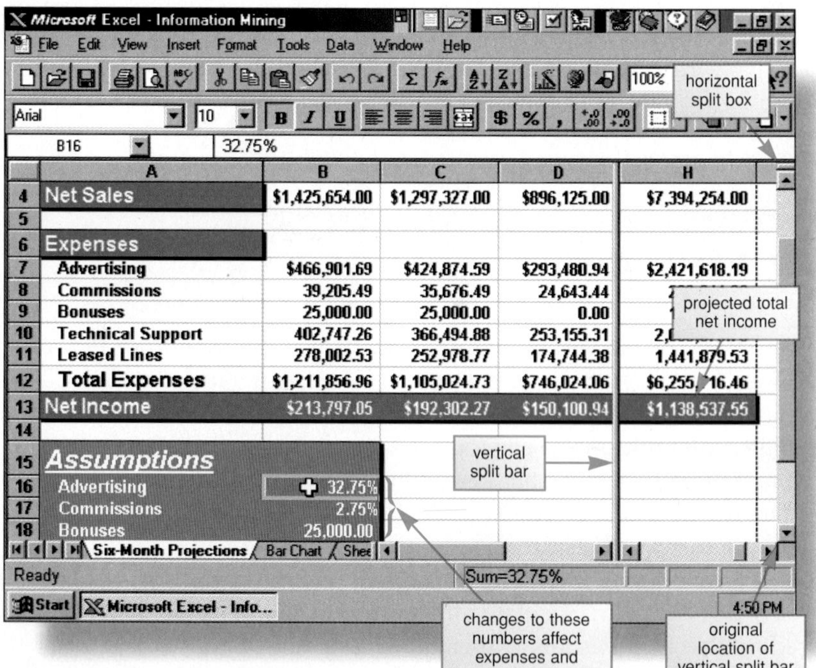

FIGURE 3-72

3 **Enter** 25.00% **in cell B16,** 1.25% **in cell B17,** 10000 **in cell B18.**

Excel immediately recalculates all the formulas in the worksheet, including the projected six-month net income in cell H13 (Figure 3-73).

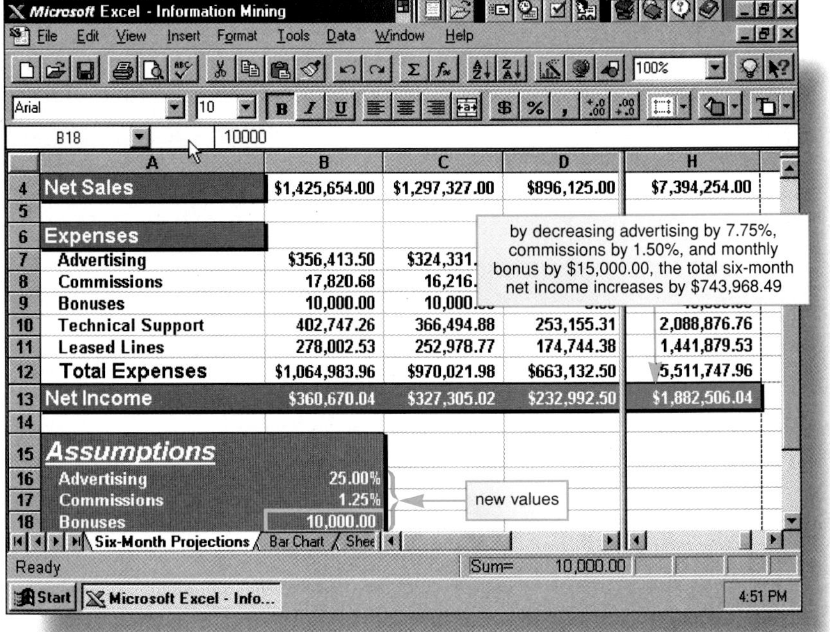

FIGURE 3-73

Each time you enter one of the new percent expenses, Excel recalculates the worksheet. This process usually takes less than one second, depending on how many calculations must be performed and the speed of your computer. Compare the projected six-month net incomes in Figures 3-73 and 3-72. By changing the values of the three assumptions (Figure 3-73), the projected six-month net income in cell H13 increases from $1,138,537.55 to $1,882,506.04. The change in the assumptions translates into an increase in the projected net income of $743,968.49 for the six-month period.

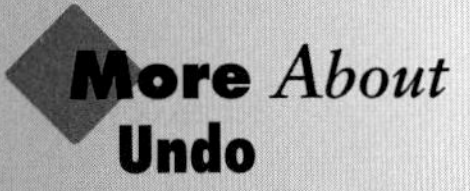

More *About* **Undo**

The Undo button is ideal for returning the worksheet to its original state after you have changed the value of a cell to answer a what-if question. Unfortunately, you can only undo the last task. Excel does not maintain a history.

Goal Seeking

If you know the result you want a formula to produce, you can use **goal seeking** to determine the value of a cell on which the formula depends. The following example reopens Information Mining and uses the **Goal Seek command** on the **Tools menu** to determine the projected advertising percentage in cell B16 that yields a projected six-month net income in cell H13 of $1,250,000.00.

To Goal Seek

1. **On the File menu click Close. Close Information Mining without saving changes. Click the Open button on the Standard toolbar and then reopen Information Mining.**

2. **Drag the vertical split box to the right of column D. Click cell H13, the cell that contains the projected six-month net income. Click Tools on the menu bar and then point to Goal Seek.**

   The vertical split bar displays to the right of column D, and the Tools menu displays (Figure 3-74).

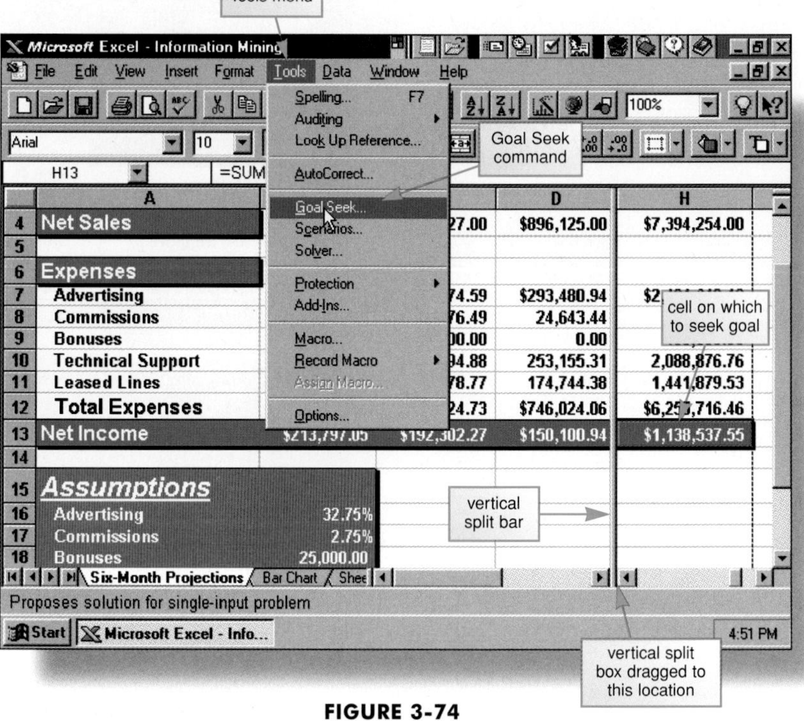

FIGURE 3-74

3. **Click Goal Seek on the Tools menu.**

   The Goal Seek dialog box displays. The Set cell box is assigned the cell reference of the active cell in the worksheet (cell H13) automatically.

4. **Type** 1,250,000 **in the To value box. Type** b16 **in the By changing cell box.**

   The Goal Seek dialog box displays as shown in Figure 3-75.

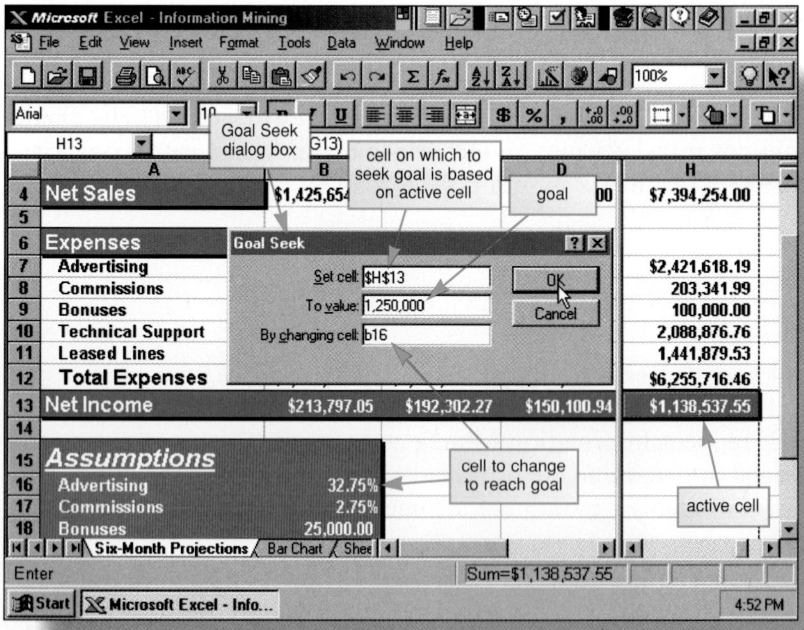

FIGURE 3-75

5 Click the OK button in the Goal Seek dialog box. When the Goal Seeking Status dialog box displays, click the OK button.

Excel immediately changes cell H13 from $1,138,537.55 to the desired value $1,250,000.00. More importantly, Excel changes the advertising assumption in cell B16 from 32.75% to 31.24% (Figure 3-76).

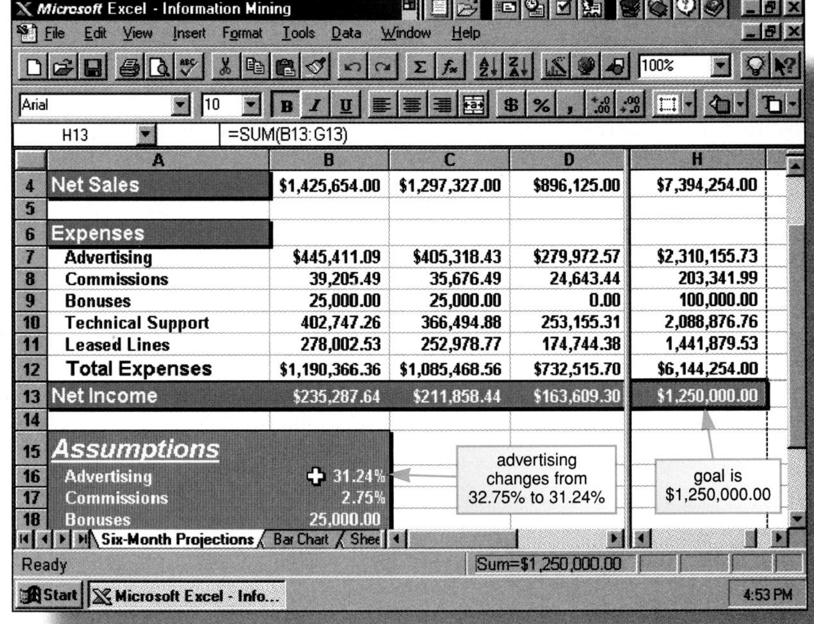

FIGURE 3-76

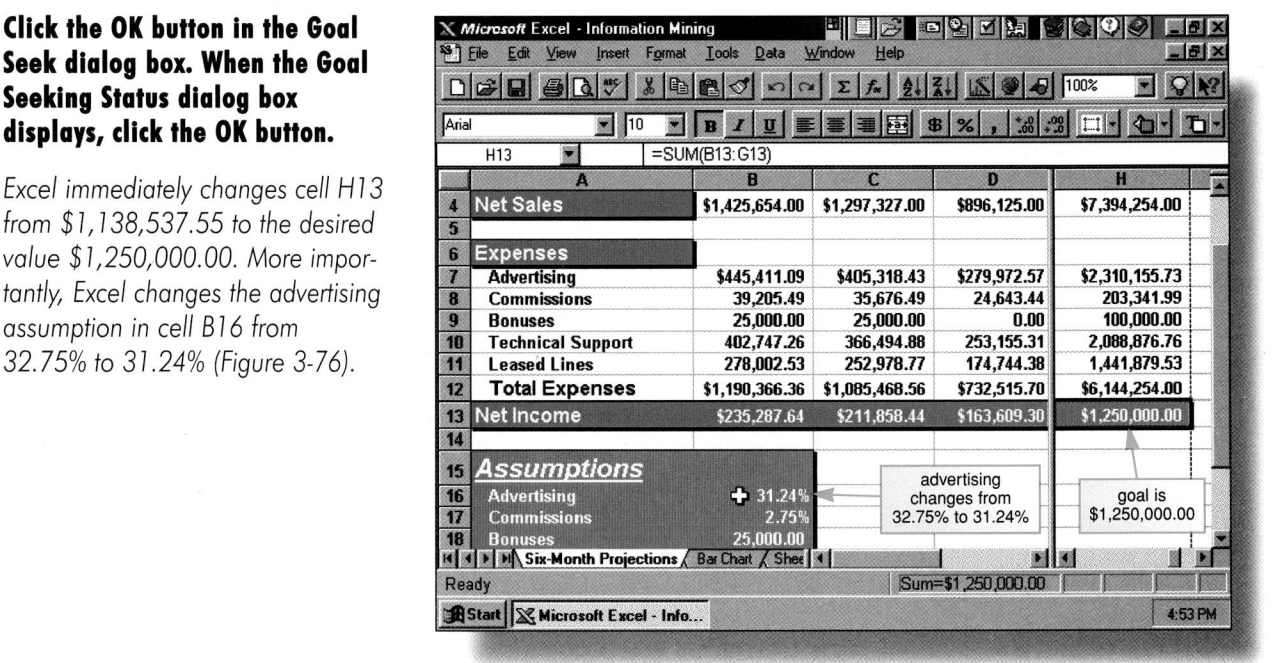

Goal seeking assumes you can change the value of only one cell referenced directly or indirectly. In this example, to change the projected six-month net income in cell H13 to $1,250,000.00, the advertising percentage in cell B16 must decrease by 1.51% from 32.75% to 31.24%.

You can see from this goal seeking example that it is not required that the cell to vary (cell B16) be directly referenced in the formula or function. For example, the projected six-month net income in cell H13 is determined from the function =SUM(B13:G13). Cell B16 is not mentioned (advertising assumption) in the function. The advertising assumption in cell B16, on which the projected monthly net incomes in row 13 are based, is referenced in the formulas in rows 7 through 12. Excel is able to goal seek on the projected six-month net income by varying the advertising assumption.

More *About* Goal Seeking

Goal seeking is a methodology in which you know what answer you want a cell's formula to be, but you do not know what value to place in a cell that is involved in the formula. You can goal seek by changing the value in a cell that is indirectly used in the formula as illustrated in Figure 3-76.

Exiting Excel

To exit Excel, complete the following steps.

TO EXIT EXCEL

Step 1: Click the Close button on the right side of the title bar.
Step 2: If the Microsoft Excel dialog box displays, click the No button.

Project Summary

With the worksheet and chart developed in this project, the CFO of Information Mining, Marissa Gold, can easily respond to any what-if questions asked by the board members the next time she presents her semi-annual projections. Questions that took several minutes to answer with paper and pencil can now be answered in a few seconds. Furthermore, computational errors are less likely to occur.

In creating the Information Mining workbook, you learned to work with worksheets that extend beyond the window. You learned how to use the fill handle to create a series. Using the Drawing button on the Standard toolbar, you learned to display hidden toolbars. You learned about the difference between absolute cell references and relative cell references and how to use the IF function. You also learned how to freeze titles, change the magnification of the worksheet, display different parts of the worksheets through panes, and improve the appearance of a chart. Finally, this project introduced you to using Excel to do what-if analyses by means of changing values in cells on which formulas depend and goal seeking.

What You Should Know

Having completed this project, you should be able to perform the following tasks:

- Add a Drop Shadow *(E 3.37)*
- Analyze Data in a Worksheet by Changing Values *(E 3.56)*
- Assign Formats to the Projected Net Sales, Expenses, and Net Income *(E 3.31)*
- Assign Formats Using the Format Cells Dialog Box *(E 3.31)*
- Change Font Size, Add Background and Font Colors, and Add Drop Shadows to Nonadjacent Selections *(E 3.39)*
- Change the Font of the Entire Worksheet to Bold *(E 3.7)*
- Change the Width of a Column *(E 3.12)*
- Check Spelling of Multiple Sheets *(E 3.51)*
- Copy a Cell's Format Using the Format Painter Button *(E 3.10)*
- Copy a Range of Cells to a Nonadjacent Paste Area *(E 3.14)*
- Copy the Projected Expenses and Totals Using the Fill Handle *(E 3.28)*
- Determine the Projected Total Expenses by Category and Total Net Income *(E 3.29)*
- Display the Drawing Toolbar *(E 3.35)*
- Dock a Toolbar at the Bottom of the Screen *(E 3.36)*
- Draw a 3-D Column Chart on a Chart Sheet *(E 3.43)*
- Enhance the 3-D Column Chart *(E 3.47)*
- Enter a Number with a Format Symbol *(E 3.18)*
- Enter an IF Function *(E 3.26)*
- Enter and Format the System Date *(E 3.21)*
- Enter Formulas Containing Absolute Cell References *(E 3.24)*
- Enter the Worksheet Titles *(E 3.8)*
- Exit Excel *(E 3.59)*
- Format the Assumptions Table *(E 3.40)*
- Format the Titles *(E 3.33)*
- Freeze Column and Row Titles *(E 3.19)*
- Goal Seek *(E 3.58)*
- Hide the Drawing Toolbar *(E 3.42)*
- Increase Column Widths and Enter Row Titles *(E 3.12)*
- Increase the Height of a Row *(E 3.37)*
- Insert Rows *(E 3.16)*
- List the Functions of Buttons on a Toolbar *(E 3.35)*
- Preview and Print the Workbook in Landscape Orientation *(E 3.51)*
- Remove the Four Panes from the Window *(E 3.55)*
- Rename the Sheet Tabs and Rearrange the Order of the Sheets *(E 3.50)*
- Shrink and Magnify the Display of a Worksheet or Chart *(E 3.53)*
- Split a Window into Four Panes *(E 3.54)*
- Start Excel *(E 3.7)*
- Unfreeze the Worksheet Titles and Save the Workbook *(E 3.29)*
- Use the Fill Handle to Create a Series of Month Names *(E 3.8)*

Test Your Knowledge

1 True/False

Instructions: Circle T if the statement is true or F if the statement is false.

T F 1. If you enter 1099 in cell B3, 1100 in cell B4, select the range B3:B4, and then drag the fill handle down to cell B10, Excel assigns cell B10 the value 1100.

T F 2. To copy the text July in cell C3 to all the cells in the range C4:C10, hold down the CTRL key while you drag the fill handle from cell C3 to cell C10.

T F 3. You can invoke the Paste command on the Edit menu by pressing the ENTER key.

T F 4. Excel has five toolbar docks.

T F 5. You can dock more than one toolbar at a toolbar dock.

T F 6. The $ in a cell reference affects only the Move command on the Edit menu.

T F 7. If you save a worksheet after changing the page setup characteristics, the next time you open the worksheet the page characteristics will be the same as when you saved it.

T F 8. You can split a window into, at most, four panes.

T F 9. D23 is an absolute reference, and $D$23 is a relative reference.

T F 10. If you assign cell A4 the IF function =IF(A5>A7, 1, 0) and cells A5 and A7 are equal to 7, then Excel displays the value 1 in cell A4.

2 Multiple Choice

Instructions: Circle the correct response.

1. If you assign cell C5 the value 23, cell G7 the value 6, and cell H6 the function =IF(C5>4*G7, "OK", "Not OK"), then __________ displays in cell H6.
   a. OK
   b. Not OK
   c. #REF!
   d. none of the above
2. Which one of the following buttons in the ChartWizard dialog boxes instructs Excel to draw the chart using the options selected thus far?
   a. Next
   b. Cancel
   c. Back
   d. Finish
3. Use function key __________ to change a relative reference in the formula bar to an absolute reference.
   a. F1
   b. F2
   c. F3
   d. F4

(continued)

A+ Test Your Knowledge

Multiple Choice *(continued)*

4. You can split the window into __________.
   a. two horizontal panes
   b. two vertical panes
   c. four panes
   d. all of the above
5. If you drag the fill handle to the right on cell G9, which contains December, then cell G10 will contain __________.
   a. December
   b. January
   c. November
   d. #REF!
6. To use the drag and drop method for copying a range of cells, the mouse pointer must point to the border of the range and change to the __________ shape.
   a. cross hair
   b. arrow
   c. block plus sign
   d. split double arrow
7. The horizontal and vertical split boxes are located __________.
   a. on the Standard toolbar
   b. on the Formatting toolbar
   c. next to the scroll arrows
   d. immediately to the left of the Select All button
8. When you insert rows in a worksheet, Excel __________ below the point of insertion to open up the worksheet.
   a. writes over the existing rows
   b. pushes up the rows
   c. reduces the height of the cells
   d. pushes down the rows
9. You cannot dock a toolbar if it contains a drop-down list box on the __________ of the window.
   a. bottom
   b. sides
   c. top
   d. in the middle
10. Which toolbar can be displayed or hidden by clicking a button on the Standard toolbar?
    a. Standard
    b. Drawing
    c. Formatting
    d. Chart

Test Your Knowledge

3 Understanding the Insert and Delete Commands and the IF Function

Instructions: Fill in the correct answers

1. Assume you want to insert four rows between rows 8 and 9.
   a. Select rows ______________________ through ______________________.
   b. On the shortcut menu, click ______________________.
2. You have data in rows 1 through 6. Assume you want to delete rows 2 through 4.
   a. Select rows ______________________ through ______________________.
   b. On the shortcut menu, click ______________________.
   c. In which row would the data from row 6 be located? ______________________
3. Which command on the shortcut menu results in formulas receiving the error message #REF! from cell referenced in the affected range? ______________________
4. Determine the truth value of the logical tests, given the following cell values: E1 = 500; F1 = 500; G1 = 2; H1 = 50; and I1 = 40. Enter true or false.
   a. E1 < 400 Truth value: ______________________
   b. F1 = E1 Truth value: ______________________
   c. 10 * H1 + I1 <> E1 Truth value: ______________________
   d. E1 + F1 >= 1000 Truth value: ______________________
   e. E1/H1 > G1 * 6 Truth value: ______________________
   f. 5 * G1 + I1 = H1 Truth value: ______________________
   g. 10 * I1 + 2 <= F1 + 2 Truth value: ______________________
   h. H1 -10 < I1 Truth value: ______________________
5. The active cell is cell F15. Write a function that assigns the value zero (0) or 1 to cell F15. Assign zero to cell F15 if the value in cell B3 is greater than the value in cell C12; otherwise assign 1 to cell F15.
   Function: ______________________
6. The active cell is cell F15. Write a function that assigns the value Credit OK or Credit Not OK to cell F15. Assign the label Credit OK if the value in cell A1 is not equal to the value in cell B1; otherwise assign the label Credit Not OK.
   Function: ______________________
7. Excel allows for nested IF functions. A nested IF function is one that contains another IF function in the value-if-true or value-if-false clauses. For example, =IF(A4>D3, IF(A2=4, "OK", "NOT OK'), "MAYBE") is a valid nested IF function. Start Excel and enter this IF function in cell B2. Enter the following sets of numbers into cells A2, A4, and D3 and write down the results in cell B2 for each: Set 1: A2=25; A4=20; D3=18; Set 2: A2=4; A4=38, Set 3= A2=4; A4=10; D3=8.

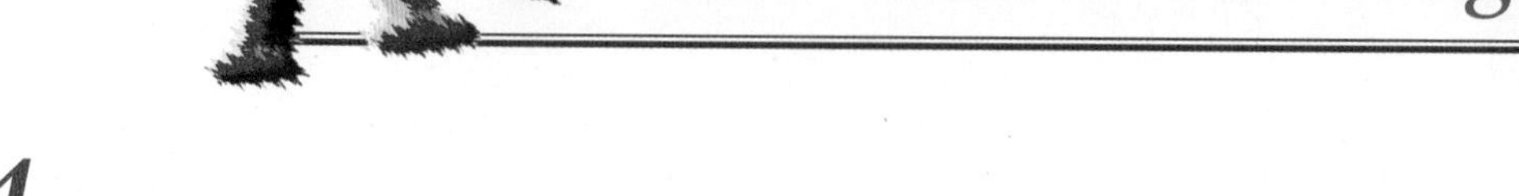

Test Your Knowledge

4 Understanding Absolute, Mixed, and Relative Referencing

Instructions: Fill in the correct answers. Use Figure 3-77 for problems 2 through 5.

1. Write cell D15 as a relative reference, absolute reference, mixed reference with the row varying, and mixed reference with the column varying.

   Relative reference: ____________________ Mixed, row varying: ____________________

   Absolute reference: ____________________ Mixed, column varying: ____________________

2. Write the formula for cell B8 that multiplies cell B1 times the sum of cells B4, B5, and B6. Write the formula so that when it is copied to cells C8 and D8, cell B1 remains absolute. Verify your formula by checking it with the values found in cells B8, C8, and D8 in Figure 3-77.

   Formula for cell B8: ____________________

3. Write the formula for cell E4 that multiplies cell A4 times the sum of cells B4, C4, and D4. Write the formula so that when it is copied to cells E5 and E6, cell A4 remains absolute. Verify your formula by checking it with the values found in cells E4, E5, and E6 in Figure 3-77.

   Formula for cell E4: ____________________

Microsoft Excel - figure 3-77

	A	B	C	D	E	F	G	H	I
1		3	5	7					
2									
3									
4	2	5	2	1	16	16			
5	3	7	3	5	30	45			
6	5	8	7	8	46	115			
7									
8		60	36	42					
9									
10		60	60	98					
11									

FIGURE 3-77

4. Write the formula for cell B10 that multiplies cell B1 times the sum of cells B4, B5, and B6. Write the formula so that when it is copied to cells C10 and D10, Excel adjusts all the cell references according to the new location. Verify your formula by checking it with the values found in cells B10, C10, and D10 in Figure 3-77.

   Formula for cell B10: ____________________

5. Write the formula for cell F4 that multiplies cell A4 times the sum of cells B4, C4, and D4. Write the formula so that when it is copied to cells F5 and F6, Excel adjusts all the cell addresses according to the new location. Verify your formula by checking it with the values found in cells F4, F5, and F6 in Figure 3-77.

   Formula for cell F4: ____________________

Use Help

1 Reviewing Project Activities

Instructions: Perform the following tasks using a computer.

1. Start Excel.
2. Double-click the Help button on the Standard toolbar to display the Help Topics dialog box.
3. Click the Contents tab. Double-click the Creating Formulas and Auditing Workbooks book.
4. Double-click the Using References book. Double-click The difference between relative and absolute references link. Read and print the information. Hand in the printout to your instructor.
5. If the Help Topics: Microsoft Excel dialog box is not on the screen, double-click the Help button on the Standard toolbar. Click the Index tab. Type `column chart` in the top box labeled 1 and then click the Display button. One at a time, click each topic in the Topics Found dialog box. Read and print the information for each topic by clicking Print Topic on the shortcut menu. To return to the Help Topics dialog box, click the Help Topic button. Hand in the printouts to your instructor.
6. If the Help Topics dialog box is not on the screen, double-click the Help button on the Standard toolbar. Click the Find tab. Type `if` in the top box labeled 1. Click IF in the middle box labeled 2, double-click IF in the bottom box labeled 3, read it, and click Print Topic on the shortcut menu. Click the Close button to close the Microsoft Excel Help window with the Help information. Hand in the printout to your instructor.
7. Double-click the Help button on the Standard toolbar. Click the Answer Wizard tab. Type `how do i goal seek` in the top box labeled 1. Click the Search button. In the bottom box labeled 2, double-click Solving problems with one or more variables under Tell Me About. One at a time, click the two links and read the Help information.

2 Expanding on the Basics

Instructions: Use Excel online Help to better understand the topics listed below. Begin each of the following by double-clicking the Help button on the Standard toolbar. If you are unable to print the Help information, then answer the questions on your own paper.

1. Double-click the Retrieving and Analyzing Data book on the Contents sheet in the Help Topics dialog box. Double-click the Solving What-If Problems book. Use the links to write a short paragraph explaining the difference between a one-variable data table and a two-variable data table. When you are finished, click the Close button and hand in your paragraph to your instructor.
2. Use the Find tab in the Help Topics: Microsoft Excel dialog box to display and then print information about the following topics and submit the printouts to your instructor: (a) freezing titles, (b) splitting a window, (c) comparison operators, (d) abramowitz.
3. Use the Answer Wizard in the Help Topics: Microsoft Excel dialog box to answer the question, *how do I fill in a series of numbers?* Answer the following related questions: (a) What types of series can Excel fill in? (b) How do I fill in a series of numbers? (c) How do I fill in a series for growth trend? (d) How do I create a custom AutoFill list?

Apply Your Knowledge

1 Creating a Series

Instructions: Start Excel. Open the workbook Create Series from the Excel folder on the Student Floppy Disk that accompanies this book. The worksheet (Figure 3-78) contains the initial values for eight different series.

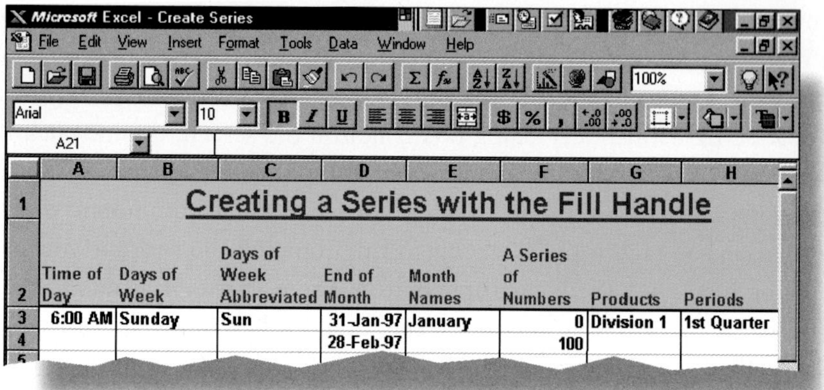

FIGURE 3-78

Use the fill handle on one column at a time to propagate the eight different series as shown in Figure 3-79 through row 17. For example, in column A, select cell A3 and drag the fill handle down to cell A17. Your final result should be 8:00 PM in cell A17. In column D, select the range D3:D4 and drag the fill handle down to cell D17. Save the worksheet using the file name Create Series 2. Print the worksheet on one page.

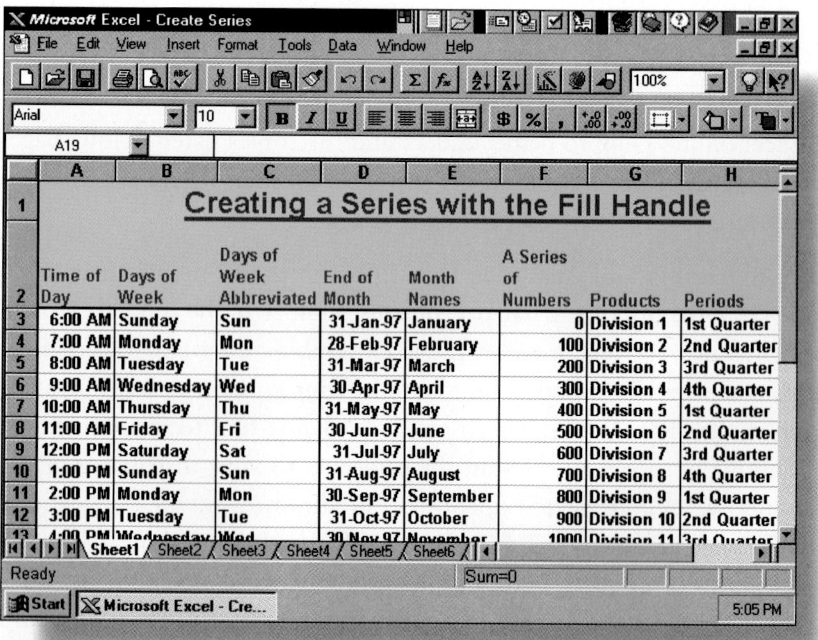

FIGURE 3-79

In the Lab

1 Pointer's Pizza and Pasta Five-Year Projected Financial Statement

Problem: You are a management trainee employed by Pointer's Pizza and Pasta. Each quarter for the first year of your employment you work in a different department. This quarter you are working for the Information Systems (IS) department. Your IS supervisor noticed from your resume that you learned Microsoft Excel in college and has requested that you build a Five-Year Projected Financial Statement based on figures available from 1996 (Figure 3-80).

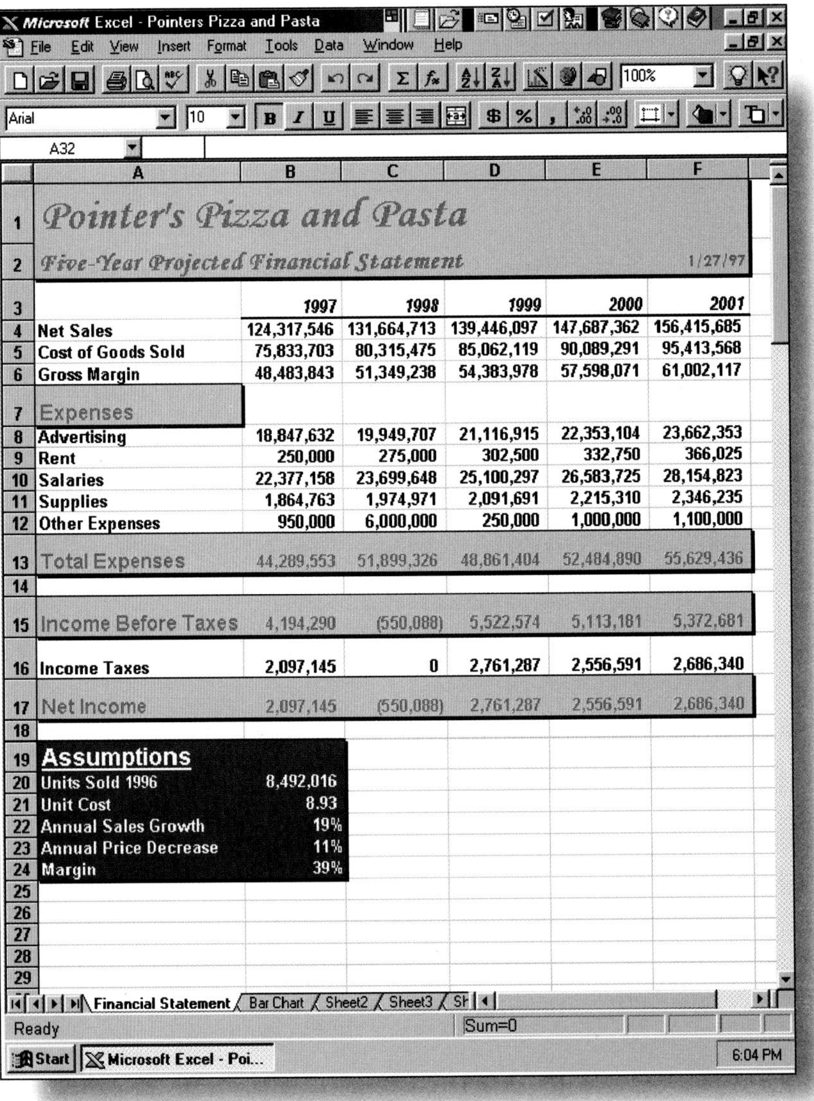

Microsoft Excel - Pointers Pizza and Pasta
File Edit View Insert Format Tools Data Window Help
100%
Arial
10
A32
A B C D E F
Pointer's Pizza and Pasta
Five-Year Projected Financial Statement 1/27/97
1997 1998 1999 2000 2001
Net Sales 124,317,546 131,664,713 139,446,097 147,687,362 156,415,685
Cost of Goods Sold 75,833,703 80,315,475 85,062,119 90,089,291 95,413,568
Gross Margin 48,483,843 51,349,238 54,383,978 57,598,071 61,002,117
Expenses
Advertising 18,847,632 19,949,707 21,116,915 22,353,104 23,662,353
Rent 250,000 275,000 302,500 332,750 366,025
Salaries 22,377,158 23,699,648 25,100,297 26,583,725 28,154,823
Supplies 1,864,763 1,974,971 2,091,691 2,215,310 2,346,235
Other Expenses 950,000 6,000,000 250,000 1,000,000 1,100,000
Total Expenses 44,289,553 51,899,326 48,861,404 52,484,890 55,629,436
Income Before Taxes 4,194,290 (550,088) 5,522,574 5,113,181 5,372,681
Income Taxes 2,097,145 0 2,761,287 2,556,591 2,686,340
Net Income 2,097,145 (550,088) 2,761,287 2,556,591 2,686,340
Assumptions
Units Sold 1996 8,492,016
Unit Cost 8.93
Annual Sales Growth 19%
Annual Price Decrease 11%
Margin 39%
Financial Statement / Bar Chart / Sheet2 / Sheet3 / Sh
Ready
Sum=0
Start
Microsoft Excel - Poi...
6:04 PM

FIGURE 3-80

(continued)

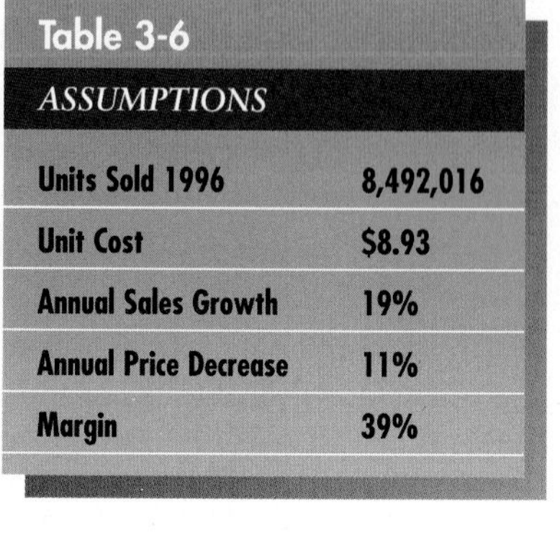

In the Lab

Pointer's Pizza and Pasta Five-Year Projected Financial Statement *(continued)*

Instructions Part 1: Do the following to create the worksheet in Figure 3-80.

Table 3-6

ASSUMPTIONS	
Units Sold 1996	8,492,016
Unit Cost	$8.93
Annual Sales Growth	19%
Annual Price Decrease	11%
Margin	39%

1. Use the Select All button and Bold button to bold the entire worksheet. Enter the worksheet titles in cells A1 and A2. Enter the system date using the NOW function in cell F2. Format the date to the m/d/yy style.
2. Enter 1997 in cell B3, 1998 in cell C3, and generate the series 1997 through 2001 in the range B3:F3 using the fill handle.
3. Enter the row titles in the range A4:A24. Change the font size in cells A7, A13, A15, and A17 to 12 point. Change the font size in cell A19 to 14 point and underline the characters in the cell.
4. Change the following column widths: A = 23.43; B through F = 11.00. Change the heights of row 3, 7, 13, 15, 16, 17 to 24.00.
5. Enter the assumptions in Table 3-6 in the range B20:B24 using format symbols where appropriate.
6. Use the Format Cells dialog box to assign the Comma style with no decimal places to the range B4:F17.
7. Complete the following entries:
   a. 1997 Net Sales (cell B4) = Units Sold 1996*(Unit Cost/(1-Margin)) or =B20*(B21/(1-B24))
   b. 1998 Net Sales (cell C4) = 1997 Net Sales*(1+Annual Sales Growth)*(1-Annual Price Decrease) or =B4*(1+$B$22)*(1-$B$23)
   c. Copy cell C4 to range D4:F4.
   d. 1997 Cost of Goods Sold (cell B5) = 1997 Net Sales-(1997 Net Sales*Margin) or =B4*(1-$B$24)
   e. Copy cell B5 to range C5:F5
   f. 1997 Gross Margin (cell B6) = 1997 Net Sales-1997 Cost of Goods Sold or =B4-B5
   g. Copy cell B6 to range C6:F6
   h. 1997 Advertising (cell B8) = 200,000+15%*1997 Net Sales or =200000+15%*B4
   i. Copy cell B8 to C8:F8
   j. 1997 Rent (cell B9) = 250,000
   k. 1998 Rent (cell C9) = 1997 Rent+10%*1997 Rent or =B9*(1+10%)
   l. Copy cell C9 to range D9:F9
   m. 1997 Salaries (cell B10) = 18%*1997 Net Sales or =18%*B4
   n. Copy cell B10 to range C10:F10
   o. 1997 Supplies (cell B11) = 1.5%*1997 Net Sales or =1.5%*B4
   p. Copy cell B11 to range C11:F11
   q. Other expenses: 1997 = $950,000; 1998 = $6,000,000; 1999 = $250,000; 2000 = $1,000,000; 2001 = $1,100,000
   r. 1997 Total Expenses (cell B13) = SUM(B8:B12)

s. Copy cell B13 to range C13:F13.
t. 1997 Income Before Taxes (cell B15) = 1997 Gross Margin-1997 Total Expenses or =B6-B13
u. Copy cell B15 to range C15:F15
v. 1997 Income Taxes (cell B16): If 1997 Income Before Expenses is less than zero, then 1997 Income Taxes equal zero, otherwise 1997 Income Taxes equal 50% * 1997 Income Before Taxes or =IF(B15<0,0,50%*B15)
w. Copy cell B16 to range C16:F16
x. 1997 Net Income (cell B17) = 1997 Income Before Taxes - 1997 Income Taxes or =B15-B16
y. Copy cell B17 to range C17:F17

8. Change the font in cell A1 to 26-point Monotype Corsiva (or a similar font). Change the font in cell A2 to 16-point Monotype Corsiva (or a similar font). Change the font in cell F2 to 10-point Century Gothic (or a similar font). Change the background and font colors and add drop shadows as shown in Figure 3-80 on page E 3.68.
9. Enter your name, course, laboratory assignment (Lab 3-1), date, and instructor name in the range A27:A31. Save the workbook using the filename Pointers Pizza and Pasta.
10. Preview and print the worksheet. Preview and print the formulas (CTRL+`) in landscape orientation using Fit to in the Page Setup dialog box. After printing the formulas version, reset the print scaling to 100%. Press CTRL+` to display the values version of the worksheet. Save the workbook again.

Instructions Part 2: Draw a 3-D column chart (Figure 3-81) that compares the projected net incomes for the years 1997 through 2001. Use the nonadjacent range B3:F3 and B17:F17. Add the chart title and format it as shown in Figure 3-81. Rename and rearrange the tabs as shown in Figure 3-81. Save the workbook using the same filename as defined in Part 1. Print both sheets.

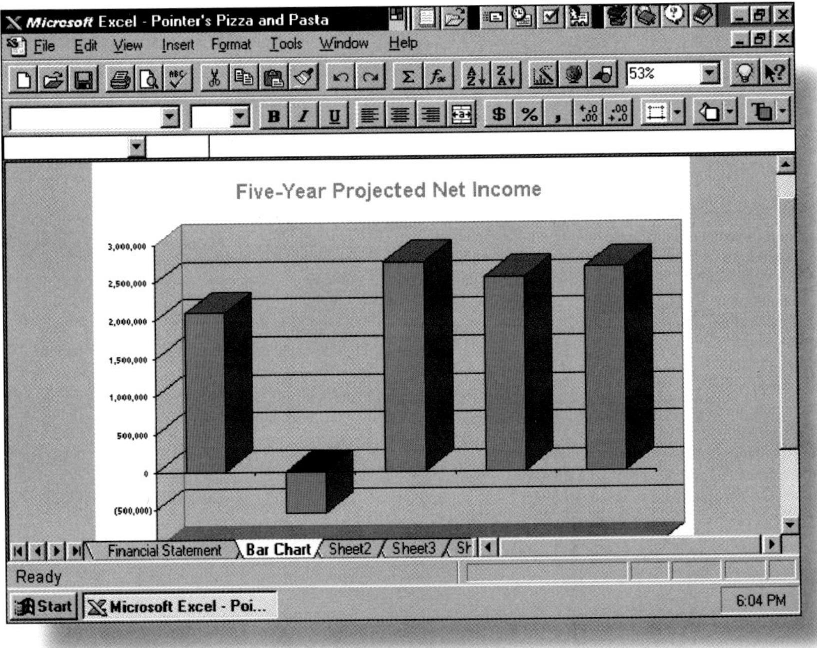

FIGURE 3-81

(continued)

In the Lab

Pointer's Pizza and Pasta Five-Year Projected Financial Statement *(continued)*

Instructions Part 3: If the 3-D column chart is on the screen, click the Financial Statement tab to display the worksheet. Divide the window into two panes by dragging the horizontal split bar between rows 6 and 7. Use the scroll bars to display both the top and bottom of the worksheet.

Using the numbers in columns 2 and 3 of Table 3-7, analyze the effect of changing the annual sales growth (cell B22) and annual price decrease (cell B23) on the annual net incomes in row 17. Print both the worksheet and chart for each case.

Table 3-7

CASE	ANNUAL SALES GROWTH	ANNUAL PRICE DECREASE	2001 RESULTING NET INCOME
1	5%	1%	$2,432,963
2	10%	-2%	$3,599,872
3	25%	10%	$3,647,473

Close the workbook without saving it, and then reopen it. Use the Goal Seek command to determine a margin (cell B24) that would result in a net income of $5,000,000 for 2001 in cell F17. You should end up with a margin in cell B24 of 42%. Print only the worksheet after the goal seeking is complete.

2 Modifying the Steel Frame House Weekly Payroll Worksheet

Problem: Your supervisor in the Payroll department has asked you to modify the payroll workbook developed in Exercise 2 of the In the Lab section in Project 2 on page E 2.73 so it appears as shown in Figure 3-82. If you did not complete Exercise 2, ask your instructor for a copy of the workbook Steel Frame House.

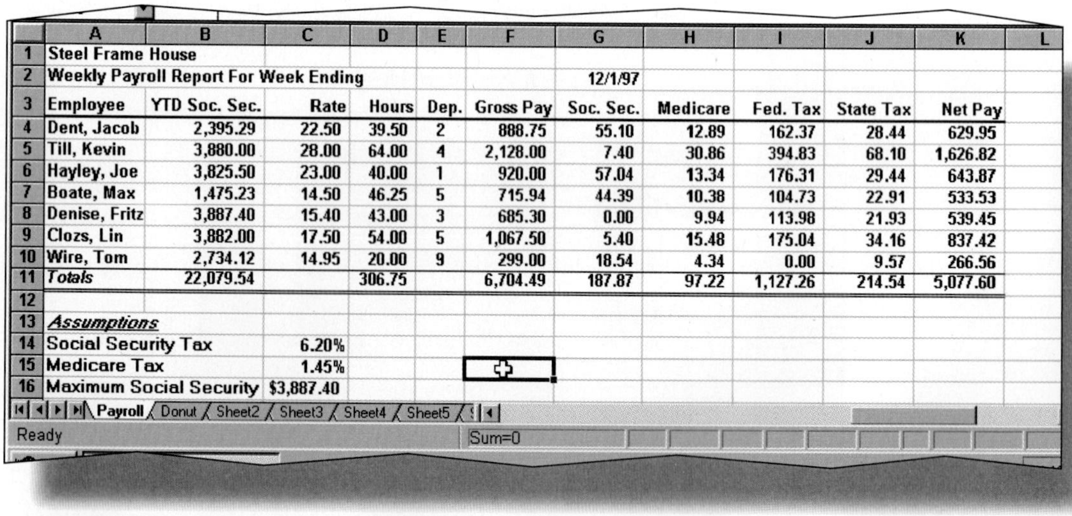

	A	B	C	D	E	F	G	H	I	J	K	L
1	Steel Frame House											
2	Weekly Payroll Report For Week Ending						12/1/97					
3	Employee	YTD Soc. Sec.	Rate	Hours	Dep.	Gross Pay	Soc. Sec.	Medicare	Fed. Tax	State Tax	Net Pay	
4	Dent, Jacob	2,395.29	22.50	39.50	2	888.75	55.10	12.89	162.37	28.44	629.95	
5	Till, Kevin	3,880.00	28.00	64.00	4	2,128.00	7.40	30.86	394.83	68.10	1,626.82	
6	Hayley, Joe	3,825.50	23.00	40.00	1	920.00	57.04	13.34	176.31	29.44	643.87	
7	Boate, Max	1,475.23	14.50	46.25	5	715.94	44.39	10.38	104.73	22.91	533.53	
8	Denise, Fritz	3,887.40	15.40	43.00	3	685.30	0.00	9.94	113.98	21.93	539.45	
9	Clozs, Lin	3,882.00	17.50	54.00	5	1,067.50	5.40	15.48	175.04	34.16	837.42	
10	Wire, Tom	2,734.12	14.95	20.00	9	299.00	18.54	4.34	0.00	9.57	266.56	
11	*Totals*	22,079.54		306.75		6,704.49	187.87	97.22	1,127.26	214.54	5,077.60	
12												
13	***Assumptions***											
14	Social Security Tax		6.20%									
15	Medicare Tax		1.45%									
16	Maximum Social Security	$3,887.40										

Payroll / Donut / Sheet2 / Sheet3 / Sheet4 / Sheet5

Ready Sum=0

FIGURE 3-82

In the Lab

The major modifications include reformatting the worksheet, time and a half for hours worked greater than 40, no federal tax if the federal tax is greater than the gross pay, and computation of the Social Security and Medicare deductions. The workbook (Steel Frame House) created earlier in Project 2 is shown in Figure 2-95 on page E 2.73.

Instructions Part 1: Open the workbook Steel Frame House created in Project 2. Perform the following tasks:

1. Use the Select All button and Clear command on the Edit menu to clear all formats.
2. Bold the entire worksheet. Delete rows 10 through 12. Insert a row above row 2. Modify the worksheet title in cell A1 so it appears as shown in Figure 3-82 on the previous page. Enter the worksheet subtitle, Weekly Payroll Report For Week Ending, in cell A2.
3. Insert a new column between columns A and B. Title the new column YTD Soc. Sec. Insert two new columns between columns F and G. Title column G in cell G3 Soc. Sec. Title column H in cell H3 Medicare. Assign the NOW function to cell G2 and format it to m/d/yy. Freeze the titles in column A and rows 1 through 3.
4. Change the column widths and row heights as follows: A = 11.00; B = 13.00; C = 9.00, D = 7.00; E = 5.00; F through K = 8.71; and row 3 = 18. Right-align the column titles in the range B3:K3.
5. Delete row 8 (Suzi, Jeff). Change Denise, Fritz's number of dependents from 5 to 3.
6. In row B, enter the YTD Social Security values listed in Table 3-8.
7. Insert two new rows immediately above the Totals row. Add the new employees listed in Table 3-9.
8. Use the Format Cells dialog box to assign a Comma style to the ranges B4:D11 and F4:K11. Center-align the range E4:E10.
9. Enter the Assumptions table in the range A13:C16 and format it as shown in Figure 3-82. Place the titles in column A and the numbers in column C.
10. Change the formulas to determine the gross pay in column F and the federal tax in column H.
    a. In cell F4, enter an IF function that applies the following logic:
       If Hours <= 40, then Gross Pay = Rate*Hours, otherwise Gross Pay = Rate*Hours+ 0. 5*Rate*(Hours–40)
    b. Copy the IF function in cell F4 to the range F5:F10.
    c. In cell I4, enter the IF function that applies the following logic:
       If (Gross Pay–Dependents*38.46) > 0, then Federal Tax = 20%*(Gross Pay–Dependents* 38.46), otherwise Federal Tax = 0
    d. Copy the IF function in cell I4 to the range I5:I10.

Table 3-8

NAME	YTD SOC. SEC.
Dent, Jacob	2,395.29
Till, Kevin	3,880.00
Hayley, Joe	3,825.50
Boate, Max	1,475.23
Denise, Fritz	3,887.40

Table 3-9

EMPLOYEE	YTD SOC. SEC.	RATE	HOURS	DEPENDENTS
Clozs, Lin	3,882.00	17. 50	54	5
Wire, Tom	2,734.12	14. 95	20	9

(continued)

In the Lab

Modifying the Steel Frame House Weekly Payroll Worksheet *(continued)*

11. An employee pays Social Security tax only if his or her YTD Social Security is less than the maximum Social Security in cell C16. Use the following logic to determine the Social Security tax for Jacob Dent in cell G4:
    If Soc. Sec. Tax*Gross Pay+YTD Soc. Sec.> Maximum Soc. Sec., then Maximum Soc. Sec.-YTD Soc. Sec., otherwise Soc. Sec. Tax*Gross Pay
12. Copy the IF function to the range G5:G10. Make sure references to the values in the Assumptions table are absolute.
13. In cell H4, enter the following formula and copy it to the range H5:H10:
    Medicare = Medicare Tax * Gross Pay
14. Copy the state tax in cell J4 to the range J5:J10.
15. In cell K4, enter the following formula and copy it to the range K5:K10:
    Net Pay = Gross Pay–(Soc. Sec.+Medicare+Fed. Tax+State Tax)
16. Determine any new totals as shown in row 11 of Figure 3-82 on page E 3.70.
17. Enter your name, course, laboratory assignment (Lab 3-2), date, and instructor name in the range A18:A22.
18. Unfreeze the titles. Save the workbook using the filename Steel House Frame 2.
19. Use the Zoom Control box on the Standard toolbar to change the view of the worksheet. One by one, select all the percents in the Zoom Control box. Change it back to 100%.
20. Preview the worksheet. Adjust column widths if number signs display in place of numbers. Print the worksheet in landscape orientation. Save the worksheet again.
21. Preview and print the formulas (CTRL+`) in landscape orientation using Fit to in the Page Setup dialog box. Close the worksheet without saving the latest changes.

Instructions Part 2: Open the workbook Steel Frame House 2. Using the range A4:A10 (category names) and the range K4:K10 (data series), draw a Donut chart (column 1, row 2 in the ChartWizard Step 2 of 5 dialog box) with the labels inside each piece (Figure 3-83). Add a chart title and format it appropriately. Rename the tabs as follows: Chart1 to Donut; Sheet1 to Payroll. Rearrange the tabs so the Payroll tab is to the left of the Donut tab. Save the workbook using the filename Steel Frame House 2. Preview and print both sheets.

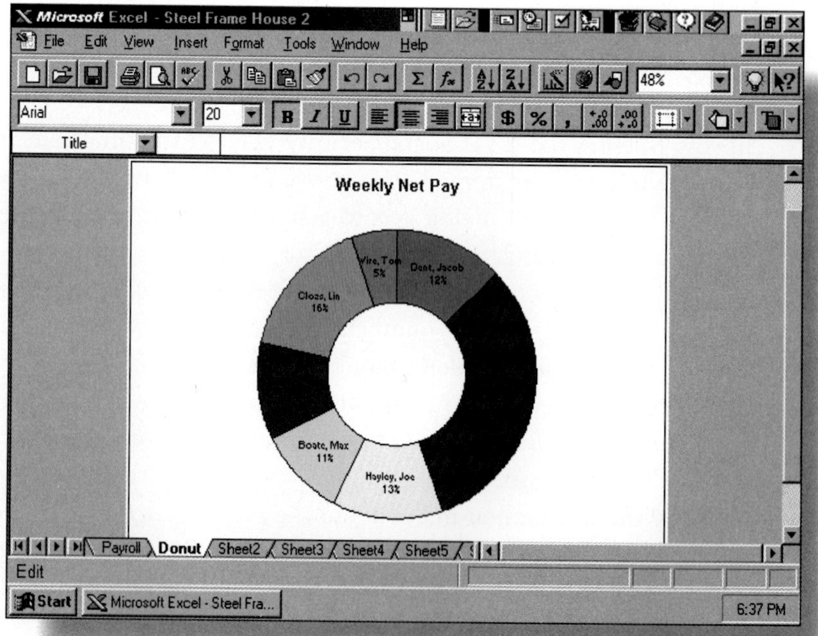

FIGURE 3-83

In the Lab

Instructions Part 3: If the Donut chart is on the screen, click the Payroll tab to display the worksheet. Using the numbers in the Table 3-10, analyze the effect of changing the Social Security tax in cell C14. Print the worksheet for each case. The first case should result in a total Social Security tax in cell G11 of $227.00. The second case should result in a total Social Security tax of $246.03.

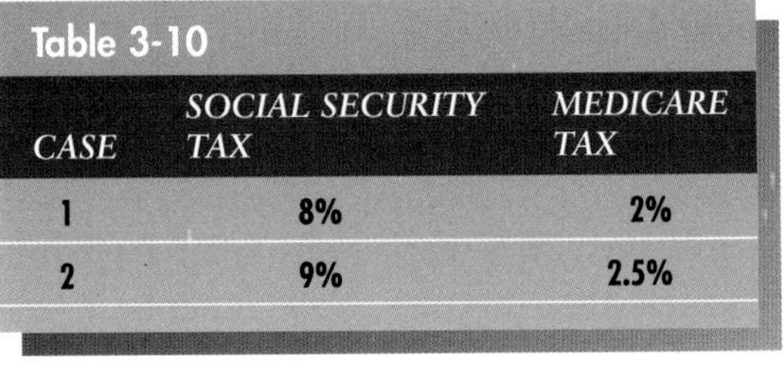

Table 3-10

CASE	SOCIAL SECURITY TAX	MEDICARE TAX
1	8%	2%
2	9%	2.5%

3 Projected Quarterly Report

Problem: You are employed as a worksheet specialist by Cryptography Inc., a leader in the field of keeping secrets known only to insiders. The company utilizes assumptions, based on past business practice, to plan for the next quarter. You have been asked to create a worksheet similar to the one shown in Figure 3-84.

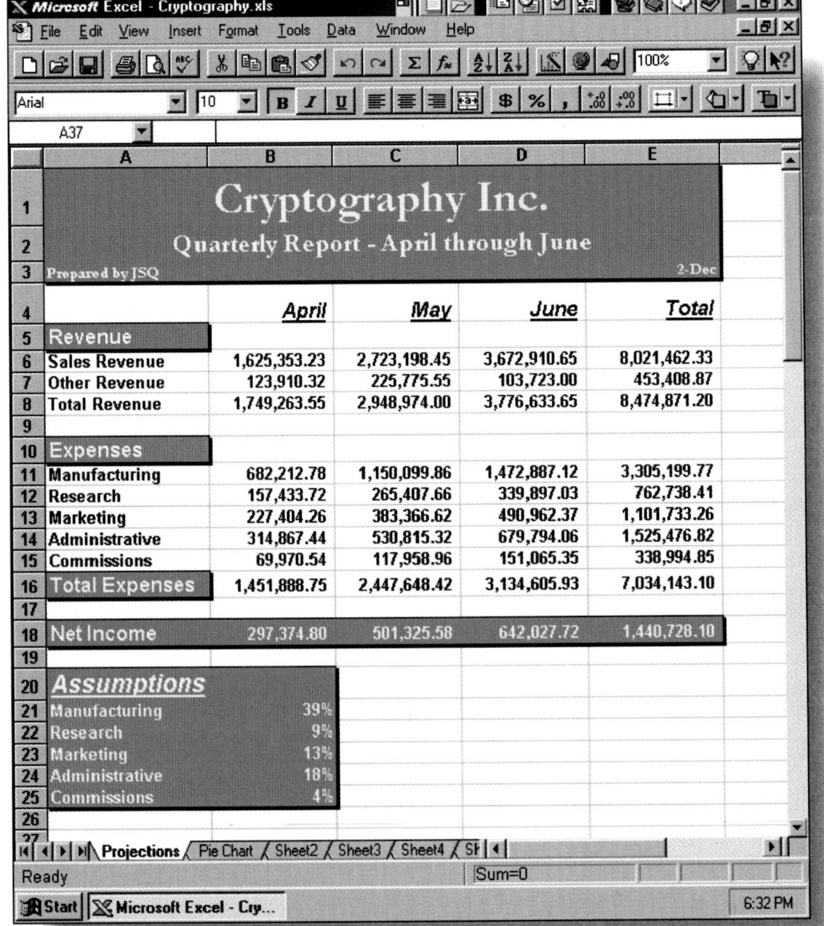

FIGURE 3-84

(continued)

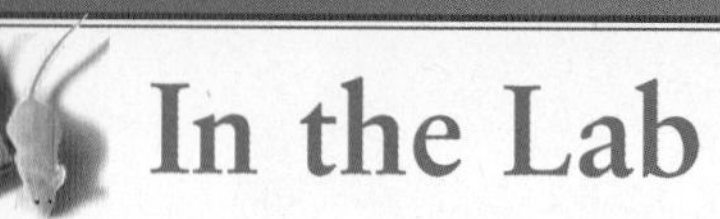

In the Lab

Projected Quarterly Report *(continued)*

Instructions Part 1: Do the following to create the worksheet shown in Figure 3-84 on the previous page.

1. Bold the entire worksheet. Enter the worksheet titles in cells A1, A2, and A3. Use your own initials in cell A3. Enter the NOW function in cell E3 and format it to 4-Mar. Enter April in cell B4 and underline, italicize, and right-align it. Use the fill handle to create the month series in row 4. Enter Total in cell E4 and use the Format Painter button on the Standard toolbar to format it the same as cell D4. Enter the row titles down through Assumptions in cell A20. Copy the row titles in the range A11:A15 to the range A21:A25.
2. Use the Select All button and change the width of all the columns to 13.71. Change the widths of column A to 18.29 and column E to 14.86. Change the height of row 4 to 24.00.
3. Enter the Assumptions values in the range B21:B25.
4. Enter the sales revenue and other revenue in Table 3-11 in the range B6:D7. Determine the totals in the range E6:E7 and B8:E8.

Table 3-11

	APRIL	MAY	JUNE
Sales Revenue	1,625,353.23	2,723,198.45	3,672,910.65
Other Revenue	123,910.32	225,775.55	103,723.00

5. Each of the expense categories in the range B11:D15 is determined by multiplying the total revenue for the month times the corresponding assumption in the Assumption table (range A20:B25). For example, the Manufacturing expense in cell B11 is equal to cell B21 times cell B8, or =B21*B8. Once the formulas are assigned to the range B11:B15, they can be copied to the range C11:D15. For the copy to work properly, however, you must make the first cell reference absolute. Thus, enter the following formulas in the designated cells: B11 = $B$21*B8; B12 = $B$22*B8; B13 = $B$23*B8; B14 = $B$24*B8; B15 = $B$25*B8.
6. Use the SUM function to determine all the totals. The net income in row 18 is equal to the total revenue for each month (row 8) minus the total expenses for each month (row 16).
7. Format the worksheet so it resembles Figure 3-84. Use Garamond font (or a similar font) in the range A1:E3.
8. Enter your name, course, laboratory assignment (Lab 3-1), date, and instructor name in the range A28:A32.
9. Save the workbook using the filename Cryptography.
10. Print the worksheet. Preview and print the formulas (CTRL+`) in landscape orientation using Fit to in the Page Setup dialog box. Press CTRL+` to display the values version of the worksheet. Save the workbook again.

Instructions Part 2: Draw a 3-dimensional pie chart (Figure 3-85) that shows the monthly contribution to the quarterly net income. That is, chart the nonadjacent ranges B4:D4 (category names) and B18:D18 (data series).

Do the following to the pie chart:

1. Add the chart title and format it as shown in Figure 3-85.
2. Explode the June slice.

In the Lab

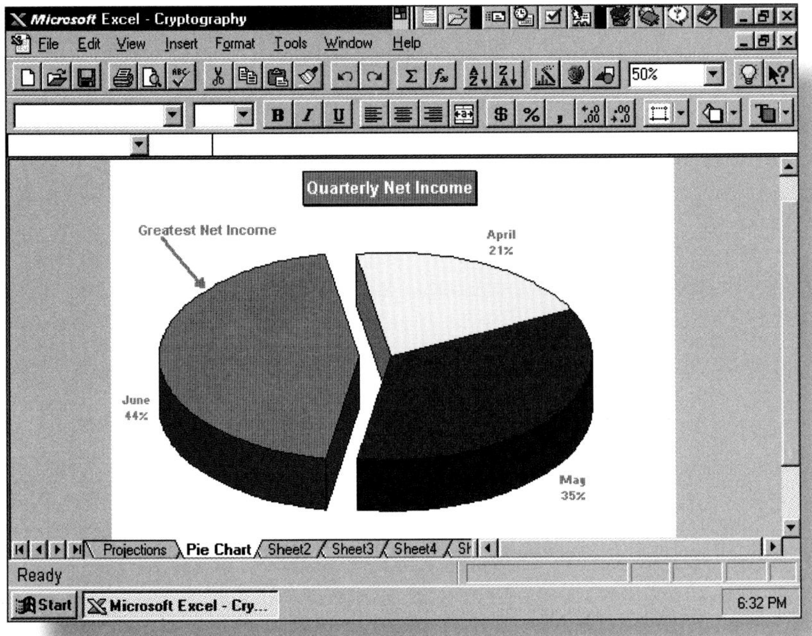

FIGURE 3-85

3. Select a slice and use the 3-D View command on the shortcut menu to change the elevation to 30° and the rotation to 350°.
4. Change the color of the slices as shown in Figure 3-85.
5. Use Help to step you through adding a text box with the phrase Greatest Net Income and an arrow pointing to the June slice. Format the text box and arrow as shown in Figure 3-85.
6. Rename the tabs as follows: Chart1 to Pie Chart; Sheet1 to Projections. Rearrange the tabs so the Projections tab is to the left of the Pie Chart tab.
7. Save the workbook using the filename Cryptography.
8. Print both sheets.

Instructions Part 3: If the 3-D pie chart is on the screen, click the Projections tab to display the worksheet shown in Figure 3-84 on page E 3.73. Using the numbers in the Table 3-12, analyze the effect of changing the assumptions in rows 21 through 25 on the quarterly net income in cell E18. Print both the worksheet and chart for each case.

You should end with the following quarterly net incomes in cell E18: Case 1 = 1,694,974.24; Case 2 = 1,271,230.68; Case 3 = 254,246.14.

Close the workbook Cryptography without saving it, and then reopen it. Use the Goal Seek command to determine the marketing percentage (cell B23) that would result in a quarterly net income of 760,000 in cell E18. You should end up with a marketing percentage of 21%. Print only the worksheet.

Table 3-12

	CASE 1	CASE 2	CASE 3
Manufacturing	35%	37%	40%
Research	10%	10%	15%
Marketing	14%	15%	17%
Administrative	16%	16%	20%
Commissions	5%	7%	5%

Cases and Places

The difficulty of these case studies varies:

◗ Case studies preceded by a single half moon are the least difficult. You are asked to create the required worksheet based on information that has already been placed in an organized form.

◗◗ Case studies preceded by two half moons are more difficult. You must organize the information presented before using it to create the required worksheet.

◗◗◗ Case studies preceded by three half moons are the most difficult. You must choose a specific topic, and then obtain and organize the necessary information before using it to create the required worksheet.

1 ◗ The Stevensville Sentinel is a small newspaper that publishes stories of local interest. Revenues are earned from subscriptions and the sale of advertising space. A fixed percentage of the proceeds is spent on marketing, payroll, commissions, production costs, and reportorial expenses. The Sentinel's editor has summarized the paper's receipts and expenditures over the past year on a bi-monthly basis as shown in Figure 3-86.

The Stevensville Sentinel
Bi-Monthly Earnings and Expenditures

Revenues:

	February	April	June	August	October	November
Subsrieptions	\$8.526.34	\$8.526.34	\$9.271.95	\$12.082.14	\$12.082.14	\$9.721.63
Advertising	\$2.500.78	\$1.762.25	\$2.134.56	\$3.455.45	\$2.987.95	\$4.234.66

Expenditures:

Marketing	20.75%	
Payroll	56.50%	
Commissions	2.25%	of advertising sales
Production Costs	13.25%	
Reportorial Expenses	3.00%	

FIGURE 3-86

With this data, you have been asked to prepare a worksheet for the next shareholder's meeting showing total revenues, total expenditures, and net incomes for each bi-monthly period. Include a chart that illustrates the net incomes. One shareholder lobbied to reduce marketing expenditures 1% and payroll costs 5%. Perform a what-if analysis with another worksheet and chart reflecting the proposed changes in expenditure assumptions. Use the concepts and techniques presented in this project to create and format the worksheets and charts.

200 MHz

Cases and Places

2 ◗ A government agency plans to conduct experiments that will result in some radioactive waste. Although the isotopes will break apart into atoms of other elements over time, agency watchdogs are concerned about containment costs while the material is still radioactive. The agency director has asked you to prepare a worksheet showing the amount of radioactive material remaining, containment costs, estimated agency appropriations, and the percentage of appropriations that will be spent on containment every year for the next decade. The director has outlined the desired worksheet as shown in Figure 3-87.

Cost of Storing Radioactive Isotopes

	Number of Years Stored			
	1	2	3 10	
Amount of Isotope X Remaining (in kg)				
Amount of Isotope Y Remaining (in kg)				
Total Remaining (in kg)				
Containment Costs				
Estimated Appropriations				
Percentage Spent on Containment				

Assumptions

Original amount of Isotope X (in kg)	700	Original amount of Isotope Y (in kg)	2,500
Half-life of Isotope X (in years)	1	Half-life of Isotope Y (in years)	0.5
Containment Cost Per Kilogram	$1,000.00	Appropriations	$5,000,000.00
Estimated Yearly Increase	8%		

FIGURE 3-87

These formulas have been supplied:

Amount Remaining = Original Amount x 0.5 (Number of Years Stored÷Half Life)
Containment Costs = Containment Cost Per Kilogram x Total Amount Remaining
Estimated Appropriations = Appropriations x (1+Estimated Yearly Increase) Number of Years Stored
Percentage Spent on Containment = Containment Costs÷Estimated Appropriations

The director has asked you to include a function that prints "Acceptable" below the percentage spent on containment whenever that percentage is less than 10%, and to goal seek on a second worksheet to determine how much of Isotope X can be used so the percentage spent on containment is always less than 15%. Use the concepts and techniques presented in this project to create and format the worksheets.

3 ◗◗ Geppetto, a woodcarver, is unhappy with the school his little boy attends ("They act as if his head were full of sawdust!" he grouses). Although the little boy has a tendency to stretch the truth, Geppetto believes if a school kept his "nose to the grindstone" eventually the boy's dreams would come true. Geppetto wants to save enough money to send his little boy to a private school. He has job orders for the next six months—$500 in July, $585 in August, $376 in September, $624 in October, $643 in November, and $775 in December. Each month Geppetto spends 33.75% of the money for materials, 2.5% for tools, 6.25% for his retirement account, and 40% for food and clothing. The remaining profits (orders - expenses) will be put aside for the boy's education. Geppetto's friend, JC, has agreed to provide an additional $50 whenever Geppetto's monthly profit exceeds $100. Geppetto has asked you to create a worksheet that shows orders, expenses, profits, and savings for the next six months, and totals for each category. On separate worksheets, Geppetto would like you to goal seek to determine a percentage for food and clothing if $1,000 is needed for the school, and then do a what-if analysis to determine the effect of reducing the percentage spent on materials to 25%. Use the concepts and techniques presented in this project to create and format the worksheets.

Cases and Places

4 ▶▶ Sweet Dreams is open year round, but most of the candy shop's production revolves around six holidays: Valentine's Day (2, 250 lb.), Easter (1,950 lb.), Mother's Day (1,150 lb.), Father's Day (975 lb.), Halloween (2,136 lb.), and Christmas (1,750 lb.). On these days, 28% of the store's output is fudge, 15% is taffy, 46% is boxed chocolate, and the remaining 11% is holiday-specific candy (such as chocolate hearts or candy canes). The fudge sells for $6.25 per pound, the taffy for $1.15 per pound, the boxed chocolate for $5.75 per pound, and holiday-specific candy for $1.35 per pound. Sweet Dreams is considering revising its production figures, and the management has asked you to create a worksheet it can use in making their decision. The worksheet should show the amount of each candy produced on a holiday, potential sales for each type of candy, total potential sales for each holiday, total candy produced for the six holidays, and total potential sales from each type of candy.

5 ▶▶▶ Ralph Nickleby, a wealthy uncle, has left you stock in several computer companies in his will. Your stock is in three major categories—hardware (5,000 shares in Apple, 11,500 shares in Compaq, 22,500 shares in IBM, and 7,000 shares in Intel), software (3,000 shares in Autodesk, 4,500 shares in Borland, 58,000 shares in Microsoft, and 6,500 shares in Symantec), and networking (2,500 shares in 3Com, 11,250 shares in Compaq, and 16,750 shares in Novell). Analysts assure you that on average, stock in the computer industry will return 5% per year for the next ten years. Using the latest stock prices, create a worksheet that organizes your computer stock portfolio and projects its annual worth for the next ten years. Group companies by major categoiies and include a total for each category.

6 ▶▶▶ Balancing budgets, a daunting task for governments at every level, also can be a significant challenge for students attending college. Whether you work part time or simply draw on a sum of money while going to school, it is necessary to equalize income and expenditures. Create and format a worksheet that reflects your monthly budget throughout the school year. Indicate the amount of money you have available each month. Hypothesize percentages for monthly expenditures (food, travel, entertainment, and so on). On the basis of these assumptions, determine expenditures for each month. Include a row for occasional, miscellaneous expenses (such as books). Ascertain the amount of money remaining at the end of each month; this amount will become part or all of the money available for the subsequent month. Perform at least one what-if analysis to examine the effect of changing one or more of the values in the worksheet.

7 ▶▶▶ Freelance workers must monitor income and business expenses carefully in order to be profitable. Painters, landscapers, consultants, and house cleaners are people who often work on a freelance basis. Interview someone who performs freelance work and build a worksheet reflecting his or her profits over the past six months. Attempt to determine the percentage of the worker's income spent on business-related expenses. Find out about any occasional expenses. With this information, and the freelance worker's income for each of the past six months, determine the worker's expenses and profits each month. Include at least one chart that illustrates an aspect of your worksheet you feel is significant—perhaps profits each month or the total money applied to every business expense.

Linking an Excel Worksheet to a Word Document

Case Perspective

Each week, the director of sales for Net Microsystems, Kevin James, sends out a memorandum to all the sales representatives in the organization showing the previous week's daily sales by office. He currently uses Word to produce the memorandum, which includes a table of the daily sales. The wording in the memorandum remains constant week to week. The table of daily sales changes each week.

Kevin recently heard of the Object Linking and Embedding (OLE) capabilities of Microsoft Office. He wants to use OLE to create the basic memorandum using Word and maintain the weekly sales in an Excel worksheet. Each week, he envisions linking the worksheet from Excel to the Word document. Once the worksheet is linked to the Word document, he can e-mail it or print it and mail it to the sales force.

As Kevin's technical assistant, you have been asked to handle the details.

Introduction

One of the more powerful features of Microsoft Office 95 is that you can incorporate parts of documents or entire documents, called **objects,** from one application into another application. For example, you can copy a worksheet created in Excel into a document created in Word (Figure 1 on the next page). In this case, the worksheet in Excel is called the **source document** (copied from) and the document in Word is called the **destination document** (copied to). Copying objects between applications can be accomplished in three ways: (1) copy and paste; (2) copy and embed; and (3) copy and link.

All of the Microsoft Office applications allow you to use these three methods to copy objects between applications. The first method uses the Copy and Paste buttons. The latter two use the Paste Special command on the Edit menu and are referred to as **Object Linking and Embedding,** or **OLE.** Table 1 on page EI 1.3 summarizes the differences among the three methods.

Copy and link is preferred over the other two methods when an object is likely to change and you want to make sure the object reflects the changes in the source document or if the object is large, such as a video clip or sound clip. Thus, if you link a worksheet to a memorandum, and update the worksheet weekly, any time you open the memorandum, the latest updates of the worksheet will display as part of the memorandum.

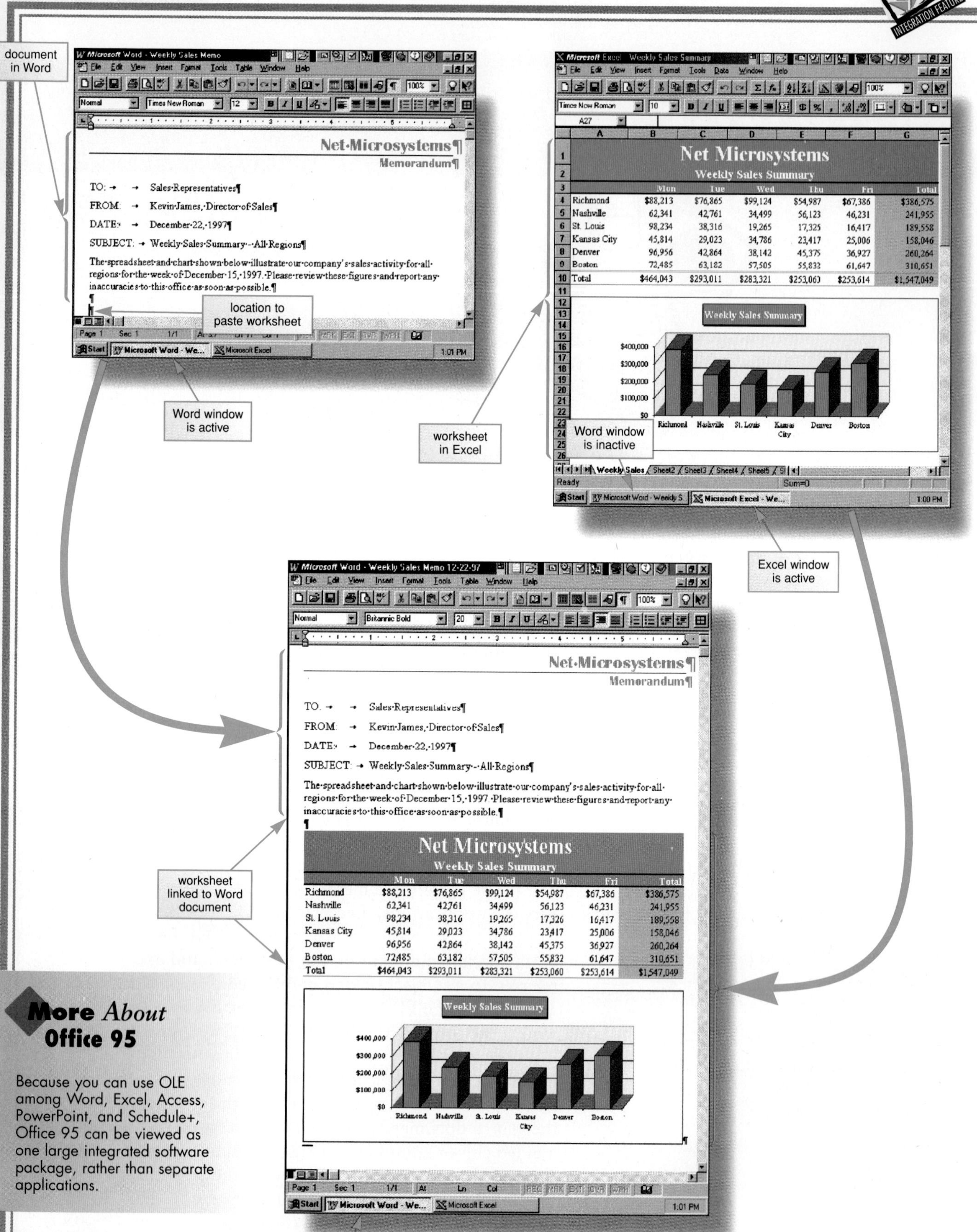

FIGURE 1

More *About* Office 95

Because you can use OLE among Word, Excel, Access, PowerPoint, and Schedule+, Office 95 can be viewed as one large integrated software package, rather than separate applications.

Because the weekly sales worksheet for Net Microsystems will change weekly, the copy and link method is the best method to use.

Table 1

METHOD	CHARACTERISTICS
Copy and paste	**The source document becomes part of the destination document. An object may be edited, but the editing features are limited to those in the destination application. An Excel worksheet becomes a Word table. If changes are made to values in the Word table, any original Excel formulas are not recalculated.**
Copy and embed	**The source document becomes part of the destination document. An object may be edited in the destination application using source editing features. The Excel worksheet remains a worksheet in Word. If changes are made to values in the worksheet with Word active, Excel formulas will be recalculated. If you change the worksheet in Excel, however, changes will not show in the Word document the next time you open it.**
Copy and link	**The source document does not become part of the destination document even though it appears to be part of it. Instead, a link is established between the two documents so that when you open the Word document, the worksheet displays as part of it. When you attempt to edit a linked worksheet in Word, the system activates Excel. If you change the worksheet in Excel, the changes also will show in the Word document the next time you open it.**

Starting Word and Excel

Both the Word document (Weekly Sales Memo) and the Excel workbook (Weekly Sales Summary) are in the Excel folder on the Student Floppy Disk that accompanies this book. The first step in linking the Excel worksheet to the Word document is both to open the document in Word and the workbook in Excel as shown in the following steps.

To Open a Word Document and an Excel Workbook

1. **Click the Start button. Click Open Office Document on the Start menu. Click 3½ Floppy [A:] in the Look in box. Open the Excel folder. Double-click the filename Weekly Sales Memo.**

   Word becomes active and the Weekly Sales Memo displays (Figure 2).

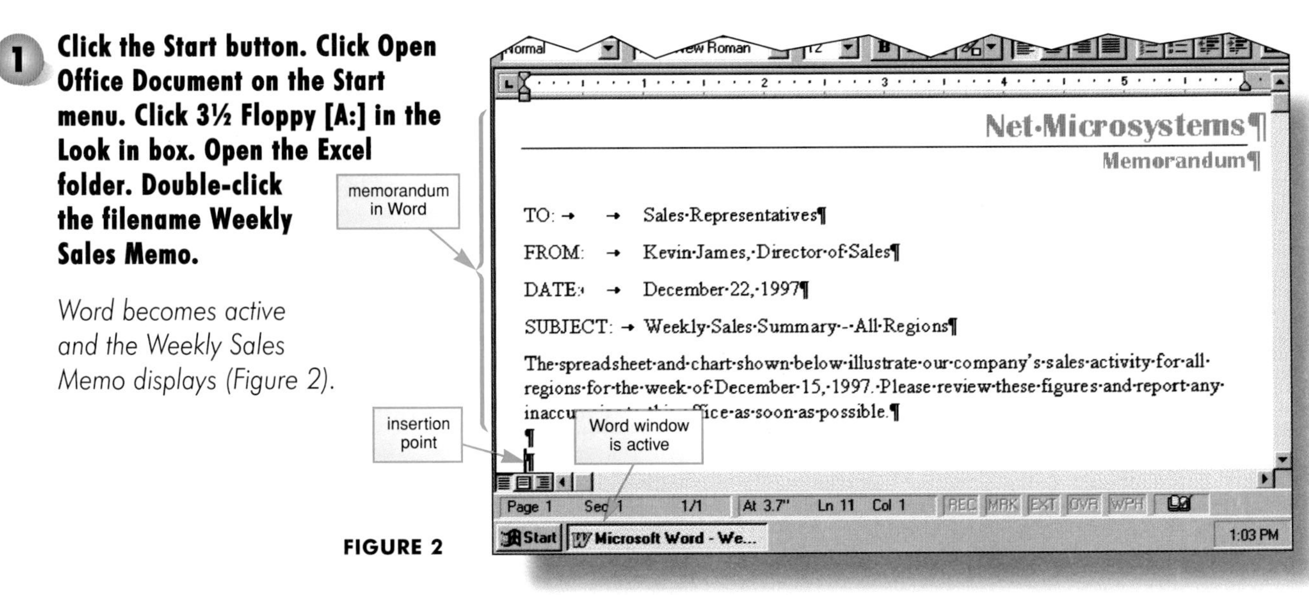

FIGURE 2

2 **Click the Start button. Click Open Office Document on the Start menu. Click 3½ Floppy [A:] in the Look in box. If necessary, open the Excel folder. Double-click the filename, Weekly Sales Summary.**

Excel becomes active and the Weekly Sales Summary workbook displays (Figure 3). At this point, Word is inactive, but still is in main memory. Excel is the active window as shown on the taskbar.

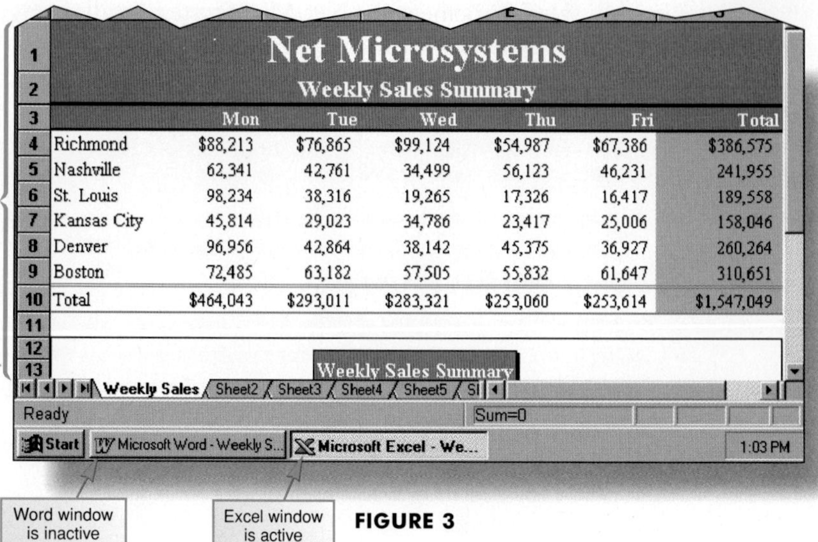

	Mon	Tue	Wed	Thu	Fri	Total
Richmond	$88,213	$76,865	$99,124	$54,987	$67,386	$386,575
Nashville	62,341	42,761	34,499	56,123	46,231	241,955
St. Louis	98,234	38,316	19,265	17,326	16,417	189,558
Kansas City	45,814	29,023	34,786	23,417	25,006	158,046
Denver	96,956	42,864	38,142	45,375	36,927	260,264
Boston	72,485	63,182	57,505	55,832	61,647	310,651
Total	$464,043	$293,011	$283,321	$253,060	$253,614	$1,547,049

FIGURE 3

OtherWays

1. On Microsoft Office Shortcut Bar, click Open a Document button

With both Word and Excel in main memory, you can switch between the applications by clicking the appropriate button on the taskbar, next to the Start button.

Linking

With both applications running, the next step is to link the Excel worksheet to the Word document as shown in the following steps.

Steps To Link the Excel Worksheet to the Word Document

1 **With the Excel window active, select the range A1:G25. Click the Copy button to place the selected range on the Clipboard.**

The range A1:G25 is selected (Figure 4).

Copy button

range A1:G25 selected

FIGURE 4

2 **Click the Microsoft Word button on the taskbar to activate the Word window. Click the last paragraph mark at the bottom of the document to position the insertion point where the worksheet will display in the document. Click Edit on the menu bar and then point to Paste Special.**

The Weekly Sales Memo document and the Edit menu display on the screen. The insertion point blinks at the bottom of the document (Figure 5).

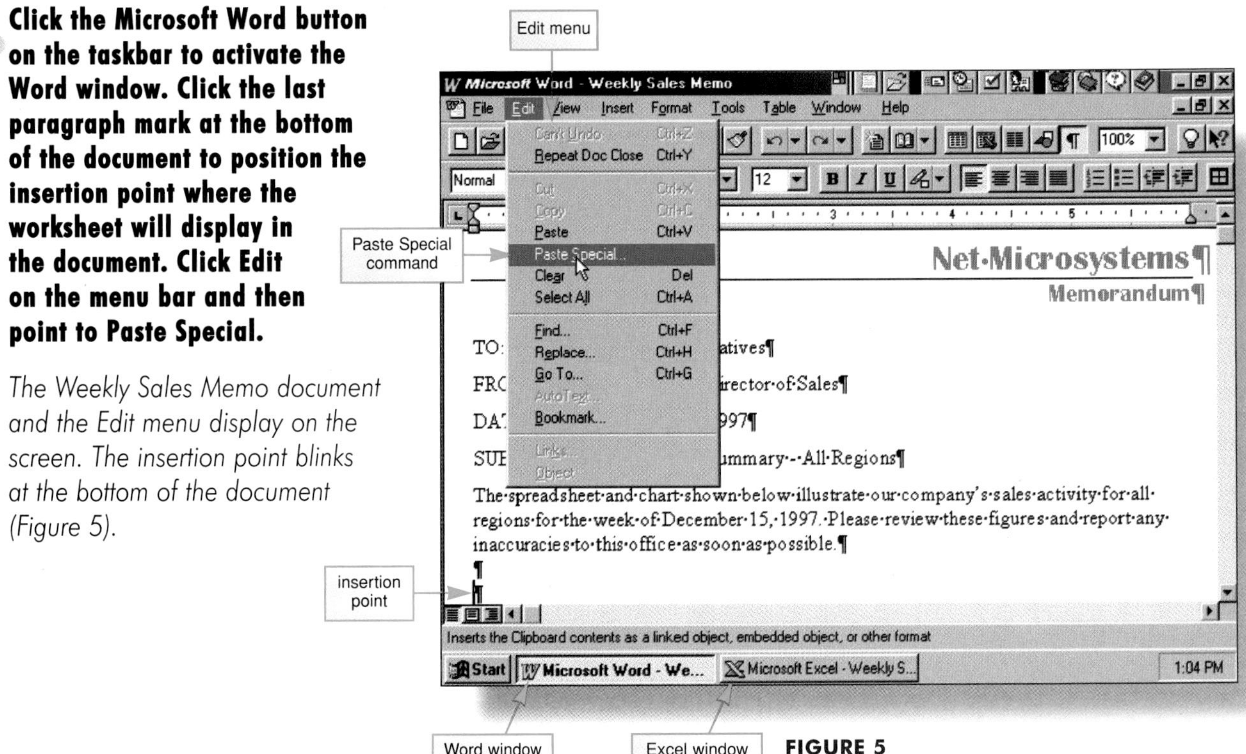

FIGURE 5

3 **Click Paste Special on the Edit menu. When the Paste Special dialog box displays, click Paste Link and then click Microsoft Excel Worksheet Object in the As box.**

The Paste Special dialog box displays as shown in Figure 6.

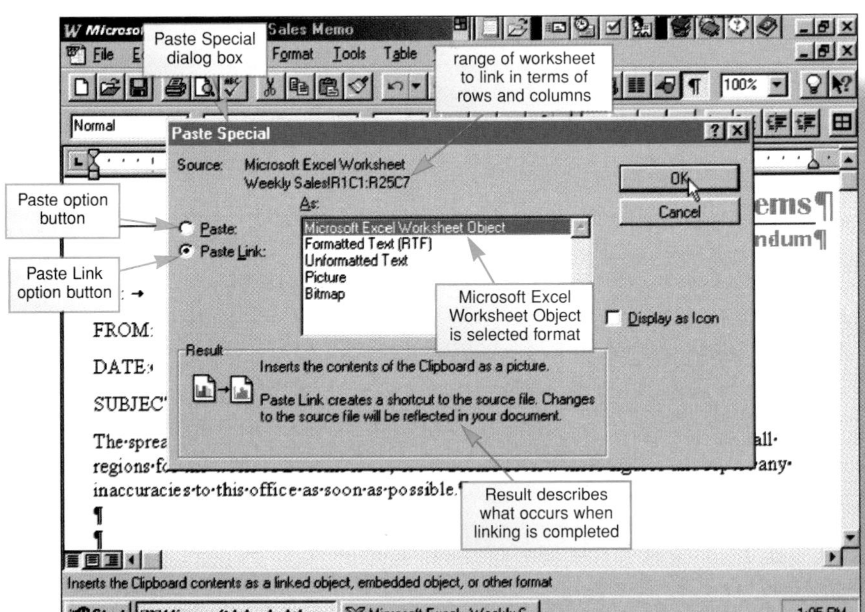

FIGURE 6

4 Click the OK button in the Paste Special dialog box.

The range A1:G25 of the worksheet displays in the Word document beginning at the location of the insertion point (Figure 7).

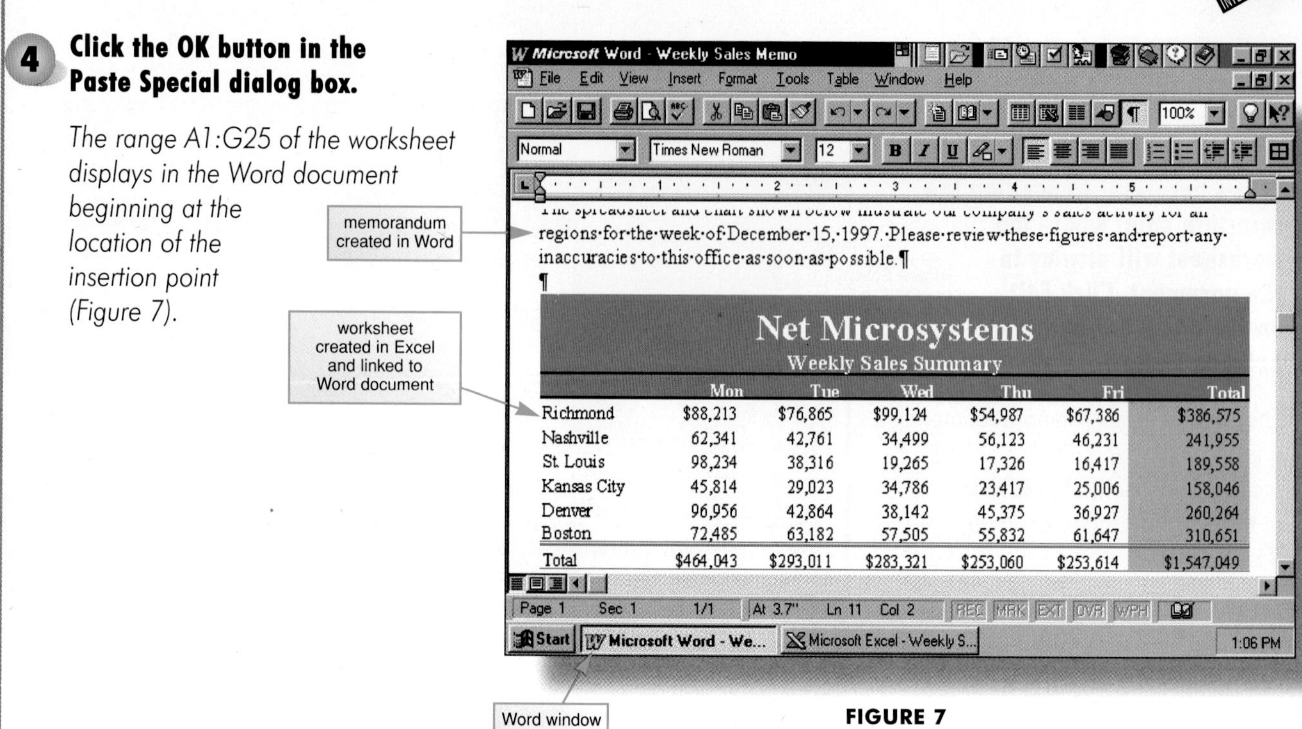

FIGURE 7

More *About* OLE

If you want to have more than one object at a time available for OLE, you can store objects to embed on the desktop, rather than using the Clipboard. When you use this technique, the objects are called **scrap**. To accomplish this task, part of the desktop must be visible behind the window of the source application. Next, right-drag the object onto the desktop. Once on the desktop, Windows displays the object as an icon. When the shortcut menu displays, click Create Scrap Here. Next, activate the destination document and drag the scrap from the desktop onto the destination document and drop it where you want it inserted. To delete a scrap from the desktop, right-click it and then click Delete.

The Excel workbook is now linked to the Word document. If you save the Word document and reopen it, the worksheet will display just as it does in Figure 7. If you want to delete the worksheet, simply click it and press the DELETE key. The next section shows how to print and save the memo with the link to the worksheet.

Printing and Saving the Word Document with the Link

To print the Word document and linked worksheet as a single document and then save it, complete the steps on the next page.

Steps To Print and Save the Memo with the Linked Worksheet

1. **With the Word window active, click the Print button on the Standard toolbar.**

   The memo and the worksheet print as one document as shown in Figure 8.

2. **Right-click the menu bar. Click Save As. Type the filename** `Weekly Sales Memo 12-22-97` **in the File name box. Click the Save button in the Save As dialog box.**

   Excel saves the Word document to your floppy disk using the filename, Weekly Sales Memo 12-22-97. The worksheet is not part of the saved file. The saved file contains a link to the workbook, Weekly Sales Memo, and information about the range to display in the Word document.

document with linked worksheet and chart printed as one entity

Net Microsystems
Memorandum

TO: Sales Representatives
FROM: Kevin James, Director of Sales
DATE: December 22, 1997
SUBJECT: Weekly Sales Summary - All Regions

The spreadsheet and chart shown below illustrate our company's sales activity for all regions for the week of December 15, 1997. Please review these figures and report any inaccuracies to this office as soon as possible.

Net Microsystems
Weekly Sales Summary

	Mon	Tue	Wed	Thu	Fri	Total
Richmond	$88,213	$76,865	$99,124	$54,987	$67,386	$386,575
Nashville	62,341	42,761	34,499	56,123	46,231	241,955
St. Louis	98,234	38,316	19,265	17,326	16,417	189,558
Kansas City	45,814	29,023	34,786	23,417	25,006	158,046
Denver	96,956	42,864	38,142	45,375	36,927	260,264
Boston	72,485	63,182	57,505	55,832	61,647	310,651
Total	$464,043	$293,011	$283,321	$253,060	$253,614	$1,547,049

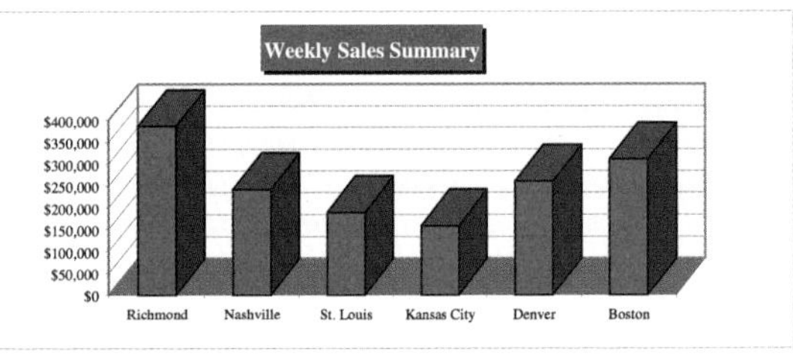

FIGURE 8

OtherWays

1. On File menu click Print, click OK button
2. Press CTRL+P, click OK button

If you exit both applications and re-open Weekly Sales Memo 12-22-97, the worksheet will display in the document even though Excel is not running. With the help of OLE, Word is able to display that portion of the linked Excel file.

The next section describes what happens when you attempt to edit the linked worksheet while Word is active.

Editing the Linked Worksheet

While the worksheet displays as part of the Word document, you can edit any of the cells in it. To edit the worksheet, double-click it. If Excel is running in main memory, the system will switch to it and display the linked workbook. If Excel is not running, the system will start it automatically and display the linked workbook. The following steps show how to change the Tuesday sales for the Boston office in cell C9 from $63,182 to $2,000.

Steps To Edit the Linked Worksheet

1 With the Word window active and the Weekly Sales Memo 12-22-97 document active, double-click the worksheet. When the Excel window becomes active, click the Maximize button.

Windows switches from Word to Excel and displays the original workbook, Weekly Sales Summary.

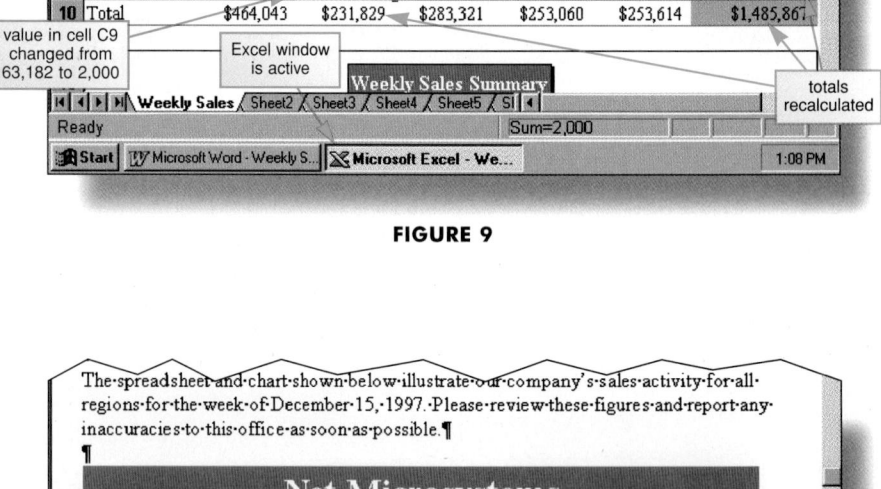

2 Click cell C9 and enter 2000 **in the cell.**

Excel recalculates all formulas in the workbook (Figure 9) and redraws the 3-D column chart.

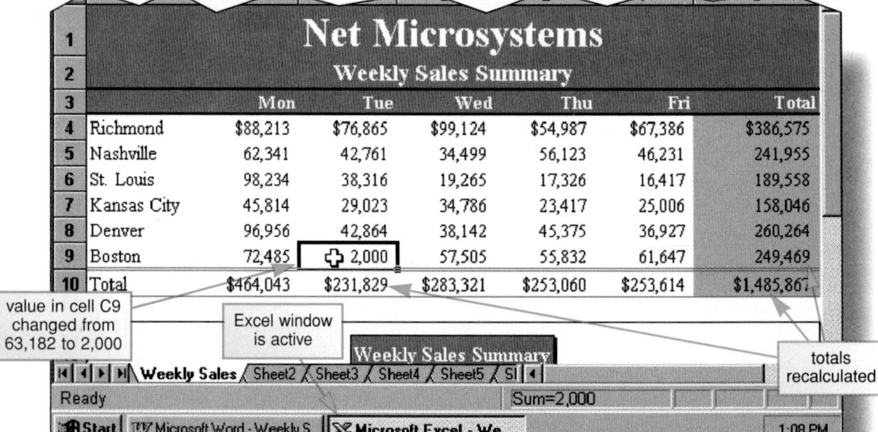

		Mon	Tue	Wed	Thu	Fri	Total
4	Richmond	$88,213	$76,865	$99,124	$54,987	$67,386	$386,575
5	Nashville	62,341	42,761	34,499	56,123	46,231	241,955
6	St. Louis	98,234	38,316	19,265	17,326	16,417	189,558
7	Kansas City	45,814	29,023	34,786	23,417	25,006	158,046
8	Denver	96,956	42,864	38,142	45,375	36,927	260,264
9	Boston	72,485	2,000	57,505	55,832	61,647	249,469
10	Total	$464,043	$231,829	$283,321	$253,060	$253,614	$1,485,867

FIGURE 9

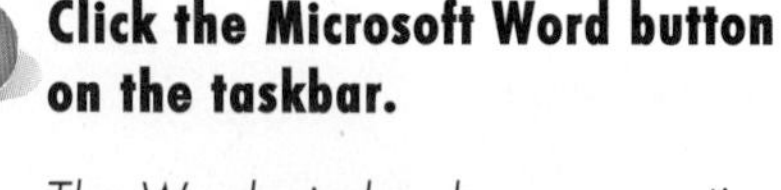

3 Click the Microsoft Word button on the taskbar.

The Word window becomes active. The Tuesday sales amount for the Boston office is the newly entered 2,000. New totals display for Tuesday sales, Boston sales, and the Total sales for the company (Figure 10).

The·spreadsheet·and·chart·shown·below·illustrate·our·company's·sales·activity·for·all·regions·for·the·week·of·December·15,·1997.·Please·review·these·figures·and·report·any·inaccuracies·to·this·office·as·soon·as·possible.¶

Net Microsystems
Weekly Sales Summary

	Mon	Tue	Wed	Thu	Fri	Total
Richmond	$88,213	$76,865	$99,124	$54,987	$67,386	$386,575
Nashville	62,341	42,761	34,499	56,123	46,231	241,955
St. Louis	98,234	38,316	19,265	17,326	16,417	189,558
Kansas City	45,814	29,023	34,786	23,417	25,006	158,046
Denver	96,956	42,864	38,142	45,375	36,927	260,264
Boston	72,485	2,000	57,505	55,832	61,647	249,469
Total	$464,043	$231,829	$283,321	$253,060	$253,614	$1,485,867

value in cell C9 changed in Excel from 63,182 to 2,000 shows in Word

new totals due to changing Tuesday sales for Boston office

Word window is active

FIGURE 10

4 Exit both applications without saving the changes.

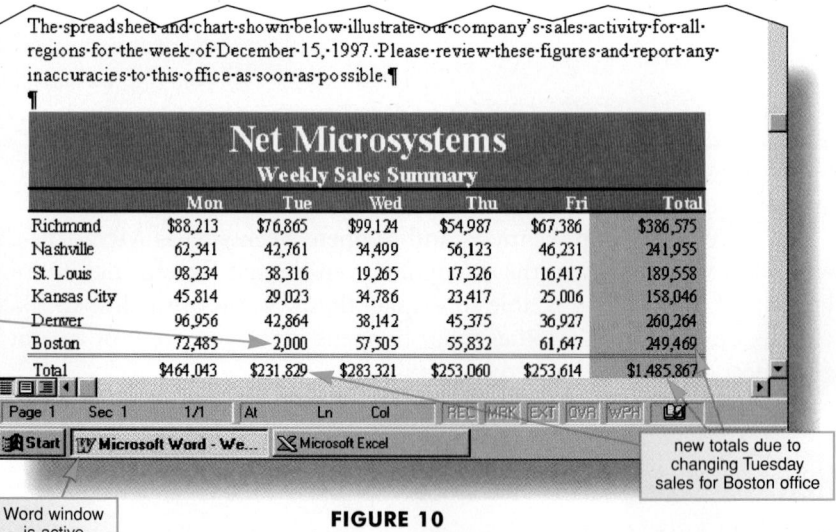

As you can see from the previous steps, when you want to edit a linked object, double-click it. Windows will activate the application and display the workbook or document from which the object came. You can then edit the object and return to the destination application. Any changes made to the object will appear in the destination document.

If you want the edited changes to the linked workbook to be permanent, you must save the workbook, Weekly Sales Summary, before exiting Excel.

Summary

With the Excel worksheet linked to the Word document, Kevin James, the director of sales, can now open the Word document each week, double-click the worksheet, and change the daily sales amounts before e-mailing the Word document or printing it and mailing it to the sales force.

This Integration Feature introduced you to linking one document to another. When you link an object to a document and save it, only a link to the object is saved with the document. You edit a linked object by double-clicking it. The system activates the application and opens the file from which the object came. If you change any part of the object and then return to the destination document, the updated object will display.

What You Should Know

Having completed this Integration Feature, you should be able to perform the following tasks:

- Edit the Linked Worksheet *(EI 1.8)*
- Link the Excel Worksheet to the Word Document *(EI 1.4)*
- Open a Word Document and an Excel Workbook *(EI 1.3)*
- Print and Save the Memo with the Linked Worksheet *(EI 1.7)*

In the Lab

1 Using Help

Instructions:

Start Excel. Double-click the Help button on the Standard toolbar to display the Help Topics: Microsoft Excel dialog box. Click the Contents tab. Double-click the Sharing Data with Other Users and Applications book. Double-click the Linking and Embedding book. Double-click and read the following links: (a) Exchanging information with other applications; (b) Share information between Office applications; and (c) Troubleshoot linking and embedding problems. Hand in one printout for each of the last two links.

2 Linking a Monthly Expense Worksheet to a Monthly Expense Memo

Problem: Your supervisor, Ms. Connie Cramer, at Dress Shoes Unlimited, sends out a monthly memo with expense figures to the regional managers. You have been asked to simplify her task by linking the monthly expense worksheet to a memo.

Instructions: Perform the following tasks.

1. One at a time, open the document Monthly Expense Memo and the workbook Monthly Expense Summary from the Excel folder on the Student Floppy Disk that accompanies this book.
2. Link the range A1:E17 to the bottom of the Monthly Expense Memo document.
3. Print and then save the document as Monthly Expense Memo 7-1-97.
4. Double-click the worksheet and increase each of the nine expense amounts by $100. Activate the Word window and print it with the new values. Close the document and workbook without saving.

3 Embedding a Monthly Expense Memo into a Monthly Expense Workbook

Problem: Your supervisor, Ms. Connie Cramer, at Dress Shoes Unlimited, has asked you to embed the Word document into the Excel workbook, rather than linking the Excel workbook to the Word document as was done in Exercise 2.

Instructions: Complete the following tasks:

1. One at a time, open the document Monthly Expense Memo and the workbook Monthly Expense Summary from the Excel folder on the Student Floppy Disk that accompanies this book.
2. Activate Excel. On the Monthly Office Expenses sheet insert 17 rows above row 1 and then select cell A1. Activate the Word document and select the entire document. Embed the Word document at the top of the worksheet on the Monthly Office Expenses sheet.
3. Print the Monthly Office Expenses sheet and then save the workbook as Monthly Expense with Memo 7-1-97.
4. With the Excel window active, double-click the embedded document and delete the first sentence. Activate the Excel window and print it with the new memo. Close the workbook and document without saving.

PROJECT FOUR

Working with Templates and Multiple Worksheets in a Workbook

PROJECT FIVE

Data Tables, Visual Basic for Applications, and Scenario Manager

PROJECT SIX

Sorting and Filtering a Worksheet Database and Creating a Data Map

INTEGRATION FEATURE

Embedding an Excel Worksheet in a Word Document Using Drag and Drop

Project 4

Microsoft Excel 7

Windows 95

Working with Templates and Multiple Worksheets in a Workbook

Objectives:

You will have mastered the material in this project when you can:

- Create and use a template
- Copy data between worksheets in a workbook
- Format ranges across multiple worksheets in a workbook
- Utilize custom format codes
- Create formulas that reference cells in different sheets in a workbook
- Summarize data using consolidation
- Add comments to cells
- Add a header or footer to a workbook
- Change the margins
- Find text in the workbook
- Replace text in the workbook

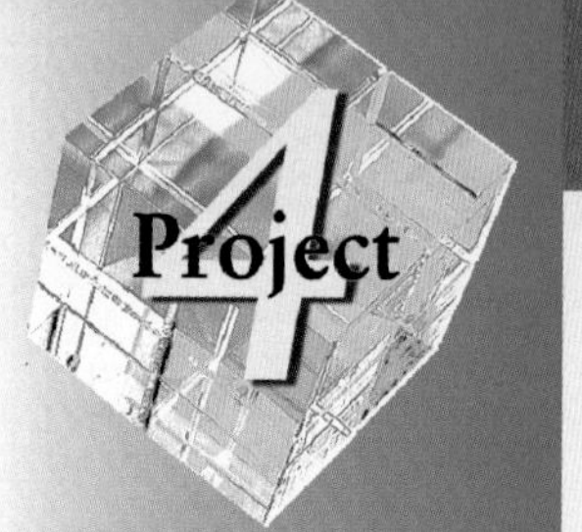

Monetary EKG: Our Financial Health

Only two percent of Americans have healthy financial outlooks, according to some financial planners. With student loans, credit card debts, and home mortgages, most individuals are on the road to financial disaster. If a family tragedy should strike, such as the death of a spouse, it is unlikely that the surviving spouse would be prepared to pay the bills and maintain the present style of living.

How much money is actually needed to face these emergencies? One way to determine monetary status is by summarizing immediate and monthly cash needs, which are contained in the reports generated by the Financial EKG Plus program used by Country Companies Insurance Group financial planners. This worksheet analysis gives a detailed review of the current financial situation, projects the amount needed to meet the family's needs, and then uses these figures in other worksheets to determine how much should be invested each month in various life insurance options to secure the added financial protection.

As in the Antietam University Budget Proposal you will be create in this Excel project, the Financial EKG uses headers and footers to

standardize the worksheet design. On each page, the forms use the company name, Country Companies Financial EKG Plus, and the current date as the header and the text, This proposal was prepared by:, and the insurance agent's name as the footer.

The agent uses the first worksheet to determine the family's immediate cash needs, which is the difference between total cash needed and total cash available. To compute cash needed, the agent enters data for the following fields in the worksheet form: last expenses (medical bills, burial expenses), debt liquidation (loans, credit cards), contingency fund (home-care, child-care), mortgage/rent payment fund (10 years rent or the mortgage balance), and the educational/vocational fund (four-year undergraduate education). The total cash available is the sum of Social Security death benefits, total liquid assets, and existing life insurance. Normally a cash shortage exists.

The agent then enters data used to compute the surviving spouse's income needs through retirement. He or she estimates how much cash the surviving spouse and child currently need to maintain their current style of living, the spouse's earnings, and Social Security benefits. The worksheet uses an average four-percent rate of growth on money and computes the total amount of cash the family will need while the child is a minor, during the blackout period between the time the child is 16 and the spouse retires, and during retirement.

When this income need is added to the cash shortage, the total represents the amount that should be invested to cover this family's financial future in time of tragedy.

The Financial EKG then uses another worksheet that references the cell containing this total cash needed. Three life insurance options are reported: term with increasing premiums, whole life with increasing premiums, and whole life with fixed premiums. For each option, the worksheet computes total premiums paid, cash value and dividends, insurance policy value, and monthly income at age 65.

These reports help a family prepare for an unexpected loss of income. Thus by using Financial EKG today, they can be on the road to a healthy family financial picture tomorrow.

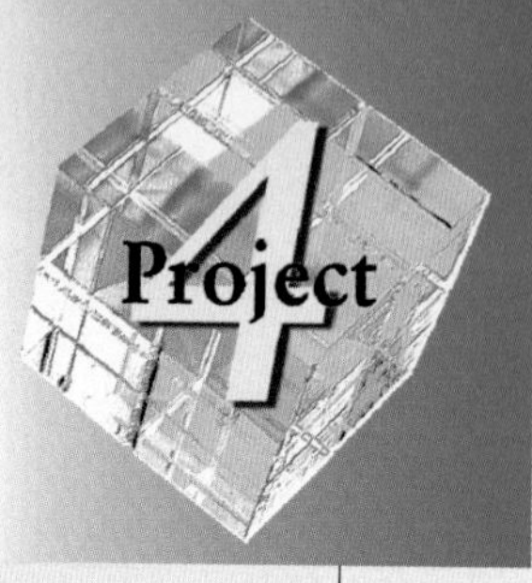

Microsoft
Excel 7
Windows 95

Working with Templates and Multiple Worksheets in a Workbook

Case Perspective

In June of each year, the controller for Antietam University, Kevin Jacob, tenders to the board of trustees a preliminary budget for the next year. The proposed budget is divided into three basic units, called services: Administrative services, Academic services, and Student services.

Each of the three units develops its own budget proposal for the upcoming year, which also includes the current year's budget and the variance between the two years. The individual budget proposals are submitted to Kevin, who then consolidates them into one budget proposal for the entire university.

In previous years, Kevin sent to the business manager of each service a budget proposal form to complete. He then used an older, two-dimensional spreadsheet package to consolidate the three budget amounts. He recently learned of the three-dimensional and template capabilities of Excel and would like to modernize his method of accumulating and summarizing the budget data. As the university's worksheet specialist, Kevin has turned the creation of the workbook over to you.

Introduction

Many business-type applications, such as the one described in the Case Perspective, require worksheet data from several worksheets in a workbook to be summarized onto one worksheet. The three-dimensional capabilities of Excel make it easy for you to complete this type of application. Worksheet data for individual units within a company can be maintained on a separate worksheet in a workbook. You use the tabs at the bottom of the Excel window to move from worksheet to worksheet. Furthermore, Excel has the capability to reference cells found on different worksheets, which allows you to easily summarize worksheet data. The process of summarizing worksheet data found on multiple worksheets is called **consolidation**.

Another important concept you will be introduced to in this project is the use of a template. A **template** is a special workbook you can use as a pattern to create new workbooks that are similar. A template usually consists of a **general format** (worksheet title, column and row titles, and numeric format) and formulas that are common to all the worksheets. For example, with the university budget proposal, the worksheets for each of the three services and the university worksheet would be identical, except for the numbers. For such an application, it is to your advantage to create a template, save it, and then copy it as many times as necessary to a workbook.

Finally, this project introduces you to using the Find and Replace commands. **The Find command** is used to quickly locate words or phrases in a workbook. The **Replace command** is used to find a word or phrase and replace it with another.

Project Four – Antietam University Budget Proposal

From your meetings with the controller, Kevin Jacob, you have accumulated the following workbook specifications.

Need: The workbook Kevin has in mind would use five worksheets — one for each of the three services, a summary worksheet for the university, and a chart sheet that includes a comparison chart comparing next year's proposed budget to this year's budget (Figure 4-1).

More About Templates

Templates can be a powerful tool for developing consistency among worksheets. Templates can contain: (1) text and graphics, such as a company name and logo; (2) formats and page layouts, such as styles and custom headers and footers; and (3) formulas and macros.

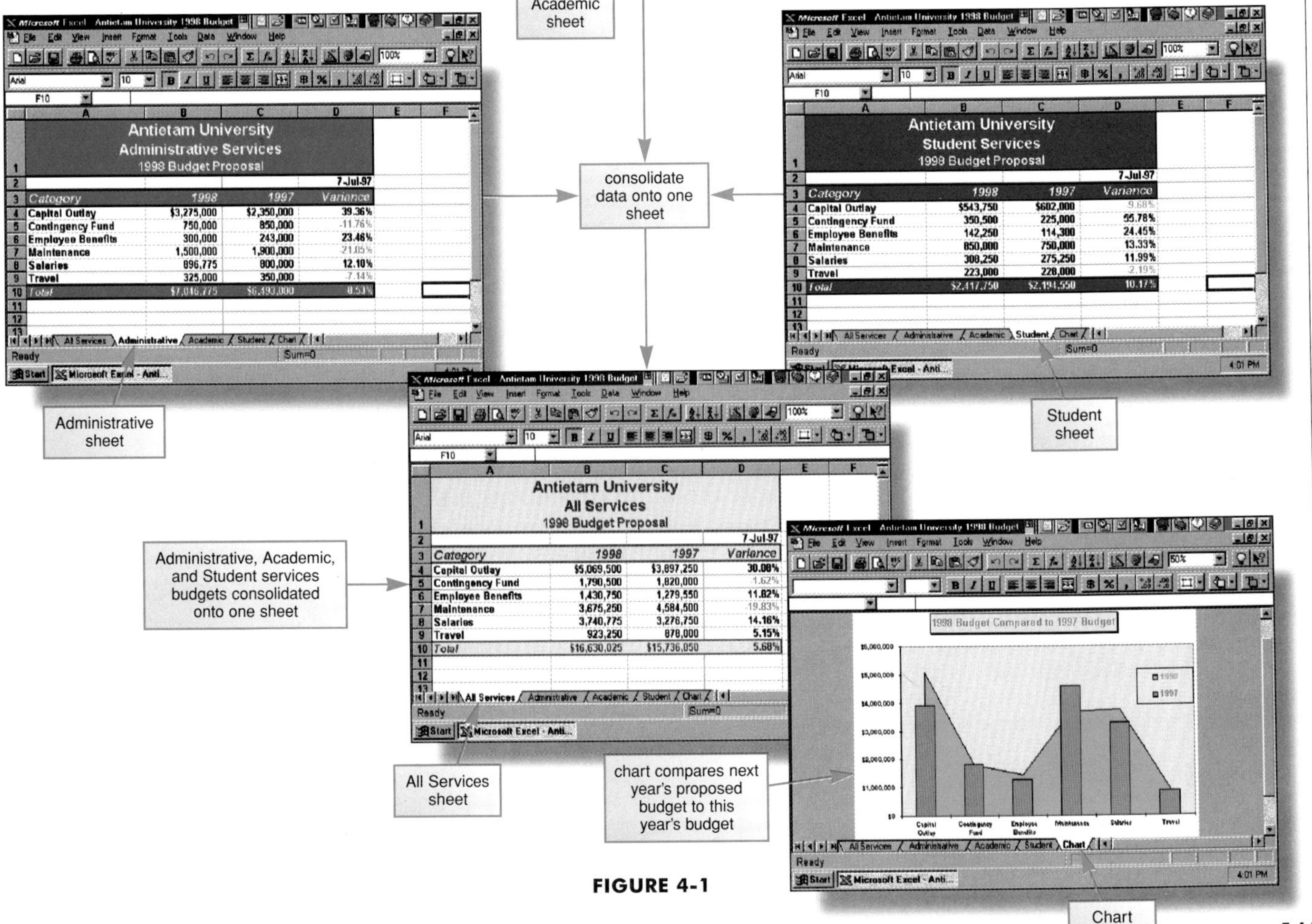

FIGURE 4-1

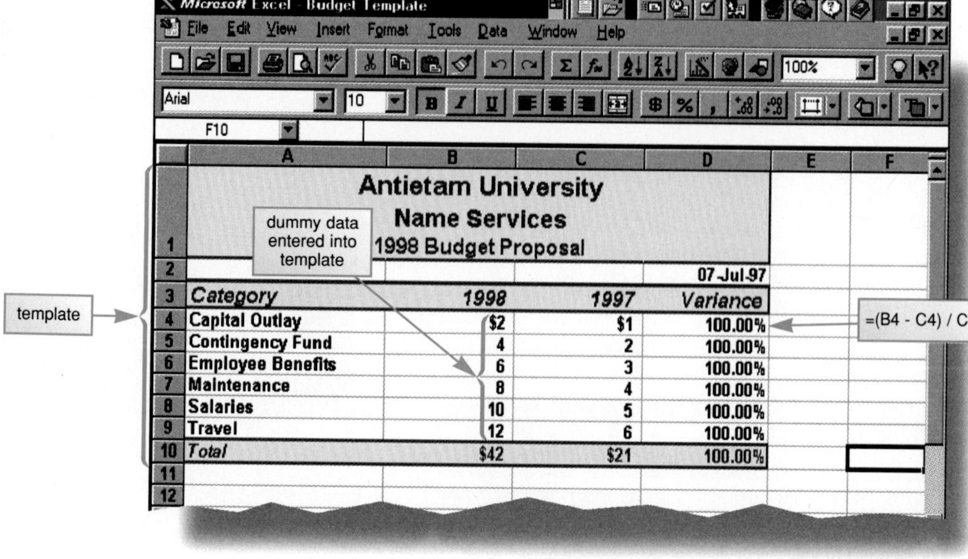

FIGURE 4-2

Because the three service worksheets and university worksheet are nearly identical, a template (Figure 4-2) will be created and then copied three times into the Antietam University Budget Proposal workbook.

Source of Data: The data will be collected from the business managers of the respective services.

Calculations: The following calculations are required for the template (Figure 4-2):

1. To determine the variance within each category (column D): Variance = (Next Year's Proposed Budget - This Year's Budget) / This Year's Budget
2. Row 10 contains totals of the six categories for next year's proposed budget (column B) and this year's budget (column C).

Once the template is used to create the four worksheets, the individual totals in columns B and C on the All Services sheet must be determined using the SUM function to sum values on the three service sheets. For example, the SUM function assigned to cell B4 on the All Services sheet in Figure 1-1 sums the values in cell B4 on the Administrative sheet, Academic sheet, and Student sheet.

Graph Requirements: Include a chart on a separate sheet that compares by category the proposed budget to last year's budget.

Template and Workbook Preparation Steps

The following preparation steps summarize how the template shown in Figure 4-2 and the workbook shown in Figure 4-1 will be developed in Project 4.

1. Start the Excel program.
2. Create the template.
   a. Assign the bold style to all the cells in the worksheet.
   b. Increase the width of columns A through D, enter the worksheet titles, row titles, column titles, and system date.
   c. Use the fill handle to enter dummy data for the 1997 budget and 1998 proposed budget. Next, determine service totals and enter the variance formulas in column D.
   d. Save the workbook as a template using the filename Budget Template.
   e. Format the template.
   f. Check spelling, save the template a second time, and then close it.

More *About* **Charts on a Template**

You can create a chart on a template. However, if you then create a workbook by copying the template to multiple worksheets, you must change the chart range on each worksheet or all the charts will refer to the first worksheet in the workbook.

3. Create the workbook.
   a. Open the template. Copy Sheet1 to Sheet2 through Sheet4. Save the workbook as Antietam University 1998 Budget.
   b. Change the worksheet titles representing each of the three services. Replace the dummy data on Sheet2 through Sheet4 with the data submitted by the business managers.
   c. Modify the worksheet title of the All Services sheet. Enter the SUM function and copy it to consolidate the data found on the three service sheets.
   d. Create a combination area and column chart on a separate sheet that compares next year's proposed budget to this year's budget. Format the chart.
   e. Add a comment to cell F1 on the All Services sheet.
   f. Add a header to the five sheets and change margins.
   g. Save, preview, and print the workbook.

The following pages contain a detailed explanation of these tasks.

> **More** *About* **Consolidation**
>
> Besides consolidating data within a single workbook, you can consolidate data across different workbooks using the Consolidate command on the Data menu. For more information, double-click the Help button on the Standard toolbar, click the Index tab, and obtain information on the topic, consolidate data.

Starting Excel

To start Excel, follow the steps you used in previous projects. These steps are summarized below:

TO START EXCEL

Step 1: Click the Start button. Click New Office Document on the Start menu. If necessary, click the General tab in the New dialog box.
Step 2: Double-click the Blank Workbook icon.

Creating the Budget Template

Learning how to use templates is important if you plan to use a similar worksheet design in your workbooks. In the case of Project 4, four sheets (Figure 4-1) are nearly identical. Thus, the first step in building the Antietam University Budget Proposal workbook is to create template that contains the labels, formulas, and formats that are found in each of the four sheets. Once the template is saved to disk, it can be used as often as required to initiate a new workbook. Many worksheet users create a template for each application they use. The templates can be as simple as containing a special font you want to use in an application to more complex entries as is the case in the template for Project 4.

You create and modify a template the same as the workbooks in past projects. The only difference between a workbook and a template is in the manner in which it is saved.

Bolding the Font and Changing Column Widths of the Template

The first step in this project is to change the font of the entire template to bold so that all entries are emphasized and change the column widths as follows: A = 22.00 and B through D = 14.00.

More About Formatting

You can apply formats to an entire workbook by clicking the Select All button and then choosing the Select All Sheets command on the shortcut menu that displays when you point to a tab and click the right mouse button.

TO BOLD THE FONT IN THE TEMPLATE AND CHANGE COLUMN WIDTHS

Step 1: Click the Select All button immediately above row heading 1 and to the left of column heading A.
Step 2: Click the Bold button on the Standard toolbar. Click cell A1.
Step 3: Point to the border between column heading A and column heading B so the pointer changes to a plus sign with two arrowheads. Drag the mouse pointer to the right until the width displayed in the Name box on the formula bar is equal to 22.00.
Step 4: Select columns B through D by pointing to column heading B and dragging though column heading D. Point to the border between column headings D and E and drag the mouse to the right until the width displayed in the Name box is 14.00.

The Bold style is assigned to all cells in the worksheet. Column A has a width of 22.00 and columns B through D have a width of 14.00.

Entering the Template Title and Row Titles

Three lines are in the template title in cell A1. To enter the three lines in one cell, press ALT+ENTER after each of the first two lines. After the third line, press the ENTER key or click the enter box in the formula bar, or press an arrow key as you have done in previous projects to complete a cell entry. The row titles are entered in the same fashion as was done in earlier projects. The following steps describe how to enter the template and row titles.

TO ENTER THE TEMPLATE TITLE AND ROW TITLES

Step 1: Click cell A1. Type `Antietam University` and press ALT+ENTER. Type `Name Services` and press ALT+ENTER. Type `1998 Budget Proposal` and press the DOWN ARROW key twice.
Step 2: With cell A3 active, type `Category` and press the DOWN ARROW key.
Step 3: Enter the remaining row titles in column A as shown in Figure 4-3.

The template title and row titles display in column A as shown in Figure 4-3.

Pressing ALT+ENTER after each line in the template title in cell A1 causes the insertion point to move down one line in the cell. This procedure allows you to control the width of each line of text entered into a cell.

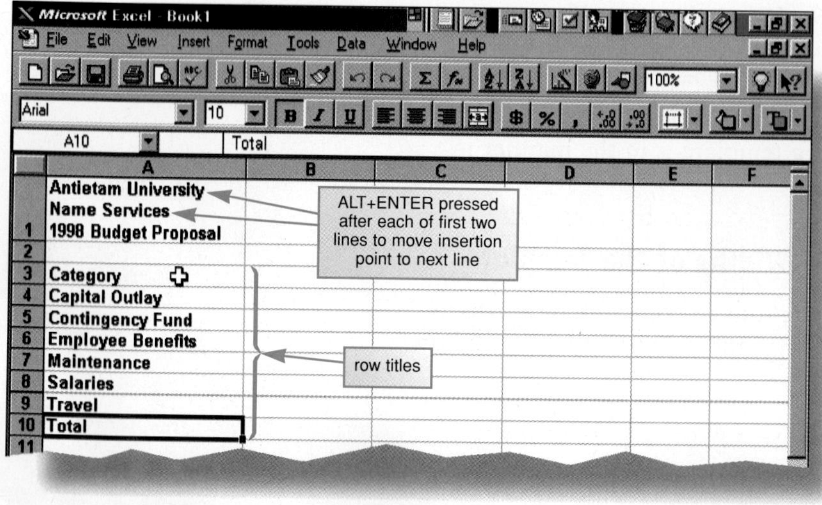

FIGURE 4-3

Entering the Template Column Titles and System Date

The next step is to enter the column titles in row 3 and the system date in cell D2. If a cell entry contains only digits, such as 1997, then Excel considers it to be numeric. Because of the method that will be used to determine the sums in column B and C and the chart range that will be selected later in this project, it is necessary that the two numeric entries in row 3 be entered as text. To enter a number as text, begin it with an apostrophe (') as shown in the following steps.

To Enter Numbers as Text, Format the Entries, and Enter the System Date

1. **Click cell B3. Type** '1998 **and press the RIGHT ARROW key. Type** '1997 **and press the RIGHT ARROW key. Type** Variance **and press the ENTER key.**

2. **Select the range B3:D3 and click the Align Right button on the Formatting toolbar.**

3. **Click cell D2. Type** =now() **and then press the ENTER key.**

   The column titles and system date display as shown in Figure 4-4.

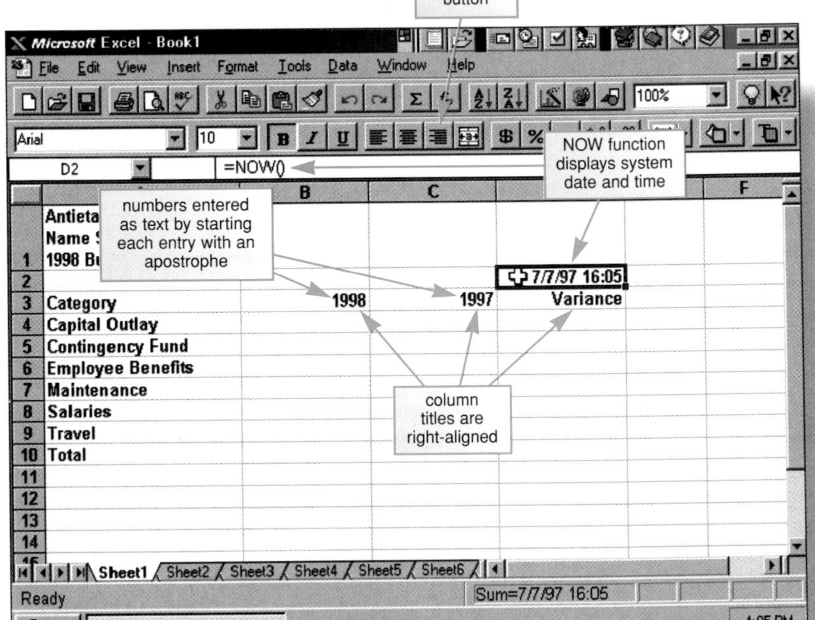

FIGURE 4-4

4. **Right-click cell D2, click Format Cells, click the Number tab, click Date in the Category box and 04-Mar-95 (or a similar format) in the Type box. Click the OK button.**

   The system date displays using the new format (Figure 4-5).

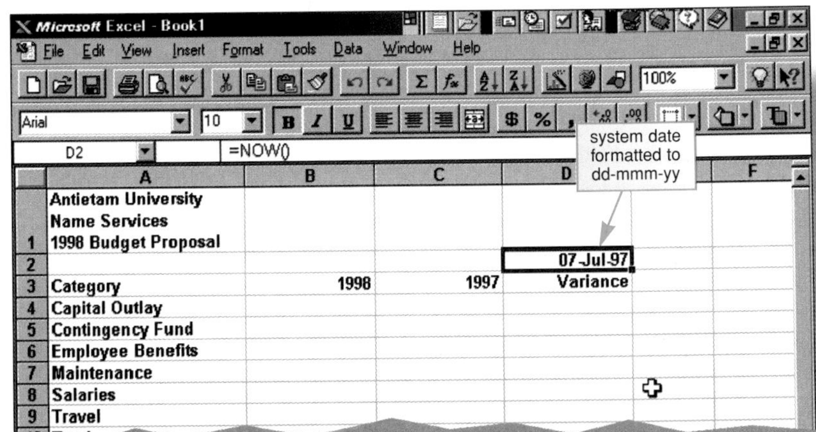

FIGURE 4-5

Entering Dummy Numbers and Summing Them in the Template

Dummy numbers are used in place of actual data in a template to verify the formulas. Usually you select simple numbers that allow you to quickly check if the formulas are generating the proper results. In Project 4, the budget category dollar amounts are entered into the range B4:C9. The following steps use the fill handle to create a series of numbers in column B that begin with 2 and increment by 2 and a series of numbers in column C that begin with 1 and increment by 1. Recall from Project 3 that to create a series you must enter the first two numbers so Excel can determine the increment amount.

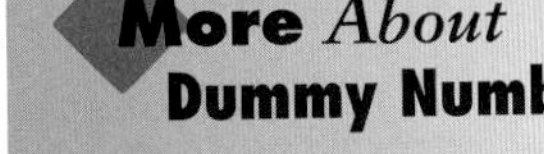

More *About* Dummy Numbers

As you develop more sophisticated workbooks, it will become increasingly important that you create good test data to ensure your workbooks are error free. The more you test a workbook, the more confident you will be in the results generated. Select test data that tests the limits of the formulas.

Steps To Enter Dummy Numbers and Sum Them in the Template

1 **Enter** 2 **in cell B4,** 4 **in cell B5,** 1 **in cell C4, and** 2 **in cell C5. Select the range B4:C5 and drag the fill handle through cells B9 and C9.**

Excel surrounds the range B4:C9 with a gray border (Figure 4-6).

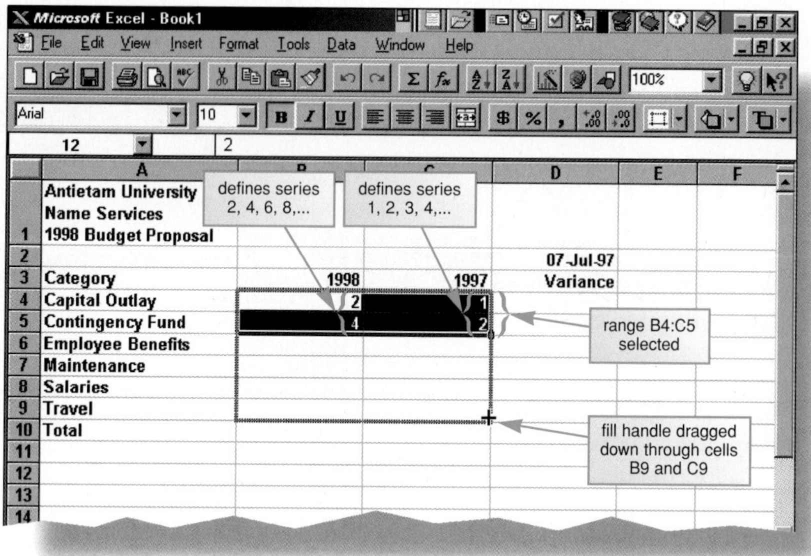

FIGURE 4-6

2 **Release the left mouse button. Select the range B10:C10 and click the AutoSum button on the Standard toolbar.**

Excel assigns the sum of the values in the range B4:B9 to cell B10 and the sum of the values in the range C4:C9 to cell C10 (Figure 4-7).

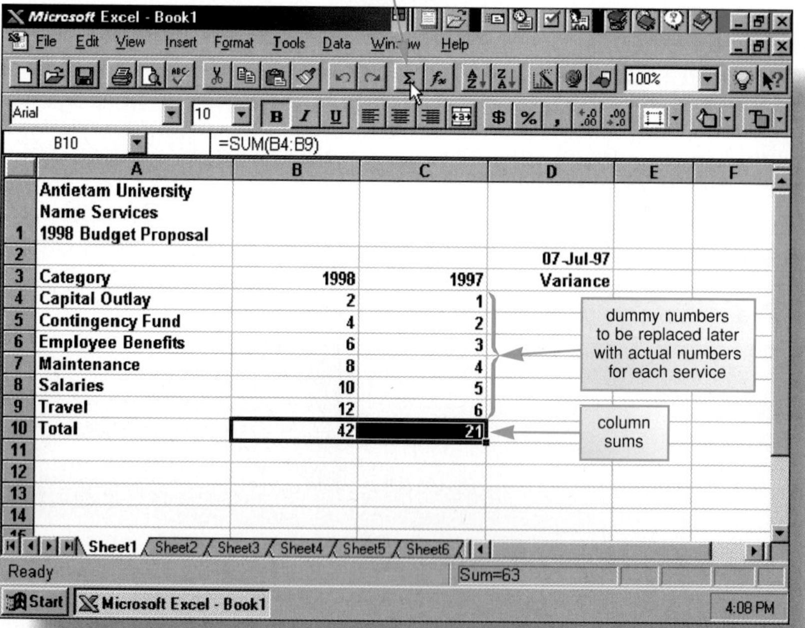

FIGURE 4-7

OtherWays

1. Select one range at a time, point to Fill on the Edit menu, click Series on the submenu, click OK button

If the column heading 1998 in cell B3 and the column heading 1997 in cell C3 were entered as numbers, then Excel would have included them in the sums. Because they were entered with an initial apostrophe, Excel considers them to be text, and therefore, does not include them in the ranges to sum in cells B10 and C10.

Entering the Variance Formula in the Template

The variances in column D (see Figure 4-1 on page E 4.7) are equal to the corresponding 1998 budget amount less the 1997 budget amount divided by the 1997 budget amount. For example, the formula to enter in cell D4 is = (B4 - C4) / C4. This formula displays a decimal result that indicates the percent increase or decrease in the 1998 budget amount when compared to the 1997 budget amount. Once the formula is entered into cell D4, it can be copied to the range D5:D10. The following steps describe how to enter the variance formula in the template.

More About Error Values

Excel displays an error value in a cell when it cannot calculate the formula. Error values always begin with # a number sign. The most common occurring error values are: #DIV/0! (trying to divide by zero); #NAME? (use of a name Excel does not recognize); #N/A (refers to a value not available); #NULL! (specifies an invalid intersection of two areas); #NUM! (uses a number incorrectly); #REF (refers to a cell that is not valid); #VALUE! (uses an incorrect argument or operand); and ##### (cell not wide enough).

TO ENTER THE VARIANCE FORMULA IN THE TEMPLATE

Step 1: Click cell D4. Type `=(B4-C4)/C4` and click the enter box or press the ENTER key.

Step 2: With cell D4 active, drag the fill handle down through cell D10. Click cell F10.

The formula is entered into cell D4 and copied to the range D5:D10 (Figure 4-8).

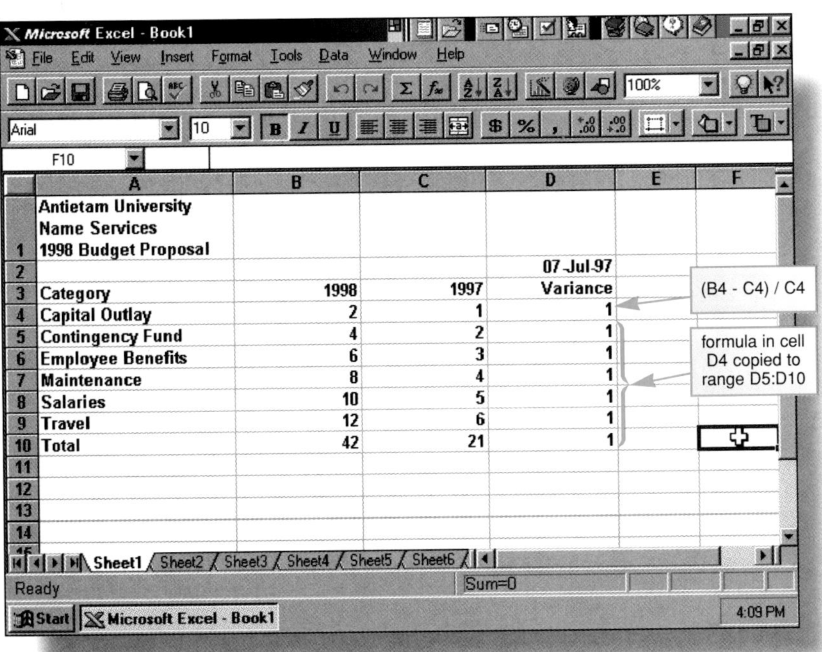

FIGURE 4-8

Excel displays a 1 in each cell in the range D4:D10 because the dummy numbers in column B are twice the corresponding numbers in column C. Thus, the 1s in column D represent a 100% proposed budget increase between 1997 and 1998. Later, when the actual budget numbers replace the dummy numbers in columns B and C, these percent values will be different. Shortly, the numbers in column D will be formatted so they display as a percent instead of a whole number.

More About File Extensions

If the MS-DOS extension .xlt shows in your title bar following the filename, it means the option not to show the MS-DOS extension is not selected on the View sheet on the Options dialog box in Explorer. You display the Options dialog box in Explorer by clicking Options on the View menu.

Saving the Template

You save a template in the same fashion you saved workbooks in previous projects, except that you select Template in the Save as type box on the Save As dialog box. The following steps save the template to drive A using the filename Budget Template.

Steps To Save a Template

1 **Click the Save button on the Standard toolbar. When the Save As dialog box displays, type** `Budget Template` **in the File name box. Click the Save as type drop-down list box arrow and click Template.**

2 **Click the Save in drop-down list box arrow and click 3 ½ Floppy [A:]. Point to the Save button.**

The Save As dialog box displays as shown in Figure 4-9.

3 **Click the Save button.**

Excel saves the template Budget Template to the floppy disk in drive A. The filename Budget Template displays in the title bar as shown in Figure 4-10.

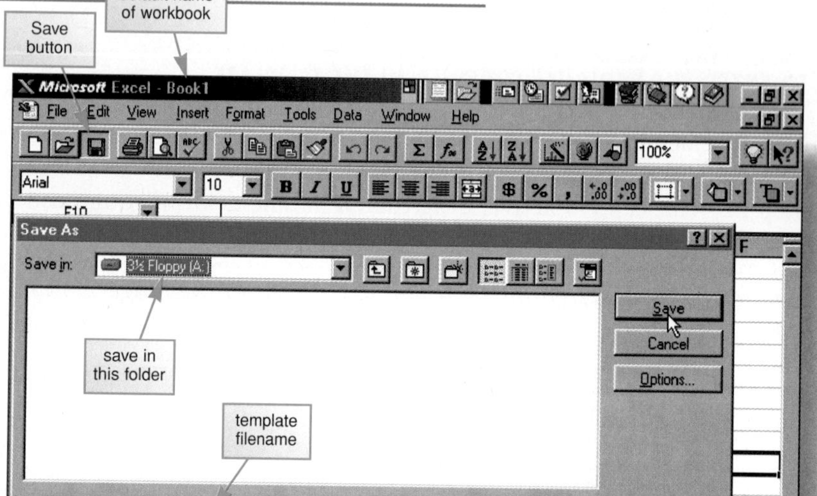

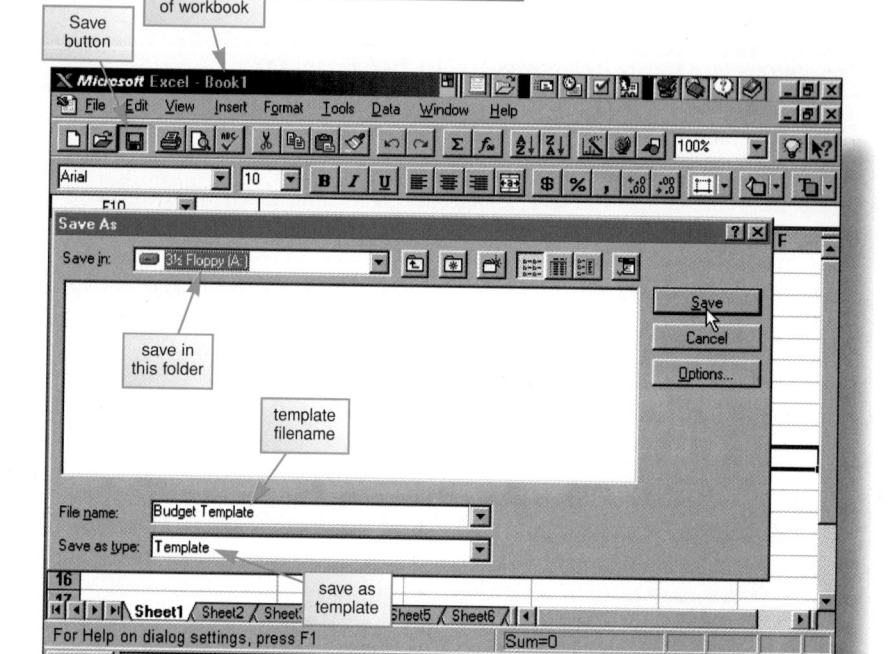

FIGURE 4-9

OtherWays

1. Right-click menu bar, click Save As, type filename, select Template in Save as type drop-down list box, type filename, select drive or folder, click OK button
2. On File menu, click Save As, type filename, select Template in Save as type drop-down list box, type filename, select drive or folder, click OK button
3. Press CTRL+S, type filename, select Template in Save as type drop-down list box, type filename, select drive or folder, click OK button

Formatting the Template

The next step is to format the template so that it appears as shown in Figure 4-10. Keep in mind that the formats selected will appear in each of the sheets for which the template is used. The following list summarizes the sequence of formatting that will be applied.

1. Change the font size of the template title in cell A1. Center cell A1 across columns A through D.
2. Italicize and change the font size of the column titles in row 3. Italicize the row title Total in cell A10.
3. Assign the background color light yellow and a medium dark red outline to the nonadjacent ranges A1:D1, A3:D3, and A10:D10.

4. Assign the Currency style to the nonadjacent ranges B4:C4 and B10:C10. Assign a Comma format to the range B5:C9.
5. Assign a Percent style to the Range D4:D10.

Formatting the Template Title

To emphasize the template title in cell A1, the font size will be changed to the following: line 1 = 16 point; line 2 = 14 point; and line 3 = 12 point. The following steps also center the template title across columns A through D.

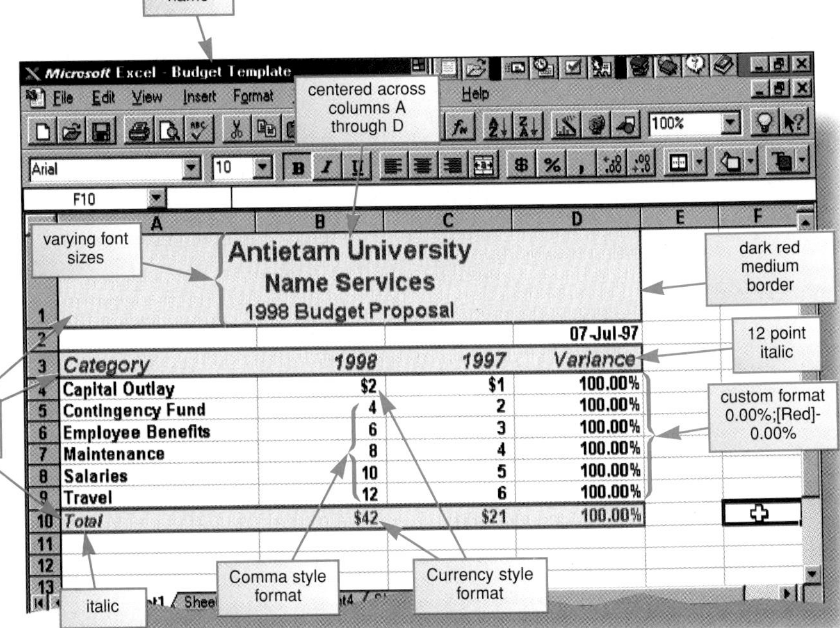

FIGURE 4-10

TO FORMAT THE TEMPLATE TITLES

Step 1: Double-click cell A1 to activate in-cell editing. Drag across the first line of text. Click the Font Size arrow on the Formatting toolbar and then click 16.

Step 2: With in-cell editing still active in cell A1, use the techniques described in Step 1 to change the font size of line 2 to 14 point and line 3 to 12 point. Click the enter box in the formula bar or press the ENTER key.

Step 3: With cell A1 active, drag through cell D1. Click the Center Across Columns button on the Formatting toolbar.

Step 4: Select the range A3:D3. Click the Font Size arrow on the Formatting toolbar and then click 12. Click the Italic button on the Formatting toolbar.

Step 5: Click cell A10 and then click the Italic button on the Formatting toolbar.

The template displays as shown in Figure 4-11.

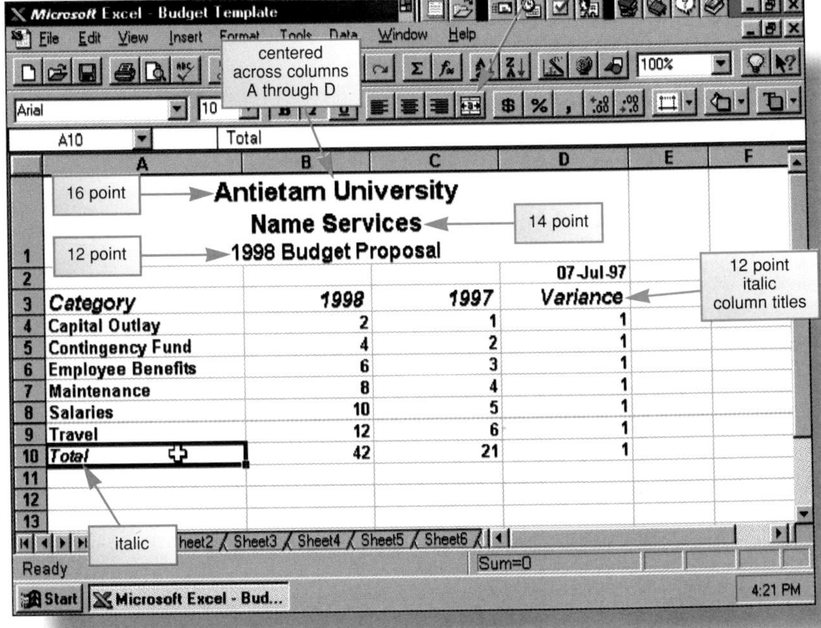

FIGURE 4-11

Changing the Background Color and Adding Outlines

To further accentuate the titles, the background color will be changed and a thick outline will be drawn around the ranges A1:D1, A3:D3, and A10:D10. You can format the ranges one at a time or, because the same format will be applied to all three ranges, you can format them at the same time using the CTRL key to select nonadjacent ranges. The following steps show how to format all three ranges at the same time.

Steps To Change the Background Color and Add Outlines

1. **Select the range A1:D1. Hold down the CTRL key and select the nonadjacent ranges A3:D3, and A10:D10. Click the Color button arrow on the Formatting toolbar.**

   A palette of colors displays (Figure 4-12).

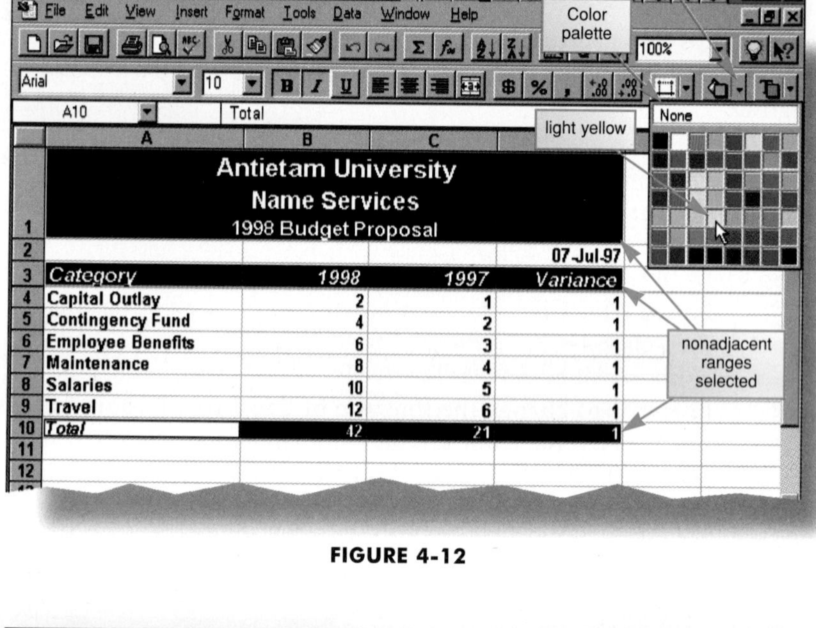

FIGURE 4-12

2. **Click light yellow (column 4, row 5 on the Color palette).**

3. **Right-click one of the selected ranges. Click Format Cells on the shortcut menu. Click the Border tab. Click the Color drop-down list box arrow and click the color dark red (column 1, row 2 on the Color palette). Click Outline in the Border area. Click the medium style (column 1, row 3) in the Style area. Point to the OK button.**

   The Border sheet in the Format Cells dialog box displays as shown in Figure 4-13.

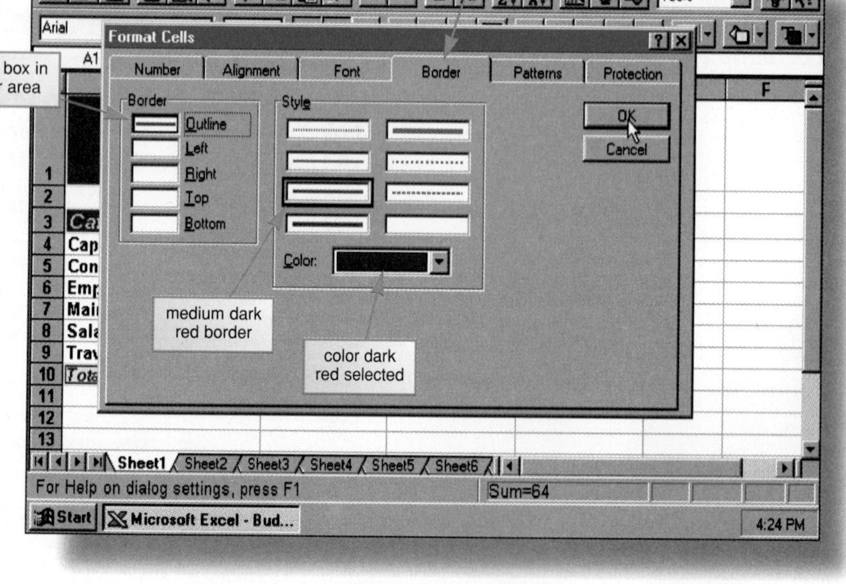

FIGURE 4-13

4 Click the OK button.

A medium dark red border surrounds the selected ranges (Figure 4-14).

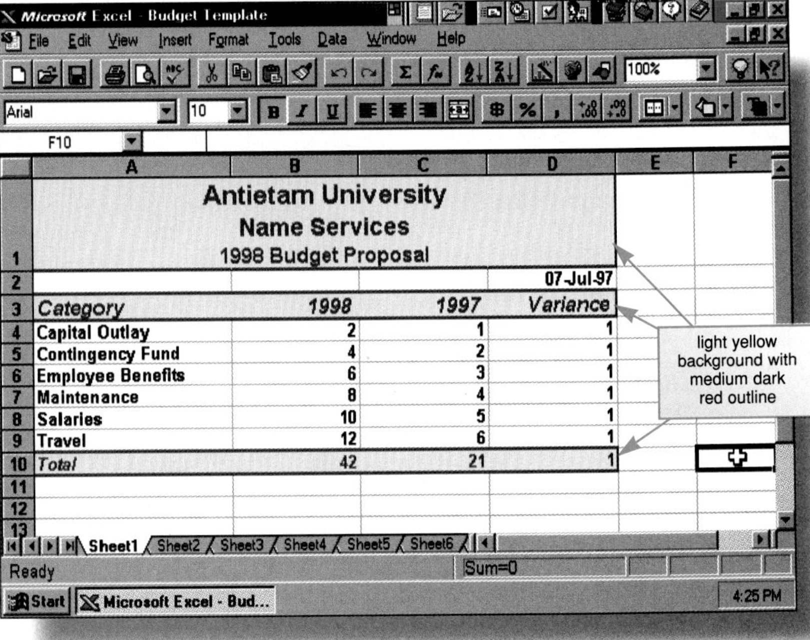

FIGURE 4-14

OtherWays

1. Click Cells on the Format menu, click Border tab, select borders, click OK button
2. Press CTRL+1, click Border tab, select borders, click OK button

Applying Number Formats From the Format Cells Dialog Box

The template in this project (see Figure 4-2 on page E 4.8) calls for following the standard accounting convention for a table of numbers by adding dollar signs to the first row of numbers (row 4) and the totals row (row 10). To accomplish this task, you could select the range and click the Currency button on the Formatting toolbar. However, the format code assigned to the selected cells would result in applying a fixed dollar sign. Recall, a fixed dollar sign always displays in the same position in a cell regardless of the number of digits in the number. The alternative to a fixed dollar sign is a floating dollar sign. A floating dollar sign always displays immediately to the left of the first significant digit. Because this project calls for using a floating dollar sign with no decimal places, it is required that a format code be selected from the Format dialog box, rather than using the Currency button.

The steps on the next page assign a Currency style with a floating dollar sign and no decimal places to the range B4:C4 and B10:C10 using the Format Cells command on the shortcut menu. The steps then use the Comma button and Decrease Decimal button on the Formatting toolbar to format the range B5:C9.

More About Formatting

Excel has formats for zip codes, phone numbers, and social security numbers. Click Special in the Category box on the Format Cells. The formats will display in the Type box. These formats will automatically add dashes in the appropriate positions. All you have to do is enter the digits.

Steps To Apply a Format Code from the Format Dialog Box

1 **Select the range B4:C4. Hold down the CTRL key and select the nonadjacent range B10:C10.**

2 **Right-click one of the two selected ranges.**

Excel displays the shortcut menu (Figure 4-15).

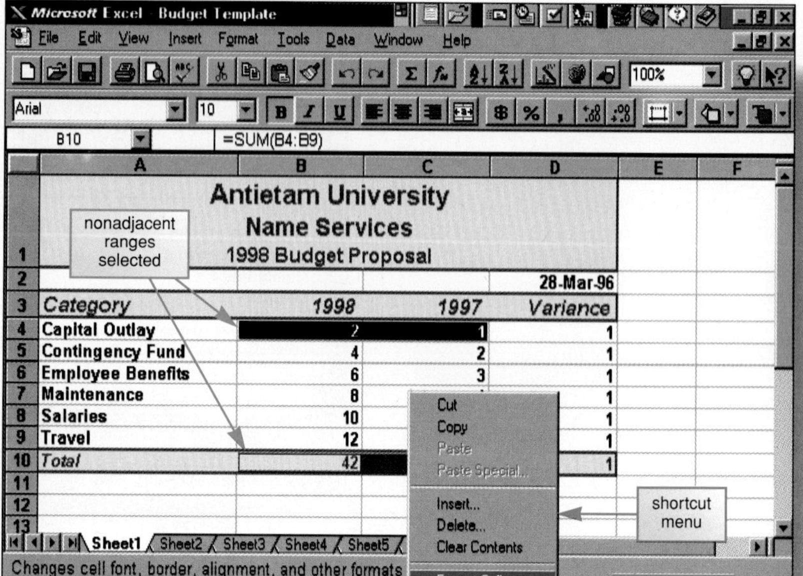

FIGURE 4-15

3 **Click Format Cells on the shortcut menu.**

4 **When the Format Cells dialog box displays, click the Number tab, click Currency in the Category box and then click the down arrow twice on the Decimal Places box so 0 displays. If necessary, click the Use $ check box to display a dollar sign, click ($1,234) in black text in the Negative Numbers box, and point to the OK button.**

The Format Cells dialog box displays as shown in Figure 4-16.

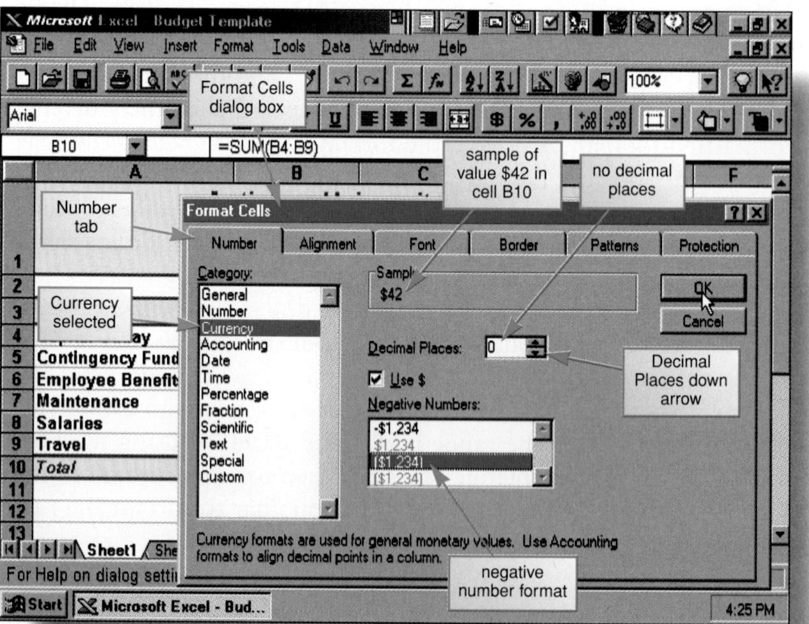

FIGURE 4-16

5 **Click the OK button in the Format Cells dialog box.**

The selected ranges display as shown in Figure 4-17.

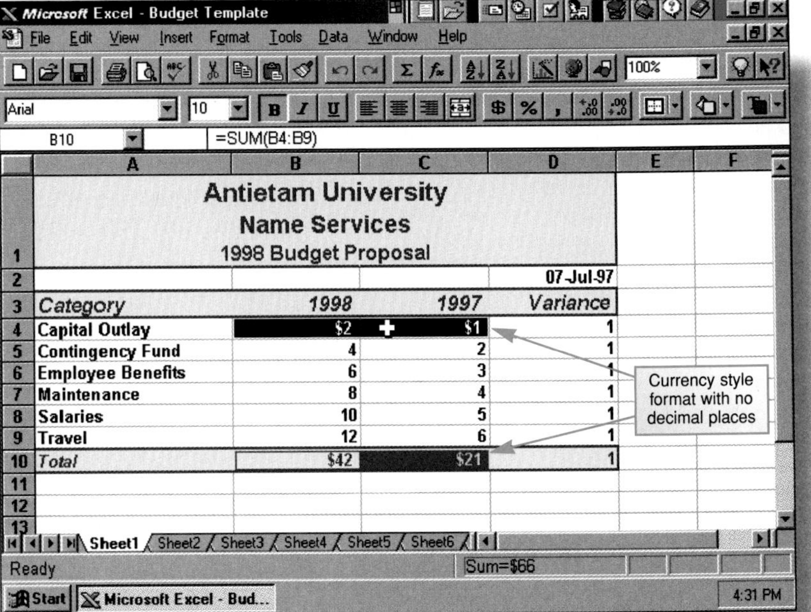

FIGURE 4-17

6 **Select the range B5:C9 and then click the Comma button on the Formatting toolbar. Next, click the Decrease Decimal button on the Formatting toolbar twice.**

Excel displays the numbers in the range B5:C9 using the Comma format with no decimal places (Figure 4-18). Later, when larger numbers are entered into the worksheets that are created from the template, the numbers will include commas.

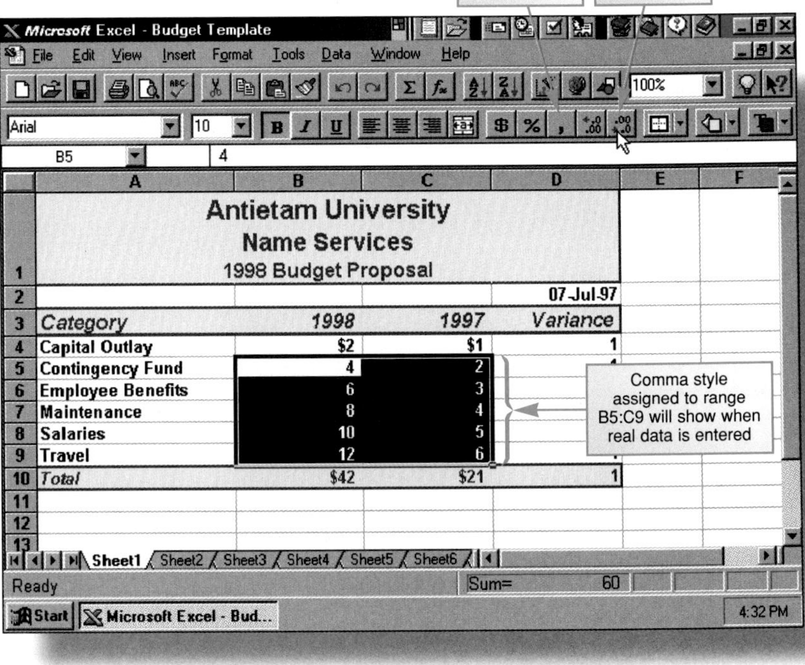

FIGURE 4-18

OtherWays

1. Click Cells on the Format menu, click Number tab, select format, click OK button
2. Press CTRL+1, click Number tab, select format, click OK button

Creating A Customized Format Code

Every format style listed in the Category box in Figure 4-16 has format codes assigned to it. A **format code** is a series of format symbols (Table 4-1) that define a format. You can view the entire list of format codes included with Excel by selecting Custom in the Category box. You can even create your own format codes or modify the customized ones provided with Excel. A format code has four sections to it: positive numbers, negative numbers, zeros, and text as shown below. Each section is divided by a semicolon.

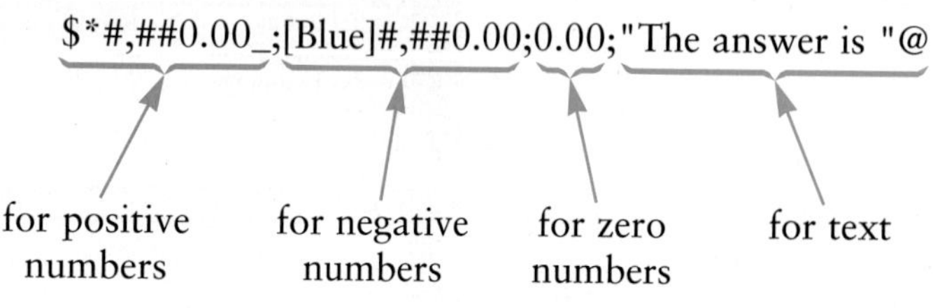

A format code need not have all four sections. For most applications, a format code will have only a positive section, and possibly a negative section.

More About Creating Customized Formats

Each format symbol within the format code has special meaning. Table 4-1 summarizes the most often used format symbols and their meanings. For additional information on creating format codes, double-click the Help button on the Standard toolbar, click the Find tab, type `format codes` in the top box labeled 1, and then double-click Custom number formats in the bottom box labeled 3.

Table 4-1

FORMAT SYMBOL	EXAMPLE OF SYMBOL	DESCRIPTION
#	###.##	Digit placeholder. If there are more digits to the right than there are number signs, Excel rounds the number. Extra digits to the left are displayed.
0 (zero)	#,##0.00	Same as number sign (#), except that if the number is less than one, Excel displays a zero in the one's place.
. (period)	#0.00	Ensures a decimal point will display in the number. Determines how many digits display to the left and right of the decimal point.
%	0.00%	Excel multiplies the value of the cell by 100 and displays a percent sign following the number.
, (comma)	#,##0.00	Displays thousands separator.
$ or - or +	$#,##0.00;($#,##0.00)	Displays a floating sign.
* (asterisk)	$* ##0.00	Displays a fixed sign ($, +, or -) to the left in the cell followed by spaces until the first significant digit.
[color]	#.##;[Red]#.##	Displays the characters in the cell in the designated color. In the example, positive numbers display in the default color and negative numbers display in red.
_	#,##0.00_)	Skips the width of the character that follows the underline.
( )	#0.00;(#0.00)	Displays negative numbers surrounded by parentheses.

The next step is to format the variances in the range D4:D10. This project requires that positive numbers in this range display using the format code 0.00%. Negative numbers display in red using a format code of 0.00% with a leading minus sign. The required format code is 0.00%;[Red]-0.00%. As shown in Figure 4-19, this format code is not available in the Percentage category in the Format Cells dialog box. Thus, it must be created manually by entering the format code in the Type box in the Format Cells dialog box.

The following steps show how to create the required customized format code by selecting a format code that is close to the desired one and then modifying it.

To Create a Custom Format Code

1 **Select the range D4:D10. Right-click the range. Click Format Cells. When the Format Cells dialog box displays, click Custom in the Category box, and then scroll to the format codes with a percent sign (%).**

2 **Click 0.00% in the list of format codes. Type** `;[Red]-0.00%` **in the Type box so 0.00%;[Red]-0.00% displays.**

The Format Cells dialog box displays as shown in Figure 4-19. Notice that Excel does display a sample of the first number in the selected range number in the Sample area.

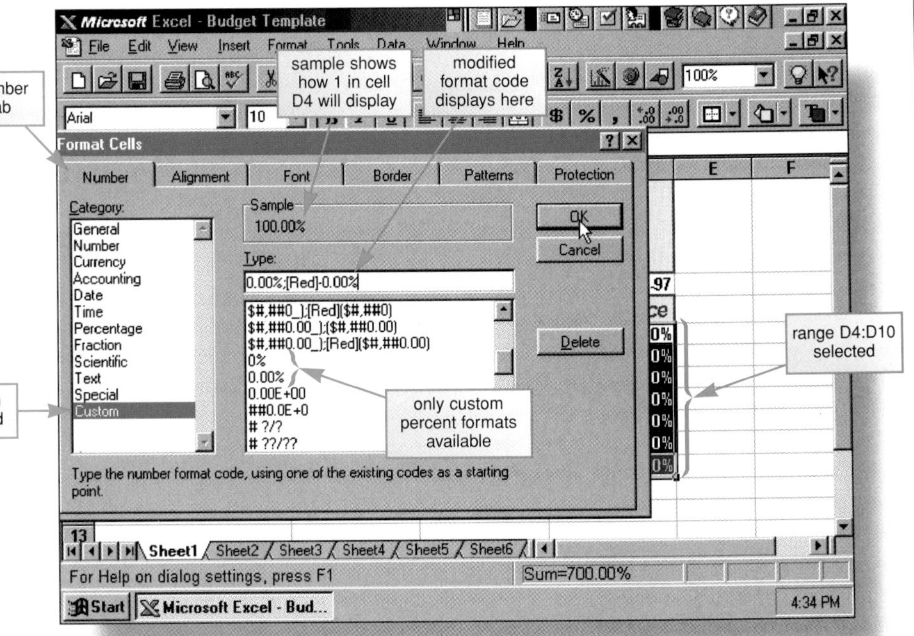

FIGURE 4-19

3 **Click the OK button, and then click cell F10.**

The dummy percents in the range D4:D10 display as shown in Figure 4-20.

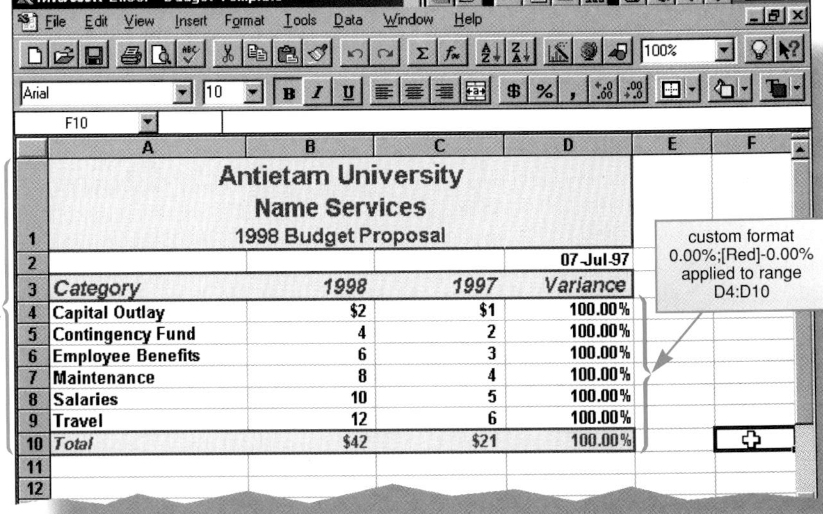

FIGURE 4-20

More About Customized Formats

When you assign a unique customized format to a cell or range of cells, Excel automatically adds the new format to the Type box on the Format Cells dialog box. Thus, if you find a need in the future to apply the same customized format, you can simply select it from the Type box. It will be listed in Custom in the Category box.

OtherWays

1. Click Cells on the Format menu, click Number tab, select format, click OK button
2. Press CTRL+1, click Number tab, select format, click OK button

More *About* **Format Codes**

Excel has the same format code capabilities as any programming language, such as COBOL.

When you create a new custom format code, Excel adds it to the bottom of the Custom list to make it available for other cells in the workbook.

Spell Check and Save Template

With the template complete, the next step is to spell check the template and then save it.

TO SPELL CHECK AND SAVE THE TEMPLATE

Step 1: Click cell A1. Click the Spelling button on the Standard toolbar. Correct any misspelled words.
Step 2: Click the Save button on the Standard toolbar. Click Close on the File menu.

Excel saves the template using the filename Budget Template. The template is closed.

More *About* **Templates**

When you click New on the File menu, any templates stored in the Xlstart folder display in the New dialog box from which you can make selections.

Alternative Uses of Templates

Before continuing and using the template to create the Antietam University 1998 Budget workbook, you should be aware of some additional uses of templates. You can specify font, formatting, column widths, or any other defaults by creating templates with the desired formats and saving them to the XLStart folder. The **XLStart folder** is called the startup directory. Templates stored in the XLStart folder are called **autotemplates**. After saving templates to this special folder, you can select any one of them by clicking the **New command** on the File menu. If you store one of the templates in the XLStart folder using the filename Book, then Excel uses the formats you assigned to it every time you start Excel.

More *About* **Opening a Workbook Automatically**

You can instruct Windows to automatically open a workbook (or template) when you turn your computer on by adding the workbook (or template) to the Startup folder. Use Explorer to copy the file to the Startup folder. The Startup folder is in the Programs folder and the Programs folder is in the Start Menu folder.

Creating a Workbook from a Template

With the template saved to disk, the second phase of this project begins. The second phase involves using the template to create the Antietam University 1998 Budget workbook shown in Figure 4-1 on page E 4.7. The following steps create and save the workbook. These steps assume that the template shown in Figure 4-20 is closed.

To Create a Workbook from a Template

1. **With Excel active, click the Open button on the Standard toolbar. If necessary, click Templates in the Files type drop-down list box. Click the Save in drop-down list and click 3½ Floppy [A:], if necessary, and then double-click Budget Template. When the template displays, click the Select All button and then click the Copy button on the Standard toolbar.**

   The template is selected as shown in Figure 4-21. The template is also on the clipboard.

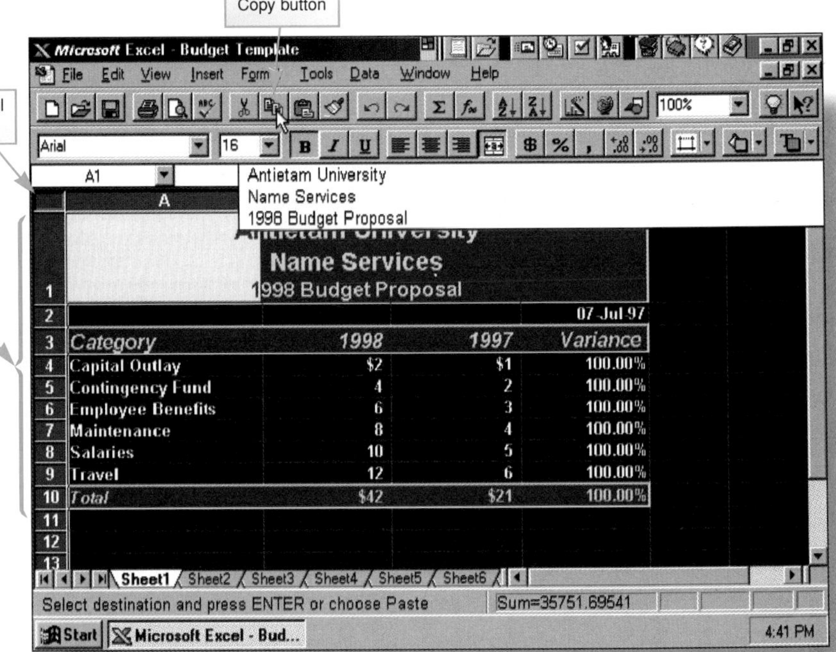

FIGURE 4-21

2. **Click the Sheet2 tab. Hold down the SHIFT key and click the Sheet4 tab. Click the Paste button on the Standard toolbar.**

   The template is copied to Sheet2 through Sheet4. Because multiple sheets are selected, the term [Group] follows the template name in the title bar (Figure 4-22).

3. **Hold down the CTRL key and click the Sheet1 tab. Click cell F10. Hold down the SHIFT key and click the Sheet1 tab.**

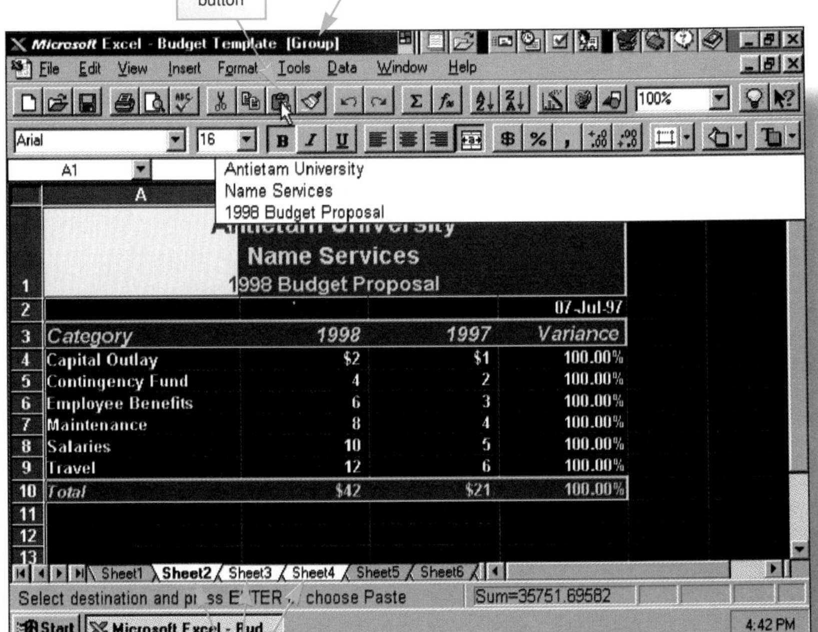

FIGURE 4-22

Click Save As on the File menu. Type `Antietam University 1998 Budget` **in the File name box. Click Microsoft Excel Workbook in the Save as type drop-down list box. If necessary, click 3 ½ Floppy [A] in the Save in drop-down list box. Click the Save button on the Save As dialog box.**

Excel saves the workbook to the floppy disk in drive A using the filename Antietam University 1998 Budget.

5 **One at a time click the Sheet1 tab, Sheet2 tab, Sheet3 tab, and Sheet4 tab.**

The four sheets are identical (Figure 4-23). Each is made up of the data and formats assigned earlier to the template.

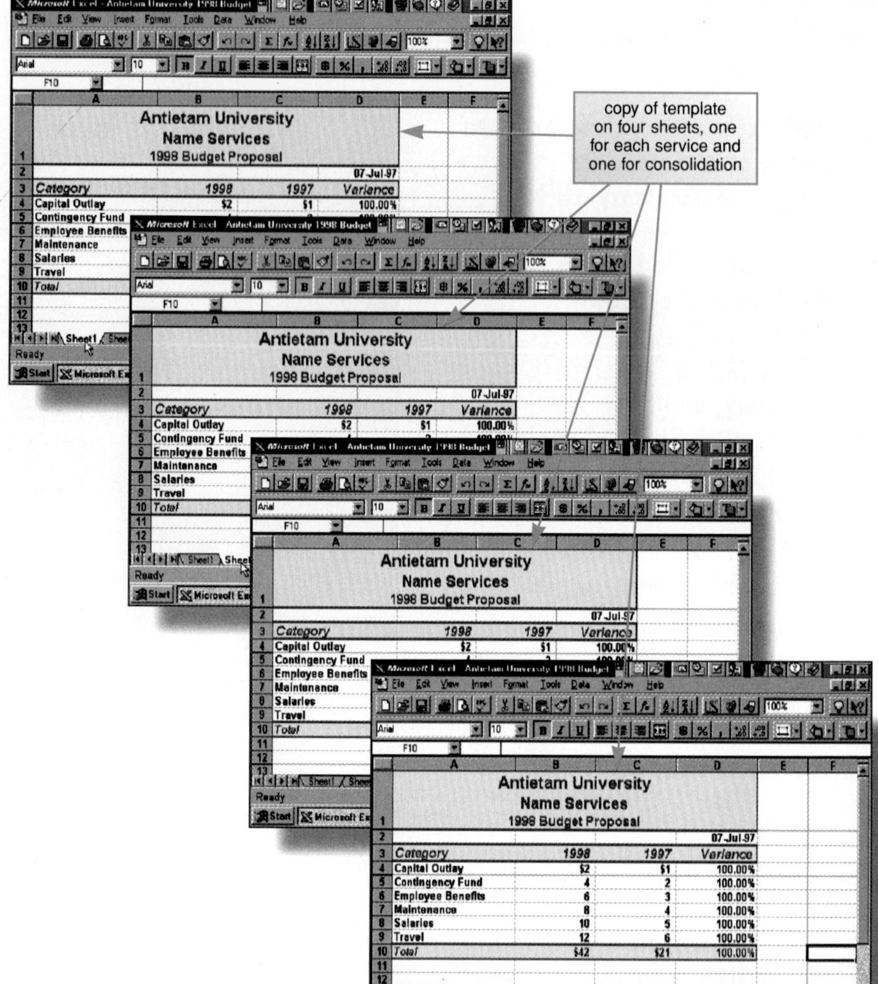

FIGURE 4-23

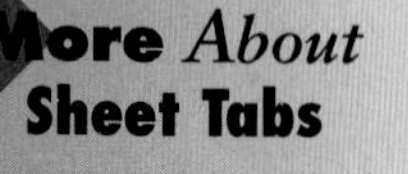

More *About* **Sheet Tabs**

If you right-click a tab, a shortcut menu displays with several commands to modify the workbook. Commands include Insert, Delete, Rename, and Move or Copy. All these commands relate to manipulating sheets in a workbook. For example, you can use this menu to insert a new sheet, delete the active sheet, rename the active sheet or move or copy the active sheet.

Modifying the Formats of Multiple Sheets

Before you enter the budget data for the individual services, perform the following steps to modify the outline and font color of the sheet titles, column titles, and total row on three sheets all at the same time. You assign formats across multiple sheets by selecting the sheets you want to affect before assigning the formats.

To Modify Formats Across Multiple Sheets

1 **Click the Sheet2 tab. Hold down the SHIFT key and click the Sheet4 tab.**

2 **Select the range A1:D1. Hold down the CTRL key and select the nonadjacent ranges A3:D3 and A10:D10. Click the Font Color button arrow and point to the color white (row 1, column 2 on the Font Color palette).**

The nonadjacent ranges are selected and the Font Color palette displays (Figure 4-24).

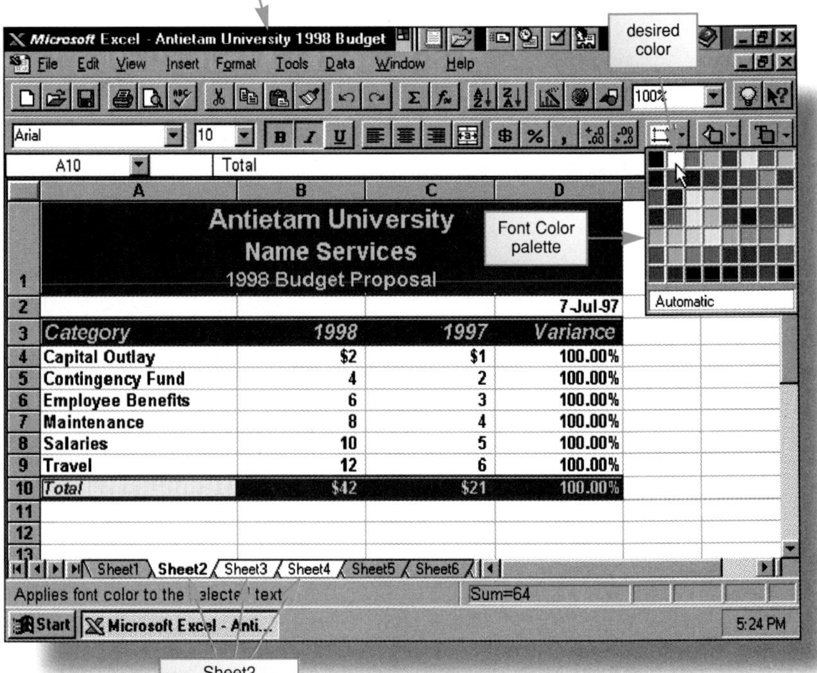

FIGURE 4-24

3 **Click the color white on the Font Color palette. Right-click one of the selected nonadjacent ranges. Click Format Cells on the shortcut menu. Click the Border tab. Click the Color drop-down list box arrow. Click Automatic (or black). Click Outline in the Border area. Click the medium border in the Style area and then point to the OK button.**

The Format Cells dialog box displays as shown in Figure 4-25.

4 **Click the OK button on the Format Cells dialog box. Click cell F10. Hold down the SHIFT key and click Sheet2. Click the Save button on the Standard toolbar.**

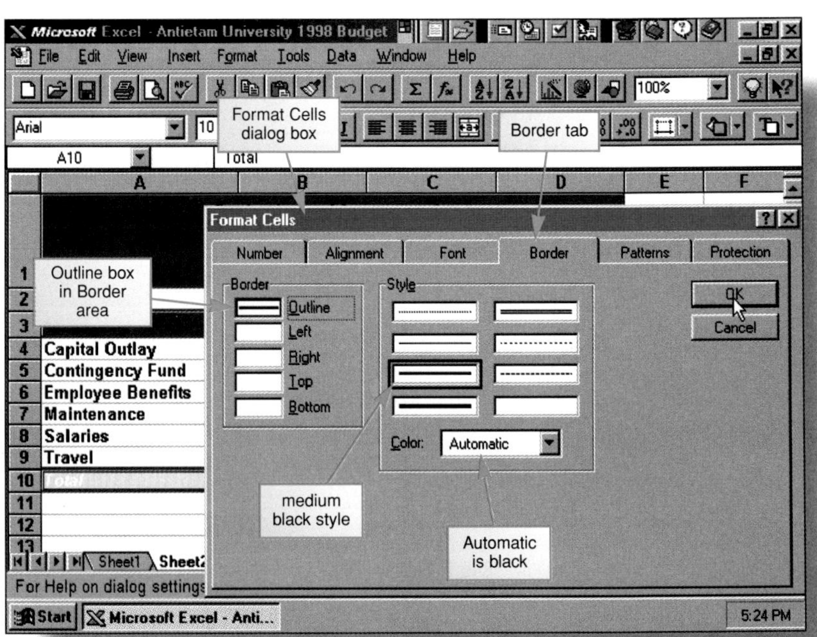

FIGURE 4-25

The outlines of the ranges A1:D1, A3:D3, and A10:D10 on sheets 2, 3, and 4 are black, and the font within these ranges is white. The latest changes to the workbook are saved.

OtherWays

1. Right-click Sheet2 tab, click ungroup sheets

The previous steps illustrate how to assign formats to multiple sheets in a workbook at the same time. You need only use the SHIFT key (or CTRL key) to select multiple sheets before assigning the formats.

Modifying the Administrative Sheet

With the skeleton of the Antietam University 1998 Budget Proposal workbook created, the next step is to modify the individual sheets. The following steps change the sheet tab title, worksheet title, and enters the Administrative services' proposed budget numbers.

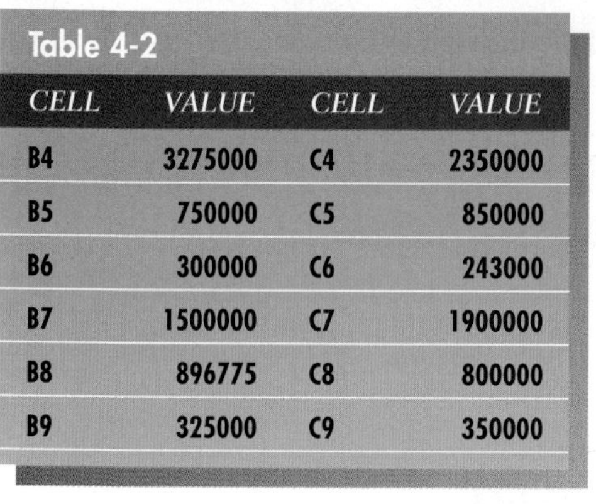

Table 4-2

CELL	VALUE	CELL	VALUE
B4	3275000	C4	2350000
B5	750000	C5	850000
B6	300000	C6	243000
B7	1500000	C7	1900000
B8	896775	C8	800000
B9	325000	C9	350000

TO MODIFY THE ADMINISTRATIVE SHEET

Step 1: Double-click the Sheet2 tab. When the Rename dialog box displays, type `Administrative` in the Name box. Click the OK button.
Step 2: Double-click cell A1, drag over Name in line 2 and type `Administrative.`
Step 3: Select the range A1:D1. Hold down the CTRL key and select the nonadjacent ranges A3:D3 and A10:D10. Click the Color button on the Formatting toolbar. Click the color green (row 2, column 2 on the Color palette).
Step 4: Enter the data in Table 4-2 in the range B4:C9.
Step 5: Click the Save button on the Standard toolbar.

The Administrative sheet displays as shown in Figure 4-26.

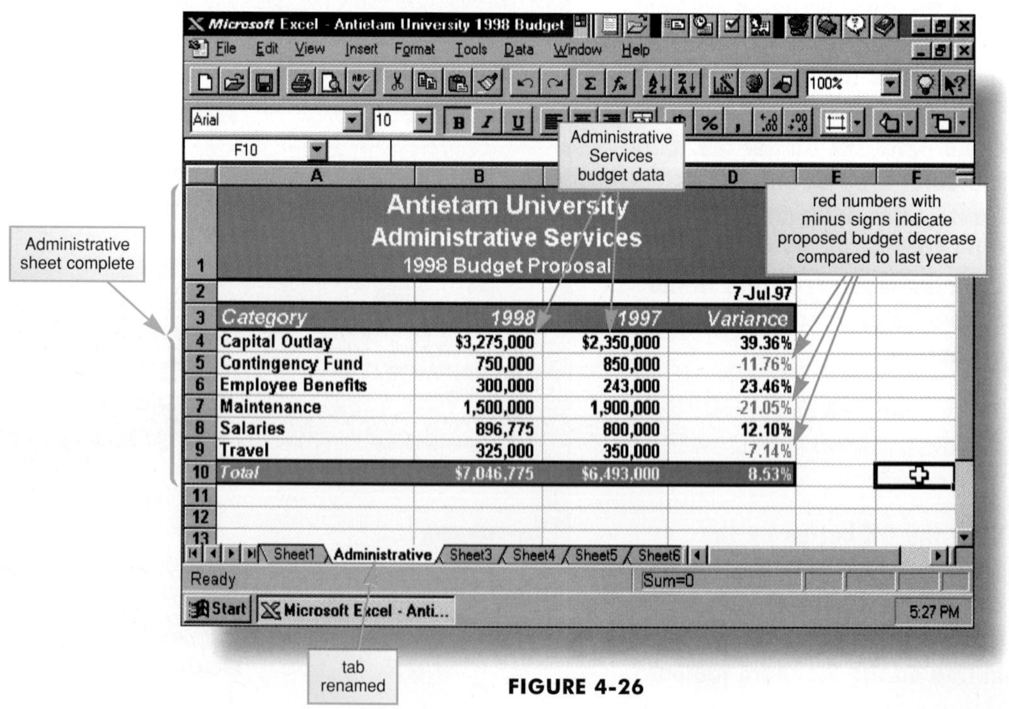

FIGURE 4-26

As you enter the new data, Excel immediately updates the variances, displaying negative variances in red.

Modifying the Academic Sheet

The following steps modify the Academic sheet.

TO MODIFY THE ACADEMIC SHEET

Step 1: Double-click the Sheet3 tab. When the Rename dialog box displays, type `Academic` in the Name box. Click the OK button.
Step 2: Double-click cell A1, drag over Name in line 2 and type `Academic`.
Step 3: Select the range A1:D1. Hold down the CTRL key and select the nonadjacent ranges A3:D3 and A10:D10. Click the Color button on the Formatting toolbar. Click the color red (row 1, column 3 on the Color palette).
Step 4: Enter the data in Table 4-3 in the range B4:C9.
Step 5: Click the Save button on the Standard toolbar.

The Academic sheet displays as shown in Figure 4-27.

Table 4-3

CELL	VALUE	CELL	VALUE
B4	1250750	C4	945250
B5	690000	C5	745000
B6	988500	C6	922250
B7	1325250	C7	1934500
B8	2535750	C8	2201500
B9	375250	C9	300000

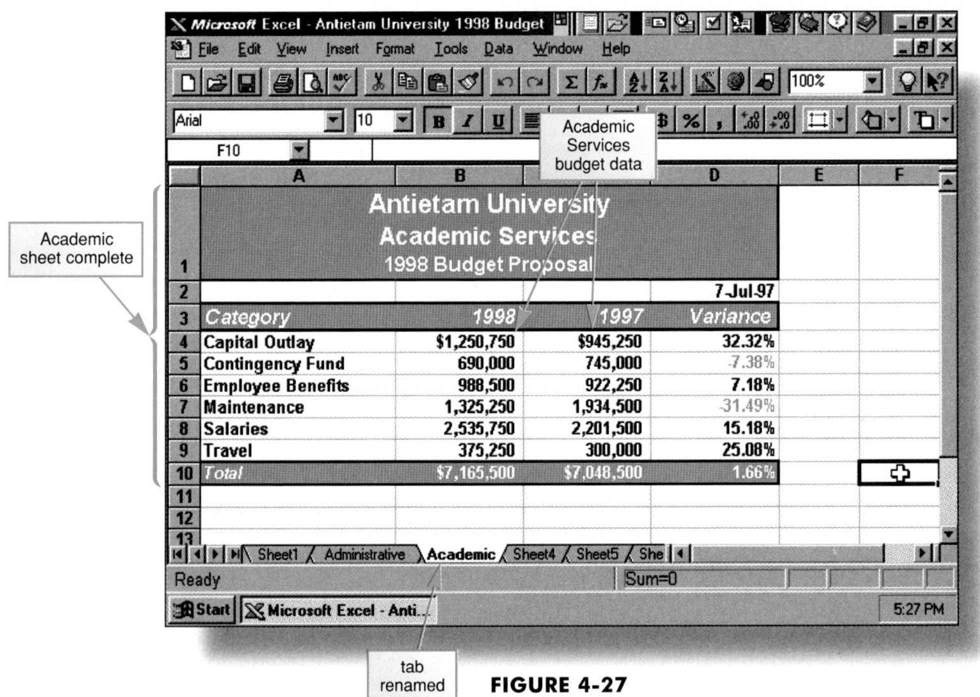

FIGURE 4-27

Modifying the Student Sheet

Like the Administrative and Academic sheets, the background color and data must be changed on the Student sheet. The steps on the next page modify the Student sheet.

More *About* **Entering Data**

You can automate entering the data in Table 4-3 by selecting the range B4:C9 before you enter the data. Excel will automatically move the active cell selection down to the next cell in the range when you press the ENTER key.

Table 4-4

CELL	VALUE	CELL	VALUE
B4	543750	C4	602000
B5	350500	C5	225000
B6	142250	C6	114300
B7	850000	C7	750000
B8	308250	C8	275250
B9	223000	C9	228000

TO MODIFY THE STUDENT SHEET

Step 1: Double-click the Sheet4 tab. When the Rename dialog box displays, type `Student` in the Name box. Click the OK button.

Step 2: Double-click cell A1, drag over Name in line 2 and type `Student`.

Step 3: Select the range A1:D1. Hold down the CTRL key and select the nonadjacent ranges A3:D3 and A10:D10. Click the Color button on the Formatting toolbar. Click the color blue (column 1, row 4 on the Color palette).

Step 4: Enter the data in Table 4-4 in the range B4:C9.

Step 5: Click the Save button on the Standard toolbar.

The Student sheet displays as shown in Figure 4-28.

With the three service sheets complete, the next step is to modify Sheet1 (All Services). However, before modifying Sheet1 it is important that you understand how to reference cells in other sheets in a workbook because this sheet contains totals of the data on the Administrative, Academic, and Student sheets.

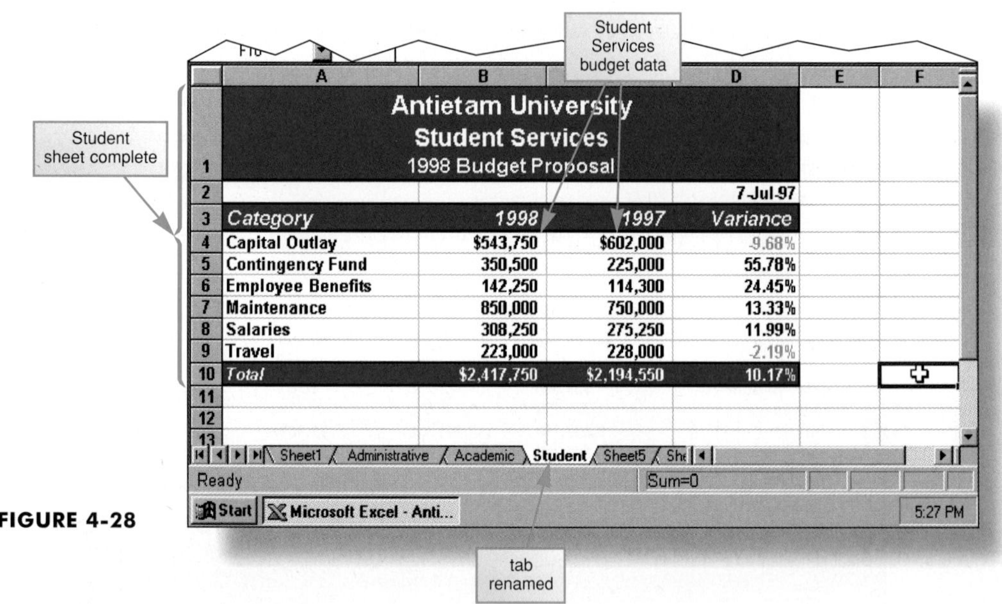

FIGURE 4-28

Referencing Cells in Other Sheets in a Workbook

To reference cells in other sheets in a workbook, you use the sheet name, also called the **sheet reference**. For example, you refer to cell B4 on the Administrative sheet in the following fashion:

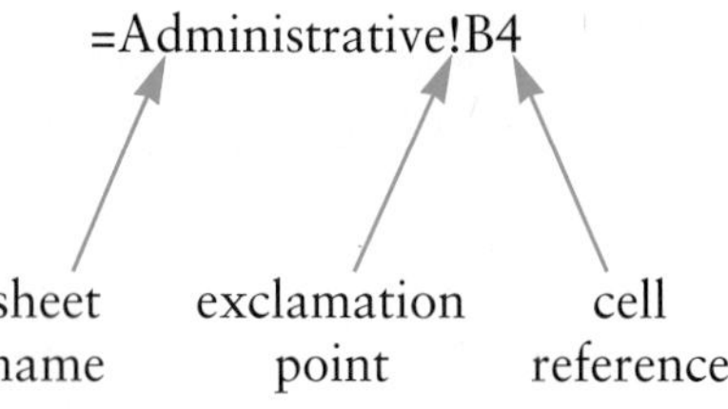

Thus, one way to add cell B4 on the last three sheets and place the sum in cell B4 of the first sheet would be to select cell B4 on the first sheet and enter:

=Administrative!B4 + Academic!B4 + Student!B4

A much quicker way to find the sum of the **three-dimensional range** is to use the SUM function as follows:

=SUM(Administrative!:Student!B4)

The SUM argument (Administrative!:Student!B4) instructs Excel to sum cell B4 on each of the last sheets (Administrative, Academic, and Student). The colon (:) between the first sheet reference and the last sheet reference indicates all sheets within the range are included. A range that spans two or more sheets in a workbook, such as Administrative!:Student!B4, is called a **3-D reference**.

A sheet reference, such as Administrative!, is always absolute. Thus, unlike a relative cell reference, when you copy formulas the sheet reference will remain constant.

Entering a Sheet Reference

You can enter a sheet reference by typing it or by clicking the sheet tab to activate it. When you click the sheet tab, Excel automatically adds the name followed by an exclamation point at the insertion point in the formula bar and activates the sheet. Next, click or drag through the cells you want to reference on the sheet.

If you are spanning sheets, click the first sheet tab, drag through the cell or range of cells, and then hold down the SHIFT key and click the last sheet tab. Excel will include the cell or range on the two sheets and all the sheets between. It will also add the colon between the first sheet and the last sheet referenced. If the sheets are not contiguous, use the CTRL key rather than the SHIFT key to select the sheets.

Modifying the All Services Sheet

The next step is to enter the SUM function in each of the cells in the range B4:C9 of Sheet1 (All Services). The SUM functions will determine the sums of the budget values for the three services by category. Thus, cell B4 on the All Services sheet will be equal to the sum of the 1998 Capital Outlay amounts in cells Administrative!B4, Academic!B4, and Student!B4. Before determining the totals, change the name of the tab from Sheet1 to All Services by performing the following steps.

TO RENAME A SHEET TAB

Step 1: Double-click the Sheet1 tab.
Step 2: When the Rename dialog box displays, type `All Services` in the Name box.
Step 3: Click the OK button.

The steps on the next page determine the totals on the All Services sheet for the six categories for the proposed 1998 budget and the 1997 budget.

Steps To Enter and Copy 3-D References on the All Services Sheet

1 With the All Services sheet active, select cell B4. Click the AutoSum button on the Standard toolbar.

The SUM function displays without a range (Figure 4-29).

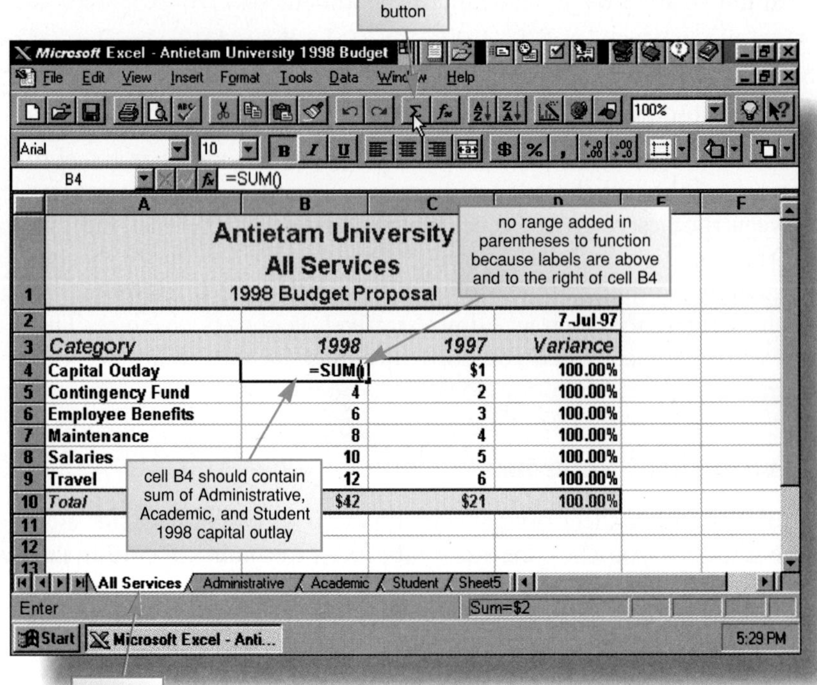

FIGURE 4-29

2 Click the Administrative tab and select cell B4. Hold down the SHIFT key and click the Student tab.

A moving border surrounds cell Administrative!B4 (Figure 4-30). All four sheet tabs are highlighted. The Administrative tab displays in bold because it is the active sheet. The SUM function displays in the formula bar.

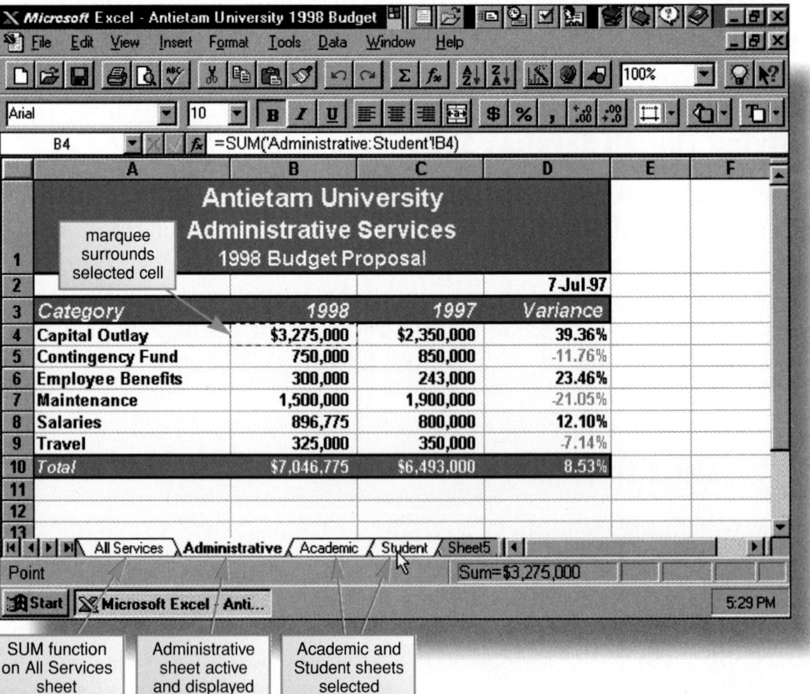

FIGURE 4-30

Click the check box in the formula bar or press the ENTER key.

The All Services sheet becomes the active sheet. The sum of the cells Administrative!B4, Academic!B4, and Student!B4 displays in cell B4 of the All Services sheet as =SUM(Administrative:Student!B4) (Figure 4-31). The SUM function assigned to cell B4 displays in the formula bar.

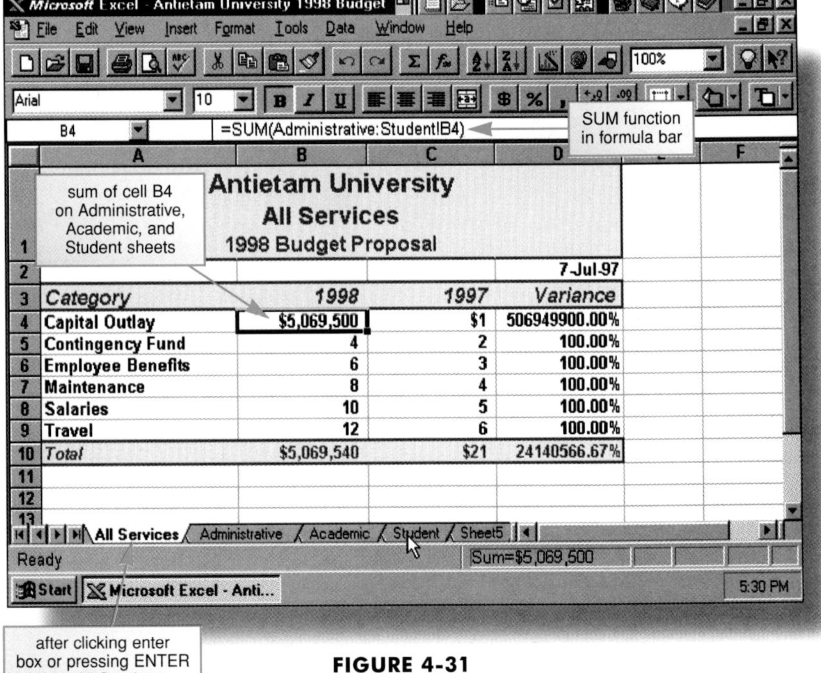

FIGURE 4-31

4 **With cell B4 active, drag the fill handle through cell C4. If necessary, select the range B4:C4 and then point to the fill handle.**

Excel copies the formula in cell B4 to cell C4 (Figure 4-32). The cell reference in the SUM function in cell C4 references cell C4 on each of the three sheets. The range B4:C4 is selected and the mouse pointer appears as a cross hair.

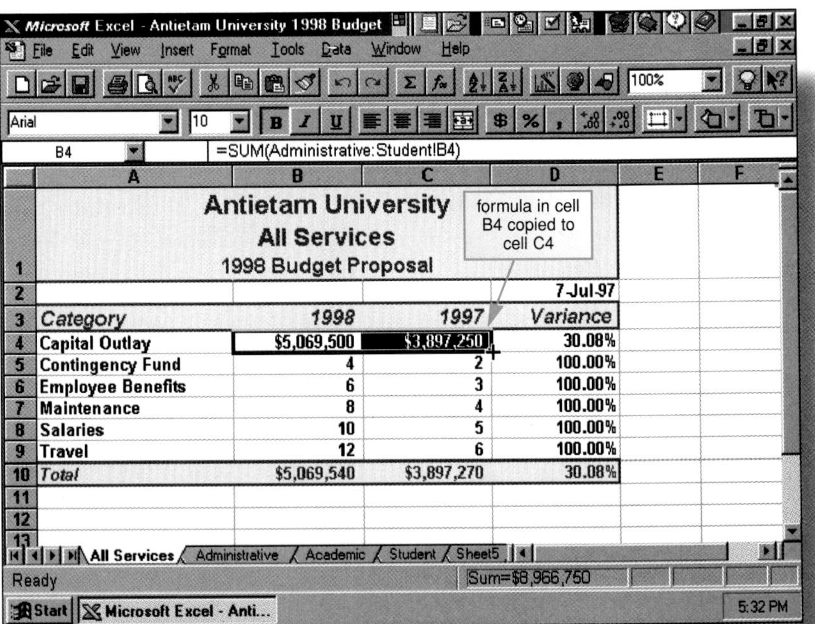

FIGURE 4-32

5 **Drag the fill handle down through cell C9 and hold.**

Excel shades the border of the paste area (Figure 4-33).

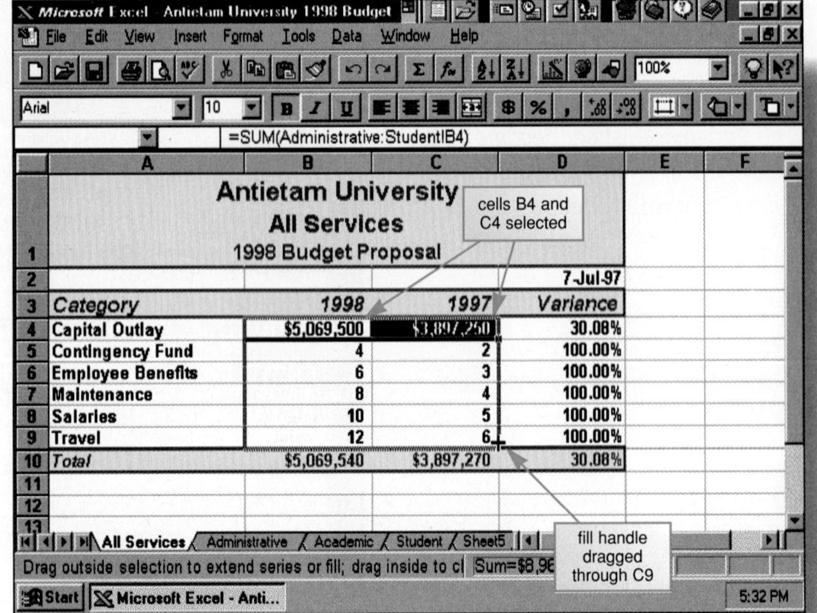

FIGURE 4-33

6 **Release the left mouse button. Select the range B5:C9. Click the Comma Style button on the Formatting toolbar, and then click the Decimal Decrease button on the Formatting toolbar twice.**

Excel copies the formulas in cells B4 and C4 to the range B5:C9 (Figure 4-34).

7 **Click the Save button on the Standard toolbar to save the workbook.**

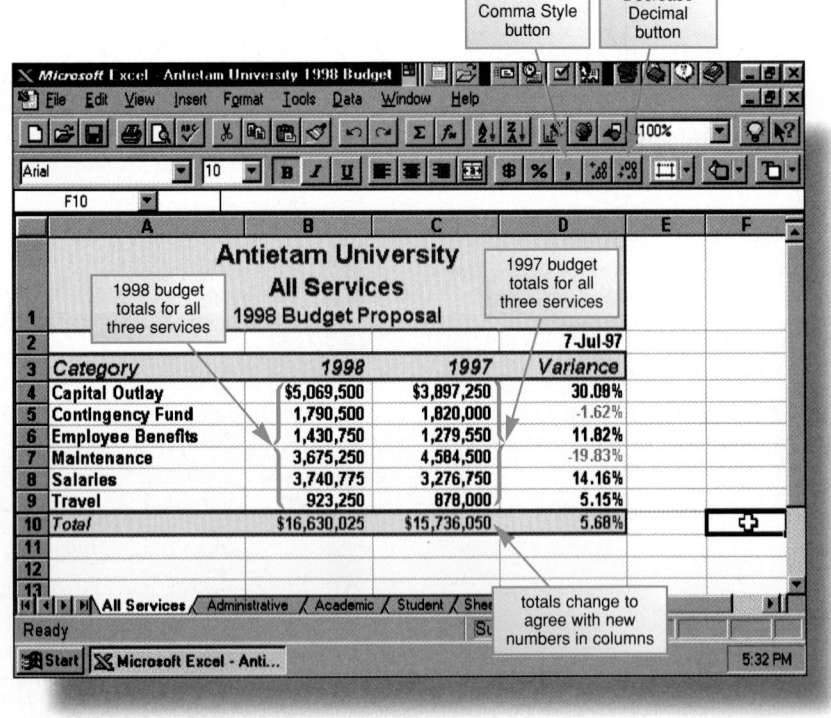

FIGURE 4-34

OtherWays

1. Click Function Wizard button, select SUM in Function Name box, click OK button
2. Click Function on Insert menu, select SUM in Function Name box, click OK button

The reason the range B5:C9 had to be reformatted is because when you copy a cell, the format is also copied. Thus, the Currency style format assigned to cell B4 earlier was copied to cell C4 and then to the range B5:C19. The four worksheets are complete. The next step is to create the comparison chart on a separate sheet, as shown in Figure 4-35.

Creating a Combination Area and Column Chart

The combination area and column chart allows you to compare two sets of numbers in one chart. The chart compares next year's proposed budget (area) to the current year's budget (column) as shown in Figure 4-35.

After creating the chart, the chart title, legends, and font along the axes are formatted. The chart is also resized and the colors of the chart are changed. Follow the steps below to create a combination area and column chart.

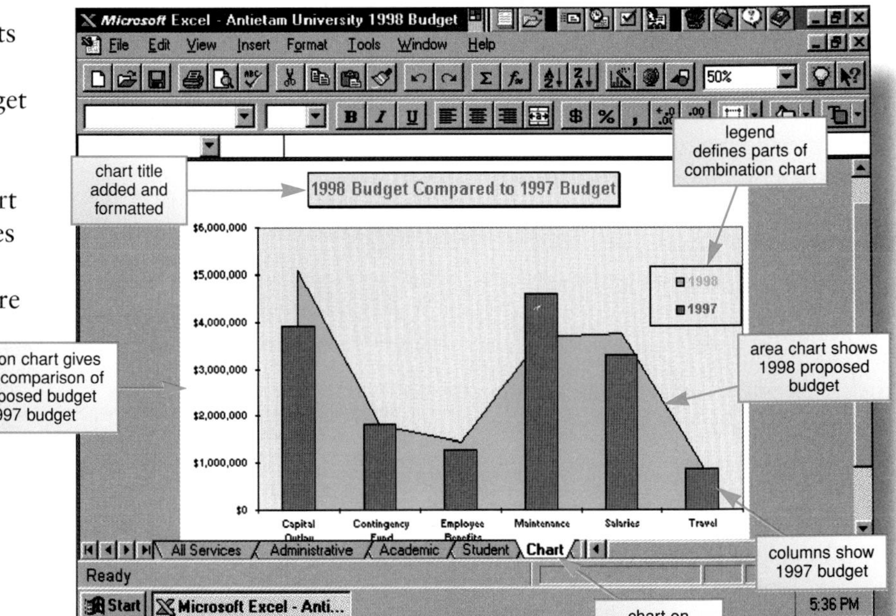

FIGURE 4-35

To Draw a Combination Area and Column Chart

1 With the All Services sheet active, select the range A3:C9. On the Insert menu, point to Chart. Point to As New Sheet on the Chart submenu.

The selected range and Chart submenu display as shown in Figure 4-36.

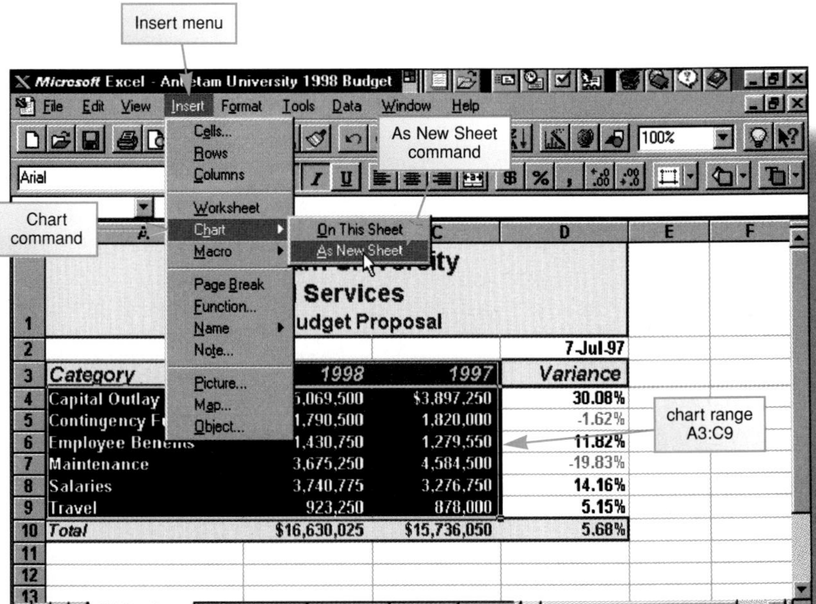

FIGURE 4-36

2 Click As New Sheet.

Excel responds by displaying the ChartWizard - Step 1 of 5 dialog box (Figure 4-37). The Range box contains the chart range, which is surrounded by a marquee on the worksheet. In the dialog box, you can change the range by typing a new one or dragging over a new range on the worksheet. A new chart sheet is added to the workbook with the tab name Chart1.

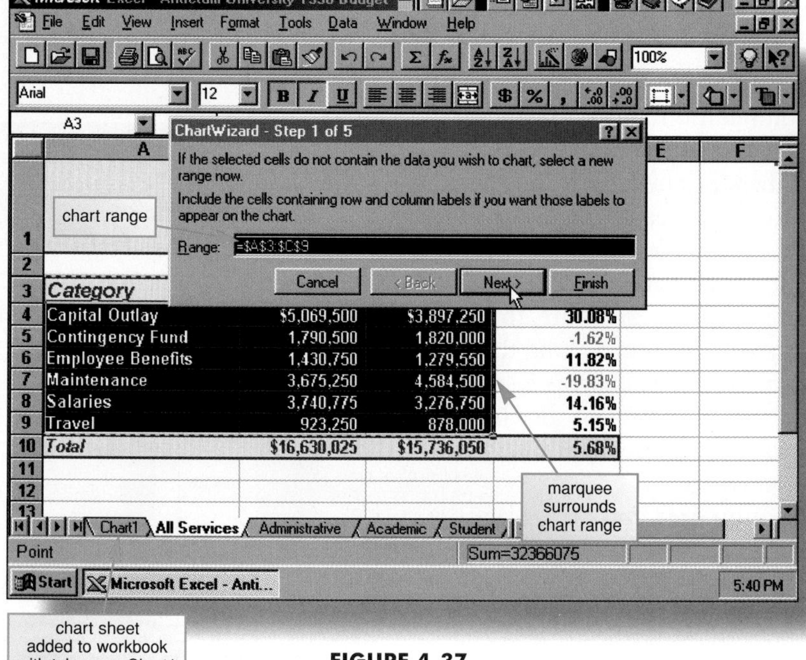

FIGURE 4-37

3 Click the Next button on the ChartWizard – Step 1 of 5 dialog box.

The ChartWizard – Step 2 of 5 dialog box displays with fifteen charts from which to choose.

4 Click Combination (column 4, row 2).

Excel highlights the combination chart (Figure 4-38).

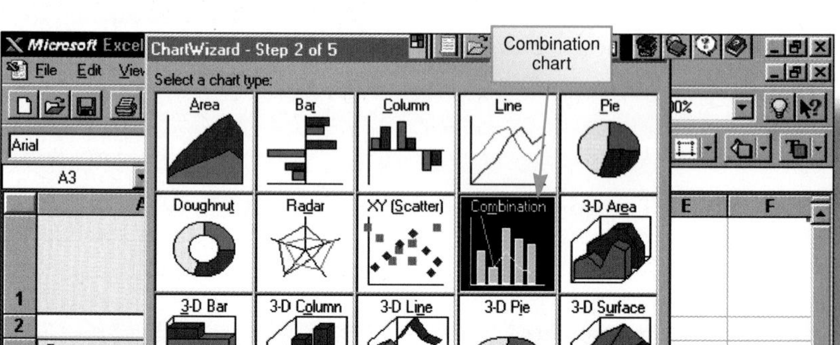
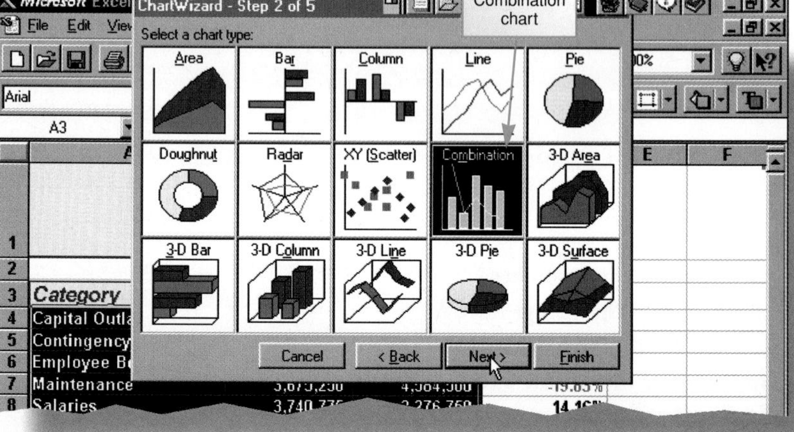
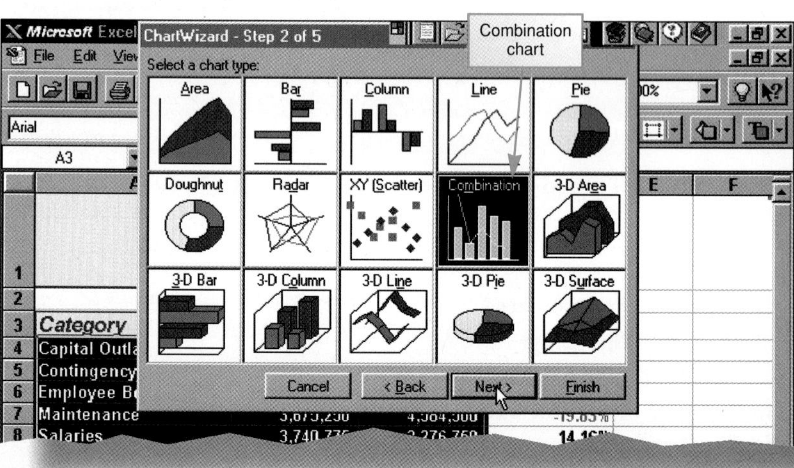

FIGURE 4-38

5 Click the Next button on the ChartWizard – Step 2 of 5 dialog box.

The ChartWizard – Step 3 of 5 dialog box displays with six different built-in combination chart formats to choose from.

6 Click format type 4, which contains area and column charts.

Excel highlights the selected combination chart format (Figure 4-39).

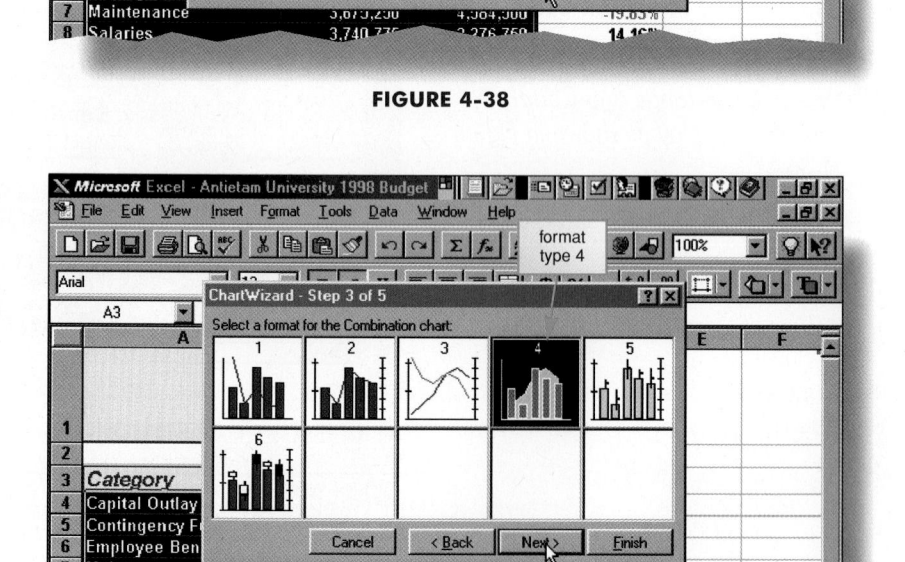

FIGURE 4-39

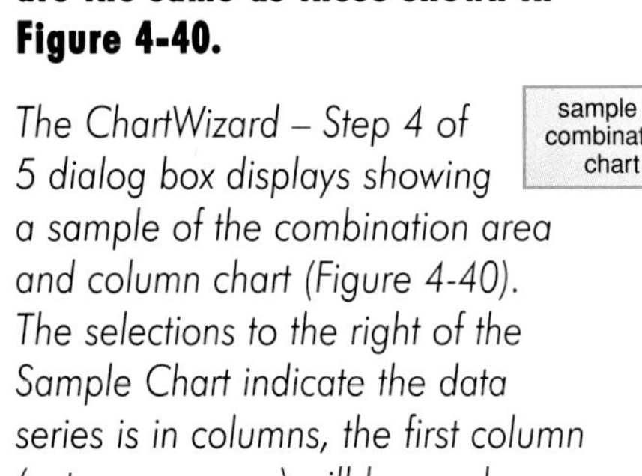

7 **Click the Next button on the ChartWizard – Step 3 of 5 dialog box. Make sure the chart settings are the same as those shown in Figure 4-40.**

The ChartWizard – Step 4 of 5 dialog box displays showing a sample of the combination area and column chart (Figure 4-40). The selections to the right of the Sample Chart indicate the data series is in columns, the first column (category names) will be used as labels on the x-axis, and the first row (1998 and 1997) will be used for the legend.

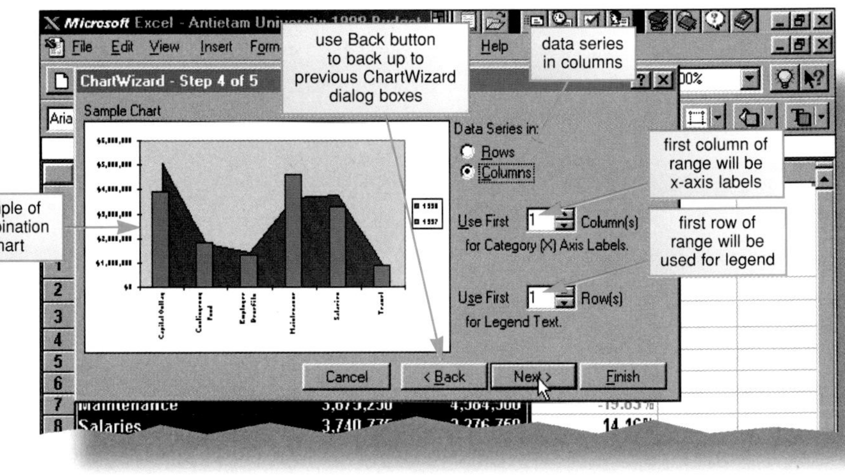

FIGURE 4-40

8 **Click the Next button on the ChartWizard — Step 4 of 5 dialog box.**

The ChartWizard - Step 5 of 5 dialog box displays on the screen. The dialog box gives you the opportunity to add a chart title.

9 **In the Chart Title box, type** `1998 Budget Compared to 1997 Budget` **as shown in Figure 4-41.**

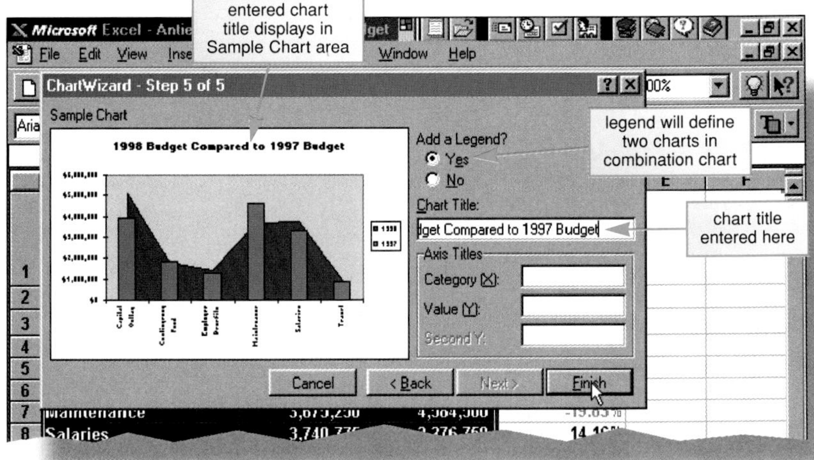

FIGURE 4-41

10 **Click the Finish button on the ChartWizard – Step 5 of 5 dialog box.**

Excel draws the combination chart on a new chart sheet added to the workbook. The tab name is Chart1 (Figure 4-42).

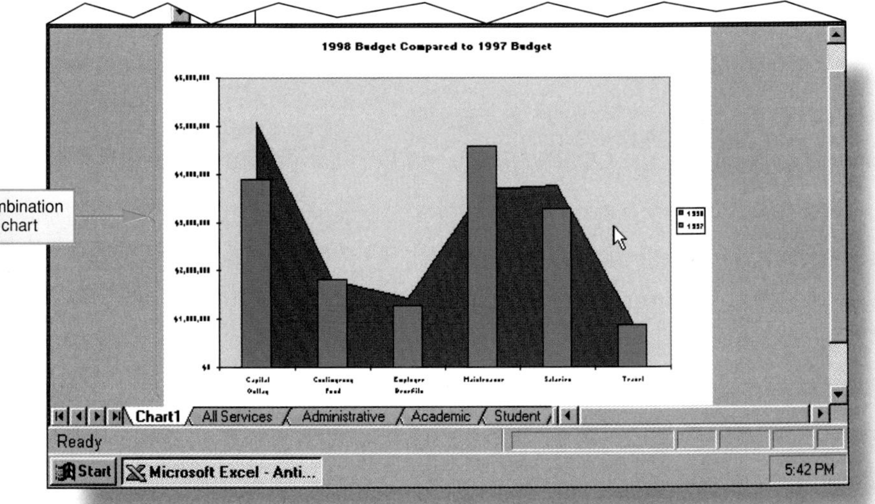

FIGURE 4-42

More *About* Combination Charts

There are six different combination charts available in Excel (Figure 4-39). The most commonly used combination charts in business are the line and column chart (format 1) and the multiple line chart (format 3).

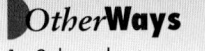

Other Ways

1. Select chart range, press F11

The combination area and column chart in Figure 4-42 compares the six budget categories proposed for the next year (B4:B9) to the six budget categories for the current year (C4:C9). The legend on the right side contains the two labels (1998 and 1997) in cells B3 and C3. When you draw a combination chart, Excel does not use the upper left cell (B3) of the chart range, even though it's part of the selected range.

Formatting the Chart Title

The following steps format the chart title so the font is red, 20 point with a light yellow background and a drop shadow surrounds it.

Steps To Format the Chart Title

1. **With the chart sheet active, click the chart title. Click the Color button arrow and then click light yellow (column 4, row 5 on the Color palette). Click the Font Size box arrow and then click 20. Click the Font Color button arrow and then click red (column 3, row 1 on the Font Color palette).**

2. **Click the Drawing button on the Standard toolbar. Dock the Drawing toolbar at the bottom of the window. Click the Drop Shadow button on the Drawing toolbar.**

   The chart title displays as shown in Figure 4-43.

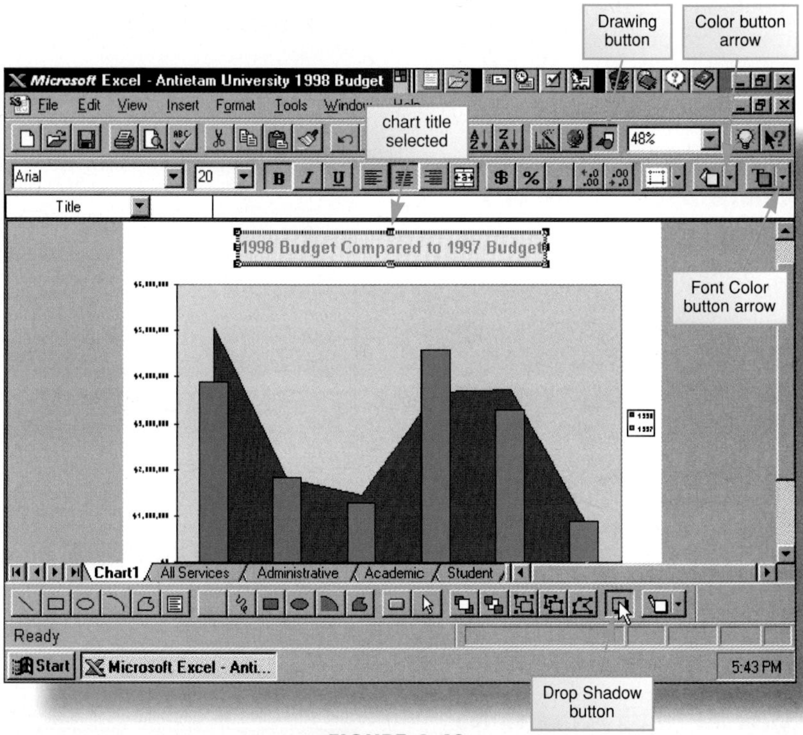

Drawing button

Color button arrow

chart title selected

Font Color button arrow

Drop Shadow button

FIGURE 4-43

3. **Click the Drawing button on the Standard toolbar to hide the Drawing toolbar.**

   The chart title displays as shown in Figure 4-44.

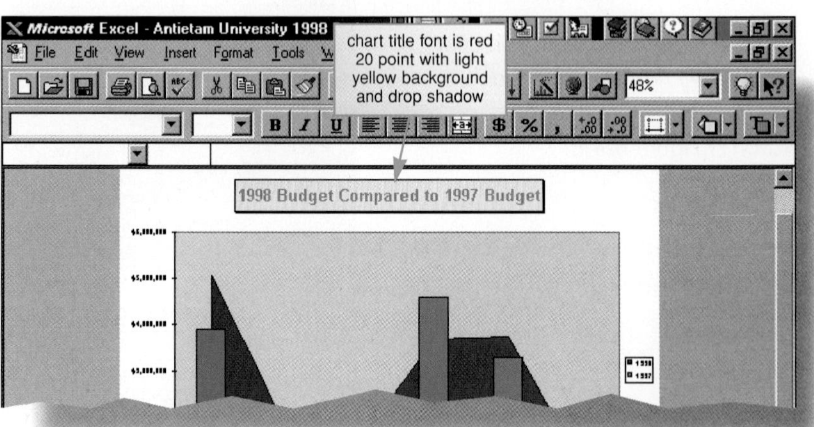

FIGURE 4-44

Other Ways

1. Right-click chart title, click Format Chart Title

Changing the Colors of the Plot Area and Data Markers

The next step is to change the colors of the plot area and data markers. The **data markers** are the columns and purple area within the plot area. The **plot area** is the rectangular gray area behind the area chart in Figure 4-44.

To Change the Colors of the Data Markers and Plot Area

1 **Click the area chart (portion colored purple). Click the Color button arrow on the Formatting toolbar. Choose light blue (column 1, row 5 on the Color palette).**

The color of the area chart changes to light blue (Figure 4-45).

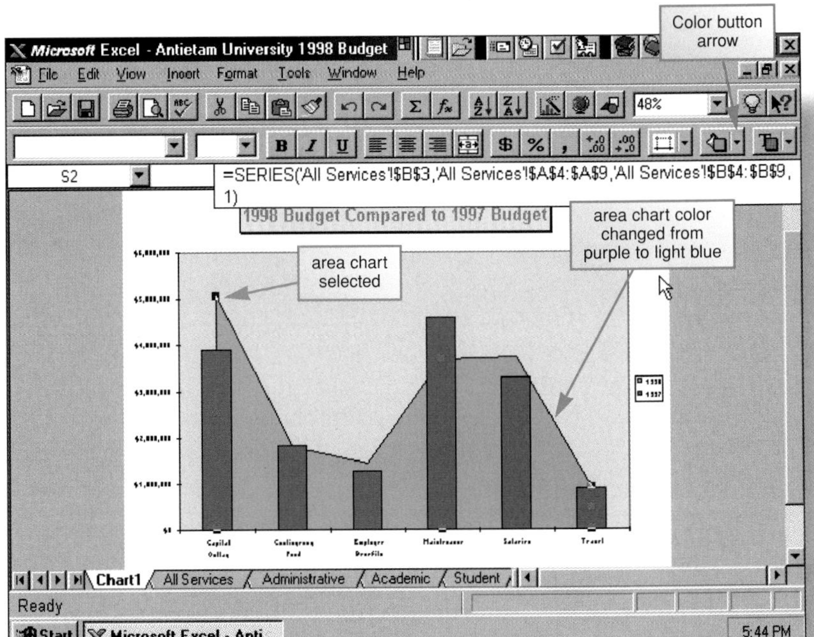

FIGURE 4-45

2 **Click one of the columns to select all of them. Click the Color button arrow on the Formatting toolbar. Choose red (column 3, row 1 on the Color palette).**

The color of the columns change to red (Figure 4-46).

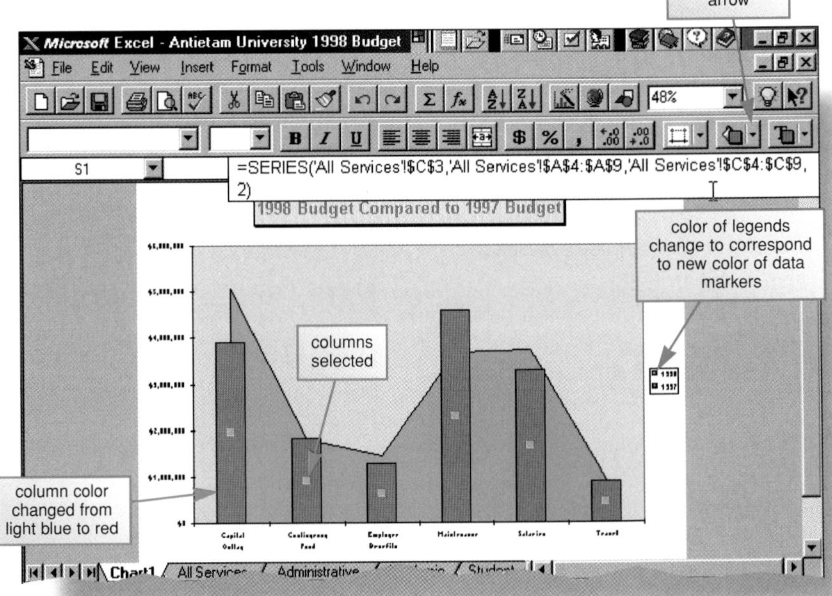

FIGURE 4-46

3 **Click the plot area, behind the area chart. Click the Color button arrow on the Formatting toolbar. Choose light yellow (column 4, row 5 on the Color palette).**

The combination area and column chart appears as shown in Figure 4-47. The plot area remains selected as indicated by the gray border.

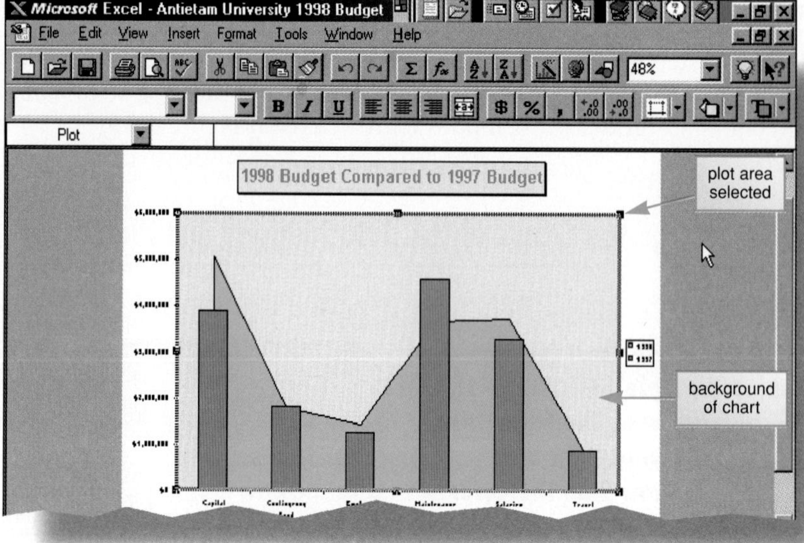

FIGURE 4-47

OtherWays

1. Right-click chart item, click appropriate command

When you change the colors of the data markers, Excel also changes the colors of the identifiers within the legend.

Resizing the Plot Area

As indicated earlier, the plot area is the rectangle behind the area chart, formed by the two axes. The following steps show how to resize the plot area.

Steps To Resize the Plot Area

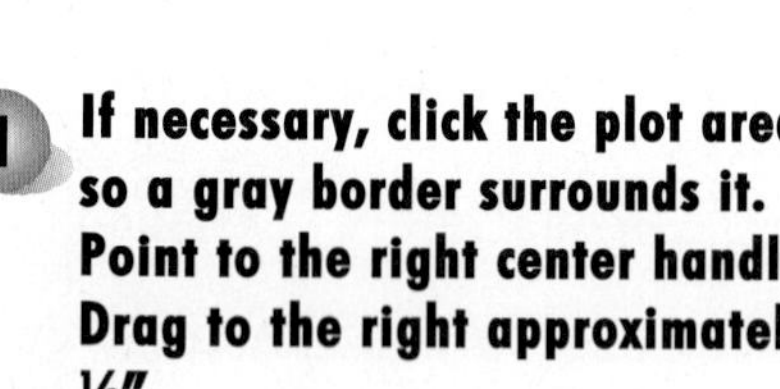

1 **If necessary, click the plot area so a gray border surrounds it. Point to the right center handle. Drag to the right approximately ½".**

The plot area increases in size (Figure 4-48).

2 **Release the left mouse button.**

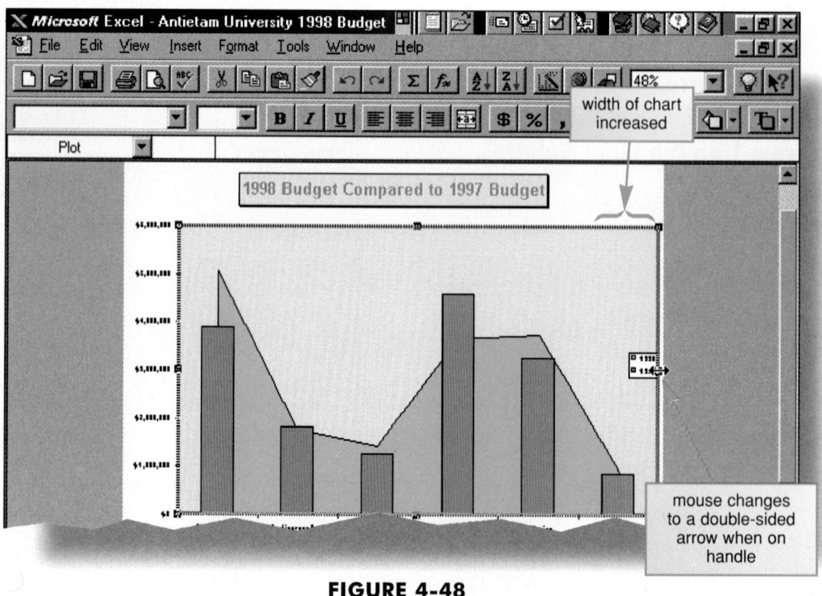

FIGURE 4-48

Compare the combination area and column chart in Figure 4-48 to Figure 4-47. Not only is the plot area wider, but Excel has proportionally increased the size of the chart.

Moving, and Resizing, and Formatting the Legend

The next step is to move, resize, and format the legend on the right side of the plot area.

Steps To Move, Resize, and Format the Legend

1 Click the legend. Drag the legend up and to the right edge of the plot area. Drag a corner to resize it to agree with Figure 4-49.

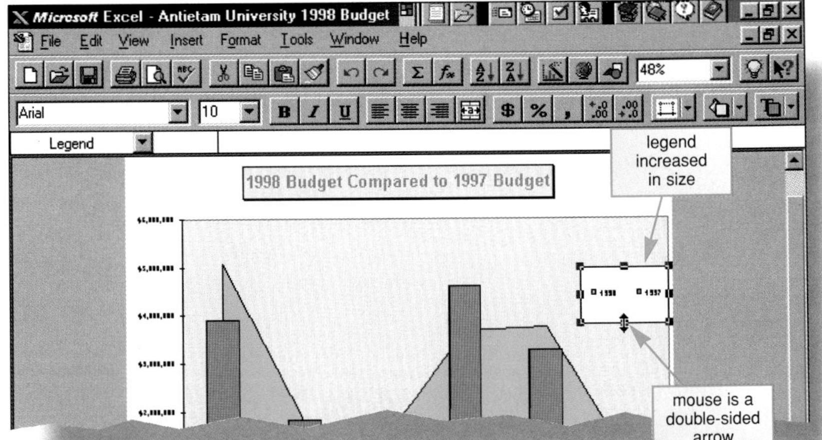

FIGURE 4-49

2 With the legend selected, click the Color button on the Formatting toolbar. Choose light yellow (column 4, row 5 on the Color palette). Click 1998. Click the Font Color button and then click light blue (column 1, row 5 on the Font Color palette). Click the Font Size box arrow and then click 16. Click 1997. Click the Font Color button and then click red (column 3, row 1 on the Font Color palette). Click the Font Size box arrow and then click 16.

The legend displays as shown in Figure 4-50.

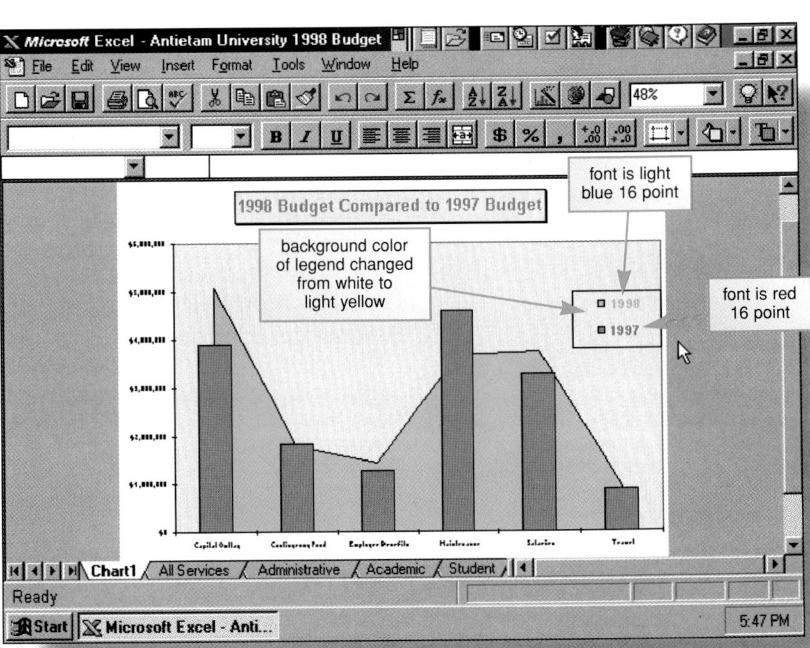

FIGURE 4-50

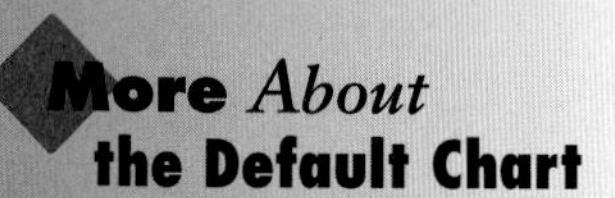

If you select a chart range and press function key F11, Excel will draw what is called the default chart on a chart sheet. Unless changed, the default chart is a two-dimensional column chart. You can change the default chart to any other type of chart by first drawing it and formatting it. You then enter a name in the Default Chart Format box on the Chart tab on the Options dialog box. You display the Options dialog box by clicking Options on the Tools menu.

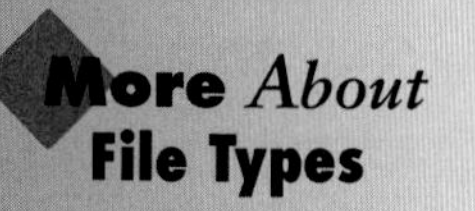

You can save Excel workbooks in a variety of formats so that the file can be opened by other application software products. For example, through the Save as type box on the Save As dialog box, you can save a workbook as text with a space separating data items, a tab separating the data items, or a comma separating the data items. You can save a workbook so it can be opened by 1-2-3, Quattro Pro, dBASE III, dBASE IV, earlier versions of Microsoft Excel, a Macintosh computer, and many other formats.

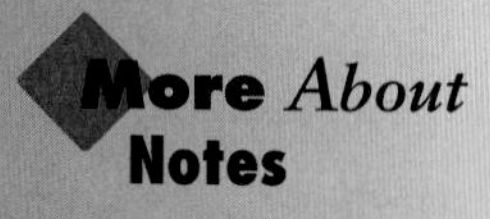

If you prefer that the note indicator (small red dot) not display in cell A1, click Options on the Tools menu and then on the View sheet click the Note Indicator check box. You can print notes assigned to cells by clicking the Notes check box on the Sheet sheet on the Print Setup dialog box.

You can move the legend to any location in the chart area, including inside the plot area.

Changing the Size of the Font on the Axes

The following steps change the font size of the labels on the x-axis and y-axis to 12 point. Depending on your printer driver, the labels along the x-axis may display and print vertically, rather than horizontally.

TO CHANGE THE SIZE OF THE FONT ON THE AXES, RENAME THE CHART1 TAB, AND SAVE THE WORKBOOK

Step 1: Click a label on the x-axis. Click the Font box arrow on the Formatting toolbar and then click 12.

Step 2: Click a label on the y-axis. Click the Font box arrow on the Formatting toolbar and then click 12.

Step 3: Double-click the Chart1 tab. Type `Chart` in the Name box on the Rename dialog box. Click the OK button. Drag the Chart tab to the right of the Student tab. Click the All Services tab.

Step 4: Click the Save button on the Standard toolbar.

The font size of the labels on the x-axis and y-axis changes from 8 point to 12 point. The Chart sheet is now positioned after the Student sheet.

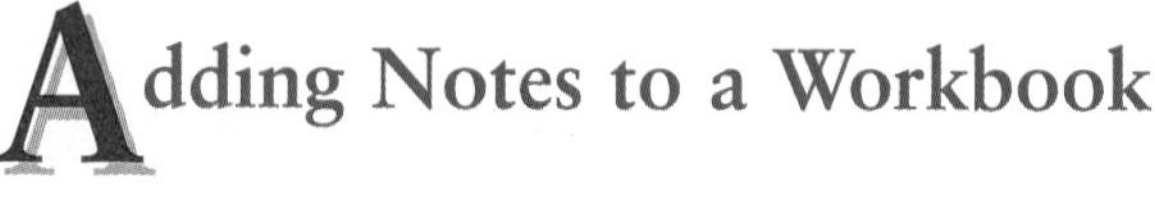

Adding Notes to a Workbook

Comments or notes in a workbook are used to describe the function of a cell, a range of cells, a sheet, or the entire workbook. Comments are used to identify workbooks and clarify entries that might otherwise be difficult to understand.

In Excel you can assign comments to any cell in the worksheet through the use of the Note command on the Insert menu. You can then point to the cell anytime you want to read the note, and Excel will display it. Overall workbook comments should include the following:

1. Worksheet title
2. Author's name
3. Date created
4. Date last modified (use N/A if it has not been modified)
5. A short description of the purpose of the worksheet

The following steps assign workbook comments to cell F1 on the All Services sheet.

To Assign a Note to a Cell

1 **Click cell F1 on the All Services sheet. Point to the Note command on the Insert menu.**

The Insert menu displays (Figure 4-51).

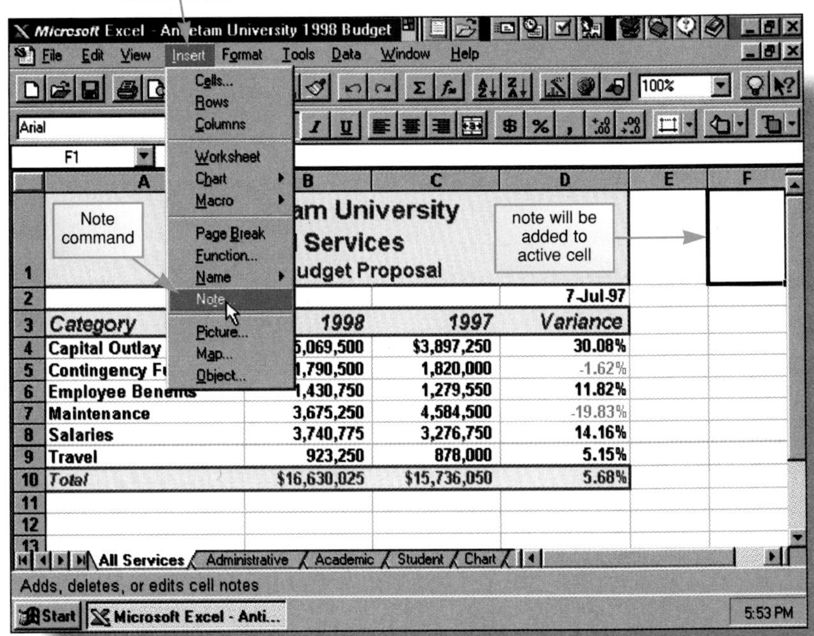

FIGURE 4-51

2 **Click Note.**

Excel displays the Cell Note dialog box. The Cell box identifies the active cell (F1). The Notes in Sheet box lists the cell locations of all notes in the active sheet.

3 **Enter the note in the Text Note box as shown in Figure 4-52. Press the ENTER key after each line.**

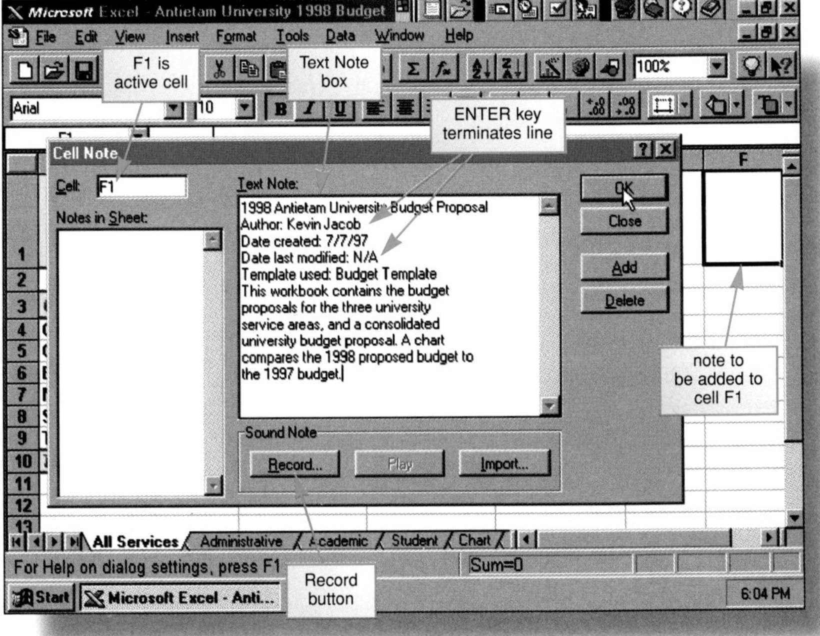

FIGURE 4-52

4 Click the OK button on the Cell Note dialog box. Point to cell F1.

*Excel adds a small red dot, called a **note indicator**, in the upper right corner of cell F1 to indicate that a note has been assigned to it (Figure 4-53). If a red dot does not appear in the cell, click Options on the Tools menu. Click the View tab and click Note Indicator. When you point to a cell with a note, Excel displays it.*

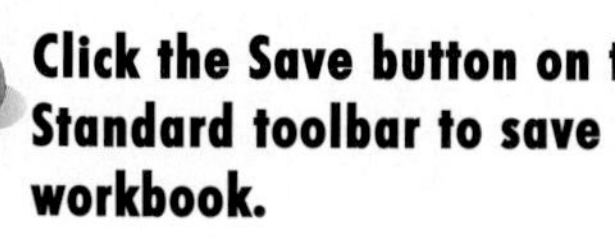

5 Click the Save button on the Standard toolbar to save the workbook.

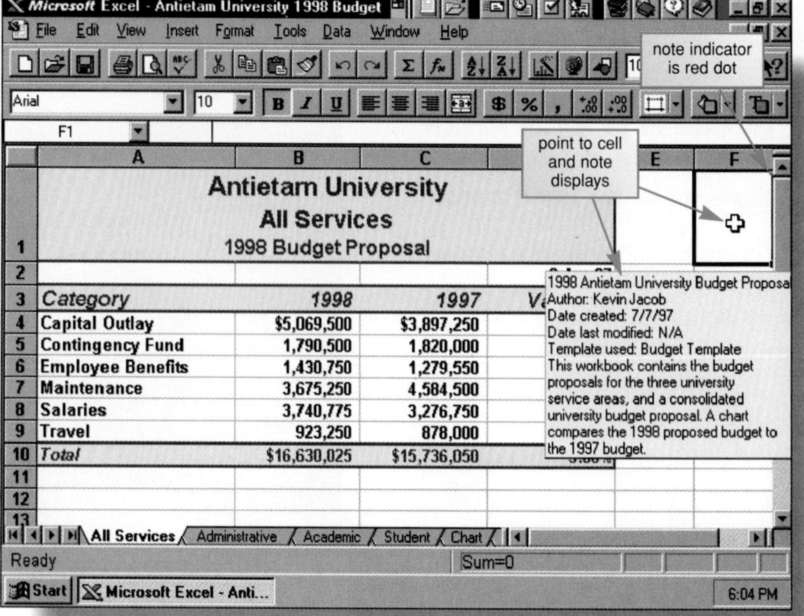

FIGURE 4-53

OtherWays

1. Press SHIFT+F2

A red dot in the upper-right corner indicates that a cell has a note attached to it (cell F1 in Figure 4-53). To read the comment or note any time, point to the cell and the note will display on the worksheet or select the cell and click the Note command on the Insert menu (or press SHIFT+F2).

Besides entering comments in the form of text, you can add an audio comment of up to two minutes to a cell if you have a sound card, a microphone, and the appropriate software. The sound note is added by clicking the **Record button** in the Cell Note dialog box (Figure 4-52 on the previous page). When a **sound note** (also called an **audio comment**) is added without a text note, the computer speaks the comment when you click Note on the Insert menu or press SHIFT+F2.

More *About* **Notes**

One of the ways to make use of the Record button (audio comments) is to incorporate instructions on how to use the workbook.

Adding a Header and Footer and Changing the Margins

A **header** is printed at the top of a every page in a printout. A **footer** is printed at the bottom of every page in a printout. By default, Excel prints the tab name as the header, .5" from the top, and the page number preceded by the word Page as a footer, .5" from the bottom. You can change the header and footer to print other types of information.

Sometimes you will want to change the margins to center a printout on the page or include additional columns and rows that would otherwise not fit. The **margins** in Excel are set to the following: Top = 1"; Bottom = 1"; Left = .75"; Right = .75".

Changing the header and footer and changing the margins are all part of the function called **page setup**. You use the Page Setup command on the shortcut menu or File menu to carry out the page setup function. It is important that you select all the sheets that contain information before you change the header, footer, or margin, or else some of the page setup characteristics will only occur on the selected sheet.

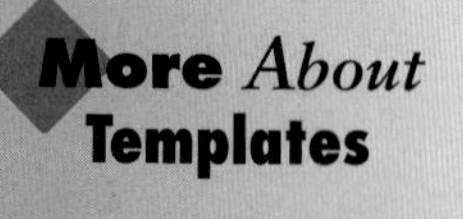

More *About* **Templates**

Applying page setup characteristics to a template will not work because they are not part of the pasted worksheets. Thus, the page setup characteristics assigned to a template will only apply to the first sheet in a workbook created by copying the template to multiple worksheets in the workbook.

You should also be aware that Excel does not copy page setup characteristics when a sheet is copied to another. Thus, assigning page setup characteristics to the template prior to copying it to form the Antietam University 1998 Budget Proposal workbook would not work.

More *About* **Headers and Footers**

You can turn off headers and footers for a printout by selecting (none) in the Header drop-down list box.

To Change the Header, Footer, and Margins

1 **With the All Services sheet active, hold down the SHIFT key and click the Chart tab. Right-click the menu bar and point to Page Setup.**

Excel displays a shortcut menu (Figure 4-54). The five tabs at the bottom of the window are selected.

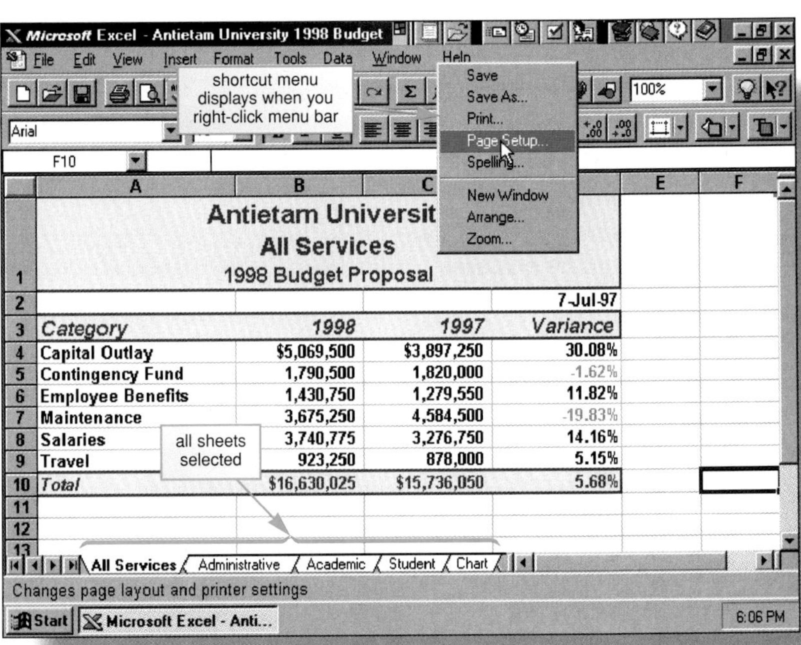

FIGURE 4-54

2 **Click Page Setup. When the Page Setup dialog box displays, click the Header/Footer tab.**

Samples of the default header and footer display (Figure 4-55).

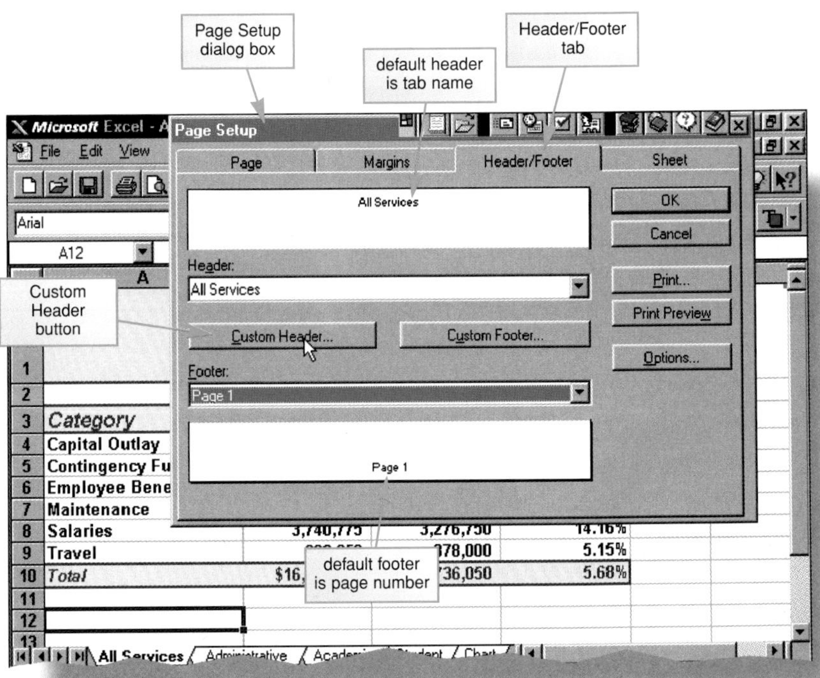

FIGURE 4-55

3 **Click the Custom Header button. When the Header dialog box displays, click in the Left Section box. Type** `Kevin Jacob, Controller` **and press the ENTER key to go to the next line. Type** `Preliminary Budget Proposal` **and click in the Center Section. If &[Tab] is not in the Center section, click the Sheet Name button in the Header dialog box. Click the Right Section box. Type** `Page` **followed by a space and click the Page Number button in the Header dialog box followed by a space. Type** `of` **followed by a space. Click the Total Pages button.**

The Header dialog box appears with the new header as shown in Figure 4-56.

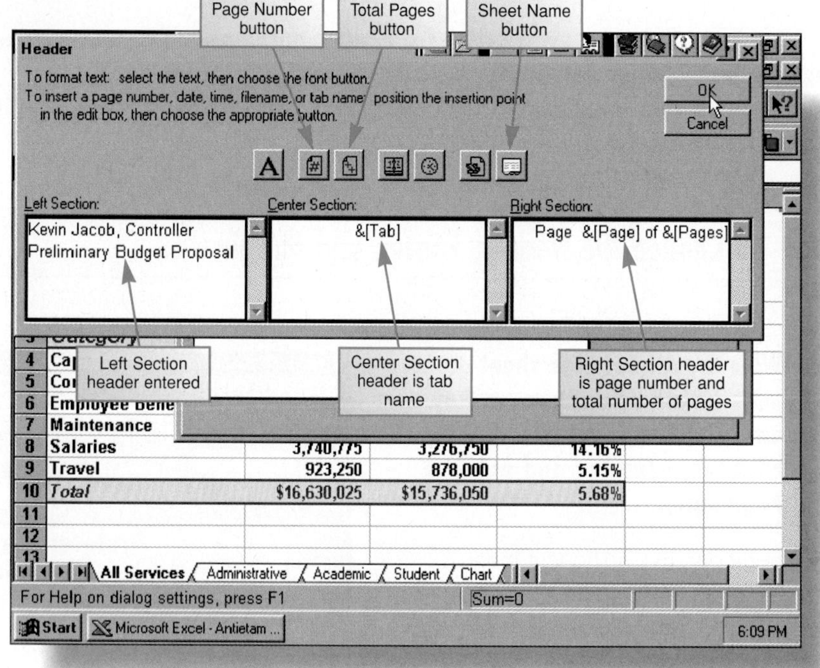

FIGURE 4-56

4 **Click the OK button in the Header dialog box. Click the Custom Footer button. Drag across the footer Page 1 and press the DELETE key to remove it. Click the OK button in the Footer dialog box.**

The Header/Footer sheet in the Page Setup dialog box appears as shown in Figure 4-57.

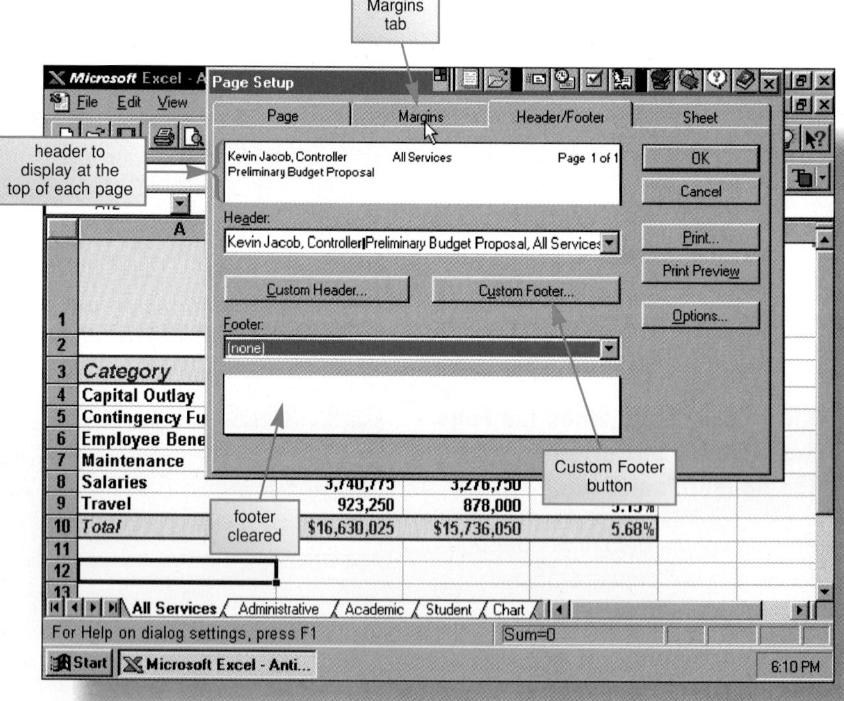

FIGURE 4-57

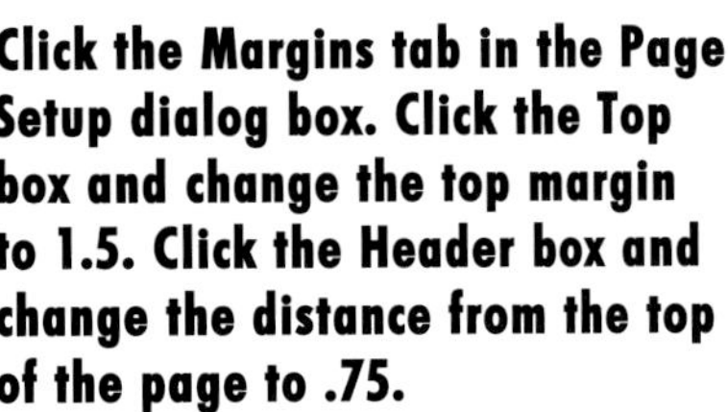

5 Click the Margins tab in the Page Setup dialog box. Click the Top box and change the top margin to 1.5. Click the Header box and change the distance from the top of the page to .75.

The Margins tab in the Page dialog box displays as shown in Figure 4-58. The Center on Page area in the lower left corner of the Margins sheet allows you to center a printout on the page.

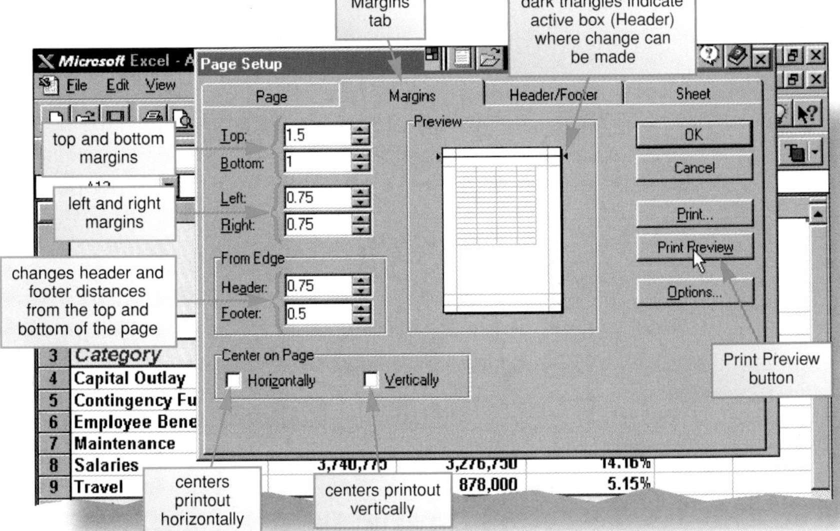

FIGURE 4-58

6 Click the Print Preview button in the Page Setup dialog box to preview the workbook.

The All Services sheet displays as shown in Figure 4-59. Although difficult to read, the header displays at the top of the page. You can choose the Zoom button to get a better view of the page. If your preview displays in landscape, click the Setup button and change the orientation on the Page tab to portrait.

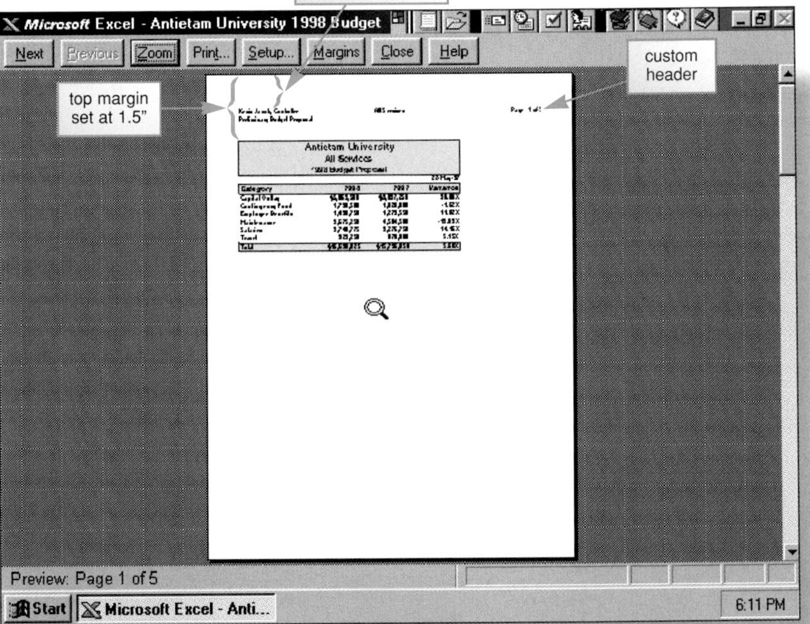

FIGURE 4-59

7 Click the Close button when you are finished reviewing the preview. Click the Save button on the Standard toolbar to save the workbook with the new print settings.

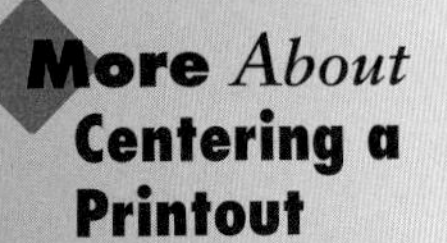

More *About* Centering a Printout

In Figure 4-59, the preview indicates that the worksheet will print beginning in the upper left corner of the paper. You can center the printout by using the check boxes in the Center on Page area of the Margins tab on the Page Setup dialog box (Figure 4-58) to center a printout horizontally, vertically, or both.

Table 4-5

BUTTON	CODE	FUNCTION
[A]		Displays the Font dialog box
[#]	&[Page]	Inserts a page number
[+]	&[Pages]	Inserts the total number of pages
[date]	&[Date]	Inserts the system date
[time]	&[Time]	Inserts the system time
[file]	&[File]	Inserts the filename of the workbook
[tab]	&[Tab]	Inserts the tab name

When you click one of the buttons in the Header dialog box (Figure 4-56 on page E 4.44), Excel enters a code into the active section. A code such as &[Page] means insert the page number. Table 4-5 summarizes the buttons, their codes, and functions in the Header or Footer dialog box.

Printing the Workbook

The following steps print the workbook.

TO PRINT THE WORKBOOK

Step 1: Ready the printer.
Step 2: If the five sheets in the workbook are not selected, click the All Services tab and then hold down the SHIFT key and click the Student tab.
Step 3: Click the Print button on the Standard toolbar.

The workbook prints as shown in Figure 4-60a and Figure 4-60b.

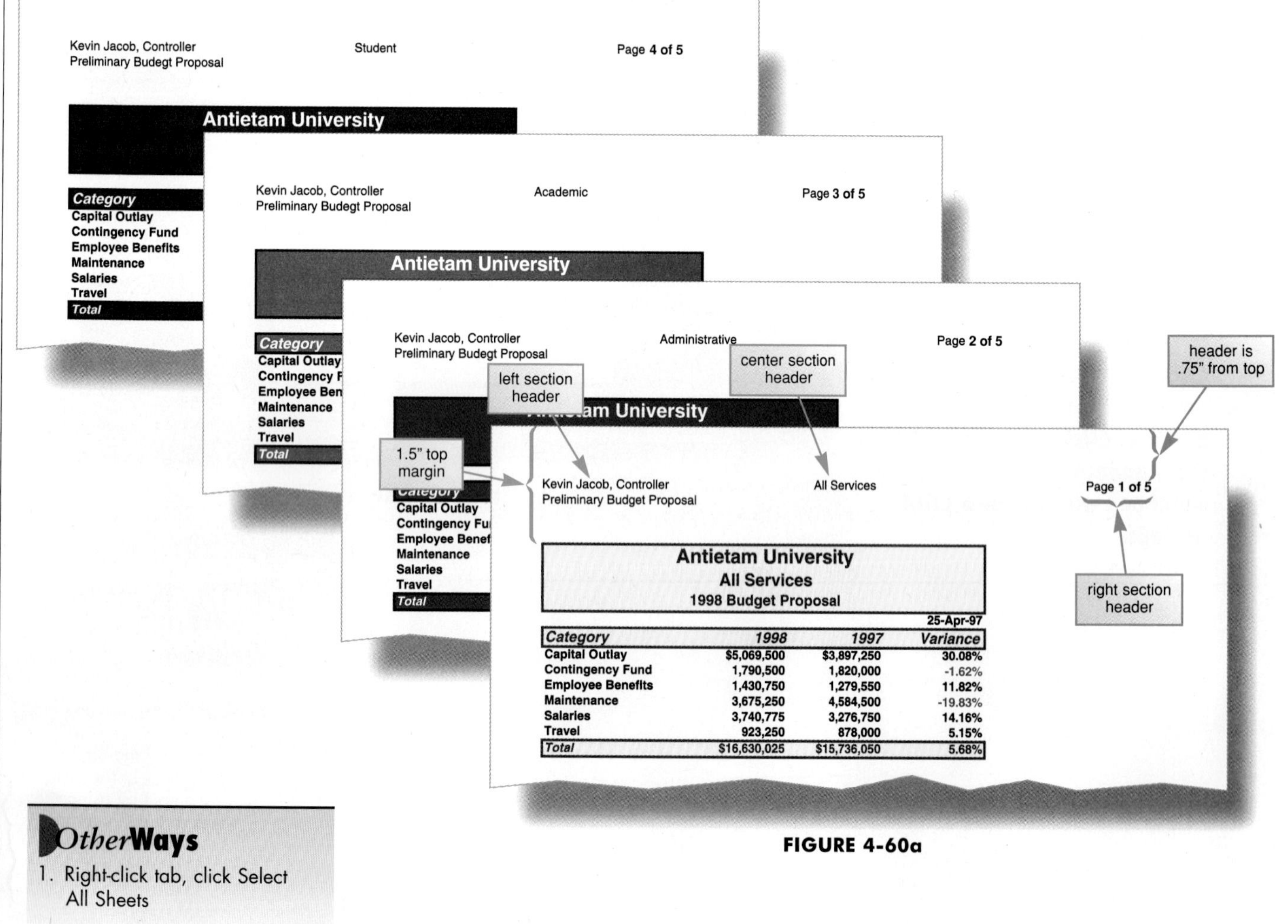

FIGURE 4-60a

OtherWays

1. Right-click tab, click Select All Sheets

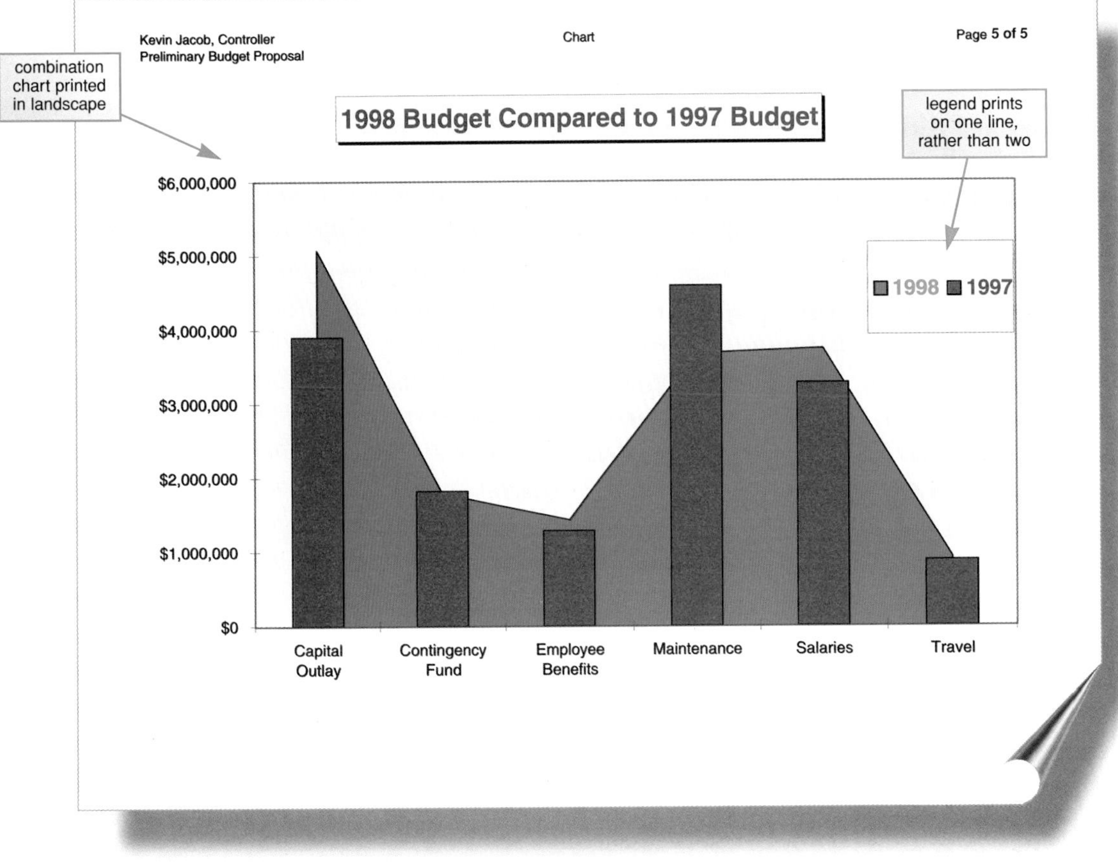

FIGURE 4-60b

Finding and Replacing Text or Numbers

You can find cells that contain specific characters by clicking Find on the Edit menu. To find and replace characters in cells, click Replace on the Edit menu.

Finding Text or Numbers

The steps on the next page show you how to find the text Main in Maintenance (cell A7) on the All Services sheet. If you select a range before invoking the Find command, Excel searches the range on the active sheet. If you select a cell, Excel searches all selected sheets. Excel searches row by row, beginning with row 1 of the active sheet. However, you can instruct Excel to search column by column by means of a check box in the Find dialog box.

More *About* **Printing Multiple Sheets**

There are three ways to print all the worksheets containing data in the workbook: (1) select all the worksheets by clicking an end sheet tab, and then holding down the SHIFT key and clicking the other end sheet tab; (2) select all the worksheets by clicking Select All on the shortcut menu that displays when you right-click a tab; (3) select the Entire Workbook option button in the Print What box on the Print dialog box.

Steps To Find Text or Numbers

1. **Hold down the SHIFT key and click the All Services tab. With cell F10 active, point to Find on the Edit menu.**

   The Edit menu displays as shown in Figure 4-61.

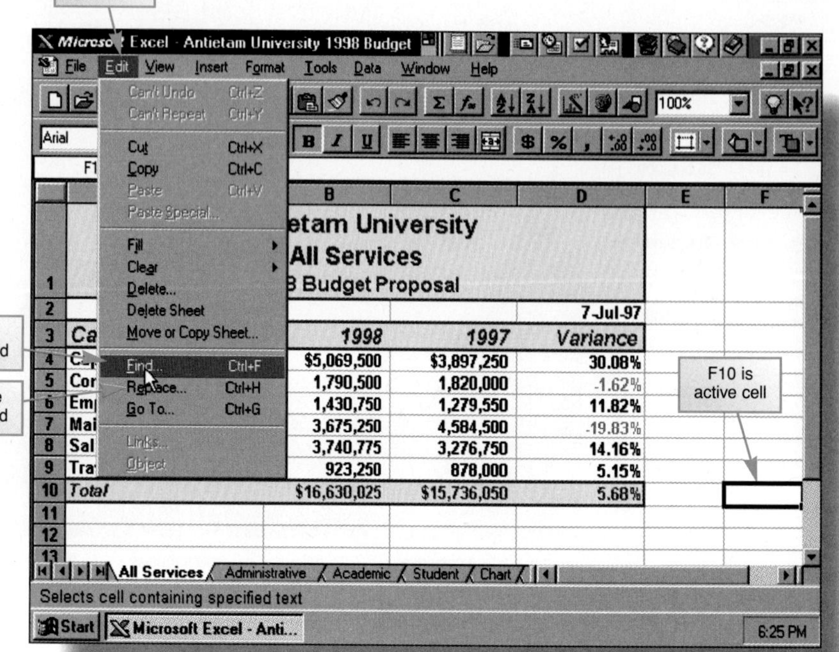

FIGURE 4-61

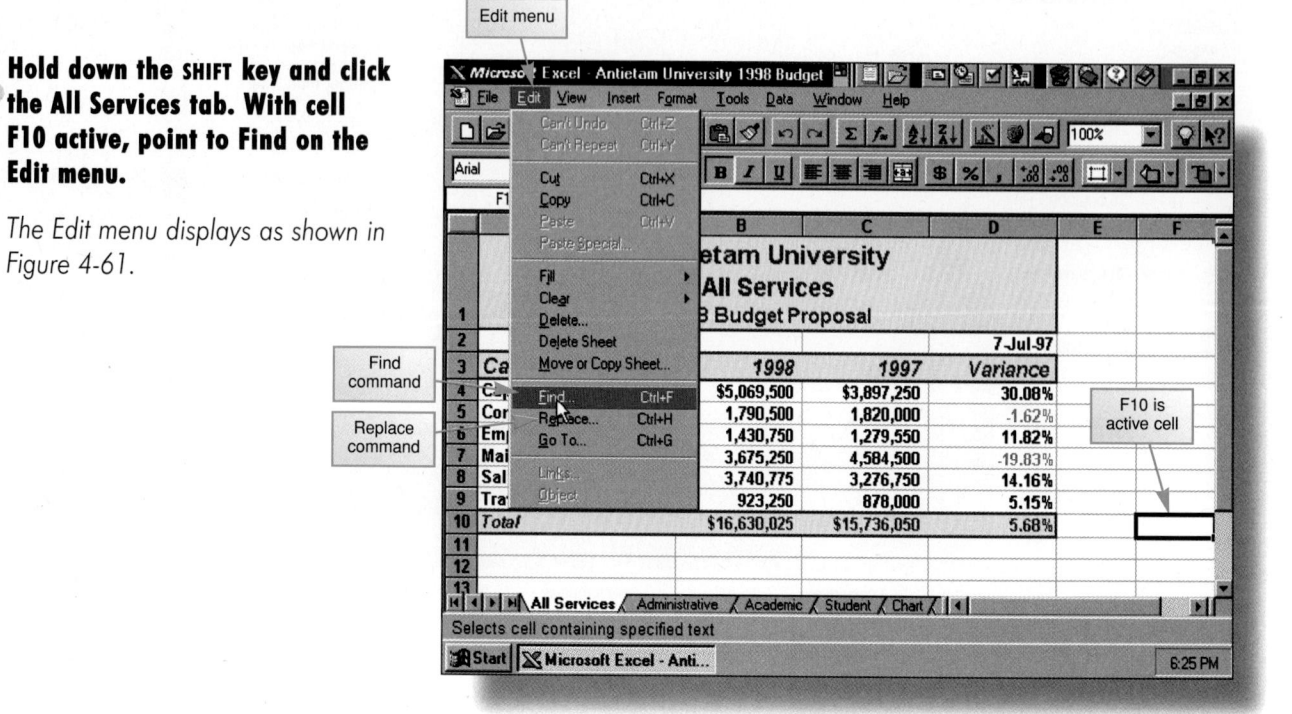

2. **Click the Find command. When the Find dialog box displays, type** `Main` **in the Find What box.**

   The Find dialog box displays as shown in Figure 4-62.

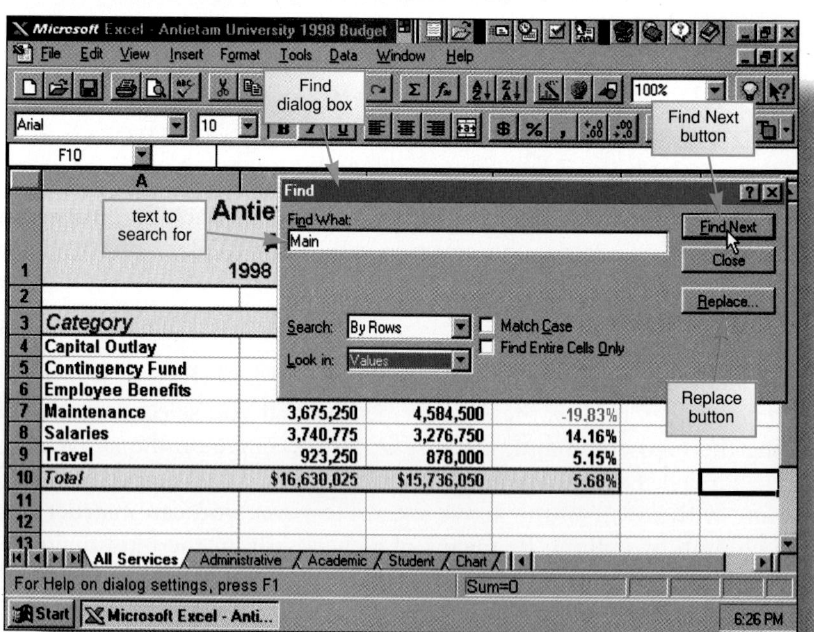

FIGURE 4-62

3 Click the Find Next button

Excel activates the first cell containing the text Main, cell A7, as shown in Figure 4-63.

4 Click the Close button to close the Find dialog box or choose the Find Next button to find the next occurrence of Main.

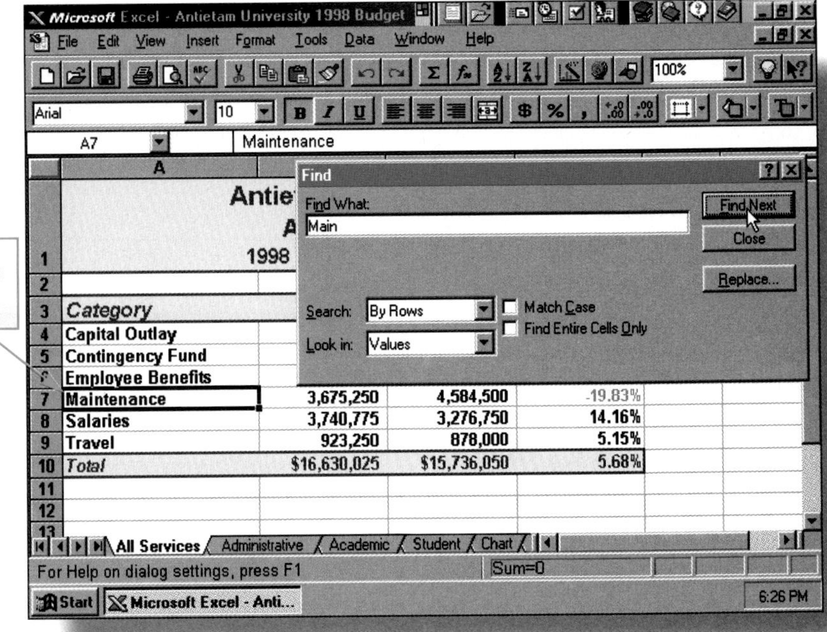

FIGURE 4-63

OtherWays

1. Press CTRL+F

You can use wildcard characters (*, or ?) to find variations of the sequence of characters typed into the Find What box. The asterisk (*) represents any number of characters in that same position. The question mark (?) represents any character in that same position. For example, if you type *ies in the Find What dialog box, Excel will stop on any cell that has text that ends with ies. If you type s?l in the Find What box, Excel will stop on any cell that has text that includes a sequence of characters with the letter s, followed by any character, followed by letter l. Table 4-6 summarizes the options found on the Find dialog box.

Table 4-6

OPTION	FUNCTION
Find Next button	Finds next occurrence.
Close button	Closes Find dialog box.
Replace button	Displays the Replace dialog box so that you can replace the occurrence.
Search box	Instructs Excel to search by rows or columns.
Look in box	Instructs Excel to search in formulas, values, or notes.
Match Case check box	Instructs Excel to be case sensitive.
Find Entire Cells Only check box	Instructs Excel to find only exact and complete matches.

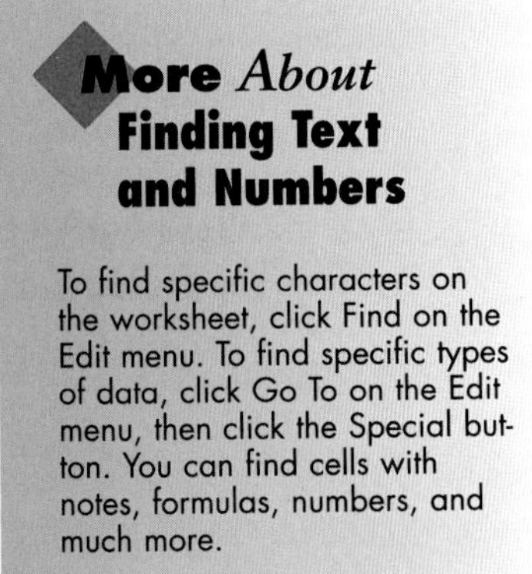

More About Finding Text and Numbers

To find specific characters on the worksheet, click Find on the Edit menu. To find specific types of data, click Go To on the Edit menu, then click the Special button. You can find cells with notes, formulas, numbers, and much more.

If you hold down the SHIFT key when you click the Find Next button, Excel reverses the direction of the search.

Replacing Text or Numbers

The following steps show you how to replace the first occurrence of Salaries with Salary on the All Services sheet.

Steps To Replace Text or Numbers

1 **With the All Services sheet selected and cell F10 active, click Replace on the Edit menu. When the Replace dialog box displays, type** `Salaries` **in the Find What box and type** `Salary` **in the Replace with box.**

The Replace dialog box displays as shown in Figure 4-64.

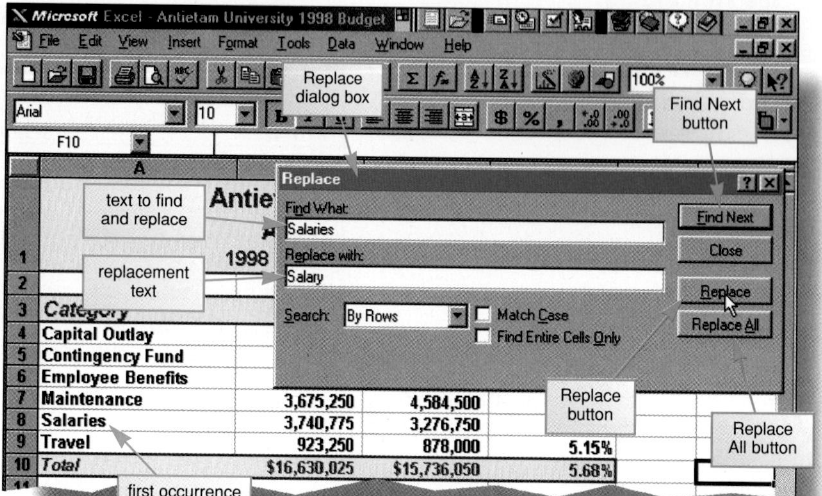

FIGURE 4-64

2 **Click the Find Next button and then click the Replace button on the Replace dialog box.**

Excel finds the first cell containing the text Salaries (cell A8) on the All Services sheet and replaces it with Salary (Figure 4-65).

3 **Click the Close button to close the Replace dialog box.**

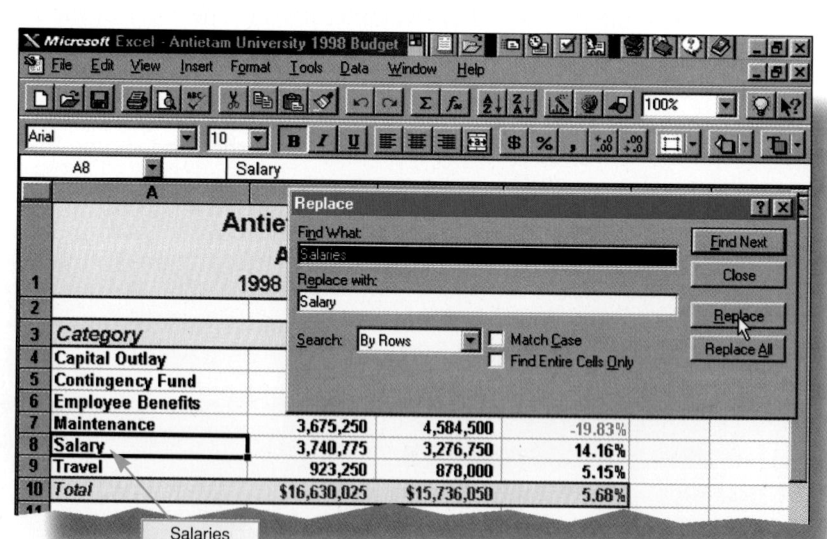

FIGURE 4-65

OtherWays

1. Press CTRL+H

The Replace All button in the Replace dialog box (Figure 4-64) causes Excel to replace all occurrences of the text in the selected sheets. The remaining options in the Replace dialog box are the same as the Find dialog box described in Table 4-6 on the previous page.

Exiting Excel

To exit Excel, follow the steps below.

TO EXIT EXCEL

Step 1: Click the Close button on the right side of the title bar.
Step 2: If the Microsoft Excel dialog box displays, click the No button.

Project Summary

Kevin Jacob, the controller for Antietam University will be pleased with the workbook developed in this project. The use of multiple sheets allows for better organization of the data. The combination area and column chart compares this year's budget to next year's proposed budget. Possibly the best aspect of the way the workbook is put together is the use of the template, because Kevin can use it in the future to add additional services or create similar workbooks.

This project introduced you to creating and using a template, customizing formats, changing chart types, and drawing and enhancing combination charts. You also learned how to reference cells in other sheets and add comments to a cell. To enhance a printout, you learned how to add a header and footer and to change margins. Finally, you learned how to find and replace text.

What You Should Know

Having completed this project, you should be able to perform the following tasks:

- Apply a Format Code from the Format Dialog Box *(E 4.18)*
- Assign a Note to a Cell *(E 4.41)*
- Bold the Font in the Template and Change Column Widths *(E 4.10)*
- Change the Background Color and Add Outlines *(E 4.16)*
- Change the Colors of the Data Markers and Plot Area *(E 4.37)*
- Change the Header, Footer, and Margins *(E 4.43)*
- Change the Size of the Font on the Axes, Rename the Chart1 Tab, and Save the Workbook *(E 4.40)*
- Create a Custom Format Code *(E 4.21)*
- Create a Workbook from a Template *(E 4.23)*
- Draw a Combination Area and Column Chart *(E 4.33)*
- Enter and Copy 3-D References on the All Services Sheet *(E 4.30)*
- Enter Dummy Numbers and Sum Them in The Template *(E 4.12)*
- Enter Numbers as Text, Format the Entries, and Enter the System Date *(E 4.11)*
- Enter the Template Title and Row Titles *(E 4.10)*
- Enter the Variance Formula in the Template *(E 4.11)*
- Exit Excel *(E 4.51)*
- Find Text or Numbers *(E 4.48)*
- Format the Chart Title *(E 4.36)*
- Format the Template Titles *(E 4.15)*
- Modify Formats Across Multiple Sheets *(E 4.25)*
- Modify the Academic Sheet *(E 4.27)*
- Modify the Administrative Sheet *(E 4.26)*
- Modify the Student Sheet *(E 4.28)*
- Move, Resize, and Format the Legend *(E 4.39)*
- Print the Workbook *(E 4.46)*
- Rename a Sheet Tab *(E 4.29)*
- Replace Text or Numbers *(E 4.50)*
- Resize the Plot Area *(E 4.38)*
- Save a Template *(E 4.14)*
- Spell Check and Save the Template *(E 4.22)*
- Start Excel *(E 4.9)*

A+ Test Your Knowledge

1 True/False

Instructions: Circle T if the statement is true or F if the statement is false.

T F 1. A template is saved the same as a workbook.

T F 2. If multiple sheets are selected and you click cell A10, then cell A10 will be active on all of the selected sheets.

T F 3. Summarizing information that appears on multiple sheets of a workbook is referred to as consolidation.

T F 4. A floating dollar sign will always appear in the same position in a cell no matter how many digits are in the number that follows it.

T F 5. A note indicator appears in the upper right corner of a cell to indicate a note has been assigned to that particular cell.

T F 6. A legend cannot be moved on the chart.

T F 7. To display the shortcut menu with commands for manipulating sheets in a workbook, right-click a tab.

T F 8. A template may be copied to the clipboard and pasted to one or more sheets in a workbook.

T F 9. A three-dimensional range is indicated in Excel functions by sheet references followed by the range on the sheet.

T F 10. Workbook headers and footers appear only on the first page of a printout.

2 Multiple Choice

Instructions: Circle the correct response.

1. Format codes are used to define formats for ______________.
   a. numbers
   b. dates
   c. text
   d. all of the above
2. To display a comment or note assigned to a cell ______________.
   a. point to the cell
   b. right-click the cell
   c. click the Show All check box on the Options dialog box
   d. double-click the cell
3. Comments are added to a workbook through the use of the ______________ command on the Insert menu.
   a. Name
   b. Note
   c. Function
   d. Object

A+ Test Your Knowledge

4. Templates, called ______________, are stored in the XLStart folder.
   a. autotemplates
   b. startup templates
   c. new templates
   d. format templates
5. Excel automatically places a ______________ at the bottom of each page in a printout.
   a. tab name
   b. filename
   c. page number
   d. date
6. The Excel function called page setup allows you to ______________.
   a. copy pages of a workbook
   b. check the spelling of a workbook
   c. change the margins of a workbook
   d. select all the sheets of a workbook
7. The symbol # in a format code represents a ______________.
   a. digit position
   b. sign
   c. decimal point
   d. comma
8. There is a maximum of ______________ sections in a format code.
   a. 2
   b. 3
   c. 4
   d. 5
9. To find all cells that contain text that begins with Wi, enter ______________ in the Find What box on the Find dialog box.
   a. Wi?
   b. Wi!
   c. Wi*
   d. can't be done
10. A header contains ______________ section(s).
    a. 4
    b. 3
    c. 2
    d. 1

Test Your Knowledge

3 Understanding 3-D References

Instructions: The workbook in Figure 4-66 is made up of five sheets labeled Item, Part 1, Part 2, Part 3, and Part 4. Write the formula or function that accomplishes each of the tasks below Figure 4-66. Assume cell A1 is active on the Item sheet. Each of the five tasks below are independent of one another.

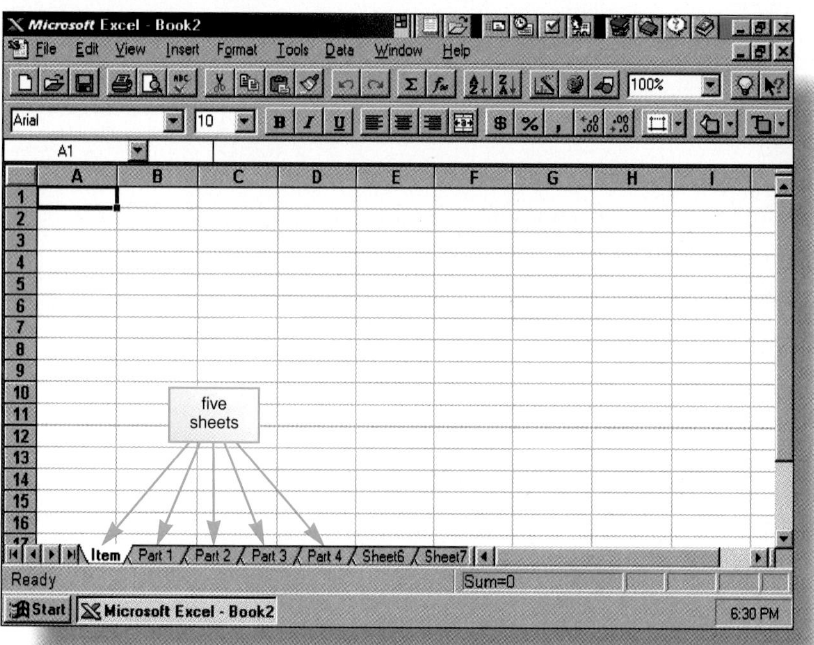

FIGURE 4-66

a. Assign Item!A1 the sum of cell B10 on each of the part sheets.

Function: ______________________________

b. Assign to cell Item!A1 the product of cell A1 on the Part 1 sheet and D5 on the Part 3 sheet.

Formula: ______________________________

c. Assign to cell Item!A1 cell H1 on the Item sheet times the quantity of cell R3 on the Part 2 sheet minus cell A6 on the Part 1 sheet.

Formula: ______________________________

d. Assign to cell Item!A1 the expression (D ^ 3 - 4 * F * H) / (4 - H) where the value of D is cell A8 on the Part 1 sheet, F is cell D3 on the Part 2 sheet, and H is cell B2 on the Part 4 sheet.

Formula: ______________________________

e. Assign to cell Item!A1 the value of cell B6 on the Part 3 sheet.

Formula: ______________________________

Test Your Knowledge

4 Working with Customized Formats

Instructions: Using Table 4-1 on page E4.20, determine the results that will display in the Results In and Color columns of Table 4-7. Assume that the column width of the cell that will display the value can hold 10 characters (including special characters). If the column width is insufficient, enter a series of 10 asterisks in the Results In column. Use the letter b to indicate positions containing blank characters.

You may want to use a PC and Excel to enter the numbers in cells (column width = 10.00) in a blank worksheet and assign the formats to determine the answers. As examples, the first two problems in the table are complete. If the number displays in a color other than black, indicate the color in the Color column, otherwise enter N/A.

Table 4-7

PROBLEM	CELL CONTENTS	FORMAT ASSIGNED	RESULTS IN	COLOR
1	37	###.00	bbbbb37.00	N/A
2	-356.23	##0.00;[Red]-##0.00	bbb-356.23	Red
3	26.217	###.##	______	____
4	-8211.63	#,##0.00;[Green]#,##0.00	______	____
5	7152.87	$ #,##0.00	______	____
6	923.21	$##,##0.00	______	____
7	99	#,##0.00;[Red](#,##0.00)	______	____
8	9	+##0.00	______	____
9	0	#,###	______	____
10	.54284	##.####	______	____
11	85231.978	$##,##0.00	______	____
12	.388	##0.00%	______	____
13	.6	$#,##0.00	______	____
14	527888425	$#,###,###	______	____
15	9	+#,##0.00	______	____

Use Help

1 Reviewing Project Activities

Instructions: Perform the following tasks using a computer.

1. Start Excel.
2. Double-click the Help button on the Standard toolbar to display the Help Topics: Microsoft Excel dialog box. Click the Contents tab. Scroll down the list of books. Double-click the Reference Information book. Double-click Microsoft Excel for Windows 95 Specifications. When the Microsoft Excel dialog box displays, click the links one at a time. Read and print them. Click the Back button to display the Microsoft Excel dialog box. Hand in the printouts to your instructor. Click the Help Topics button to return to the Help Topics: Microsoft Excel dialog box.
3. If the Help Topics: Microsoft Excel dialog box is not on the screen, double-click the Help button on the Standard toolbar. Click the Find tab. Type `format codes` in the top box labeled 1. Double-click Basic number format codes in the bottom box labeled 3. Read and print the information. Click the Help Topics button. Hand in the printout to your instructor.
4. If the Help Topics: Microsoft Excel dialog box is not on the screen, double-click the Help button on the Standard toolbar. Click the Index tab. Type `3-D references` in the top box labeled 1. Double-click 3-D references in the bottom box labeled 2. Double-click the links one at a time. Read and print the information. Click the Help Topics button and continue double-clicking 3-D references until you have gone through all the links. Hand in the printouts to your instructor.
5. Open any workbook from the Excel folder on the Student Floppy Disk that accompanies this book. Double-click the Help button on the Standard toolbar. Click the Answer Wizard tab. Obtain information on the following topic: How do I find text? Click Find text or numbers in the lower box labeled 2. Step through the tutorial.

2 Expanding on the Basics

Instructions: Perform the following tasks using a computer.

1. Start Excel.
2. Double-click the Help button on the Standard toolbar to display the Help Topics: Microsoft Excel dialog box. Click the Contents tab. Double-click the Changing the Appearance of Your Page book. Double-click the Page Breaks book. One at a time, double-click the Insert Page Breaks and remove Page Breaks links. Read and print the information (include all links). Hand in the printouts to your instructor.
3. If the Help Topics: Microsoft Excel dialog box is not on the screen, double-click the Help button on the Standard toolbar. Use the Index tab to collect information on the following topics: .XLT files, adding sound notes, and headers and footers. Hand in one printout on each topic to your instructor.
4. If the Help Topics: Microsoft Excel dialog box is not on the screen, double-click the Help button on the Standard toolbar. Use the Find tab to collect information on the IF function. Hand in one printout on IF, AND, OR, and logical functions.

Apply Your Knowledge

1 Consolidating Data in a Workbook

Instructions: Follow the steps on the next page to consolidate the four quarterly payroll sheets into the Annual Totals sheet in the workbook Annual Payroll. The Annual Totals sheet should appear as shown in the lower screen in Figure 4-67.

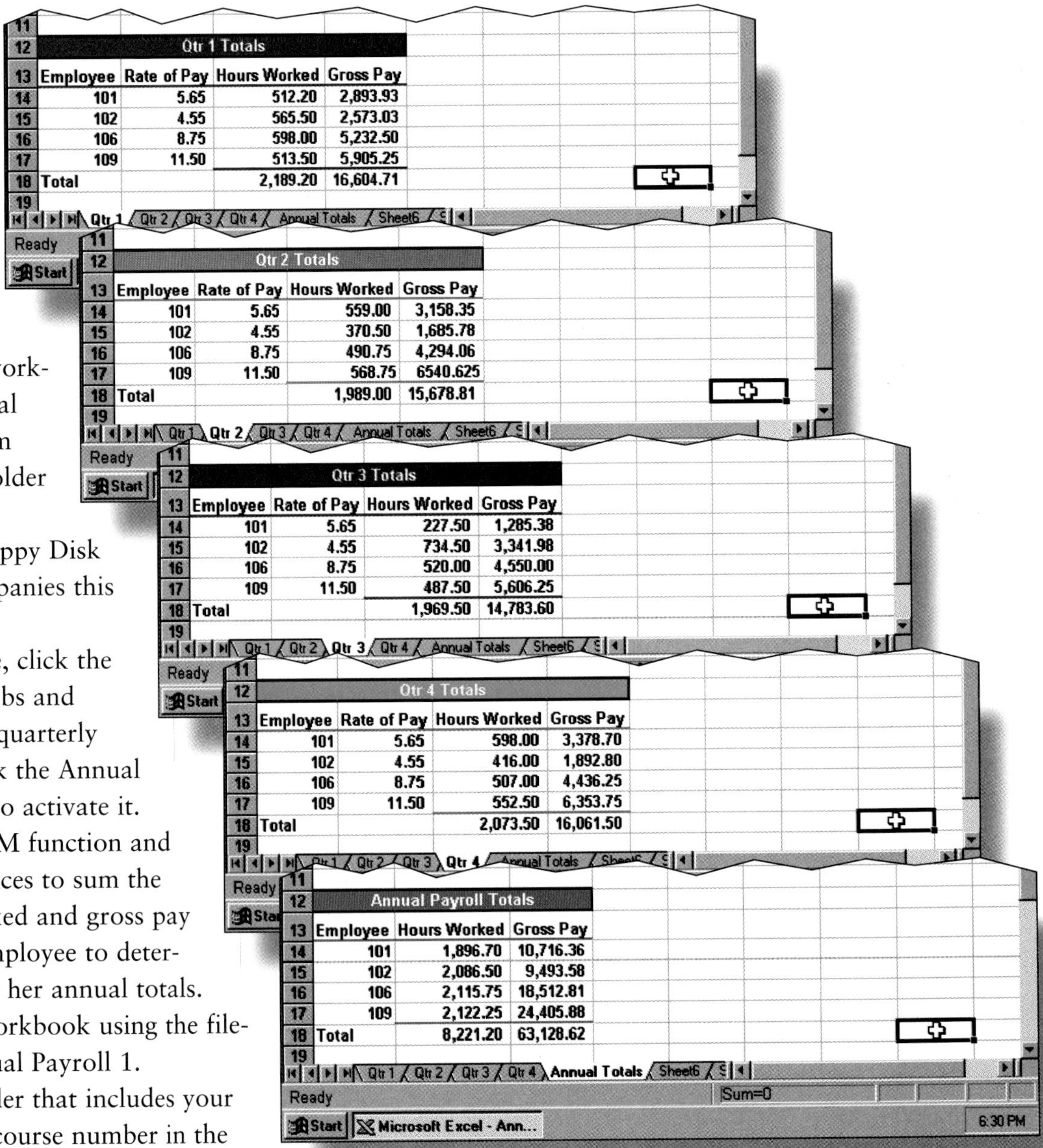

	Qtr 1 Totals			
13	Employee	Rate of Pay	Hours Worked	Gross Pay
14	101	5.65	512.20	2,893.93
15	102	4.55	565.50	2,573.03
16	106	8.75	598.00	5,232.50
17	109	11.50	513.50	5,905.25
18	Total		2,189.20	16,604.71

	Qtr 2 Totals			
13	Employee	Rate of Pay	Hours Worked	Gross Pay
14	101	5.65	559.00	3,158.35
15	102	4.55	370.50	1,685.78
16	106	8.75	490.75	4,294.06
17	109	11.50	568.75	6540.625
18	Total		1,989.00	15,678.81

	Qtr 3 Totals			
13	Employee	Rate of Pay	Hours Worked	Gross Pay
14	101	5.65	227.50	1,285.38
15	102	4.55	734.50	3,341.98
16	106	8.75	520.00	4,550.00
17	109	11.50	487.50	5,606.25
18	Total		1,969.50	14,783.60

	Qtr 4 Totals			
13	Employee	Rate of Pay	Hours Worked	Gross Pay
14	101	5.65	598.00	3,378.70
15	102	4.55	416.00	1,892.80
16	106	8.75	507.00	4,436.25
17	109	11.50	552.50	6,353.75
18	Total		2,073.50	16,061.50

	Annual Payroll Totals		
13	Employee	Hours Worked	Gross Pay
14	101	1,896.70	10,716.36
15	102	2,086.50	9,493.58
16	106	2,115.75	18,512.81
17	109	2,122.25	24,405.88
18	Total	8,221.20	63,128.62

FIGURE 4-67

1. Open the workbook Annual Payroll from the Excel folder on the Student Floppy Disk that accompanies this book.
2. One by one, click the first four tabs and review the quarterly totals. Click the Annual Totals tab to activate it.
3. Use the SUM function and 3-D references to sum the hours worked and gross pay for each employee to determine his or her annual totals.
4. Save the workbook using the filename Annual Payroll 1.
5. Add a header that includes your name and course number in the Left section, the computer laboratory exercise number (Apply 4-1) in the Center section, and the system date and your instructor's name in the Right section. Print the workbook. Save the workbook with the new page setup.

In the Lab

1 Creating a Company Template

Problem: You are a summer intern in the Information Systems department at Northeast Airlines. Your specialty is designing workbooks. The company uses a Groupware product that allows people to share information across a computer network. Your supervisor has instructed you to create a company-specific template for employees to open when they use Excel (Figure 4-68).

Instructions: The template should include the following:

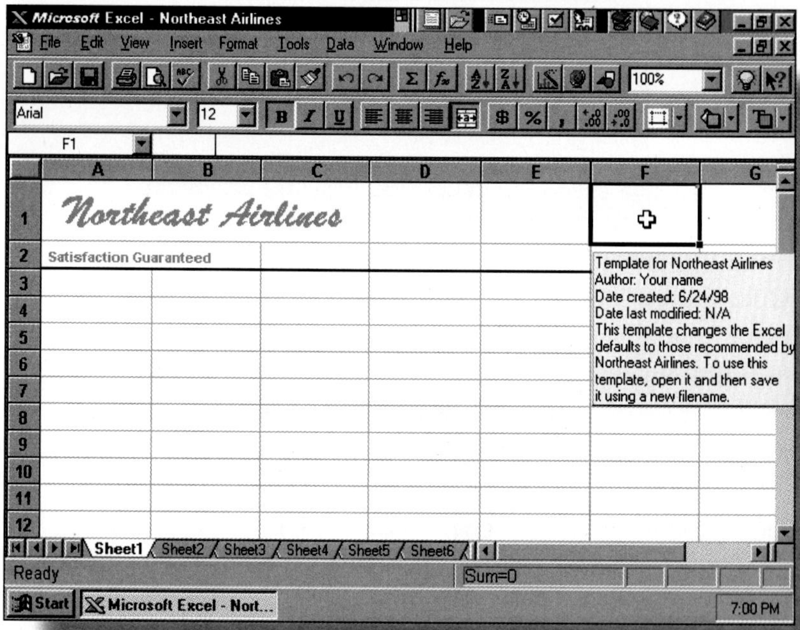

1. Assign the Comma format to all cells. Change the font of all cells to 12-point. Increase all column widths to 12. (Hint: Click the Select All button to make these changes.)
2. Add a note to cell F1 identifying the template and its purpose as shown in Figure 4-68. Include your name as the author, and substitute the currnt date for the one shown in the figure.
3. Enter the titles in cells A1 and A2 as shown in Figure 4-68. Change the font in cells A1 and A2 to Lucida Calligraphy (or a similar font). In cell A1, change the font size and color to 26 point red. In cell A2, change the font size to 8 point and the color to blue. Draw a heavy bottom border across the range A2:F2.
4. Enter your name, course, computer laboratory assignment (Lab4-1), date, and instructor name in the range A8:A12.
5. Save the template using the filename Northeast Airlines Template. You must select Template in the Save as type box in the Save As dialog box when you save the template.
6. Print the template and note. To print the note, click Note on the Sheet tab in the Page Setup dialog box. The note will print on a separate sheet. After the note prints, click Note to toggle off printing the note.
7. Close the template. Open the template. Save the template as a regular workbook using the filename Northeast Airlines. Make sure the Save as type box is set to Excel Workbook. Close the Northeast Airlines workbook.

FIGURE 4-68

In the Lab

2 Using a Template to Create a Multiple-Sheet Sales Analysis Workbook

Problem: MegaTronics Center has three outlets in Los Angeles, Chicago, and New York. Each outlet sells products to walk-ins, by telephone, by mail, or by fax. The Information Systems service generates a year-end sales analysis workbook from a template. The workbook contains four sheets, one for each of the three outlets and one for the company. The Company Totals sheet displays as shown in Figure 4-69 on the next page.

The template (Megatronics Template) is stored in the Excel folder on the Student Floppy Disk that accompanies this book. You have been assigned the task of creating the year-end sales analysis workbook from the template.

Instructions: Perform the following tasks:

1. Open the template MegaTronics Template from the folder Excel on the Student Floppy Disk. One at a time, paste the template to Sheet2, Sheet3, and Sheet4. Save the workbook using the filename MegaTronics Annual Sales Analysis. Make sure the Save as type box is set to Excel Workbook.
2. Enter the data in Table 4-8 on the next page onto the three outlet sheets. Before entering the data on each sheet, rename the sheet tabs (Company Totals, Los Angeles, Chicago, New York). Change the title in cell A1 on each sheet. Choose different background colors for each sheet.

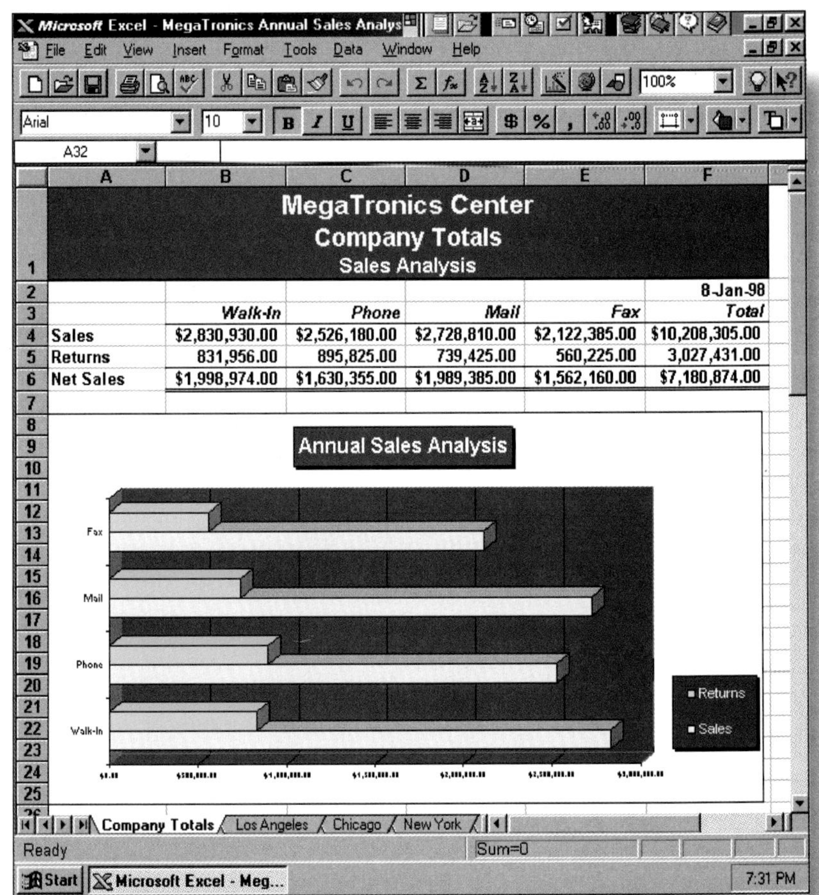

FIGURE 4-69

Table 4-8

		LOS ANGELES	CHICAGO	NEW YORK
Walk-In	Sales	1005360	929120	896450
	Returns	408350	126250	297356
Phone	Sales	792800	754730	978650
	Returns	425900	123150	346775
Mail	Sales	1040500	753210	935100
	Returns	123000	211675	404750
Fax	Sales	876140	592345	653900
	Returns	132650	235125	192450

(continued)

In the Lab

Using a Template to Create a Multiple-Sheet Sales Analysis Workbook *(continued)*

3. On the Company Totals sheet, use the SUM function, 3-D references, and the fill handle to total the corresponding cells on the three outlet sheets. The Company Totals sheet should resemble the top of Figure 4-69. Save the workbook by clicking the Save button on the Standard toolbar.
4. Create the embedded 3-D column chart (Figure 4-69) in the range A8:F25 on the Company Totals sheet. Chart the range A3:E5 on the Company Totals sheet. Format the chart as shown in Figure 4-69. Click the Save button on the Standard toolbar to save the workbook.
5. Select all four sheets. Change the header to include your name, course, computer laboratory exercise (Lab 4-2), date, and instructor name. Change the footer to include the page number and total pages. Print the entire workbook. Save the workbook with the new page setup.

3 Creating and Using a Consolidated Profit Forecast Template

Problem: The consulting firm you work for has assigned you to be the lead workbook specialist on their account with College Ware to create a Profit Forecast workbook. College Ware has outlets in two major cities, Seattle and Baltimore. The workbook is to include a worksheet and pie chart for each outlet and a summary worksheet with a pie chart for the company.

Instructions Part 1: Do the following:

1. Create the template in Figure 4-70. The column widths are as follows: A = 19.00; B through E = 12.00; and F = 13.00. Bold all cells. Change the font in the title in cell A1 to Old Bookman Old Style (or a similar font). The font in the first line of the title is 26 points. The font in the second line is 16 points. Draw a light bottom border on row 3. Italicize and right-align the column titles. Italicize the label Profit in cell A6. Draw a single light top border and a double light bottom border on row 6.
2. Enter the row headings. Italicize Profit in cell A6. Enter the dummy data shown in Figure 4-70 into the Assumptions table in the range B9:E12. Format the table as shown in Figure 4-70. Enter all percents with a trailing percent sign (%). Format cell B9 to a Currency style with a floating dollar sign and two decimal places. Format the range B10:E12 to a Percentage style with two decimal places. Add the colors shown in Figure 4-70.
3. All the values that display in rows 4 through 6 are based on the assumptions in rows 9 through 12. A surcharge is added to the expenses whenever the Qtr Growth rate is negative. Use the formulas on the next page.
   a. Sales in cell B4: =B9
   b. Sales in cell C4: =B4*(1+C10)
   c. Copy cell C4 to the range D4:E4
   d. Expenses in cell B5: =IF(B10 < 0, B4*(B11+B12), B4*B11)
   e. Profit in cell B6: =B4-B5
   f. Copy the range B5:B6 to C5:E6
   g. Use the SUM function to determine totals in column F

In the Lab

4. Create the 3-D pie chart that shows the contribution of each quarter to the total profit as shown in Figure 4-70. Use the chart range B3:E3 and B6:E6. Change the data labels in the pie chart to two decimal places by using the Format Data Labels command on the shortcut menu. Explode the Qtr 4 slice and rotate the pie chart as shown in Figure 4-70.
5. Save the template using the filename College Ware Template. Make sure the Save as type box is set to Template. Close the template.
6. Open the template. Copy the template to Sheet2 and Sheet3. Save the workbook using the filename College Ware. Make sure the Save as type box is set to Excel Workbook.
7. Rename the tabs to All Stores, Seattle, and Baltimore. Change the assumptions for Seattle to the following: Qrt1 Sales Amount (cell B9) = $875,300; Qtr2 Growth Rate (cell C10) = 3%; Qtr3 Growth Rate (cell D10) = -2.5%; Qtr4 Growth Rate (cell E10) = 1.5%; Qtr Expense Rate (cells B11 through E11) = 52%, 54.5%, 48.75%, and 54%; Surcharge (cells B12 through E12) = 2%, 1.75%, 3.5%, and 2.25%. Change the assumptions for Baltimore to the following: Qrt1 Sales Amount (cell B9) = $962,000; Qtr2 Growth Rate (cell C10) = -3%; Qtr3 Growth Rate (cell D10) = 2%; Qtr4 Growth Rate (cell E10) = 4.75%; Qtr Expense Rate (cells B11 through E11) = 51%, 49.5%, 51%, and 57%; Surcharge (cells B12 through E12) = 1%, 2.25%, 1.75%, and 2%. If necessary, use best fit to increase the size of the columns so the numbers display.
8. Delete the Assumptions table from the All Stores sheet. Use 3-D references and the fill handle to determine totals on the All Stores Sheet. You should end up with the following totals in column F on the summary sheet: Sales = $7,392,040.58; Expenses = $3,914,821.53; and Profit = $3,477,219.05. If necessary, change th formulas.

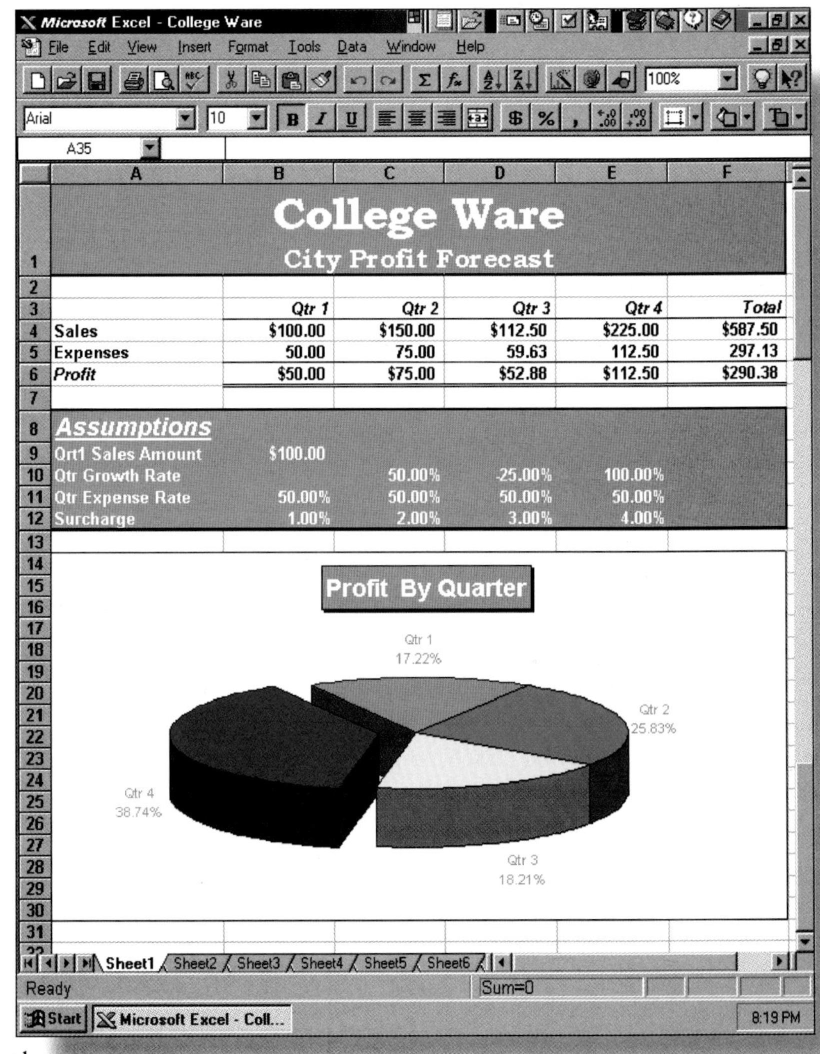

FIGURE 4-70

(continued)

In the Lab

Creating and Using a Consolidated Profit Forecast Template *(continued)*

9. Change the chart range so that each pie chart refers to the data on the same sheet. (Hint: One at a time, activate the charts on the Seattle and Baltimore sheets. Click the ChartWizard button and change the range in the ChartWizard dialog box so that the range reflects the active sheet.)
10. Save the workbook by clicking the Save button on the Standard toolbar.
11. Select all three sheets. Change the header to include your name, course, computer laboratory exercise (Lab 4-3), date, and instructor name. Change the footer to include the page number and total pages. Print the workbook.
12. Save the workbook by clicking the Save button on the Standard toolbar.

Instructions Part 2: Decrease each of the quarter expense rates (B11:E11) for both cities by 2.5%. You should end up with a total profit of $3,662,020.07 in cell F6 of the All Stores sheet.

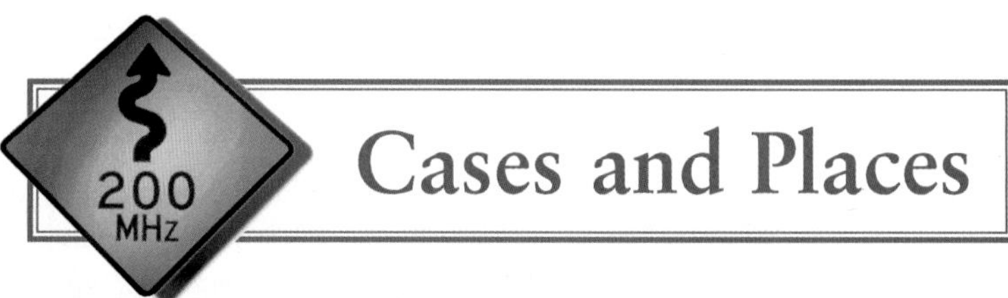

Cases and Places

The difficulty of these case studies varies:

◗ Case studies preceded by a single half moon are the least difficult. You are asked to create the required worksheet based on information that has already been placed in an organized form.
◗◗ Case studies preceded by two half moons are more difficult. You must organize the information presented before using it to create the required worksheet
◗◗◗ Case studies preceded by three half moons are the most difficult. You must decide on a specific topic, then obtain and organize the necessary information before using it to create the required worksheet.

1 ◗ Rob Rally, tennis coach, has jotted notes on three players (Figure 4-71) based on a recent match. Make a template that Coach Rally can use to evaluate his players. Include each statistic, the percentage of winners (winners /total shots), the percentage of errors (errors /total shots), and what Coach Rally calls the "success rate" (percentage of winners - percentage of errors). Use the template to develop a worksheet for each player.

Cases and Places

200 MHz

Tom Topspin	Total	Winners	Errors
Forehand	216	45	24
Backhand	172	24	24
Volley	12	0	9
Service	96	15	3
Service Return	114	24	15
Suzi Slice	**Total**	**Winners**	**Errors**
Forehand	138	54	42
Backhand	147	63	21
Volley	36	18	3
Service	114	21	0
Service Return	108	60	9
Larry Lob	**Total**	**Winners**	**Errors**
Forehand	192	36	12
Backhand	168	24	39
Volley	102	84	3
Service	72	33	6
Service Return	96	30	42

FIGURE 4-71

GRANT STREET	
Individual applications	$48,812
Integrated packages	40,135
Entertainment software	52,912
System software	12,769
Learning aids	8,562
Supplies	34,215

FIGRUE 4-72

LEXINGTON AVENUE	
Individual applications	$42,864
Integrated packages	63,182
Entertainment software	52,345
System software	15,278
Learning aids	11,397
Supplies	24,921

FIGRUE 4-73

2 ◗ Progressive Programs sells computer software and supplies. Merchandise is divided into six categories based on profit margin: individual application packages (15%), integrated application packages (10%), system software (19%), entertainment software (17%), learning aids (8%), and supplies (20%). Last year's sales data has been collected for the Grant Street and Lexington Avenue Stores as shown in Figures 4-72 and Figures 4-73.

Develop a template that can be used to determine marketing strategies for next year. Include sales, profit margins, profits (sales x profit margin), total sales, total profits, and functions to determine the most and least profitable categories. Use the template to create a worksheet for each outlet, a consolidated worksheet for the entire company, and a chart reflecting the company's profits by category.

3 ◗◗ Beaverton's public safety division is made up of three departments — Fire, Police, and Streets & Sanitation. The departments have submitted figures comparing expenditures this year to anticipated expenditures next year in four categories (Figure 4-74 on the next page). Develop a template that can be used to prepare each department's budget and the division's consolidated total budget. Include this year's costs, next year's anticipated costs, and the variance [(anticipated costs - this year's costs) ÷ this year's costs/ for each expenditure. Indicate totals where appropriate. Construct a chart comparing the division's expenditures this year and next.

Cases and Places

FIGURE 4-74

	FIRE DEPT.		POLICE DEPT.		STREETS & SANITATION DEPT.	
	THIS YEAR	NEXT YEAR	THIS YEAR	NEXT YEAR	THIS YEAR	NEXT YEAR
Equipment	$33,675	$ 35,000	$ 36,575	$ 28,000	$43,250	$36,500
Maintenance	$35,300	$ 30,500	$ 12,000	$ 14,500	$14,500	$13,700
Miscellaneous Expenses	$21,500	$ 27,500	$ 24,850	$ 21,900	$22,800	$18,500
Salaries and Benefits	$94,300	$109,900	$153,850	$187,000	$66,950	$80,500

4 ▶▶ Tri-Quality International is parent to two companies — Modern Elek and Analog Haven. Last year, Modern Elek's and Analog Haven's assets, respectively, were: $211,000 and $123,000 (cash); $72,500 and $63,500 (accounts receivable); $179,150 and $213,500 (marketable securities); $459,000 and $357,000 (inventory); and $213,000 and $114,000 (equipment). Each company's liabilities were: $62,500 and $51,500 (notes payable); $212,850 and $179,150 (accounts payable); and $73,000 and $49,500 (income tax payable). The stockholders' equity for each company was: $585,200 and $625,100 (common stock) and $780,100 and $327,750 (retained earnings). Create a template that can be used to show each company's assets, total assets, liabilities, total liabilities, stockholder's equity, total stockholders' equity, and total liabilities and stockholders' equity. Use the template to develop a balance sheet for each company, and a consolidated worksheet for Tri-Quality International.

5 ▶▶▶ When an instructor teaches the same course to more than one class, similar standards are commonly used to assign grades in each. The instructor might apportion a specific *weight* to performance on different tasks (assignments, quizzes, reports, exams, and so on), and then use the weighted performances in a formula to determine final grades. Find out how an instructor at your school measures student achievement. Create a template to determine final grades with any necessary formulas and functions. Then, discuss it with the instructor and make any required revisions. Use a *hypothetical* class to test the template.

6 ▶▶▶ Video rental stores frequently group the tapes into categories. The popularity of different categories of tapes may vary depending on the day of the week. Visit a video rental store. List six categories of videotapes and the price of renting a tape in each category. Develop a template that can be used to study daily rentals. Include the number of tapes rented in each category, the income from each category, the total number of tapes rented in the six categories, and the total income. Using your template and information gathered from the store's records, produce worksheets showing rental patterns for at least three days. Create a consolidated worksheet based on the data from the three days and construct a chart illustrating the consolidated data.

7 ▶▶▶ Meteorologists can use worksheets to summarize weekly weather conditions. For each day of the week, these worksheets might have data on such factors as low temperature, high temperature, median temperature, humidity, and precipitation. Develop a template that can be used to study weekly weather conditions. Have at least six factors for each day of the week and use functions to find weekly averages, highs, and lows where appropriate. Include a chart on the template that illustrates one weather factor. Use your template to record and chart weather data for at least two weeks. Create a consolidated worksheet based on the two weeks.

Microsoft Excel 7

Windows 95

Data Tables, Visual Basic for Applications, and Scenario Manager

Objectives:

You will have mastered the material in this project when you can:

- Assign a name to a cell and refer to the cell in a formula by using the assigned name
- Determine the monthly payment of a loan using the financial function PMT
- State the purpose of the FV and PV functions
- Enter a series of percents using the fill handle
- Build a data table to analyze data in a worksheet
- Write a macro in Visual Basic to automate data entry in your worksheet
- Use the Macro Recorder to create a macro
- Execute macros
- Analyze worksheet data by changing values and goal seeking
- Use Excel's Scenario Manager to record and save different sets of what-if assumptions and the corresponding results of formulas
- Protect and unprotect cells

The HOME *Stretch* Nears

Worksheets Help Home Buyers Achieve the American Dream

Part of the American Dream includes owning a home. With current corporate downsizing, fluctuating interest rates, and salary freezes, this dream often remains just that — a desire that seems unattainable.

Creative lending institutions, however, work with customers' purse strings to explore various mortgage options. They often use worksheets resembling the First Bank Loan Analysis in this Excel project that evaluate data by applying financial functions and displaying scenarios to guide consumers.

For example, Citibank uses two worksheets to help potential borrowers: the Client Affordability Analysis determines the maximum loan amount based on the customers' income and CitiShowcase displays scenarios showing the annual income and down payments required to qualify for various mortgage options.

Home shoppers, particularly first-time buyers, often do not know whether they have a sufficient down payment and adequate income to purchase a home. Then they need to know maximum sales prices of homes they can afford. To provide this information, a Citibank loan officer retrieves the Client Affordability

THE AMERICAN DREAM A DREAM COME TRUE

THE AMERICAN DREAM A DREAM COME TRUE THE AMERICAN DREAM A DREAM COME TRUE THE AMERICAN DREAM

Analysis form on a notebook computer and interviews the clients. The officer asks the amount of annual income, monthly debt, and down payment and simultaneously inputs the figures in unprotected worksheet cells. Then the officer inputs current interest rates for particular loans, such as 8.75 percent on a 30-year fixed rate.

At this point, the worksheet program uses financial functions to determine the maximum loan amounts and monthly payments based on the clients' data. For example, a client with an annual income of $45,000 and a down payment of $15,000 can afford a maximum loan of $101,000 and monthly payments of $1,050 if his or her housing expenses, including home insurance, taxes, association dues, and mortgage insurance, do not exceed the optimal 28 percent of the total gross income.

If this client has an approximate sales price in mind, the worksheet will use this figure to determine if the property is affordable. For example, if the home is priced at $150,000, the worksheet computes that this price, coupled with other property expenses, amounts to 35.73 percent of the total gross income. Strictly speaking, the client does not qualify for a mortgage on this home.

These figures then are referenced in the CitiShowcase mortgage options analysis, which displays 12 scenarios. Using the $150,000 home, the worksheet computes the annual income required to obtain 30-year fixed, 15-year fixed, and adjustable-rate mortgages with down payments of 25, 20, 10, and 5 percent. For example, the client needs an annual income of $40,365 and a 25 percent down payment of $37,500 to obtain a 30-year fixed mortgage with an interest rate of 8.75 percent and monthly payments of $1,111. Another scenario on the CitiShowcase report indicates that the client needs to earn $57,525 with a 10-percent down payment of $15,000 to obtain a 15-year fixed mortgage at 8.25 percent with monthly payments of $1,583.

Citibank, like most lenders, uses these worksheets as a starting point to help potential borrowers explore mortgage options. In an attempt to qualify the client for the mortgage, the loan officer considers compensating factors, such as a clean credit history, verifiable job offers, and length of time since graduation, particularly for first-time buyers. The worksheets, together with the clients' financial picture, can help make the American Dream come true.

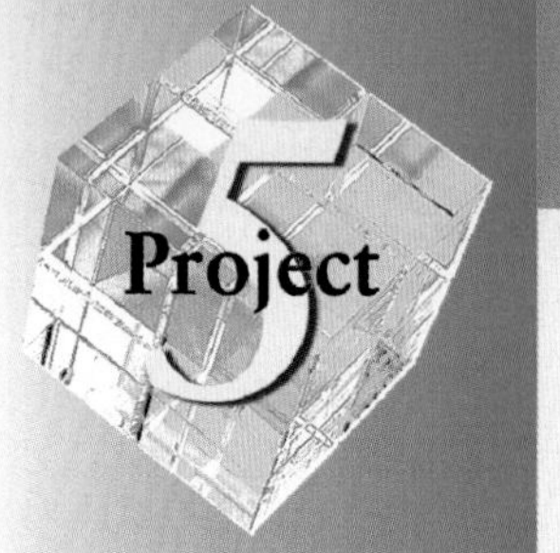

Microsoft Excel 7
Windows 95

Data Tables, Visual Basic for Applications, and Scenario Manager

Case Perspective

Sueann Weddington is vice president of financial services for First Bank, whose motto is *The people with ideas*. Sueann has taken the motto to heart and recently obtained permission to computerize the loan department. Her intent is to have the loan officers generate instant loan information, including the monthly payment, total interest, and total cost of a proposed loan when the loan applicant comes in for an interview. The applicant can then take home a printed copy of the information to review.

Sueann recently took a one-day course on Microsoft Excel at the local community college and has some idea of its potential. For example, she learned that Excel has many financial functions and what-if tools. She also learned that macros can be written to ensure that occasional users, such as the loan officers, can be guided through a task without much chance of making a serious mistake. As Sueann's part-time technical specialist, she has asked you to create a workbook that will generate the desired loan information at the click of a button, while ensuring that the loan officers will not render the worksheet useless by entering data into the wrong cells.

Introduction

Two of the most powerful internal aspects of Excel are its repertoire of functions and its capability to analyze worksheet data or answer what-if questions. In Project 2 you were introduced to some of the statistical functions, such as AVERAGE, MAX, and MIN. In this project you will learn about the financial functions, namely the PMT function, which allows you to determine a monthly payment for a loan.

In Project 3 you learned how to analyze data by using Excel's recalculation feature and goal seeking. This project revisits these two methods of analyzing data and describes two additional methods — data tables and Scenario Manager. A **data table** is a powerful what-if tool because it can automate your data analyses and organize the answers returned by Excel. The data table in Figure 5-1 answers eleven different what-if questions. The questions pertain to the effect the eleven different interest rates in column D have on the monthly payment, total interest, and total cost.

The macro in Figure 5-2 on page E 5.6, is made up of a series of Visual Basic statements that are executed when you click the New Loan button (Figure 5-1). Visual Basic statements tell Excel to carry out an operation, such as select a range or clear the selection. Creating a macro is a form of **programming**. The programming language you use with Excel 5 is called **Visual Basic for Applications** or **VBA**.

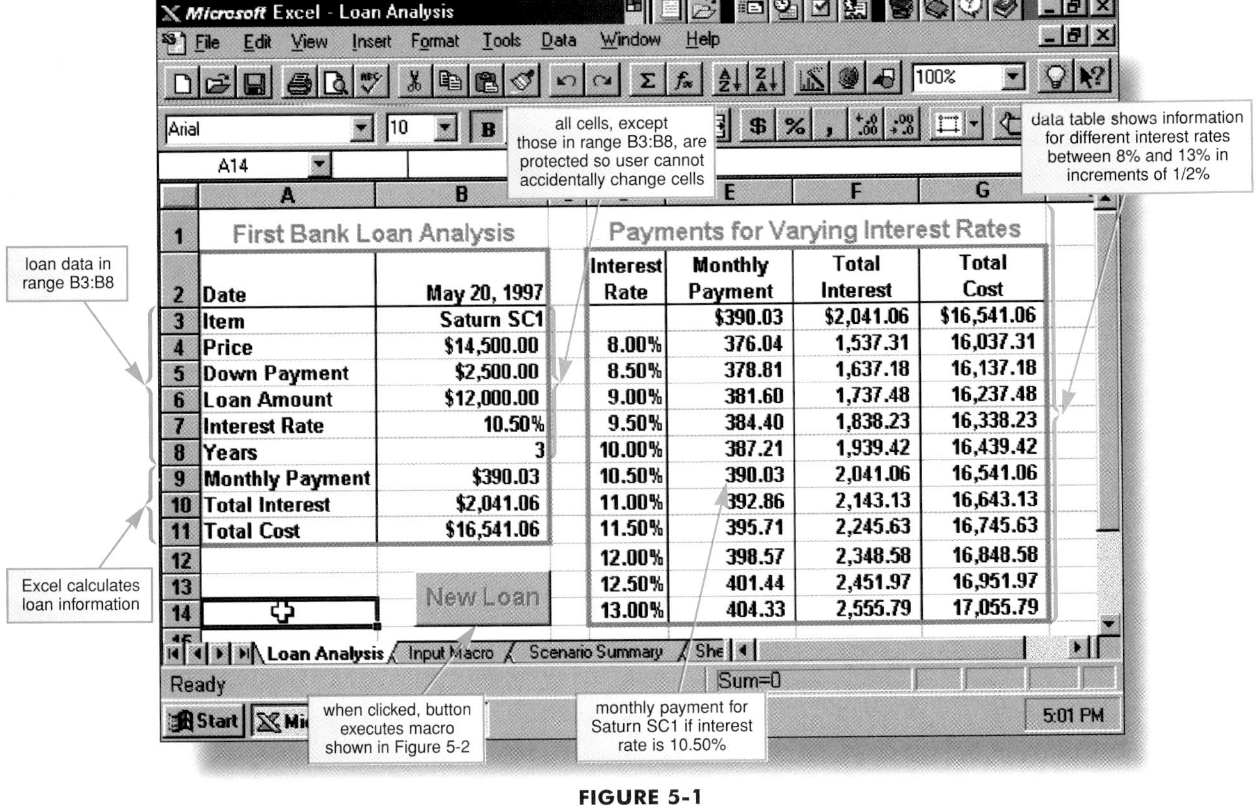

FIGURE 5-1

This project also introduces you to cell protection. Cell protection ensures that you don't inadvertently change values that are critical to the worksheet.

> **More** *About*
> **Solution Templates**
>
> There are a set of ten templates available with Excel that provide solutions to many common business and financial problems. To view the templates, click New on the File menu and then click the Spreadsheet Solutions tab. One template, called Loan Manager, offers a partial solution to the problem being solved in this project.

Project Five – First Bank Loan Analysis

From your meeting with Sueann Weddington you have determined the following need, source of data, calculations, and special requirements.

Need: An easy-to-read worksheet (Figure 5-1) that determines the monthly payment, total interest, and total cost for a loan. A button on the worksheet that executes a macro (Figure 5-2) requesting that the loan officer enter the new loan data. A macro that prints the worksheet in landscape orientation. A worksheet that summarizes what-if questions. The latter is called a **Scenario Summary worksheet**, which allows a user to easily compare various loan data combinations on a separate sheet in the workbook.

Source of Data: The data (item, price of item, down payment, interest rate, and term) is determined by the loan officer and customer when they initially meet to discuss the loan.

Calculations: The following calculations must be made for each loan (see column B in Figure 5-1):

Loan Amount = Price – Down Payment
Use the Excel function PMT to determine the monthly payment
Total Interest = 12 × Years × Monthly Payment – Loan Amount
Total Cost = 12 × Years x Monthly Payment + Down Payment

The data table, which involves calculations, will be created using the Table command on the Data menu

Special Requirements: Protect the worksheet in such a way that the loan officers cannot mistakenly enter data into the wrong cells. Include a macro that automatically prints the loan information in landscape orientation and then resets the print orientation to portrait.

More *About* Visual Basic for Applications

Most analysts agree that Microsoft's plan is to have all of its major applications (Word, Excel, Access, and PowerPoint) using or being controlled by Visual Basic for Applications (Figure 5-2). Thus, what you learn in this project will eventually apply to other applications as well. Today, Visual Basic is the most widely used Windows programming language.

The proposed worksheet (Figure 5-1) that will be built in this project to satisfy Sueann Weddington's needs include four distinct sections: (1) a loan analysis section in the range A1:B11; (2) a button in the range B13:B14, labeled New Loan, which when clicked executes the macro in Figure 5-2; (3) a data table in the range D1:G14 that can be used to show the effect of different interest rates on the monthly payment, total interest, and total cost of the loan; and (4) a Scenario Summary worksheet, which will be shown and discussed later in this project.

The loan analysis section on the left in Figure 5-1 answers the following question: What is the monthly payment (cell B9), total interest (cell B10), and total cost (cell B11) for a Saturn SC1 (cell B3) that costs $14,500.00 (cell B4), if the down payment is $2,500.00 (cell B5), the interest rate is 10.50% (cell B7), and the term of the loan is 3 years (cell B8)? As shown in Figure 5-1, the monthly payment is $390.03 (cell B9), the total interest is $2,041.06 (cell B10), and the total cost of the Saturn SC1 is $16,541.06 (cell B11). Excel determines the monthly payment in cell B9 through the use of the PMT function. Formulas are used to calculate the total interest and total cost. The Loan Analysis section of the worksheet can determine the answers to loan questions for the First Bank loan department as fast as a loan officer can enter the loan data in the range B3:B8.

The function of the button labeled New Loan in the range B13:B14 (Figure 5-1) is to automate the entry of loan data. The button executes the macro in Figure 5-2, which simplifies the loan data entry in cells B3 through B8. Using a button that executes a macro to enter the loan data is especially helpful for users who know little about computers and worksheets. The macro itself is created on a separate sheet in the workbook.

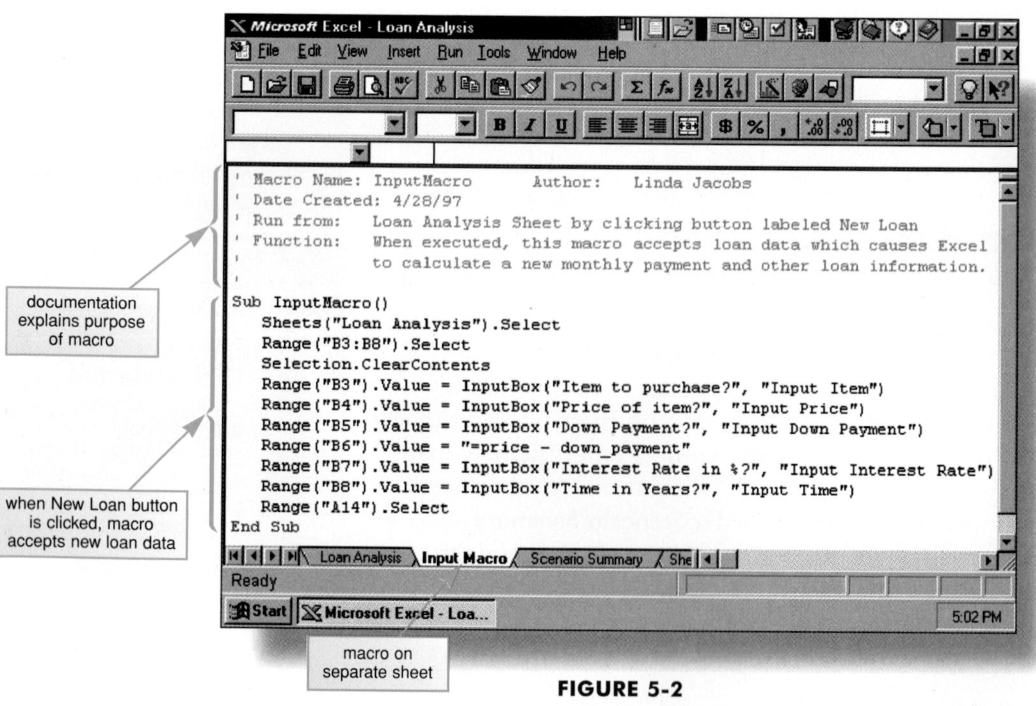

FIGURE 5-2

The third section of the worksheet in Figure 5-1 is the data table on the right side of the screen. Each time a loan officer enters new loan data into the worksheet, the data table recalculates new values for the monthly payment, total interest, and total cost for the different interest rates in column D.

Preparation Steps

The following preparation steps summarize how the workbook will be developed in Project 5.

1. Start Excel.
2. Enter the worksheet title and row titles for the loan analysis section.
3. Save the workbook.
4. Enter the system date and loan data.
5. Create names for the cells with data.
6. Determine the monthly payment, total interest, and total cost.
7. Enter the data table title and column titles for the data table section.
8. Create a series of varying interest rates for the data table.
9. Assign to the data table the formulas that are to be analyzed.
10. Create the data table using the Table command.
11. Create a Visual Basic macro to accept the loan data. Assign the macro to a button.
12. Use the Macro Recorder to create a macro to print the worksheet.
13. Print the worksheet using the recorded macro.
14. Use the Scenarios command to create a Scenario Summary worksheet.
15. Protect the worksheet.
16. Save the workbook and exit Excel.

Starting Excel

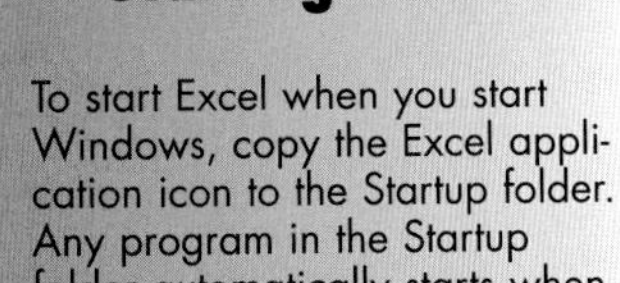

More *About* **Starting Excel**

To start Excel when you start Windows, copy the Excel application icon to the Startup folder. Any program in the Startup folder automatically starts when Windows starts.

To start Excel, Windows 95 must be running. Perform the following steps to start Excel.

TO START EXCEL

Step 1: Click the Start button on the taskbar.
Step 2: Click New Office Document. If necessary, click the General tab in the New dialog box.
Step 3: Double-click the Blank Workbook icon.

An alternative to Steps 1 and 2 is to click the Start a New Document button on the Microsoft Office Shortcut Bar.

Changing the Font of the Entire Worksheet

The first step in this project is to change the font of the entire worksheet to bold. A bold font causes the characters in the worksheet stand out.

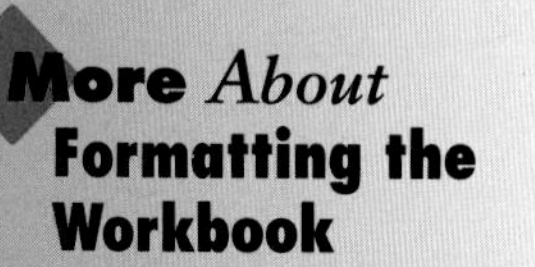

More *About* **Formatting the Workbook**

To assign formats to all the cells in all the worksheets in a workbook, click the Select All button, then right-click a tab and click the Select All Sheets. Next, assign the formats. To deselect the sheets, hold down the SHIFT key and click the Sheet1 tab. You also can select a cell or a range of cells and then select all sheets to assign formats to a cell or a range of cells on all the sheets in a workbook.

TO CHANGE THE FONT OF THE ENTIRE WORKSHEET

Step 1: Click the Select All button immediately above row heading 1 and to the left of column heading A (Figure 5-3).
Step 2: Click the Bold button on the Formatting toolbar.

As you enter text and numbers in the worksheet, they will display in bold.

Entering the Worksheet Title, Row Titles, and System Date

The next step is to enter the Loan Analysis section title, row titles, and system date. To make the worksheet easier to read, the width of columns A and B and the height of rows 1 and 2 will be increased. The worksheet title will also be changed from 10 point to 12 point. The following steps describe how to complete these tasks.

TO ENTER THE WORKSHEET TITLE, ROW TITLES, AND SYSTEM DATE

Step 1: Click cell A1. Type `First Bank Loan Analysis` and then click the enter box or press the ENTER key.
Step 2: With cell A1 active, click the Font Size arrow on the Formatting toolbar and then click 12. Click the Font Color button arrow on the Formatting toolbar and then click the color green (column 2, row 2 on the Font Color palette).
Step 3: Position the mouse pointer on the border between row headings 1 and 2 and drag down until the height of row 1 in the Name box in the formula bar is 21.00.
Step 4: Click cell A2 and type `Date` as the row title.
Step 5: Position the mouse pointer on the border between row headings 2 and 3 and drag until the height of row 2 in the Name box in the formula bar is 27.00.
Step 6: Enter the following row titles:

Cell	Entry	Cell	Entry	Cell	Entry
A3	`Item`	A4	`Price`	A5	`Down Payment`
A6	`Loan Amount`	A7	`Interest Rate`	A8	`Years`
A9	`Monthly Payment`	A10	`Total Interest`	A11	`Total Cost`

Step 7: Select columns A and B. Position the mouse pointer on the border between column headings B and C and drag until the width of column B in the Name box is 16.00.
Step 8: Click cell B2. Type `=now()` and click the enter box or press the ENTER key.
Step 9: With the mouse pointer within cell B2, right-click and then click Format Cells on the shortcut menu. When the Format Cells dialog box displays, click the Number tab, click Date in the Category box, click March 4, 1995 in the Type box, and click the OK button.
Step 10: Click the Save button on the Standard toolbar. Save the workbook using the filename Loan Analysis.

The worksheet title, row titles, and system date display as shown in Figure 5-3.

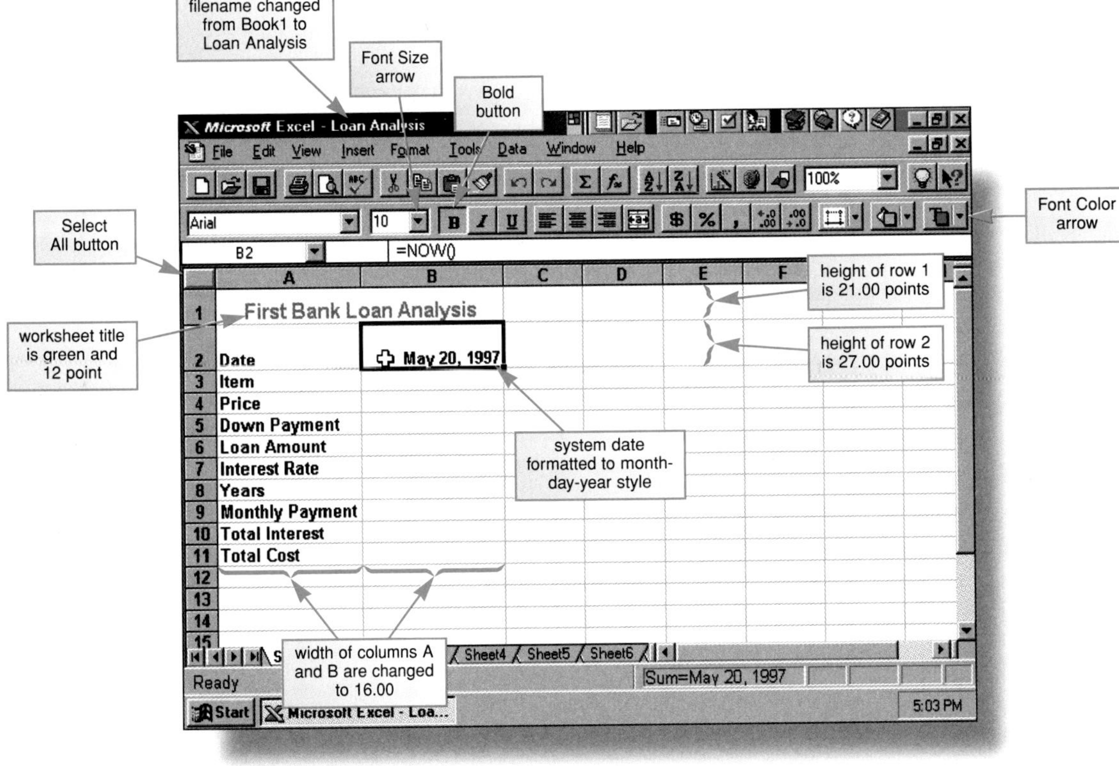

FIGURE 5-3

Outlining and Adding Borders to the Loan Analysis Section of the Worksheet

An outline is used to box an area of the worksheet so that it stands out. In this case, the outline is used to visually separate the loan analysis in the range A1:B11 from the data table in the range D1:G14. Light borders are also used within the outline to further subdivide the loan analysis text and numbers as shown in Figure 5-1 on page E5.5. The following steps describe how to draw an outline and borders.

TO DRAW AN OUTLINE AND BORDERS

Step 1: Select the range A2:B11. With the mouse pointer within the selected range, right-click to display the shortcut menu.

Step 2: Click Format Cells on the shortcut menu. When the Format Cells dialog box displays, click the Border tab (Figure 5-4 on the next page). Click the Color arrow. Click the color green (column 2, row 2 on the palette). Click the regular border in the Style box (column 1, row 3). Click the Outline box in the Border area. Click the OK button.

Step 3: Select the range A2:B2. Click the Border button arrow on the Formatting toolbar. Click the bottom border (column 2, row 1 on the Border palette). Select the range A2:A11. Click the Border button arrow on the Formatting toolbar. Click the right border (column 4, row 1 on the Border palette). Click cell B13 to deselect the range A2:A11.

The loan analysis section is outlined in green. The section has a black border dividing row 2 from the rest of the rows and a right border dividing the two columns (Figure 5-4 on the next page).

More *About* **Shortcut Menus**

Excel requires that you point to the object (cell, range, toolbar) on the screen when you right-click to display the corresponding shortcut menu. For example, if you select the range A1:D5, and right-click with the mouse pointer on cell F10, then the shortcut menu pertains to cell F10, and not the range A1:D5.

More About the Mouse

Are you a lefty? Left-handed users can change the functions of the left and right mouse buttons. Double-click My Computer on the desktop, double-click the Control Panel icon, double-click the Mouse icon in Control Panel, click the Left-handed option, and click the OK button.

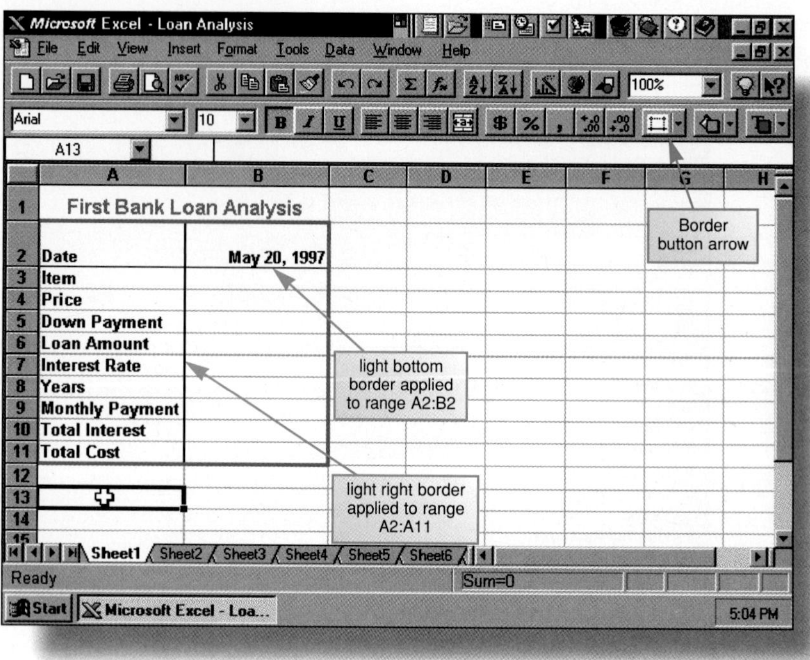

FIGURE 5-4

Entering the Loan Data

According to the worksheet in Figure 5-1 on page E 5.5, the item to be purchased, the price of the item, down payment, interest rate, and number of years until the loan is paid back are entered into cells B3 through B5 and cells B7 and B8. These five values make up the loan data. The following steps describe how to enter the loan data.

TO ENTER THE LOAN DATA

Step 1: Click cell B3. Type `Saturn SC1` and then with cell B3 still active, click the Align Right button on the Formatting toolbar. Click cell B4 and type `14500` as the price of the automobile. Click cell B5 and type `2500` as the down payment.

Step 2: Click cell B7. Type `10.50%` as the interest rate. Click cell B8 and type `3` as the number of years.

The loan data displays in the worksheet as shown in Figure 5-5. The interest rate is formatted to the Percentage style with two decimal places because the percent sign (%) was appended to 10.50 when it was entered into cell B7.

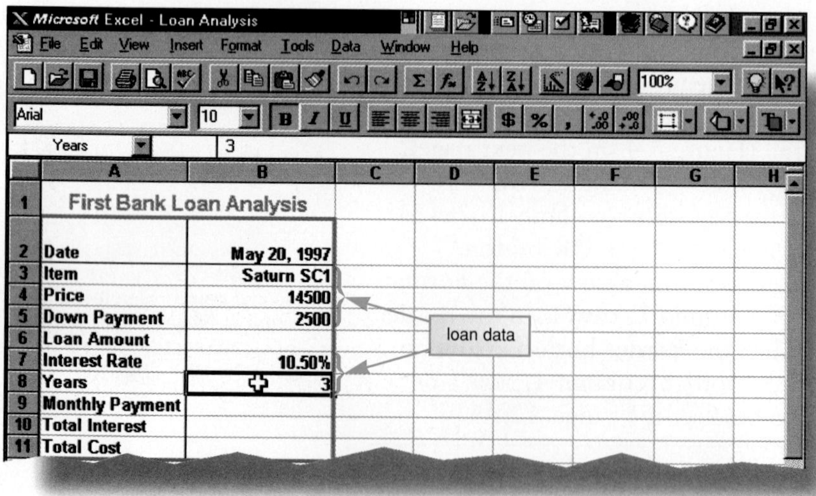

FIGURE 5-5

The four remaining entries in the Loan Analysis section of the worksheet, loan amount (cell B6), monthly payment (cell B9), total interest (cell B10), and total cost (cell B11) require formulas that reference cells B4, B5, B7, and B8. The formulas will be entered referencing names assigned to cells rather than cell references.

Creating Cell Names Based on Row Titles

Naming a cell that you plan to reference in a formula helps make the formula easier to read and remember. For example, the loan amount in cell B6 is equal to the price in cell B4 minus the down payment in cell B5. Therefore, according to what you learned in the earlier projects, you can write the loan amount formula in cell B6 as =B4 - B5. However, by assigning the corresponding row titles in column A as the names of cells B4 and B5, you can write the loan amount formula as =Price – Down_Payment. This formula is clearer and easier to remember than =B4 - B5.

To name cells, you select the range that encompasses the row titles that include the names and the cells to be named (A4:B11) and then use the **Name command** on the Insert menu.

In the following steps, each row title in the range A4 to A11 is assigned to the adjacent cell in column B. Because the date in cell B2 and the item in cell B3 will not be referenced in formulas, it is not necessary to include them in the range.

More About Names

Tired of writing formulas that make no sense when you read them because of cell references? Then the Name command is for you. This command allows you to assign names to cells. You can then use the names, such as Price, rather than the cell reference, such as B4, in the formulas you create.

Steps To Create Cell Names

1 Select the range A4:B11. Point to Name on the Insert menu and then point to Create on the Name submenu.

The range A4:B11 is selected and Excel displays the Name submenu (Figure 5-6).

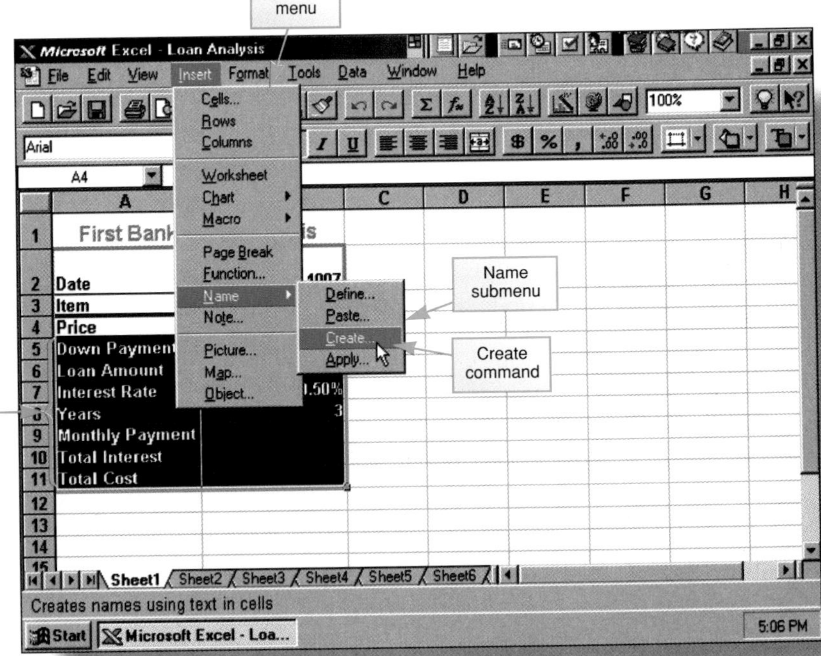

FIGURE 5-6

2 Click Create on the Name submenu.

Excel displays the Create Names dialog box (Figure 5-7). Excel automatically selects the Left Column box in the Create Names dialog box, because the general direction of the range in Step 1 is downward.

3 Click the OK button on the Create Names dialog box.

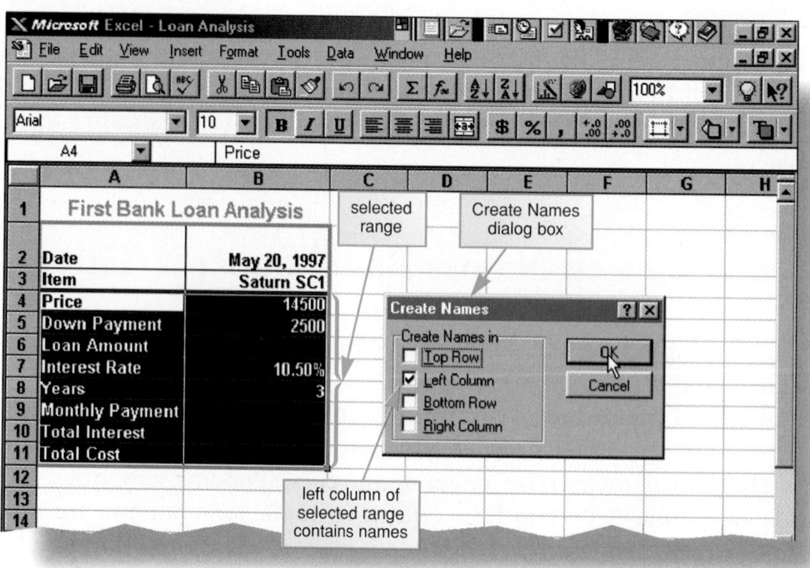

FIGURE 5-7

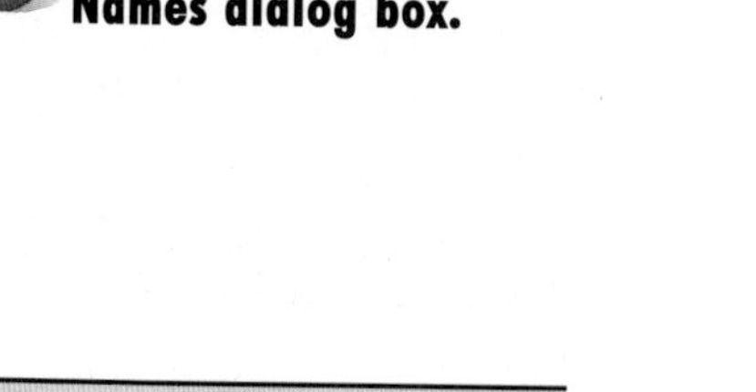

OtherWays

1. Select range, press CTRL+SHIFT+F3

You can now use the names in the range A4:A11 in formulas to reference the adjacent cells in the range B4:B11. Excel is not case-sensitive with respect to names of cells. Hence, you can enter the names of cells in formulas in uppercase or lowercase. Some names, such as Down Payment in cell A5, include a space because they are made up of two words. To use a name in a formula that is made up of two or more words, you replace any space with the underscore character (_). For example, Down Payment is written as down_payment when you want to reference the adjacent cell B5.

Consider these three additional points regarding the assignment of names to cells:

1. A name can be a minimum of one character or a maximum of 255 characters.
2. If you want to assign a name that is not a text item in an adjacent cell, use the Define command on the Name submenu in Figure 5-6 or select the cell or range and type the name in the Name box in the formula bar.
3. The worksheet names display in alphabetical order in the Name box when you click the Name box arrow (Figure 5-8).

More *About* **the Length of Names**

Although names of cells can be up to 255 characters, you want to make them shorter because formulas are also limited to 255 characters.

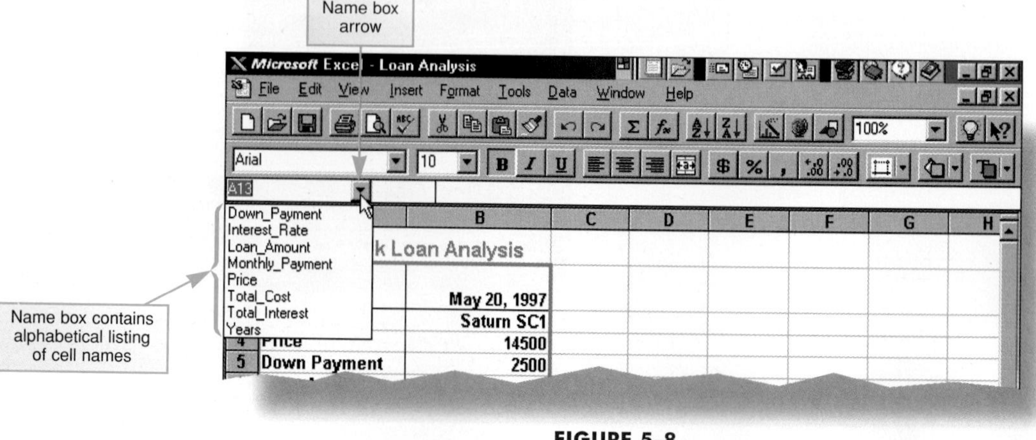

FIGURE 5-8

Using the Name Box and Point Mode to Enter a Formula

The next step is to enter the formula =Price – Down_Payment in cell B6. You can enter the formula as you have in the previous projects by using the keyboard and Point mode. However, the Name box offers an alternative to Point mode which allows you to point to the names of cells, rather than to the cells themselves. The following steps show how to use Point mode and the Name box to enter the formula =Price – Down_Payment in cell B6.

More *About* **Names**

You can create row and column names at the same time if you have a worksheet with column titles and row titles. Simply select the column titles and row titles along with the cells to name, then click both Top Row and Left Column in the Create Names dialog box. Finally click the OK button. Then you can use the column title and row title separated by a space to refer to the intersecting cell.

To Enter the Loan Amount Formula Using the Name Box

1 **Click cell B6. Type = and then click the Name box arrow in the formula bar.**

The Name box displays with Loan_Amount selected because the cell it names (cell B6) is the active cell (Figure 5-9).

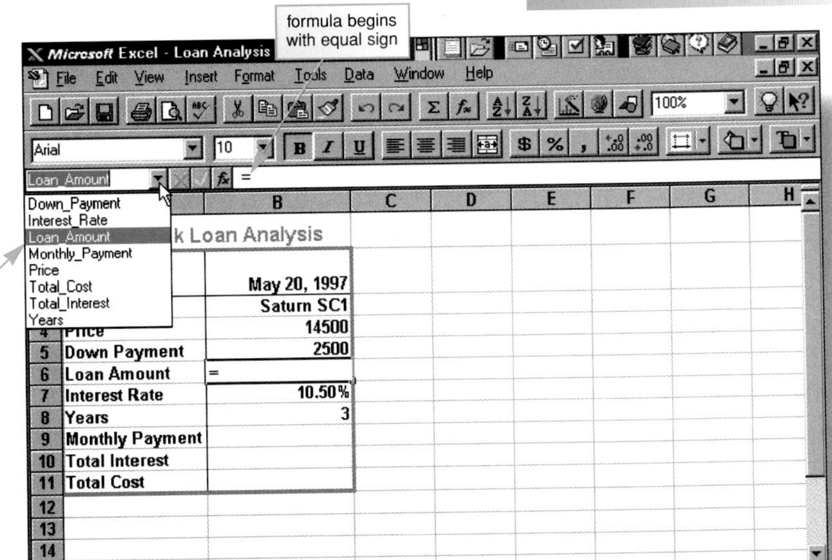

FIGURE 5-9

2 **Click the name Price in the Name drop-down list box. Press the SPACEBAR, type - (minus sign), and press the SPACEBAR. Click the Name box arrow.**

The first term in the formula displays in the formula bar and in cell B6 (Figure 5-10). Pressing the spacebar inserts spaces before and after the minus sign for readability.

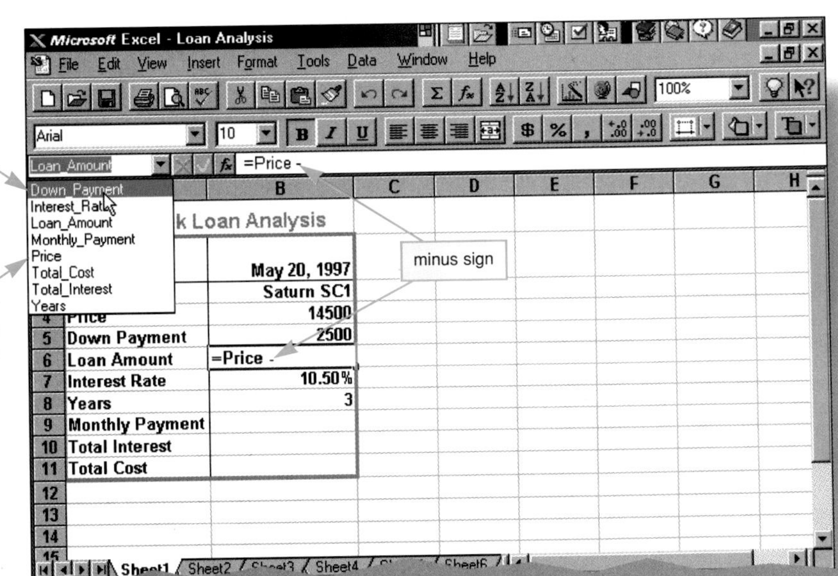

FIGURE 5-10

3 Click the name Down_Payment in the Name drop-down list box. Click the enter box or press the ENTER key.

Excel assigns the formula =Price – Down_Payment to cell B6 and displays the result of the formula (12000) in cell B6 (Figure 5-11).

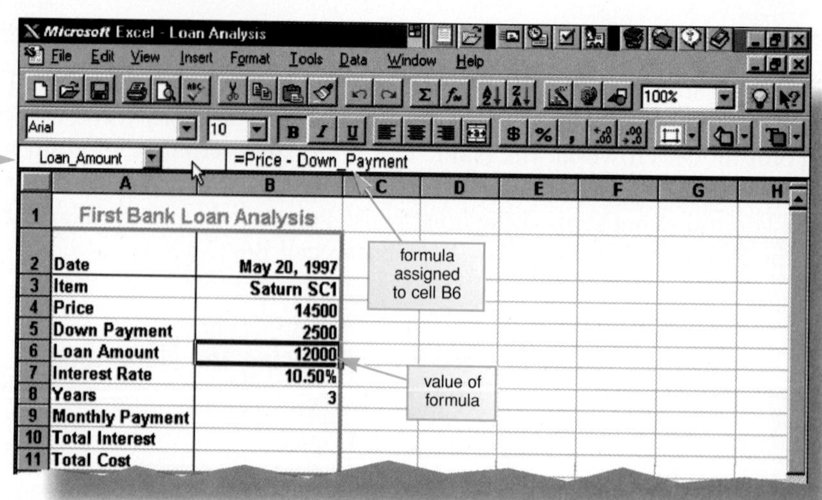

FIGURE 5-11

OtherWays

1. Press F3 to enter names in formula
2. Type formula using cell references, rather than using cell names

When cell B6 is selected, Excel displays the name of the cell (Loan_Amount) in the Name box rather than the cell reference B6. Besides using the Name box to assign names in formulas, you can click a name in the Name drop-down list box to activate the cell it names. For example, to activate cell B9, click Monthly_Payment in the Name drop-down list box.

Formatting to Currency Style with a Floating Dollar Sign

The nonadjacent ranges B4:B6 and B9:B11 should be formatted to the Currency style with a floating dollar sign. The following steps describe how to accomplish this task.

To Format to Currency Style with a Floating Dollar Sign

1 Select the range B4:B6. Hold down the CTRL key and select the range B9:B11. With the mouse pointer within one of the selected ranges, right-click to display the shortcut menu. Click Format Cells on the shortcut menu. When the Format Cells dialog box displays, click the Number tab. Click Currency in the Category box and then click the fourth format in the Negative Numbers box.

The Format Cells dialog box displays as shown in Figure 5-12.

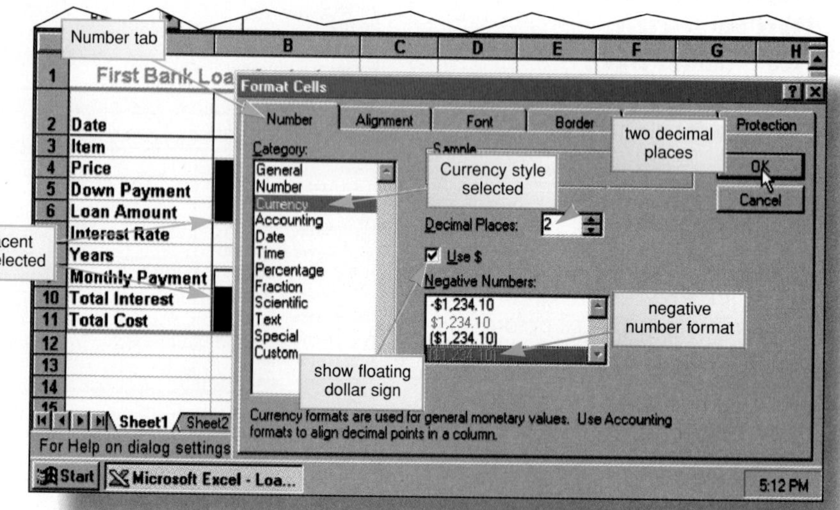

FIGURE 5-12

2 Click the OK button on the Format Cells dialog box.

The price, down payment, and loan amount in the range B4:B6 have been formatted to Currency style and display as shown in Figure 5-13. When numbers display in the range B9:B11 later, they will display using the Currency style.

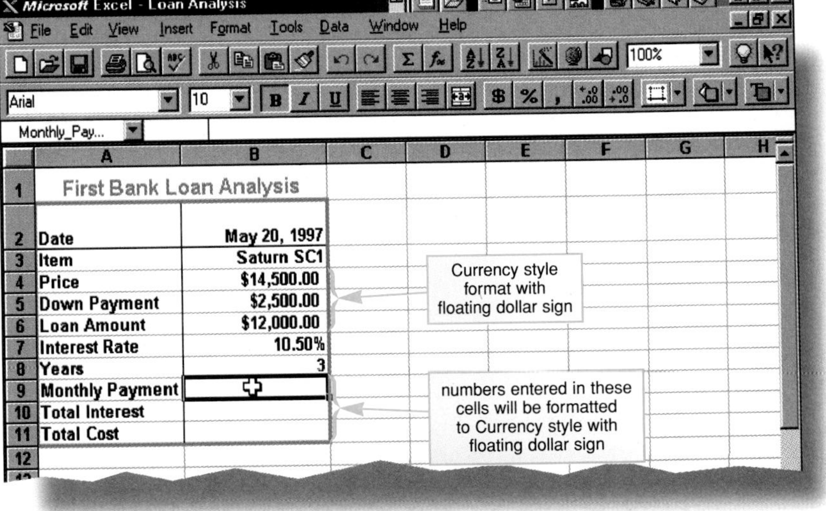

FIGURE 5-13

OtherWays

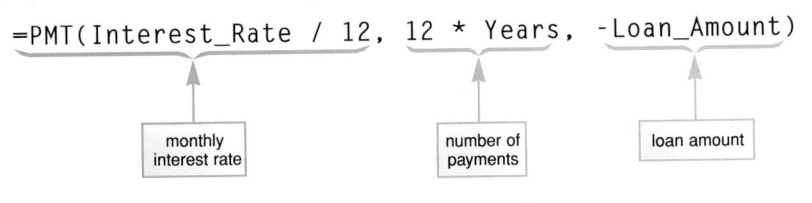

1. On Format menu click Cells, click Number tab, click Currency in the Category list box, click desired negative number format, click OK button
2. Press CTRL+1, click Number tab, click Currency in the Category list box, click desired negative number format, click OK button
3. Press CTRL+SHIFT+$

An alternative to formatting the numbers to the Currency style as described in the previous steps is to enter the numbers in the desired format. For example, the number 18500 could have been entered earlier as $18,500.00 and the Currency style with a floating dollar sign would have been automatically assigned to the cell. The same can be said for the remaining dollar amounts entered earlier. A third alternative is to enter the dollar amount in cell B4 with the dollar sign and comma, and then use the Format Painter button on the Standard toolbar to format the remaining cells containing dollar amounts.

Determining the Monthly Payment

You can use Excel's PMT function to determine the monthly payment (cell B9) on the basis of the loan amount (cell B6), the interest rate (cell B7), and the term of the loan (cell B8). The general form of the **PMT function** is =PMT(rate, payments, loan amount)where rate is the interest rate per payment period, payments is the number of payments, and loan amount is the amount of the loan. Rate, payments, and loan amount are called **arguments**.

In the worksheet in Figure 5-13, cell B7 is equal to the annual interest rate. However, loan institutions calculate the interest, which is their profit, on a monthly basis. Thus, the first value in the PMT function is Interest_Rate / 12 (cell B7 divided by 12) rather than Interest_Rate (cell B7). The number of payments (or periods) is equal to 12 * Years (12 times cell B8) because there are 12 months, or 12 payments, per year.

Excel considers the value returned by the PMT function to be a debit and, therefore, returns a negative number as the monthly payment. To display the monthly payment as a positive number precede the loan amount with a negative sign. Thus, the loan amount is equal to -Loan_Amount. The PMT function for cell B9 becomes the following:

```
=PMT(Interest_Rate / 12, 12 * Years, -Loan_Amount)
```

monthly interest rate — number of payments — loan amount

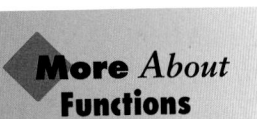

More About Functions

Functions operate on data, called arguments, that are inserted between parentheses. Functions return to a cell a value, much the same way a formula returns a value.

The following steps use the PMT function to determine the monthly payment in cell B7.

TO ENTER THE PMT FUNCTION

Step 1: Click cell B9. Type `=pmt(interest_rate / 12, 12 * years, -loan_amount)` as the function.

Step 2: Click the enter box on the formula bar or press the ENTER key.

Excel displays the monthly payment $390.03 in cell B9 (Figure 5-14) for a loan amount of $12,000.00 (cell B6) with an annual interest rate of 10.50% (cell B7) for three years (cell B8). With cell B9 active, the PMT function displays in the formula bar.

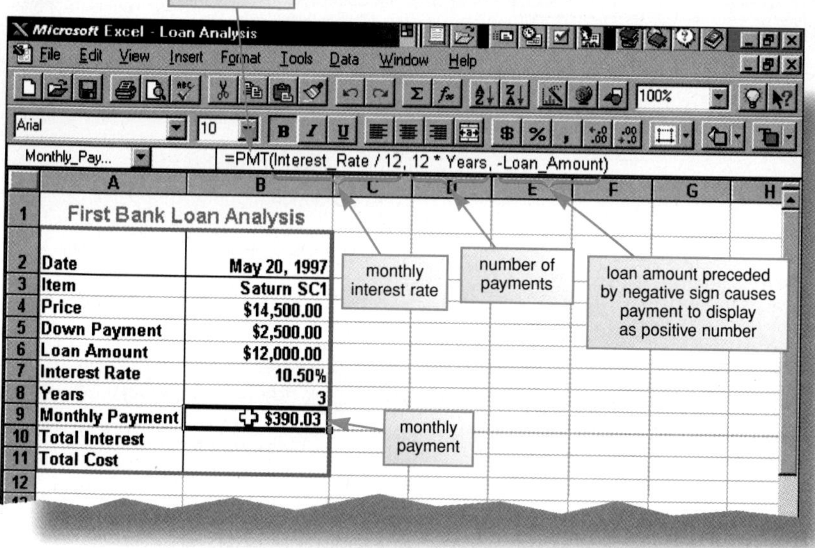

FIGURE 5-14

The PMT function could have been entered using the Function Wizard button on the Standard toolbar. Furthermore, Point mode could have been used in Step 1 along with the Name box in the formula bar to select the cells representing the rate, payment, and loan amount.

Besides the PMT function, Excel has over 50 additional **financial functions** to help you solve the most complex finance problems. These functions save you from entering long, complicated formulas to obtain the results you require. Table 5-1 summarizes three of the most frequently used financial functions.

Table 5-1

FUNCTION	DESCRIPTION
FV(rate, periods, payment)	Returns the future value of an investment based on periodic, constant payments, and a constant interest rate
PMT(rate, periods, loan amount)	Returns the periodic payment of a loan
PV(rate, periods, payment)	Returns the present value of an investment made up of a series of payments

Determining the Total Interest and Total Cost

The next step is to determine the total interest (the loan institution's profit) and the borrower's total cost of the item being purchased. The total interest (cell B10) is equal to:

12 * Years * Monthly_Payment - Loan_Amount

The total cost of the item to be purchased (cell B11) is equal to:

12 * Years * Monthly_Payment + Down_Payment

To enter the total interest and total cost formulas, perform the following steps.

TO DETERMINE THE TOTAL INTEREST AND TOTAL COST, AND SAVE THE WORKBOOK

Step 1: Click cell B10. Use Point mode and the Name box to enter the formula `=12 * years * monthly_payment - loan_amount` to determine the total interest.

Step 2: Click cell B11. Use Point mode and the Name box to enter the formula `=12 * years * monthly_payment + down_payment` to determine the total cost.

Step 3: Click the Save button on the Standard toolbar to save the workbook using the filename Loan Analysis.

Excel displays a total interest of $2,041.06 in cell B10 and a total cost of $16,541.06 in cell B11 for the Saturn SC1 (Figure 5-15).

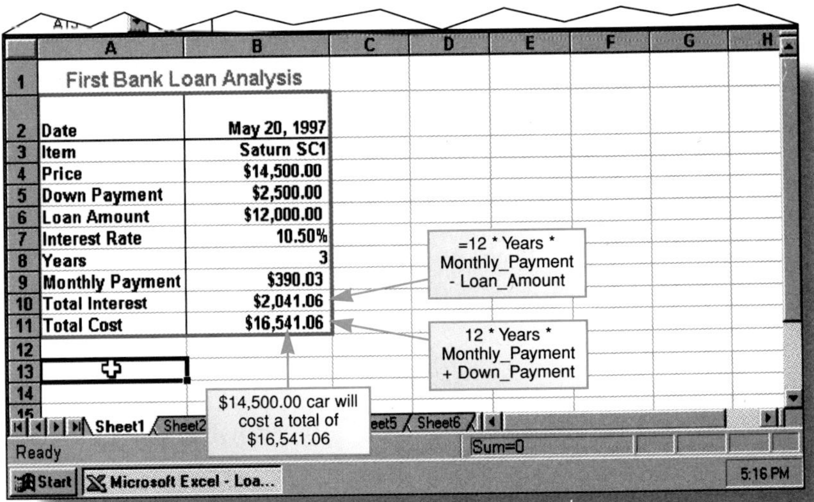

FIGURE 5-15

With the Loan Analysis section of the worksheet complete, you can determine the monthly payment, total interest, and total cost for any reasonable loan data. After entering the data table in the next section, alternative loan data will be entered to illustrate Excel's recalculation feature.

Using a Data Table to Analyze Worksheet Data

The next step is to build the Data Table section of the worksheet in the range D1:G14. A **data table** is a range of cells that shows the answers to formulas in which different values have been substituted.

You have already seen that if a value is changed in a cell referenced elsewhere in a formula in the worksheet, Excel immediately recalculates and stores the new value in the cell assigned the formula. What if you want to compare the results of the formula for several different values? It would be unwieldy to write down or remember all the answers to the what-if questions. A data table becomes useful in this situation because it will automatically organize the answers in the worksheet for you.

Data tables are built in an unused area of the worksheet. You may vary one or two values and display the results of the specified formulas in table form. The right side of Figure 5-16 illustrates the makeup of a one-input data table. With a **one-input data table**, you vary one cell reference (in this project, cell B7, the interest rate) and Excel fills the table with the results of one or more formulas (in this, project monthly payment, total interest, and total cost).

More About Data Tables

Data tables have one purpose, and that is to organize the answers to what-if questions. You can create two kinds of data tables. The first type involves changing one input value to see the resulting effect on one or more formulas. The second type involves changing two input values to see the resulting effect on one formula.

More *About* Data Tables

The data table you see in Figure 5-17 is relatively small. You can continue the series of percents to the bottom of the worksheet and insert additional formulas to the right in row 3 to create as large a data table as you want.

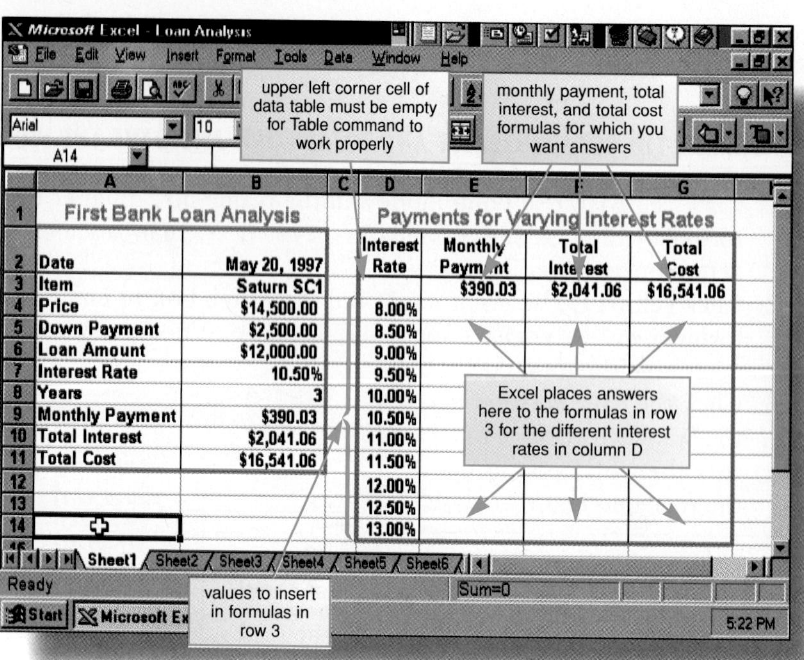

FIGURE 5-16

The interest rates that will be used to analyze the loan formulas in this project range from 8.00% to 13.00% in increments of 0.5%. The data table (Figure 5-17) illustrates the impact of varying the interest rate on three formulas: the monthly payment (cell B9), total interest paid (cell B10), and the total cost of the item to be purchased (cell B11).

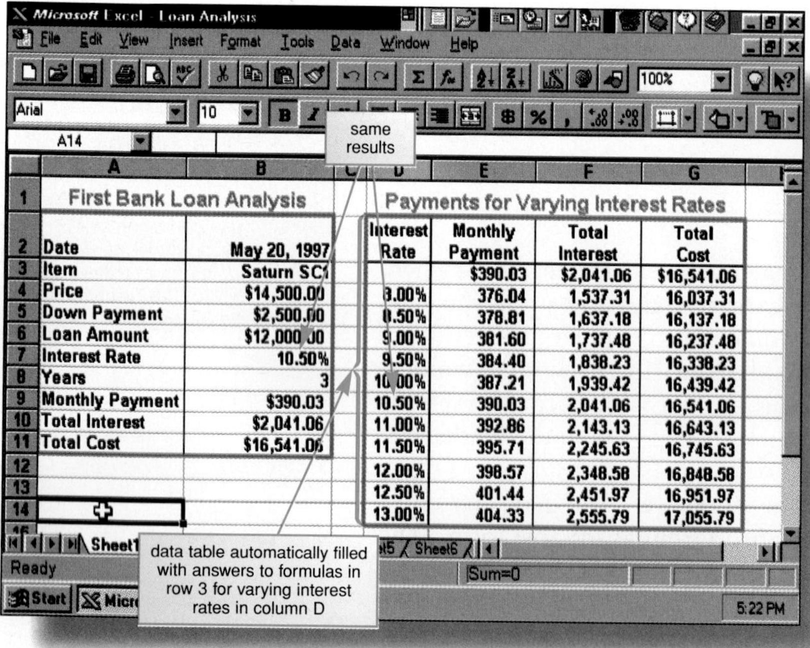

FIGURE 5-17

The following sections use these steps to construct the data table in Figure 5-17 as follows: (1) adjust the widths of columns C through G; (2) enter the data table title and column titles in the range D1:G2; (3) use the data fill handle to enter the varying interest rates in column D; (4) enter the formulas in the range E3:G3 for which the data table is to determine answers; (5) use the **Table command** on the **Data menu** to define the range D3:G14 as a data table and identify the interest rate in cell B7 as the **input cell**, the one that varies; and (6) outline the data table to highlight it.

In the steps that follow, the columns are set to specific widths so the data table will fit in the same window with the Loan Analysis section. You may have to adjust the column widths after the numbers and text are assigned to the cells. Numbers that are larger than their cell will display as number signs (#) across the cell.

When you design a worksheet, you make the best possible estimate of column widths and then adjust them as required.

TO ENTER THE DATA TABLE TITLE AND COLUMN TITLES

Step 1: Use the mouse to change the widths of columns C through G as follows: C = 3.00; D = 6. 71; and E, F, and G = 11.29.

Step 2: Click cell D1 and type `Payments for Varying Interest Rates` as the data table title.

Step 3: With cell D1 active, click the Font Size arrow on the Formatting toolbar and choose 12. Click the Font Color button on the Formatting toolbar to change the font to the color green.

Step 4: Select the range D2:G2 and enter the following values:

Cell	Entry
D2	`Interest` ALT+ENTER `Rate`
E2	`Monthly` ALT+ENTER `Payment`
F2	`Total` ALT+ENTER `Interest`
G2	`Total` ALT+ENTER `Cost`

Pressing ALT+ENTER *instructs Excel to continue the entry on the next line of the cell.*

Step 5: With the range D2:G2 selected, click the Center button on the Formatting toolbar.

The data table title and column headings display as shown in Figure 5-18.

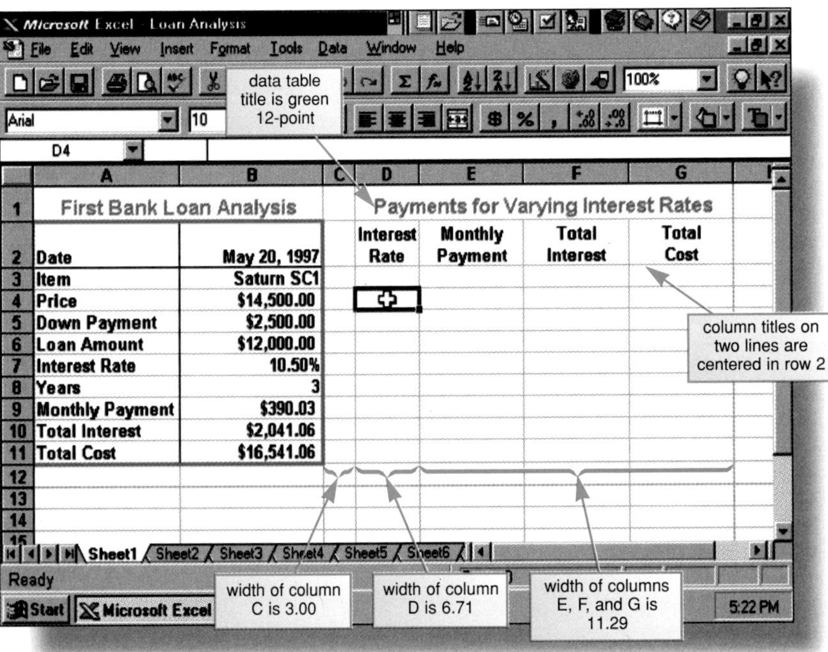

FIGURE 5-18

More *About* **Data Tables**

The most common error made by beginning Excel users when creating a one-input data table is to not leave the upper left cell in the data table blank (see Figure 5-16). A value in this cell tells Excel that you are trying to create a two-input data table, which requires a formula in the upper left cell of the data table rather than a number.

Creating a Percent Series Using the Fill Handle

The next step is to create the percent series in column D using the fill handle.

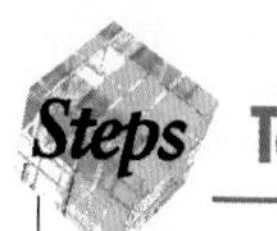

To Create a Percent Series Using the Fill Handle

1. **Click cell D4 and enter** `8.00%` **as the first number in the series. Select cell D5 and enter** `8.50%` **as the second number of the series.**

2. **Select the range D4:D5 and point to the fill handle. Drag the fill handle down to cell D14 and hold.**

   Excel shades the border of the paste area (Figure 5-19).

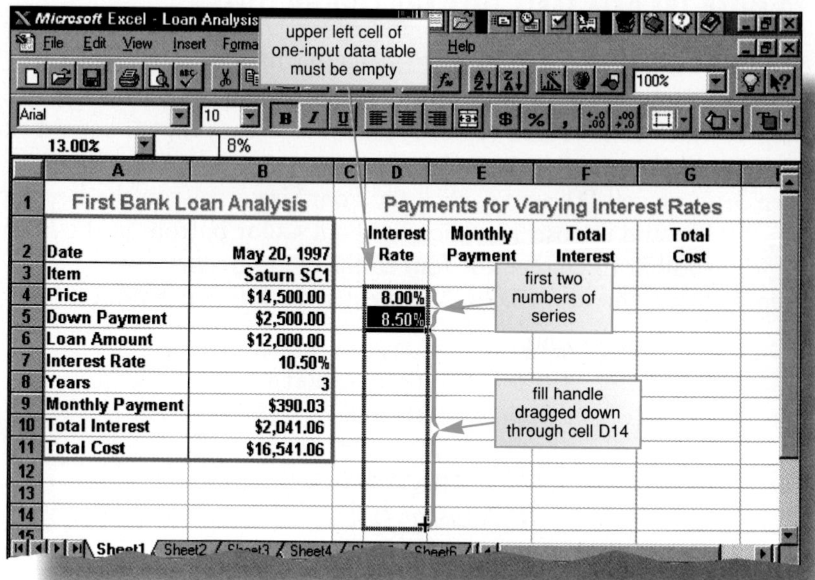

FIGURE 5-19

3. **Release the mouse button. Click cell E3.**

   Excel generates the series of numbers 8.00% to 13.00% in increments of 0.5% in the range D4:D14 (Figure 5-20).

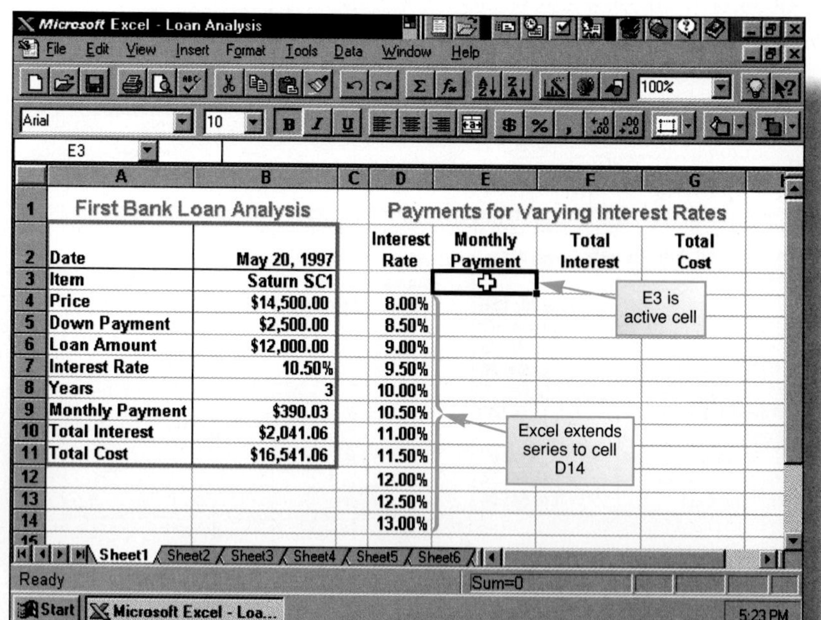

FIGURE 5-20

OtherWays

1. Enter initial values, select initial values and range to fill, click Fill on Edit menu, click Series, click Columns, click Linear, click OK button
2. Enter initial values, select initial values, right-drag fill handle through range to fill, click Fill Series on shortcut menu

The percents in column D are the values Excel uses to compute the formulas entered at the top of the data table in row 3. Notice that the series beginning with 8.00% in column D was not started in cell D3 because the cell immediately above the series and to the left of the formulas in the data table (Figure 5-16 on page E 5.18) must be empty for a one-input data table.

Entering the Formulas in the Data Table

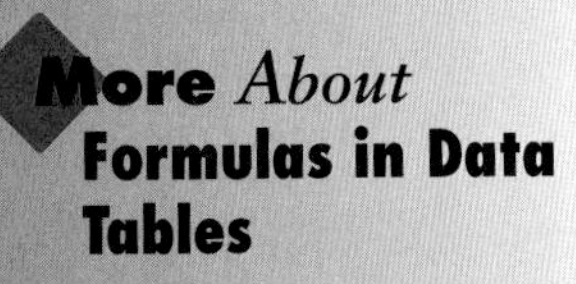

More *About* **Formulas in Data Tables**

Any experienced Excel user will tell you that to enter the formulas at the top of the data table, you should enter the cell reference or name of the cell preceded by an equal sign. This ensures that if you change the original formula in the worksheet, Excel will automatically change the corresponding formula in the data table.

The next step in creating the data table is to enter the three formulas in cells E3, F3, and G3. The three formulas are the same as the monthly payment formula in cell B9, the total interest formula in cell B10, and the total cost formula in cell B11.

Excel provides three ways to enter these formulas in the data table: (1) retype the formulas in cells E3, F3, and G3; (2) copy cells B9, B10, and B11 to cells E3, F3, and G3, respectively; or (3) enter the formulas =Monthly_Payment in cell E3, =Total_Interest in cell F3, and enter =Total_Cost in cell G3. Recall that earlier in this project cells B9 through B11 were assigned names.

Using the names preceded by an equal sign to define the formulas in the data table has two advantages: (1) it is more efficient; and (2) if you change any of the formulas in the range B9:B11, the formulas at the top of the data table are automatically updated. The following steps describe how to enter and format the formulas in the data table.

TO ENTER AND FORMAT THE FORMULAS IN THE DATA TABLE

Step 1: With cell E3 active, use Point mode and the Name box to enter `=Monthly_Payment` and then press the RIGHT ARROW key.
Step 2: Use Point mode and the Name box to enter `=Total_Interest` and then press the RIGHT ARROW key.
Step 3: Use Point mode and the Name box to enter `=Total_Cost` in cell E5.
Step 4: Select cell B4. Click the Format Painter button on the Standard toolbar. Drag across the range E3:G3. Release the mouse button.

The results of the formulas display in the range E3:G3 (Figure 5-21).

The formulas could have been entered using cell references rather than cell names

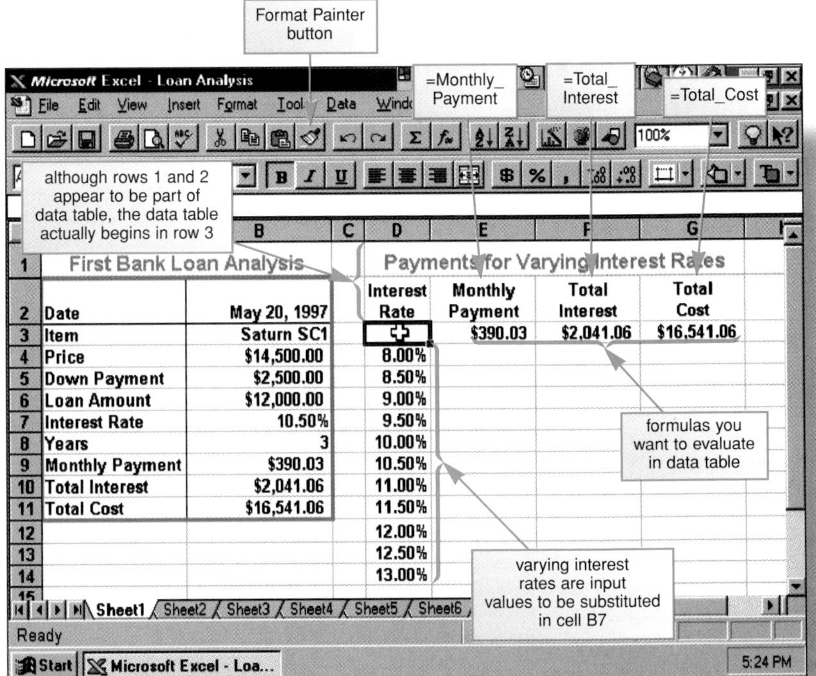

FIGURE 5-21

Defining the Data Table

After creating the interest rates in column D and assigning the formulas in row 3, the next task is to define the range D3:G14 as a data table, as shown in the steps on the next page.

To Define a Range as a Data Table

1 **Select the range D3:G14. Click the Data menu and then point to Table.**

*Excel displays the Data menu (Figure 5-22). The column headings in the range D1:G2 are **NOT** part of the data table, even though they identify the columns in the table.*

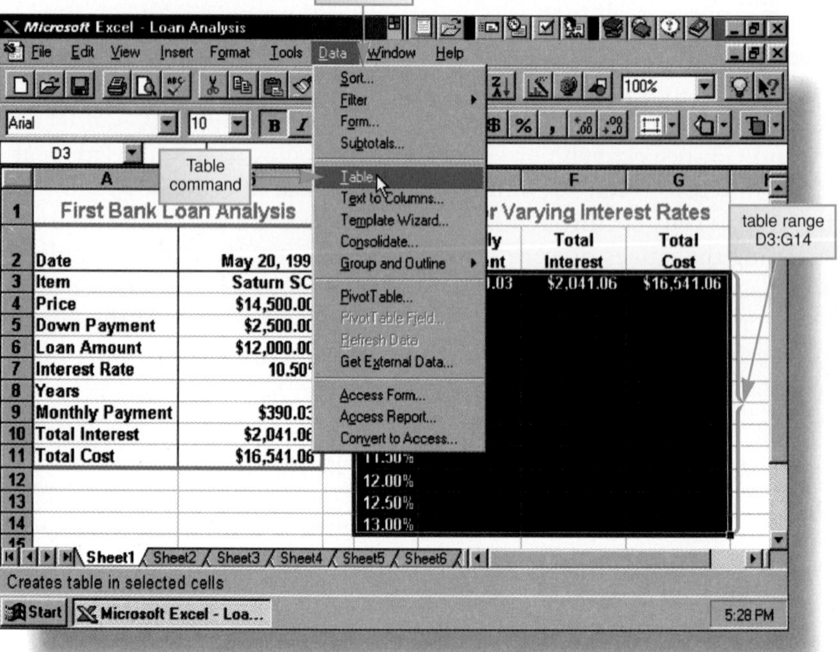

FIGURE 5-22

Click Table on the Data menu. When the Table dialog box displays, click the Column Input Cell box. Click cell B7 or type B7 **to identify the input cell.**

*A marquee surrounds the selected input cell B7 and Excel assigns cell B7 to the Column Input Cell box on the **Table dialog box** (Figure 5-23).*

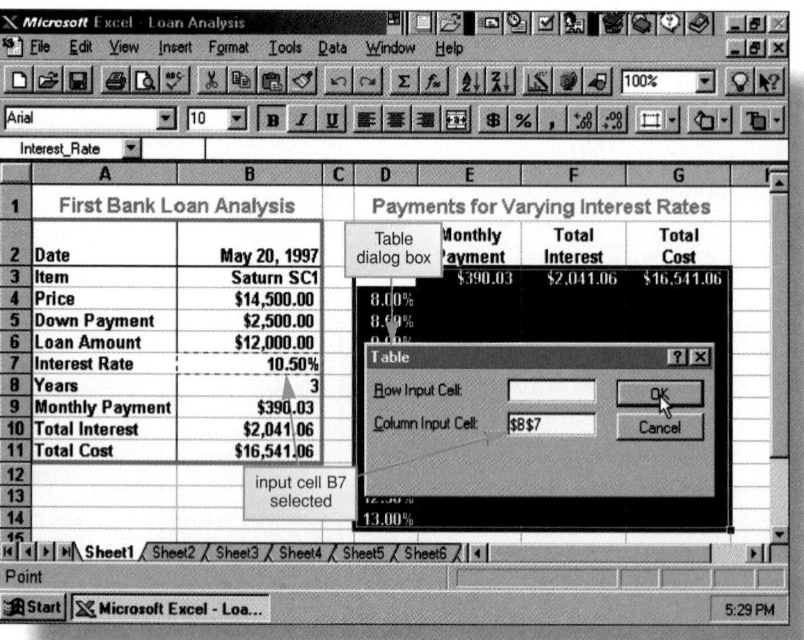

FIGURE 5-23

3 Click the OK button.

Excel immediately fills the data table by calculating the three formulas at the top of the data table for each interest rate in column D (Figure 5-24).

	A	B	C	D	E	F	G
1	First Bank Loan Analysis			Payments for Varying Interest Rates			
2	Date	May 20, 1997		Interest Rate	Monthly Payment	Total Interest	Total Cost
3	Item	Saturn SC1			$390.03	$2,041.06	$16,541.06
4	Price	$14,500.00		8.00%	376.0363855	1537.309879	16037.30988
5	Down Payment	$2,500.00		8.50%	378.8104491	1637.176167	16137.17617
6	Loan Amount	$12,000.00		9.00%	381.5967919	1737.484509	16237.48451
7	Interest Rate	10.50%		9.50%	384.3953969	1838.234288	16338.23429
8	Years	3		10.00%	387.2062463	1939.424868	16439.42487
9	Monthly Payment	$390.03		10.50%	390.0293221	2041.055594	16541.05559
10	Total Interest	$2,041.06		11.00%	392.8646054	2143.125795	16643.12579
11	Total Cost	$16,541.06		11.50%	395.7120772	2245.634779	16745.63478
12				12.00%	398.5717178	2348.581839	16848.58184
13				12.50%	401.4435069	2451.966249	16951.96625
14				13.00%	404.327424	2555.787265	17055.78727

FIGURE 5-24

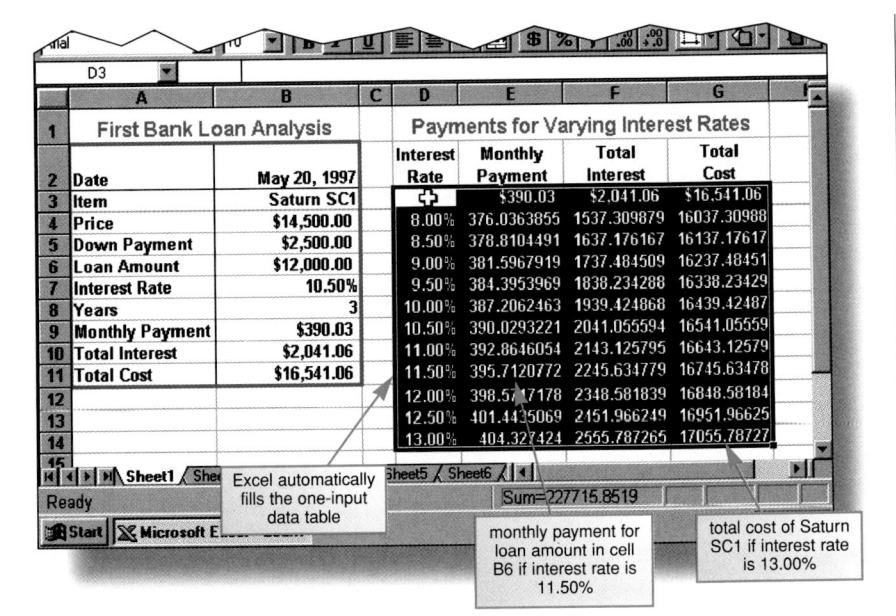

In Figure 5-24, the data table displays the monthly payment, total interest, and total cost for the interest rates in column D. For example, if the interest rate is 9.00% (cell D6) rather than 10.50% (cell B7), the monthly payment is $381.60 (cell E6) rather than $390.03 (cell B9). If the interest rate is 13.00% (cell D14), then the total cost of the Saturn SC1 is approximately $17,055.79 (cell G14), rather than $16,541.06 (cell B11). Thus, a 2.50% increase in the interest rate results in a $514.73 increase in the total cost of the Saturn SC1.

Formatting the Data Table

The next step is to format the data table to improve its readability. Perform these tasks to outline and format the data table and save the workbook.

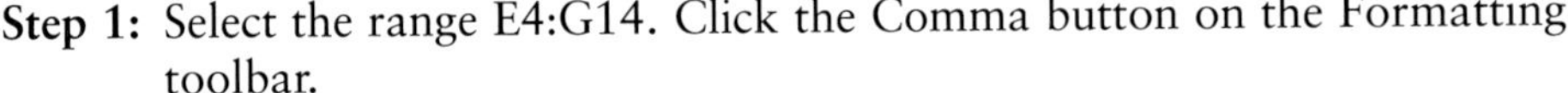

TO OUTLINE AND FORMAT THE DATA TABLE AND SAVE THE WORKBOOK

Step 1: Select the range E4:G14. Click the Comma button on the Formatting toolbar.
Step 2: Select the range D2:G14. Right-click the selected range.
Step 3: Click Format Cells on the shortcut menu. When the Format Cells dialog box displays, click the Border tab.
Step 4: Click the Color button arrow on the Formatting toolbar. Select green (column 2, row 2 on the palette). Click the regular border in the Style box (column 1, row 3). Click Outline in the Border box. Click the OK button.
Step 5: Select the range D2:G2. Click the Borders button arrow on the Formatting toolbar. Click the light bottom border (column 2, row 1 on the palette).
Step 6: Select the range D2:F14. Click the Borders button arrow on the Formatting toolbar. Click the light right border (column 4, row 1 on the palette).

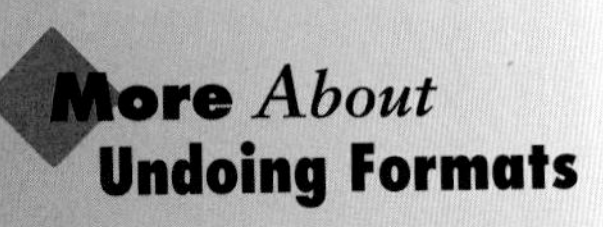

More *About* Undoing Formats

If you started to assign formats to a range and then realize you made a mistake and want to start over, select the range, click Style on the Format menu, click Normal in the Style Name drop-down list box, and click the OK button.

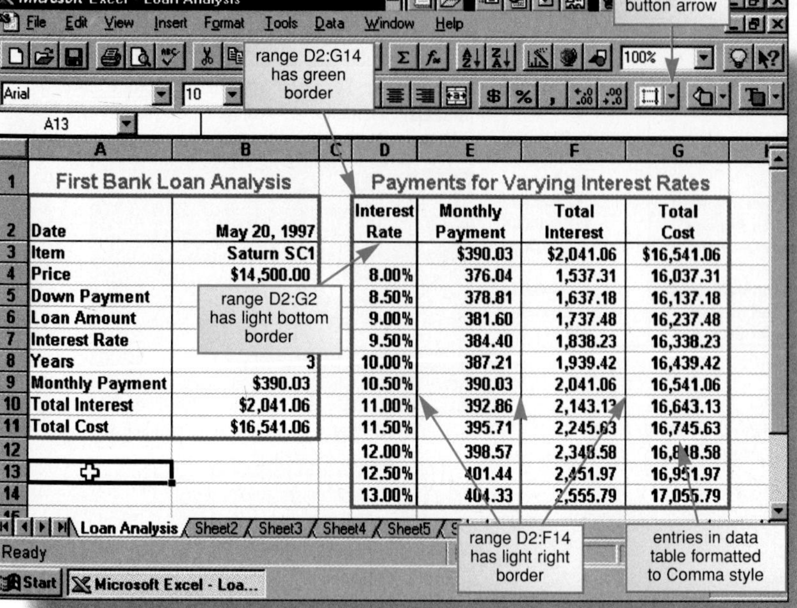

FIGURE 5-25

Step 7: Double click the Sheet1 tab. When the Rename Sheet dialog box displays, type `Loan Analysis` and then click the OK button.

Step 8: Click the Save button on the Standard toolbar to save the workbook using the filename Loan Analysis.

The worksheet displays as shown in Figure 5-25.

The following list details important points you should know about data tables:

1. The input-cell must be a cell reference in the formula(s) you are analyzing.
2. You can have as many active data tables in a worksheet as you want.
3. You delete a data table as you would any other item on a worksheet. That is, you select the data table and then press the DELETE key.
4. For a data table with one varying value, the cell in the upper left corner of the table (cell D3 in Figure 5-25) must be empty.
5. To add formulas to a one-input data table, enter them in adjacent cells in the same row as the current formulas (row 3 in Figure 5-25) and define the entire range as a data table by using the Table command on the Data menu.
6. A one-input data table can vary only one value (such as the interest rate), but can analyze as many formulas as you desire.

Entering New Loan Data

With the loan analysis and data table sections of the worksheet complete, you can use them to generate new loan information. For example, assume you want to purchase a $198,250.00 house. You have $38,500.00 for a down payment and want the loan for 15 years. First Bank is currently charging 8.50% interest for a 15-year loan. The following steps show how to enter the new loan data.

TO ENTER NEW LOAN DATA

Step 1: Click cell B3. Type `House` and press the DOWN ARROW key.
Step 2: In cell B4, type `198250` and press the DOWN ARROW key.
Step 3: In cell B5, type `38500` and press the DOWN ARROW key twice.
Step 4: In cell B7, type `8.50%` and press the DOWN ARROW key.
Step 5: In cell B8, type `15` and click the enter box or press the ENTER key. Click cell A14.

Excel automatically recalculates the loan information in cells B6, B9, B10, B11, and the data table (Figure 5-26).

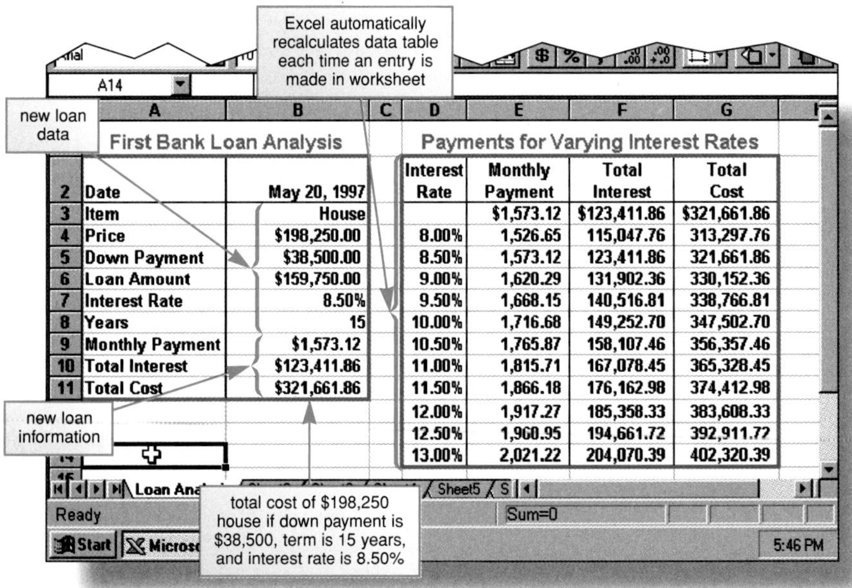

	A	B
1	First Bank Loan Analysis	
2	Date	May 20, 1997
3	Item	House
4	Price	$198,250.00
5	Down Payment	$38,500.00
6	Loan Amount	$159,750.00
7	Interest Rate	8.50%
8	Years	15
9	Monthly Payment	$1,573.12
10	Total Interest	$123,411.86
11	Total Cost	$321,661.86

Payments for Varying Interest Rates

Interest Rate	Monthly Payment	Total Interest	Total Cost
	$1,573.12	$123,411.86	$321,661.86
8.00%	1,526.65	115,047.76	313,297.76
8.50%	1,573.12	123,411.86	321,661.86
9.00%	1,620.29	131,902.36	330,152.36
9.50%	1,668.15	140,516.81	338,766.81
10.00%	1,716.68	149,252.70	347,502.70
10.50%	1,765.87	158,107.46	356,357.46
11.00%	1,815.71	167,078.45	365,328.45
11.50%	1,866.18	176,162.98	374,412.98
12.00%	1,917.27	185,358.33	383,608.33
12.50%	1,960.95	194,661.72	392,911.72
13.00%	2,021.22	204,070.39	402,320.39

FIGURE 5-26

You can use the Loan Analysis worksheet to calculate the loan information for any reasonable loan data. As you can see from Figure 5-26, the monthly payment for the house is $1,573.12 (cell B9). The total interest (First Bank's profit) is $123,411.86 (cell B10). The total cost of the $198,250.00 house is $321,661.86 (cell B11).

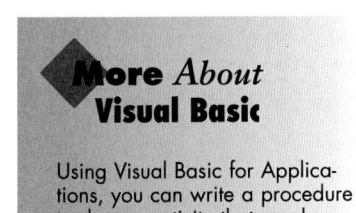

More *About* **Visual Basic**

Using Visual Basic for Applications, you can write a procedure to do any activity that you have done thus far in Excel.

Creating a Macro to Automate Loan Data Entry

A **macro** is made up of a series of Visual Basic statements that tell Excel how to complete a task. A macro such as the one in Figure 5-27 is used to automate routine workbook tasks, such as entering new data into a worksheet. Macros are almost a necessity for worksheets that are built to be used by people who know little or nothing about computers and worksheets.

For example, in the previous section loan data for buying a house was entered to calculate new loan information. However, the user who enters the data must know what cells to select and how much loan data is required to obtain the desired results. To facilitate entering the loan data, a worksheet and macro can be constructed so the user simply clicks a button to execute the macro. The instructions that make up the macro (Figure 5-27) then guide the user through entering the required loan data in the range B3:B8.

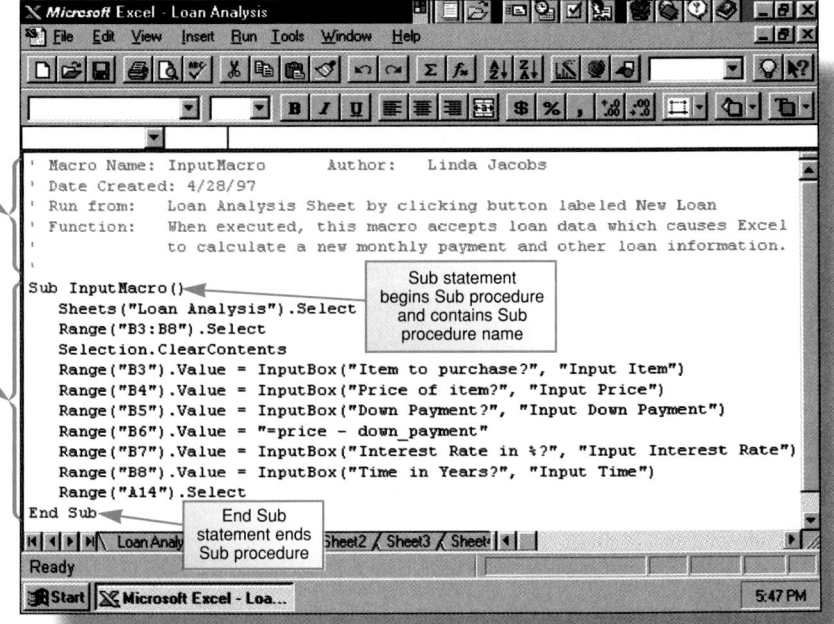

Microsoft Excel - Loan Analysis

Visual Basic comments

Visual Basic Sub procedure

Sub statement begins Sub procedure and contains Sub procedure name

End Sub statement ends Sub procedure

```
' Macro Name: InputMacro       Author:    Linda Jacobs
' Date Created: 4/28/97
' Run from:     Loan Analysis Sheet by clicking button labeled New Loan
' Function:     When executed, this macro accepts loan data which causes Excel
'               to calculate a new monthly payment and other loan information.
'
Sub InputMacro()
    Sheets("Loan Analysis").Select
    Range("B3:B8").Select
    Selection.ClearContents
    Range("B3").Value = InputBox("Item to purchase?", "Input Item")
    Range("B4").Value = InputBox("Price of item?", "Input Price")
    Range("B5").Value = InputBox("Down Payment?", "Input Down Payment")
    Range("B6").Value = "=price - down_payment"
    Range("B7").Value = InputBox("Interest Rate in %?", "Input Interest Rate")
    Range("B8").Value = InputBox("Time in Years?", "Input Time")
    Range("A14").Select
End Sub
```

Ready

Start | Microsoft Excel - Loa... 5:47 PM

FIGURE 5-27

Visual Basic Statements

Visual Basic for Applications is a powerful programming language that you can use to execute most of the workbook activity described so far in this book. Visual Basic statements (or **Visual Basic code)** are entered on a **module sheet. Visual Basic statements** are instructions to Excel. In the case of Project 5, all the statements are entered into a single **Sub procedure.** A Sub procedure begins with a **Sub statement** and ends with an **End Sub statement** (Figure 5-27).

The Sub statement includes the name of the Sub procedure. In Project 5, the procedure name used is InputMacro, but it could have been any name containing up to 255 characters. This procedure name is important because it is used later to run the macro.

Remark statements begin with the word **Rem** or an apostrophe ('). In Figure 5-27, there are six remark lines prior to the Sub statement. Because these remarks contain overall procedure documentation they are optionally placed above the Sub statement. Rem statements have no effect on the execution of a macro.

Table 5-2 Visual Basic

STATEMENTS	DESCRIPTION
Rem or '	Initiates a comment
Sub name ()	Begins a Sub procedure
Sheets("sheet name").Select	Selects the worksheet to affect
Range("range").Select	Selects a range
Selection.ClearContents	Clears the selected range
Range("cell").Value	Assigns the value following the equal sign to the cell
InputBox("Message", "Title of Dialog Box")	Displays Message in a dialog box with the title, Title of Dialog Box
End Sub	Ends a Sub procedure

This project is concerned with using the seven Visual Basic statements and one Visual Basic function listed in Table 5-2. InputBox is a **function**, rather than a statement, because it returns a value to the Sub procedure.

Planning a Macro

When you execute a macro, Excel steps through the Visual Basic statements one at a time beginning at the top of the Sub procedure. Excel bypasses any statements that begin with Remark, Rem or an apostrophe ('). Thus, when you plan a macro you should remember that the order in which you place the statements in the procedure determines the sequence of execution.

Once you determine what the macro should do, write it out on paper. Then, before entering the macro into the computer, put yourself in the position of Excel and step through the instructions and see how it affects the worksheet. Testing a macro before entering it is an important part of the development process called **desk checking.**

You should add comments before each procedure because they help you remember the purpose of the macro at a later date.

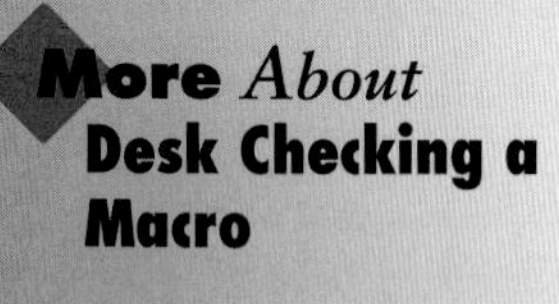

More *About* **Desk Checking a Macro**

Getting into the habit of desk checking macros can save you time and money. To desk check a macro, obtain a printout of the macro, open the workbook, and step through each instruction manually. Make corrections and step through the macro again and again until you generate the correct results manually.

Inserting a Module Sheet

You write a macro on a module sheet, which is a blank sheet with no cells. You insert a module sheet by using the Macro command on the Insert menu. The following steps show how to insert a macro sheet.

Steps To Insert a Module Sheet

1 Point to Macro on the Insert menu. Point to Module on the Macro submenu.

Excel displays a cascading menu (Figure 5-28).

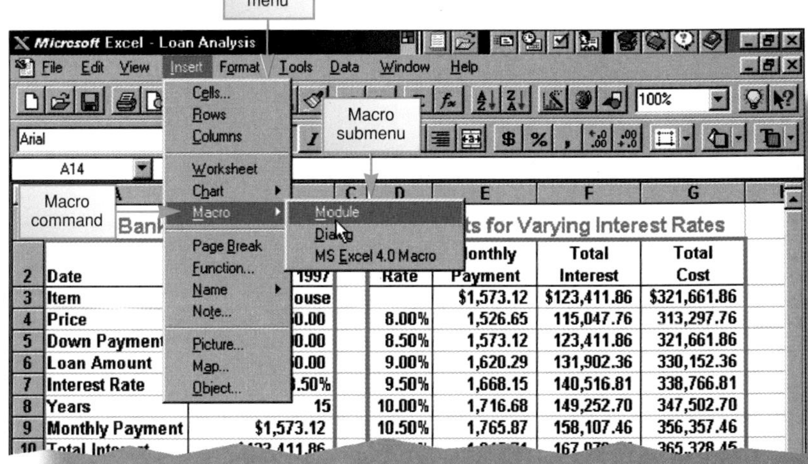

FIGURE 5-28

2 Click Module on the Macro submenu.

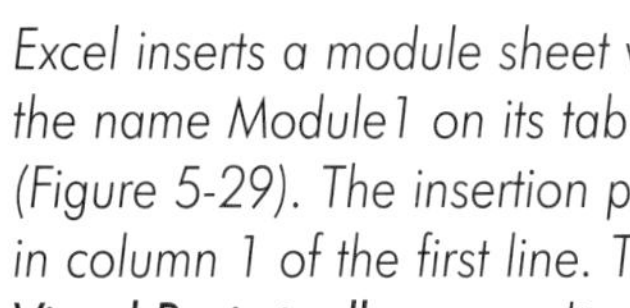

Excel inserts a module sheet with the name Module1 on its tab (Figure 5-29). The insertion point is in column 1 of the first line. The **Visual Basic toolbar** *may display in the window. The buttons on the Visual Basic toolbar will be discussed shortly.*

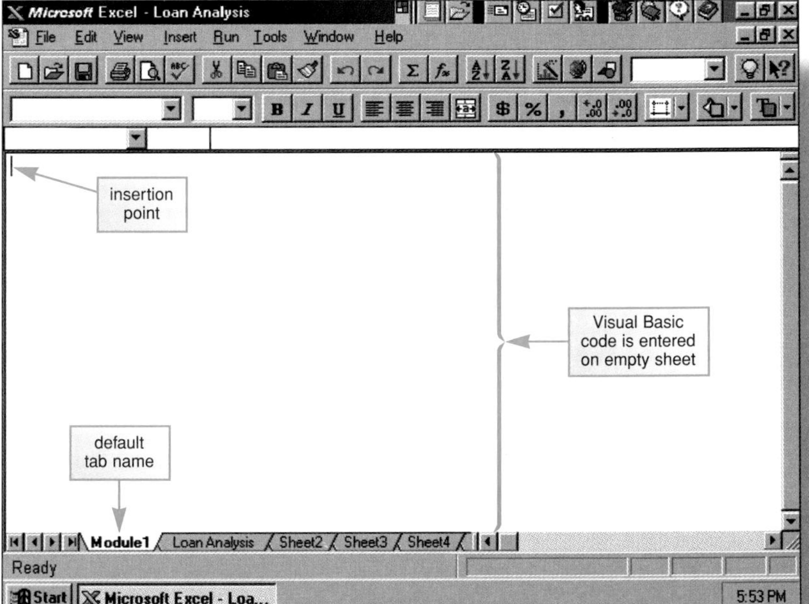

FIGURE 5-29

Entering the Macro on the Module Sheet

You enter a macro by typing the lines of Visual Basic code (statements) the same way you would if you were using word processing software. The macro editor is a full-screen editor. Thus, you can move the insertion point to previous lines to make corrections. At the end of a line, you press the ENTER key or use the DOWN ARROW key to move to the next line. If you make a mistake in a statement and notice it, use the arrow keys and the DELETE or BACKSPACE key to correct it.

Each time you type a line and move the insertion point to the next line, Excel checks the syntax of the statement. If you overlook an error, such as a missing parenthesis, Excel displays the line in red along with a dialog box to alert you that the previous statement is in error. When you are finished entering the macro, move to another sheet by clicking a sheet tab.

The following steps describe how to enter a macro on a module sheet.

To Enter a Macro on a Module Sheet

1 Type the six Rem statements as shown in Figure 5-30. Remember to begin each line with an apostrophe (').

Excel automatically displays the remark lines in green.

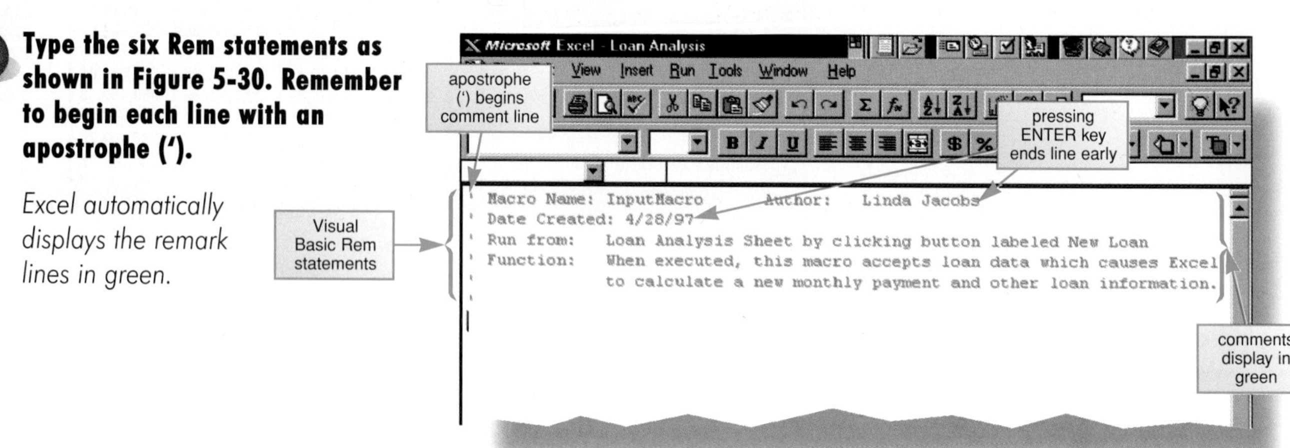

FIGURE 5-30

2 Type the Sub procedure as shown in Figure 5-31. For clarity, indent all lines between the Sub statement and End Sub statement by three spaces. There can be no spaces between the object, for example, Range ("B3"), the period (.), and the property, for example Value. Double-click the Module1 tab. When the Rename Sheet dialog box displays, type `Input Macro`**. Click the OK button.**

3 Drag the Input Macro tab and position it between the Loan Analysis and Sheet2 tabs.

The module sheet displays as shown in Figure 5-31.

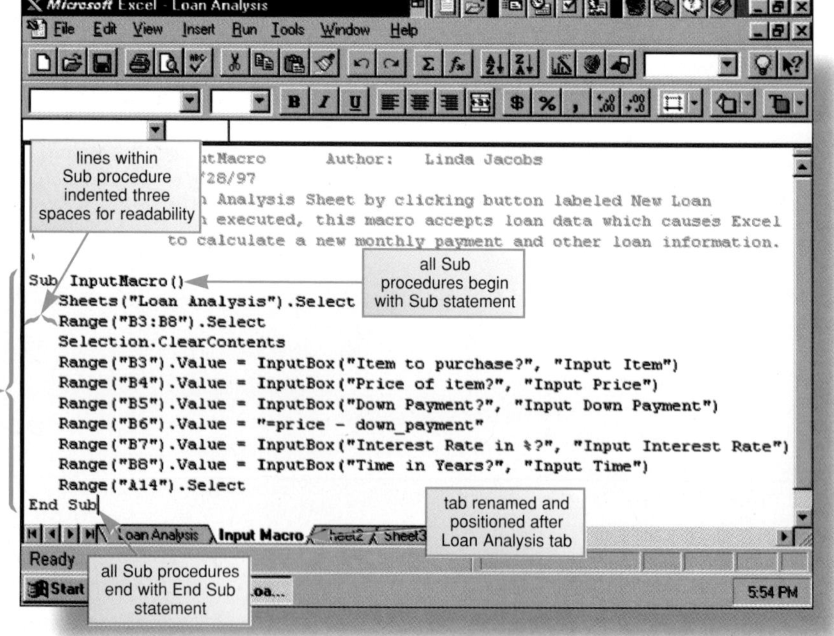

FIGURE 5-31

More About Macros and Visual Basic Statements

When the module sheet is active, Excel may display a Visual Basic toolbar. The toolbar displays if it displayed the last time a module sheet was active. Figure 5-32 describes the function of each button on the Visual Basic toolbar. Once you begin writing macros on your own, you will find these buttons to be handy, especially for testing macros.

Visual Basic for Applications is capable of much more than is presented here. You should notice, however, the basic makeup of a Visual Basic statement. For example, each of the statements within the Sub procedure includes a period. On the left side of the period you instruct Excel which object on the worksheet you want to affect. An **object** can be a cell, a range, a chart, a button, the worksheet, or the workbook. On the right side of the period, you tell Excel what activity to perform on the object. The right side of the period is called the **property**. For example,

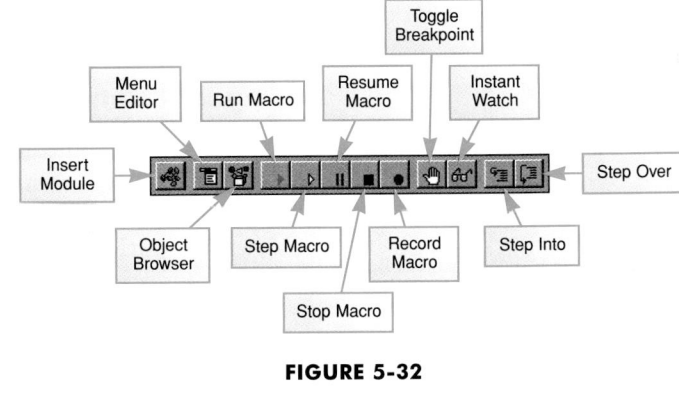

Toggle Breakpoint
Menu Editor
Run Macro
Resume Macro
Instant Watch
Insert Module
Step Over
Object Browser
Step Macro
Record Macro
Step Into
Stop Macro

FIGURE 5-32

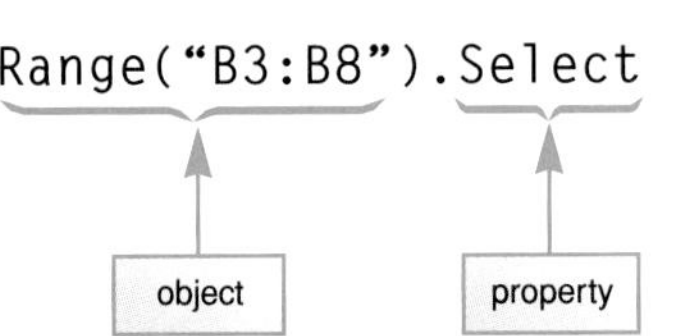

Thus, when Excel executes the statement Range("B3:B8"). Select, the range B3:B8 (object) is selected (property), as if you used the mouse to drag across the range B3:B8 in the worksheet. Several of the statements in Figure 5-31 contain equal signs. An equal sign instructs Excel to make an assignment to a cell. For example,

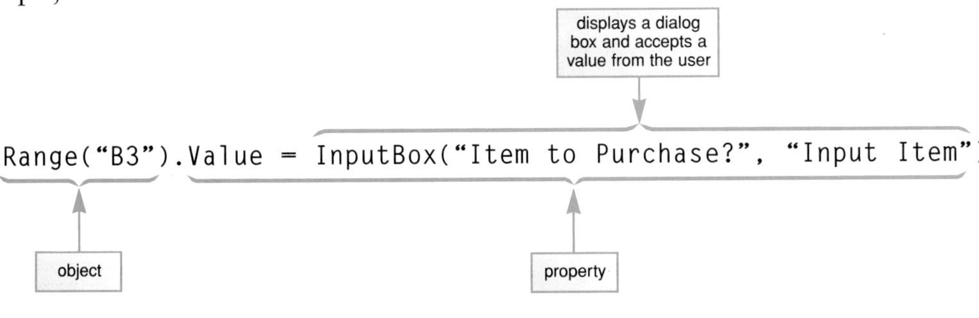

When executed as part of the macro, this Range.Value statement assigns to cell B3 the value entered by the user in response to the dialog box.

Because the second and third statement in the Sub procedure clears the range B3:B8, the formula in cell B6 has to be reentered. When executed, the seventh statement in the Sub procedure:

```
Range("B6").Value = "=price - down_payment"
```

reenters the formula =price - down_payment in cell B6.

The next to the last statement in the Sub procedure selects cell A14, the same as if you clicked on cell A14 in the worksheet. Finally, the last statement in the Sub procedure in Figure 5-31, End Sub, ends the Sub procedure and control returns to the worksheet from which the Sub procedure was executed.

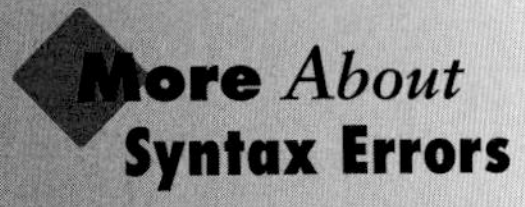

More *About* **Syntax Errors**

Syntax errors include misspelled words, improper spacing, and grammatical errors. One of the most common syntax errors in writing VBA is to place spaces around the period that separates the object from the property. The period must be the only separator between the object and property.

More *About* Buttons on a Toolbar

Each button on a toolbar has macro-like instructions assigned to it. For example, when you click the Save button on the Standard toolbar, the macro-like instructions assigned to the button executes and steps you through saving the workbook. You can add a new button to a toolbar and assign it a macro. For more information, see the Other Ways at the bottom of the next page.

Using a macro is a two-step process. First, you enter the macro on a module sheet as was done in the previous set of steps. Next, you execute it. You can execute a macro in several ways. For example, you can click the Run Macro button on the Visual Basic toolbar (Figure 5-32). Another way is to create a button on the worksheet or on a toolbar, assign the macro to it, and then click the button. In this project, the macro will be assigned to a button on the worksheet.

Adding a Button to the Worksheet to Execute a Macro

You create the button by using the Button tool on the Drawing toolbar. You size and locate a button in the same way you did a chart in the earlier projects. You then assign the macro to the button by using the name in the Sub statement (InputMacro). Finally, you change the name on the button by editing it. The following steps show how to create a button and assign to it the macro InputMacro. Recall, that InputMacro was the name placed earlier in the Sub statement (see Figure 5-31 on page E 5.28).

Steps To Add a Button to the Worksheet and Assign a Macro to It

1. **Click the Loan Analysis tab to activate the worksheet. Click the Drawing button on the Standard toolbar. Dock the Drawing toolbar at the bottom of the screen.**

2. **Click the Create Button button on the Drawing toolbar. Drag the mouse pointer (a plus sign) from the top of cell B13 to the lower right corner of cell B14 and hold, as shown in Figure 5-33.**

   Excel draws a light border around the button area.

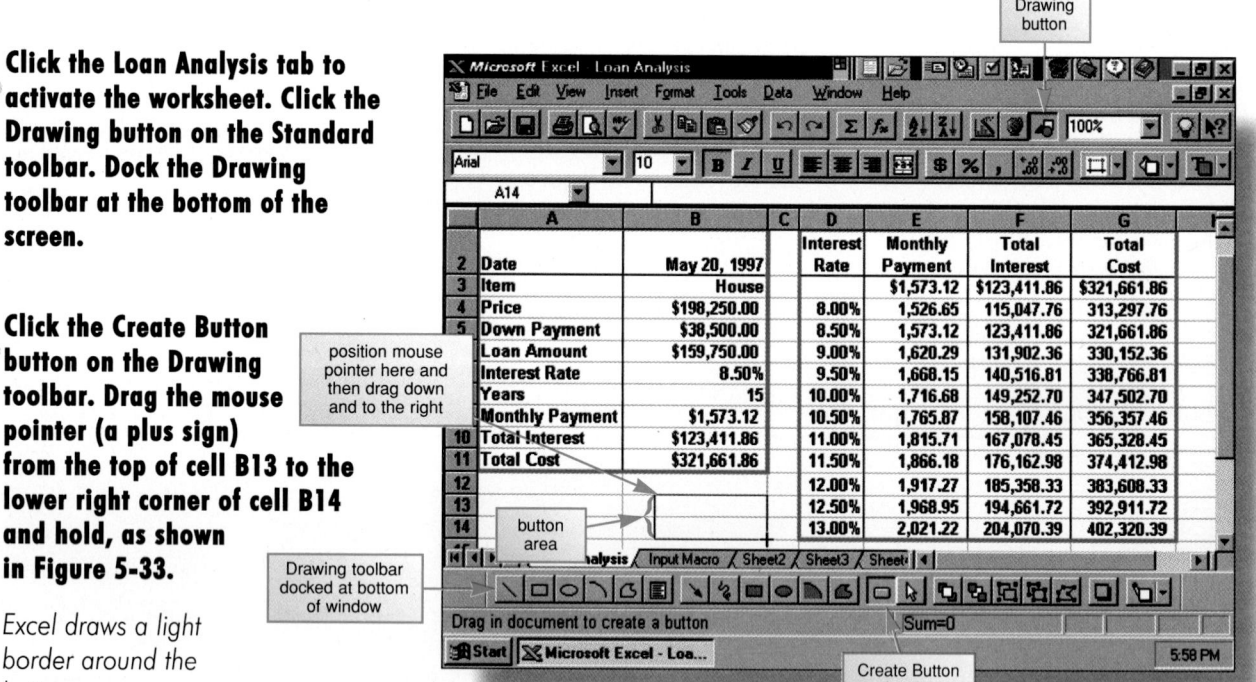

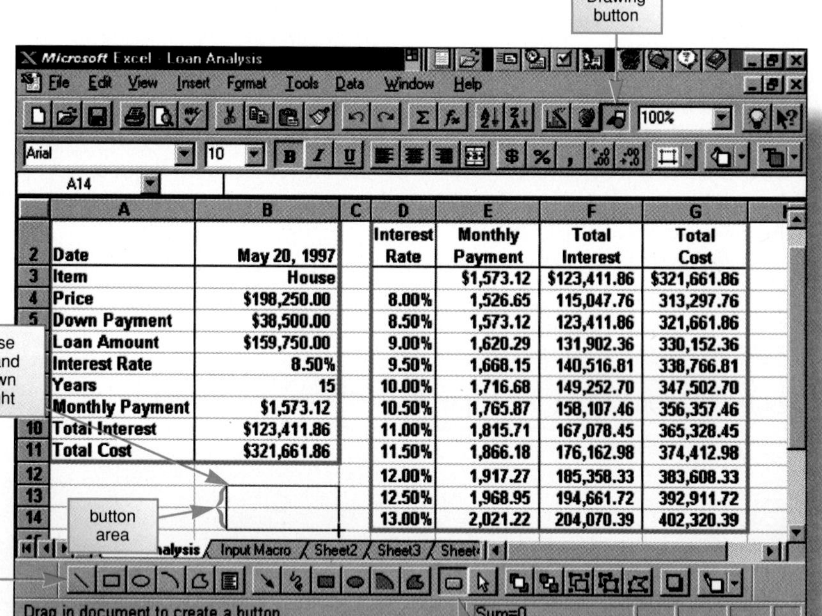

FIGURE 5-33

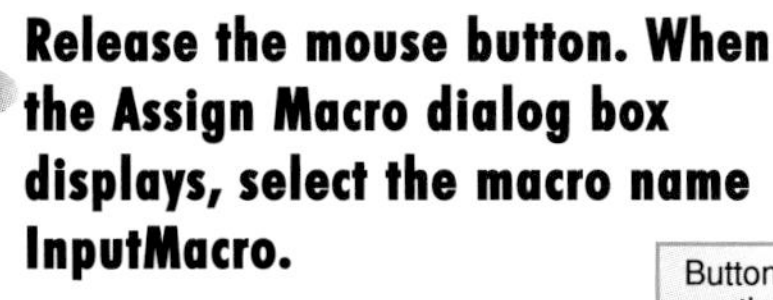

3 Release the mouse button. When the Assign Macro dialog box displays, select the macro name InputMacro.

Excel displays the button with the title Button 1 and also displays the ***Assign Macro dialog box*** *(Figure 5-34). The button's handles and shaded border indicate you can resize the button on the worksheet after the Assign Macro dialog box is closed.*

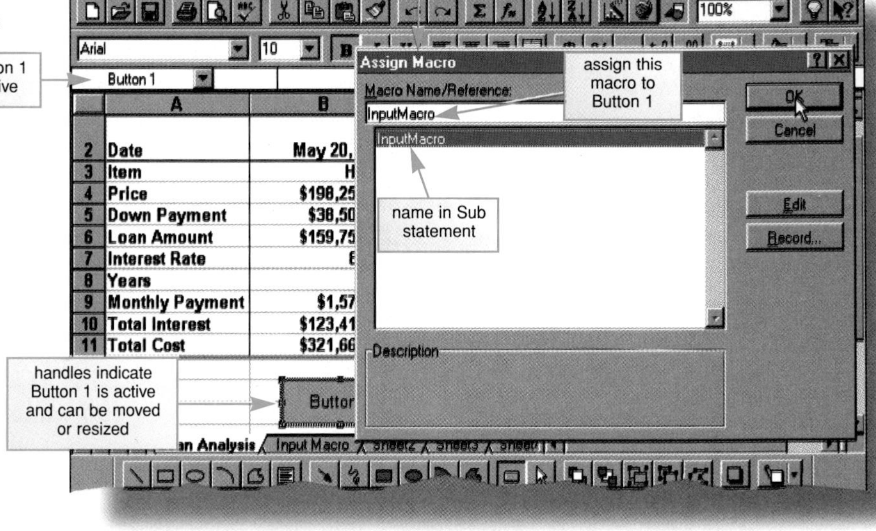

FIGURE 5-34

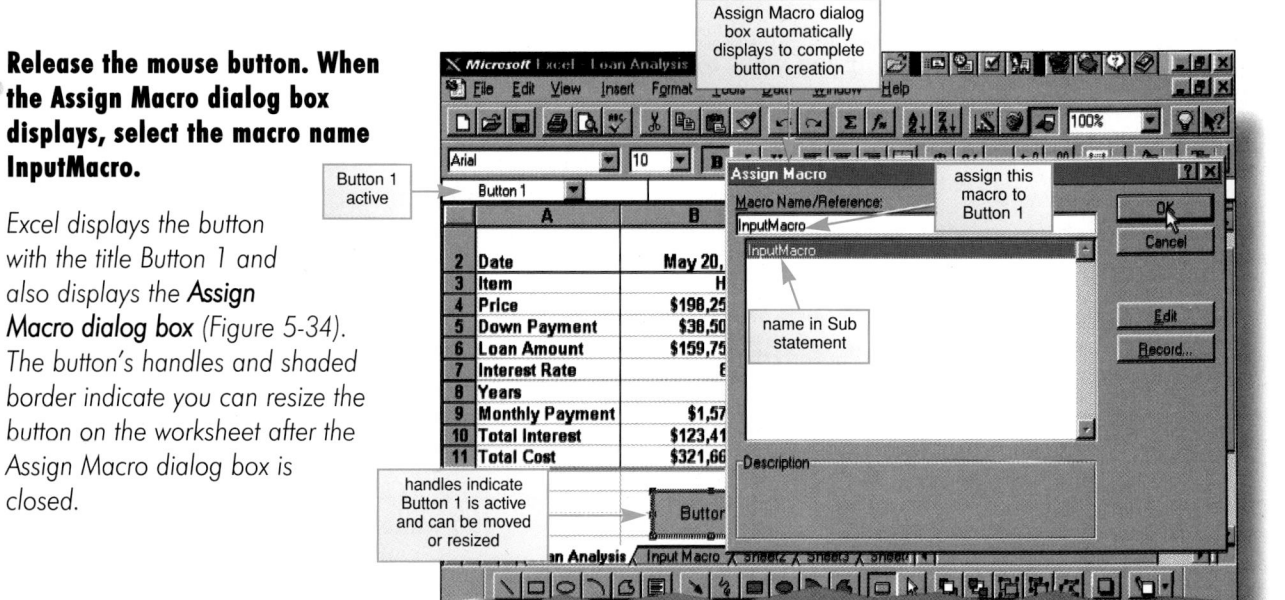

4 Click the OK button. Click the Drawing button on the Standard toolbar to close the Drawing toolbar. Drag across the button title, Button 1, and type `New Loan` **as the new button title. Drag across the button title, click 12 in the Font drop-down list box on the Formatting toolbar, click the Bold button, click the Font Color button arrow, and click the color red (column 3, row 1 on the Font Color palette).**

5 Select cell A14 to lock in the new button title. Click the Save button on the Standard toolbar to save the workbook using the filename Loan Analysis.

The button with the title New Loan displays in the range B13:B14 on the worksheet (Figure 5-35).

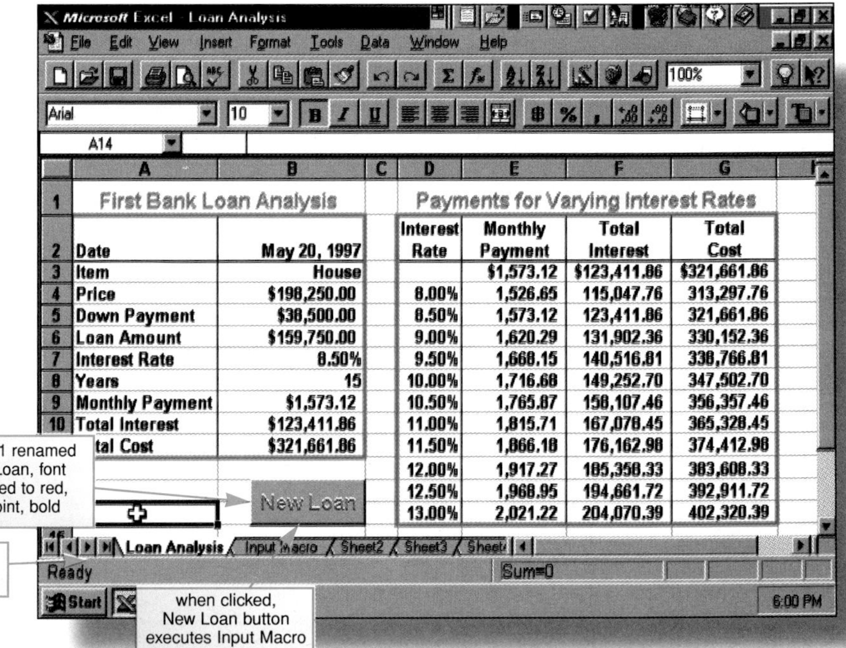

FIGURE 5-35

OtherWays

1. Right-click toolbar, click Customize, click Custom in Categories box, drag any button in dialog box on to worksheet or toolbar, select macro, click OK button

More *About*
Executing Macros

During the testing phase, never execute a macro without first saving the workbook. If a save operation is part of the macro, then save the workbook under another name. A runaway macro can ruin a workbook.

If you want to resize or change the name of the button anytime after Step 5, hold down the CTRL key and click the button. Once the button is surrounded by the shaded border and handles, you can modify it. You can also choose the **Assign to Macro command** from the Tools menu or shortcut menu to assign a different macro to the button. When you finish editing the button, click any cell to deselect it.

Executing the Macro

The next steps are to enter the loan data. You should be aware that when the macro executes, the second and third statements clear the range. Thus, any formula in the worksheet that includes the operation of division may result in the display of the diagnostic message **#DIV/0!** in the cell. Follow these steps to enter the loan data for a 32' Sailboat priced at $68,750. Assume the customer plans to make a down payment of $21,000 and wants the loan for seven years. First Bank is charging 11.5% interest.

Steps To Execute the Macro and Enter New Loan Data

1. **Click the New Loan button. When Excel displays the Input Item dialog box with the prompt message Item to purchase?, type** `32' Sailboat` **(Figure 5-36).**

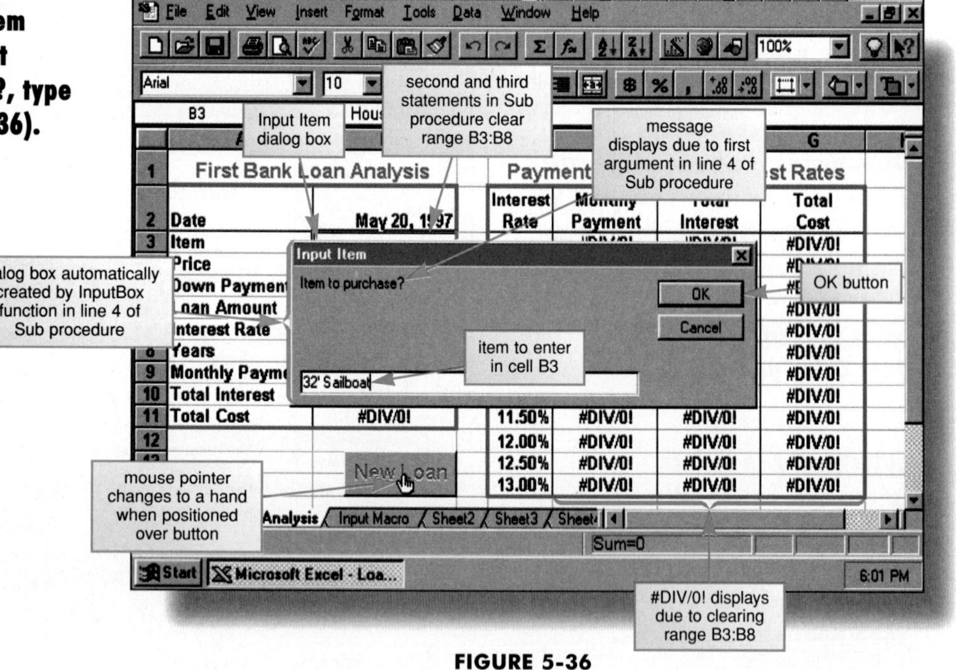

FIGURE 5-36

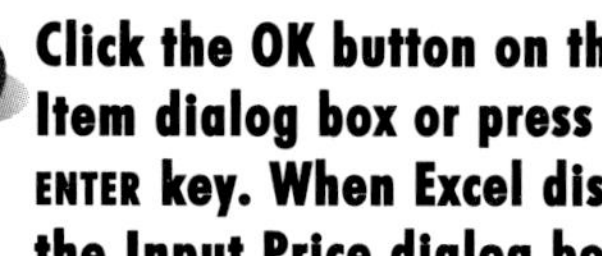

Click the OK button on the Input Item dialog box or press the ENTER key. When Excel displays the Input Price dialog box with the prompt message Price of item?, type 68750 **(Figure 5-37).**

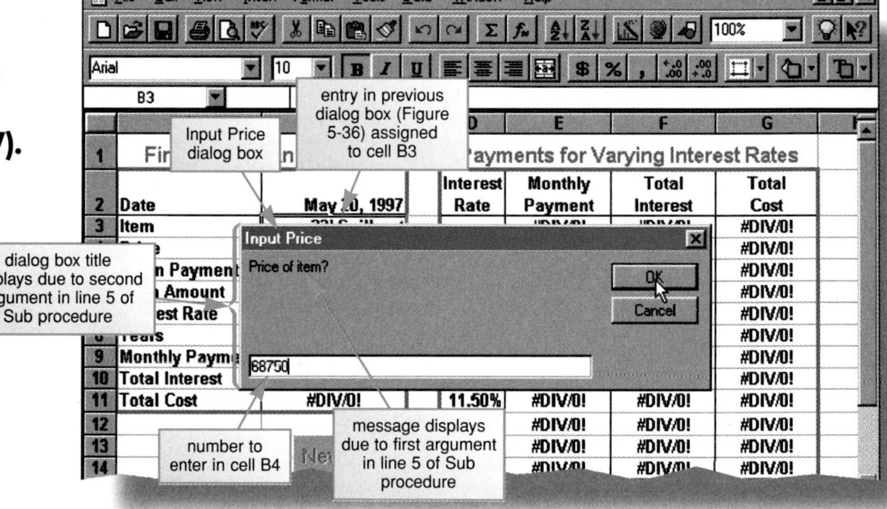

FIGURE 5-37

Click the OK button on the Input Price dialog box. When Excel displays the Input Down Payment dialog box with the prompt message Down Payment?, type 21000 **(Figure 5-38).**

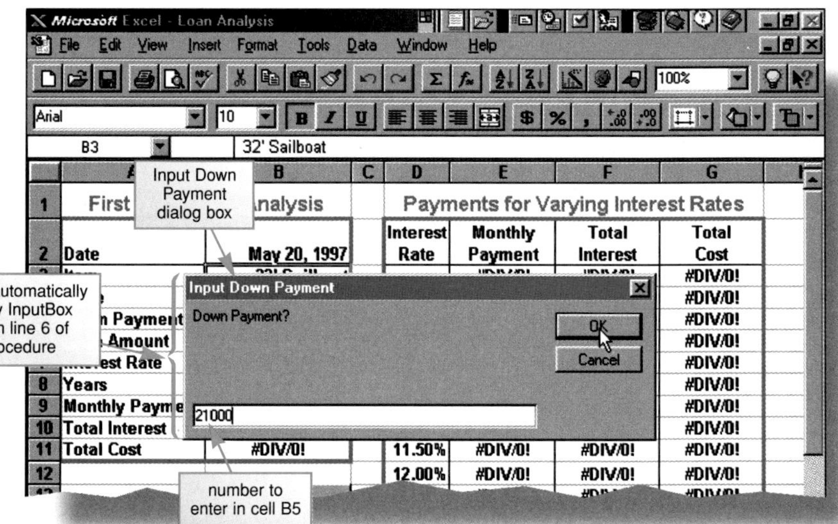

FIGURE 5-38

Click the OK button on the Input Down Payment dialog box. When Excel displays the Input Interest Rate dialog box with the prompt message Interest Rate in %?, type 11.50% **(Figure 5-39).**

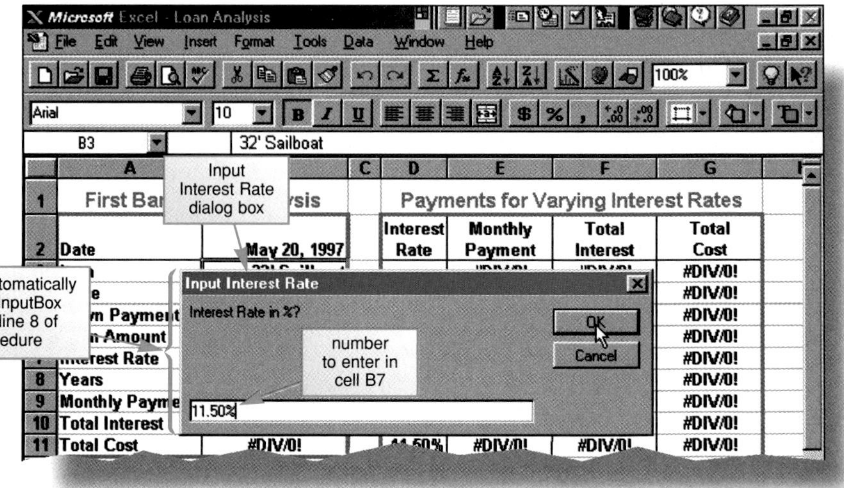

FIGURE 5-39

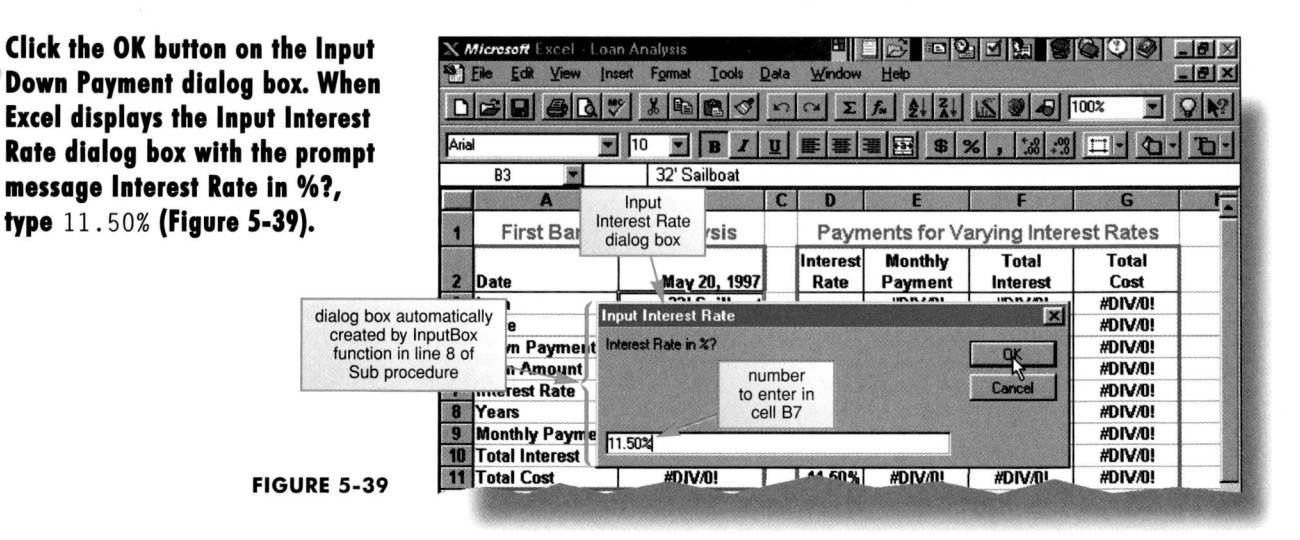

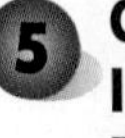

Click the OK button on the Input Interest Rate dialog box. When Excel displays the Input Time dialog box with the prompt message Time in Years?, type 7 **(Figure 5-40).**

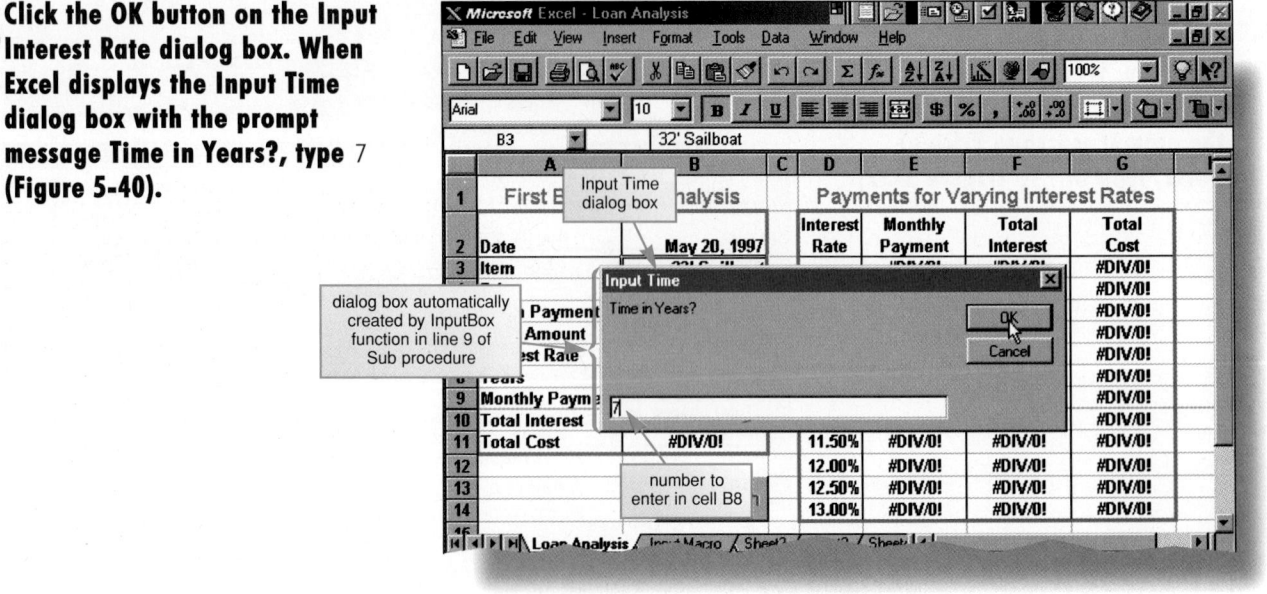

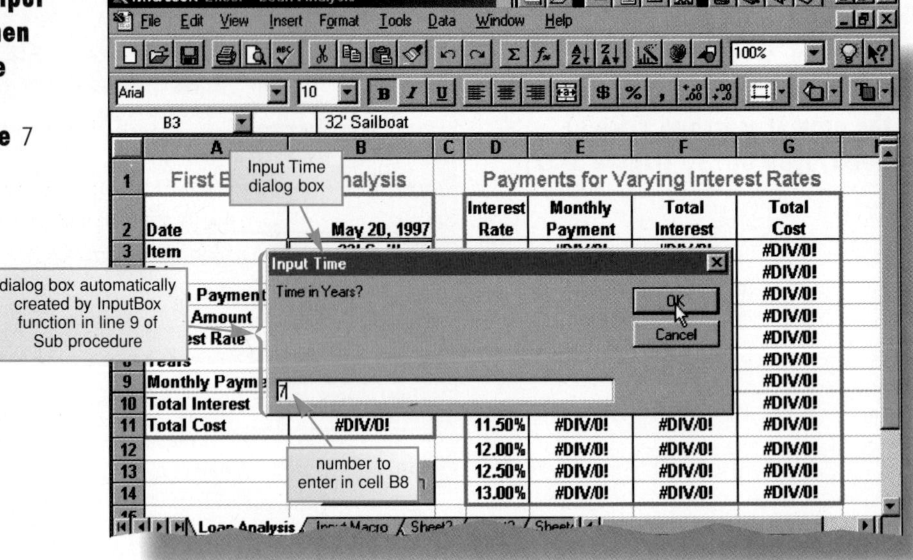

FIGURE 5-40

6 Click the OK button on the Input Time dialog box.

Excel recalculates the loan information for the new loan data and cell A14 is the active cell (Figure 5-41).

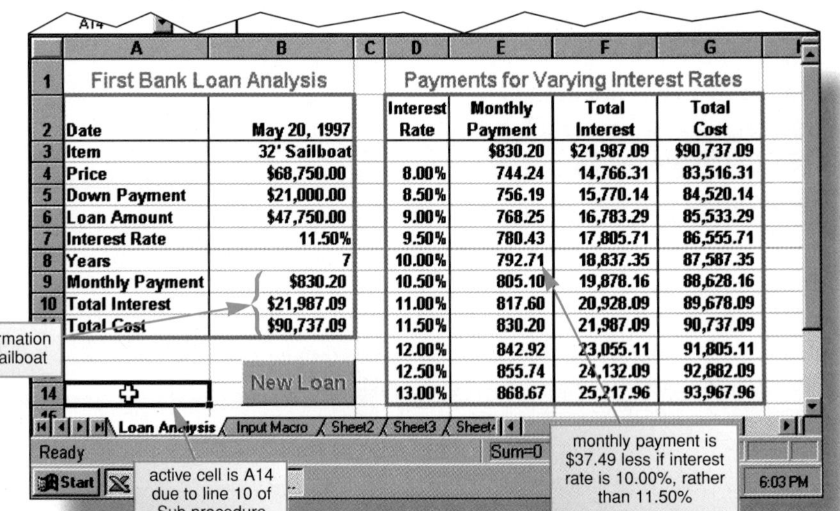

FIGURE 5-41

OtherWays

1. On Tools menu, click Macro, double-click macro name
2. On Visual Basic toolbar click Run Macro button

Figure 5-41 shows that the monthly payment is $830.20 (cell B9), the total interest is $21,987.09 (cell B10), and the total cost is $90,737.09 (cell B11) for the 32' Sailboat. Furthermore, Excel automatically recalculates new results in the data table (range D3:G14) for the new loan data.

You can see the significance of using a macro to accept the loan data, especially if the loan officers know little about computers. Each time the New Loan button is clicked, the macro guides the user through entering the loan data and placing it in the correct cells.

Recording a Macro

Excel has a **Macro Recorder** that creates a macro automatically from the actions you perform and commands you choose. The Macro Recorder can be turned on, during which time it records your activities, and then turned off to terminate the recording. The steps you perform during the time it is recording, can be **played back** (executed) as often as you want. Thus, the Macro Recorder is like a tape recorder, in that it records everything you do to a workbook over a period of time. The instructions are recorded on a sheet, called Module1, that is automatically added as the last sheet in the workbook. Once the macro is recorded, you can do one of the following to play it back:

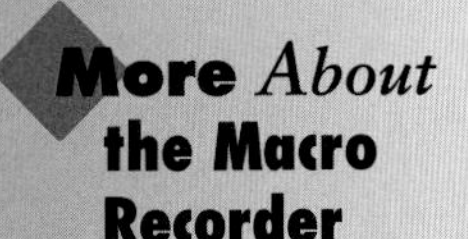

Record short procedures you can call and use from a main procedure. This makes your code easier to manage, reuse, and debug.

1. Assign the macro to a button on the worksheet as was done earlier in this project, and click the button.
2. Assign the macro to a custom button on a toolbar and click the button.
3. Click the **Macro command** on the Tools menu.
4. Click the **Run Macro button** on the Visual Basic toolbar.
5. Add a command to the Tools menu that plays back the macro and then click the command.
6. Assign the macro to a graphic, such as a chart, so that when you click it the macro plays back.

The following series of steps shows you how to record a macro to print the Loan Analysis worksheet in landscape orientation and then return the orientation to portrait. To guard against macro catastrophes, the workbook is saved before invoking the Macro Recorder.

The macro recorder is a neat tool for discovering Visual Basic programming methods. But there are limitations to recording macros. You cannot record the following: (1) conditional branches; (2) looping structures; (3) calculated selections and references; (4) some built-in functions and dialog boxes; and, (5) custom dialog boxes. You can, however, enhance your recorded macros by editing them.

TO RECORD A MACRO TO PRINT THE LOAN ANALYSIS WORKSHEET IN LANDSCAPE

Step 1: Click the Save button on the Standard toolbar to save the workbook using the filename Loan Analysis.

Step 2: Point to Record Macro on the Tools menu, and then click Record New Macro on the Record Macro submenu.

Step 3: When the Record New Macro dialog box displays, type the macro name `PrintLandscape` in the Macro Name box.

Step 4: Click the OK button.

*Excel displays the **Stop Macro button** in its own toolbar and displays the message Recording on the status bar at the bottom of the screen. The Macro Recorder is on and whatever actions you perform are recorded.*

Step 5: Complete the following actions:
a. Right-click the menu bar
b. Click Page Setup on the shortcut menu
c. When the Page Setup dialog box displays, click the Page tab
d. Click Landscape and then click the Print button
e. Click the OK button on the Print dialog box
f. Right-click the menu bar
g. Click Page Setup on the shortcut menu
h. Click Portrait and then click the OK button

Step 6: Click the Stop Macro button.

More *About* **Viewing a Recorded Macro**

You can view the macro that the Macro Recorder created by clicking the Right Tab Scroll button and when the Module1 tab appears, click it. If you click the Module1 tab, you can see the PrintLandscape macro is 70 Visual Basic statements long.

You are able to step through the actions and see the results as the macro is recorded. If you recorded the wrong actions, click Macro on the Tools menu. When the **Macro dialog box** displays, click the name of the macro (PrintLandscape) and then click the Delete button.

More About Hiding a Macro Sheet

Worried about users changing a macro on you? One quick solution is to hide the macro sheet so both the tab and sheet don't show. You hide a macro sheet by first clicking the macro sheet's tab and then pointing to Sheet on the Edit menu. When the Sheet submenu displays, click Hide. The macro will still execute, even though its hidden. For a worksheet, the Hide command is available through the Sheet command on the Format menu. You unhide a sheet by clicking the Unhide command on the Sheet submenu.

Playing Back a Recorded Macro

The following steps show you how to play back the recorded macro PrintLandscape.

TO PLAY BACK A RECORDED MACRO

Step 1: Click Macro on the Tools menu.
Step 2: When the Macro dialog box displays, double-click PrintLandscape in the Macro Name/Reference box.
Step 3: Click the Save button to save the workbook using the filename Loan Analysis.

The Excel window blinks as the macro is executed. The report prints as shown in Figure 5-42.

Loan Analysis

First Bank Loan Analysis

Date	April 24, 1997
Item	Saturn SC1
Price	$14,500.00
Down Payment	$2,500.00
Loan Amount	$12,000.00
Interest Rate	10.50%
Years	3
Monthly Payment	$390.03
Total Interest	$2,041.06
Total Cost	$16,541.06

Payments for Varying Interest Rates

Interest Rate	Monthly Payment	Total Interest	Total Cost
	$390.03	$2,041.06	$16,541.06
8.00%	376.04	1,537.31	16,037.31
8.50%	378.81	1,637.18	16,137.18
9.00%	381.60	1,737.48	16,237.48
9.50%	384.40	1,838.23	16,338.23
10.00%	387.21	1,939.42	16,439.42
10.50%	390.03	2,041.06	16,541.06
11.00%	392.86	2,143.13	16,643.13
11.50%	395.71	2,245.63	16,745.63
12.00%	398.57	2,348.58	16,848.58
12.50%	401.44	2,451.97	16,951.97
13.00%	404.33	2,555.79	17,055.79

FIGURE 5-42

More About the Personal Macro Workbook

To record a macro that you always want available, click Options in the Record New Macro dialog box, and then click Personal Macro Workbook. The Personal Macro Workbook is a hidden workbook that is always open. Give macros you record into this workbook meaningful names.

Goal Seeking to Determine the Down Payment for a Specific Monthy Payment

If you know the result that you want a formula to produce, you can use goal seeking to determine the value of a cell on which the formula depends. The following example uses the Goal Seek command to determine the down payment so that the monthly payment for the 32' Sailboat will be exactly $650.00.

Steps To Determine the Down Payment for a Specific Monthly Payment Using Goal Seek

1. **Click cell B9, the cell with the monthly payment amount. Click Goal Seek on the Tools menu. When the Goal Seek dialog box displays, type** 650 **in the To value box. Select the By changing cell box. In the worksheet, click cell B5.**

   The Goal Seek dialog box displays as shown in Figure 5-43. The first entry on the dialog box indicates the cell on which you want to seek a goal (cell B9), the second box indicates the specific value you are seeking ($650.00), and the third box indicates the cell to vary (cell B5).

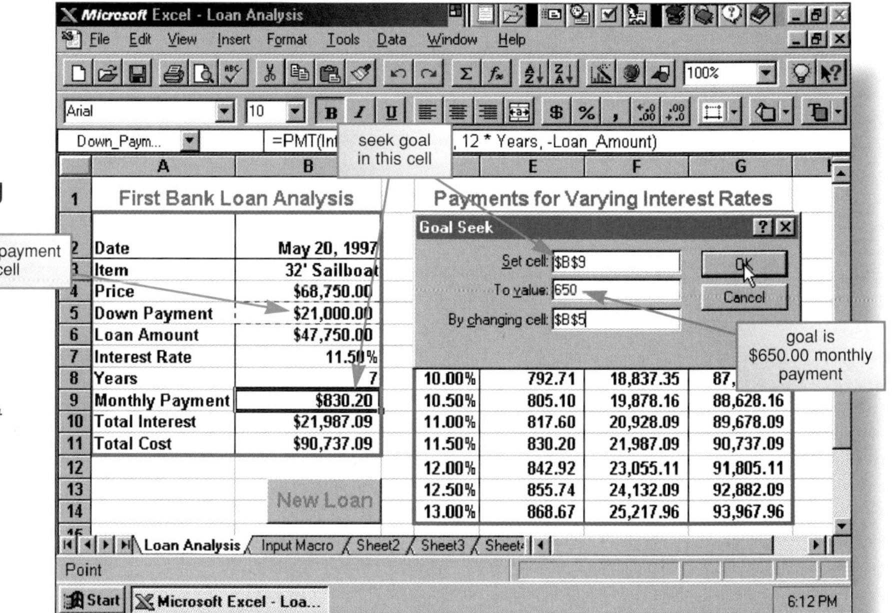

FIGURE 5-43

2. **Click the OK button.**

   Excel displays the Goal Seek Status dialog box indicating an answer has been found. Excel also changes the monthly payment in cell B9 to the goal ($650.00) and changes the down payment in cell B5 to $31,364.59 (Figure 5-44).

3. **Click the Cancel button on the Goal Seek Status dialog box to undo the changes to the worksheet.**

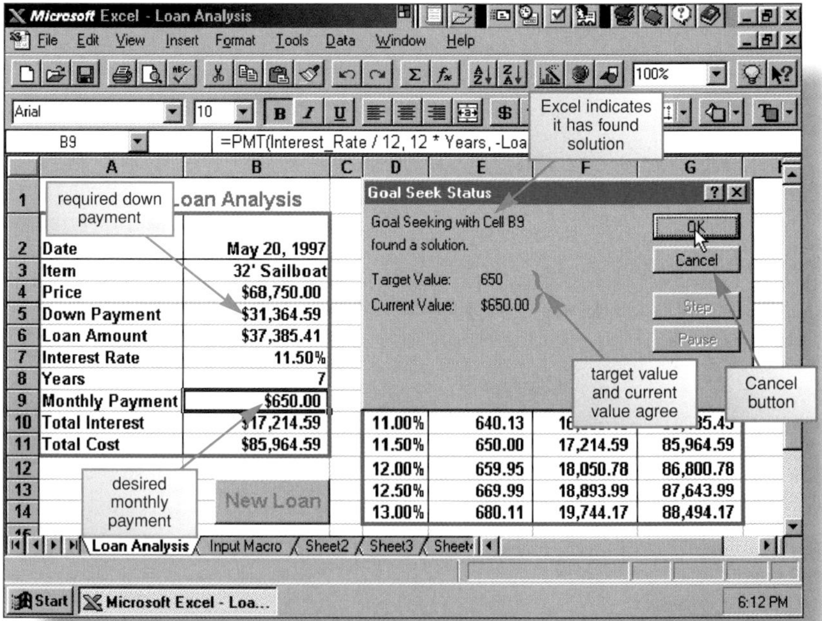

FIGURE 5-44

Thus, according to Figure 5-44, if the 32' Sailboat costs $68,750.00, the interest rate is 11.50%, the term is 7 years, and you want to pay exactly $650.00 a month, then you must make a down payment of $31,364.59.

In this goal seeking example it is not required that the cell to vary be directly referenced in the formula or function. For example, the monthly payment formula in cell B9 is =PMT(interest_rate / 12, 12 * years, loan_amount). The down payment is not mentioned in the PMT function. However, because the loan amount, which is referenced in the PMT function, is based on the down payment, Excel is able to goal seek on the monthly payment by varying the down payment.

If you had clicked the OK button in Step 3 on the previous page, then Excel would have permanently made the changes to the worksheet based on the goal seek activity. If you decided to click the OK button, rather than the Cancel button, you could reset the worksheet to the values displayed prior to goal seeking by clicking the Undo button on the Standard toolbar, or by clicking Undo Goal Seek on the Edit menu. However, these undoing procedures will work only if executed prior to completing the next activity.

Using Scenario Manager to Analyze Data

More *About* **Scenario Manager**

Worksheets are primarily used for what-if analysis. You enter values into cells and instantaneously the results change in the dependent cells. As you continue to change values in the key cells, you lose the previous results. If you want to go back, you have to reenter the data. Scenario manager allows you to store the different sets of values (called scenarios) so that you can easily redisplay them with a few clicks of the mouse button. Each scenario can have up to 32 sets of changing cells for each scenario.

An alternative to using a data table to analyze worksheet data is to use Excel's Scenario Manager. The **Scenario Manager** allows you to record and save different sets of what-if assumptions (data values) called scenarios. For example, earlier in this project (Figure 5-26 on page E 5.25) a monthly payment of $1,573.12 was determined for the following loan data: Item — House; Price —$198,250.00; Down payment — $38,500.00; Interest Rate — 8.50%; and Years —15. One scenario for the house loan might be: "What is the monthly payment, total interest, and total cost if the interest rate is the same (8.50%) but the number of years changes from 15 to 30?" Another scenario might be: "What is the monthly payment, total interest, and total cost if the interest rate is increased by 2% to 10.50% and the number of years remains at 15?" Each set of values represents a what-if assumption. The primary uses of Scenario Manager are to:

1. Create different scenarios with multiple sets of changing cells.
2. Build a summary worksheet that contains the different scenarios.
3. View the results of each scenario on your worksheet.

The following sections show how to use the Scenario Manager for each of the procedures just listed. Once you create the scenarios, you can instruct Excel to build the summary worksheet. The summary worksheet that the Scenario Manager generates is actually an outlined worksheet (Figure 5-45) that you can print and manipulate like any other worksheet. An **outlined worksheet** is one that contains symbols (buttons) above and to the left which allow you to collapse and expand row and columns.

Before illustrating the Scenario Manager, click the New Loan button and enter the loan data for the house as described in Figure 5-26 on page E 5.25.

The following steps create the two scenarios and the Scenario Summary worksheet shown in Figure 5-45 by using the **Scenarios command** on the Tools menu. The worksheet illustrates the monthly payment, total interest, and total cost for two scenarios and for the current values in the Loan Analysis worksheet. The current interest rate equals 8.50% and the current years equal 15 (Figure 5-46). The first scenario sets the interest rate to 8.50% and the number of years to 30. The second scenario sets the interest rate to 10.50% and the number of years to 15.

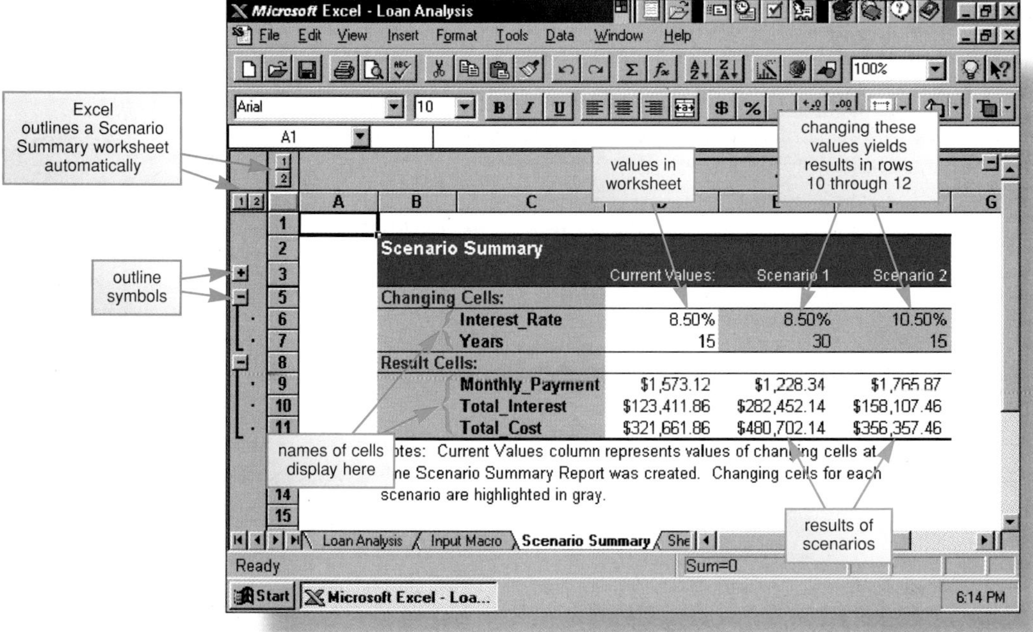

FIGURE 5-45

To Create Scenarios and a Scenario Summary Worksheet

1 **Point to Scenarios on the Tools menu (Figure 5-46).**

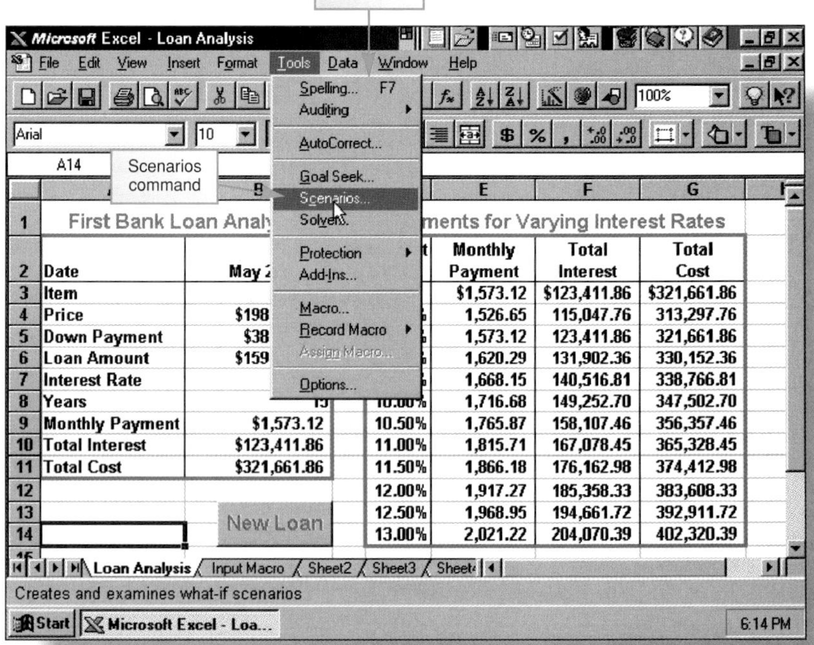

FIGURE 5-46

Click Scenarios.

The Scenario Manager dialog box displays informing you there are no scenarios defined (Figure 5-47).

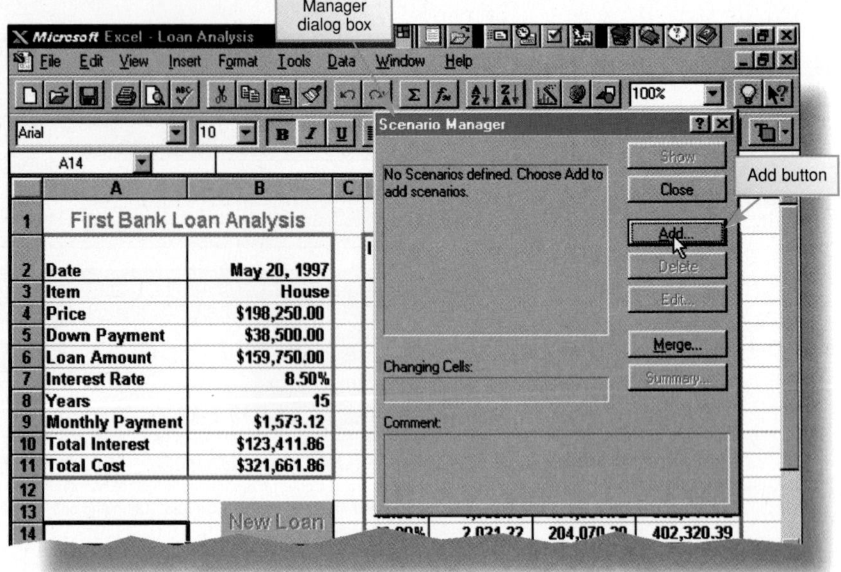

FIGURE 5-47

3 Click the Add button to add a scenario. When the Add Scenario dialog box displays, type `Scenario 1` **in the Scenario Name box, click the Changing Cells box, and drag over the range B7:B8 on the worksheet to assign B7:B8 to the Changing Cells box.**

*Excel displays a moving border around the cells in the worksheet to change (interest rate in cell B7 and years in cell B8) and assigns the range B7:B8 to the Changing Cells box in the **Add Scenario dialog box** (Figure 5-48).*

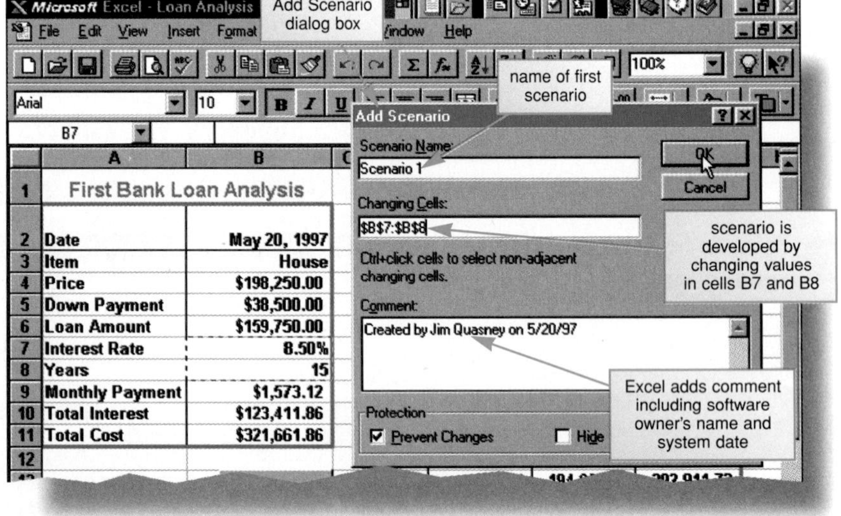

FIGURE 5-48

Click the OK button on the Add Scenario dialog box. When the Scenario Values dialog box displays, click the Years box and type 30 **to enter the years.**

*The **Scenario Values dialog box** displays as shown in Figure 5-49.*

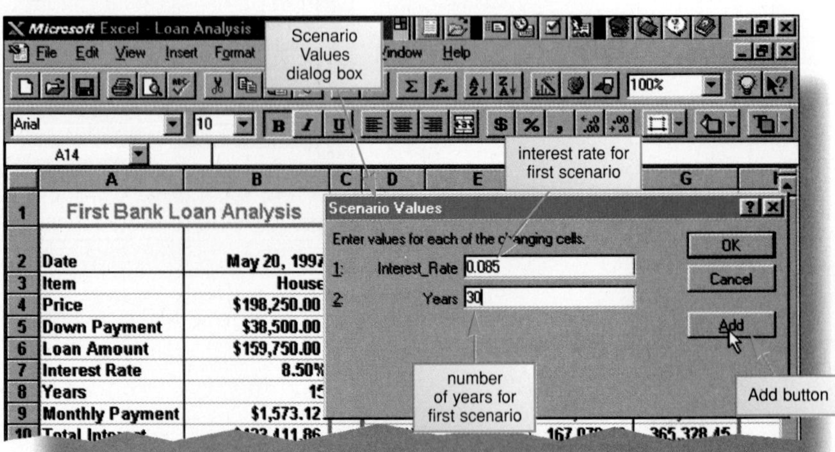

FIGURE 5-49

5 **Click the Add button in the Scenario Values dialog box to add the second scenario. When the Add Scenario dialog box displays, type** `Scenario 2` **in the Scenario Name box.**

The Add Scenario dialog box displays as shown in Figure 5-50. Excel automatically assigns the range $B$7:$B$8 to the Changing Cells box because this range was used in the prior scenario.

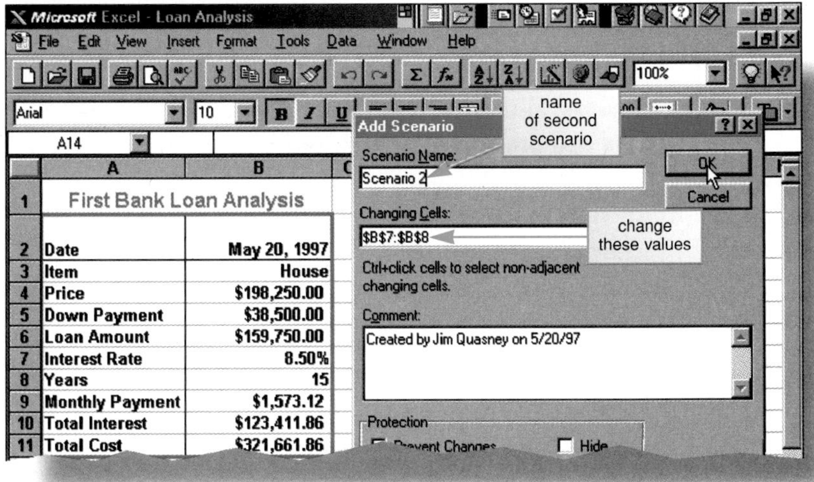

FIGURE 5-50

6 **Click the OK button on the Add Scenario dialog box. When the Scenario Values dialog box displays, type** `10.50%` **in the Interest_Rate box and** `15` **in the Years box.**

The Scenario Values dialog box displays as shown in Figure 5-51.

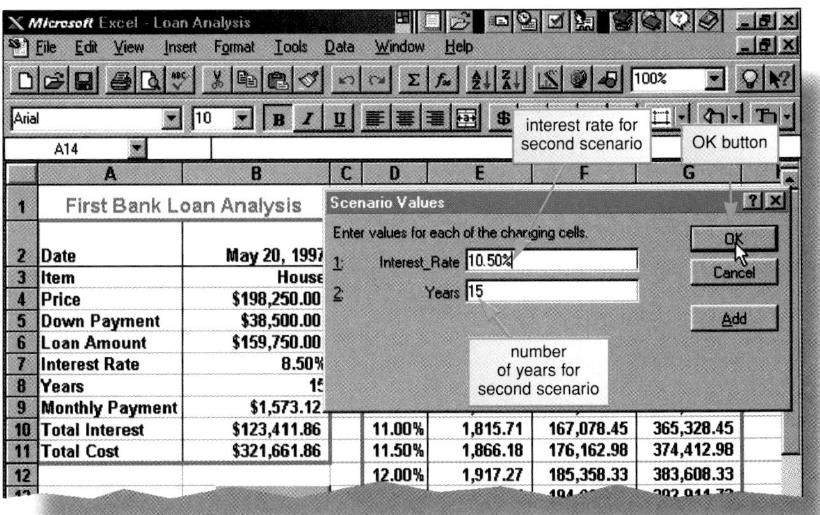

FIGURE 5-51

7 **Because this is the last scenario to create, click the OK button on the Scenario Values dialog box.**

The Scenario Manager dialog box displays with the two named scenarios (Figure 5-52).

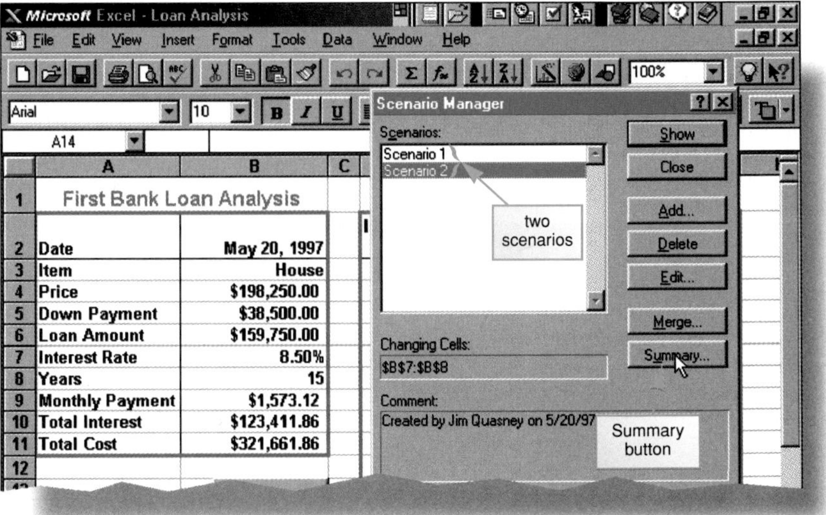

FIGURE 5-52

8 **Click the Summary button on the Scenario Manager dialog box. When the Scenario Summary dialog box displays, click the Result Cells box and drag over the range B9:B11 to indicate the cells for which you want results.**

The Scenario Summary dialog box displays as shown in Figure 5-53.

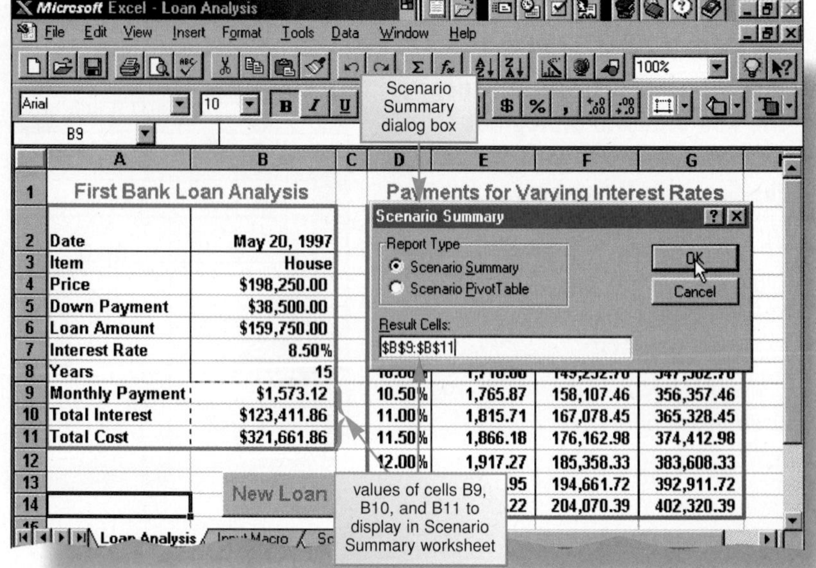

FIGURE 5-53

9 **Click the OK button on the Scenario Summary dialog box. Drag the Scenario Summary sheet tab to the immediate right of the Input Macro tab.**

The Scenario Summary worksheet displays as shown in Figure 5-54.

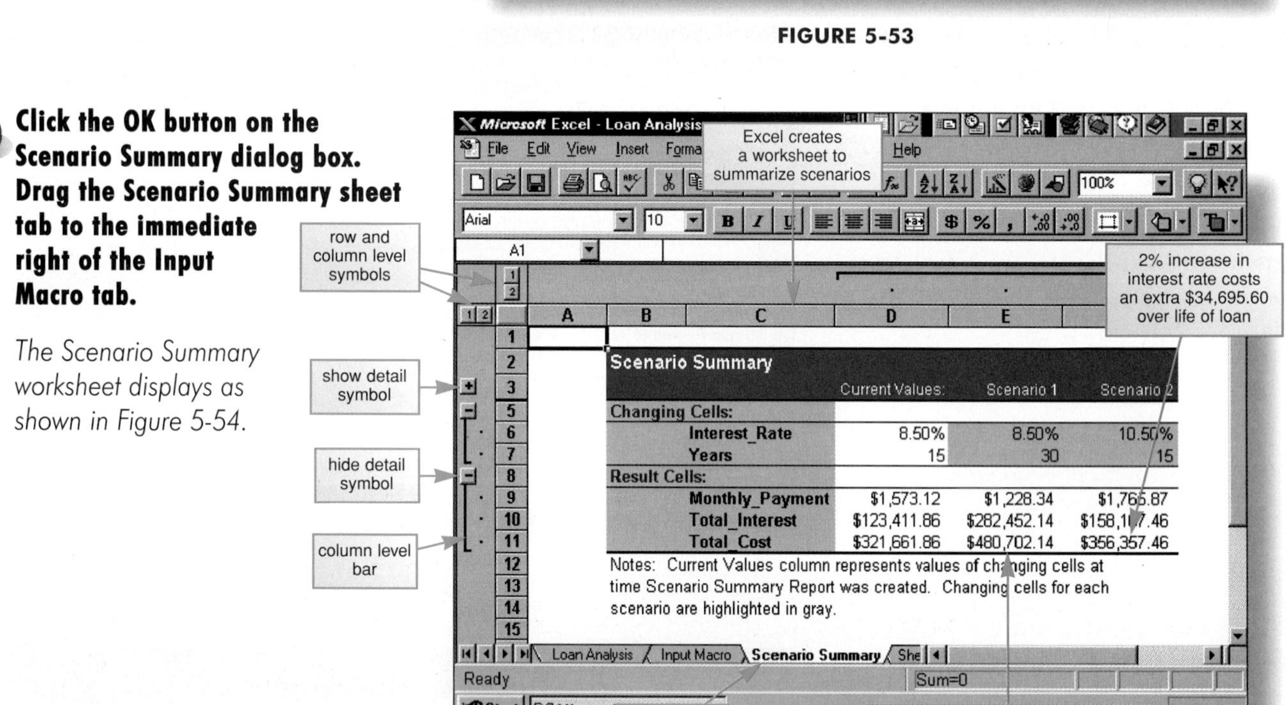

FIGURE 5-54

The Scenario Summary worksheet in Figure 5-54 shows the results of the current values (column D) in the Loan Analysis worksheet and two scenarios in columns E and F. Compare the Scenario 1 column to the Current Values column. In the Scenario 1 column, the interest rate is the same as in the Current Values column, but the length of time is 30 years rather than 15 years. Because the loan is for twice the length of time, the monthly payment is $344.78 less per month, but the total cost of the loan increases by $159,040.28 to $480,702.14.

In the Scenario 2 column of Figure 5-54, the number of years is the same as the Current Values column, but the interest rate is 2% greater. The 2% change increases the monthly payment by $192.75 per month and the total cost of the house to $356,357.46 or $34,695.60 more than the loan data in the Current Values column.

Working with an Outlined Worksheet

Excel automatically outlines the Scenario Summary worksheet. The **Outline symbols** display above the worksheet and to the left (Figure 5-54). You click the outline symbols to expand or collapse the worksheet. For example, if you click the **show detail symbol** Excel displays additional rows or columns that are summarized on the displayed row or column. If you click a **hide detail symbol**, Excel hides any detail rows that extend through the length of the corresponding **row level bar** or **column level bar**.

You can also expand or collapse a worksheet by clicking the **row level** or **column level** symbols above and to the left of row title 1. An outline is especially useful when working with large worksheets. To remove an outline, point to **Group and Outline** on the Data Menu, then click **Clear Outline** on the Group and Outline submenu.

More *About* Outlined Worksheets

You can outline any worksheet by clicking Auto Outline on the Group and Outline submenu. You display the Group and Outline submenu by pointing to Group and Outline on the Data menu.

Applying Scenarios Directly to the Worksheet

When you work with scenarios, it is not necessary to create the Scenario Summary Report worksheet shown in Figure 5-54. You can create the scenarios following the first seven steps of the previous example and then use the Show button on the Scenario Manager dialog box (Figure 5-52 on page 5.41) to apply the scenarios directly to the worksheet for which they were created. The following steps show how to apply the two scenarios created earlier directly to the worksheet.

To Apply Scenarios Directly to the Worksheet

1 Click the Loan Analysis tab. Click Scenarios on the Tools menu.

The Scenario Manager dialog box displays (Figure 5-55).

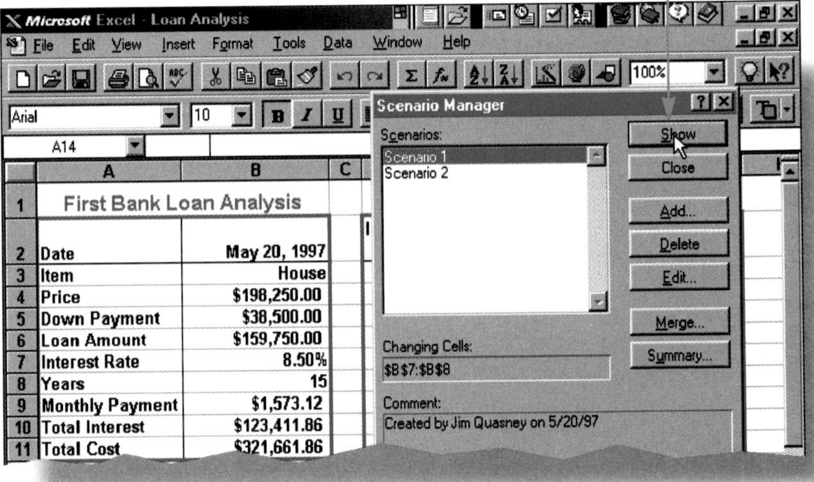

FIGURE 5-55

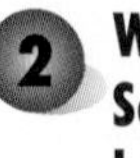

With Scenario 1 selected in the Scenarios box, click the Show button.

Excel inserts the numbers from Scenario 1 into the worksheet and recalculates all formulas (Figure 5-56). The entries in the range B7:B11 have changed so that they agree with the results in column E of the Scenario Summary Report worksheet shown in Figure 5-54.

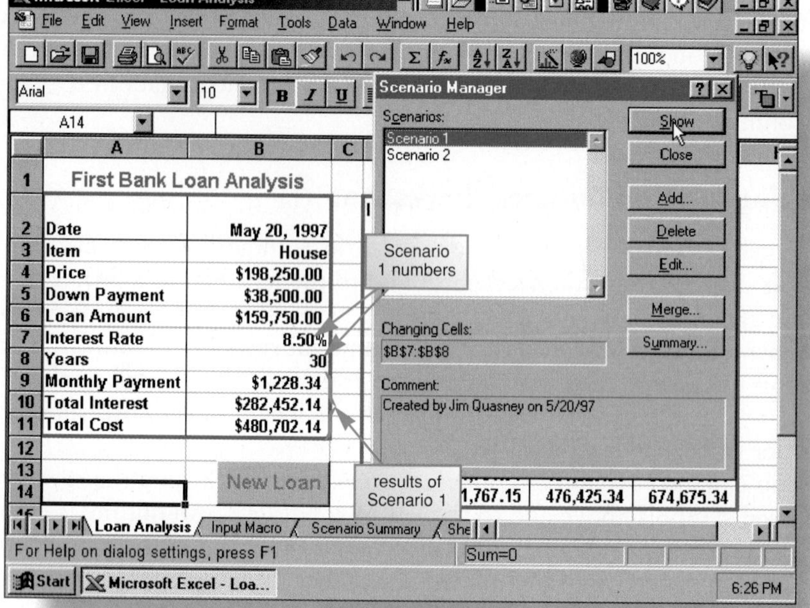

FIGURE 5-56

Click Scenario 2 in the Scenarios box in the Scenario Manager dialog box. Click the Show button.

Excel inserts the numbers from Scenario 2 into the worksheet and recalculates all formulas (Figure 5-57). Here again, the results in the worksheet agree exactly with column F of the Scenario Summary Report worksheet shown in Figure 5-54.

Click the Close button on the Scenario Manager dialog box. Enter 8.50% in cell B7 and 15 in cell B8, so the original results in Figure 5-55 display.

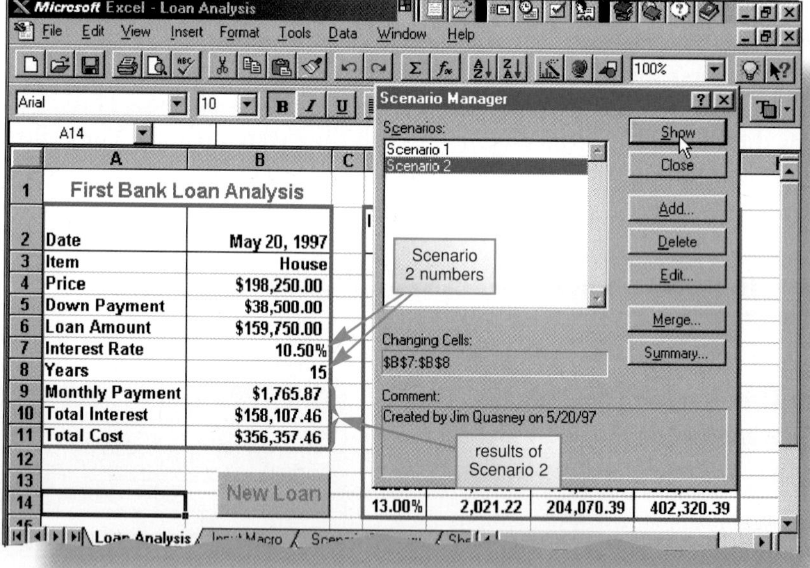

FIGURE 5-57

You can undo the scenario results by clicking the Undo button on the Standard toolbar or by clicking Undo Show on the Edit menu. If desired, you can then click the Redo button on the Standard toolbar or click Redo Show on the Edit menu to redisplay results of the scenario on the worksheet.

Scenario Manager is an important what-if tool for organizing your assumptions. Using Scenario Manager, you can define different scenarios with up to 32 changing cells per scenario. Once you have entered the scenarios, you can show them one by one as illustrated in the previous example, or you can create the Scenario Summary worksheet described earlier.

Protecting the Worksheet

When you build a worksheet that will be used by people who know little or nothing about computers and worksheets, it is important that you protect the cells in the worksheet that you do not want changed, namely the cells that contain text and formulas. In the loan analysis worksheet (Figure 5-58) the user should be allowed to change only five cells: the item in cell B3; the price in cell B4; the down payment in cell B5; the interest rate in cell B7; and the years in cell B8. Also, because of the way the command macro assigned to the New Loan button works, cell B6 should be unprotected. The remaining cells in the worksheet should be protected so that they cannot be changed by the user.

More *About* **Protecting Worksheets**

You can move from one unprotected cell to another in a worksheet by using the TAB and SHIFT+TAB keys.

When you create a new worksheet, all the cells are unprotected. **Unprotected cells**, or **unlocked cells**, are cells whose values you can change at any time, as opposed to **protected cells**, or **locked cells**, that you cannot change. If a cell is protected and the user attempts to change its value, Excel displays a dialog box with a message indicating the cells are protected.

You should protect cells only after the worksheet has been fully tested and displays the correct results. Protecting a worksheet is a two-step process:

1. Select the cells you want to leave unprotected and change their cell protection settings to unprotected.
2. Protect the entire worksheet.

At first glance, these steps may appear to be backwards. However, once you protect the entire worksheet you cannot change anything including the protection of individual cells. Thus, you identify first the cells you want to leave unprotected and then protect the entire worksheet.

The following steps show how to protect the loan analysis worksheet.

Steps To Protect a Worksheet

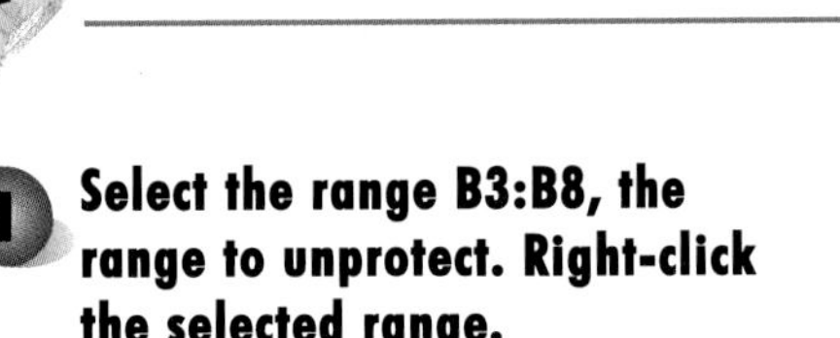

1 Select the range B3:B8, the range to unprotect. Right-click the selected range.

Excel displays the shortcut menu (Figure 5-58).

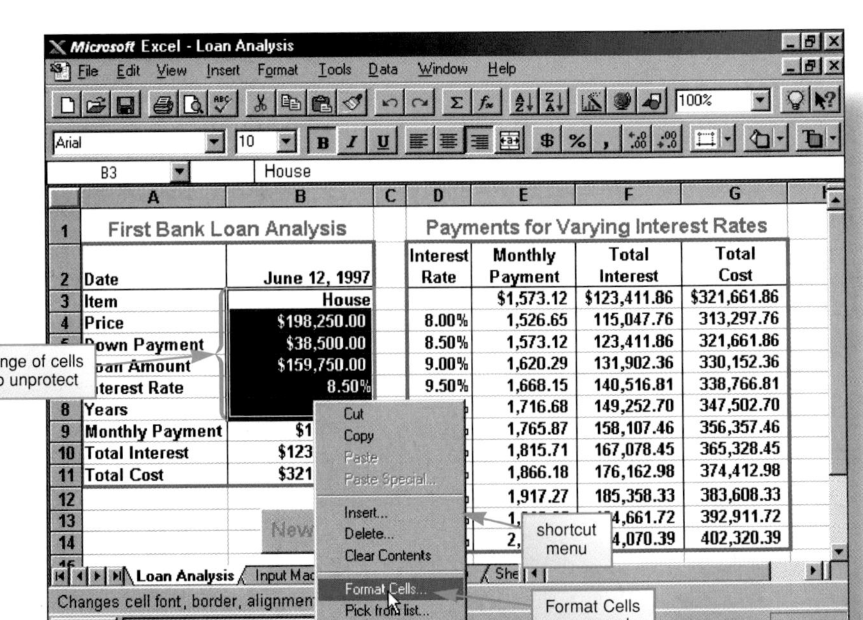

FIGURE 5-58

Click Format Cells on the shortcut menu. When the Format Cells dialog box displays, click the Protection tab. Click Locked.

The ***Protection tab*** *in the Format Cells dialog box displays with the check mark removed from the* ***Locked check box*** *(Figure 5-59).*

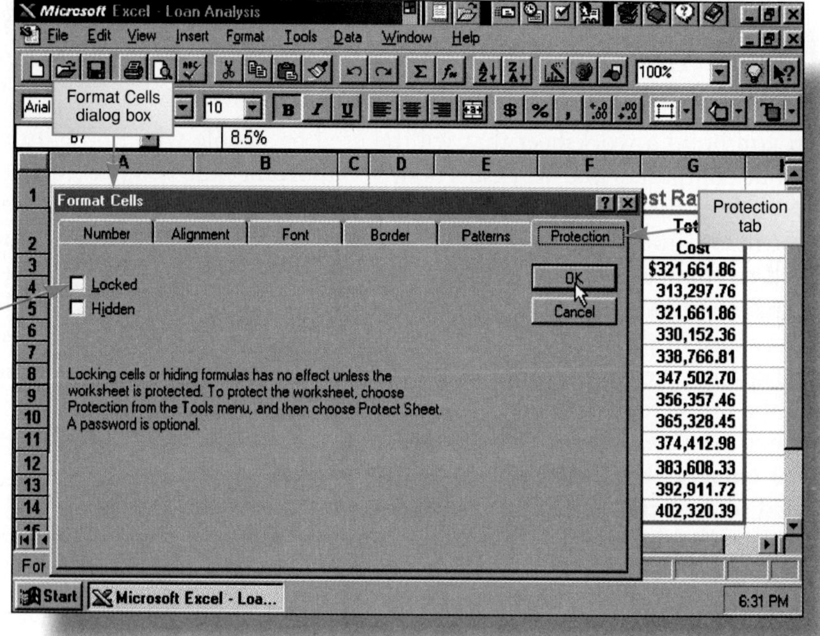

FIGURE 5-59

3 Click the OK button. Point to Protection on the Tools menu.

Excel displays the Tools menu and Protection submenu (Figure 5-60).

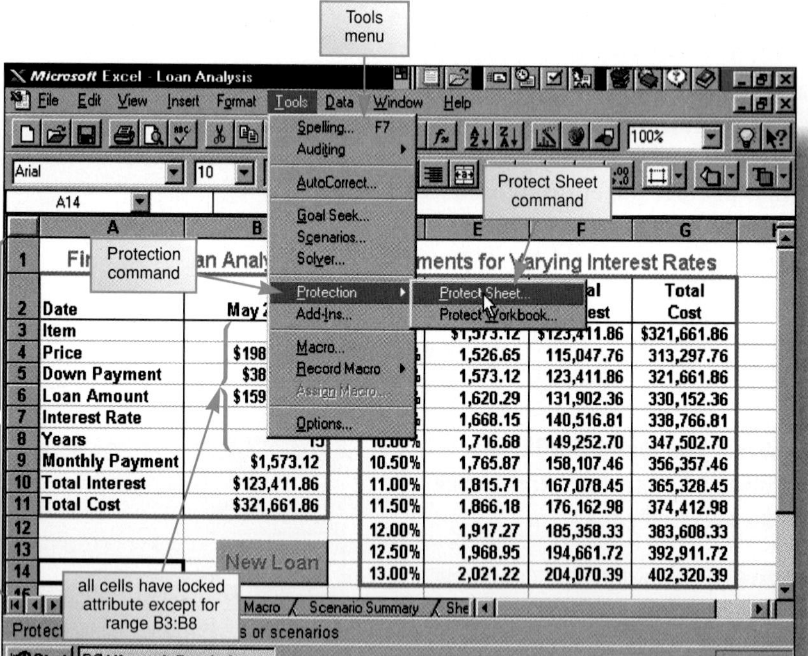

FIGURE 5-60

4 Click Protect Sheet on the Protection submenu.

*Excel displays the **Protect Sheet dialog box** (Figure 5-61).*

5 Click the OK button. Click the Save button on the Standard toolbar to save the protected workbook.

All the cells in the worksheet are protected, except for the range B3:B8. The range B3:B8 encompasses the cells in which you enter new loan data.

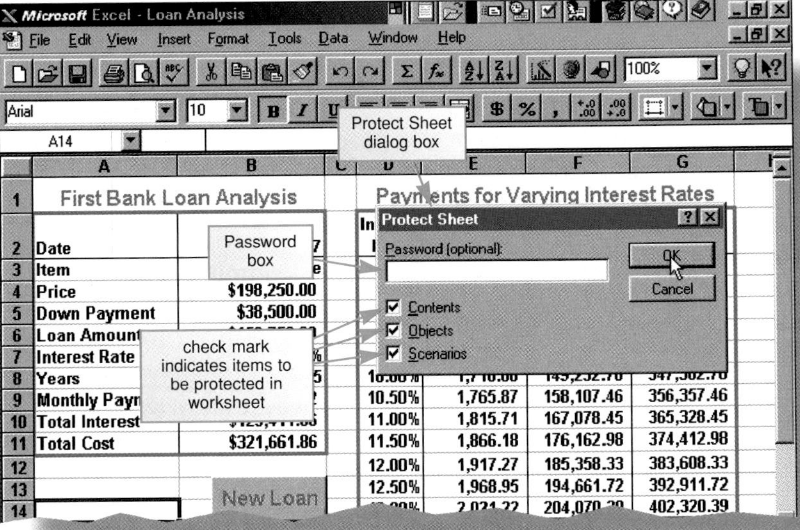

FIGURE 5-61

You can add a password in the Protect Sheet dialog box in Figure 5-61. You add a password when you want to keep others from changing the worksheet from protected to unprotected. You can also click any of the three check boxes (Contents, Objects, and Scenarios) shown in Figure 5-61 to unprotect them. Contents refers to the entries in the worksheet. Objects are charts and buttons. Scenarios refer to those scenarios associated with the worksheet being protected.

The protection pertains only to the active worksheet. If you want to protect additional sheets, select them before you begin the protection process or use **Protect Workbook** on the Protection submenu that displays (Figure 5-60) when you point to Protection on the Tools menu.

With the worksheet protected, you can still execute the macro InputMacro by clicking the New Loan button at any time because the cells referenced (B3:B8) by the macro are unprotected. However, if you attempt to change any protected cell, Excel displays a dialog box with a diagnostic message. For example, attempt to change the row title Item in cell A3. When you type the first character with cell A3 selected, Excel responds by displaying a diagnostic message in a dialog box. If you want to change any cells in the worksheet such as titles or formulas, unprotect the document by pointing to Protection on the Tools menu, and then click **Unprotect Sheet** from the Protection submenu.

More About Protecting Scenarios

To prevent others from making changes to your scenario, click the Prevent Changes check box (Figure 5-48 on page E 5.40). You also will have to activate sheet protection. You must clear the Prevent Changes check box or remove sheet protection before you edit or delete a scenario.

Exiting Excel

To exit Excel, follow the steps below.

TO EXIT EXCEL

Step 1: Click the Close button on the right side of the title bar.
Step 2: If the Microsoft Excel dialog box displays, click the No button.

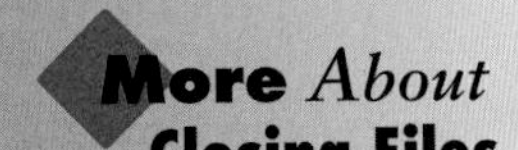

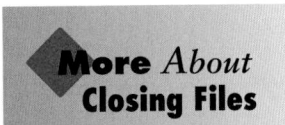

More About Closing Files

If you have multiple workbooks opened, you can close them all at the same time by holding down the SHIFT key when you click the File menu. The Close command changes to Close All. Click Close All and Excel will close all open workbooks.

Project Summary

The workbook developed in this project will handle all of Suann Weddington's requirements for the loan department at First Bank. The macro created to accept loan data and the protection features of Excel ensure that the loan officers will not change values in the wrong cells. The loan information, including the data table and Scenario Summary worksheet, is easy to read, which will improve customer relations. Finally, the macro created to print the worksheet will simplify providing the customer with a copy.

In this project you learned how to apply the PMT function to determine the monthly payment of a loan. You also learned how to analyze data by creating a data table and working with the Scenario Manager. This project explained how macros are used to automate worksheet tasks, and you learned how to build a macro that accepts loan data. Once the macro was built, it was assigned to a button in the worksheet. The button was then used to execute the macro. You also learned how to record a macro and play it back. Finally, you learned how to protect a document so a user can change only the contents of unprotected cells.

What You Should Know

Having completed this project, you should be able to perform the following tasks:

- Add a Button to the Worksheet and Assign a Macro to It *(E 5.30)*
- Apply Scenarios Directly to the Worksheet *(E 5.43)*
- Change the Font of the Entire Worksheet *(E 5.8)*
- Create a Percent Series Using the Fill Handle *(E 5.20)*
- Create Cell Names *(E 5.11)*
- Create Scenarios and a Scenario Summary Worksheet *(E 5.39)*
- Define a Range as a Data Table *(E 5.22)*
- Determine the Down Payment for a Specific Monthly Payment Using Goal Seek *(E 5.37)*
- Determine the Total Interest and Total Cost, and Save the Workbook *(E 5.17)*
- Draw an Outline and Borders *(E 5.29)*
- Enter a Macro on a Module Sheet *(E 5.28)*
- Enter and Format the Formulas in the Data Table *(E 5.21)*
- Enter New Loan Data *(E 5.24)*
- Enter the Data Table Title and Column Titles *(E 5.19)*
- Enter the Loan Amount Formula Using the Name Box *(E 5.13)*
- Enter the Loan Data *(E 5.10)*
- Enter the PMT Function *(E 5.16)*
- Enter the Worksheet Title, Row Titles, and System Date *(E 5.8)*
- Execute the Macro and Enter New Loan Data *(E 5.32)*
- Exit Excel *(E 5.47)*
- Format to Currency Style with a Floating Dollar Sign *(E 5.14)*
- Insert a Module Sheet *(E 5.27)*
- Outline and Format the Data Table and Save the Workbook *(E 5.23)*
- Play Back a Recorded Macro *(E 5.36)*
- Protect a Worksheet *(E 5.45)*
- Record a Macro to Print the Loan Analysis Worksheet in Landscape *(E 5.35)*
- Start Excel *(E 5.7)*

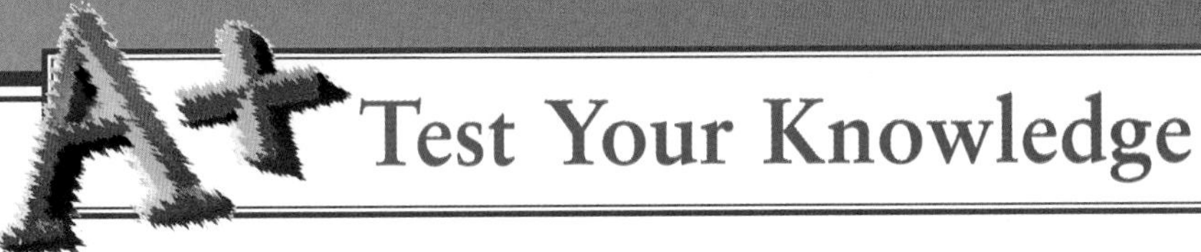

Test Your Knowledge

1 True/False

Instructions: Circle T if the statement is true or F if the statement is false.

T F 1. If cell B4 is named Balance and cell B5 is named Payment, then the formula =B4 - B5 can be written as =Balance - Payment.
T F 2. A data table is a cell that answers what-if questions.
T F 3. The cell you vary in a one-input data table is called the input cell.
T F 4. Use the Open command on the File menu to create a new macro sheet.
T F 5. A macro consists of a series of Visual Basic statements.
T F 6. A module sheet has cells similar to a worksheet.
T F 7. The Create Button button is on the Standard toolbar.
T F 8. When executed, the macro function InputBox causes a dialog box to display.
T F 9. When you open a new worksheet it is unprotected.
T F 10. Select the cells to unprotect after you protect the entire worksheet.

2 Multiple Choice

Instructions: Circle the correct response.

1. If payments are to be made on a monthly basis and the length of the loan is given in years, then __________ for the period argument in the PMT function.
   a. multiply years by 12
   b. divide years by 12
   c. enter years
   d. multiply years by 365
2. When the name of a cell is made up of two or more words, replace the spaces between the words with __________ when you use the name in a formula.
   a. minus signs (–)
   b. number signs (#)
   c. circumflexes (^)
   d. underscores (_)
3. Use the __________ function to determine a monthly payment on a loan.
   a. FV
   b. PMT
   c. PV
   d. NOW
4. A worksheet that summarizes what-if questions is called a(n)__________.
   a. scenario
   b. outlined worksheet
   c. Report worksheet
   d. Scenario Summary worksheet
5. In a one-input data table, the input cell __________.
   a. must be referenced directly or indirectly in the formula(s) at the top of the data table
   b. is the upper-left corner cell of the worksheet
   c. is a range of cells
   d. must be defined on the macro sheet
6. In a macro, use the __________ property to assign a value to a cell.
   a. Assign
   b. Clear
   c. Select
   d. Value

(continued)

A+ Test Your Knowledge

Multiple Choice *(continued)*

7. After creating a module sheet, return to the worksheet by __________.
   a. using the Window menu
   b. clicking the worksheet tab
   c. clicking the Open command on the File menu
   d. entering the End Sub statement
8. To name a cell, use the __________ command on the Insert menu.
   a. Name c. Apply Names
   b. Paste Function d. Paste Name
9. Data tables are usually created __________.
   a. in an unused area of the worksheet c. in a cell
   b. on a toolbar d. on a chart sheet
10. For a one-input data table to work properly, the input cell must be __________.
    a. a cell reference in the formula you are using
    b. on another worksheet
    c. blank
    d. the upper left cell in the data table

3 Understanding Macro Functions

Instructions: Assume a macro sheet is open. In the space provided, write the Visual Basic statement that completes the specified task.

1. Select the range B12:C13 on the worksheet: ____________________
2. Clear the selected range: ____________________
3. Accept a value from the user and assign it to cell C14 in the worksheet: ____________________
4. Assign the formula =C4 - D3 to cell B12 in the worksheet: ____________________
5. End the Sub procedure: ____________________
6. Select cell B16: ____________________

4 Understanding Functions, Data Analysis, and Worksheet Protection

Instructions: Answer the following.

1. Write a function to determine the monthly payment (PMT function) on a loan of $134,000.00, over a period of 15 years, at an annual interest rate of 9.2%. Make sure the function returns the monthly payment as a positive number.
2. Write a function to determine the future value (FV function) of a $250.00 a month investment for 15 years if the interest rate is fixed at 7.25% and compounded monthly.
3. Explain the difference between a protected cell and an unprotected cell. How do you change the contents of a cell that is protected?

Use Help

1 Reviewing Project Activities

Instructions: Perform the following tasks using a computer.

1. Start Excel.
2. Double-click the Help button on the Standard toolbar to display the Help Topics: Microsoft Excel dialog box. Click the Contents tab. Double-click the Creating Formulas and Auditing Workbooks book. Double-click the Working with Names book. Double-click the link Using Names in Formulas. Click each link and read the information. Click the Help Topics button. Double-click the Naming formulas and constants in formulas link. Read and print the information and hand it in to your instructor. Do the same for the Names cells link. Close the Help window.
3. If the Help Topics: Microsoft Excel dialog box is not on the screen, double-click the Help button on the Standard toolbar. Click the Find tab. Type `financial` in the top box labeled 1. Double-click Financial Functions in the bottom box labeled 3. Read and print the information. Click the Help Topics button. Hand in the printout to your instructor.
4. If the Help Topics: Microsoft Excel dialog box is not on the screen, double-click the Help button on the Standard toolbar. Click the Index tab. Type `Visual Basic` in the top box labeled 1. Under Visual Basic code in the bottom box labeled 2, one at a time double-click (1) copying from Help Examples; and (2) debugging. Click the links and read the information.
5. If the Help Topics: Microsoft Excel dialog box is not on the screen, double-click the Help button on the Standard toolbar. Click the Answer Wizard tab. Obtain information on the following topic: How do I create a Scenario Summary report? Read and print the information and hand it in to your instructor.

2 Expanding on the Basics

Instructions: Perform the following tasks using a computer.

1. Start Excel.
2. Double-click the Help button on the Standard toolbar to display the Help Topics: Microsoft Excel. Click the Contents tab. Double-click the Retrieving and Analyzing Data book. Double-click the Solving What-If Problems book. Double-click the Fill in a one-variable, column-oriented data table and Fill in a two-variable data table links. Read and print the information (include all links). Hand in the printouts to your instructor.
3. If the Help Topics: Microsoft Excel dialog box is not on the screen, double-click the Help button on the Standard toolbar. Use the Index tab to collect information on the following topics: goal seeking, data tables, and looping in Visual Basic. Hand in one printout on each topic to your instructor.
4. If the Help Topics: Microsoft Excel dialog box is not on the screen, double-click the Help button on the Standard toolbar. Use the Find tab to collect information on debugging Visual Basic code and the most frequently asked questions about Visual Basic. Hand in one printout on each topic to your instructor.

Apply Your Knowledge

1 Assigning a Command Macro to a Button and Protecting a Worksheet

Instructions: Start Excel and perform the following tasks:

1. Open the workbook Net Dial Inventory (Figure 5-62) from the Excel folder on the Student Floppy Disk.
2. Click the Accept Total Items tab and print the macro (Figure 5-63). Briefly explain the function of each of the five Visual Basic statements between Sub and End Sub. Click the Inventory Listing tab. Click the Drawing button on the Standard toolbar to display the Drawing toolbar. Add the button shown in Figure 5-62. Assign the macro titled InputMacro to the button. Change the title of the button to Acceptable Total Items.
3. Use the Format Cells command on the shortcut menu to unprotect cell C9. Use the Protection command on the Tools menu to protect the worksheet. Try to enter a value in any cell other than C9. What happens? Write your answer at the bottom of the macro printout.
4. Click the Acceptable Total Items button and enter 100000. The words in the Excessive Parts column (column F) change based on the value entered. Print the worksheet. Press CTRL+` and print the formulas version of the worksheet. Press CTRL+` to display the values version. Use the button to enter 189000. Print the worksheet.
5. Save the worksheet as Net Dialing Inventory 2.

Net Dial Inventory

Plant	Item 1	Item 2	Item 3	Total	Excessive Items
Seattle	43,129	45,120	37,165	125,414	NO
Houston	70,532	65,219	43,865	179,616	YES
Boston	22,143	65,982	34,910	123,035	NO
Total	135,804	176,321	115,940	428,065	
Acceptable Total Items:		148,000		May 25, 1997	

Acceptable Total Items

FIGURE 5-62

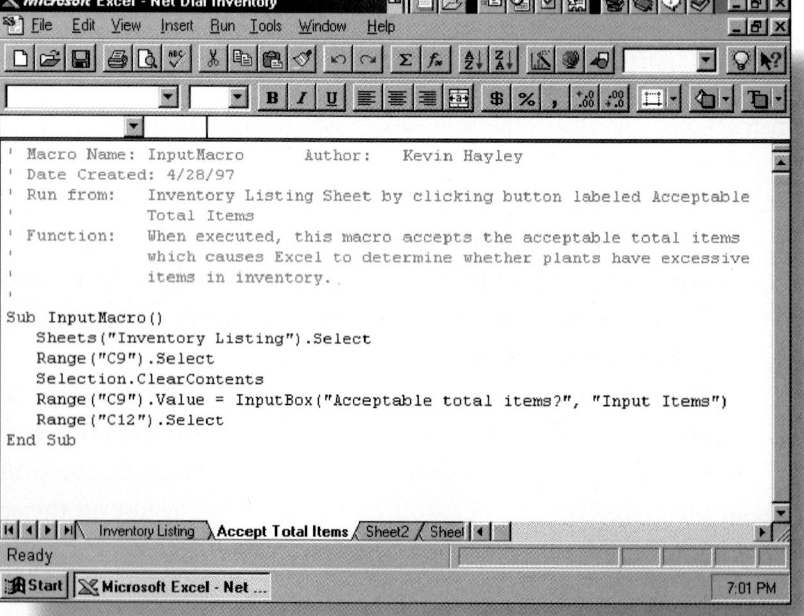

```
' Macro Name: InputMacro      Author:   Kevin Hayley
' Date Created: 4/28/97
' Run from:    Inventory Listing Sheet by clicking button labeled Acceptable
'              Total Items
' Function:    When executed, this macro accepts the acceptable total items
'              which causes Excel to determine whether plants have excessive
'              items in inventory.
'
Sub InputMacro()
   Sheets("Inventory Listing").Select
   Range("C9").Select
   Selection.ClearContents
   Range("C9").Value = InputBox("Acceptable total items?", "Input Items")
   Range("C12").Select
End Sub
```

FIGURE 5-63

In the Lab

1 Determining the Monthly Mortgage Payment

Problem: You are a part-time consultant for a loan company. You have been asked to build a worksheet (Figure 5-64 on the next page) that determines the monthly payment and includes a one-input data table that shows the monthly payment, total interest, and total cost for a loan for varying years. The worksheet will be used by loan officers who know little about computers and worksheets. Thus, create a macro (Figure 5-65 on the next page) that will guide the user through entering the loan data. Assign the macro to a button on the worksheet.

Instructions: With a blank workbook on the screen, perform the following tasks:

1. Bold the entire worksheet. Change the column widths to the following: A = 14.57; B = 18.00; C = 5.00; D = 16.57; E = 11.86; and F = 11.57.
2. Enter the Monthly Loan section of the worksheet in the first 5 rows. Change the title of the worksheet in cell A1 to 14 point and center it across columns A through E. Create names for the range B2:B4 and E2:E4 using the Name command on the Insert menu. Use the names in the columns on the left of each range.
3. Enter the following loan data: Item = 1997 Chevy Van; Price = $22,500; Down Payment = $3,500; Interest Rate = 9.90%; and Years = 5. Format the ranges B3:B4 and E2:E4 as shown in Figure 5-64.
4. Assign cell E4 the following formula using Point mode and the Name box in the formula bar: =PMT(Interest_Rate / 12, 12 * Years, -Loan_Amount)
5. Enter the Payments for the Varying Years section of the worksheet. Assign cell D8 the formula =Monthly_Payment, cell E8 the formula =12 * Years * Monthly_Payment + Down_Payment, and cell F8 the formula =E8 – Price. Use the fill handle to create the series in the range C9:C18. Create a data table in the range C8:F18 using the Table command on the Data menu. Use cell E3 as the input cell.
6. Change the name of the tab for the worksheet to Monthly Payment. Add your name, course, computer laboratory assignment number (Lab5-1), date, and instructor name in column A beginning in cell A15. Save the worksheet using the filename Monthly Loan Payment. Print the worksheet. Press CTRL+` and print the formulas version. Press CTRL+` to display the values version.
7. Use the Macro command on the Insert menu to create the macro in Figure 5-65. Change the name of the tab for the macro to Input Macro. Print the macro.
8. Click the Monthly Payment tab. Display the Drawing toolbar. Create the button shown below the Loan Payment section in column A of Figure 5-64. Assign the macro InputMacro to the button. Hide the Drawing toolbar. Unprotect the range B2:B4 and E2:E3. Protect the worksheet. Click the Save button on the Standard toolbar to save the worksheet.
9. Use the newly created button to determine the monthly payment for the following loan data and print the worksheet for each data set: (a) Item = House; Price = $250,000; Down Payment = $55,000; Interest Rate = 10.50%; and Years =15; (b) Item = Mobile Home Price = $75,800; Down Payment = $12,500; Interest Rate = 8.25%; and Years = 10. The Monthly Payment for (a) is $2,155.53 and for (b) $776.39.

(continued)

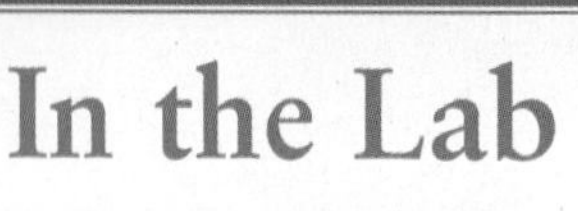

Determining the Monthly Mortgage Payment *(continued)*

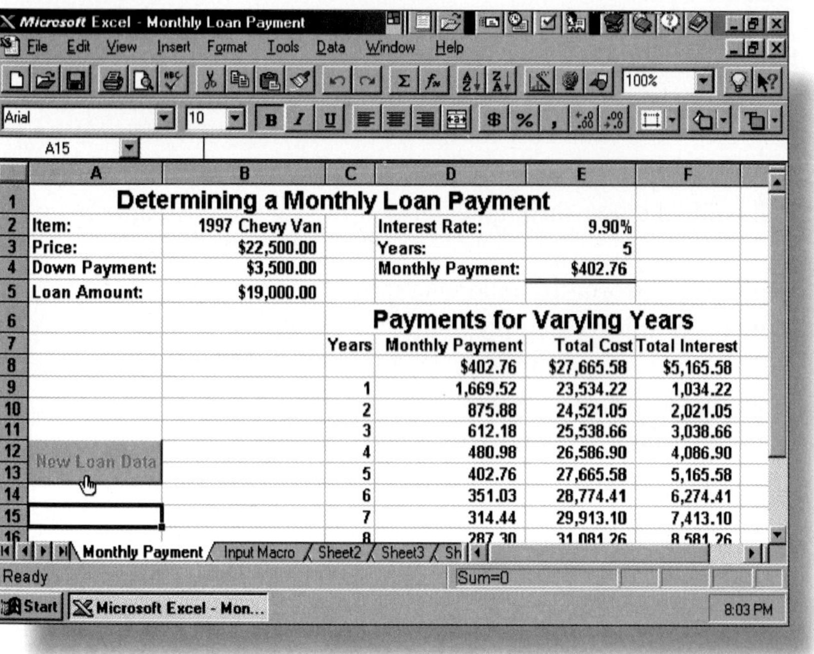

FIGURE 5-64

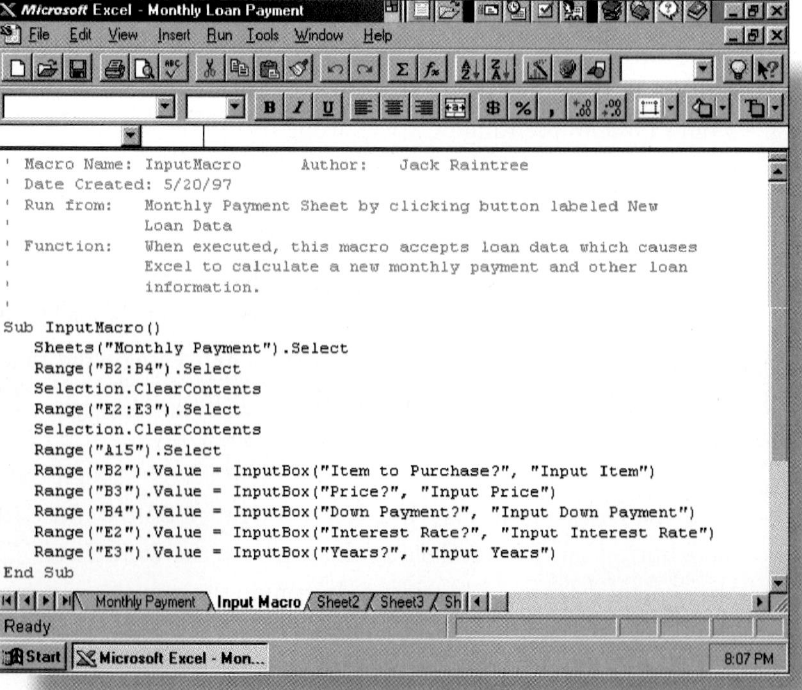

FIGURE 5-65

2 Determining the Future Value of an Investment

Problem: The Insurance company you work for is in need of a Future Value worksheet that its agents can use with a portable computer when they visit clients. A future value computation tells the user what a constant monthly payment is worth after a period of time if the insurance company pays a fixed interest rate.

An agent survey indicates they want a worksheet similar to the one in Figure 5-66 on the next page that includes not only a future value computation, but also a **two-input data table** that determines future values for varying interest rates and monthly payments. The survey indicates that the agents know little about computers and worksheets. Thus, you must create a macro (Figure 5-67 on the next page) that will guide the agent through entering the future value data. Assign the macro to a button. Protect the worksheet so that the agents can change values only in the cells that contain the data required to compute the future value.

Instructions: With a blank workbook on the screen, perform the following tasks:

1. Bold the entire worksheet. Change the column widths of the entire worksheet to 16.14.
2. Enter the Future Value Computations section of the worksheet (A1:E4). Assign cell B2 the NOW function so it displays the system date. Format the system date so it appears as shown in Figure 5-66. Enter the following data in cells B3, B4, and E2: Monthly Payment (B2) = $125.00; Interest Rate (B3) = 6.75%; and Years (E2) = 25. Create names for the range B3:B4 and E2:E4 using the columns to the left. Assign cell E3 the following formula:
   =FV(Interest_Rate / 12, 12 * Years, -Monthly_Payment)
   Assign cell E4 the following formula:
   =12 * Years * Monthly_Payment
3. Enter the Varying the Interest Rate and Monthly Payment data table. Assign cell A7 the entry =Future_Value. Assign cells B7, C7, D7, and E7 the following monthly payments: $100.00, $150.00, $200.00, and $250.00, respectively. Use the fill handle to create the series in the range A8:A15. Create a data table in the range A7:E15 using the Table command from the Data menu. Use cell B3 as the row input cell and cell B4 as the column input cell. Rename the Sheet1 tab Future Values.
4. Add your name, course, computer laboratory assignment number (Lab5-2), date, and instructor name in column A beginning in cell A19. Save the workbook using the filename Future Value. Print the worksheet with the future value data shown in Figure 5-66. Press CTRL+` and print the formulas version of the worksheet. Press CTRL+` to display the values version.
5. Use the Macro command on the Insert menu to create the macro in Figure 5-67. Rename the tab Input Data. Print the macro.
6. Click the Future Values tab. Display the Drawing toolbar. Create the button shown in cell A1 in Figure 5-66. Assign the macro InputMacro to the button. Hide the Drawing toolbar. Unprotect the ranges B3:B4, cell E2, and the range B7:E7. Protect the worksheet. Click the Save button on the Standard toolbar to save the workbook.

(continued)

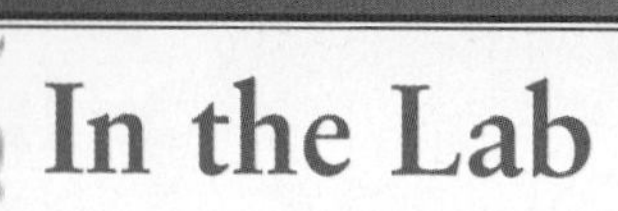

Determining the Future Value of an Investment *(continued)*

7. Use the New Data button in cell A1 (Figure 5-66) to determine the future value for the following data and print the worksheet for each data set: (a) Monthly Payment = $300.00; Interest Rate = 8.00%; Years = 20. Also make the following changes: cell B7 = $400; C7 = $500; D7 = $600; E7 = $700. (b) Monthly Payment = $25.00; Interest Rate = 7.25%; Years = 10. Also make the following changes: cell B7 = $50; C7 = $75; D7 = $100; E7 = $125. The future value in cell E3 for (a) is $176,706.12 and for (b) $4,387.17.

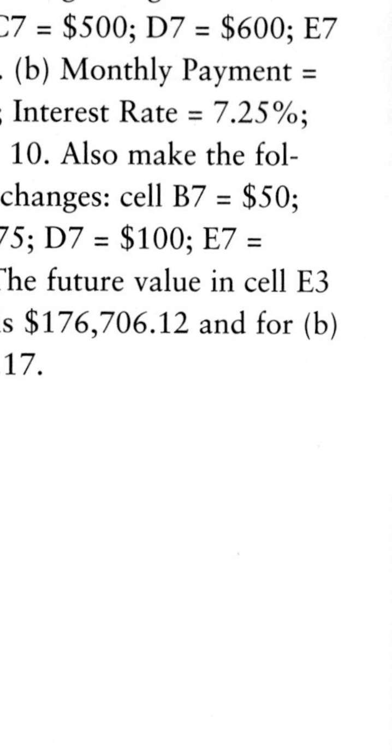

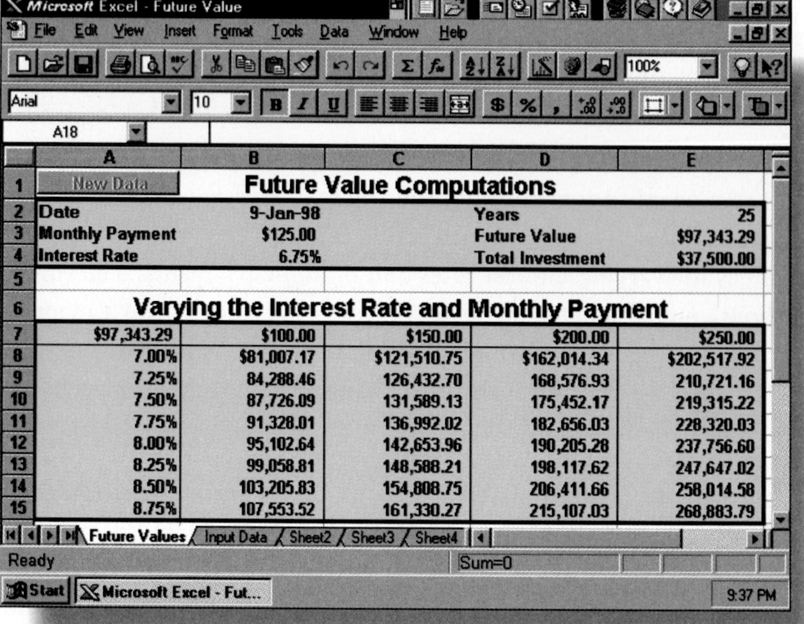

FIGURE 5-66

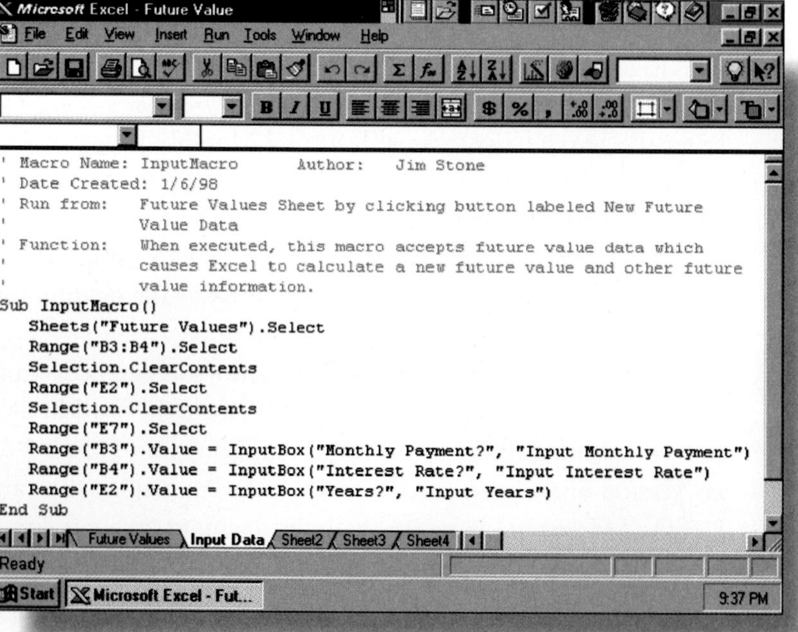

FIGURE 5-67

In the Lab

3 Building an Amortization Table and Analyzing Data

Problem: Each student in your Office Automation course is assigned a "live project" with a local company. You have been assigned to the J. B. Richardson Loan Company to generate the loan information worksheet in Figure 5-68 on the next page and the Scenario Summary worksheet in Figure 5-69 on the next page. The president also wants you to demonstrate the goal seeking capabilities of Excel.

Instructions: With a blank workbook on the screen, perform the following tasks:

1. Bold the entire worksheet. Enter the worksheet title in cell A1 and increase its font size to 16. Enter the text in the ranges A2:A4 and D2:D4. Use the Name command on the Insert menu to name the cells in the ranges B2:B4 and E2:E4 using the columns to the left. Enter $267,500.00 in cell B2, $52,000.00 in cell B3, 8.45% in cell E2, and 30 in cell E3 (Figure 5-68). In cell B4, enter the formula: =Price - Down_Pymt. In cell E4, enter the PMT function:

   =PMT(Rate / 12, 12 * Years, – Loan_Amount)
2. Increase the widths of columns A through E to 15.00. Center the worksheet title over the range A1:E1. Color the background of the range A2:E4 and add a heavy outline to the range.
3. Enter the column titles for the amortization schedule in the range A5:E5. An amortization schedule is a tabular report that shows the gradual extinguishment of a loan. Use the fill handle to generate the years in the range A6:A35.
4. Assign the formulas and functions to the cells indicated in Table 5-3.
5. Copy cell B7 to the range B8:B35. Copy the range C6:E6 to the range C7:E35. Draw the borders shown in Figure 5-68. Rename the sheet tab Loan Information.
6. Save the workbook using the filename Richardson Loan Company. Print the worksheet with the loan data and loan information in Figure 5-68. Press CTRL+` and print the formulas version of the worksheet. Press CTRL+` to display the values version.
7. Unprotect the ranges B2:B4 and E2:E3. Protect the worksheet. Save the worksheet.
8. Use Excel's goal seeking capabilities to determine the down payment required for the loan data in Figure 5-68 if the monthly payment is set to $1,500.00. The down payment that results for a monthly payment of $1,500.00 is $71,517.06. Print the worksheet with the new monthly payment of $1,500.00. Change the down payment in cell B3 back to $52,000.00.

Table 5-3

CELL	FORMULA OR FUNCTION
B6	=Loan_Amount
C6	=IF(A6 <= Years, PV(Rate / 12, 12 * (Years - A6), -Monthly_Pymt), 0)
D6	=B6 - C6
E6	=IF(B6 > 0, 12 * Monthly_Pymt - D6, 0)
B7	=C6
D36	=SUM(D6:D35)
E36	=SUM(E6:E35)
E37	=Down_Pymt
E38	=D36 + E36 + E37

(continued)

In the Lab

Building an Amortization Table and Analyzing Data *(continued)*

9. Unprotect the worksheet. Name cell E36 Total_Interest by using the Name command from the Insert menu, and then using the Define command from the cascading menu. Use the same command to assign the name Total_Cost to cell E38. These names will show up in the Scenario Summary worksheet in the next step. Protect the worksheet.
10. Use Scenario Manager to create a Scenario Summary worksheet (Figure 5-69) for the following scenarios: (1) Interest Rate = 8.45% and Years = 15; (2) Interest rate = 10.00% and Years = 15; and (3) Interest Rate = 10.00% and Years = 30. After the Scenario Summary worksheet displays, move the Scenario Summary tab to the immediate right of the Loan Information tab. Print the Scenario Summary worksheet. Activate the Loan Information worksheet and save the workbook.

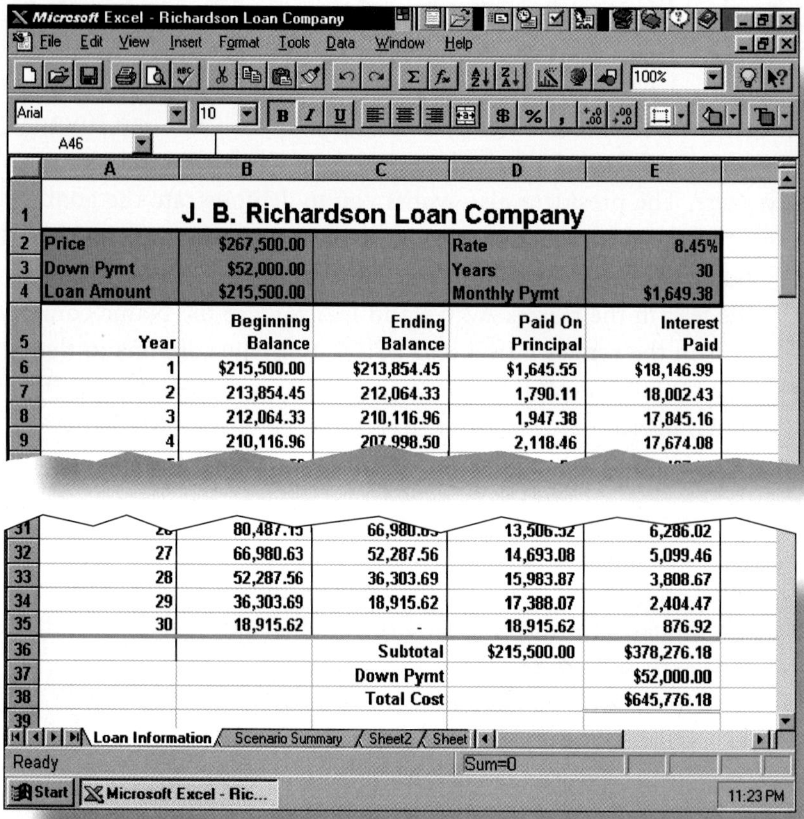

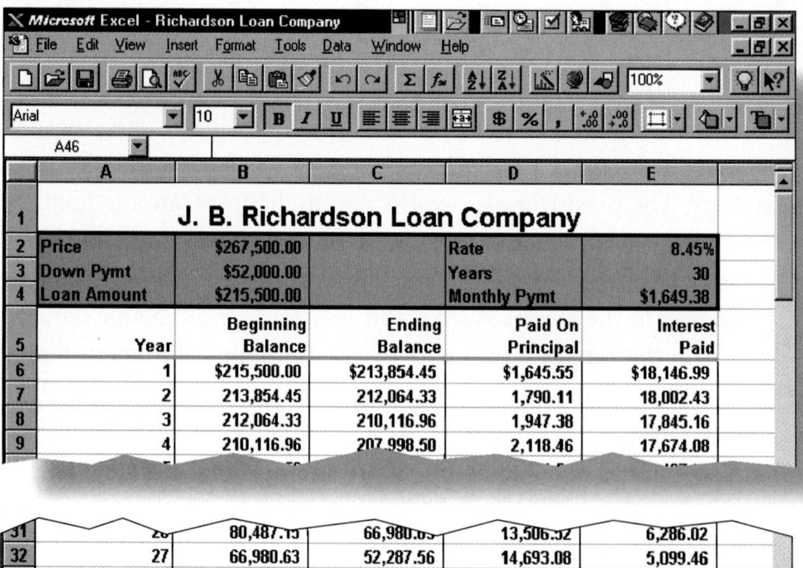

FIGURE 5-68

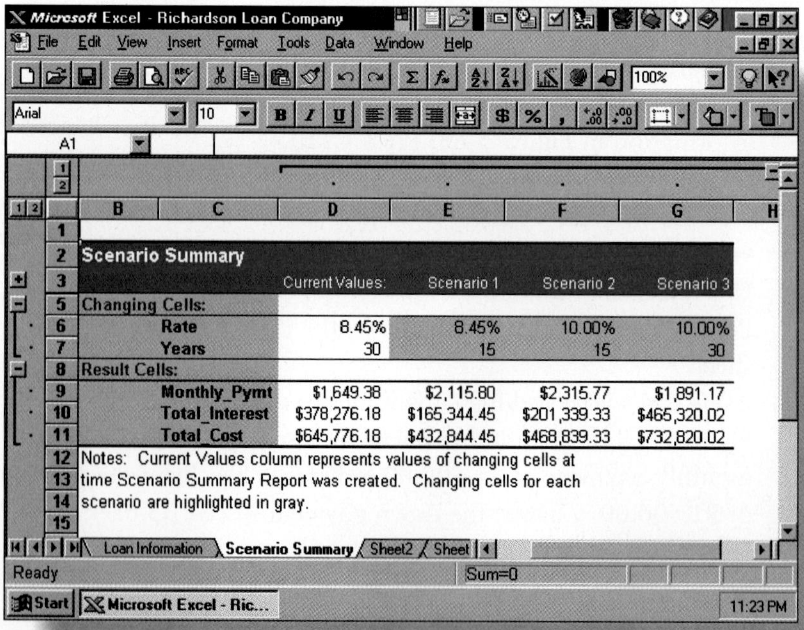

Scenario Summary		Current Values:	Scenario 1	Scenario 2	Scenario 3
Changing Cells:					
	Rate	8.45%	8.45%	10.00%	10.00%
	Years	30	15	15	30
Result Cells:					
	Monthly_Pymt	$1,649.38	$2,115.80	$2,315.77	$1,891.17
	Total_Interest	$378,276.18	$165,344.45	$201,339.33	$465,320.02
	Total_Cost	$645,776.18	$432,844.45	$468,839.33	$732,820.02

Notes: Current Values column represents values of changing cells at time Scenario Summary Report was created. Changing cells for each scenario are highlighted in gray.

FIGURE 5-69

Cases and Places

The difficulty of these case studies varies:

◗ Case studies preceded by a single half moon are the least difficult. You are asked to create the required worksheet based on information that has already been placed in an organized form.

◗◗ Case studies preceded by two half moons are more difficult. You must organize the information presented before using it to create the required worksheet.

◗◗◗ Case studies preceded by three half moons are the most difficult. You must decide on a specific topic, then obtain and organize the necessary information before using it to create the required worksheet.

1 ◗ The value of an asset frequently declines over time. When the value falls at a steady rate, the loss each year is called **straight-line depreciation (SLN)**. Depreciation is considered a business expense. Straight-line depreciation is based on an asset's initial cost, how long it can be used (called useful life), and the price at which it eventually can be sold (called salvage value). Louis Quatorze, president of Versailles Landscape, recently purchased a new truck. Louis wants a worksheet that uses a financial function to show the truck's straight-line depreciation (SLN) and a formula to determine the annual rate of depreciation. Louis has supplied the following information: Cost: $36,584; Salvage: $10,000; Life: 6 years; and Rate of depreciation: SLN / Cost.

Louis is not sure how much he will be able to sell the truck for. Create a data table that shows straight-line depreciation and rate of depreciation for salvage costs from $6,000 to $14,000, in one-thousand-dollar-increments.

2 ◗ Laius and Jocasta's dream for their son Eddie is that one day he will attend their alma mater, Thebes College. For the next ten years, they plan to make monthly deposits to a savings account at a local bank. The account pays 6% annual interest, compounded monthly. Create a worksheet for the parents that uses a financial function to show the future value (FV) of their investment and a formula to determine the percentage of the college's tuition saved. Laius and Jocasta have supplied the following information: Tuition: $80,000; Rate (per month): 6% / 12; Nper (number of monthly payments): 10 * 12; Pmt (payment each period): $200; and Percentage of tuition saved: FV /Tuition.

Laius and Jocasta are not sure how much they will be able to save each month. Create a data table that shows the future value and percentage of tuition saved for monthly payments from $100 to $500, in fifty-dollar increments.

3 ◗◗ The Rousseau Rural School is offering its faculty a generous retirement package. Julie Emile has acceped the proposal, but before moving to warmer climes she wants to settle her account with the school credit union. Julie has four years remaining on a car loan, with an interest rate of 5% and $250 each month. The credit union is willing to accept the present value (PV) of the loan. Develop a worksheet showing how much Julie must pay. Because it anticipates other retiring pedagogues will want to pay off their loans, the credit union also would like a macro to determine the present value of any loan based on the interest rate, number of years remaining, and payment each period. Attach the macro to a button on the worksheet.

Cases and Places

4 ▶▶ Tired of living in a tiny apartment, Alice and Ralph have decided to save for the down payment on a house. Their neighbor, Ed, who works for the sewer authority, promises he can get the pair an annual interest rate of 11% through a special city annuity program. Ralph would like a worksheet that determines how much their monthly payment (PMT) must be so that in two years the value of the account is $15,000. Alice realizes Ralph is full of grand schemes that often go awry, so in case Ralph's plans change she has asked that a macro be written to find a monthly payment based on varying interest rates, number of years, and/or future values. Attach the macro to a button on the worksheet.

5 ▶▶▶ Although it is difficult to save money while going to school, students find having a small nest egg after graduation is a real boon, allowing them to wait for just the right job opportunity. Visit a local financial institution and obtain data on its savings account interest rate. With this information, prepare a worksheet that shows the future value (FV) of a savings account based on the amount of money you can afford to save each month and the length of time remaining until commencement. Create a data table on the worksheet that illustrates the future value of your savings using a range of monthly payments, in reasonable increments, from well below what can be spared to far above what could ever be managed.

6 ▶▶▶ For most people, buying a car not only means finding one they like, it also entails finding one they can afford. Many dealerships offer financing plans to prospective buyers. Visit an automobile dealership and locate your favorite car. Talk to a salesperson about the cost, down payment, amount that must be borrowed, annual loan interest rate, and length of time for which the loan runs. With this information, develop a worksheet to calculate your monthly payment (PMT). Consider a number of cars before making a decision, and then write a macro that ascertains the monthly payment for any car based on the car's cost, required down payment, interest rate, and payment periods. Attach the macro to a button on the worksheet.

7 ▶▶▶ Some things "hold their value;" that is, they are worth almost as much after years have passed as they were when brand new. How well does computer equipment hold its value? Using old magazines, find the original selling price of at least one personal computer and two or more peripheral devices (printers, keyboards, and so on). Visit a vendor that deals with used computer equipment and find out how much would be paid for each item today. Develop a worksheet that uses the original price, value today, and number of years that have passed to compute the straight-line depreciation (SLN) for each item. Write a macro that finds the straight-line depreciation of any item based on the item's initial cost, salvage value (value today), and useful life to date. Attach the macro to a button on the worksheet. Try to discover what type of computer equipment holds its value best, and see if you can guess why.

Microsoft Excel 7

Windows 95

Sorting and Filtering a Worksheet Database and Creating a Data Map

Objectives:

You will have mastered the material in this project when you can:

- Create a database
- Use a data form to display records, add records, delete records, and change field values in a database
- Sort a database on one field or multiple fields
- Display automatic subtotals
- Use a data form to find records that meet comparison criteria
- Filter data to display records in a database that meet comparison criteria
- Use the advanced filtering features to display records in a database that meet comparison criteria
- Apply database functions to generate information about the database
- Use the VLOOKUP function to look up a value in a table
- Create and format a Data Map
- Analyze a database using a pivot table

Security for the Future

Are You Prepared?

Economic security is an age-old concern. Despite years of dedicated loyalty to a company, workers fear losing their incomes due to injuries. Having sufficient funds for retirement is worrisome, especially when lifetimes may exceed 90 years in the near future. Only 30 percent of Americans, however, are set for retirement at age 55.

The Social Security program was created during the Great Depression to address economic security fears. Today, 95 percent of Americans are protected by the program, and nearly one in five receives Social Security benefits. More than 90 percent of senior citizens receive these funds. In addition, 13 million Americans of all ages receive Social Security disability and survivors benefits as compensation for losing a source of family income when severe injury or death strikes.

Social Security works by using pooled resources, much like an insurance program does. Workers contribute money that is invested in a trust fund. Since the inception of the program, more than $4.5 trillion has been paid into the system, and more than $4.1 trillion has been dispersed. Benefits generally are based on the amount a worker has contributed to the program during his or her career.

The Social Security Administration maintains a database that has a record for every person with a Social Security number. Similar to the Sales Representative Database you will create in this Excel project, the SSA database has records that contain fields to store such data as Social Security number, last name, first name, gender, birth date, length of time the worker contributed Social Security funds, wages, date of death, date of disability, and birth date of widow or widower.

The data in these fields can be analyzed in computations, just as you will learn to do in this Excel project. For example, the SSA determines the total number of people who have received or are receiving various benefits and the average amount they receive. Also, the agency uses the data to manage its trust fund by predicting demands for benefits. By filtering records based on birth date, it can determine people who will reach retirement age each year and the amount of benefits they will draw. Using these figures, the SSA realizes that without taking any action, in 2019 the interest and tax revenues generated from the trust funds will be insufficient to meet these retirees' financial demands. If the agency then begins drawing on the trust fund principal, which is expected to grow to $3.3 trillion in 2019, that principal will be exhausted during the next ten years.

Anyone with a Social Security number can call the SSA 800 number to use this database to compute a Personal Earnings and Benefit Estimate Statement that shows Social Security earnings history and estimates how much has been paid in Social Security taxes. It also estimates future benefits and tells how to qualify for them. In addition, the SSA distributes a comparable interactive PC-compatible program, ANYPIA, that allows users to compute these estimates themselves. For details, visit the SSA's home page on the Internet at: http://www.ssa.gov/

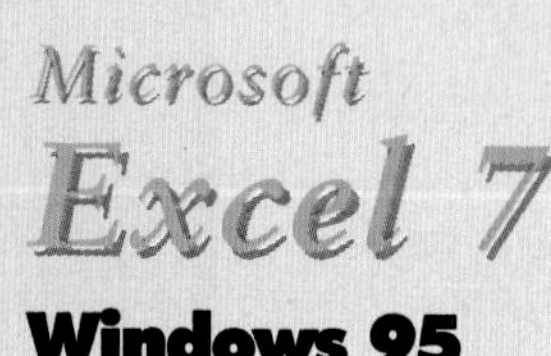

Windows 95

Sorting and Filtering a Worksheet Database and Creating a Data Map

Case Perspective

MedsForU is a small, up and coming Pharmaceutical company that specializes in skin-care products. Tina Capsol is the national sales manager for MedsForU. She has a dozen sales representatives spread equally between four states: California, Texas, Illinois, and New York. Tina recently purchased a laptop computer and Microsoft Office, which she plans to use to analyze the sales force as she travels between offices.

Tina is most familiar with Excel. She plans to use it to create, maintain, and query a database consisting of the MedsForU sales force. She has learned through online help that a pivot table can be used to obtain different summary views of the data in the database. She also wants to create a data map of the United States that shows the states covered by the sales force and quota comparisons between this year's sales quota and last year's sales quota for each state. Tina has assigned you the challenge of creating the database, pivot table, and data map. She also wants you to demonstrate how to query the database using Excel's database capabilities and how to use the VLOOKUP function.

Introduction

In this project you will learn about the database capabilities of Excel. A **worksheet database**, also called a **database** or **list**, is an organized collection of data. For example, telephone books, grade books, and lists of company employees are databases. In these cases, the data related to a person is called a record, and the data items that make up a record are called **fields**. In a list of company employees, some of the fields could be name, hire date, age, and gender.

A worksheet's row and column structure can easily be used to organize and store a database (Figure 6-1). Each row of a worksheet can be used to store a record and each column can store a field. Additionally, the column titles at the top of the worksheet are used as **field names** to identify each field.

Once you enter a database onto a worksheet, you can use Excel to:

1. add and delete records
2. change the values of fields in records
3. sort the records so that they appear in a different order
4. determine subtotals for numeric fields
5. display records that pass comparison criteria
6. analyze data using database functions
7. summarize information about the database using a **pivot table**

This project illustrates all seven of these database capabilities, as well as how to create a data map.

Project Six – MedsForU Sales Representative Database

FIGURE 6-1

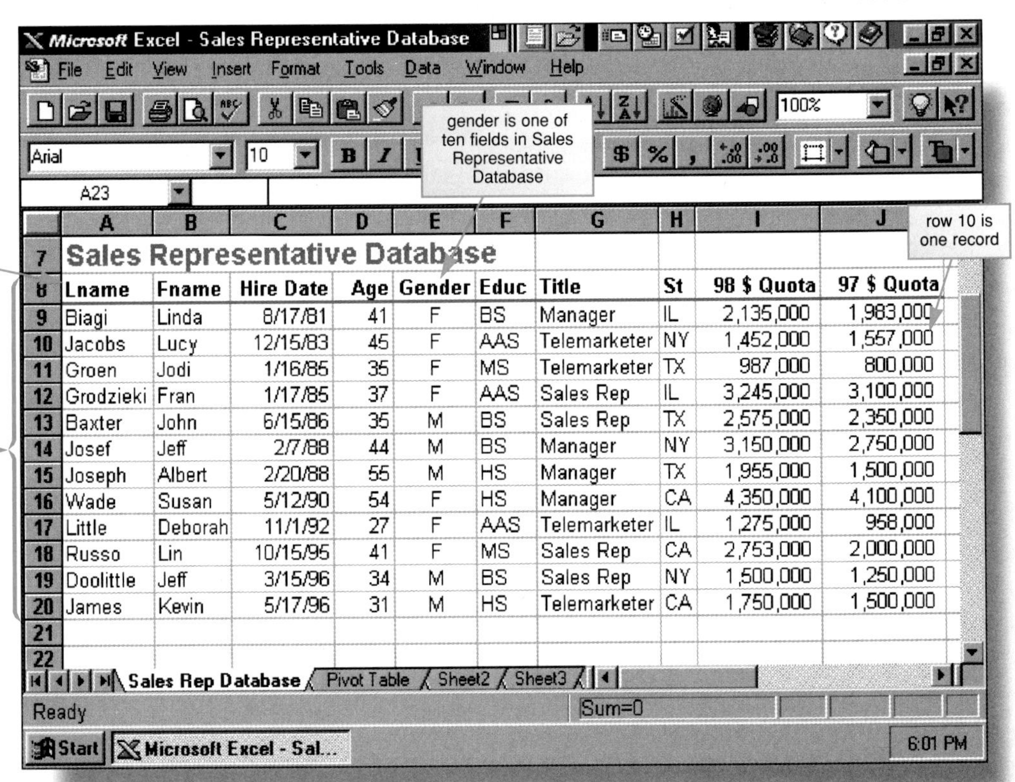

From your meeting with Tina Capsol, you have determined the following needs, source of data, and graph specifications.

Need: Create a sales representative database (Figure 6-1). The field names, columns, types of data, and column widths are described in Table 6-1. Because the database is visible on the screen, it is important that it be readable. Therefore, some of the column widths in Table 6-1 are determined from the field names and not the maximum length of the data.

Once the sales representative database is entered onto the worksheet, it is to be sorted and manipulated to illustrate how quickly information can be generated. One way to generate information from a database is to create a pivot table (Figure 6-2 on the next page). A pivot table gives you the capability to summarize data in the database and then rotate the table's row and column titles to show different views of the summarized data.

Table 6-1

COLUMN TITLES (FIELD NAMES)	COLUMN	TYPE OF DATA	COLUMN WIDTH
Lname	A	Text	9.00
Fname	B	Text	7.00
Hire Date	C	Date	9.00
Age	D	Numeric	5.00
Gender	E	Text	7.00
Educ	F	Text	5.00
Title	G	Text	11.00
St	H	Text	3.00
98 $ Quota	I	Numeric	11.00
97 $ Quota	J	Numeric	11.00

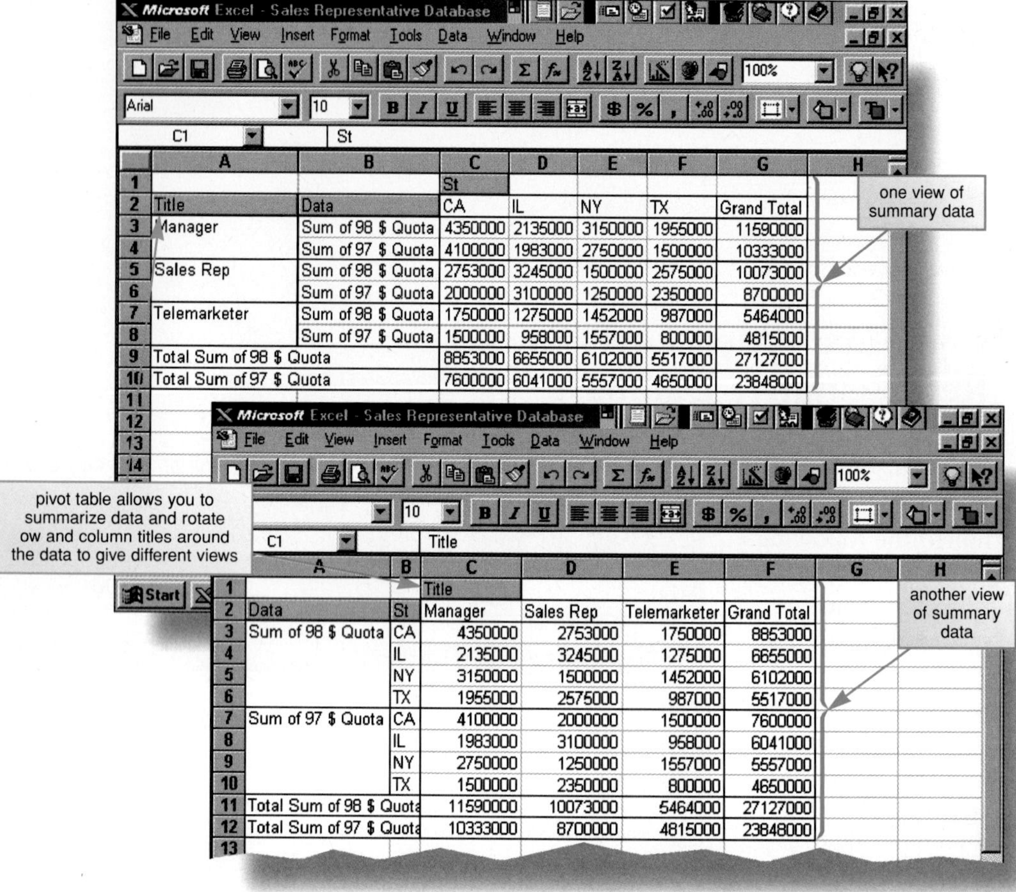

FIGURE 6-2

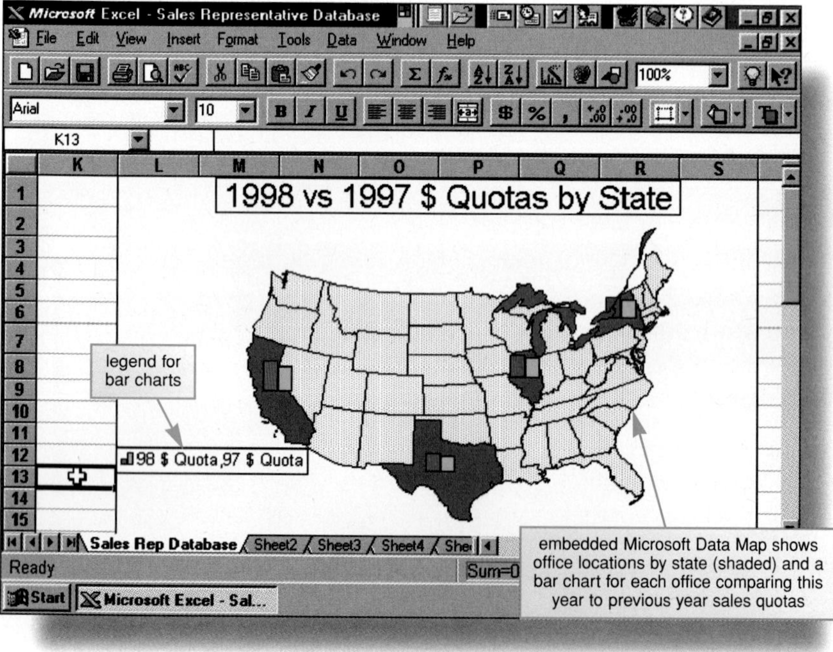

FIGURE 6-3

Source of Data: The Human Resources department will supply the required data.

Graph Specifications: Create a data map of the United States (Figure 6-3) that shows the states covered by the sales force and quota comparisons between this year's sales quota and last year's sales quota for each state with a sales representative.

Project Steps

The following tasks will be completed in this project.

1. Start the Excel program.
2. Enter and format the database title and column titles.
3. Assign the column titles in row 8 and the row immediately below it the name Database. Save the workbook.
4. Enter the data into the database using a data form.
5. Display sales representative records using a data form.
6. Sort the records in the database.
7. Determine quota subtotals.
8. Use a data form to display records one at a time that meet a comparison criteria.
9. Filter the database using the AutoFilter command.
10. Filter the database using the Advanced Filter command.
11. Extract employee records from the database that meet comparison criteria.
12. Apply database functions to the database to generate information.
13. Create and format a data map.
14. Create and manipulate a pivot table.
15. Save the workbook.
16. Exit Excel.

The following pages contain a detailed explanation of each of these steps.

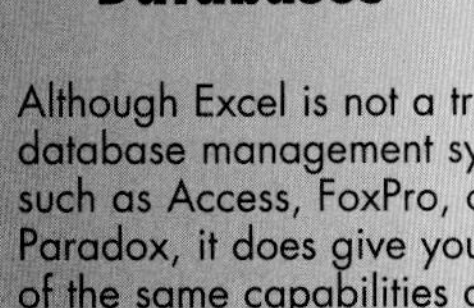

More About Databases

Although Excel is not a true database management system, such as Access, FoxPro, or Paradox, it does give you many of the same capabilities as these dedicated systems. For example, in Excel you can create a database; add, change, and delete data in the database; sort data in the database; query the database; and create forms and reports.

Starting Excel

To start Excel, follow the steps below.

TO START EXCEL

Step 1: Click the Start button. Click Start a New Document on the Start menu.

Step 2: Double-click the Excel workbook icon on the Start a New Document dialog box.

Creating the Database

Three steps are involved in creating a database in Excel: (1) set up the database; (2) assign the range containing the database a name; and (3) enter the data into the database. These steps are similar to those you would follow with a more traditional database package, such as Access, FoxPro, or Paradox. The following pages illustrate these three steps for creating the MedsForU sales representative database.

Setting Up the Database

Setting up the database involves assigning field names to a row in the worksheet and changing the column widths so the data will fit in the columns. Although Excel does not require a database title, it is a good practice to include one on the worksheet to show where the database begins. The steps on the next page also change the name of the Sheet1 tab to Sales Rep Database and saves the workbook using the filename Sales Representative Database.

More *About*
Setting Up the Database

Always leave several rows empty above the database on the worksheet to set up a criteria area for querying the database. Some experienced Excel users also leave several columns to the left empty, beginning with column A, for additional worksheet activities. A range of blanks rows or columns on the side of a database is called a moat of cells.

TO SET UP THE DATABASE

Step 1: Use the mouse to change the column widths as follows: A = 9.00, B = 7.00, C = 9.00, D = 5.00, E = 7.00, F = 5.00, G = 11.00, H = 3.00, I = 11.00, and J = 11.00.

Step 2: Click cell A7. Type `Sales Representative Database` and then click the enter box or press the ENTER key.

Step 3: With cell A7 active, click the Font Size button on the Formatting toolbar then click 14. Position the mouse pointer on the border between row heading 7 and row heading 8. When the mouse pointer changes to a plus sign with two arrows, drag down until 18.00 displays in the Name box in the formula bar.

Step 4: Enter the column titles in row 8 as shown in Figure 6-4. Change the height of row 8 to 15.00. Select the range A7:J8. Click the Bold button on the Formatting toolbar. Click the Font Color button on the Formatting toolbar and click teal (column 6, row 2 on the Font Color palette).

Step 5: Select the range A8:J8. Right-click the selected range. Click Format Cells. Click the Border tab. Click the Color arrow in the Style area and then click teal (column 6, row 2 on the palette). Click the regular border in the Style area (column 1, row 3). Click the Bottom box in the Border area. Click the OK button.

Step 6: Click column heading E to select the entire column. Click the Center button on the Formatting toolbar so that all entries in column E will be centered. Click column heading I and drag through column heading J to select both columns. Click the Comma Style button on the Formatting toolbar. Click the Decrease Decimal button on the Formatting toolbar twice so that all entries in columns I and J will display using the Comma style with zero decimal places. Click cell A10.

Step 7: Double click the Sheet1 tab at the bottom of the screen. When the Rename Sheet dialog box displays, type `Sales Rep Database` and then click the OK button.

Step 8: Click the Save button on the Standard toolbar. When the Save As dialog box displays, type `Sales Representative Database` in the Filename box. Click drive A in the Save in box and then click the Save button on the Save As dialog box.

The worksheet displays as shown in Figure 6-4.

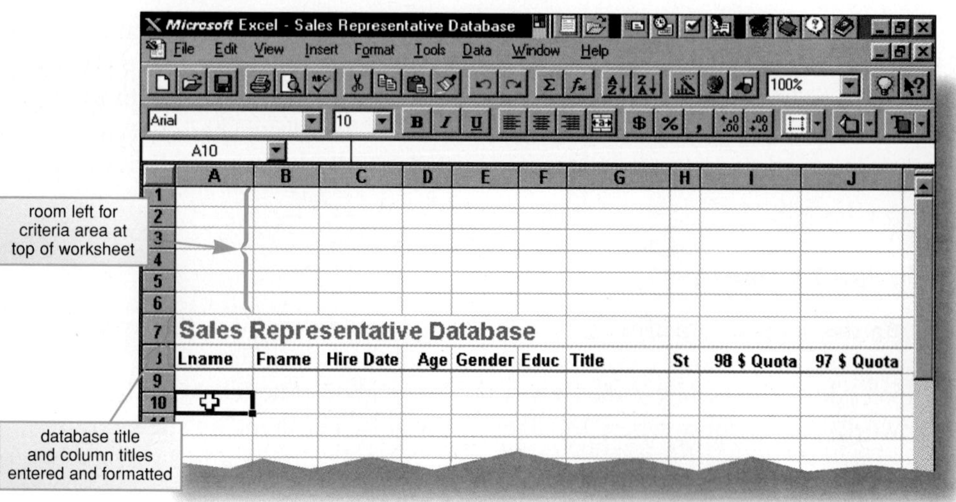

FIGURE 6-4

Naming a Database

Although Excel can usually identify a **database range** on a worksheet without any qualifications, it is best to give it the name Database. Using the name Database eliminates any confusion when commands are entered to manipulate the database. Thus, to create the MedsForU sales representative database shown in Figure 6-1, you define the name Database to be the range A8:J9 by selecting the range and typing Database in the Name box in the formula bar. The range assigned to the name Database encompasses the column titles (row 8) and one blank row (row 9) below the column titles. The blank row is for expansion of the database. As records are added using a **data form**, Excel automatically expands the range of the name Database to encompass the last record.

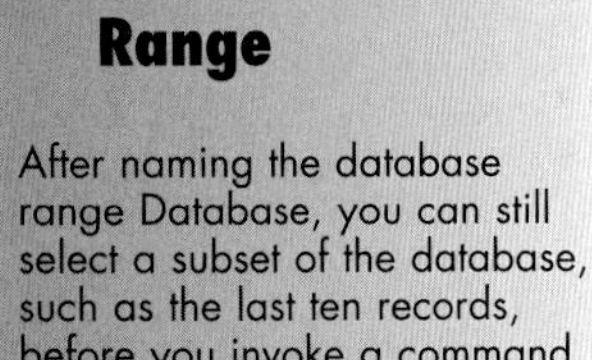

More *About* **the Database Range**

After naming the database range Database, you can still select a subset of the database, such as the last ten records, before you invoke a command and Excel will only manipulate the data in the selected range.

TO NAME THE DATABASE

Step 1: Select the range A8:J9. Click the Name box and type `Database` as the name for the selected range.
Step 2: Press the ENTER key.

The worksheet displays as shown in Figure 6-5.

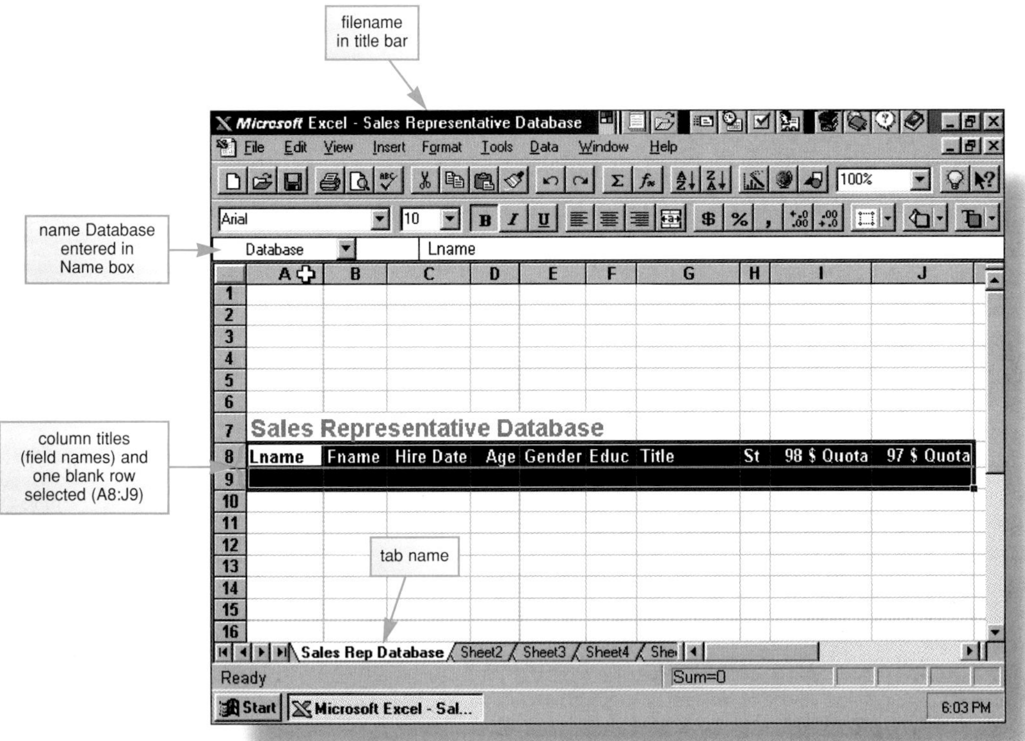

FIGURE 6-5

Entering Records into the Database Using a Data Form

After defining the name Database to be two rows long, a data form is used to enter the personnel records. A data form is a dialog box in which Excel includes the field names in the database and corresponding boxes in which you enter the field values. The following steps add the sales representative records to the database as shown in Figure 6-1 on page E 6.5.

Steps To Enter Records into a Database Using a Data Form

1 Click cell A9 to deselect the range A8:J9. Point to Form on the Data menu.

The Data menu displays as shown in Figure 6-6.

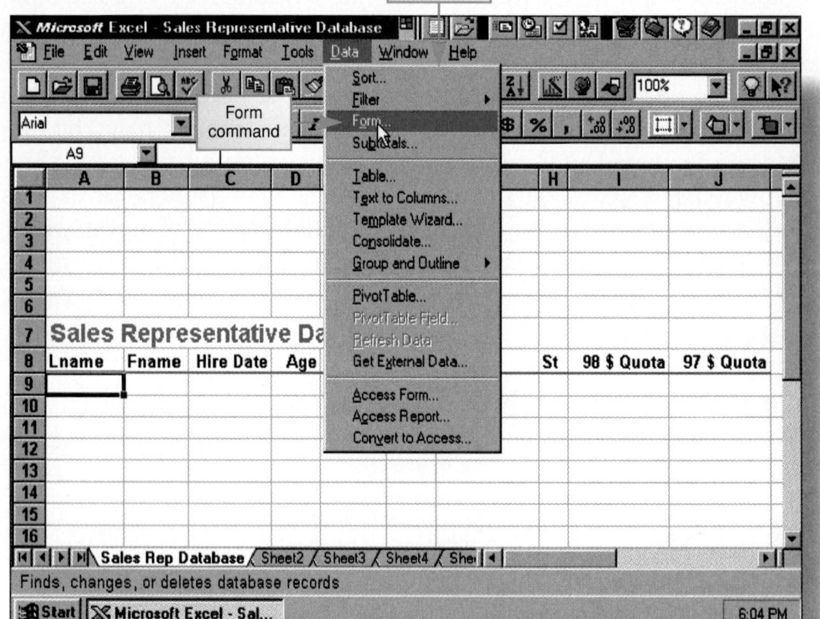

FIGURE 6-6

Click Form.

Excel displays the data form (Figure 6-7) with the worksheet title Sales Rep Database in the title bar. The data form automatically includes the field names and corresponding boxes for entering the field values. Excel selects the field names in the range A8:J8 because it is at the top of the range named Database.

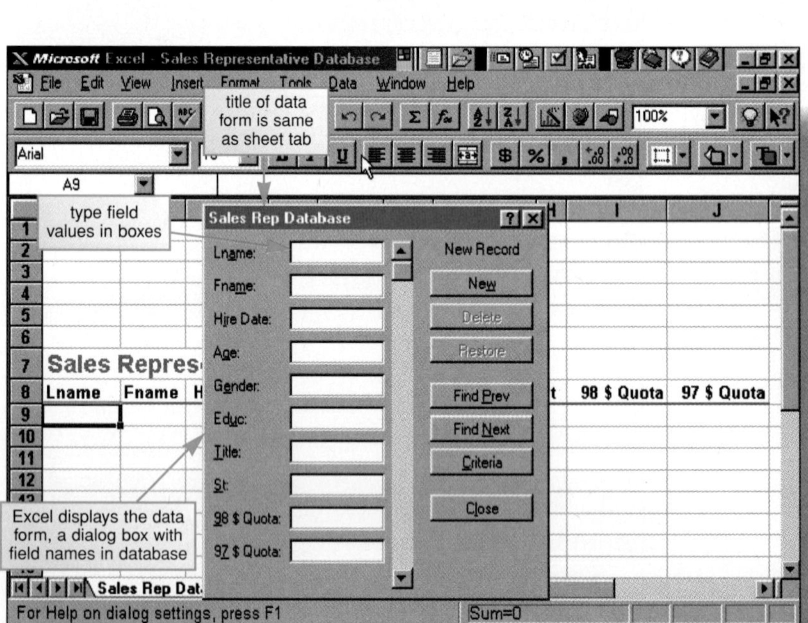

Enter the first sales representative record into the data form as shown in Figure 6-8. If you make a mistake, use the mouse or the TAB key to move the insertion point down to the next box and the SHIFT+TAB keys to move the insertion point to the previous box in the data form.

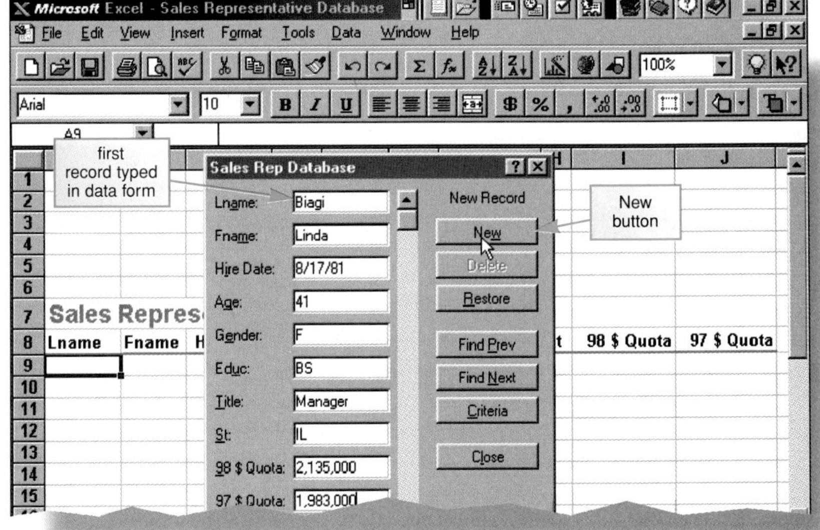

FIGURE 6-8

4 Click the New button on the data form. Type the second sales representative record in the data form.

Excel adds the first sales representative record to row 9 in the database range on the worksheet, and the second record displays on the data form (Figure 6-9).

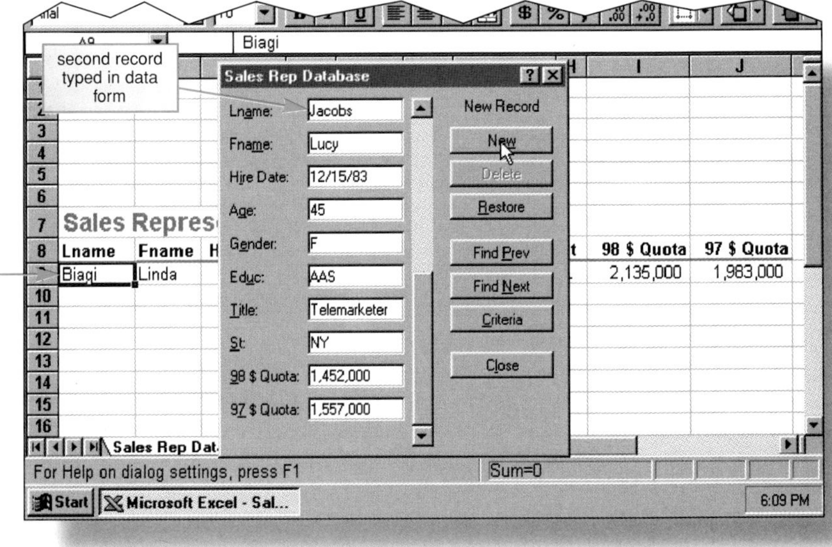

FIGURE 6-9

5 Click the New button on the data form to enter the second personnel record. Enter the next nine sales representative records in rows 11 through 19 of Figure 6-1 on page E 6.5 using the data form. Type the last sales representative record in row 20 of Figure 6-1 in the data form.

Excel enters the records into the database range as shown in Figure 6-10. The last record displays on the data form.

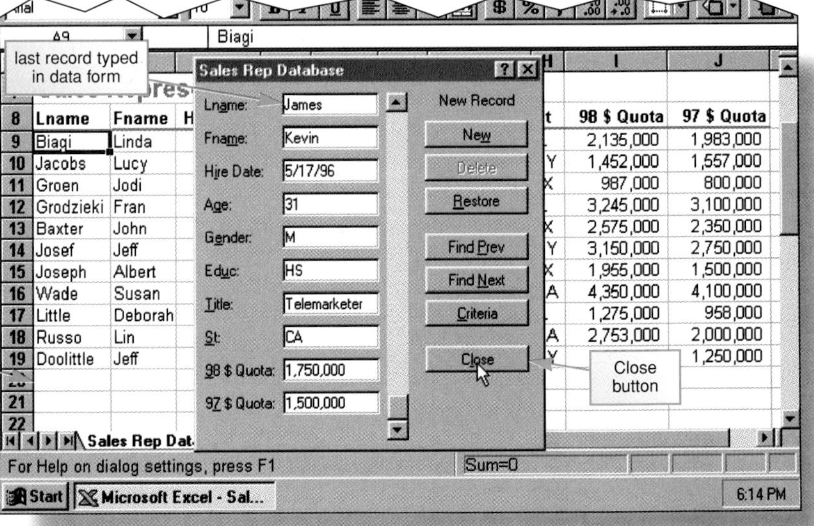

FIGURE 6-10

6 With the last record typed in the data form, click the Close button to complete the record entry. Click the Save button on the Standard toolbar to save the workbook using the filename Sales Representative Database.

The data form closes and the MedsForU sales representative database displays as shown in Figure 6-11.

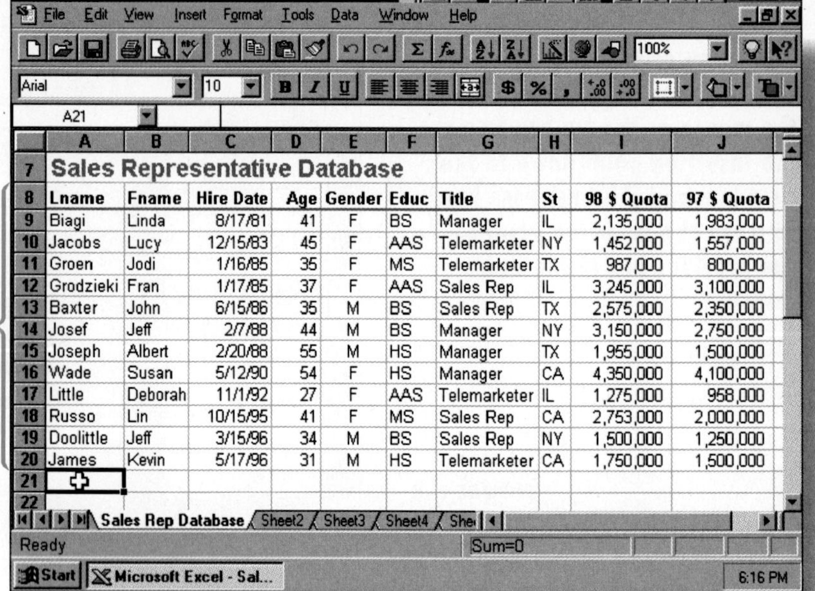

	A	B	C	D	E	F	G	H	I	J
7	Sales Representative Database									
8	Lname	Fname	Hire Date	Age	Gender	Educ	Title	St	98 $ Quota	97 $ Quota
9	Biagi	Linda	8/17/81	41	F	BS	Manager	IL	2,135,000	1,983,000
10	Jacobs	Lucy	12/15/83	45	F	AAS	Telemarketer	NY	1,452,000	1,557,000
11	Groen	Jodi	1/16/85	35	F	MS	Telemarketer	TX	987,000	800,000
12	Grodzieki	Fran	1/17/85	37	F	AAS	Sales Rep	IL	3,245,000	3,100,000
13	Baxter	John	6/15/86	35	M	BS	Sales Rep	TX	2,575,000	2,350,000
14	Josef	Jeff	2/7/88	44	M	BS	Manager	NY	3,150,000	2,750,000
15	Joseph	Albert	2/20/88	55	M	HS	Manager	TX	1,955,000	1,500,000
16	Wade	Susan	5/12/90	54	F	HS	Manager	CA	4,350,000	4,100,000
17	Little	Deborah	11/1/92	27	F	AAS	Telemarketer	IL	1,275,000	958,000
18	Russo	Lin	10/15/95	41	F	MS	Sales Rep	CA	2,753,000	2,000,000
19	Doolittle	Jeff	3/15/96	34	M	BS	Sales Rep	NY	1,500,000	1,250,000
20	James	Kevin	5/17/96	31	M	HS	Telemarketer	CA	1,750,000	1,500,000
21										
22										

FIGURE 6-11

***Other* Ways**

1. Enter data the same as you entered worksheet data in previous projects

The data form was illustrated here because it is considered to be a more accurate and reliable method of data entry, and it automatically extends the range of the name Database.

Moving From Field to Field on a Data Form

To move from field to field on a data form in Figure 6-10, you can use the TAB key as described earlier in Step 3, or you can hold down the ALT key and press the key that corresponds to the underlined letter in the name of the field to which you want to move. An underlined letter in a field name is called an **access key**. Thus, to select the field titled Fname in Figure 6-10 you can hold down the ALT key and press the M key (ALT+M) because m is the access key for the field name Fname.

More *About* Entering Data

If you decide to enter the data into the database as you entered worksheets in past projects, you will notice Excel entering data automatically for you, based on the data entered into the column. For example, in the St column in Figure 6-11, if you type the letter c in cell H21, Excel will enter CA into the cell. You also can right-click an empty cell under a list of items in a column and click the Pick from list command. Excel will give you a list of items in the column from which you can pick to assign to cell H21.

Reviewing the Appearance of the MedsForU Sales Representative Database

You should notice the following about the data shown in Figure 6-11:

1. In column C, the dates are right-justified because Excel treats dates as numbers.
2. Excel formats the dates to the m/d/yy style when you enter them in the form m/d/yy.
3. The Gender codes in column E are centered because in Step 6 on page E 6.8 column E was assigned the center format, which means all values in column E will be centered as they are entered.

4. The quota entries in columns I and J display using the Comma style with no decimal places because in Step 6 on page E 6.8 columns I and J were assigned this format.

Guidelines to Follow When Creating a Database

Table 6-2 lists some guidelines to use when creating a database in Excel.

Table 6-2
DATABASE SIZE AND LOCATION IN WORKBOOK
1. Do not enter more than one database per worksheet.
2. Maintain at least one blank row between a database and other worksheet entries.
3. Do not store other worksheet entries in the same rows as your database.
4. Define the name Database to be the database range.
5. A database can have a maximum of 256 fields and 16,384 records on a worksheet.
COLUMN TITLES (FIELD NAMES)
1. Place column titles in the first row of the database.
2. Do not use blank rows or rows with dashes to separate the column titles from the data.
3. Apply a different format to the column titles and data. For example, bold the column titles and display the data below the column titles using a regular style. Varying the format between the column titles and data is necessary only if you do not assign the name Database to the database range.
4. Column titles (field names) can be up to 255 characters in length.
CONTENTS OF DATABASE
1. Each column should have similar data. For example, employee gender should be in the same column for all employees.
2. Do not use spaces in data to improve readability.
3. Format the data to improve readability, but do not vary the format in a column.

Using a Data Form to View Records and Change Data

At any time while the worksheet is active, you can use the Form command on the Data menu to display records, add new records, delete records, and change the data in records. When a data form is initially opened, Excel displays the first record in the database. To display the fifth record as shown in Figure 6-12 on the next page, click the Find Next button until the fifth record displays. Each time you click the Find Next button, Excel advances to the next record in the database. If necessary, you can use the Find Prev button to back up to a previous record. You can also use the UP ARROW key, the DOWN ARROW key, or the vertical scroll bar to the left of the buttons to move between records.

FIGURE 6-12

To change data in a record, you first display it on a data form. Next, you select the fields to change. Finally, you use the DOWN ARROW key or the ENTER key to confirm the field changes. If you change field values on a data form and then select the Find Next button to move to the next record, the field changes will not be made.

To add a new record, click the New button on the data form. A data form always adds the new record to the bottom of the database, which increases the range assigned to the name Database. To delete a record, you first display it on a data form and then click the Delete button. Excel automatically moves all records below the deleted record up one row.

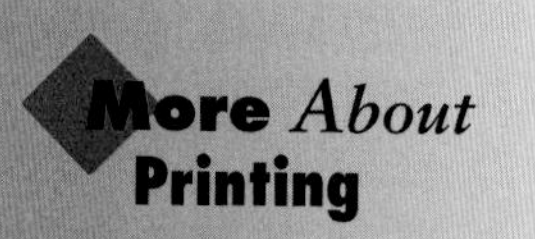

You also can print the database or any portion of it by selecting the desired range and clicking Selection in the Print What area on the Print dialog box.

Printing a Database

You can print the database using the same procedures you followed in earlier projects. If there is data on the worksheet that is not part of the database you want to print, then follow these steps to print only the database.

TO PRINT A DATABASE

Step 1: Right-click the menu bar at the top of the screen to display the shortcut menu.
Step 2: Click Page Setup on the shortcut menu. Click the Sheet tab. Type `Database` in the Print Area box.
Step 3: Click the OK button.
Step 4: Ready the printer and click the Print button on the Standard toolbar.

If you want to print the entire worksheet, remove the name Database from the Print area box on the Sheet tab in the Page Setup dialog box.

Sorting a Database

The data in a database is easier to work with and more meaningful if the records are arranged in sequence on the basis of one or more fields. Arranging records in sequence is called **sorting**. Data is in **ascending sequence** if it is ordered from lowest to highest, earliest to most recent, or alphabetically. For example, the records were entered into the MedsForU sales representative database beginning with the earliest hire date to the most recent hire date. Thus, the database in Figure 6-11 is sorted in ascending sequence by hire date. Data that is in sequence from highest to lowest in value is in **descending sequence**.

You sort by clicking the **Sort Ascending button** or **Sort Descending button** on the Standard toolbar or by clicking **Sort** on the Data menu. If you are sorting on a single field (column), use one of the Sort buttons on the Standard toolbar. If you are sorting on multiple fields, use the Sort command on the Data menu. Make sure you select a cell in the field on which to sort before you click the button. The field you select to sort the records on is called the **sort key**. The first sort example reorders the records by last name.

More *About*
Sorting

If a column you are sorting on contains numbers, text, and blanks, then Excel uses the following order of priority: numbers from smallest to largest positive; text; and blanks.

Sorting the Database by Last Name in Ascending Sequence

Follow these steps to sort the records.

To Sort the Database by Last Name in Ascending Sequence

Steps

1 **Click cell A9 and point to the Sort Ascending button on the Standard toolbar (Figure 6-13).**

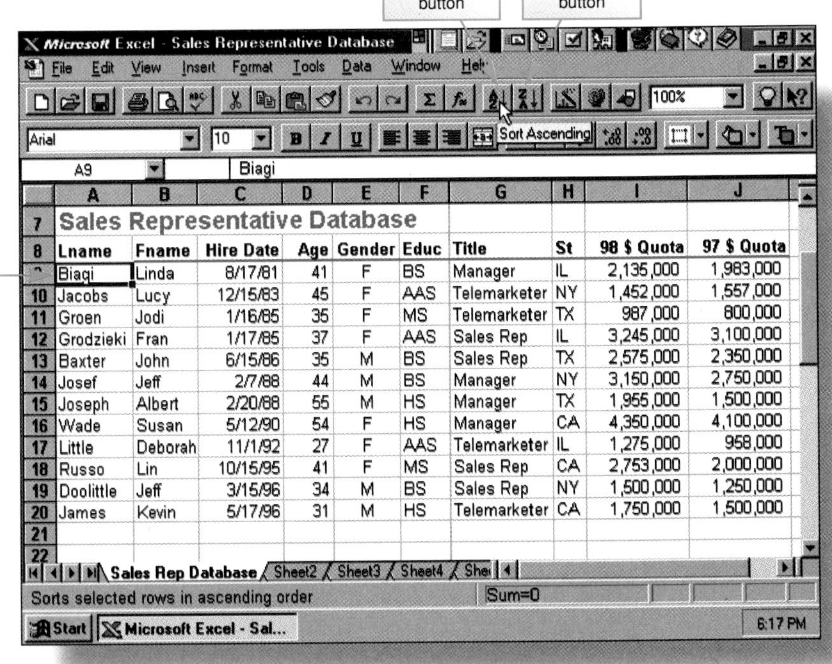

2 Click the Sort Ascending button.

Excel sorts the database by last name in ascending sequence (Figure 6-14).

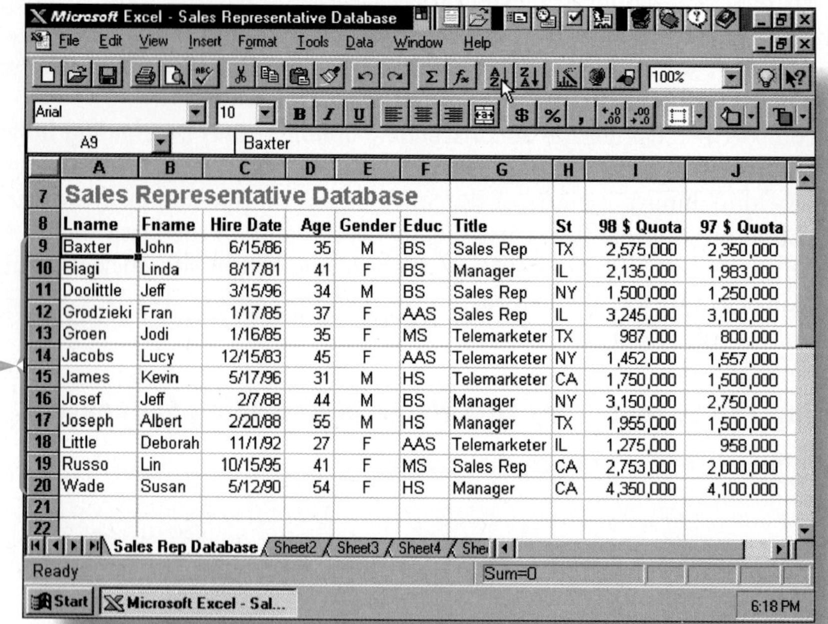

	A	B	C	D	E	F	G	H	I	J
7	Sales Representative Database									
8	Lname	Fname	Hire Date	Age	Gender	Educ	Title	St	98 $ Quota	97 $ Quota
9	Baxter	John	6/15/86	35	M	BS	Sales Rep	TX	2,575,000	2,350,000
10	Biagi	Linda	8/17/81	41	F	BS	Manager	IL	2,135,000	1,983,000
11	Doolittle	Jeff	3/15/96	34	M	BS	Sales Rep	NY	1,500,000	1,250,000
12	Grodzieki	Fran	1/17/85	37	F	AAS	Sales Rep	IL	3,245,000	3,100,000
13	Groen	Jodi	1/16/85	35	F	MS	Telemarketer	TX	987,000	800,000
14	Jacobs	Lucy	12/15/83	45	F	AAS	Telemarketer	NY	1,452,000	1,557,000
15	James	Kevin	5/17/96	31	M	HS	Telemarketer	CA	1,750,000	1,500,000
16	Josef	Jeff	2/7/88	44	M	BS	Manager	NY	3,150,000	2,750,000
17	Joseph	Albert	2/20/88	55	M	HS	Manager	TX	1,955,000	1,500,000
18	Little	Deborah	11/1/92	27	F	AAS	Telemarketer	IL	1,275,000	958,000
19	Russo	Lin	10/15/95	41	F	MS	Sales Rep	CA	2,753,000	2,000,000
20	Wade	Susan	5/12/90	54	F	HS	Manager	CA	4,350,000	4,100,000

FIGURE 6-14

OtherWays

1. Click Sort on Data menu, click field name in Sort By drop-down list box, click OK

Sorting the Database by Last Name in Descending Sequence

Follow these steps to sort the records.

TO SORT THE DATABASE BY LAST NAME IN DESCENDING SEQUENCE

Step 1: Click cell A9.
Step 2: Click the Sort Descending button on the Standard toolbar.

Excel sorts the sales representative database by last name in descending sequence (Figure 6-15).

Sort Descending button

Microsoft Excel - Sales Representative Database

A9 Wade

records sorted by last name in descending sequence

	A	B	C	D	E	F	G	H	I	J
7	Sales Representative Database									
8	Lname	Fname	Hire Date	Age	Gender	Educ	Title	St	98 $ Quota	97 $ Quota
9	Wade	Susan	5/12/90	54	F	HS	Manager	CA	4,350,000	4,100,000
10	Russo	Lin	10/15/95	41	F	MS	Sales Rep	CA	2,753,000	2,000,000
11	Little	Deborah	11/1/92	27	F	AAS	Telemarketer	IL	1,275,000	958,000
12	Joseph	Albert	2/20/88	55	M	HS	Manager	TX	1,955,000	1,500,000
13	Josef	Jeff	2/7/88	44	M	BS	Manager	NY	3,150,000	2,750,000
14	James	Kevin	5/17/96	31	M	HS	Telemarketer	CA	1,750,000	1,500,000
15	Jacobs	Lucy	12/15/83	45	F	AAS	Telemarketer	NY	1,452,000	1,557,000
16	Groen	Jodi	1/16/85	35	F	MS	Telemarketer	TX	987,000	800,000
17	Grodzieki	Fran	1/17/85	37	F	AAS	Sales Rep	IL	3,245,000	3,100,000
18	Doolittle	Jeff	3/15/96	34	M	BS	Sales Rep	NY	1,500,000	1,250,000
19	Biagi	Linda	8/17/81	41	F	BS	Manager	IL	2,135,000	1,983,000
20	Baxter	John	6/15/86	35	M	BS	Sales Rep	TX	2,575,000	2,350,000

FIGURE 6-15

Returning the Database to its Original Order

Follow these steps to change the sequence of the records back to their original order by hire date in ascending sequence.

TO RETURN THE DATABASE TO ITS ORIGINAL ORDER

Step 1: Click cell C9.
Step 2: Click the Sort Ascending button on the Standard toolbar.

Excel reorders the records in their original sequence by hire date (Figure 6-16).

You can also undo a sort operation by doing one of the following:

1. Click the Undo button on the Standard toolbar.
2. Choose the Undo Sort command on the Edit menu.

These two procedures will work only if you have not entered any commands since the sort operation. For example, after sorting by last name in descending sequence, if you click the Undo button on the Standard toolbar, Excel displays the records in their most recent order, which was last name in ascending sequence. If you click the Undo button a second time, Excel displays the records by last name in descending sequence. Thus, the Undo button does not allow you to revert to an original order once multiple sorts have taken place.

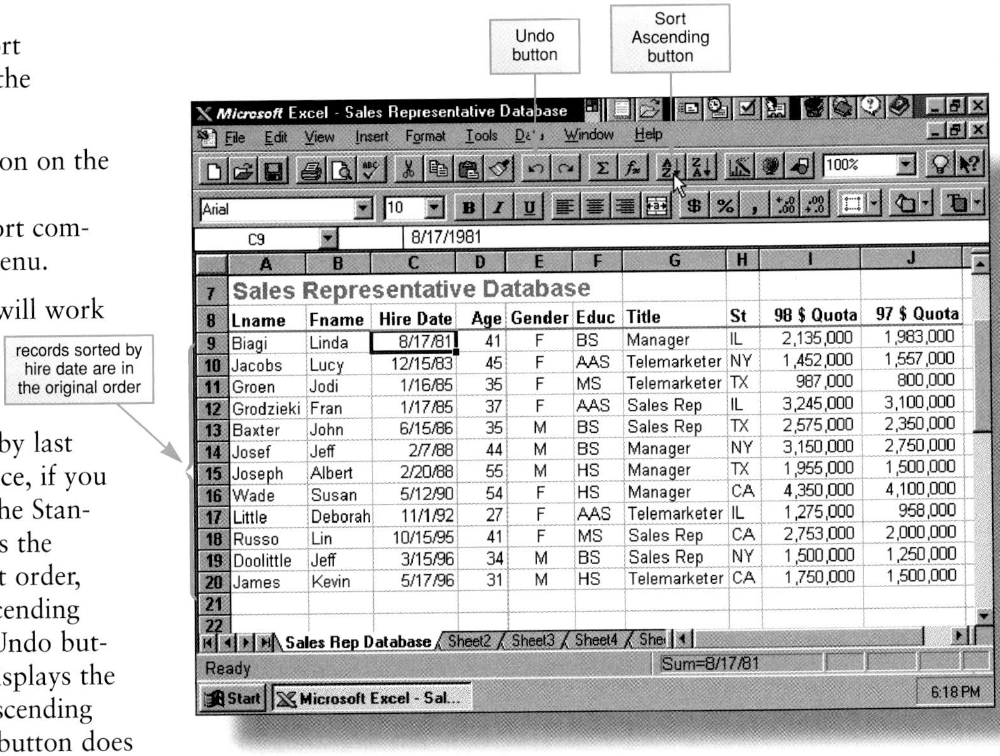

Undo button
Sort Ascending button
records sorted by hire date are in the original order

Microsoft Excel - Sales Representative Database

C9 — 8/17/1981

Sales Representative Database

Lname	Fname	Hire Date	Age	Gender	Educ	Title	St	98 $ Quota	97 $ Quota
Biagi	Linda	8/17/81	41	F	BS	Manager	IL	2,135,000	1,983,000
Jacobs	Lucy	12/15/83	45	F	AAS	Telemarketer	NY	1,452,000	1,557,000
Groen	Jodi	1/16/85	35	F	MS	Telemarketer	TX	987,000	800,000
Grodzieki	Fran	1/17/85	37	F	AAS	Sales Rep	IL	3,245,000	3,100,000
Baxter	John	6/15/86	35	M	BS	Sales Rep	TX	2,575,000	2,350,000
Josef	Jeff	2/7/88	44	M	BS	Manager	NY	3,150,000	2,750,000
Joseph	Albert	2/20/88	55	M	HS	Manager	TX	1,955,000	1,500,000
Wade	Susan	5/12/90	54	F	HS	Manager	CA	4,350,000	4,100,000
Little	Deborah	11/1/92	27	F	AAS	Telemarketer	IL	1,275,000	958,000
Russo	Lin	10/15/95	41	F	MS	Sales Rep	CA	2,753,000	2,000,000
Doolittle	Jeff	3/15/96	34	M	BS	Sales Rep	NY	1,500,000	1,250,000
James	Kevin	5/17/96	31	M	HS	Telemarketer	CA	1,750,000	1,500,000

Sales Rep Database / Sheet2 / Sheet3 / Sheet4
Ready — Sum=8/17/81
Start — Microsoft Excel - Sal... — 6:18 PM

FIGURE 6-16

Sorting the Database on Multiple Fields

Excel allows you to sort a maximum of three fields at a time. The sort example that follows uses the Sort command on the Data menu to sort the MedsForU sales representative database by the 1998 dollar quotas (column I) within education (column F) within gender (column E). In this case, gender is the **major sort key** (Sort By field), education is the **intermediate sort key** (1st Then By field), and the 1998 dollar quota filed is the **minor sort key** (2nd Then By field). The first two keys will be sorted in ascending sequence. The 1998 dollar quota field will be sorted in descending sequence.

The phrase, *sort by 1998 dollar quota within education within gender*, means that the records are arranged in ascending sequence by gender code. Within gender, the records are arranged in ascending sequence by education code. Within education, the records are arranged in descending sequence by 1998 dollar quota.

The following steps describe how to sort a database on multiple fields.

To Sort the Database on Multiple Fields

1 Click any cell in the database and then point to Sort on the Data menu.

The Data menu displays as shown in Figure 6-17.

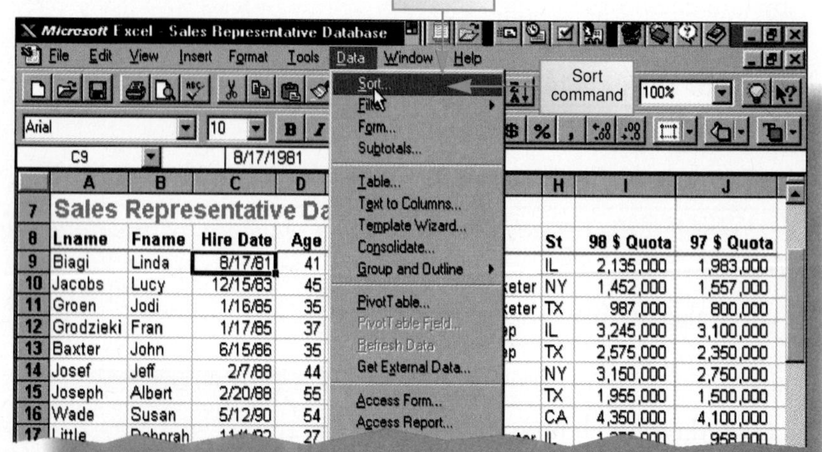

FIGURE 6-17

2 Click Sort. When the Sort dialog box displays, click the Sort By arrow.

The Sort By drop-down list shows the field names in the database (Figure 6-18).

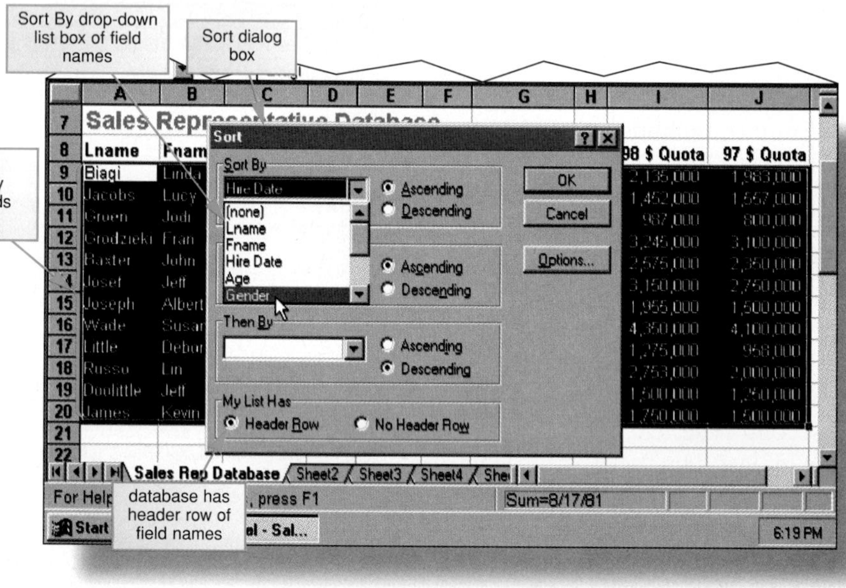

Sort By drop-down list box of field names

Sort dialog box

Excel automatically selects records in database

database has header row of field names

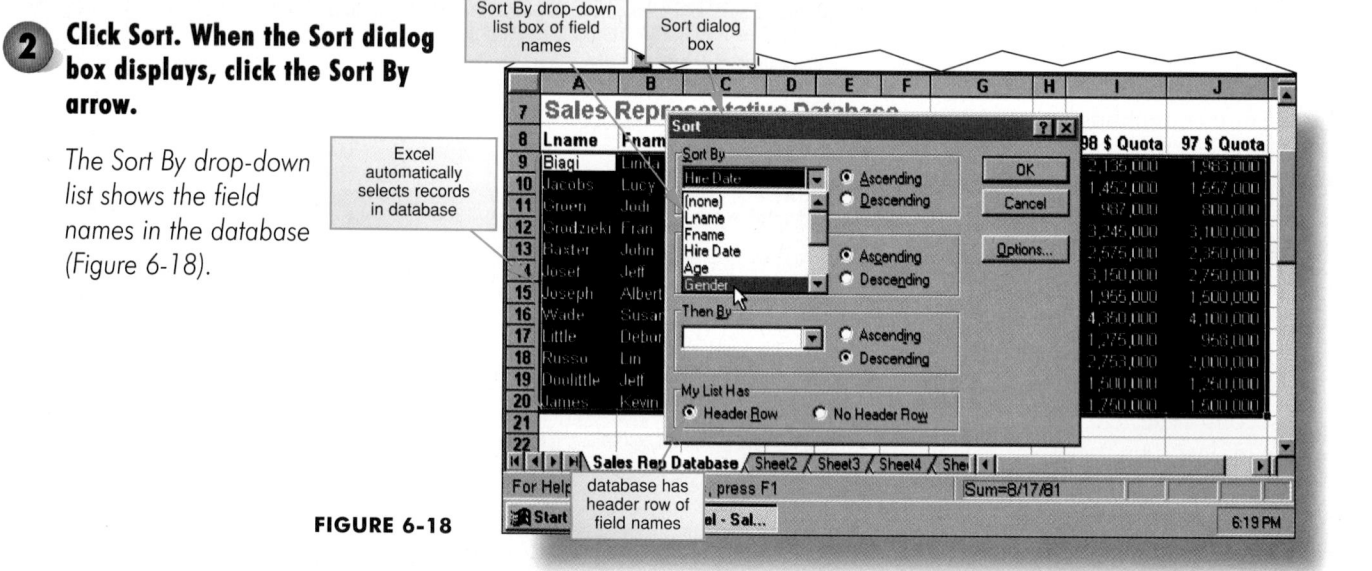

FIGURE 6-18

3 Click Gender in the Sort By drop-down list. Click the first Then By arrow and then click Educ. Click the 2nd Then By arrow and then click 98 $ Quota. Click Descending in the 2nd Then By area.

The Sort dialog box displays as shown in Figure 6-19.

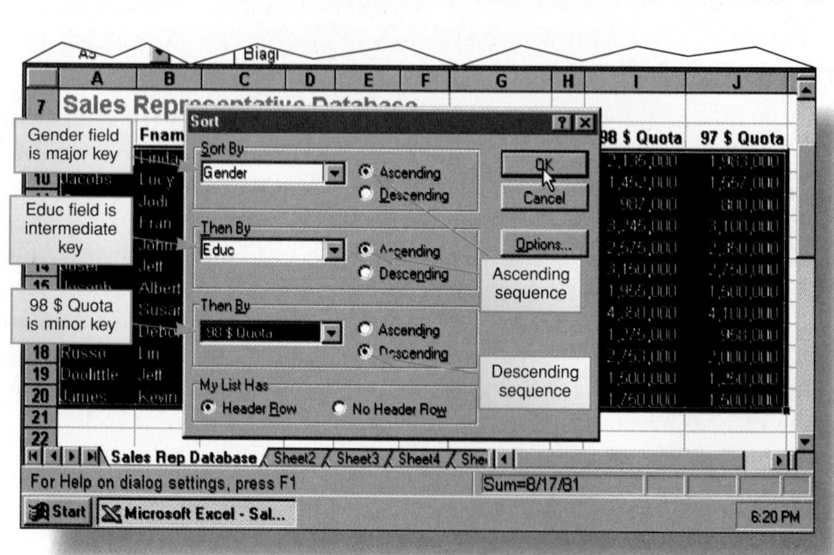

FIGURE 6-19

4 Click the OK button in the Sort dialog box.

Excel sorts the sales representative database by the 1998 dollar quotas within education within gender as shown in Figure 6-20.

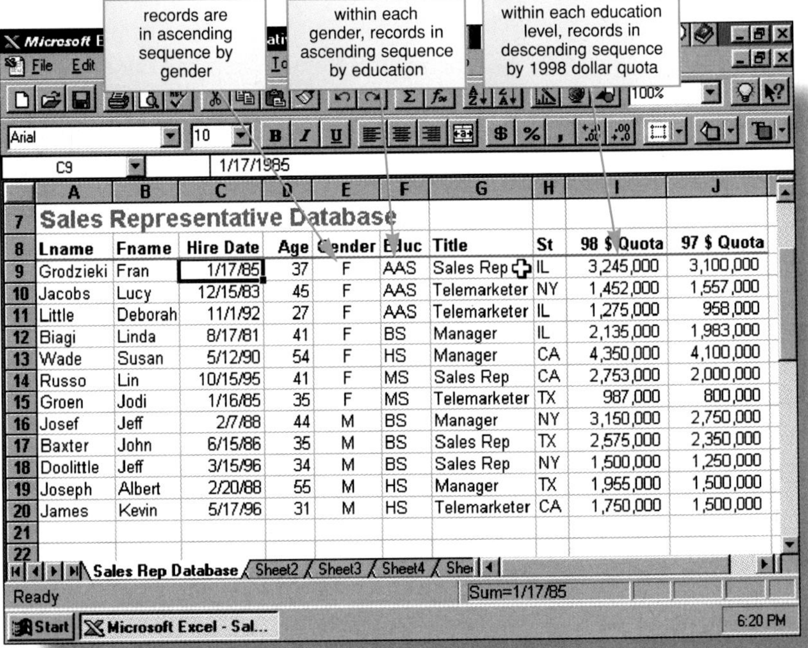

Lname	Fname	Hire Date	Age	Gender	Educ	Title	St	98 $ Quota	97 $ Quota
Grodzieki	Fran	1/17/85	37	F	AAS	Sales Rep	IL	3,245,000	3,100,000
Jacobs	Lucy	12/15/83	45	F	AAS	Telemarketer	NY	1,452,000	1,557,000
Little	Deborah	11/1/92	27	F	AAS	Telemarketer	IL	1,275,000	958,000
Biagi	Linda	8/17/81	41	F	BS	Manager	IL	2,135,000	1,983,000
Wade	Susan	5/12/90	54	F	HS	Manager	CA	4,350,000	4,100,000
Russo	Lin	10/15/95	41	F	MS	Sales Rep	CA	2,753,000	2,000,000
Groen	Jodi	1/16/85	35	F	MS	Telemarketer	TX	987,000	800,000
Josef	Jeff	2/7/88	44	M	BS	Manager	NY	3,150,000	2,750,000
Baxter	John	6/15/86	35	M	BS	Sales Rep	TX	2,575,000	2,350,000
Doolittle	Jeff	3/15/96	34	M	BS	Sales Rep	NY	1,500,000	1,250,000
Joseph	Albert	2/20/88	55	M	HS	Manager	TX	1,955,000	1,500,000
James	Kevin	5/17/96	31	M	HS	Telemarketer	CA	1,750,000	1,500,000

FIGURE 6-20

OtherWays

1. Click a cell in the 98 $ Quota column, click Sort Descending button, click a cell in the Educ column, click Sort Ascending button, click a cell in the Gender column, click Sort Ascending button

In Figure 6-20, the records are in ascending sequence by the gender codes (F or M) in column E. Within each gender code, the records are in ascending sequence by the education codes (AAS, BS, HS, MS) in column F. Finally, within the education codes, the 1998 dollar quotas are in descending sequence in column I. Remember, if you make a mistake in a sort operation, you can reorder the records into their original sequence by immediately clicking the Undo button on the Standard toolbar.

Because Excel sorts the database using the current order of the records, the previous example could have been completed by sorting on one field at a time, beginning with the least important one.

Sorting with More than Three Fields

Excel allows you to sort on more than three fields by sorting two or more times. The most recent sort takes precedence. Hence, if you plan to sort on four fields, you sort on the three least important keys first and then sort on the major key. If you want to sort on fields Lname within Title within St within Gender, you first sort on Lname (2nd Then By field) within Title (1st Then By field) within St (Sort By field). After the first sort operation is complete, you finally sort on the Gender field by clicking one of the cells in the Gender column and then clicking the Sort Ascending button on the Standard toolbar.

More About Sorting

Some Excel users use the fill handle to create a series in an additional field in the database that is used only to reorder the records into their original sequence.

Displaying Automatic Subtotals in a Database

Displaying **automatic subtotals** is a powerful tool for summarizing data in a database. Excel requires only that you sort the database on the field on which you want subtotals to be based, and then use the **Subtotals command** on the Data menu. The field you sort on, prior to invoking the Subtotals command, is called the **control field**. When the control field changes, Excel displays a subtotal for the numeric fields you select in the Subtotal dialog box. For example, if you sort on the St (state) field and request subtotals on the 98 $ Quota and 97 $ Quota fields, then Excel displays a subtotal for each quota field every time the St field changes, and quota grand totals for the entire database.

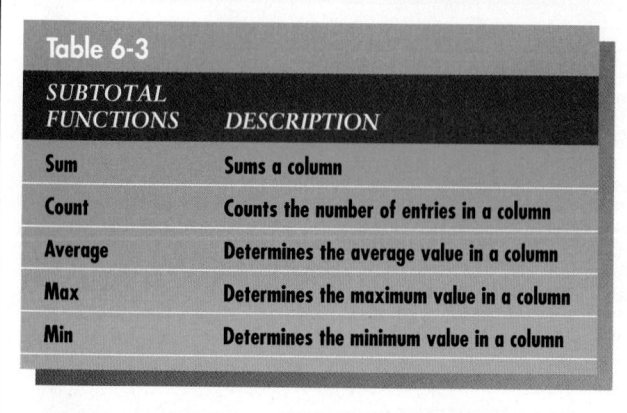

Table 6-3

SUBTOTAL FUNCTIONS	DESCRIPTION
Sum	Sums a column
Count	Counts the number of entries in a column
Average	Determines the average value in a column
Max	Determines the maximum value in a column
Min	Determines the minimum value in a column

In the Subtotal dialog box you select the subtotal function you want to use. The subtotal functions most often used are listed in Table 6-3.

Besides displaying subtotals, Excel also creates an outline for the database. The following example shows you how to display quota subtotals by state. Because the insertion of subtotals increases the number of rows, the Zoom control box on the Standard toolbar is used to display the entire database. Follow the steps to display subtotals in a database.

Steps To Display Subtotals in a Database

1 Select cell H9. Click the Sort Ascending button on the Standard toolbar.

The MedsForU sales representative database displays by state in ascending sequence as shown in Figure 6-21.

FIGURE 6-21

2 Point to Subtotals on the Data menu.

The Data menu displays as shown in Figure 6-22.

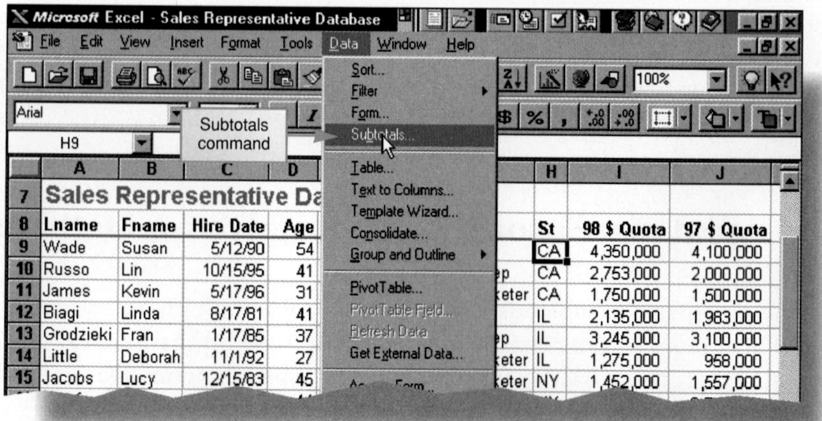

FIGURE 6-22

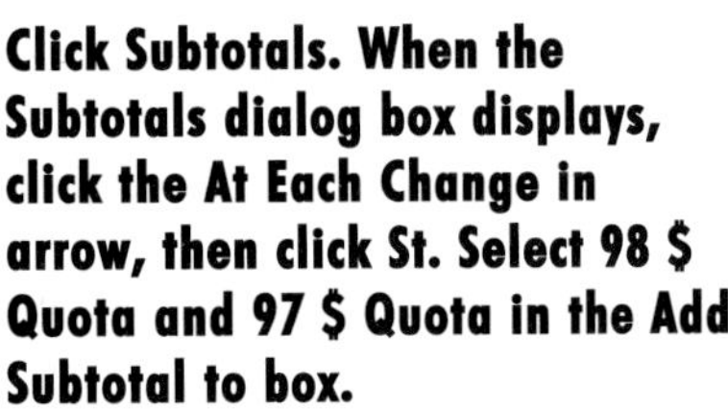

3 Click Subtotals. When the Subtotals dialog box displays, click the At Each Change in arrow, then click St. Select 98 $ Quota and 97 $ Quota in the Add Subtotal to box.

The Subtotal dialog box displays as shown in Figure 6-23. The At Each Change in box contains the St field. The Use Function box contains Sum by default. In the Add Subtotal to box, both 98 $ Quota and 97 $ Quota are selected.

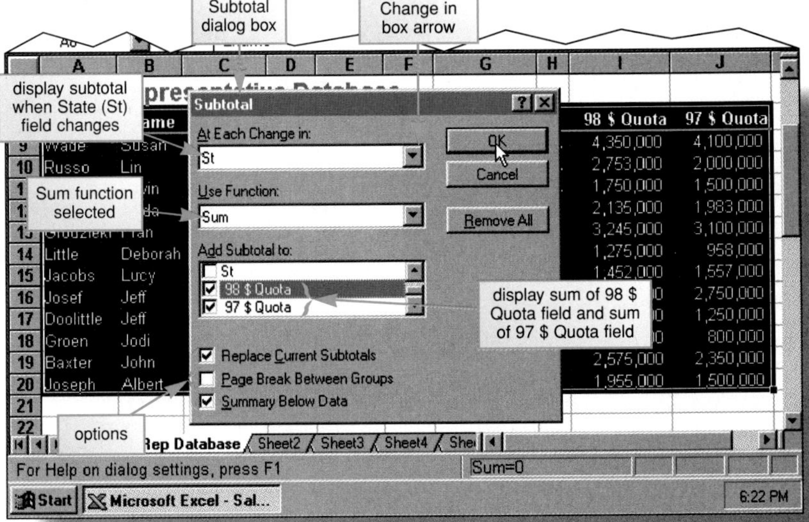

FIGURE 6-23

4 Click the OK button. Double-click the right border of column heading H to change the column width to best fit.

Excel inserts new rows in the MedsForU sales representative database. Each new row contains quota subtotals for each state (Figure 6-24). The database is now outlined and extends beyond the window.

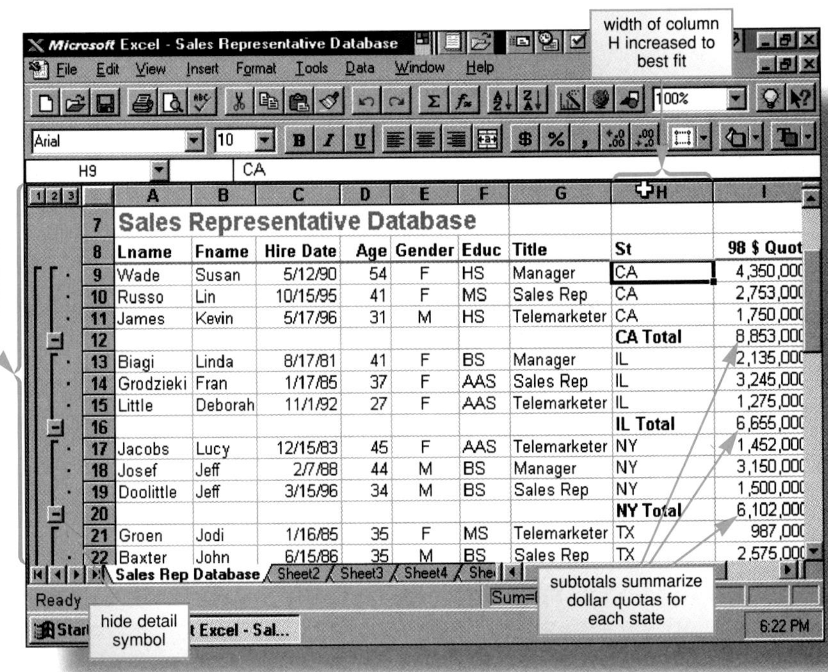

FIGURE 6-24

As shown in Figure 6-24, Excel has added subtotal rows in the middle of the database. Names for each subtotal row are derived from the state names. Thus, in row 12 the text CA Total precedes the actual quota totals for California.

> **More About Sort Options**
>
> You can sort left to right across rows by clicking the Options button in the Sort dialog box (Figure 6-18 on page E 6.18) and then clicking Sort Left to Right in the Orientation area. You also can select case sensitive, which would sort lowercase letters ahead of the same capital letters for an ascending sort.

Zooming Out on a Worksheet and Hiding and Showing Detail Data in a Subtotaled Database

The following steps show how to use the Zoom Control box on the Standard toolbar to reduce the size of the display so that all records and fields show. The steps also illustrate how to use the outline features of Excel to display only the total rows.

To Zoom Out on a Worksheet to Hide and Show Detail Data in a Subtotaled Database

1 **Click the Zoom Control box arrow on the Standard toolbar. Click 75%. If necessary, change widths of columns I and J to best fit.**

Excel displays the worksheet in reduced form so that all the rows and columns in the database, including the subtotals and grand total, display (Figure 6-25).

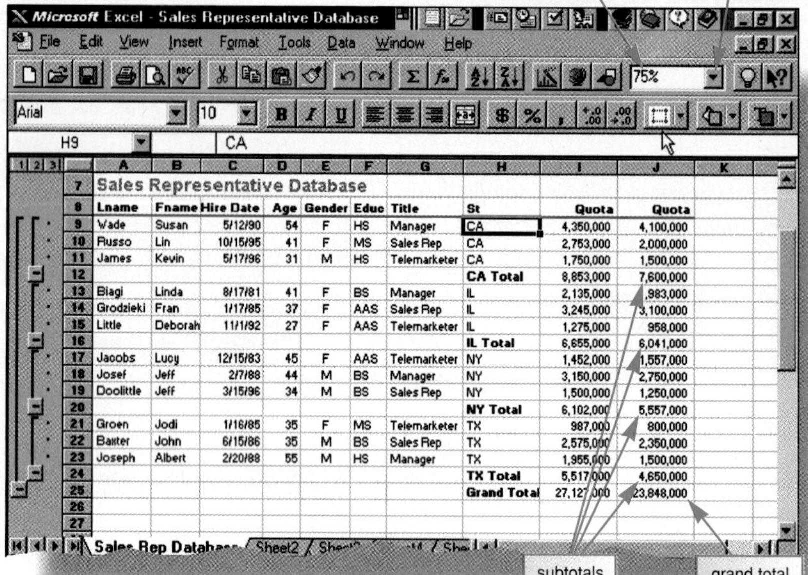

FIGURE 6-25

2 **Click the row level 2 symbol next to the Select All button on the left side of the screen to hide all detail rows.**

Excel displays only the subtotal and grand total rows (Figure 6-26).

3 **Click the row level 3 symbol next to the Select All button on the left side of the screen to display hidden detail rows. Click the Zoom Control box arrow and then click 100% in the drop-down list.**

Excel displays the worksheet in normal size (Figure 6-24 on Page E 6xx).

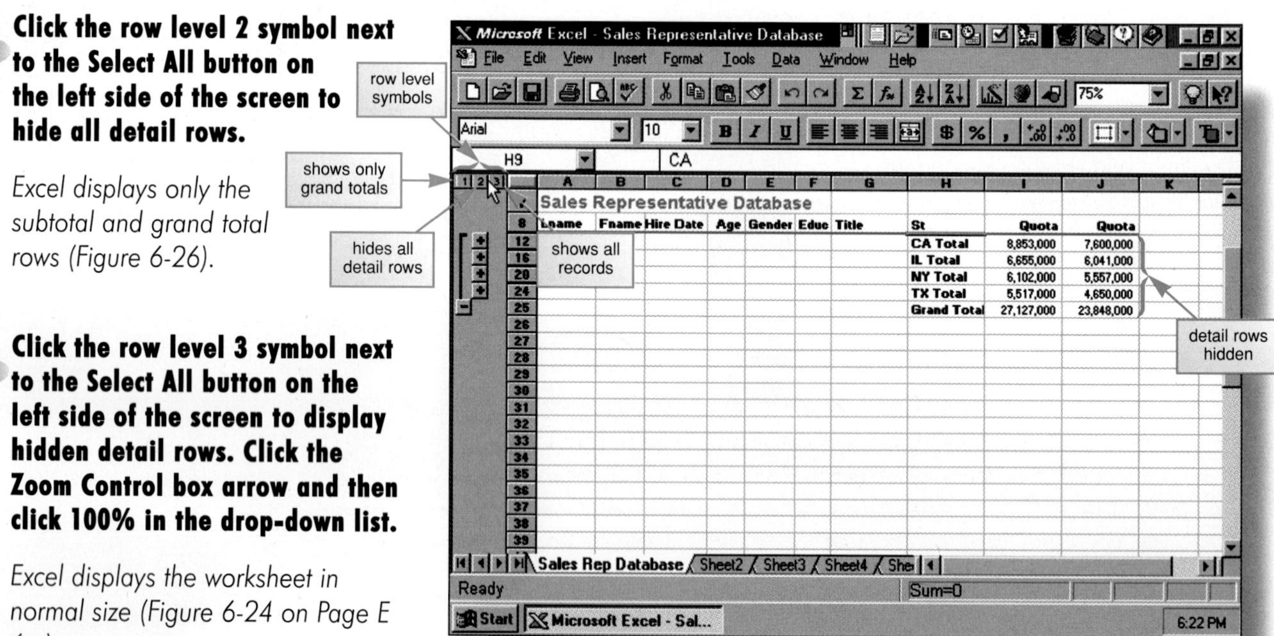

FIGURE 6-26

*Other*Ways

1. Click Zoom on the View menu to shrink or magnify the display
2. Click the minus or plus signs in the outline on the left side of the screen to hide or show detail data

By utilizing the outlining features of Excel, you can quickly hide and show detail data.

Removing Subtotals from the Database

Excel provides two ways to remove subtotals and the accompanying outline from a database. First, you can click the Undo button on the Standard toolbar or use the Undo Subtotals command on the Edit menu if you have not entered any commands since creating the subtotals. Second, you can click the Remove All button in the Subtotal dialog box. The following steps show how to use the Remove All button to remove subtotals from a database.

More About Outlining

When you hide data using the outline features, you can chart the resulting rows and columns as if they were adjacent to one another. Thus, in Figure 6-26 you can chart the salary subtotals as an adjacent range even though they are not in adjacent rows when the worksheet displays in normal form.

To Remove Subtotals from a Database

1 Click Subtotals on the Data menu.

Excel selects the sales representative database and displays the Subtotal dialog box (Figure 6-27).

2 Click the Remove All button on the Subtotals dialog box.

Excel removes all total rows and the outline from the database so that it displays as shown previously in Figure 6-21 on page E 6.20.

3 Reset any column widths that were changed so they agree with Table 6-1 on page E 6.5.

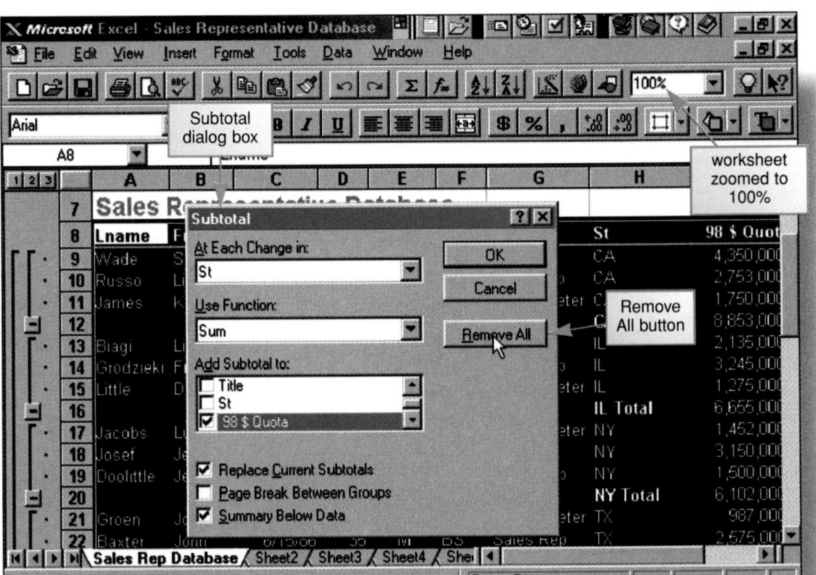

FIGURE 6-27

From the previous sections, you can see how easy it is to add and remove subtotals from a database. This allows you to quickly generate the type of information that database users require to help them make decisions about products or company direction.

Before moving on to the next section, follow the steps on the next page to sort the MedsForU sales representative database in its original sequence, which was by hire date in ascending sequence.

TO SORT THE DATABASE BY HIRE DATE

Step 1: Click cell C9.
Step 2: Click the Sort Ascending button on the Standard toolbar.

The records in the MedsForU sales representative database are sorted into ascending sequence by hire date (Figure 6-16 on page E 6.17).

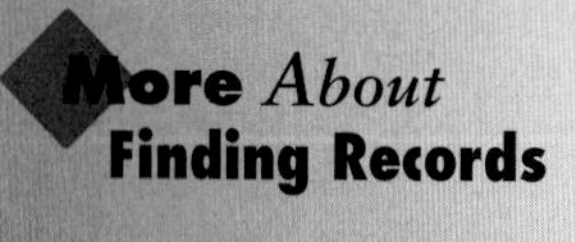

More *About* **Finding Records**

Excel is not case sensitive. That is, Excel considers uppercase and lowercase characters in the comparison criteria to be the same. For example, =m is the same as =M.

Finding Records Using a Data Form

To find records in the database that pass a test made up of **comparison criteria,** you can use the Find Prev and Find Next buttons together with the Criteria button on the data form. Comparison criteria are one or more conditions that include the field names and entries in the corresponding boxes on a data form. For example, you can instruct Excel to find and display only those records that pass the test:

Age >= 35 **AND** Gender = F **AND** Education <> BS **AND** 98$Quota > 1,500,000

For a record to display on the data form, it has to pass ALL four parts of the test. Finding records that pass a test is useful for viewing specific records, as well as maintaining the database. When a record that passes the test displays on the data form, you can change the field values or delete it from the database.

You use the same relational operators (=, <, >, >=, <=, and <>) to form the comparison criteria on a data form that you used to formulate conditions in IF functions. The following steps illustrate how to use a data form to find records that pass the test described above.

Steps To Find Records Using a Data Form

1 Click Form on the Data menu.

The first record in the MedsForU sales representative database displays on a data form (Figure 6-28).

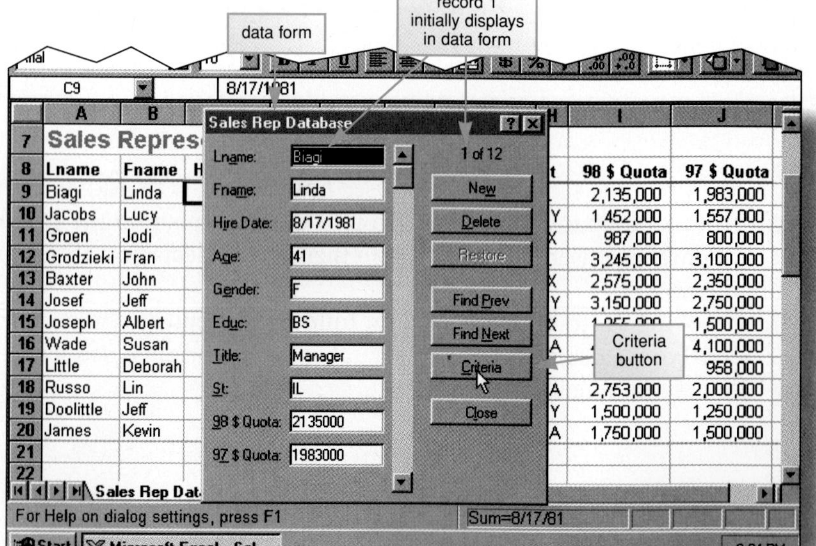

FIGURE 6-28

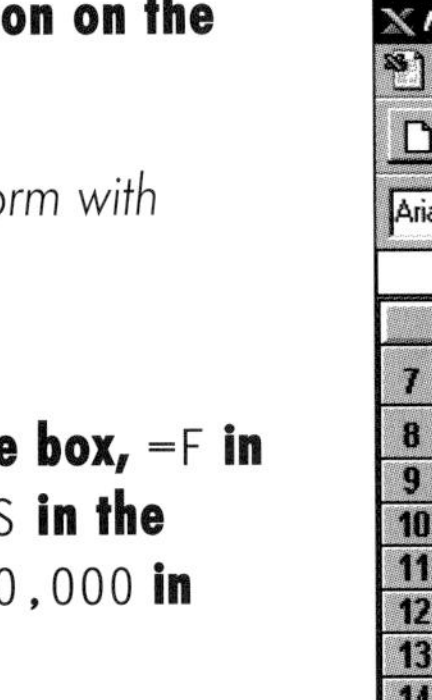

2 Click the Criteria button on the data form.

Excel displays a data form with blank boxes.

3 Type >=35 in the Age box, =F in the Gender box, <>BS in the Educ box, and >1,500,000 in the 98 $ Quota box.

The data form displays with the comparison criteria as shown in Figure 6-29.

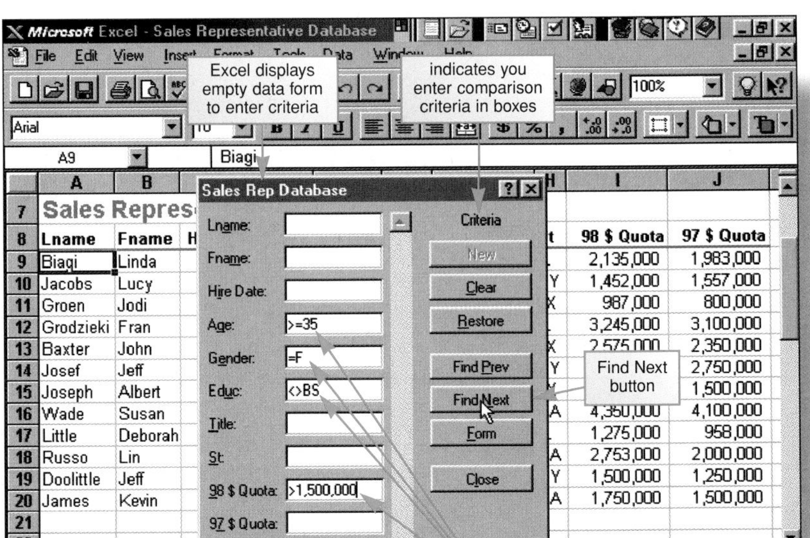

FIGURE 6-29

4 Click the Find Next button on the data form.

Excel immediately displays the fourth record in the database because it is the first record that passes the test (Figure 6-30). Ms. Fran Grodzieki is a 37 year old female with an AAS degree whose 98 $ Quota is $3,245,000. The first 3 records in the sales representative database failed the test.

5 Use the Find Next and Find Prev buttons to display other records (Ms. Susan Wade and Ms. Lin Russo) in the database that pass the test. When you are finished displaying records, click the Close button on the data form.

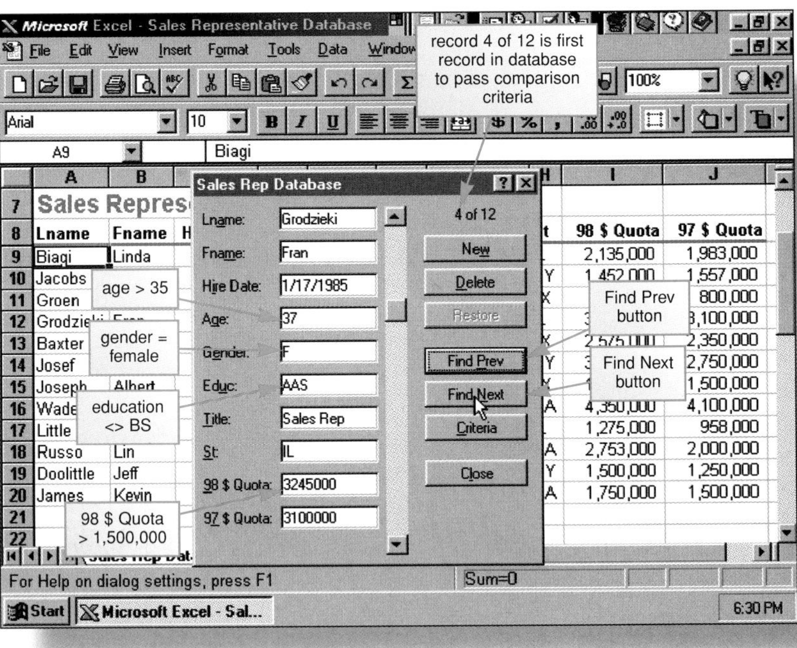

FIGURE 6-30

Three records in the personnel database pass the test: record 4 (Ms. Fran Grodzieki), record 8 (Ms. Susan Wade), and record 10 (Ms. Lin Russo). Each time you click the Find Next button, Excel displays the next record that passes the test. You can also use the Find Prev button to display the previous record that passed the test.

In Figure 6-29, no blank characters appear between the relational operators and the values. Leading or trailing blank characters have a significant impact on text comparisons. For example, there is a big difference between =M and =   M.

Using Wildcard Characters in Comparison Criteria

For text fields, you can use **wildcard characters** to find records that share certain characters in a field. Excel has two wildcard characters, the question mark (?) and the asterisk (*). The **question mark** represents any single character in the same position as the question mark. For example, if the comparison criteria for Lname (last name) is =Wa?e, then any last name passes the test that has the following: Wa as the first two characters, any third character, and the letter e as the fourth character. Wade (record 8 in row 16) passes this particular test.

Use the **asterisk** in a comparison criteria to represent any number of characters in the same position as the asterisk. Jo*, *e, Ru*o, are examples of valid text with the asterisk wildcard character. Jo* means all text that begins with the letters Jo. Josef (record 6 in row 14) and Joseph (record 7, row 15) pass the test. The second example, *e, means all text that ends with the letter e. Wade (record 8, in row 16), Little (record 9 in row 17), and Doolittle (record 11 in row 19) pass the test. The third example, Ru*o, means all text that begins with the letters Ru and ends with the letter o. Only Russo (record 10 in row 18) passes the test.

More *About* **Comparison Criteria**

An alternative to using the * at the end of a letter or phrase is to use the >= relational operator. For example, A* is the same as >=A.

Using Computed Criteria

A **computed criteria** involves using a formula in a comparison criteria. For example, the computed criterion formula =Age > 98 $ Quota / 1000 in the Age field on a data form finds all records whose Age field is less than the corresponding 98 $ Quota field divided by 1000.

Filtering a Database Using AutoFilter

An alternative to using a data form to find records that pass a test is to use AutoFilter. Whereas the data form displays one record at a time, **AutoFilter** enables you to display all the records that meet a criteria as a subset of the database. AutoFilter hides records that do not pass the test, displaying only those that do pass the test.

You apply AutoFilter to a database by pointing to Filter on the Data menu and then clicking AutoFilter on the Filter submenu. Excel responds by adding drop-down arrows directly on the field names at the top of the database in row 8. Clicking a drop-down arrow displays a list box of the unique items in the field (column). If you select an item from the list, Excel immediately hides records that do not contain the item. The item you select from the drop-down list is called the **filter criterion**. If you select an item from a second field, Excel displays a subset of the first subset.

The following steps show how to use AutoFilter to display those records in the MedsForU sales representative database that pass the following test:

Gender = M **AND** Educ = HS

Steps To Apply AutoFilter to a Database

1 Select any cell in the database. Point to Filter on the Data menu and then point to AutoFilter on the Filter submenu (Figure 6-31).

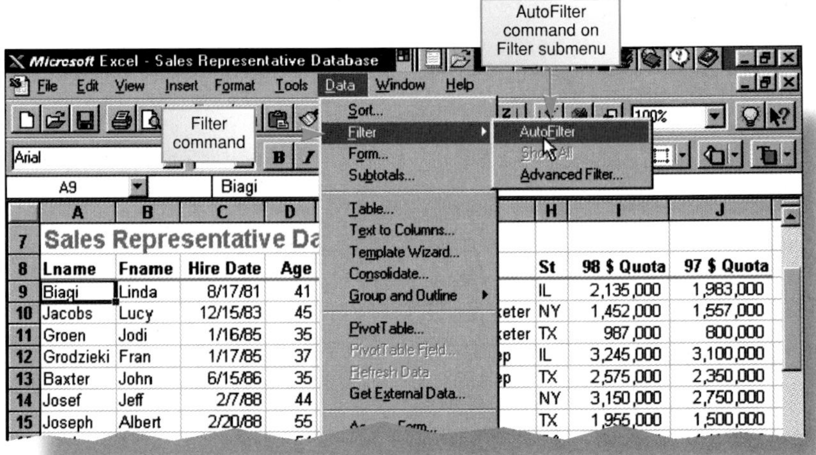

FIGURE 6-31

2 Click AutoFilter.

Drop-down arrows appear to the right of each field name in row 8 (Figure 6-32).

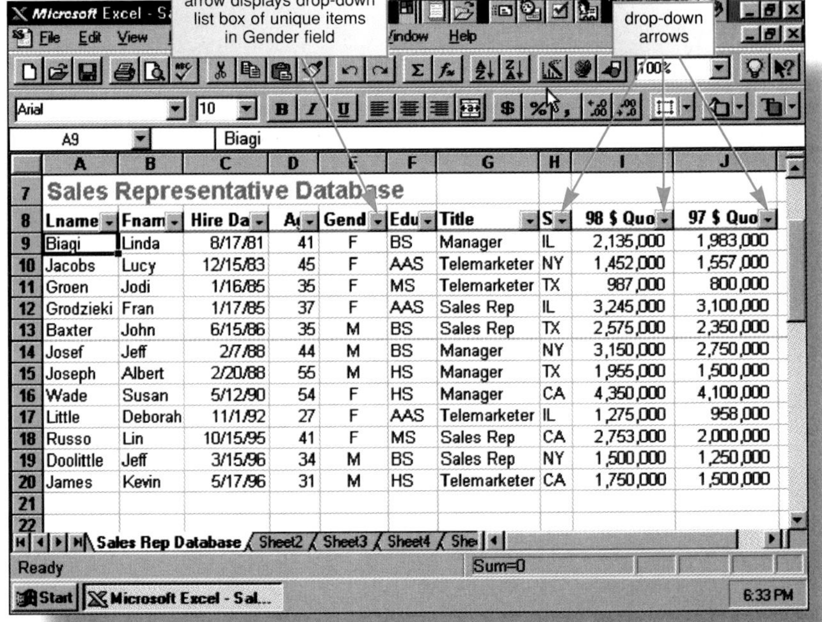

FIGURE 6-32

3 Click the Gender drop-down arrow and point to M in the drop-down list box.

A list of the entries F and M in the Gender field display (Figure 6-33). (All), (Top 10...), (Custom...), (Blanks), and (NonBlanks) are found in every AutoFilter drop-down list. When you first click AutoFilter on the Filter submenu, the filter criteria for each field in the database is set to All. Thus, all records display.

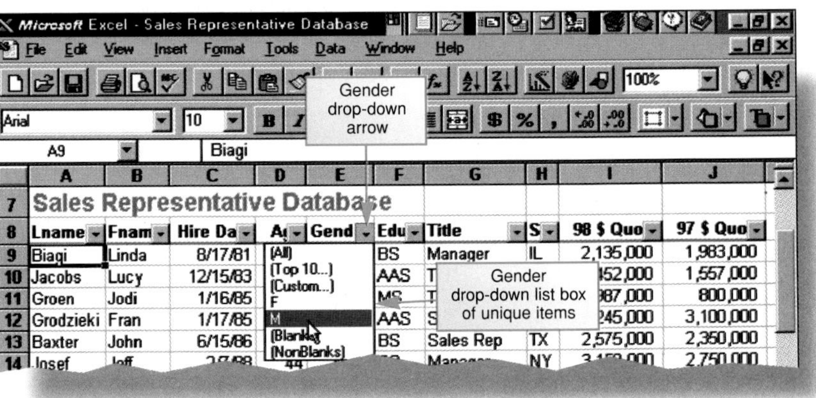

FIGURE 6-33

Click M in the Gender drop-down list box. Click the Educ drop-down arrow and point to HS in the drop-down list box.

Excel hides all records representing females. Thus, only records representing males display (Figure 6-34). The Educ drop-down list of entries displays.

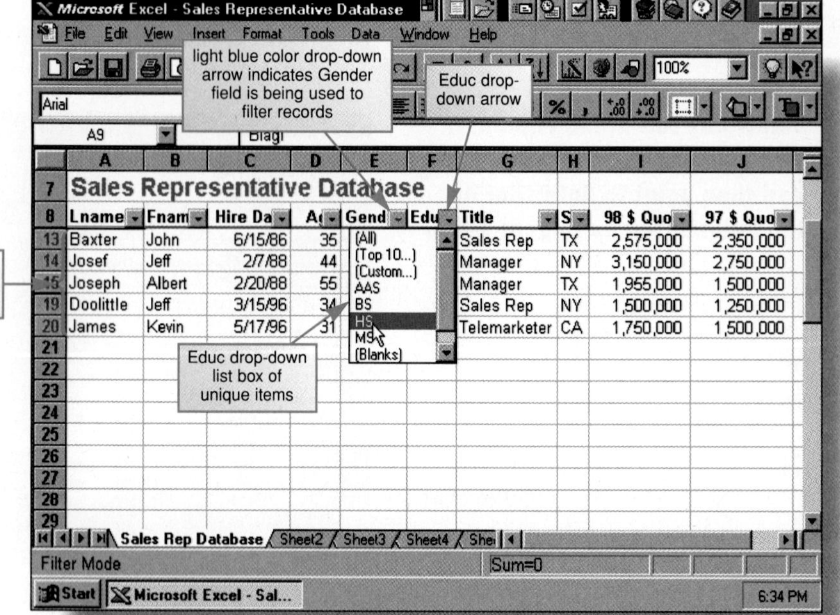

FIGURE 6-34

5 **Click HS from the Educ drop-down list.**

Excel hides all records representing males that do not have HS in the Educ field. Only two records pass the filter criterion Gender = M AND Educ = HS (Figure 6-35).

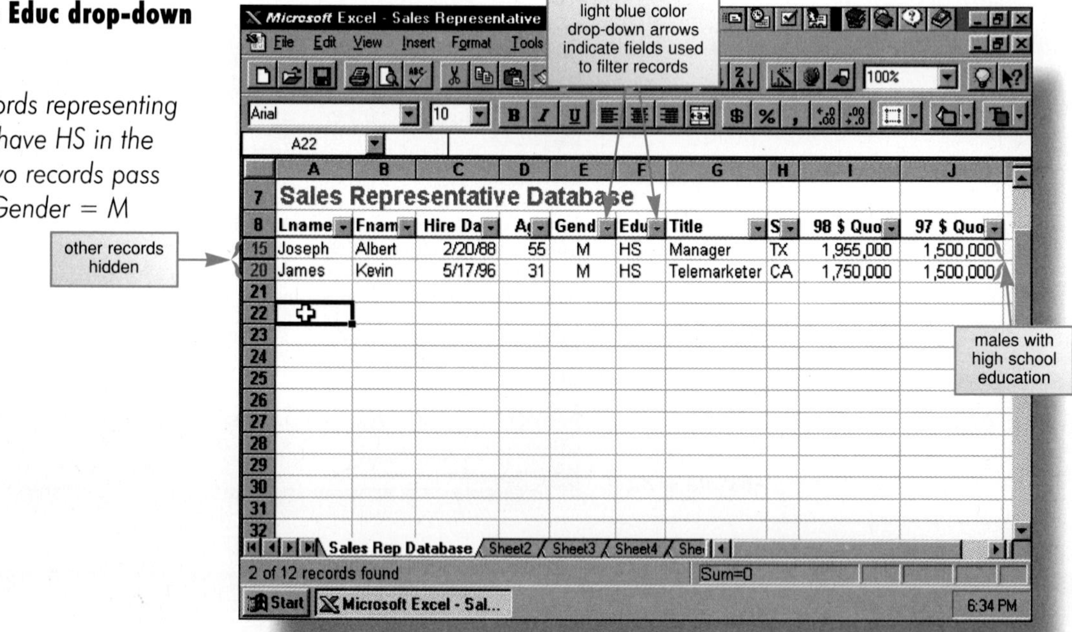

FIGURE 6-35

When you select a second filter criteria, Excel adds it to the first. Hence, in the case of the previous steps, each record must pass two tests to display as part of the final subset of the database. Listed below are some important points regarding AutoFilter.

1. When AutoFilter is active, Excel displays the row headings and drop-down arrows used to establish the filter in blue.
2. If you have multiple lists (other columns of data) on the worksheet, select a cell within the database prior to invoking AutoFilter.

3. If a single cell is selected prior to applying AutoFilter, Excel assigns drop-down arrows to all field names in the database. If you select certain field names, Excel assigns arrows to only the selected field names.
4. To find rows with blank cells in a field, select Blanks from the drop-down list box for that field. To find rows with nonblank cells in a field, select the NonBlanks option from the drop-down list box for that field.
5. To remove a filter criteria for a single field, select the All option from the drop-down list box for that field.
6. If you plan to have Excel determine automatic subtotals for a filtered database, apply AutoFilter first and then apply Subtotals, because Excel does not recalculate after selecting the filter criteria.

Removing AutoFilter

AutoFilter is like a toggle switch. Click it once and Excel adds the drop-down arrows to the field names in the database. Click it again and Excel removes the drop-down arrows from the field names and shows all records in the database. If you want to keep the drop-down arrows, but display all the records, click the Show All command on the Filter submenu.

The following steps show how to display all records and remove the drop-down arrows from the field names by clicking AutoFilter on the Filter submenu.

To Remove AutoFilter

1 Select a cell in the database. Point to Filter on the Data menu and then point to AutoFilter on the Filter submenu.

The Data menu and Filter submenu display as shown in Figure 6-36.

2 Click AutoFilter.

All the records in the MedsForU sales representative database display.

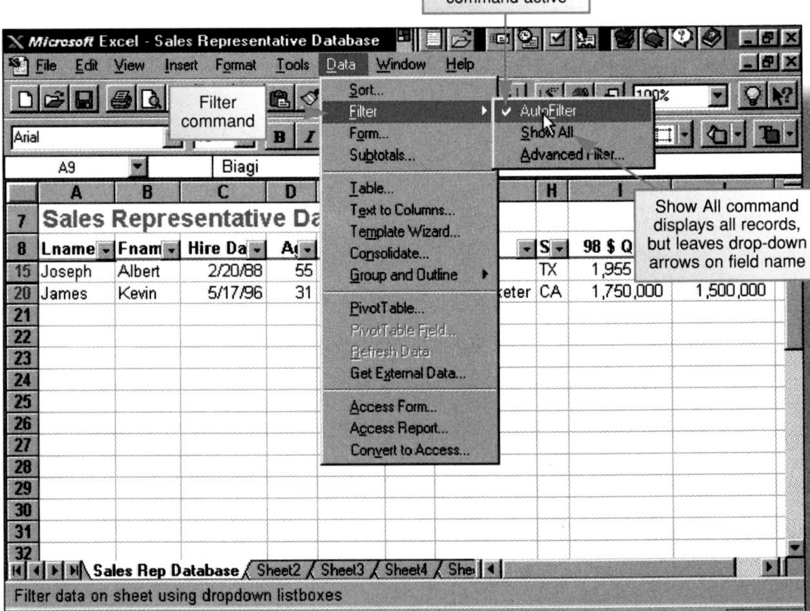

FIGURE 6-36

Entering Custom Criteria with AutoFilter

One of the options available in all the drop-down list boxes is (Custom...). **(Custom...)** allows you to enter custom criteria, such as multiple options in a drop-down list box and ranges of numbers. The following steps show how to display records in the MedsForU sales representative database that represent employees whose ages are in the range 40 to 50 inclusive (40 < Age < 50).

Steps To Enter Custom Criteria

1 Point to Filter on the Data menu and then click AutoFilter on the Filter submenu. Click the Age drop-down arrow in row 8 and point to (Custom...) in the drop-down list box.

The Age drop-down list displays (Figure 6-37).

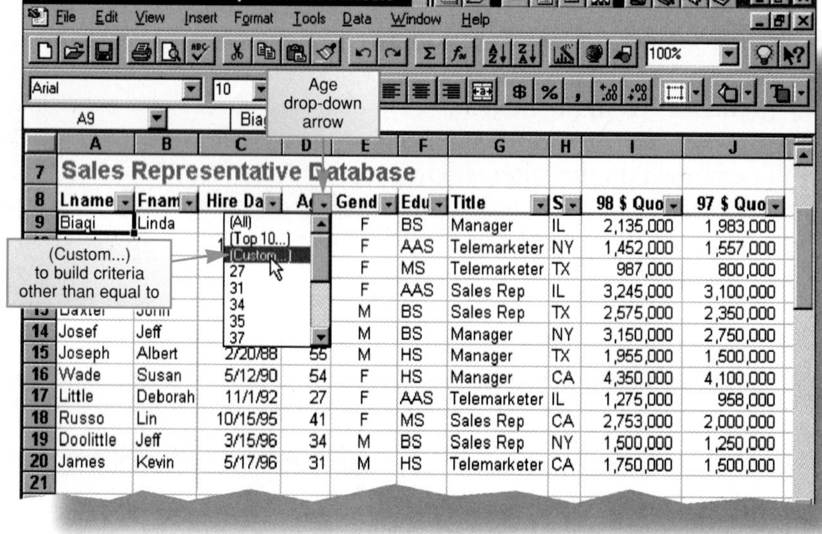

FIGURE 6-37

2 Click (Custom...) in the drop-down list box. When the Custom AutoFilter dialog box displays, select the >= relational operator in the top left box. Type 40 **in the top right box. Select the <= relational operator in the bottom left box. Type** 50 **in the bottom right box.**

The Custom AutoFilter dialog box displays as shown in Figure 6-38.

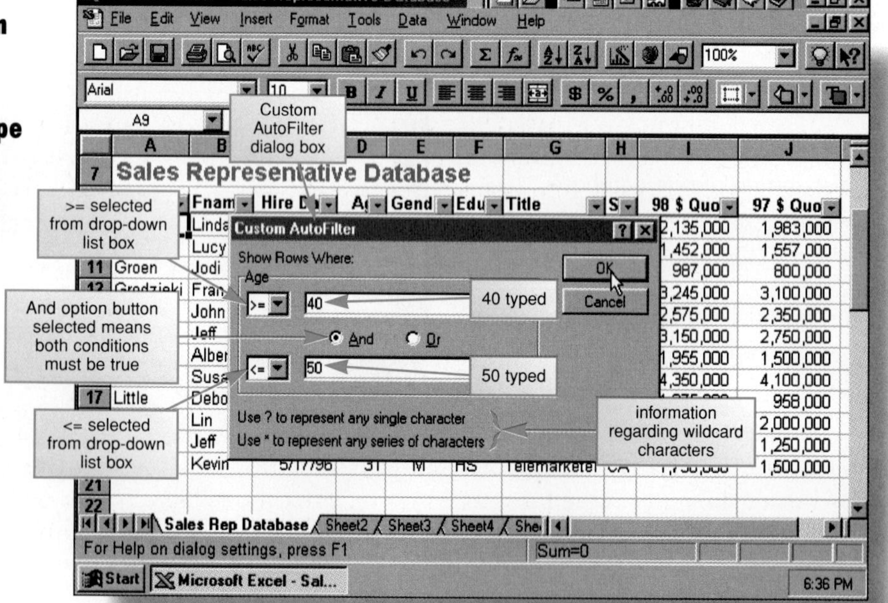

FIGURE 6-38

3 **Click the OK button in the Custom AutoFilter dialog box.**

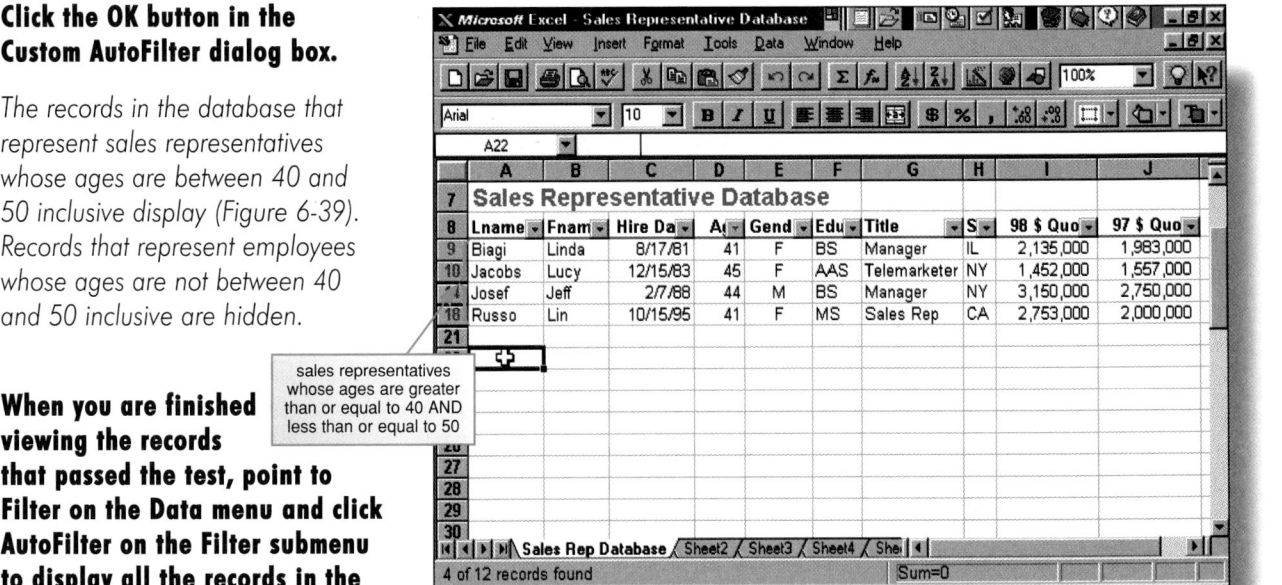

The records in the database that represent sales representatives whose ages are between 40 and 50 inclusive display (Figure 6-39). Records that represent employees whose ages are not between 40 and 50 inclusive are hidden.

4 **When you are finished viewing the records that passed the test, point to Filter on the Data menu and click AutoFilter on the Filter submenu to display all the records in the database.**

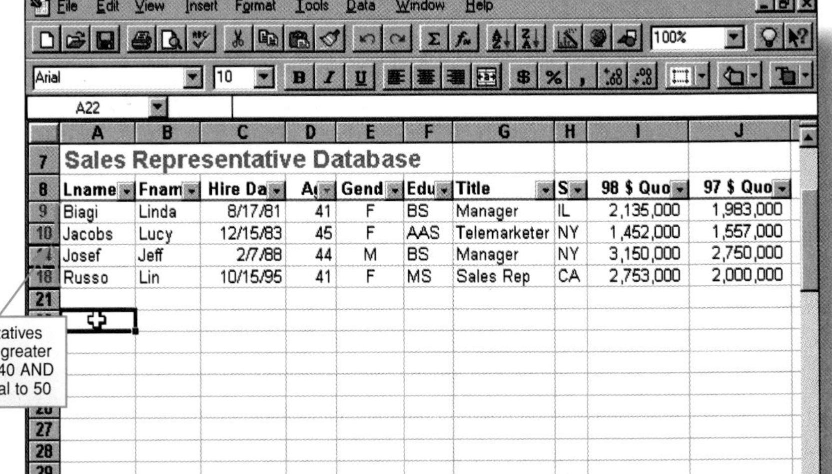

FIGURE 6-39

In Figure 6-38, you can select the And or Or operator in the Custom AutoFilter dialog box to indicate that both parts of the criteria must be true (And) or only one of the two must be true (Or). Use the And operator when the custom criteria is continuous over a range of values, such as Age greater than or equal to 40 **AND** less than or equal to 50 inclusive (40 < = Age < = 50). Use the Or operator when the custom criteria is not continuous, such as Age less than or equal to 40 **OR** greater than or equal to 50 (40 > = Age > = 50).

More *About* **Logical Operators**

AND means each and every one of the comparison criteria must be true. OR means only one of the comparison criteria must be true.

Using a Criteria Range on the Worksheet

Rather than use a data form or AutoFilter to establish criteria, you can set up a **criteria range** on the worksheet and use it to manipulate records that pass the comparison criteria. Using a criteria range on the worksheet involves two steps:

1. Create the criteria range and name it Criteria.
2. Use the Advanced AutoFilter command on the Filter submenu (Figure 6-36 on page E 6.29).

Creating a Criteria Range on the Worksheet and Naming it Criteria

To set up a criteria range, you copy the database field names to another area of the worksheet, preferably above the database in case the database is expanded downward or to the right in the future. Next, you enter the comparison criteria in the row immediately below the field names in the criteria range. Then you use the Name box to name the criteria range Criteria. The following steps show how to set up criteria in the range A2:J3 to find records that pass the test:

Age > 40 **AND** Gender = F **AND** Educ = AAS

Steps To Set Up a Criteria Range on the Worksheet

1 **Select the database title and field names in the range A7:J8. Click the Copy button on the Standard toolbar. Select cell A1. Press the ENTER key to copy the contents of the Clipboard to the paste area A1:J2. Change the title in cell A1 from Sales Representative Database to Criteria Area. Type** `>35` **in cell D3. Type** `F` **in cell E3. Type** `AAS` **in cell F3.**

The worksheet displays as shown in Figure 6-40.

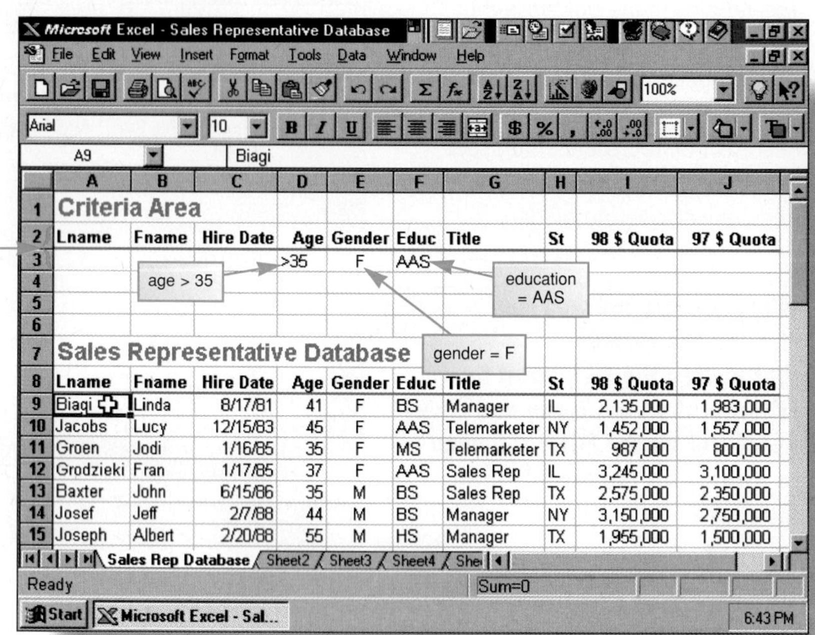

	A	B	C	D	E	F	G	H	I	J
1	Criteria Area									
2	Lname	Fname	Hire Date	Age	Gender	Educ	Title	St	98 $ Quota	97 $ Quota
3				>35	F	AAS				
4										
5										
6										
7	Sales Representative Database									
8	Lname	Fname	Hire Date	Age	Gender	Educ	Title	St	98 $ Quota	97 $ Quota
9	Biagi	Linda	8/17/81	41	F	BS	Manager	IL	2,135,000	1,983,000
10	Jacobs	Lucy	12/15/83	45	F	AAS	Telemarketer	NY	1,452,000	1,557,000
11	Groen	Jodi	1/16/85	35	F	MS	Telemarketer	TX	987,000	800,000
12	Grodzieki	Fran	1/17/85	37	F	AAS	Sales Rep	IL	3,245,000	3,100,000
13	Baxter	John	6/15/86	35	M	BS	Sales Rep	TX	2,575,000	2,350,000
14	Josef	Jeff	2/7/88	44	M	BS	Manager	NY	3,150,000	2,750,000
15	Joseph	Albert	2/20/88	55	M	HS	Manager	TX	1,955,000	1,500,000

FIGURE 6-40

2 **Select the range A2:J3. Click in the Name box in the formula bar and type** `Criteria`**. Press the ENTER key.**

The name Criteria is defined to be the range A2:J3. The Advanced AutoFilter command will automatically recognize the range named Criteria as the criteria range.

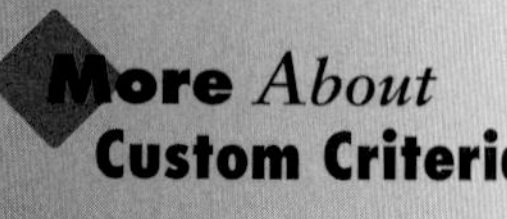

More About Custom Criteria

As with comparison criteria in data forms, you can use wildcard characters (?, *) to build the custom criteria as described at the bottom of the Custom AutoFilter dialog box in Figure 6-38 on page E 6.30. If the comparison criteria calls for searching for a question mark (?) or asterisk (*), precede either one with a tilde (~). For example, to search for the text What?, enter What~? in the comparison criteria.

Here are some important points to remember about setting up a criteria range:

1. Do not begin a test for equality involving text with an equal sign (= F) because Excel will assume the F is a range name rather than text.
2. If you include a blank row in the criteria range (for example, rows 2 and 3 and the blank row 4), all records will pass the test.
3. To ensure the field names in the criteria range are spelled exactly the same as in the database, use the Copy command to copy the database field .names to the criteria range as was done in the previous steps.
4. The criteria range is independent of the criteria set up on a data form.

Displaying Records that Meet a Criteria Using the Advanced Filter Command

The Advanced Filter command is similar to the AutoFilter command, except that it does not add drop-down arrows to the field names. Rather, it uses the comparison criteria set up on the worksheet in a criteria range (A2:J3). Follow these steps to display the records in the personnel database that pass the test (Age > 40 **AND** Gender = F **AND** Educ = AAS) defined in the previous set of steps and shown in Figure 6-40.

Steps To Display Records Using the Advanced Filter

1 **Click cell A9. Point to Filter on the Data menu and then point to Advanced Filter on the Filter submenu.**

The Data menu and Filter submenu display as shown in Figure 6-41.

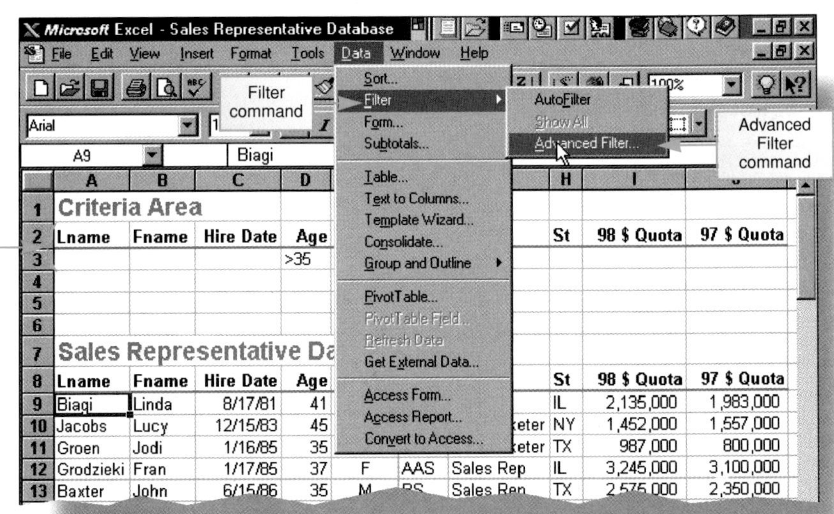

FIGURE 6-41

2 **Click Advanced Filter.**

The Advanced Filter dialog box displays (Figure 6-42). In the Action area, the Filter the List, in-place option is selected automatically. Excel also selects the database (A8:J20) in the List Range box, because the active cell (cell A9) is within the database range. Excel also selects the criteria range (A2:J3) in the Criteria Range box, because it is assigned the name Criteria.

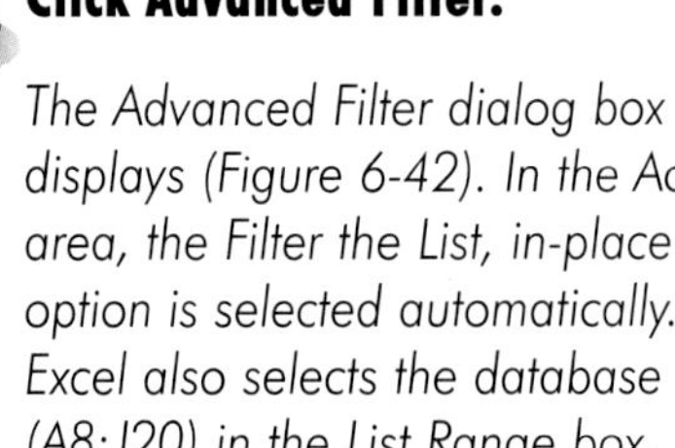

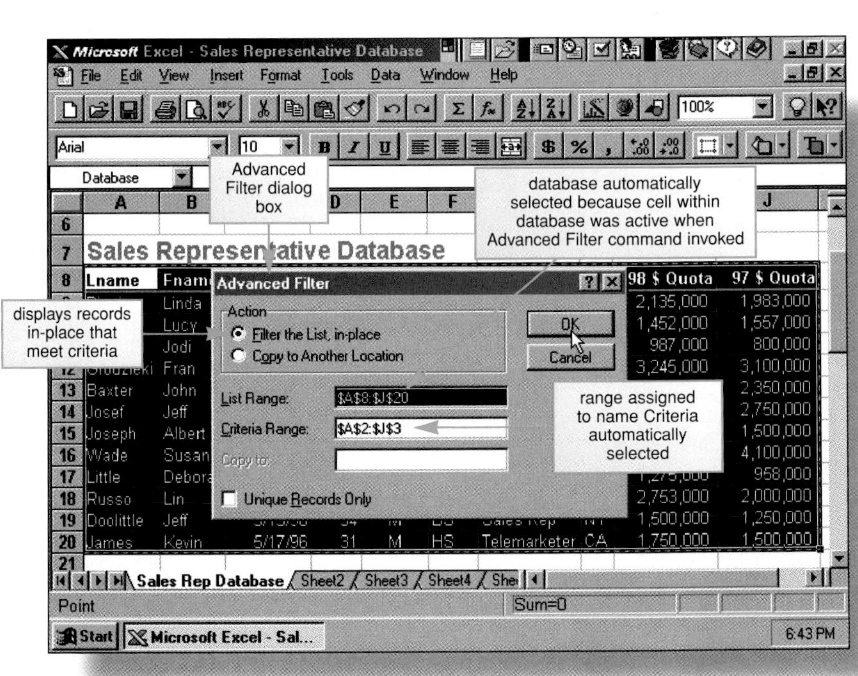

FIGURE 6-42

Click the OK button on the Advanced Filter dialog box.

Excel hides all records that do not meet the comparison criteria, leaving only two records on the worksheet (Figure 6-43). Lucy Jacobs (row 10) and Fran Grodzieki (row 12) are the only two employees in the sales representative database who are older than 35, female, and have an AAS degree.

	A	B	C	D	E	F	G	H	I	J
1	Criteria Area									
2	Lname	Fname	Hire Date	Age	Gender	Educ	Title	St	98 $ Quota	97 $ Quota
3				>35	F	AAS				
4										
5										
6										
7	Sales Representative Database									
8	Lname	Fname	Hire Date	Age	Gender	Educ	Title	St	98 $ Quota	97 $ Quota
10	Jacobs	Lucy	12/15/83	45	F	AAS	Telemarketer	NY	1,452,000	1,557,000
12	Grodzieki	Fran	1/17/85	37	F	AAS	Sales Rep	IL	3,245,000	3,100,000

criteria
records that meet criteria
blue indicates database is filtered
age > 35
gender = F
education = AAS
2 of 12 records found
Sum=0
Start
Microsoft Excel - Sal...
6:44 PM

FIGURE 6-43

More *About*
Printing a Criteria Range

You can print the criteria range by entering the name Criteria in the Print Area box on the Sheet tab in Print Area box on the Sheet tab on the Page Setup dialog box.

The Advanced Filter command displays a subset of the database in the same fashion as the AutoFilter command. The primary difference between the two is that the Advanced Filter command allows you to create more complex comparison criteria. This is possible because the criteria range can be as many rows long as necessary, which allows for many sets of comparison criteria.

To display all the records in the MedsForU sales representative database, perform the following steps:

TO DISPLAY ALL RECORDS IN THE DATABASE

Step 1: Point to Filter on the Data menu.
Step 2: Click Show All on the Filter submenu.

All the records in the database display.

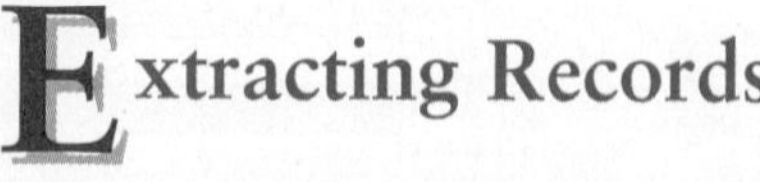

Extracting Records

If you select the Copy to Another Location in the Action area of the Advanced Filter dialog box (Figure 6-42), Excel copies the records to another part of the worksheet, rather than displaying a subset of the database. The location where the records are copied is called the **extract range.** The extract range is set up in a manner similar to the way the criteria range was set up earlier. Once the records that pass the test in the criteria range are **extracted** (copied), you can manipulate and print them as a group.

Creating the Extract Range

To create an extract range, copy the field names of the database to an area on the worksheet, preferably well below the database range. Next, name the range containing the field names Extract by using the Name box. Finally, use the Advanced Filter command to extract the records. The following steps show how to set up an extract range below the MedsForU sales representative database and extract records that meet the criteria in the Criteria Area (Figure 6-43): Age > 35 **AND** Gender = F **AND** Educ = AAS.

To Create an Extract Range on the Worksheet and Extract Records

1 Select the database title and field names in the range A7:J8. Click the Copy button on the Standard toolbar. Select cell A24. Press the ENTER key to copy the contents of the Clipboard to the paste area A24:J25. Change the title in cell A24 from Sales Representative Database to Extract Area. Select the range A25:J25. Type the name `Extract` **in the Name box in the formula bar and press the ENTER key. Click cell A20 so a cell in the database is active. Point to Filter on the Data menu and then point to Advanced Filter on the Filter submenu.**

The worksheet displays as shown in Figure 6-44. The name Extract is assigned only the field names in row 25. Excel will automatically copy the records to the rows below the range named Extract.

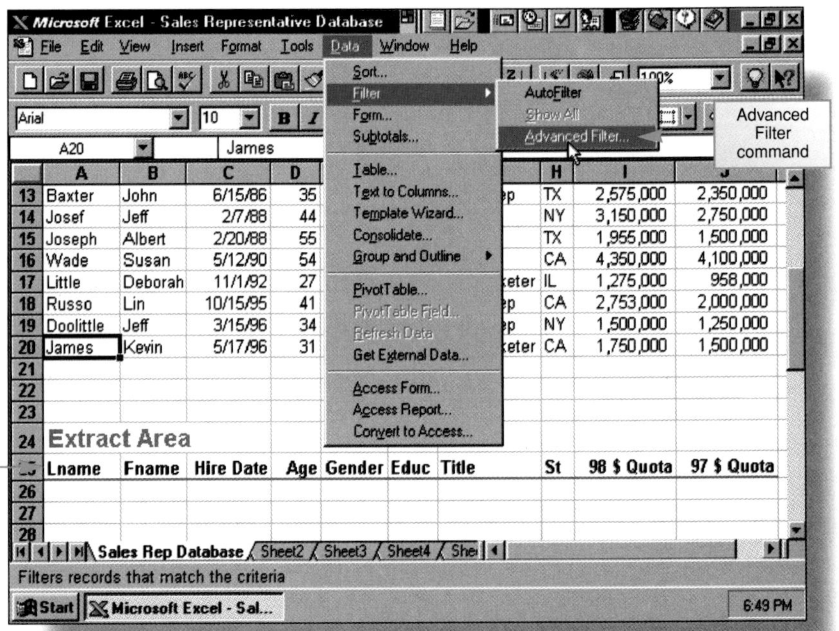

FIGURE 6-44

Click Advanced Filter on the Filter submenu. When the Advanced Filter dialog box displays, select the Copy to Another Location option in the Action area.

The Advanced Filter dialog box displays (Figure 6-45). Excel automatically assigns the range A8:J20 to the List Range box because the active cell is within the range of the database. It also assigns the range named Criteria (A2:J3) to the Criteria Range box and the range named Extract (A25:J25) to the Copy to box.

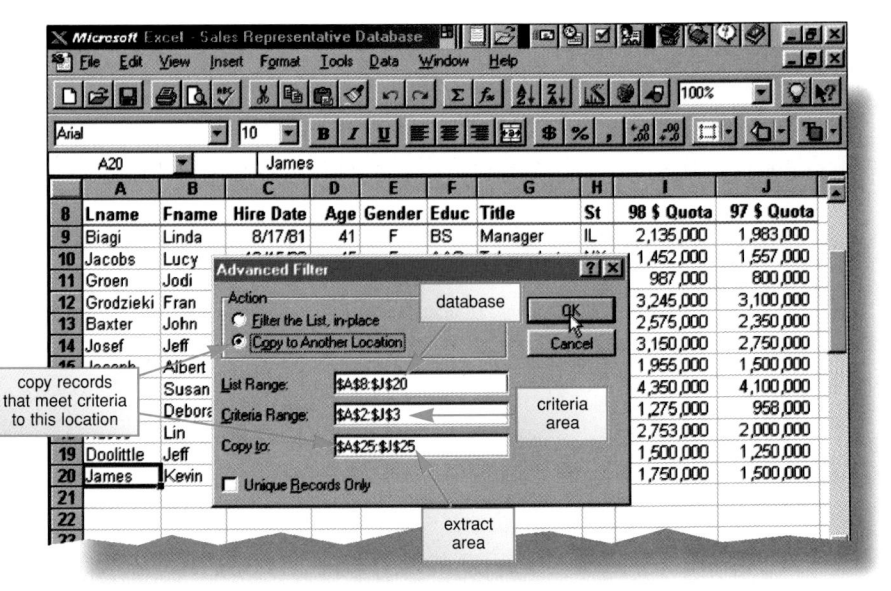

FIGURE 6-45

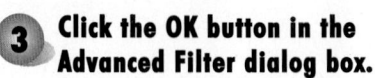

Click the OK button in the Advanced Filter dialog box.

Excel copies the records from the MedsForU Sales Representative database that pass the test described in the criteria range (see Figure 6-43) to the extract range (Figure 6-46).

records that meet criteria age > 35, gender = F, and education = AAS

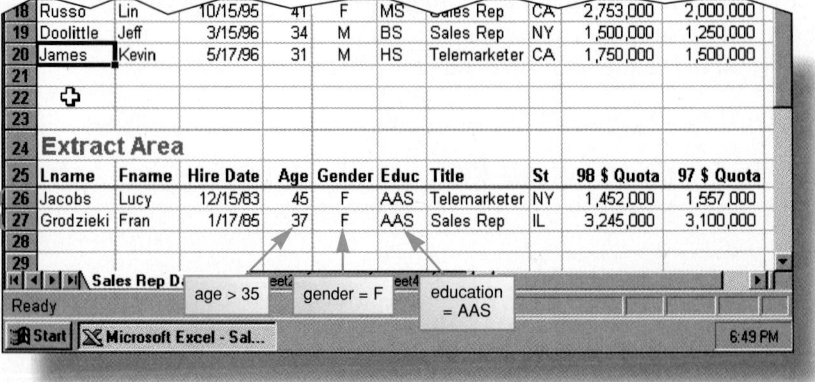

FIGURE 6-46

When you set up the extract range, you do not have to copy all the field names in the database to the proposed extract range. You can copy only those field names you want, and they can be in any order. You can also type the field names rather than copy them, but it is not recommended.

When you invoke the Advanced Filter command and select the Copy to Another Location option, Excel clears all the cells below the field names in the extract range. Hence, if you change the comparison criteria in the criteria range and invoke the Extract command a second time, Excel clears the original extracted records before it copies the records that pass the new test.

In the previous example, the extract range was defined as a single row containing the field names (A25:J25). When you define the extract range as one row long (the field names), any number of records can be extracted from the database because Excel will use all the rows below row 25 to the bottom of the worksheet. The alternative is to define an extract range with a fixed number of rows. However, if you define a fixed-size extract range and more records are extracted than there are rows available, Excel displays a dialog box with a diagnostic message indicating the extract range is full.

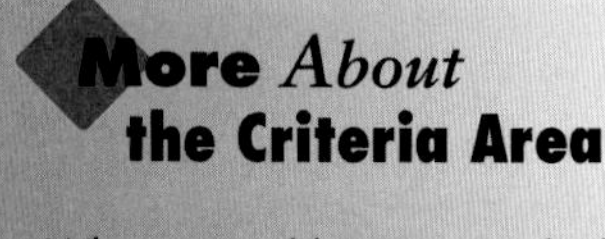

More *About* **the Criteria Area**

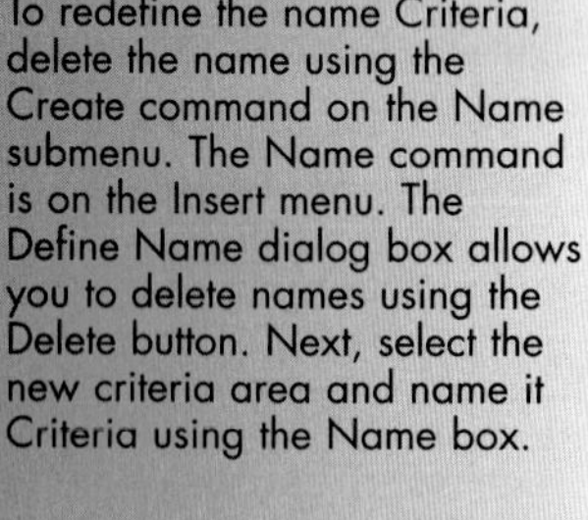

When you add items in multiple rows to a Criteria area, you must redefine the range of the name Criteria before you use it. To redefine the name Criteria, delete the name using the Create command on the Name submenu. The Name command is on the Insert menu. The Define Name dialog box allows you to delete names using the Delete button. Next, select the new criteria area and name it Criteria using the Name box.

More About Comparison Criteria

The way you set up the comparison criteria in the criteria range determines the records that will pass the test when you use the Filter command. Different examples of comparison criteria are described in this section.

A Blank Row in the Criteria Range

If the criteria range contains a blank row, then all the records in the database pass the test. For example, the blank row in the criteria range in Figure 6-47 causes all records to pass the test.

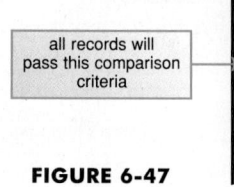

all records will pass this comparison criteria

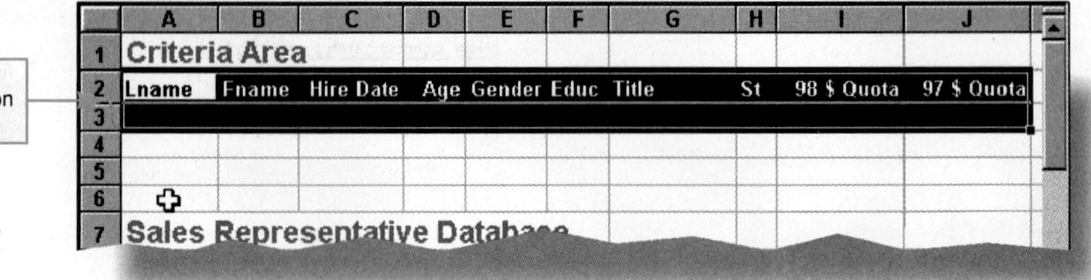

FIGURE 6-47

Using Multiple Comparison Criteria with the Same Field

If the criteria range contains two or more entries under the same field name, then records that pass either comparison criterion pass the test. For example, the criteria range in Figure 6-48 causes all records that represent sales representatives that have an AAS degree **OR** a BS degree to pass the test.

If an **AND** applies to the same field name (Age > 50 **AND** Age <55) then you must duplicate the field name (Age) in the criteria range. That is, add the field name Age to column K, which is to the right of the 97 $ Quota field. Then delete the name Criteria by using the Name command on the Insert menu, and redefine the name Criteria in the reference area to include the second Age field.

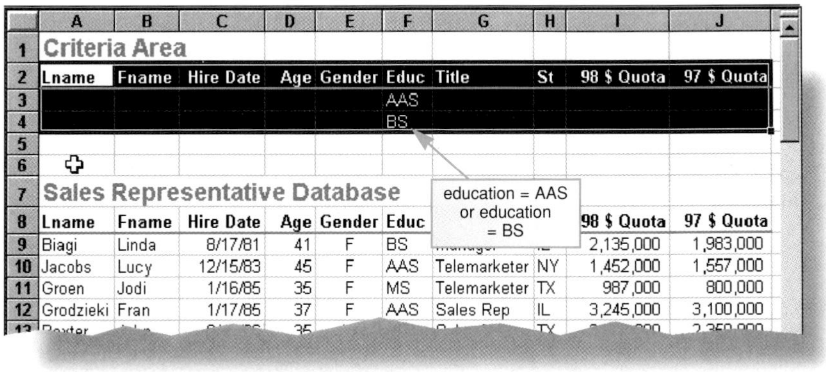

	A	B	C	D	E	F	G	H	I	J
1	Criteria Area									
2	Lname	Fname	Hire Date	Age	Gender	Educ	Title	St	98 $ Quota	97 $ Quota
3						AAS				
4						BS				
5										
6										
7	Sales Representative Database									
8	Lname	Fname	Hire Date	Age	Gender	Educ			98 $ Quota	97 $ Quota
9	Biagi	Linda	8/17/81	41	F	BS			2,135,000	1,983,000
10	Jacobs	Lucy	12/15/83	45	F	AAS	Telemarketer	NY	1,452,000	1,557,000
11	Groen	Jodi	1/16/85	35	F	MS	Telemarketer	TX	987,000	800,000
12	Grodzieki	Fran	1/17/85	37	F	AAS	Sales Rep	IL	3,245,000	3,100,000

education = AAS or education = BS

FIGURE 6-48

Comparison Criteria in Different Rows and Under Different Fields

When the comparison criteria under different field names are in the same row, then records pass the test only if they pass all the comparison criteria. If the comparison criteria for the field names are in different rows, then the records must pass only one of the tests. For example, in the criteria range in Figure 6-49, all records that represent sales representatives who are greater than 60 years old **OR** have a 98 $ Quota greater than $1,500,000 pass the test.

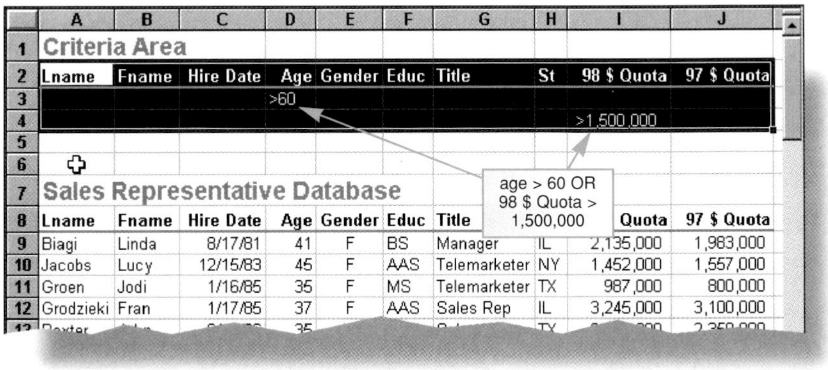

	A	B	C	D	E	F	G	H	I	J
1	Criteria Area									
2	Lname	Fname	Hire Date	Age	Gender	Educ	Title	St	98 $ Quota	97 $ Quota
3				>60						
4									>1,500,000	
5										
6										
7	Sales Representative Database									
8	Lname	Fname	Hire Date	Age	Gender	Educ	Title		Quota	97 $ Quota
9	Biagi	Linda	8/17/81	41	F	BS	Manager	IL	2,135,000	1,983,000
10	Jacobs	Lucy	12/15/83	45	F	AAS	Telemarketer	NY	1,452,000	1,557,000
11	Groen	Jodi	1/16/85	35	F	MS	Telemarketer	TX	987,000	800,000
12	Grodzieki	Fran	1/17/85	37	F	AAS	Sales Rep	IL	3,245,000	3,100,000

age > 60 OR 98 $ Quota > 1,500,000

FIGURE 6-49

Using Database Functions

Excel has 12 database functions that you can use to evaluate numeric data in a database. One of the functions is called the DAVERAGE function. As the name implies, you use the **DAVERAGE function** to find the average of numbers in a database field that pass a test. This function serves as an alternative to finding an average using the Subtotals command on the Data menu. The general form of the DAVERAGE function is

=DAVERAGE(database, "field name", criteria range)

where database is the name of the database, field name is the name of the field in the database, and criteria range is the comparison criteria or test to pass.

In the steps on the next page, the DAVERAGE function is used to find the average age of the females and the average age of the males in the MedsForU sales representative database.

More *About*
Database Functions

Database functions are useful when working with lists of data, such as the one in this project. Remembering the function arguments and their order within parentheses is not easy. Thus, it is recommended that you use the Function Wizard button on the Standard toolbar to assign a database function to your worksheet.

TO USE THE DAVERAGE DATABASE FUNCTION

Step 1: With the Sales Representative Database workbook open, type the field name Gender twice, once in cell A40 and again in cell B40. Type the code for females F in cell A41. Type the code for males M in cell B41.

Step 2: Type `Average Female Age = = = = =>` in cell A43. Type `Average Male Age = = = = = = =>` in cell A44.

Step 3: Type the database function `=daverage(database, "Age", A40:A41)` in cell D43.

Step 4: Type the database function `=daverage(database, "Age", B40:B41)` in cell D44.

Excel computes and displays the average age of the females in the sales representative database (40) in cell D43 and the average age of the males in the sales representative database (39.8) in cell D44 (Figure 6-50).

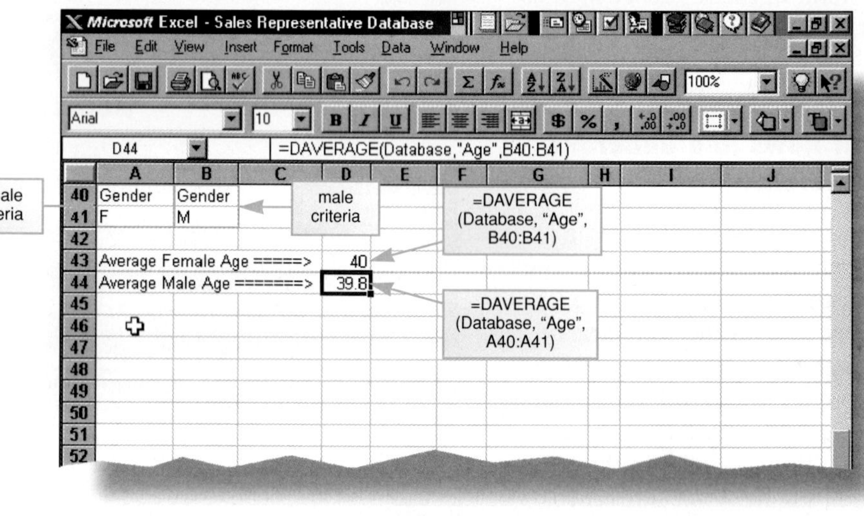

FIGURE 6-50

In Figure 6-50, the first value (database) in the function references the MedsForU sales representative database defined earlier in this project (A8:J20). The second value ("Age") identifies the field on which to compute the average. Excel requires that you surround the field name with quotation marks unless the field has been assigned a name through the Name box. The third value (A40:A41 for the female average) defines the criteria range.

Other database functions that are similar to the functions described in previous projects include the DCOUNT, DMAX, DMIN, and DSUM functions. For a complete list of the database functions, click the Function Wizard button on the Standard toolbar. When the FunctionWizard - Step 1 of 2 dialog box displays, click Database in the Function Category list box. The database functions display in the Function Name list box.

Using Excel's Lookup Functions

The HLOOKUP and VLOOKUP functions are useful for looking up values in tables, such as tax tables, discount tables, parts tables, and grade scale tables. Both functions look up a value in a table and return a corresponding value from the table to the cell assigned the function. The HLOOKUP function is used when the table direction is horizontal, or across the worksheet. The VLOOKUP function is used when a table direction is vertical, or down the worksheet. The VLOOKUP function is by far the most often used, because most tables are vertical. Therefore, the VLOOKUP function will be illustrated in this section.

Assume Tina Capsol, national sales manager for MedsForU, wants to grade the sales representatives on the percent of the 98 dollar quota met thus far by state, which is illustrated in Table 6-4. Tina uses the grading scale shown in Table 6-5. Using the information from these two tables, the states would grade out as follows: CA = F; IL = A; NY = C; and TX = B.

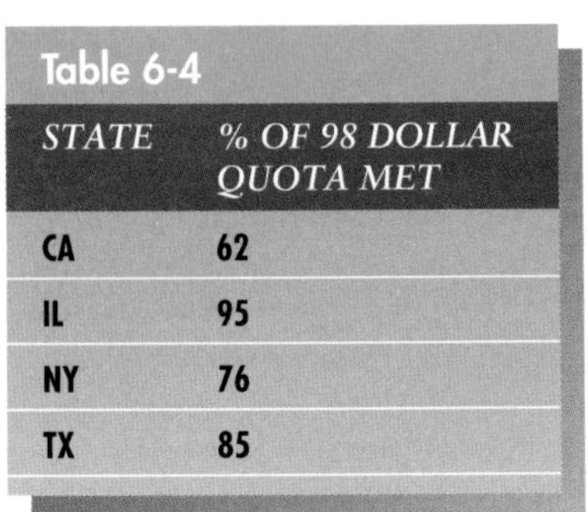

Table 6-4

STATE	*% OF 98 DOLLAR QUOTA MET*
CA	62
IL	95
NY	76
TX	85

In the example in this section, the VLOOKUP function will use the total state percent of 98 dollar quota met in Table 6-4 (called the **search argument**) and lookup the grade in Table 6-5. The VLOOKUP function searches the leftmost column (called the **table arguments**) of a table for a particular value, and returns the value from the specified column (called the **table values**). In this example, the table values are the grade.

The general form of the VLOOKUP function is:

VLOOKUP(search argument, table range, column number),

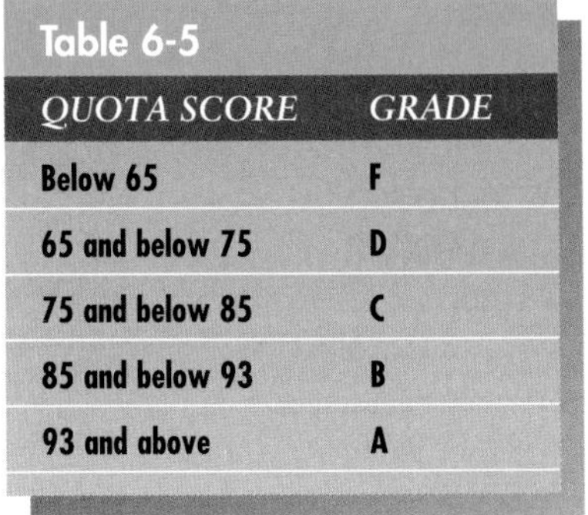

Table 6-5

QUOTA SCORE	*GRADE*
Below 65	F
65 and below 75	D
75 and below 85	C
85 and below 93	B
93 and above	A

where search argument is the value to be found in the first column of the table (called lookup-value); table range is the range of the table of information in which data is looked up (called table-array); and column number is the column number of the table values, counting from the left column of the table (called Cd-index-num).

For the VLOOKUP function to work correctly, it is necessary that the search arguments in the table to be searched be in ascending sequence, because the VLOOKUP function will return a table value based on the search argument being less than or equal to the table arguments. Thus, if the percent of sales quota met is 77%, then a grade of C is returned by the VLOOKUP function because 77% is greater than or equal to 75% and less than 85%, which is the minimum percent for a grade of B.

The following steps show how to enter the two tables of information shown in Tables 6-4 and 6-5 and use the VLOOKUP function to determine the letter grades for each state in the MedsForU sales representative database.

TO CREATE A LOOKUP TABLE AND USE THE VLOOKUP FUNCTION

Step 1: Type `State` in cell A50, `% of 98 $ Quota` in cell B50, press ALT+ENTER after 98, and type `Grade` in cell C50.

Step 2: Type `CA` in cell A51, 62 in cell B51, `IL` in cell A52, 95 in cell B52, `NY` in cell A53, 76 in cell B53, TX in cell A54, and 85 in cell B54.

Step 3: Type `Quota Score` in cell E50, press ALT+ENTER after Quota, and type `Grade` in cell E50.

Step 4: Type `0` in cell E51, `F` in cell F51, 65 in cell E52, `D` in cell F52, 75 in cell E53, `C` in cell F53, 85 in cell E54, `B` in cell F54, 93 in cell E55, and `A` in cell F55.

Step 5: Type `=VLOOKUP(B51, E51:F55, 2)` in cell C51. Use the fill handle to copy the function to the range C52:C54.

The VLOOKUP function returns the grades shown in column C from the table of grades in columns E and F for the corresponding grades in column B (Figure 6-51 on the next page).

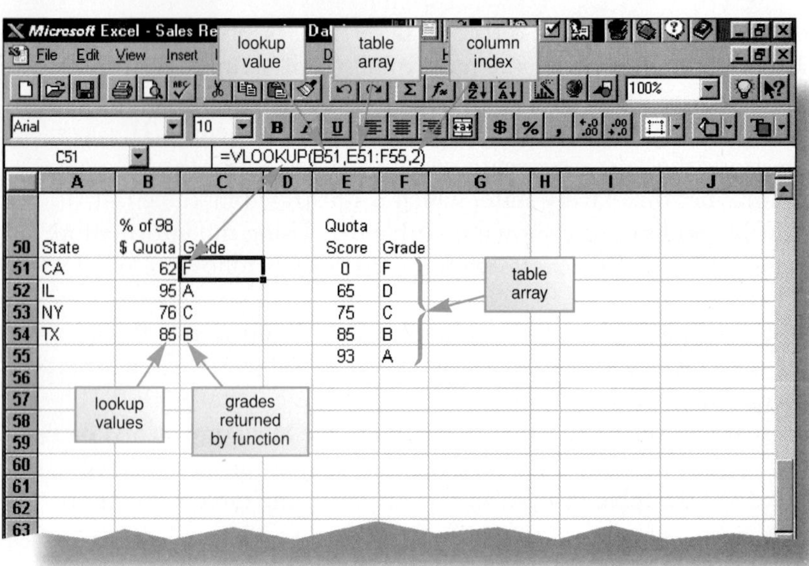

FIGURE 6-51

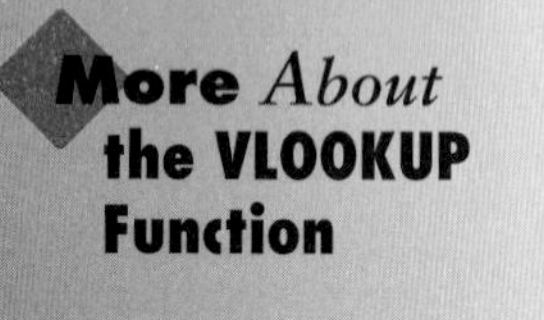

More *About* **the VLOOKUP Function**

A score less than the least table argument (zero in Figure 6-51) will return an error message (#N/A) to the cell assigned the VLOOKUP function.

In Figure 6-51, any percent of 98 dollar quota met below 65 returns a grade of F. Thus, CA receives a grade of F because its percent of 98 dollar quota met is 62%. A percent of 65 is required to move up to the next letter grade. IL receives a grade of A because its percent of 98 quota met is 95%. Any percent of 93 or greater returns a letter grade of A.

From the example in Figure 6-51, you can see that the VLOOKUP function is not searching for a table argument that matches the search argument exactly. The VLOOKUP function begins the search at the top of the table and works downward. As soon as it finds the first table argument greater than the search argument, it returns the previous table value. For example, when it searches the table with the CA score of 62%, it determines the score is less than 65% in the first column in the table and returns the grade of F from the second column in the table, which actually corresponds to 0 in the table. Thus, the letter grade of F is returned for any value greater than or equal to 0 (zero) and less than 65.

Creating a Data Map

Microsoft Excel includes a mapping feature, called **Microsoft Data Map**, you can use it to see the relationships between numbers and geographic regions. With a few clicks of the mouse, you can embed as an OLE object in your worksheet, a **data map** of any location in the world and then format it. For example, you can add

labels, text, and pins to a data map to display and analyze the sales representative quotas by state. Figure 6-52 shows the data map required for this project. It is a data map of the 48 contiguous states in the United States. The four states with MedsForU offices are highlighted in gray. The column chart on top of each of the four states compares the 98 dollar quota to the 97 dollar quota.

To use the mapping feature of Excel, you select a range of cells on your worksheet that includes geographic data, such as countries or states, and then click the Map button on the Standard toolbar. When the mouse pointer changes to a cross hair, drag it to an open area on your worksheet to define the data map location and size.

The data you plan to use to create a data map must be in columnar form with the names or abbreviations of the states (or countries) in the left-most column. For example, the data shown in Table 6-6 could be used to create a data map. Before clicking the Map button, you select the range encompassing the rows and columns, including the column titles Country and Employees.

Excel determines which countries to include on the map from the left column in Table 6-6. The data in the second column could then be used to format the map to emphasize the numbers and their corresponding countries.

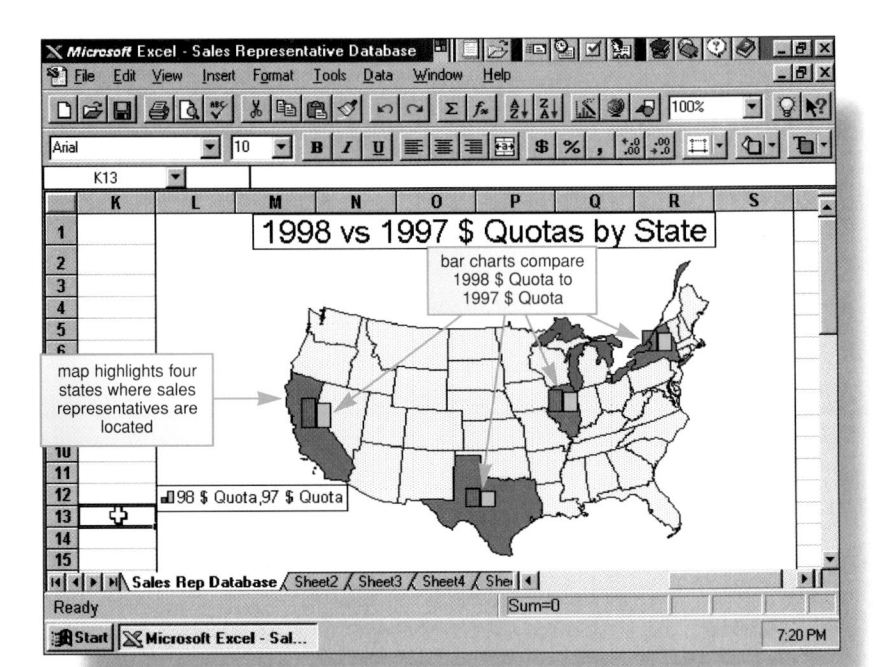

FIGURE 6-52

Creating the Data Map

Follow the steps below to create a data map in the range L1:S17 using the right three columns (H8:J20) of the MedsForU sales representative database.

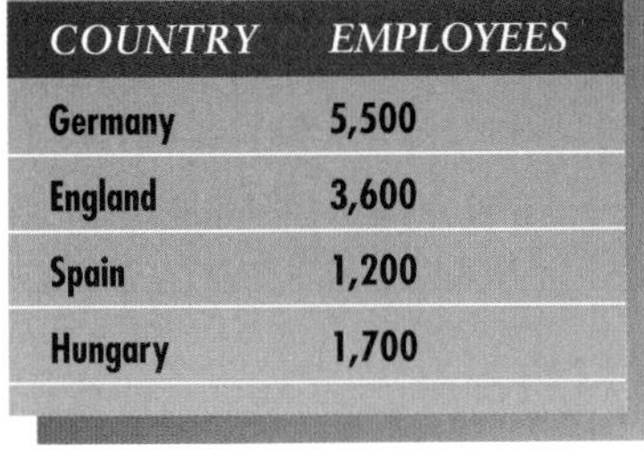

Table 6-6

COUNTRY	EMPLOYEES
Germany	5,500
England	3,600
Spain	1,200
Hungary	1,700

Steps To Create a Data Map

1 Select the range H8:J20 and point to the Map button on the Standard toolbar.

Excel highlights the selected range (Figure 6-53).

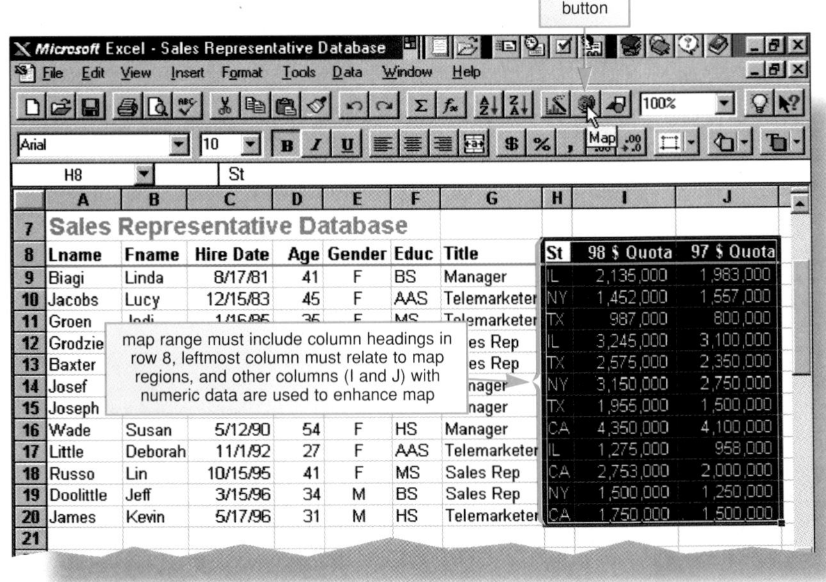

FIGURE 6-53

Click the Map button. Use the scroll bars to display cell L1. Point to the upper left corner of cell L1. Hold down the ALT key and drag to the lower right corner of cell S17 and hold.

The map location L1:S17 is surrounded by a marquee (Figure 6-54).

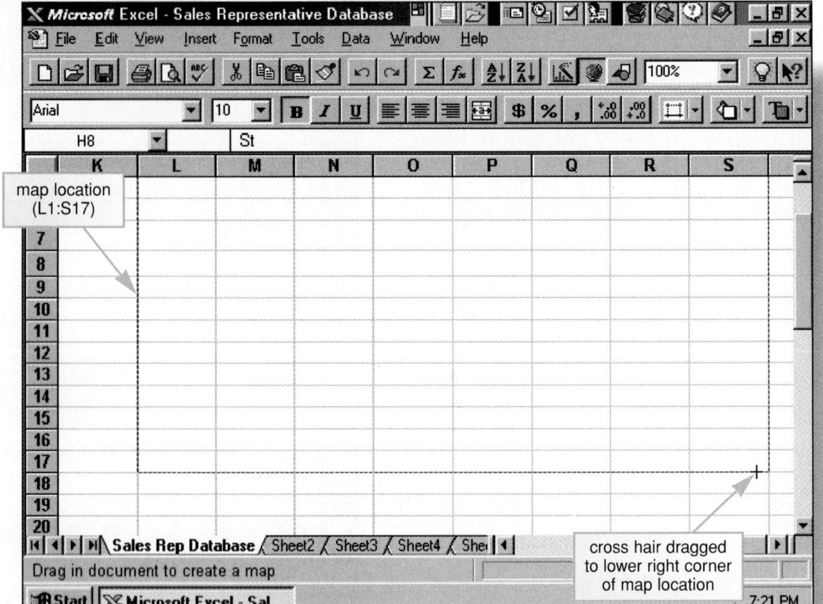

FIGURE 6-54

3 **Release the left mouse button.**

The Microsoft Data Map menu bar and toolbar display at the top of the screen in place of the Excel menu bar and toolbar, a thick gray border surrounds the map location indicating it is active, and the Multiple Maps Available dialog box displays (Figure 6-55).

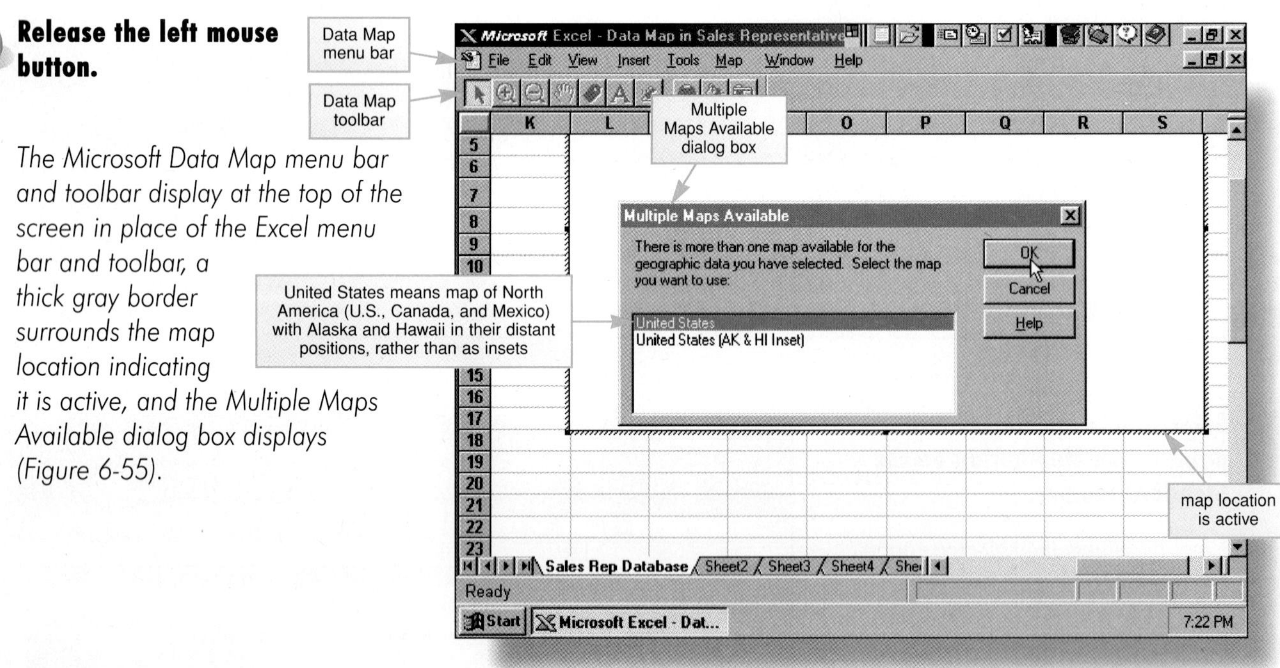

FIGURE 6-55

4 With United States highlighted, click the OK button.

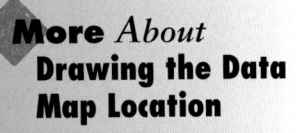

Microsoft Data Map draws a map of North America (Canada, United States, and Mexico) and displays the Data Map Control dialog box (Figure 6-56). The four states with sales representatives (California, Illinois, Texas, and New York) display in varying shades.

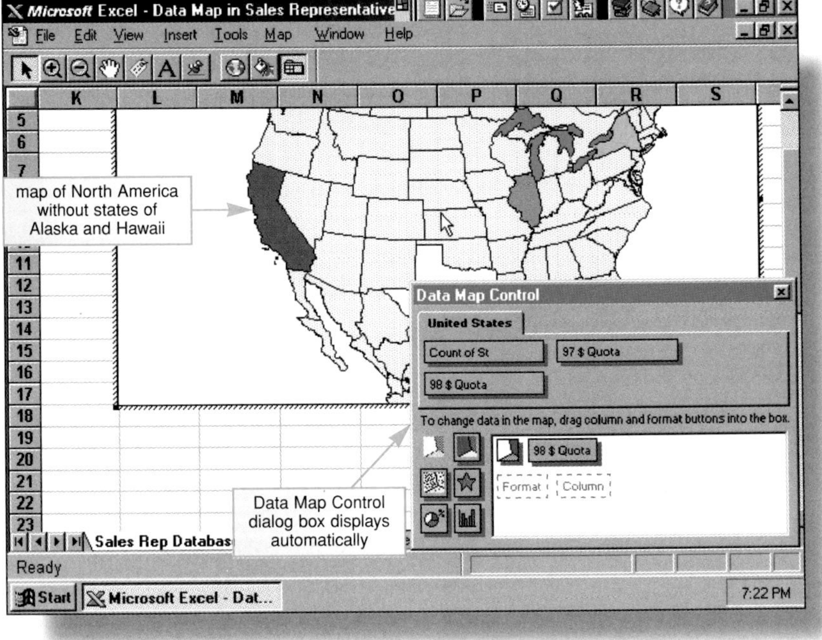

FIGURE 6-56

The basic data map is complete. The data map soon will be formatted so that it appears as shown in Figure 6-52 on page E 6.41. When the data map is active (the gray border indicates it is active) the menu and toolbar at the top of the screen can be used to manipulate the data map. The function of the buttons on the **Data Map toolbar** are described in Figure 6-57. When you first create a data map, two of the buttons on the toolbar are recessed (active) – Select Objects and Show/Hide Data Map Control.

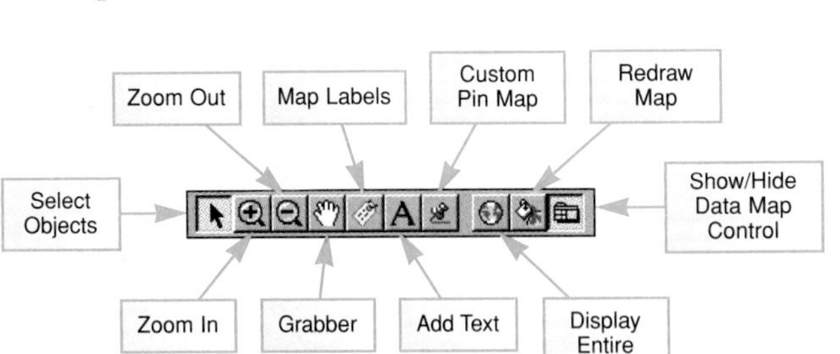

FIGURE 6-57

When the **Select Objects button** is recessed, you can select items within the data map location, such as legends and the data map title, and move and format them. When the **Show/Hide Data Map Control button** is recessed, the Data Map Control dialog box displays, which allows you to format the data map. The **Grabber button** allows you to grab the data map and move it. This button is especially useful when the data map is zoomed out and you want to see hidden parts.

More *About*
Drawing the Data Map Location

Holding down the ALT key while you drag to define the data map location instructs Excel to snap the data map location to the nearest gridline on the worksheet. Thus, in Figure 6-54, the rectangular box defining the data map location is lined up on gridlines.

Deleting the Data Map

If the data map you draw is not correct and you want to start over, click a cell outside the data map location and then click the data map location to select it. A light border, rather than a heavy gray border will surround the data map location when it is selected. Press the DELETE key and Excel will delete the embedded map. You can not delete the data map as long as it is active (with a gray border). An embedded object, such as the data map, is either selected or active. When it is **selected** (light border), you can resize, move, or delete it. When the embedded object is **active**, you can change its features and format it.

More *About* Data Map Features

There are additional characteristics you can add to a data map, such as major highways, cities, airports, lakes, or a combination of these. Right-click the data map and click Add Feature on the shortcut menu. If you are using a data map to communicate a point to a group of people, it is best to keep it simple as shown in Figure 6-52 on page E 6.41, rather than stack multiple characteristics on the same data map.

Changing the Map's Features

The Features command on the shortcut menu allows you to add or delete countries from the active data map. In the case of the data map in Figure 6-52 on page E 6.41, Canada and Mexico are not necessary because sales are limited to the United States. The following steps show you how to change the features of the map.

Steps To Change the Features of the Data Map

1 **Right-click the data map and then point to Features.**

The shortcut menu displays as shown in Figure 6-58.

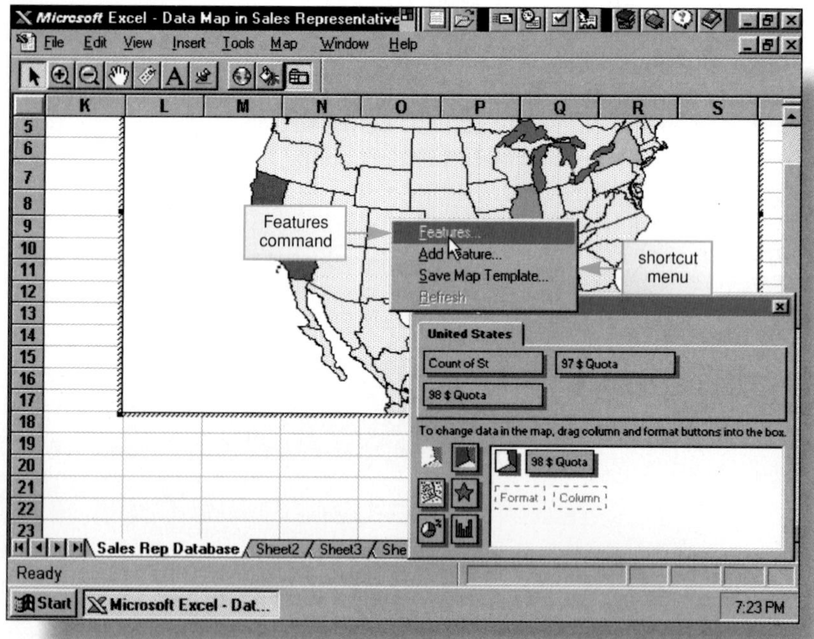

FIGURE 6-58

2 Click Features. When the Map Features dialog box displays, click Canada, Canada Lakes, and Mexico to remove their check marks from the Visible box.

The Map Features dialog box displays as shown in Figure 6-59.

3 Click the OK button.

The data map displays without Mexico, Canada, and Canada Lakes (Figure 6-60 on page E 6.46).

FIGURE 6-59

OtherWays

1. Click Features on Map menu, click categories to remove, click OK button
2. Right-click data map, click Features, highlight map feature in Visible box on Map Features dialog box, click Remove button, click OK button

Formatting the Data Map and Adding Column Charts

The Data Map Control dialog box, which displays when the data map is first created (Figure 6-58), is used to format the map and add charts. The Data Map Control dialog box is divided into three areas, **Data column** buttons area, Map format buttons area, and Work area. The **Data column buttons area** includes a button for each column heading at the top of the range (H8:J20) used to create the data map. The **Map format buttons area** includes six format buttons as described in Table 6-7. The **Work area** in the Data Map Control dialog box is where you drag buttons from the other two areas to format the data map.

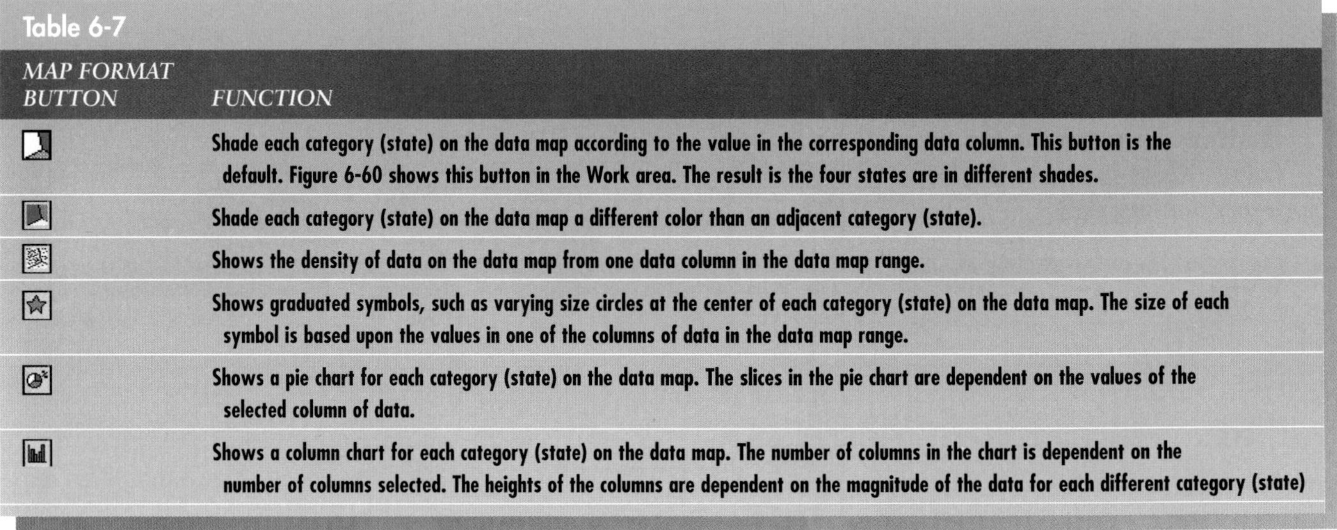

Table 6-7

MAP FORMAT BUTTON	*FUNCTION*
	Shade each category (state) on the data map according to the value in the corresponding data column. This button is the default. Figure 6-60 shows this button in the Work area. The result is the four states are in different shades.
	Shade each category (state) on the data map a different color than an adjacent category (state).
	Shows the density of data on the data map from one data column in the data map range.
	Shows graduated symbols, such as varying size circles at the center of each category (state) on the data map. The size of each symbol is based upon the values in one of the columns of data in the data map range.
	Shows a pie chart for each category (state) on the data map. The slices in the pie chart are dependent on the values of the selected column of data.
	Shows a column chart for each category (state) on the data map. The number of columns in the chart is dependent on the number of columns selected. The heights of the columns are dependent on the magnitude of the data for each different category (state)

As shown in Figure 6-52 on page E 6.41, this project calls for the same shading for each of the four states with offices (CA, IL, TX, and NY). By default Microsoft Data Map activates the Value Shading button in the work area. This button shades the states based on the first numeric column in the data map range, column I (98 $ Quota). To shade the four states the same, drag the Count of St button on top of the 98 $ Quota button in the Work area of the Data Map Control dialog box. When you drag one button on top of another in the Work area, the dragged button replaces the current button. Finally, drag the Column chart button, then the 98 $ Quota button and the 97 $ Quota button on to the Work area to draw the column charts. The following steps describe how to format the data map.

To Format the Data Map

1 Point to the Count of St button in the Data Column button area of the Data Map Control dialog box.

The mouse pointer changes to a hand grabbing a handle (Figure 6-60).

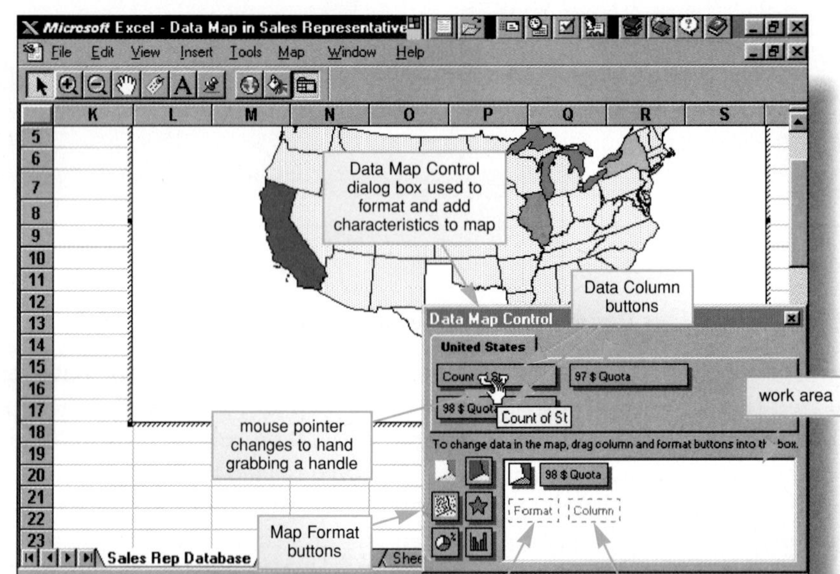

FIGURE 6-60

2 Drag the Count of St button on top of the 98 $ Quota button in the Work area. Point to the Column Chart button in the Map format buttons area.

Microsoft Data Map shades the four states the same (Figure 6-61).

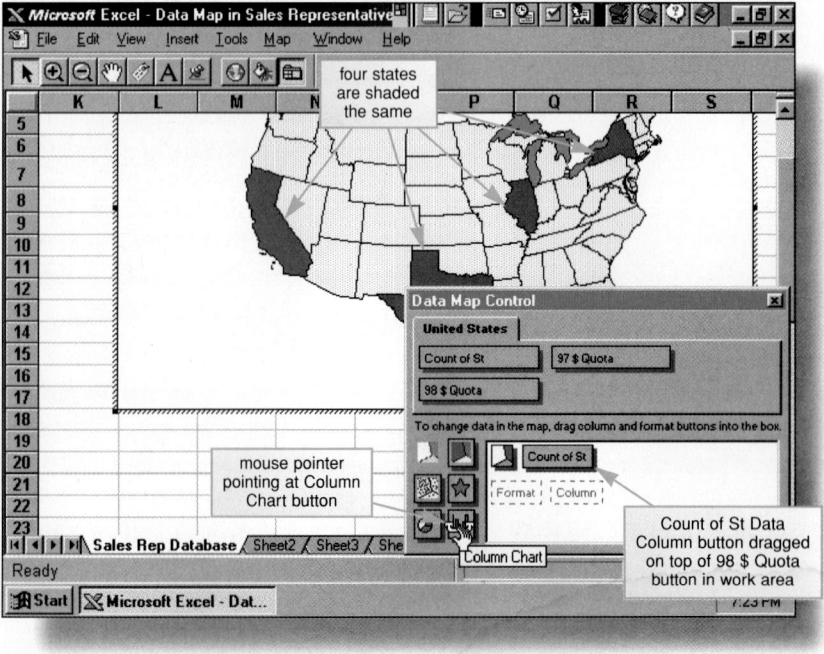

FIGURE 6-61

3 **Drag the Column Chart button onto the word Format in the Work area. One by one, drag the 98 Quota button and the 97 $ Quota button onto the word column. Point to the Show/Hide Data Map Control button on the toolbar.**

The Work area on the Data Map Control displays as shown in Figure 6-62. Each of the four states with offices are assigned a column chart on the data map. The leftmost column represents the sum of the 98 $ Quota for a given state. The rightmost column chart represents the 97 $ Quota values.

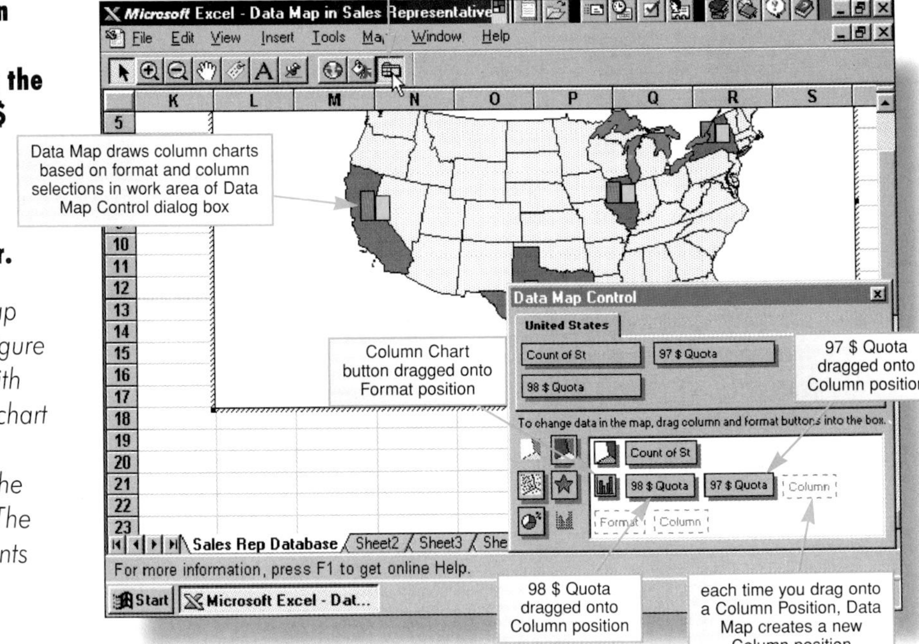

FIGURE 6-62

4 **Click the Show/Hide Data Map Control button. Click the Shade legend in the lower right corner of the data map location.**

The Data Control dialog box disappears. The data map displays with two legends in the lower right corner of the data map location. One legend defines the shading and the other defines the column charts. The Shade legend is selected (Figure 6-63).

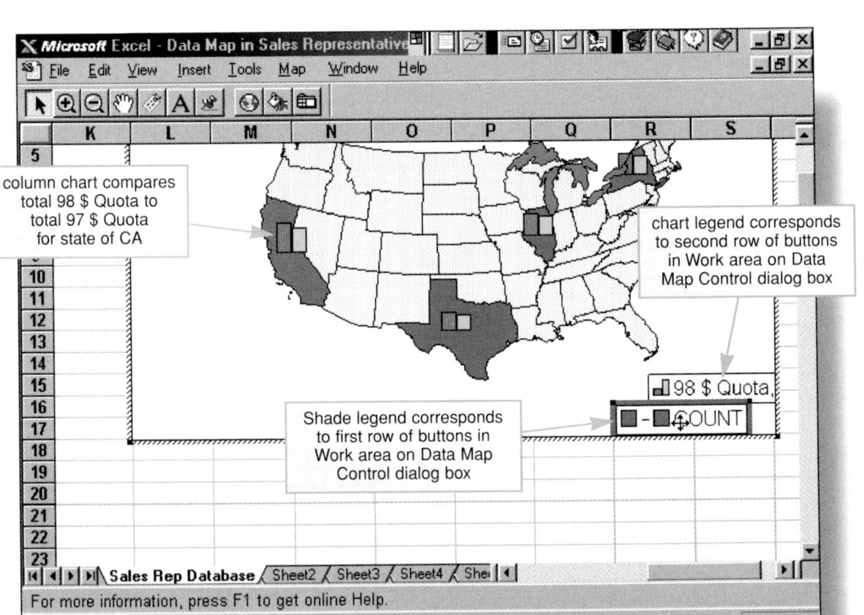

FIGURE 6-63

Press the DELETE key to delete the Shade legend. Drag the Column Chart legend immediately below the state of California and then resize it as shown in Figure 6-64. Scroll up so cell L1 displays. Point to the immediate left of the letter N in North America and click twice. Enter the title shown in Figure 6-64. Resize and center the new data map title. Click cell K13 to deactivate the data map. Click the Save button on the Standard toolbar.

The data map is complete.

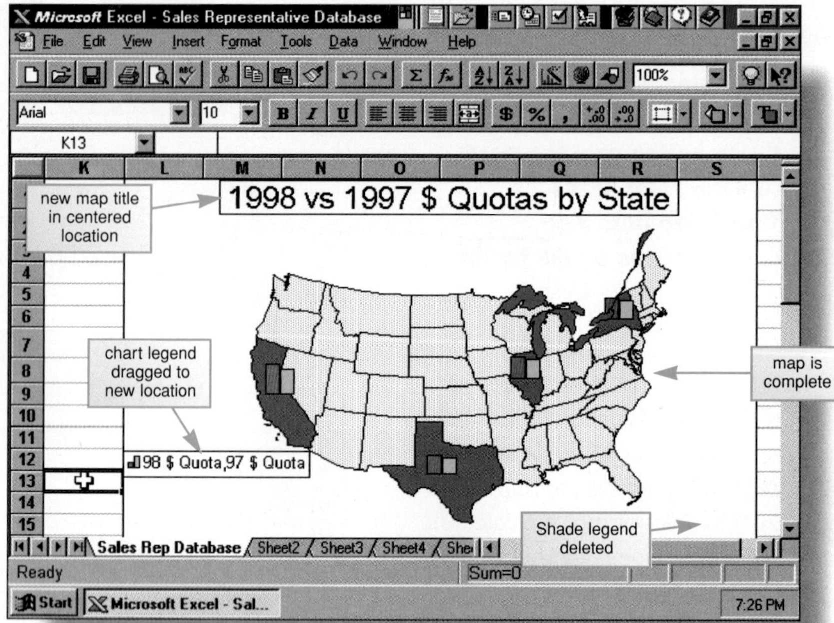

FIGURE 6-64

More *About*
Formatting the Data Map Title

You can format the data map title in the same way you formatted chart titles. Right-click the data map title and click Format Font on the shortcut menu.

As you can see from Figure 6-64, you can create sophisticated data maps with just a few clicks of the mouse button.

Creating a Pivot Table to Analyze Data

A pivot table gives you the capability of summarizing data in the database and then rotating the table's row and column titles to give different views of the summarized data. You usually create a pivot table on another sheet in the same workbook containing the database you are analyzing, although you can create it on the same sheet containing the data.

The **PivotTable command** on the Data menu starts the **PivotTable Wizard**, which guides you through creating a pivot table. The PivotTable Wizard does not modify the database in any way. It uses the data in the database to generate information, similar to the way the Scenario Manager command worked in Project 5.

The pivot table to be created in this project is shown in Figure 6-65. The table summarizes 1997 and 1998 dollar quota information by title and state for the MedsForU sales representative database built earlier in this project. To create the pivot table in Figure 6-65, you need select only four fields from the database when requested by the PivotTable Wizard: row field, column field, and two data fields.

In Figure 6-65, the row field, Title, is Manager, Sales Rep, and Telemarketer. The column field, St, is CA, IL, NY, and TX. The two data fields are 98 $ Quota and 97 $ Quota.

Grand total sales automatically display for the row and column fields in rows 9 and 10 and in column G. For example, from the table in Figure 6-65 you can see in the 98 $ Quota totals for Managers in column G are $11,590,000 and $10,333,000, respectively. Cells G9 and G10 show the grand totals for each year's dollar quota.

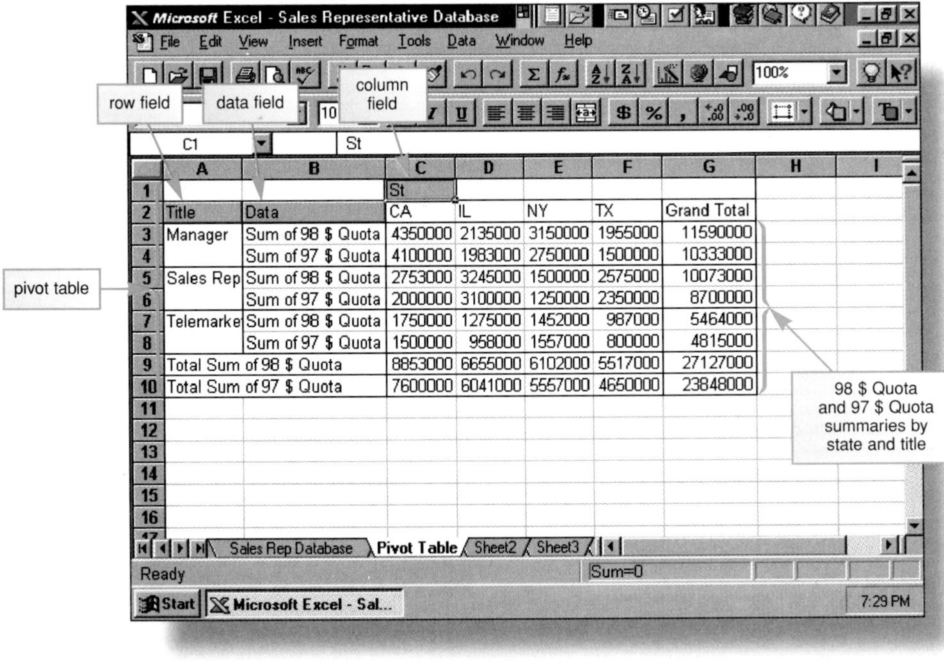

FIGURE 6-65

More About Pivot Tables

The pivot table is one of the most powerful analytical tools available in Excel. Pivot tables are used to show the relationships among the data in a list or a database. These tables allow you to use drag and drop to examine the data from different views.

The data analysis power of pivot tables is found in its ability to allow you to view the data by interchanging or pairing up the row and column fields by dragging the buttons located over cells A2, B2, and C1 in Figure 6-65. The process of rotating the field values around the data fields will be discussed later in this project.

To create the pivot table shown in Figure 6-65, perform the following steps.

To Create a Pivot Table

1 Point to PivotTable on the Data menu (Figure 6-66).

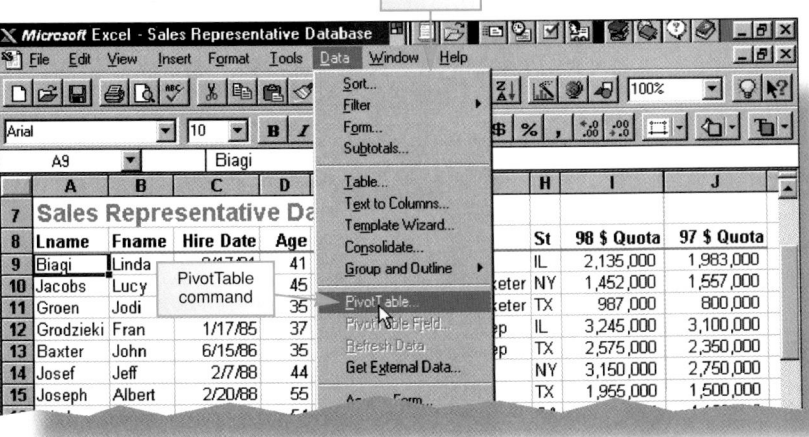

FIGURE 6-66

Click PivotTable.

The PivotTable Wizard - Step 1 of 4 dialog box displays (Figure 6-67). The option Microsoft Excel List or Database is selected automatically.

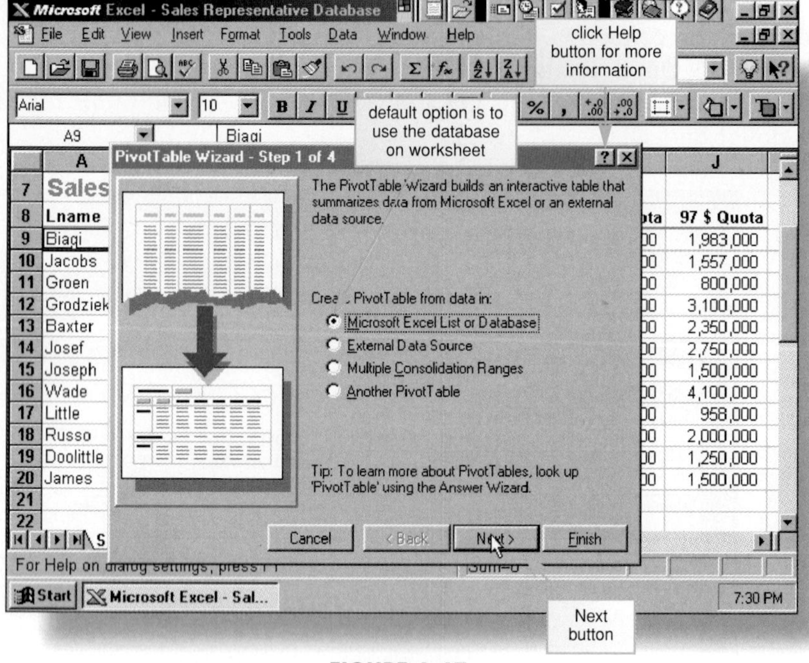

FIGURE 6-67

3 Click the Next button.

Excel displays the PivotTable Wizard - Step 2 of 4 dialog box with Database (A8:J20) automatically selected in the Range box (Figure 6-68). The database on the worksheet is surrounded by a marquee.

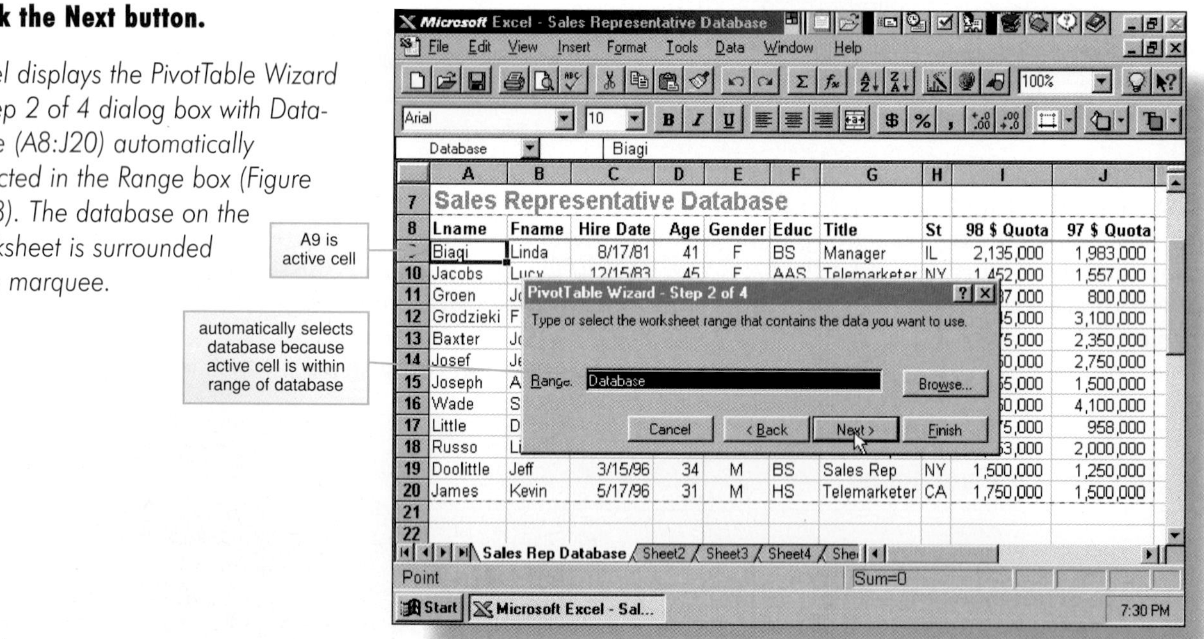

FIGURE 6-68

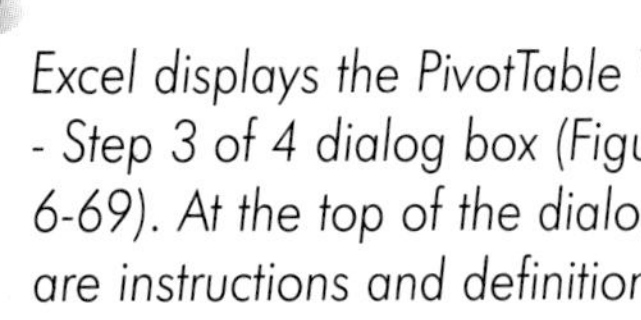

4 Click the Next button.

Excel displays the PivotTable Wizard - Step 3 of 4 dialog box (Figure 6-69). At the top of the dialog box are instructions and definitions that help you create the pivot table. On the right side of the dialog box are buttons, one for each field in the MedsForU sales representative database. You drag these buttons to locations (ROW, COLUMN, and DATA) in the middle of the dialog box.

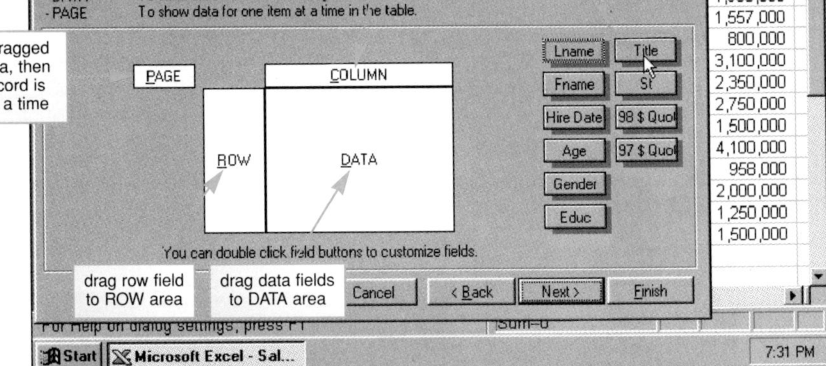

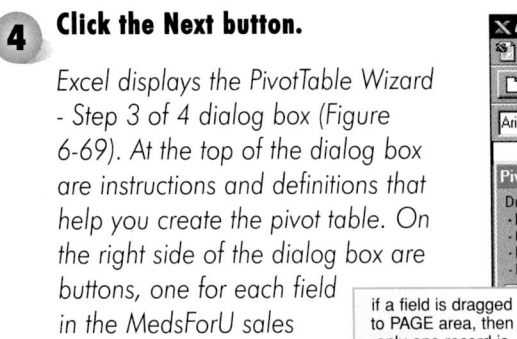

FIGURE 6-69

5 Drag the Title button to the ROW area. Drag the St button to the COLUMN area. Drag the Sum of 98 $ Quota and Sum of 97 $ Quota buttons to the DATA area.

The PivotTable Wizard - Step 3 of 4 dialog box displays as shown in Figure 6-70.

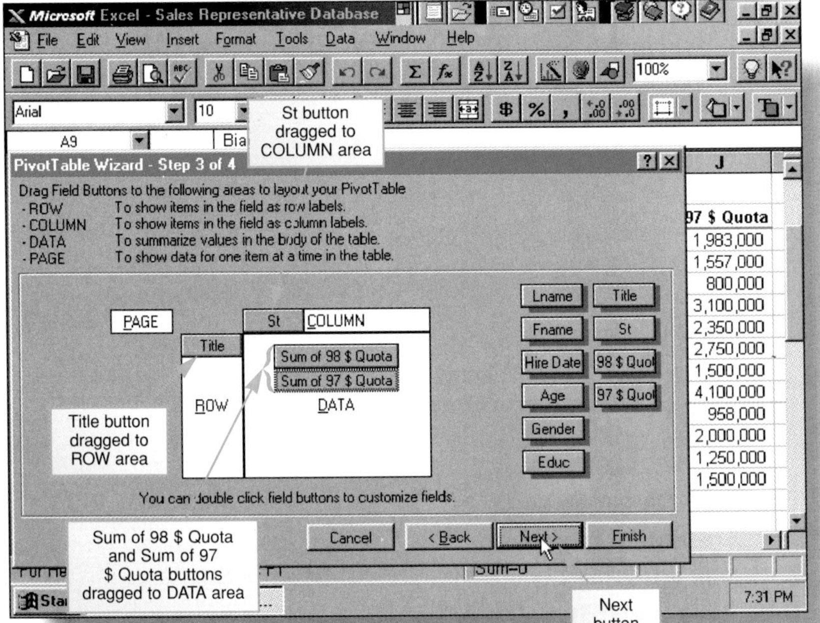

FIGURE 6-70

Click the Next button. With the PivotTable Starting Cell box selected, press the DELETE key.

The PivotTable Wizard - Step 4 of 4 dialog box displays (Figure 6-71). At the top right corner of the dialog box, Excel's starting location for the pivot table is blank and the pivot table name is PivotTable1. When you leave the Pivot Table Starting Cell box blank, Excel automatically creates the pivot table on a new sheet in the workbook.

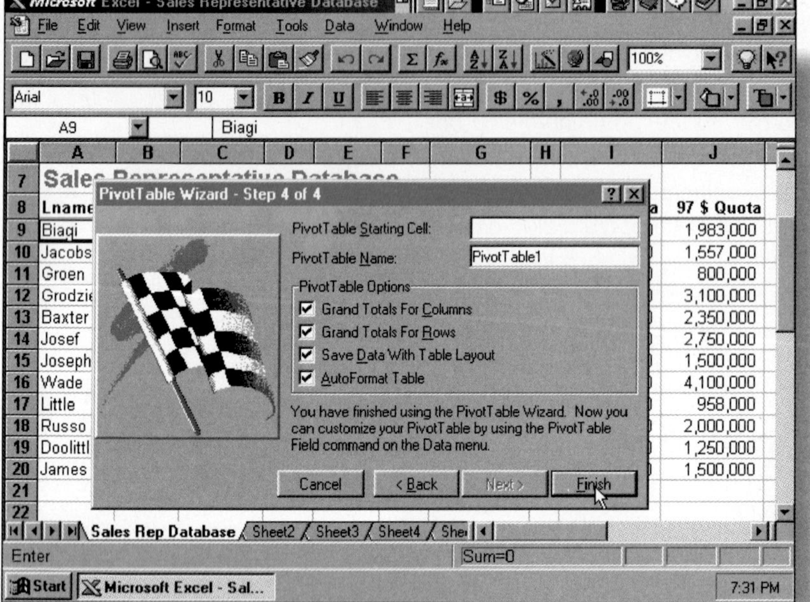

FIGURE 6-71

7 Click the Finish button. Double-click the sheet tab and rename it Pivot Table. Drag the Pivot Table tab to the immediate right of the Sales Rep Database tab.

Excel creates and displays the pivot table on a new sheet as shown in Figure 6-72. The pivot table summarizes the 1997 and 1998 dollar quotas by title and state.

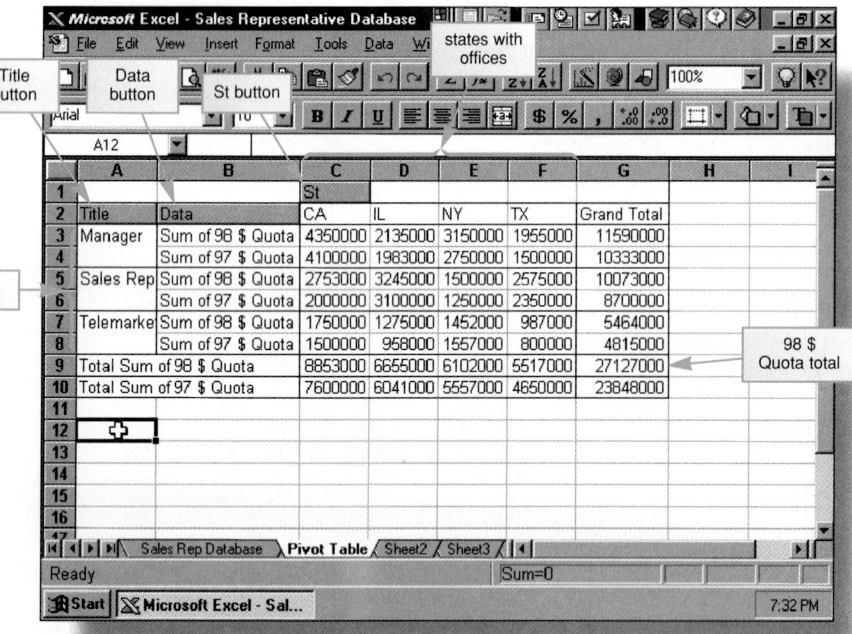

	A	B	C	D	E	F	G
1			St				
2	Title	Data	CA	IL	NY	TX	Grand Total
3	Manager	Sum of 98 $ Quota	4350000	2135000	3150000	1955000	11590000
4		Sum of 97 $ Quota	4100000	1983000	2750000	1500000	10333000
5	Sales Rep	Sum of 98 $ Quota	2753000	3245000	1500000	2575000	10073000
6		Sum of 97 $ Quota	2000000	3100000	1250000	2350000	8700000
7	Telemarke	Sum of 98 $ Quota	1750000	1275000	1452000	987000	5464000
8		Sum of 97 $ Quota	1500000	958000	1557000	800000	4815000
9	Total Sum of 98 $ Quota		8853000	6655000	6102000	5517000	27127000
10	Total Sum of 97 $ Quota		7600000	6041000	5557000	4650000	23848000

FIGURE 6-72

8 Click the Save button on the Standard toolbar to save the workbook using the filename Sales Representative Database.

Once the pivot table is created you can treat it like any other worksheet. Thus, you can print or chart a pivot table. If you update the data in the personnel database, click Refresh Data on the Data menu or shortcut menu to update the corresponding pivot table.

Changing the View of a Pivot Table

You can rotate the row and column fields around the data field by dragging the buttons on the pivot table from one side of the data to another. For example, if you drag the St button to the lower left corner of the Data button so that the mouse displays as a vertical table, and then drag the Title button to the top of the first row of data so that the mouse pointer displays as a horizontal table, you change the view of the pivot table to the one in Figure 6-73.

If you drag the Title button to the left of the Data button, and then drag the St button on top of the column A heading so that the mouse pointer changes to three bars, you get the view shown in Figure 6-74. Each time you change the view of the pivot table, Excel gives you a new look at the same data. Notice that the State button has a box arrow. Click the box arrow to display and select another state whose totals you wish to view.

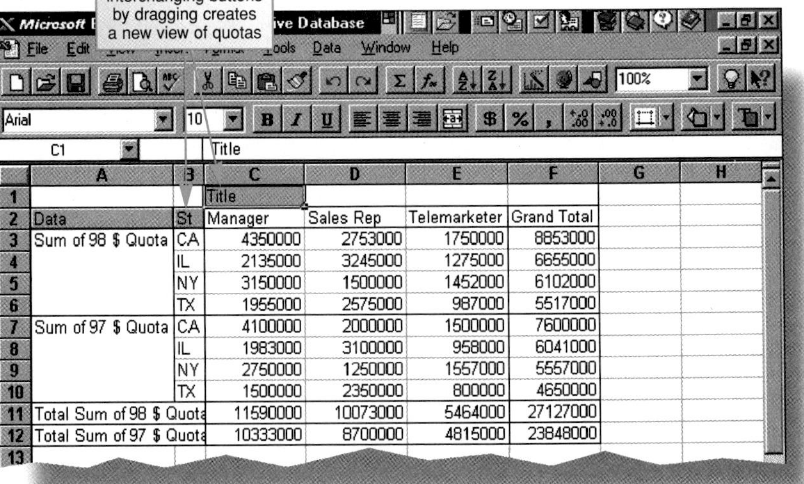

FIGURE 6-73

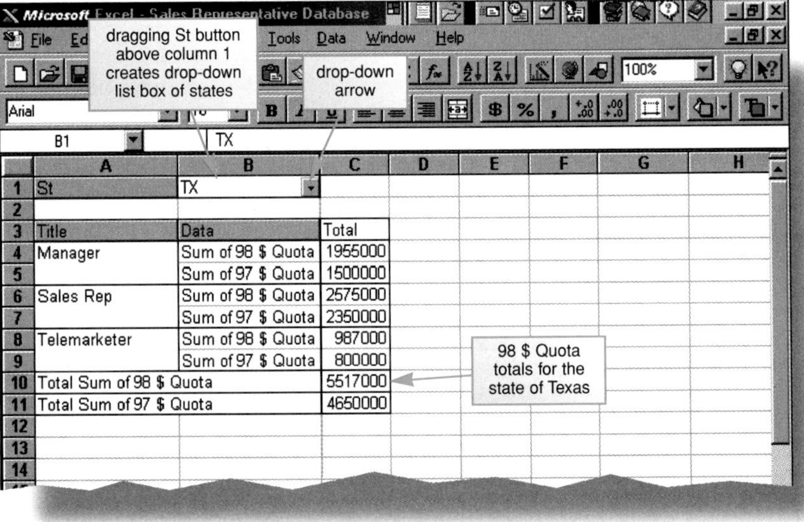

FIGURE 6-74

Query and Pivot Toolbar

When you create a pivot table, Excel may display the Query and Pivot toolbar shown in Figure 6-75. The buttons on the toolbar allow you to quickly modify the appearance of the pivot table. You can also use the buttons to reenter the PivotTable Wizard and refresh the data after updating the database with which the pivot table is associated.

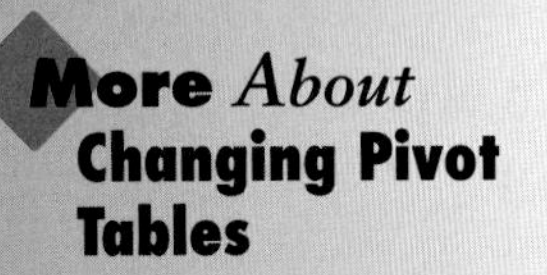

More About Changing Pivot Tables

At any time while the workbook containing a pivot table is active, you can click the tab of the sheet containing the Pivot Table, click Pivot table on the Data menu to display the PivotTable Wizard - Step 3 of 4 dialog box (Figure 6-70 on page E 6.51). This dialog box serves as an alternative to using drag and drop to change the view of the pivot table.

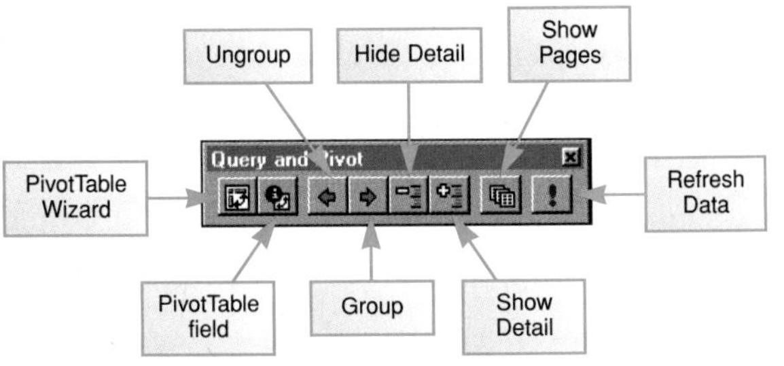

FIGURE 6-75

Exiting Excel

The project is complete. To exit Excel, follow the steps below.

TO EXIT EXCEL

Step 1: Click the Close button on the right side of the title bar.
Step 2: If the Microsoft Excel dialog box displays, click the No button.

Project Summary

The MedsForU sales representative database and pivot table created in this project will allow Tina Capsol, the national sales manager, to generate information that will help her make decisions regarding the sales force. She can also use the data map for presentations to the company's management teams, as well as to potential customers interested in knowing more about the company.

In this project you learned how to create, sort, and query a database. Creating a database involves naming a range Database. You can then add, change, and delete records in the database through a data form. Sorting a database can be done using the Sort Ascending and Sort Descending buttons on the Standard toolbar or by using the Sort command on the Data menu.

Once a database is sorted you can use the Subtotals command on the Data menu to generate subtotals that display within the database range. Filtering a database involves displaying a subset of the database or copying (extracting) records that pass a test. This project also showed you how to use database functions and lookup functions. Finally, you learned how to create and format data maps and how to use pivot tables to analyze data in a database.

What You Should Know

Having completed this project, you should be able to perform the following tasks:

- Apply AutoFilter to a Database *(E 6.27)*
- Change the Features of a Data Map *(E 6.44)*
- Create a Data Map *(E 6.41)*
- Create a Lookup Table and Use the VLOOKUP Function *(E 6.39)*
- Create a Pivot Table *(E 6.49)*
- Create an Extract Range on the Worksheet and Extract Records *(E 6.35)*
- Display All Records in the Database *(E 6.34)*
- Display Records Using the Advanced Filter *(E 6.33)*
- Display Subtotals in a Database *(E 6.20)*
- Enter Custom Criteria *(E 6.30)*
- Enter Records into a Database Using a Data Form *(E 6.10)*
- Exit Excel *(E 6.54)*
- Find Records Using a Data Form *(E 6.24)*
- Format a Data Map *(E 6.46)*
- Name a Database *(E 6.9)*
- Print a Database *(E 6.14)*
- Remove AutoFilter *(E 6.29)*
- Remove Subtotals from a Database *(E 6.23)*
- Return a Database to Its Original Order *(E 6.17)*
- Set Up a Criteria Range on the Worksheet *(E 6.32)*
- Set Up the Database *(E 6.8)*
- Sort the Database by Hire Date *(E 6.24)*
- Sort the Database by Last Name in Ascending Sequence *(E 6.15)*
- Sort the Database by Last Name in Descending Sequence *(E 6.16)*
- Sort the Database on Multiple Fields *(E 6.18)*
- Start Excel *(E 6.7)*
- Use the DAVERAGE Database Function *(E 6.39)*
- Zoom Out on a Worksheet to Hide and Show Detail Data in a Subtotaled Database *(E 6.22)*

Test Your Knowledge

1 True/False

Instructions: Circle T if the statement is true or F if the statement is false.

T F 1. The series of numbers 1, 2, 3, 4, 5, 6 is in ascending sequence.

T F 2. The column headings in a database are treated the same as a record in the database.

T F 3. When you name a database using the Name box in the formula bar, select the column headings (field names) and the cells in the row immediately below the field names.

T F 4. Excel allows you to sort on up to three fields at a time.

T F 5. The wildcard character asterisk (*) only can be used at the end of text that is part of the comparison criteria.

T F 6. In the phrase "sort age within seniority within trade," age is the intermediate key.

T F 7. You have five minutes to click the Undo button on the Standard toolbar to undo a sort.

T F 8. The VLOOKUP function is used to look up the average of numbers in a database field that pass a test.

T F 9. Data map is a term used to describe the column headings in a database.

T F 10. A pivot table is used to summarize data and display different views of the data.

2 Multiple Choice

Instructions: Circle the correct response.

1. Click PivotTable on the Data menu to create a __________.
   a. summary table within the workbook
   b. chart
   c. database
   d. scenario
2. If you make a mistake and sort a database on the wrong field, immediately click _________ on the Edit menu.
   a. Clear
   b. Replace
   c. Repeat Sort
   d. Undo Sort
3. To copy all records that pass a test defined in a criteria range, click _________ on the Filter submenu.
   a. Advanced Filter
   b. Filter
   c. Subtotals
   d. Show All

(continued)

A+ Test Your Knowledge

Multiple Choice *(continued)*

4. With a data form active and criteria defined, use the ________ button to display the former record in the database that passed the test.
   a. Find Next
   b. Find Prev
   c. New
   d. Close
5. Which one of the following commands adds box arrows to all the field names at the top of the database?
   a. Subtotals
   b. Filter
   c. Form
   d. Pivot Table
6. To set up a criteria range that will cause the Filter command to process all records, include a(n) ________ in the criteria range.
   a. blank cell immediately below the first field name
   b. blank cell immediately below each field name
   c. asterisk under all field names
   d. =" " under all field names
7. A database field name referenced in a database function must be surrounded by ________.
   a. colons (:)
   b. quotation marks (")
   c. brackets ({})
   d. apostrophes (')
8. When a data form is first opened, Excel displays the ________ record in the database.
   a. least
   b. previously displayed
   c. first
   d. last
9. To select a field in a database to sort on when the Sort dialog box displays, enter the ________ in the Sort By box.
   a cell reference of any cell in the field (column)
   b. cell reference of the field (column) in the first record
   c. cell reference of the field (column) in the last record
   d. all of the above will work
10. Which one of the following characters, when used in comparison criteria, represents any character in the same position?
   a. question mark (?)
   b. tilde (~)
   c. number sign (#)
   d. asterisk (*)

Test Your Knowledge

3 Understanding Sorting

Instructions: Write down the sort order of the records in the personnel database in Figure 6-76. Use the term *within* to describe the sort order. For example, minor field within intermediate field within major field. Also indicate the sequence (ascending or descending) of each field.

Order: ________ within ________ within ________
Field(s) in ascending sequence: ________
Field(s) in descending sequence: ________

4 Understanding Comparison Criteria

Instructions: Assume that the figures that accompany each of the following six problems make up the criteria range. Fill in the comparison criteria to select records from the database in Figure 6-76 according to these problems. So that you better understand what is required for this assignment, the answer is given for the first problem.

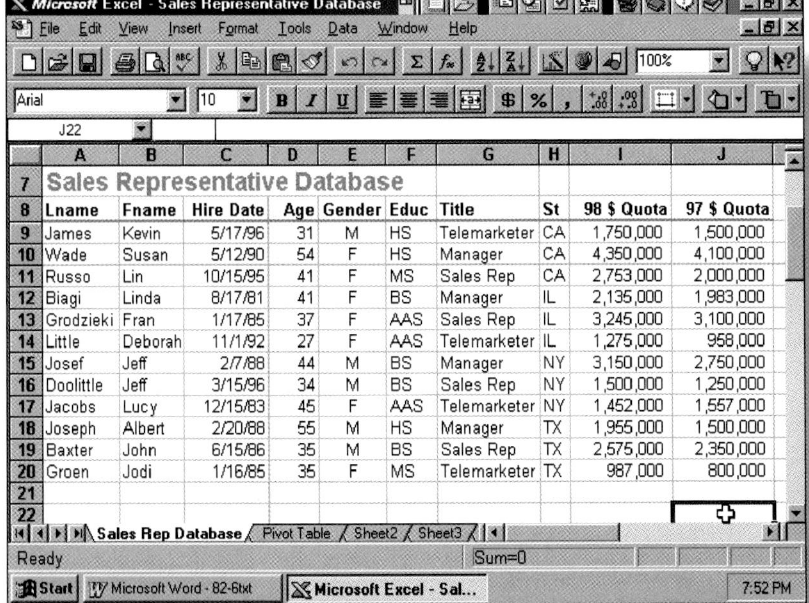

	A	B	C	D	E	F	G	H	I	J
7	Sales Representative Database									
8	Lname	Fname	Hire Date	Age	Gender	Educ	Title	St	98 $ Quota	97 $ Quota
9	James	Kevin	5/17/96	31	M	HS	Telemarketer	CA	1,750,000	1,500,000
10	Wade	Susan	5/12/90	54	F	HS	Manager	CA	4,350,000	4,100,000
11	Russo	Lin	10/15/95	41	F	MS	Sales Rep	CA	2,753,000	2,000,000
12	Biagi	Linda	8/17/81	41	F	BS	Manager	IL	2,135,000	1,983,000
13	Grodzieki	Fran	1/17/85	37	F	AAS	Sales Rep	IL	3,245,000	3,100,000
14	Little	Deborah	11/1/92	27	F	AAS	Telemarketer	IL	1,275,000	958,000
15	Josef	Jeff	2/7/88	44	M	BS	Manager	NY	3,150,000	2,750,000
16	Doolittle	Jeff	3/15/96	34	M	BS	Sales Rep	NY	1,500,000	1,250,000
17	Jacobs	Lucy	12/15/83	45	F	AAS	Telemarketer	NY	1,452,000	1,557,000
18	Joseph	Albert	2/20/88	55	M	HS	Manager	TX	1,955,000	1,500,000
19	Baxter	John	6/15/86	35	M	BS	Sales Rep	TX	2,575,000	2,350,000
20	Groen	Jodi	1/16/85	35	F	MS	Telemarketer	TX	987,000	800,000
21										
22										

FIGURE 6-76

1. Select records that represent female sales representatives greater than 45 years old.

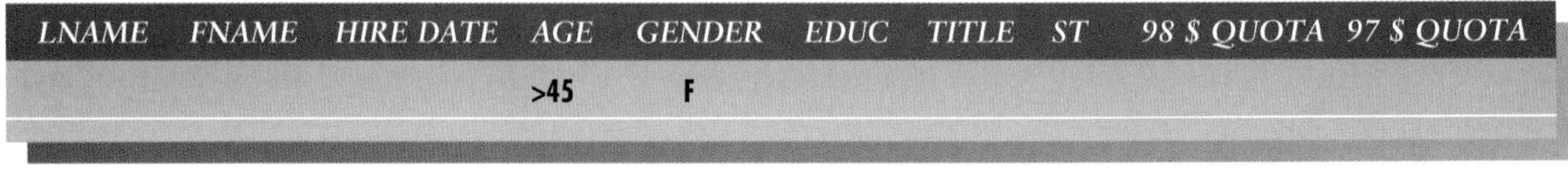

LNAME	FNAME	HIRE DATE	AGE	GENDER	EDUC	TITLE	ST	98 $ QUOTA	97 $ QUOTA
			>45	F					

2. Select records that represent sales representatives whose title is Telemarketer or Manager.

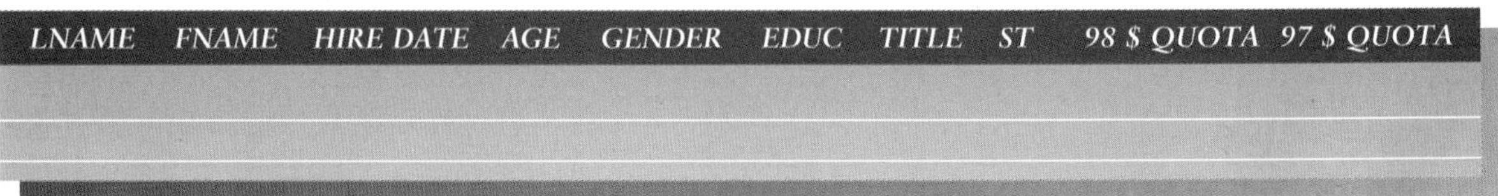

LNAME	FNAME	HIRE DATE	AGE	GENDER	EDUC	TITLE	ST	98 $ QUOTA	97 $ QUOTA

(continued)

A+ Test Your Knowledge

Understanding Comparison Criteria *(continued)*

3. Select records that represent sales representatives whose last names begin with "Jo," education is BS, and are assigned to the California office.

LNAME	FNAME	HIRE DATE	AGE	GENDER	EDUC	TITLE	ST	98 $ QUOTA	97 $ QUOTA

4. Select records that represent male sales representatives who are at least 40 years old and were hired before 1/1/93.

LNAME	FNAME	HIRE DATE	AGE	GENDER	EDUC	TITLE	ST	98 $ QUOTA	97 $ QUOTA

5. Select records that represent male sales representatives or sales representatives who are at least 49 years old.

LNAME	FNAME	HIRE DATE	AGE	GENDER	EDUC	TITLE	ST	98 $ QUOTA	97 $ QUOTA

6. Select records that represent female managers who are at least 29 years old and whose last names begin with the letter B.

LNAME	FNAME	HIRE DATE	AGE	GENDER	EDUC	TITLE	ST	98 $ QUOTA	97 $ QUOTA

Use Help

1 Reviewing Project Activities

Instructions: Perform the following tasks using a computer:

1. Start Excel. Double-click the Help button on the Standard toolbar to display the Help Topics: Microsoft Excel dialog box. Click the Contents tab. Double-click the Retrieving and Analyzing Data book. Double-click the Managing Lists book. Double-click the Sorting book. Double-click the Sort a list link. Click the last two links under What do you want to do? Read and print the information and hand it in to your instructor. Do the same for the Filtering Data book. Double-click the Filter a list link. Read and print the information and hand it in to your instructor. Close the Help window.
2. If the Help Topics: Microsoft Excel dialog box is not on the screen, double-click the Help button on the Standard toolbar. Click the Find tab. Type data map in the top box labeled 1. Double-click Microsoft Data Map in the bottom box labeled 3. Read and print the information. Click the Help Topics button. Hand in the printout to your instructor.
3. If the Help Topics: Microsoft Excel dialog box is not on the screen, double-click the Help button on the Standard toolbar. Click the Index tab. Type `pivottable` as one word in the top box labeled 1. Scroll down in the bottom box labeled 2 and double-click the word, creating, under PivotTables. One at a time double-click (1) Analyzing data with a PivotTable and (2) Create a PivotTable to analyze data. Click the links and read the information. Print the information for the second one and hand it in to your instructor.
4. If the Help Topics: Microsoft Excel dialog box is not on the screen, double-click the Help button on the Standard toolbar. Click the Answer Wizard tab. Obtain information on the following topic: How do I look up data? Read and print the information regarding the VLOOKUP function and hand it in to your instructor.

2 Expanding on the Basics

Instructions: Perform the following tasks using a computer:

1. Start. Excel. Double-click the Help button on the Standard toolbar to display the Help Topics: Microsoft Excel. Click the Contents tab. Double-click the Outlining a Worksheet book. Double-click the Summarizing data in an outline link. Click each link and read the information.
2. If the Help Topics: Microsoft Excel dialog box is not on the screen, double-click the Help button on the Standard toolbar. Use the Index tab to collect information on the following topics: database functions, data forms, and filtering data. Hand in one printout on each topic to your instructor.
3. If the Help Topics: Microsoft Excel dialog box is not on the screen, double-click the Help button on the Standard toolbar. Use the Find tab to collect information on inserting subtotals in a list. Hand in one printout on the topic to your instructor.

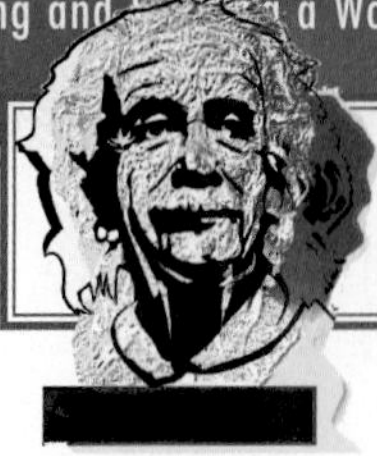

Apply Your Knowledge

1 Filtering a Database

Instructions: Start Excel. Open the workbook TeleMar Personnel Database from the Excel folder on the Student Floppy Disk that accompanies this book. The worksheet displays with the drop-down arrows as shown in Figure 6-77. Step through each filter exercise in Table 6-8 and print the results for each.

To complete a filter exercise, select the appropriate box arrow and option. Use the (Custom...) option for field names that do not contain the appropriate selections in filter exercises 3, 4, 5, 7, and 9. After you print the filtered list solution for each, choose the Show All command on the Filter cascading menu before you begin another filter exercise. When you are finished with the last filter exercise, remove the box arrows by clicking the AutoFilter command on the Filter submenu. You should end up with the following number of records: 1 = 2; 2 = 4; 3 = 1; 4 = 1; 5 = 4; 6 = 2; 7 = 7; 8 = 0; 9 = 1; and 10 = 10.

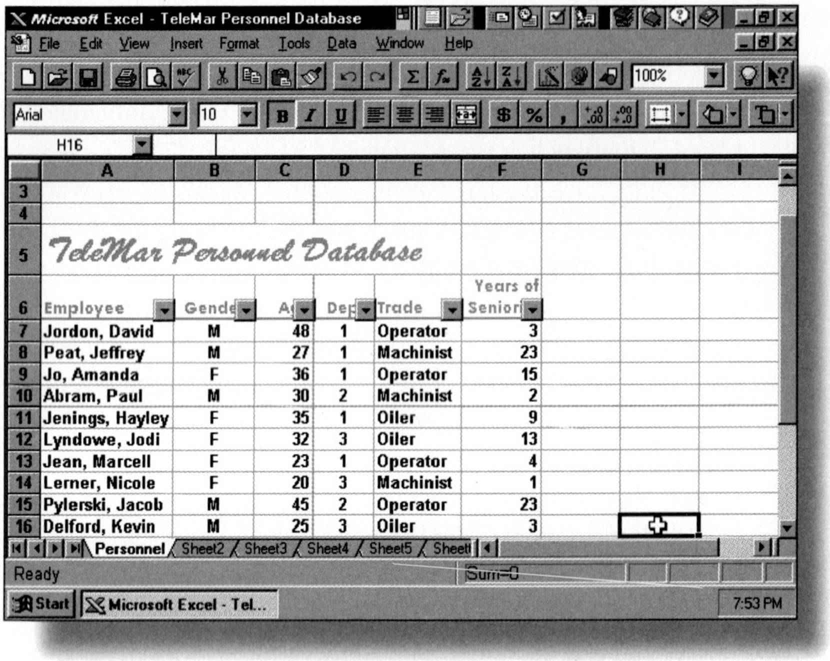

Microsoft Excel - TeleMar Personnel Database

TeleMar Personnel Database

	A	B	C	D	E	F
6	Employee	Gender	Age	Dept	Trade	Years of Seniority
7	Jordon, David	M	48	1	Operator	3
8	Peat, Jeffrey	M	27	1	Machinist	23
9	Jo, Amanda	F	36	1	Operator	15
10	Abram, Paul	M	30	2	Machinist	2
11	Jenings, Hayley	F	35	1	Oiler	9
12	Lyndowe, Jodi	F	32	3	Oiler	13
13	Jean, Marcell	F	23	1	Operator	4
14	Lerner, Nicole	F	20	3	Machinist	1
15	Pylerski, Jacob	M	45	2	Operator	23
16	Delford, Kevin	M	25	3	Oiler	3

FIGURE 6-77

Table 6-8

FILTER	EMPLOYEE	GENDER	AGE	DEPT	TRADE	SENIORITY
1		M		1		
2	Begins with J					
3			>35 and <45			
4		F			Operator	>10
5						>10 and <25
6				3	Oiler	
7				1 or 2		
8		F		2		
9		M	>30	2		
10	All	All	All	All	All	All

In the Lab

1 Building and Sorting a Database and Determining Subtotals

Problem: Spider Web, Inc., an Internet company you work for, has asked you to create a sales report database (Figure 6-78) and then generate subtotal information as shown in Figure 6-79 on the next page.

Part 1 Instructions: Create the database shown in Figure 6-78 using the techniques developed in this project. In particular, enter and format the database title and field names in rows 1 and 2. Use Desdemona bold font (or a similar font) for the titles. Point size is 20 for the database title and 12 for the column titles. Name the range A2:E3 Database. Use a data form to enter the data in rows 3 through 15. Enter your name, course number, laboratory assignment (Lab 6-1), date, and instructor name in the range A20:A24. Save the workbook using the filename Spider Web.

Part 2 Instructions: Sort the database according to the six sort problems below. Print the database for each sort problem. Save the workbook with each sort solution using the filename Spider Web x, where x is the sort problem number. For each sort problem, open the original workbook Spider Web.

1. Sort the database into ascending sequence by division.
2. Sort the database by department within district within division. All three sort keys are to be in ascending sequence.
3. Sort the database by district within division. Both sort keys are to be in descending sequence.
4. Sort the database by salesperson within department within district within division. All four sort keys are to be in ascending sequence.
5. Sort the database into descending sequence by sales.
6. Sort the database by department within district within division. All three sort keys are to be in descending sequence.

Microsoft Excel - Spider Web

SPIDER WEB SALES REPORT

	A	B	C	D	E
2	DIVISION	DISTRICT	DEPARTMENT	SALESPERSON	SALES
3	3	2	2	302	1,432,516.60
4	1	1	1	316	6,723,190.50
5	3	1	3	213	1,839,201.77
6	1	1	2	111	3,718,294.93
7	2	2	2	301	1,120,391.33
8	1	2	2	210	2,324,156.45
9	1	2	3	102	1,994,019.12
10	1	2	2	211	798,621.40
11	2	1	1	409	4,657,341.23
12	1	2	1	215	4,867,212.00
13	2	1	1	435	2,564,738.20
14	2	1	3	315	1,342,516.12
15	2	2	2	123	2,109,283.00

Spider Web / Sheet2 / Sheet3 / Sheet4 / Sheet5 / She

Ready Sum=0

Start Microsoft Excel - Spi... 8:00 PM

FIGURE 6-78

Part 3 Instructions: One at a time, close all the workbooks created in Part 2 by holding down the SHIFT key and clicking Close All on the File menu. Next, open the workbook Spider Web (Figure 6-78) created in Part 1. Sort the database by department within district within division. Select ascending sequence for all three sort keys. Use the Subtotals command on the Data menu to generate subtotals by division. Click 75% in the Zoom Control box on the Standard toolbar so the worksheet appears as shown in

(continued)

In the Lab

Building and Sorting a Database and Determining Subtotals *(continued)*

Figure 6-79. Change column E to best fit. Print the database with the subtotals. Use the Subtotals command to remove the subtotals. Click 100% in the Zoom drop-down list box on the Standard toolbar. Close the workbook without saving it.

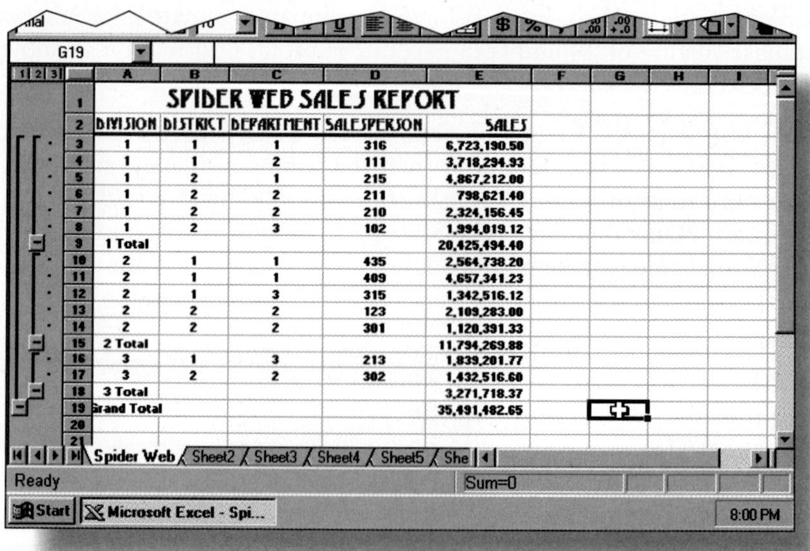

	A	B	C	D	E
1	SPIDER WEB SALES REPORT				
2	DIVISION	DISTRICT	DEPARTMENT	SALESPERSON	SALES
3	1	1	1	316	6,723,190.50
4	1	1	2	111	3,718,294.93
5	1	2	1	215	4,867,212.00
6	1	2	2	211	798,621.40
7	1	2	2	210	2,324,156.45
8	1	2	3	102	1,994,019.12
9	1 Total				20,425,494.40
10	2	1	1	435	2,564,738.20
11	2	1	1	409	4,657,341.23
12	2	1	3	315	1,342,516.12
13	2	2	2	123	2,109,283.00
14	2	2	2	301	1,120,391.33
15	2 Total				11,794,269.88
16	3	1	3	213	1,839,201.77
17	3	2	2	302	1,432,516.60
18	3 Total				3,271,718.37
19	Grand Total				35,491,482.65

FIGURE 6-79

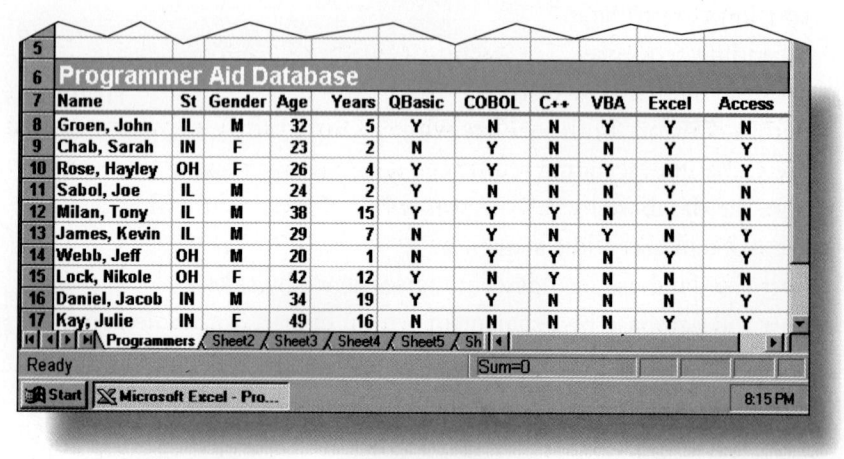

2 Building, Sorting, and Filtering a Database of Prospective Programmers

Problem: You are an Applications Software Specialist for Programmer Aid, Inc. You have been assigned the task of building the Prospective Programmer database shown in Figure 6-80. Create the database beginning in row 6 of the worksheet. Use the field information shown in Table 6-9.

Part 1 Instructions: Perform the following tasks:

1. Bold the entire worksheet. Change the column widths as described in the preceding table. Enter the database title and column titles (field names) as shown in Figure 6-80. Use the Name box in the formula bar to define the name Database as the range A7:K8. Use the Form command on the Data menu to display a data form to enter the ten records.
2. Enter your name, course, computer laboratory exercise (Lab 6-2), date, and instructor name in the range A35:A39. Print the worksheet. Save the workbook using the filename Programmer Aid.

Programmer Aid Database

	Name	St	Gender	Age	Years	QBasic	COBOL	C++	VBA	Excel	Access
8	Groen, John	IL	M	32	5	Y	N	N	Y	Y	N
9	Chab, Sarah	IN	F	23	2	N	Y	N	N	Y	Y
10	Rose, Hayley	OH	F	26	4	Y	Y	N	Y	N	Y
11	Sabol, Joe	IL	M	24	2	Y	N	N	N	Y	N
12	Milan, Tony	IL	M	38	15	Y	Y	Y	N	Y	N
13	James, Kevin	IL	M	29	7	N	Y	N	Y	N	Y
14	Webb, Jeff	OH	M	20	1	N	Y	Y	N	Y	Y
15	Lock, Nikole	OH	F	42	12	Y	N	Y	N	N	N
16	Daniel, Jacob	IN	M	34	19	Y	Y	N	N	N	Y
17	Kay, Julie	IN	F	49	16	N	N	N	N	Y	Y

FIGURE 6-80

In the Lab

3. Sort the records in the database into ascending sequence by name. Print the sorted version.
4. Sort the records in the database by age within gender. Select ascending sequence for the gender code and ascending sequence for the age. Print the sorted version. Close the workbook without saving it.

Table 6-9

COLUMN HEADINGS (FIELD NAMES)	COLUMN	TYPE OF DATA	COLUMN WIDTH
Name	A	Text	13
State	B	Text	3
Gender	C	Text	7
Age	D	Numeric	4
Years	E	Numeric	7
Qbasic	F	Text	8
COBOL	G	Text	8
C++	H	Text	5
VBA	I	Text	6
Excel	J	Text	7
Access	K	Text	9

Part 2 Instructions: Open the workbook Programmer Aid (Figure 6-80). Use the Criteria button on a data form to enter the comparison criteria for the following tasks. Use the Find Next button on the data form to find the records that pass the comparison criteria. Write down and submit the names of the prospective programmers who pass the comparison criteria for items a through d. Close the data form after each query and then reopen it by clicking the Data Form command on the Data menu. You should end up with the following number of records for items a through d: a = 1; b = 1; c = 2; d = 1.

a. Find all records that represent prospective programmers who are female and can program in C++.
b. Find all records that represent prospective programmers who can program in QBasic and VBA and can use Access.
c. Find all records that represent prospective male programmers who are at least 26 years old and can use Excel.
d. Find all records that represent prospective programmers who live in IL and can program in COBOL and VBA.
e. All prospective programmers who did not know C++ were sent to a seminar on the software package. Use the Find Next button to locate the records of these programmers and change the Excel field entry on the data form from the letter N to the letter Y. Make sure you press the ENTER key or press the DOWN ARROW key after changing the letter. Save the database using the filename Programmer Aid A. Print the worksheet. Close Programmer Aid A.

Part 3 Instructions: Open the workbook Programmer Aid. Use the AutoFilter command on the Filter submenu and redo Part 2 a, b, c, and d. Use the Show All command on the Filter submenu before starting items b, c, and d. Print the worksheet for each problem. Change the laboratory exercise number in the range A30:A34 to Lab 6-23x, where x is the problem letter. Click the AutoFilter command on the Filter submenu to remove the box arrows. Close the workbook without saving it.

(continued)

Building, Sorting, and Filtering a Database of Prospective Programmers *(continued)*

Part 4 Instructions: Open the workbook Programmer Aid created in Part 1. Add a criteria range by copying the database title and field names (A7:K8) to A1:K2. Change cell A1 to Criteria Area. Use the Name box in the formula bar to name the criteria range (A1:K2) Criteria. Add an extract range by copying the database title and field names (A7:K8) to A21:K22. Change cell A21 to Extract Area. Use the Name box in the formula bar to name the extract range (A1:K2) Extract. The top of your worksheet should look similar to the top screen in Figure 6-81.

Use the Advanced Filter command on the Filter submenu to extract records that pass the tests in items 1 through 5 below. Change the laboratory exercise number in the range A30:A34 to Lab6-24x, where x is the problem letter. Print the entire worksheet after each extraction.

	A	B	C	D	E	F	G	H	I	J	K
1	Criteria Area										
2	Name	St	Gender	Age	Years	QBasic	COBOL	C++	VBA	Excel	Access
3			M								
4											
5											
6	Programmer Aid Database										
7	Name	St	Gender	Age	Years	QBasic	COBOL	C++	VBA	Excel	Access
8	Groen, John	IL	M	32	5	Y	N	N	Y	Y	N
9	Chab, Sarah	IN	F	23	2	N	Y	N	N	Y	Y
10	Rose, Hayley	OH	F	26	4	Y	Y	N	Y	N	Y
11	Sabol, Joe	IL	M	24	2	Y	N	N	N	Y	N
12	Milan, Tony	IL	M	38	15	Y	Y	Y	N	Y	N
13	James, Kevin	IL	M	29	7	N	Y	N	Y	N	Y
14	Webb, Jeff	OH	M	20	1	N	Y	Y	N	Y	Y
15	Lock, Nikole	OH	F	42	12	Y	N	Y	N	N	N

Programmers / Sheet2 / Sheet3 / Sheet4 / Sheet5 / Sh
Ready Sum=0
Start Microsoft Excel - Pro... 8:25 PM

FIGURE 6-81

1. Extract the records that represent prospective programmers who are male (Figure 6-82).
2. Extract the records that represent prospective programmers who can program in QBasic and cannot program in C++.
3. Extract the records that represent prospective female programmers who are at least 30 years old and can use Excel.
4. Extract the records that represent prospective programmers who know Excel and Access.
5. Extract the records that represent prospective programmers who do not know how to use any programming language (QBasic, COBOL, C++, and VBA). Save the workbook using the filename Programmer Aid B. Close the workbook.

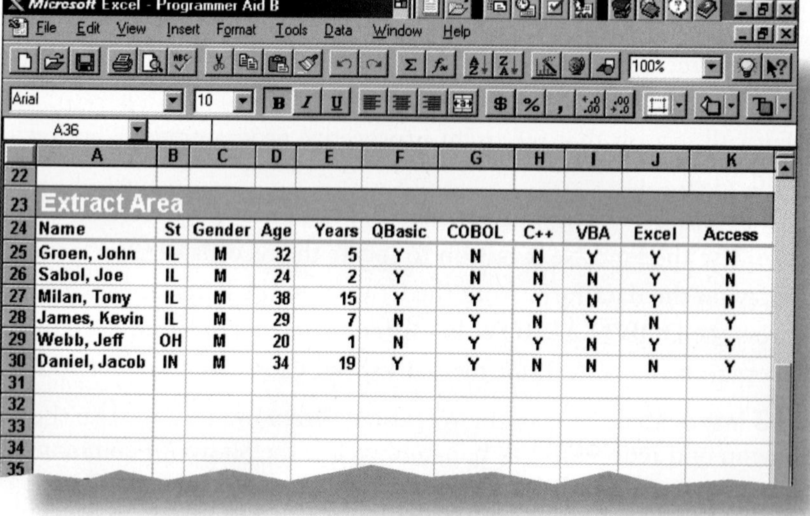

	A	B	C	D	E	F	G	H	I	J	K
22											
23	Extract Area										
24	Name	St	Gender	Age	Years	QBasic	COBOL	C++	VBA	Excel	Access
25	Groen, John	IL	M	32	5	Y	N	N	Y	Y	N
26	Sabol, Joe	IL	M	24	2	Y	N	N	N	Y	N
27	Milan, Tony	IL	M	38	15	Y	Y	Y	N	Y	N
28	James, Kevin	IL	M	29	7	N	Y	N	Y	N	Y
29	Webb, Jeff	OH	M	20	1	N	Y	Y	N	Y	Y
30	Daniel, Jacob	IN	M	34	19	Y	Y	N	N	N	Y

FIGURE 6-82

In the Lab

Part 5 Instructions: Open the workbook Programmer Aid created in Part 1. Draw a data map of the United States (Figure 6-83) that highlights the states where the prospective programmers live. Select the range B7:B17 as the basis for the data map. Use the data map location M1:T17. Save the workbook using the filename Programmer Aid C.

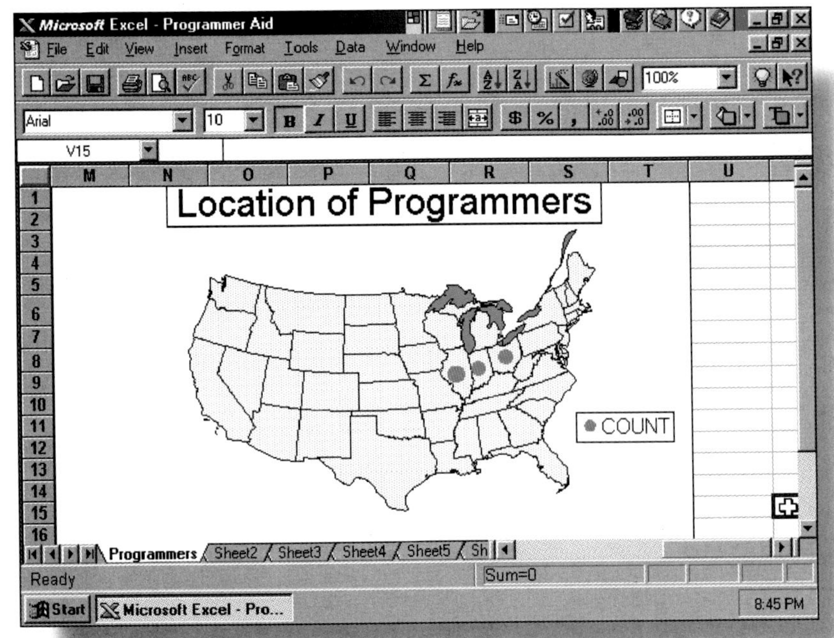

FIGURE 6-83

3 Finding Subtotals and Creating a Pivot Table for an Order Entry Database

Problem: You are employed as a spreadsheet specialist in the order entry department of Davis Sports, Inc. You have been assigned to do the following:

1. Develop an order entry database that keeps track of the outstanding orders (Figure 6-84).
2 Display subtotals of the number ordered and amount (Figure 6-85 on the next page).
3. Create a pivot table for summarizing the amount (Figure 6-86 on the next page).

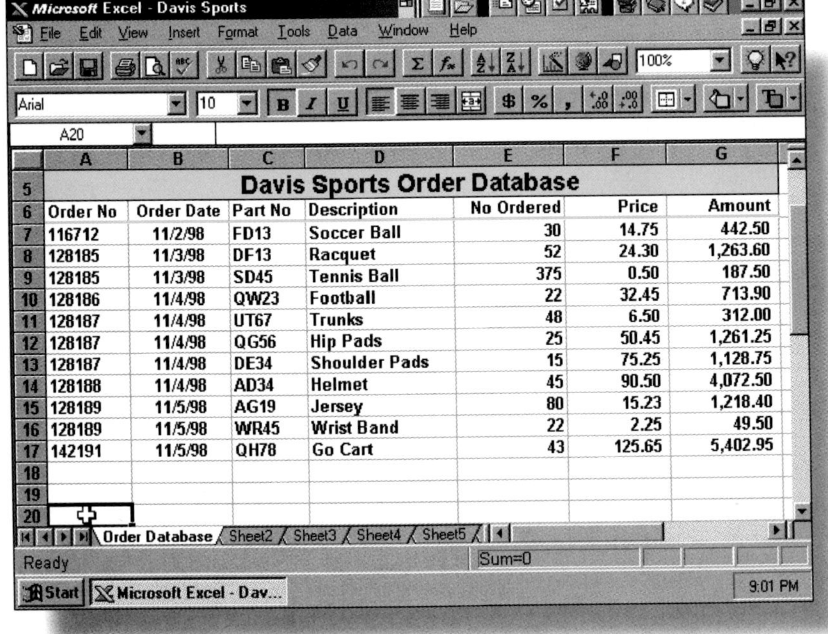

Davis Sports Order Database

Order No	Order Date	Part No	Description	No Ordered	Price	Amount
116712	11/2/98	FD13	Soccer Ball	30	14.75	442.50
128185	11/3/98	DF13	Racquet	52	24.30	1,263.60
128185	11/3/98	SD45	Tennis Ball	375	0.50	187.50
128186	11/4/98	QW23	Football	22	32.45	713.90
128187	11/4/98	UT67	Trunks	48	6.50	312.00
128187	11/4/98	QG56	Hip Pads	25	50.45	1,261.25
128187	11/4/98	DE34	Shoulder Pads	15	75.25	1,128.75
128188	11/4/98	AD34	Helmet	45	90.50	4,072.50
128189	11/5/98	AG19	Jersey	80	15.23	1,218.40
128189	11/5/98	WR45	Wrist Band	22	2.25	49.50
142191	11/5/98	QH78	Go Cart	43	125.65	5,402.95

FIGURE 6-84

Part 1 Instructions: Do the following to create the database shown in the range A5:G17 in Figure 6-84.

1. Change the font of the worksheet to bold. Change the column widths to the following: A = 9, B = 11, C = 8, D = 16, E = 12, F = 11, G = 12. Enter and format the database heading and field names in the range A5:G7. Center entries in column B. Align the field names as shown in row 6 in Figure 6-84.

(continued)

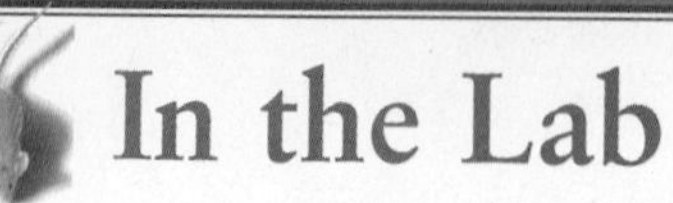

In the Lab

Finding Subtotals and Creating a Pivot Table For on Order Entry Database *(continued)*

2. Enter the first record without using a data form. Enter the formula =E8 * F8 in cell G8. Define the name Database as the range A6:G7. Use a data form to enter the remaining order records.
3. Enter your name, course, computer laboratory exercise (Lab6-3a), date, and instructor name in the range A20:A24.
4. Save the workbook using the filename Davis Sports. Use the Page Setup command on the File menu or shortcut menu to change the left and right margins to 0.5. Print the worksheet. Click the Save button on the Standard toolbar to save the workbook.

Part 2 Instructions: Do the following to develop the subtotals shown in Figure 6-85.

1. Select a cell within the range of Database. Click the Subtotals command on the Data menu and determine totals for the Amounts fields by the Order No field.
2. Change the magnification of the worksheet to 75% (Figure 6-85).
3. Print the worksheet.
4. Hide detail records so that only total rows display. Print the worksheet.
5. Change the magnification back to 100%. Use the Subtotals command on the Data menu to remove subtotals.

	A	B	C	D	E	F	G
5	Davis Sports Order Database						
6	Order No	Order Date	Part No	Description	No Ordered	Price	Amount
7	116712	11/2/98	FD13	Soccer Ball	30	14.75	442.50
8	116712 Total						442.50
9	128185	11/3/98	DF13	Racquet	52	24.30	1,263.60
10	128185	11/3/98	SD45	Tennis Ball	375	0.50	187.50
11	128185 Total						1,451.10
12	128186	11/4/98	QV23	Football	22	32.45	713.90
13	128186 Total						713.90
14	128187	11/4/98	UT67	Trunks	48	6.50	312.00
15	128187	11/4/98	QG56	Hip Pads	25	50.45	1,261.25
16	128187	11/4/98	DE34	Shoulder Pads	15	75.25	1,128.75
17	128187 Total						2,702.00
18	128188	11/4/98	AD34	Helmet	45	90.50	4,072.50
19	128188 Total						4,072.50
20	128189	11/5/98	AG19	Jersey	80	15.23	1,218.40
21	128189	11/5/98	WR45	Wrist Band	22	2.25	49.50
22	128189 Total						1,267.90
23	142191	11/5/98	QH78	Go Cart	43	125.65	5,402.95
24	142191 Total						5,402.95
25	Grand Total						16,052.85

FIGURE 6-85

Part 3 Instructions: Using the Order database, create the pivot table shown in Figure 6-86 on a separate worksheet. The table summarizes dollar amount information by order number and order date. Use the Pivot Table command to create the pivot table. Print the pivot table. Drag the Order No and Order Date buttons around on the pivot table to obtain different views of the information. Save the workbook using the filename Davis Sports A.

	A	B	C	D	E	F
1	Sum of Amount	Order Date				
2	Order No	11/2/98	11/3/98	11/4/98	11/5/98	Grand Total
3	116712	442.5	0	0	0	442.5
4	128185	0	1451.1	0	0	1451.1
5	128186	0	0	713.9	0	713.9
6	128187	0	0	2702	0	2702
7	128188	0	0	4072.5	0	4072.5
8	128189	0	0	0	1267.9	1267.9
9	142191	0	0	0	5402.95	5402.95
10	Grand Total	442.5	1451.1	7488.4	6670.85	16052.85

FIGURE 6-86

Cases and Places

The difficulty of these case studies varies:

◗ Case studies preceded by a single half moon are the least difficult. You are asked to create the required worksheet based on information that has already been placed in an organized form.

◗◗ Case studies preceded by two half moons are more difficult. You must organize the information presented before using it to create the required worksheet.

◗◗◗ Case studies preceded by three half moons are the most difficult. You must decide on a specific topic, then obtain and organize the necessary information before using it to create the required worksheet.

1 ◗ Academic classes, like individuals, may have distinct personalities and characteristics. A database can help reveal a class's idiosyncrasies. Create a Student Database with information collected from your classmates. Use the following field names: Lname, Fname, Age, Gender, Home State, Class (Freshman, Sophomore, Junior, Senior, Graduate Student), Major, and Credit Hours Earned. Sort the database in ascending order by last name. Sort again by age within gender within major. Sort the database by class. Display subtotals for the number of credit hours earned by students in each class. Use a data form to find all female students who have earned more than sixteen credit hours and whose home state is the same as that in which your school is located.

2 ◗ A class database can be used to locate students with specific attributes. Create the Student Database described in case study 1. Use wildcard characters to find all students who have the same last initial as yours. Use AutoFilter to find all male students who are in the same class as you and have the same major. Set up a criteria range on the worksheet. Use the Advanced AutoFilter to locate the records of all Juniors or Seniors who are more than twenty-one years old, and copy the records to an extract range. Use the DAVERAGE function to find the average age of male and female students. Create and format a data map that illustrates the home states of students in the class.

3 ◗◗ A typical video rental store carries more than 5,000 movie titles. With that many titles available, it may be difficult to remember specific movies you have seen. Visit a video store or library and create a Video Cassette Database with the following information: movie title, year made, move type (suspense, drama, comedy, and so on), director, producer, number of academy awards, and rental cost. Sort the database in ascending order by movie title. Sort again by number of academy awards within year made within director. Sort the database by movie type. Display subtotals for the rental cost of videos by type. Use a data form to find all comedies released before 1990 that earned at least one academy award.

Cases and Places

4 ▸▸ A video database can be used to identify movies that have certain qualities. Create the Video Cassette Database described in case study 3. Use AutoFilter to find all dramas directed by Steven Spielberg that have won at least one academy award. Set up a criteria range on the worksheet. Use the Advanced AutoFilter to locate the titles of all drama and suspense films that were released after 1995, and copy the records to an extract range. Create a lookup table that gives a letter grade to a movie based on the number of academy awards won (0 = F, 1 = D, 2 = C, 3 or 4 = B, 5 or more = A). Use the VLOOKUP function to assign letter grades to each movie. Create a pivot table that summarizes rental cost by movie type and director.

5 ▸▸▸ In order to maintain a balanced collection, art museums and galleries must have a detailed knowledge of the artwork they possess. Visit a local museum or gallery and create an art collection database that contains records for twenty different pieces of work. Use at least six fields (artist name, title of work, type of work, style, year created, value, and so on). Sort the database in various ways and explain how each sort order might be valuable. Display automatic subtotals for the value of different types of work. Use a data form, AutoFilter, and criteria range to find specific works. Use the DAVERAGE function to find the average value of works by each artist. Create a pivot table that summarizes values by artist and type of work.

6 ▸▸▸ Sportswriters often use databases when comparing athletes. Create an athlete database that contains records for twenty different players. Use at least six fields (player name, sport, age, birthplace, earnings, and so on). Sort the database in various ways and explain how each sort order might be valuable. Display automatic subtotals for player earnings based on the sport played. Use a data form, AutoFilter, and criteria range to find specific athletes. Decide on a field that could be used to compare the athletes. Create a lookup table that assigns letter grades to athletes based on the criteria you have chosen. Using the VLOOKUP function, give a grade to each athlete. Create and format a data map showing the birthplaces of the athletes.

7 ▸▸▸ Retailers of *big-ticket* items, such as automobiles, furniture, or appliances, need an in-depth knowledge of their inventories to satisfy the demands of potential customers. Visit a retailer that deals in high-cost merchandise and create an inventory database. Use at least six fields (item name, type of item, color, cost, place of manufacture, and so on). Sort the database in various ways and explain how each sort order might be valuable. Display automatic subtotals for the costs of different types of items. Use a data form, AutoFilter, and criteria range to find specific items. Use the DAVERAGE function to find the average cost for different items. Create and format a data map showing where the items were manufactured.

Embedding an Excel Worksheet in a Word Document Using Drag and Drop

Case Perspective

Several years ago, Ted Schroeder talked a few of his friends into starting the Cycle Stock Club. Each club member pitches in $100 a month. The money then is invested in the stock market based on recommendations made by the members and voted on at their monthly meetings. Members are expected to research an assigned company and come to the meeting with their buy and sell recommendations.

Ted serves as treasurer of the club. Each month he sends the members a letter summarizing the club's end-of-month financial status. Recently, the club passed the $150,000 mark. Because of their good fortune, the members voted unanimously to purchase for Ted a laptop computer with Microsoft Office and trading software. The trading software will help reduce the club's broker costs and allow better tracking of their investments. Ted also would like to use Word to create the monthly letter and Excel to create an end-of month financial summary. Ted knows little about Microsoft Office and has asked you to show him how to create the documents. He would especially like to join the letter and worksheet together in one document.

Introduction

In the earlier Excel Integration Feature, you were introduced to using the Copy button on the Standard toolbar and the Paste Special command on the Edit menu to link a worksheet, also called the source document, to a Word document, also called the destination document. This Integration Feature shows you how to use the OLE features of Microsoft Office to **embed**, rather than link, a worksheet into a Word document using **drag and drop** techniques (Figure 1 on the next page). Table 1 summarizes the difference between linking and embedding.

Table 1

METHOD	*CHARACTERISTICS*
Embed	**Source document becomes part of the destination document. The object may be edited in the destination application using source editing features. If you modify the worksheet in Excel, changes will not show in the Word document the next time you open it.**
Link	**Source document does not become part of the destination document even though it appears to be part of it. Instead, a link is established between the two documents so that when you open the Word document, the worksheet displays as part of it. When you attempt to edit a linked worksheet in Word, the system activates Excel. If you change the worksheet in Excel, the changes will show in the Word document the next time you open it.**

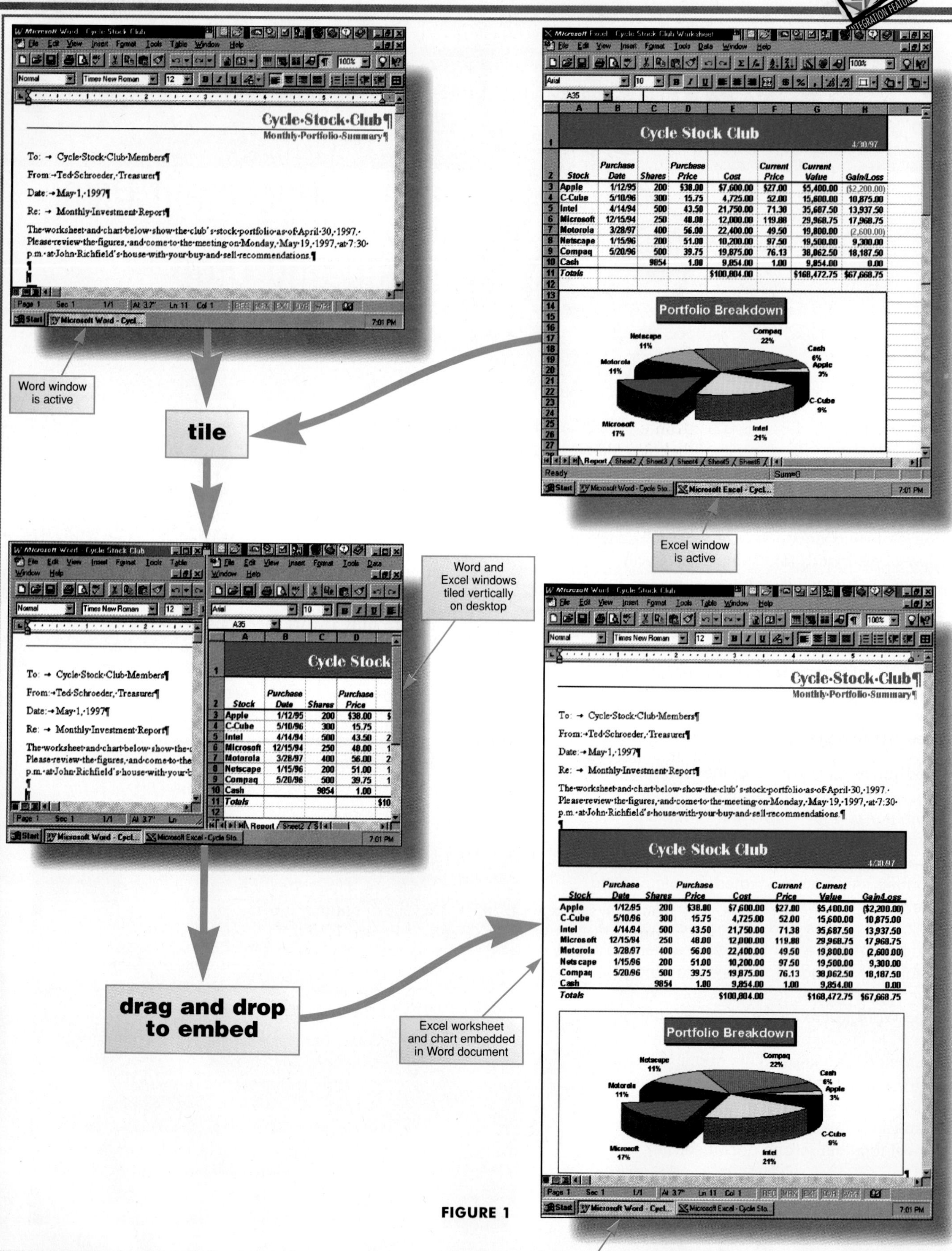

Word window is active
tile
Excel window is active
Word and Excel windows tiled vertically on desktop
drag and drop to embed
Excel worksheet and chart embedded in Word document
Word window is active

FIGURE 1

Starting Word and Excel

Both the Word document (Cycle Stock Club) and the Excel workbook (Cycle Stock Club Worksheet) are in the Excel folder on the Student Floppy Disk that accompanies this book. The first step in embedding the Excel worksheet into the Word document is to open both the document in Word and the workbook in Excel as shown in the following steps.

TO OPEN A WORD DOCUMENT AND AN EXCEL WORKBOOK

Step 1: Click the Start button on the taskbar. Click Open Office document on the Start menu. Click 3½ Floppy [A:] in the Look in box and then click the Excel folder. Double-click the filename Cycle Stock Club.

Word becomes active and the document Cycle Stock Club displays as shown in the upper left screen in Figure 1.

Step 2: Click the Start button on the taskbar. Click Open Office document on the Start menu. Click 3½ Floppy [A:] in the Look in box and then click the Excel folder. Double-click the filename Cycle Stock Club Worksheet.

Excel becomes active and the workbook Cycle Stock Club Worksheet displays as shown in the upper right screen of Figure 1. At this point, Word is inactive, but still in main memory.

Step 3: Click the Microsoft Word button on the taskbar to activate Word.

Word becomes the active window.

More *About* **Starting Applications**

You can start an application through Explorer by double-clicking the filename. For example, if you display the contents of the Excel folder on the Student Floppy Disk in Explorer, then you can double-click the Word document Cycle Stock Club to start Word and open the document. You can do the same with the Excel workbook Cycle Stock Club Worksheet to start Excel and open the workbook.

Windows 95 automatically activates an application when you open it and deactivates the application that was previously active. As described in Step 3, with both Word and Excel in main memory, you can click the application button on the taskbar to activate the corresponding application.

Tiling Applications on the Desktop

To drag and drop information from one application to another, both applications must be running and visible on your screen (lower left screen of Figure 1). The applications can be tiled to make them visible at the same time. **Tiling** is the process of arranging open applications in smaller windows to fit side by side on the desktop. When tiled, each application displays in its own window. Follow the steps on the next page to tile the two applications on the desktop in preparation for dragging and dropping the Excel worksheet onto the Word document.

To Tile the Applications on the Desktop

1 Right-click an open area on the taskbar between the Microsoft Excel button and the Tray status area.

A shortcut menu displays (Figure 2). Although the Word document displays on the screen, its corresponding button on the taskbar is no longer recessed because the displayed shortcut menu is associated with Windows, not Word.

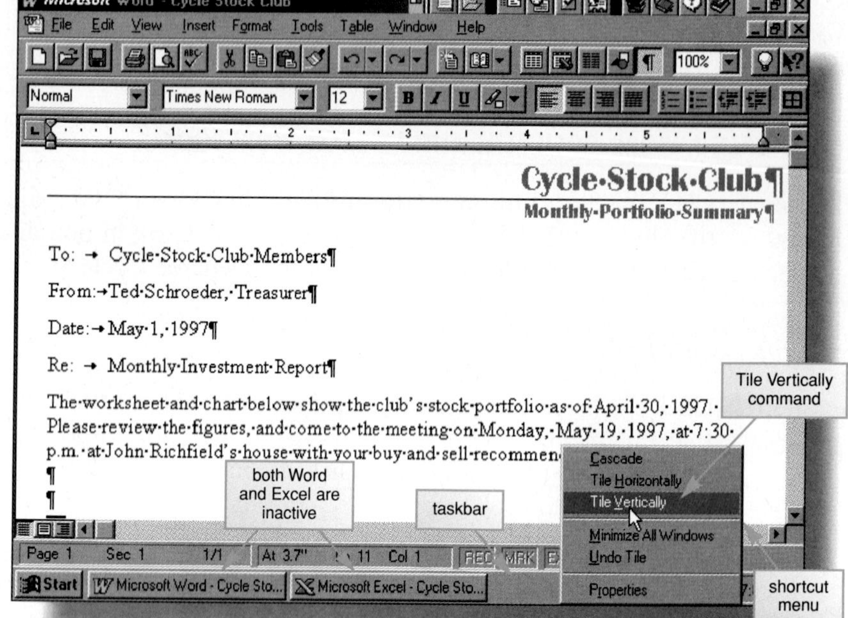

FIGURE 2

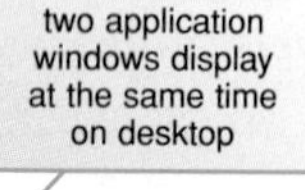

2 Click Tile Vertically.

Windows displays each open application in its own window on the desktop. In this case, the Word document and Excel worksheet display, side by side, in two vertical windows (Figure 3). When the applications are tiled, each window has its own title bar, status bar, Minimize button, Maximize button, Close button, and scroll bars.

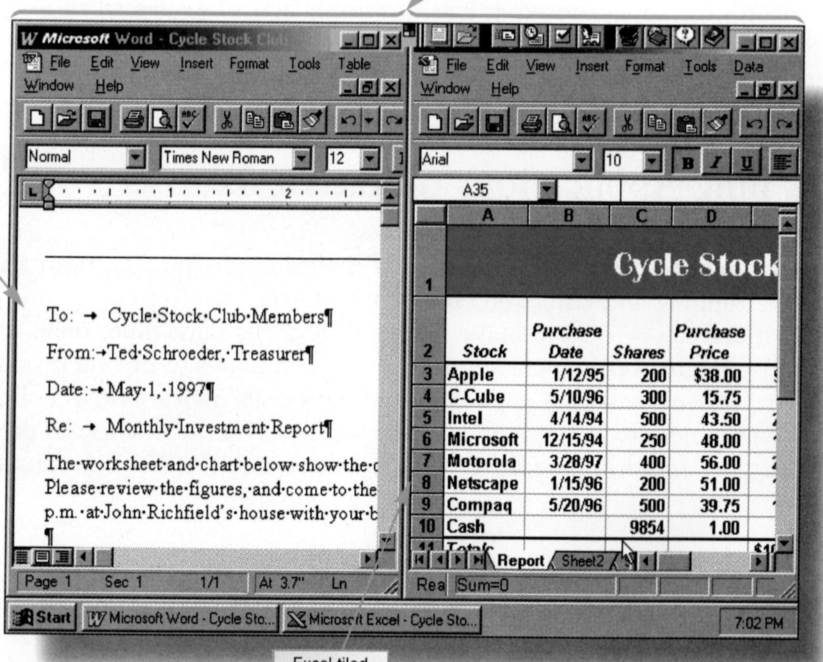

FIGURE 3

OtherWays

1. Right-click taskbar, type V

In addition to tiling applications vertically, Windows can tile horizontally and cascade the applications. To tile horizontally, click **Tile Horizontally** on the shortcut menu (Figure 2). The windows display across the desktop. To cascade, click **Cascade** on the shortcut menu. When the windows **cascade**, they overlap so each title bar is visible. When the applications are cascaded, you can bring any application window to the top of the desktop by clicking any part of its window.

You can switch back and forth among vertical tiling, horizontal tiling, and cascade by right-clicking the taskbar and then clicking the appropriate command on the shortcut menu.

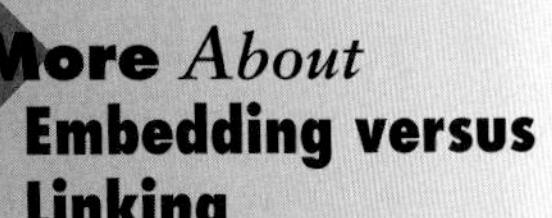

More *About* Embedding versus Linking

When you embed an Excel worksheet into a Word document, the size of the Word document increases by approximately the size of the Excel worksheet. If you link, rather than embed, the size of the Word document will increase in size only by a few thousand bytes.

Embedding Using Drag and Drop

With each application in its own window on the desktop, the next step is to embed the Excel worksheet into the Word document using drag and drop as shown in the following steps.

Steps To Embed Using Drag and Drop

1. **With the Excel window active, select the range A1:H27. Point to the border of the selected range so the mouse pointer changes to a block arrow, and then hold down the CTRL key.**

The worksheet and pie chart are selected and the mouse pointer is a block arrow with a plus sign above and to the right (Figure 4).

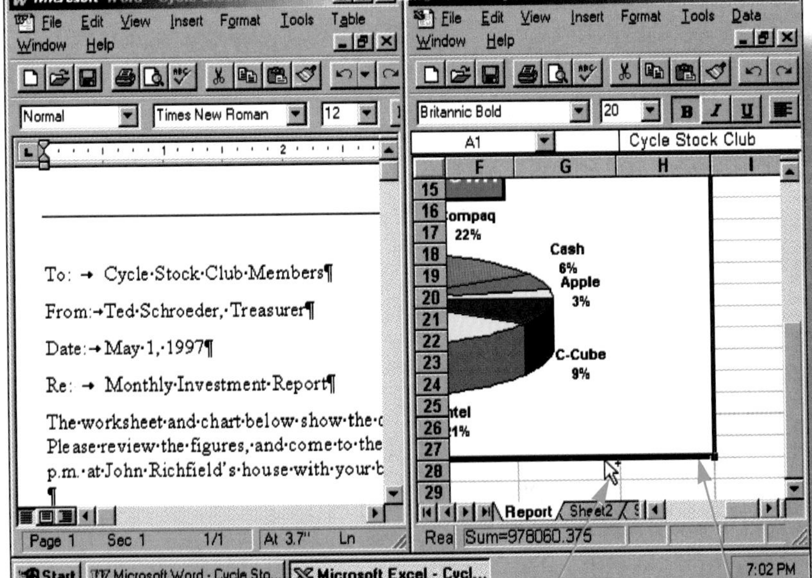
Excel window is active
mouse pointer is block arrow and plus sign when you point to a border of the selected range and then hold down the CTRL key
range A1:H27, which includes worksheet and chart, is selected

FIGURE 4

INTEGRATION FEATURE

2 While holding down the CTRL key, drag the mouse to the last paragraph mark in the Word window and hold.

The mouse pointer changes to a block arrow and a plus sign in a square with a shadow in the Word document (Figure 5).

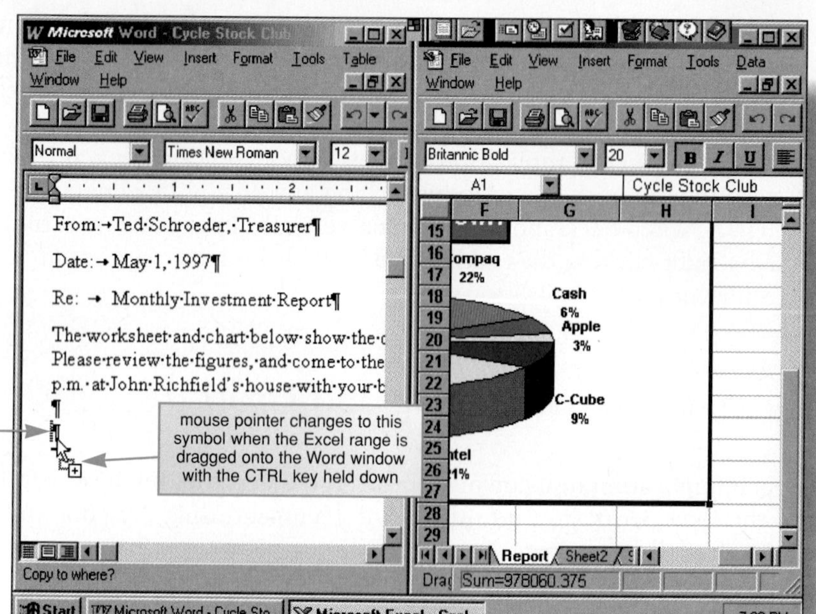
drop object here
mouse pointer changes to this symbol when the Excel range is dragged onto the Word window with the CTRL key held down

FIGURE 5

3 Release the mouse button.

The system embeds the range A1:H27 of the worksheet into the Word document beginning at the location of the insertion point, and the embedded range displays in the Word window (Figure 6). The worksheet also remains intact in the Excel window.

worksheet and chart embedded in Word document

worksheet and chart in Excel is copied, rather than moved, and thus displays in both windows

Word window is active

FIGURE 6

OtherWays

1. Select range to embed in source document, click Copy button on Standard toolbar, click point of insertion in destination document, on Edit menu click Paste Special, click Paste, click OK button

The Excel worksheet is now embedded in the Word document. If you drag the worksheet onto the Word document without holding down the CTRL key, the worksheet is *moved* to the Word document, rather than copied to the Word document. The next section shows how to undo the tile so the Word document with the embedded worksheet displays in a maximized window.

Undoing Tiling of the Applications on the Desktop

Once you are finished with the Excel window, you can undo tiling so the Word document displays in a maximized window.

To Undo Tiling of the Applications on the Desktop

1. **Click within the Word window to ensure it is the active application.**

2. **Right-click an open area on the taskbar between the Microsoft Excel button and the Tray status area.**

   A shortcut menu displays (Figure 7).

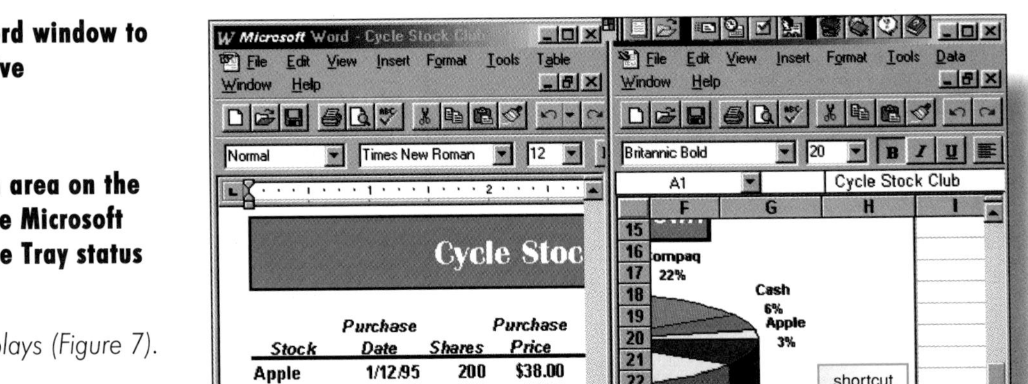

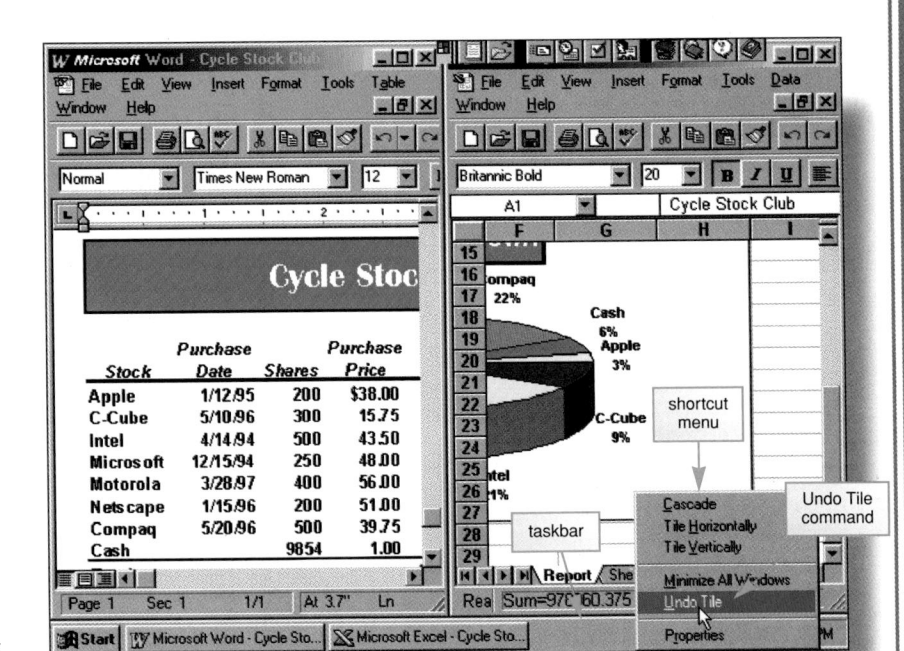

FIGURE 7

3. **Click Undo Tile. When Word displays in a maximized window, scroll to the top of the document.**

   The embedded worksheet displays at the bottom of the Word window (Figure 8).

4. **Click the Microsoft Excel button on the taskbar. Click the Maximize button on the title bar. Click the Close button on the title bar. Do not save the changes.**

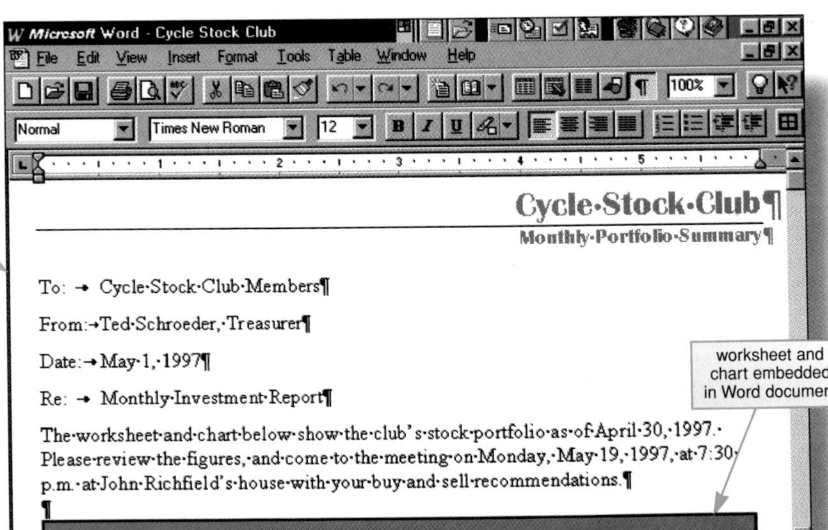

FIGURE 8

OtherWays

1. Click Maximize button on Excel title bar, click Close button, click Maximize button on Word title bar

More *About* Embedding Objects as Icons

You can embed an object in a destination document as an icon using the Copy button on the Standard toolbar in the source document and the Paste Special command on the Edit menu in the destination document. If you embed as an icon, then the user double-clicks the icon in the destination document to start the source application and display the document.

If you embed an object, such as the Excel worksheet, and the results are not what you expected, click the Undo button on the Standard toolbar or click Undo on the Edit menu. If you entered other commands between the time you embedded the object and your decision to remove the object, click the embedded object to select it and then press the DELETE key.

Saving and Printing the Word Document with the Embedded Worksheet

With the Word window maximized, the next step is to save and print the Word document with the embedded worksheet.

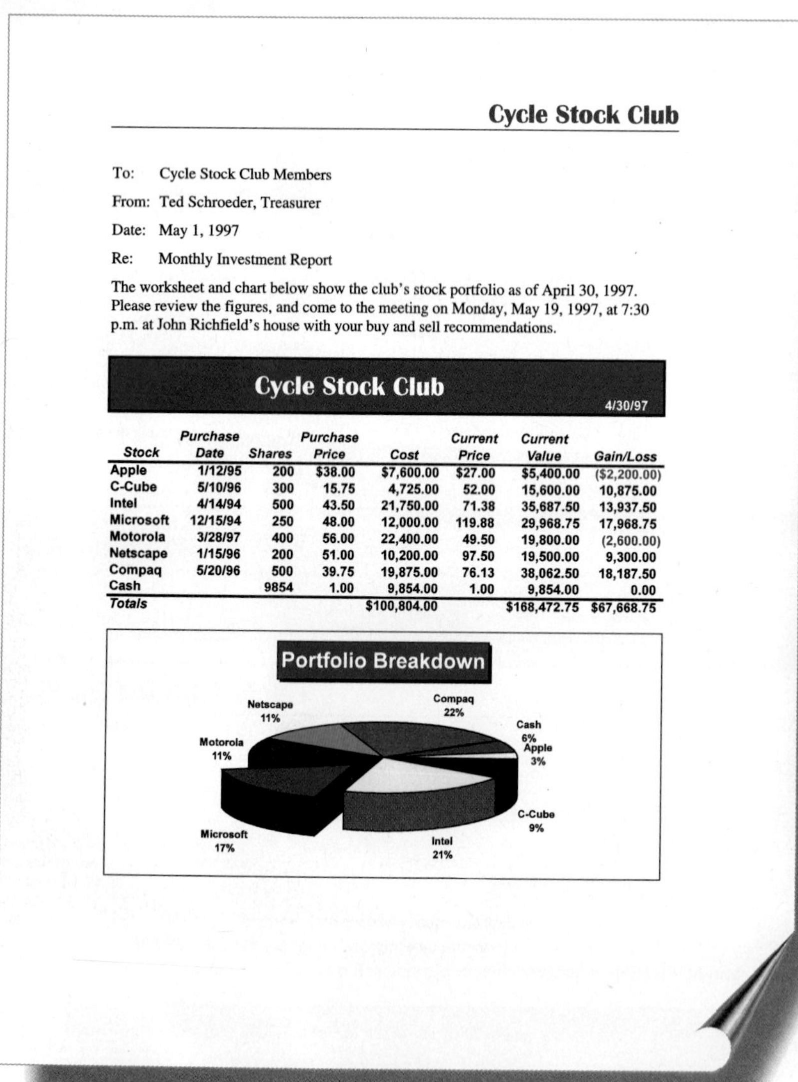

Cycle Stock Club

To: Cycle Stock Club Members

From: Ted Schroeder, Treasurer

Date: May 1, 1997

Re: Monthly Investment Report

The worksheet and chart below show the club's stock portfolio as of April 30, 1997. Please review the figures, and come to the meeting on Monday, May 19, 1997, at 7:30 p.m. at John Richfield's house with your buy and sell recommendations.

Cycle Stock Club 4/30/97

Stock	Purchase Date	Shares	Purchase Price	Cost	Current Price	Current Value	Gain/Loss
Apple	1/12/95	200	$38.00	$7,600.00	$27.00	$5,400.00	($2,200.00)
C-Cube	5/10/96	300	15.75	4,725.00	52.00	15,600.00	10,875.00
Intel	4/14/94	500	43.50	21,750.00	71.38	35,687.50	13,937.50
Microsoft	12/15/94	250	48.00	12,000.00	119.88	29,968.75	17,968.75
Motorola	3/28/97	400	56.00	22,400.00	49.50	19,800.00	(2,600.00)
Netscape	1/15/96	200	51.00	10,200.00	97.50	19,500.00	9,300.00
Compaq	5/20/96	500	39.75	19,875.00	76.13	38,062.50	18,187.50
Cash		9854	1.00	9,854.00	1.00	9,854.00	0.00
Totals				$100,804.00		$168,472.75	$67,668.75

FIGURE 9

TO SAVE AND PRINT THE WORD DOCUMENT WITH THE EMBEDDED WORKSHEET

Step 1: With Word active, click File on the menu bar and then click Save As. Type the filename `Cycle Stock Club with Worksheet` in the File name text box. Click the Save in box arrow and then click 3½ Floppy [A:], if necessary. Click the Save button in the Save As dialog box.

The document with the embedded worksheet is saved on your floppy disk using the filename Cycle Stock Club with Worksheet.

Step 2: Click the Print button on the Standard toolbar.

The memorandum prints as shown in Figure 9.

If you exit and then start Word and re-open Cycle Stock Club with Worksheet, the worksheet will display in the Word document even though Excel is not running, because the worksheet is part of the Word document. The next section describes what occurs when you attempt to edit the embedded worksheet while Word is active.

Summary

With the Excel worksheet embedded into the Word document, Ted Schroeder can easily open the letter with the embedded worksheet each month, make the appropriate modifications, and send the letter to the Cycle Stock Club members.

This Integration Feature introduced you to embedding an object into a document using tiling and drag and drop techniques. When you embed an object into a document and save it, the destination document increases in size by the size of the object. You edit an embedded object by double-clicking it.

What You Should Know

Having completed this Integration Feature, you should be able to perform the following tasks:

- Edit an Embedded Worksheet in a Word Document *(EI 2.9)*
- Embed Using Drag and Drop *(EI 2.5)*
- Open a Word Document and an Excel Workbook *(EI 2.3)*
- Save and Print the Word Document with the Embedded Worksheet *(EI 2.8)*
- Tile the Applications on the Desktop *(EI 2.4)*
- Undo Tiling of the Applications on the Desktop *(EI 2.7)*

In the Lab

1 Using Help

Instructions: Perform the following tasks using a computer.

Start Excel. Double-click the Help button on the Standard toolbar to display the Help Topics: Microsoft Excel dialog box. Click the Index tab. Type `embed` in the top box labeled 1. Double-click the subtopic creating and inserting under the topic embedded objects in the lower box labeled 2 to display the Topics Found dialog box. Hand in one printout for the following topics: (a) Drag and drop information between applications; and (b) Link or embed selected information from an existing file.

2 Embedding a Monthly Expense Worksheet into a Monthly Expense Memo

Problem: You have been assigned the task of embedding a monthly expense worksheet into a memo.

Instructions: Perform the following tasks.

1. One at a time, open the document Monthly Expense Memo and the workbook Monthly Expense Summary from the Excel folder on the Student Floppy Disk that accompanies this book. Tile the two applications on the desktop.
2. Drag and drop the range A1:E17 at the bottom of the Monthly Expense Memo document.
3. Print and then save the document as Monthly Expense 7-1-97.
4. Double-click the worksheet and increase each of the nine expense amounts by $200. Print the document with the new values. Close the document and workbook without saving them.

3 Embedding a Monthly Expense Memo as an Icon in a Monthly Expense Workbook

Problem: You now are asked to embed the Word document as an icon in the Excel workbook.

Instructions: Complete the following tasks:

1. One at a time, open the document Monthly Expense Memo and the workbook Monthly Expense Summary from the Excel folder on the Student Floppy Disk that accompanies this book. Tile the two applications on the desktop.
2. Click within the Word window and select the entire document. Use the Copy button on the Standard toolbar in Word and Paste Special on the Edit menu in Excel to embed the Word document as an icon. Position the icon beginning in cell G1. Make sure you click Display as Icon in the Paste Special dialog box.
3. Print the Monthly Office Expenses sheet and then save the workbook as Monthly Expense 7-1-97.
4. With the Excel window active, double-click the icon representing the embedded document and delete the second sentence. Print the revised memo. Close the workbook and document without saving them.

Index

NOTE TO READER: *This index contains references for Projects 1 through 6 of the book, Microsoft Excel 7 for Windows 95: Complete Concepts and Techniques. The same references can be used for Excel Projects 1 through 3 in the book, Microsoft Office 95: Introductory Concepts and Techniques, and Excel Projects 4 through 6 in the book, Microsoft Office 95: Advanced Concepts and Techniques.*